PRINCIPLES OF REAL ESTATE PRACTICE IN MARYLAND

1st Edition

I0053173

Stephen Mettling
David Cusic
Jane Somers

PERFORMANCE PROGRAMS COMPANY

© 2021 by Performance Programs Company
6810 190th Street East, Bradenton, FL 34211
info@performanceprogramscompany.com
www.performanceprogramscompany.com

ISBN: 978-0915777730

Table of Contents

Section II : Maryland Principles, Practices and Laws

PREFACE

**About
the text**

Principles of Real Estate Practice in Maryland contains the essentials of the national and Maryland real estate law, principles, and practices necessary for basic competence as a real estate professional and as mandated by Maryland license law. It is based on our highly successful and popular national publication, **Principles of Real Estate Practice**, which is in use in real estate schools nationwide.

The text is tailored to the needs of the pre-license student. It is designed to

- make it easy for students to learn the material
- prepare students for numerous career applications
- stress practical, as well as theoretical, skills and knowledge.

It is streamlined, direct and to-the-point. It includes multiple learning reinforcements. It has a student-oriented organization, both within each chapter and from chapter to chapter. Its examples and exercises are grounded in the authors' many years in real estate education.

**Inside
the cover**

Each chapter begins with an overview of the main section heads covered in the chapter. As each of these heads is expanded, the subheads are displayed in the margin. Key terms are printed in bold type the first time they are used and defined. The chapters conclude with a study aid called the "Snapshot Review," which compresses the main points of the chapter into one or two pages. At the end of the chapter section are tests on each chapter. The answer key following the tests refers to the page in the text that explains the correct answer. The book is also provided with a special section on real estate math, a practice exam covering national and state topics reflecting the content of the state licensing examination, and two glossaries of real estate terminology.

**About the
authors**

For over forty years, Stephen Mettling and David Cusic have operated one of the nation's most successful custom training organizations specializing in real estate program development. Mr. Mettling has also served as vice president and author for a major real estate training and publishing organization. Under various capacities, he has managed the acquisition, development, and sale of national real estate textbooks and publications, as well as directed the country's largest affiliated group of real estate schools.

Mr. Cusic, an author and educator with international real estate training experience, has been engaged in vocation-oriented education since 1966. Specializing in real estate training since 1983, he has developed numerous real estate training programs for corporate and institutional clients around the country.

Jane Somers has been a writer and educator for more than 30 years. She has directed the academic programs for a multi-campus college and has in recent years become an accomplished developer of online and classroom real estate curricula for a national real estate licensing organization, specializing in state licensing laws. Ms. Somers is also active in condominium association management and has served as president of a condominium owners association for ten years.

1 The Real Estate Business

Real Estate Professions
Real Estate Brokerage
Professional Organizations
Regulation and Licensing

REAL ESTATE PROFESSIONS

Real estate activities
Professional specialties
Property type specialization

In its broadest sense, the real estate industry is the largest single industry in the American economy. Within it one might include the construction industry, itself often considered our country's largest business. In addition, the real estate industry may be said to include the creation, management, and demolition of every residence and business facility in the nation: offices, warehouses, factories, stores, and special purpose buildings such as hospitals and government facilities. The real estate business would include as well the managing of all the undeveloped land in the country: national parks, forests, and the vast quantity of unused federal property.

Real estate professionals are individuals and business organizations whose *sole enterprise is performing a real estate-related service or function.* A wide range of professions is available to persons wishing to enter the real estate business.

Real estate activities

Real estate professionals perform the following property-related functions:

▸ creation and improvement
▸ management and maintenance
▸ demolition
▸ investment ownership
▸ regulation
▸ transfer

Creation and improvement. Creating real properties from raw land involves capital formation, financing, construction contracting, and regulatory approvals. The key parties involved in this aspect of the business are generally the developer, the landowner, and the mortgage lender. Also involved are market analysts, architects, engineers, space planners, interior designers, and construction subcontractors.

Experts who manage the legal aspects of the development project include real estate attorneys, title companies, surveyors, property insurance companies, and government regulatory officials. The brokerage community, with the assistance of professional appraisers, usually handles the ownership and leasing transactions that occur over the many phases of development.

Management and maintenance. All real estate, whether raw land or improved property, must be managed and maintained. The two principal types of managers are property managers and asset managers. Property managers and their staff oversee specific properties on behalf of the owners, making sure the condition of the property and its financial performance meet specific standards.

Asset managers oversee groups of properties, or portfolios. Their role is to achieve the investment objectives of the owners as opposed to managing day-to-day operations.

Maintenance personnel include engineers, systems technicians, janitorial staff, and other employees needed to maintain the property's condition.

Demolition. Demolition experts in conjunction with excavation and debris removal experts serve to remove properties that are no longer economically viable from the market.

Investment ownership. A specialized niche in the real estate business is the real estate investor who risks capital in order to buy, hold, and sell real properties. In contrast to property owners whose primary interest is in some other business, the real estate investor focuses on identifying and exploiting real estate investment opportunities for profit. The real estate investor provides capital and liquidity to the real estate market.

Regulation. All real estate is to some degree regulated by government. The principal areas of regulation are usage, taxation, and housing administration. Professional regulatory functions include public planners, zoning administrators, building inspectors, assessors, and administrators of specific federal statutes such as Federal Fair Housing Laws.

Transfer. Rights and interests in real estate can be bought, sold, assigned, leased, exchanged, inherited, or otherwise transferred from one owner to another. Real estate brokers and the brokers' salespeople are generally centrally involved in such transfers. Other professional participants are mortgage brokers, mortgage bankers, appraisers, insurers, and title companies.

Professional specialties

In summary, the six primary functional areas are populated by professionals with the following specialties.

Exhibit 1.1 Professions in Real Estate

Creating	developers public and private planners architects building contractors space planners mortgage lenders and bankers title and escrow companies insurers real estate brokers and agents	market analysts surveyors engineers public and private inspectors mortgage brokers securities companies attorneys appraisers
Managing & Maintaining	property managers maintenance engineers technicians corporate managers	asset managers maintenance
Destroying	demolition contractors	excavators
Holding	investors	corporate managers
Regulating	assessors zoning administrators	public planners building inspectors
Transferring	brokers and agents lenders and bankers title and escrow companies insurers	appraisers mortgage brokers attorneys surveyors

Property type specialization

In addition to specializing by function, many professionals also specialize in the type of property they work with. According to the purpose of ownership, properties are classified as residential, commercial, or investment properties.

Residential property refers to property that is owned and used for habitation. Such properties may be further classified in terms of how many families they are designed to house, whether they are attached to other units or detached, and so forth.

Commercial property generally refers to retail and office properties, but may also include industrial real estate. The term "commercial" relates to the fact that the property can potentially generate income from a business's usage.

Investment property refers to any property that is held by its owners for investment purposes. All classifications of property may be investment properties. Generally, however, the term does not refer to owner-occupied residences, even though such properties constitute an investment. Apartments, condominiums, cooperatives, and single-family homes may be considered as investment property if non-occupants own the property for investment purposes. These properties are also referred to as residential income properties.

According to use, the following classifications of real properties are commonly accepted.

Exhibit 1.2 Classifications of Real Estate by Use

residential	industrial
residential income	farm and ranch
office	special purpose
retail	land

These categories are not absolute, since properties often have overlapping uses. A bank, for example, may have retail as well as office operations. An industrial distribution facility may include extensive office space. A retail center may contain offices.

Special purpose properties include publicly or privately owned recreational facilities, government buildings, churches and schools, and so on.

REAL ESTATE BROKERAGE

Forms of specialization
Skills and knowledge

Most newly licensed practitioners choose to begin their real estate careers in residential brokerage.

Primary real estate brokerage activities involve performance of one or more of the following tasks:

▶ locating a buyer for a seller
▶ locating a seller for a buyer
▶ locating a tenant for a landlord
▶ locating a landlord for a tenant

A seller, buyer, landlord or tenant hires a broker to procure the opposite party to the sale or lease transaction. To help get the job done, the broker hires licensed agents as assistants. The brokerage company, in its simplest form, consists of a broker and the broker's agents, who together work to locate buyers, sellers, tenants and landlords for the broker's clients.

Forms of specialization

In the modern brokerage environment, brokers and agents specialize along the following lines:

> ► property type
> ► geographical area
> ► type of transaction
> ► type of client
> ► type of relationship

One's choice of specialization is influenced by competitive factors in the market and by perceived opportunities.

Property type. Since different properties have different features and potential buyers, brokers commonly choose to specialize in a property type. Thus there are:

> ► residential agents
> ► commercial agents (office, retail)
> ► industrial agents
> ► land agents

Geographical area. Brokers and agents must maintain current, accurate data on properties. It is not possible to keep track of every property in larger markets. Therefore, one must create an area of geographical specialization. One's area may be defined by natural barriers; by streets and highways; or by a certain set of subdivisions.

Type of transaction. The principal types of transaction are sales, leases and subleases, exchanges, and options.

Each form of transaction involves particular legal documents and considerations. As a result, many agents, particularly commercial agents, specialize in a type of transaction. For example, in an urban commercial property market, agents generally specialize in either leases or sales.

Type of client. Brokers increasingly represent buyers and tenants as well as sellers and landlords. Since conflicts of interest may be involved, many brokers restrict their business to representing either buyers and tenants or sellers and landlords exclusively.

Some brokers and agents also specialize according to the type of business their clients are in or their motivations for the transaction. Thus one finds brokers who focus exclusively on hospitals, or fast food chains, or executive relocations.

Type of relationship. In recent years, many brokers have specialized in providing advisory services to clients instead of the traditional transaction-based, commission-compensated services. In the advisory relationship, the broker works on identified real estate tasks or projects in exchange for a fee, salary, or retainer. The fee advisor may or may not focus on completing a transaction.

Some of the individual brokerage services that one might perform for a pre-set fee are:

- ▶ comparative price analysis
- ▶ database search
- ▶ prospect screening
- ▶ site analysis

Skills and knowledge

Professionals in the brokerage business must have a broad range of real estate knowledge and skills. Agents must develop a thorough awareness of their local market and the properties within it. In addition, agents must develop a proficiency with the economics of real estate: prices, financing, closing costs, and so forth. Equally important are "people" skills: communicating with clients and responding to their needs.

Exhibit 1.3 Skills and Knowledge in Real Estate Brokerage

Knowledge	Skills
local market conditions	financial qualification
local properties	market analysis
real estate principles	marketing practices
real estate law	ethical practices
value estimation	liability management
real estate financing	data management
investment principles	selling
license laws	time management
related math calculations	communication
closing procedures	writing
	basic computer operation

PROFESSIONAL ORGANIZATIONS

There are trade organizations within the real estate industry that support and promote virtually every form of business specialization. Benefits of membership include training programs, professional designations, and communication channels for keeping abreast of events and laws. Trade organization membership also generally enhances one's business image in the eyes of clients and the public at large.

Some of the major trade organizations, institutes and related professional designations are listed below.

Exhibit 1.4 Real Estate Trade Organizations and Designations

American Society of Appraisers
www.appraisers.org

American Society of Home Inspectors
www.ashi.com

Building Owners and Managers Association
www.boma.org

CCIM Institute
www.ccim.com

    Certified Commercial-Investment Member (CCIM)

Corenet Global
www.corenetglobal.org

    Master of Corporate Real Estate (MCR)

Counselors of Real Estate
www.cre.org

    Counselor of Real Estate (CRE)

Institute of Real Estate Management
www.irem.org

    Certified Property Manager (CPM)

International Association of Assessing Officers
www.iaao.org

International Council of Shopping Centers
www.icsc.org

Mortgage Bankers Association of America
www.mbaa.org

    Certified Mortgage Banker (CMB)

National Association of Exclusive Buyer's Agents
www.naeba.org

National Association of Home Builders
www.nahb.org

NAIOP Commercial Real Estate Development Association
www.naiop.org

National Association of Real Estate Brokers
www.nareb.com

National Association of Realtors
www.nar.realtor

    Graduate, Realtors Institute (GRI)
    Certified International Property Specialist (CIPS)

Real Estate Educators Association
www.reea.org

Realtors Land Institute
www.rliland.com

    Accredited Land Consultant (ALC)

Society of Industrial and Office Realtors

www.sior.com

The Appraisal Institute
www.appraisalinstitute.org

    Member, Appraisal Institute (MAI)
    Senior Residential Appraiser (SRA)

Women's Council of Realtors
www.wcr.org

    Performance Management Network (PMN)

REGULATION AND LICENSING

Regulation of business practices
Real estate license laws

Regulation of business practices

The real estate industry is regulated by every level of government. Federal and state statutes, as well as a large body of court decisions, generally referred to as common law, circumscribe how real estate can be developed, managed, and transferred.

Among the laws most relevant to agents and brokers are those relating to:

- agency
- contracts
- disclosure
- environmental impact
- fair housing

In addition to federal, state, and local laws and regulations, the real estate industry is, to a degree, self-regulated by the codes of ethical conduct propounded by the industry's many trade organizations. For example, the National Association of Realtors® Code of Ethics not only reflects the law but sets an even higher standard of performance for member brokers and agents.

It is imperative for new practitioners to understand and abide by the many laws which regulate the industry.

Real estate license laws

State real estate license laws comprise the primary body of laws and regulations governing real estate brokerage practice. License laws in each state specify who must obtain a license to practice real estate and set the requirements for obtaining and maintaining the license. License laws also define critical aspects of real estate brokerage, including

- procedures for handling escrow deposits and fees
- procedures for advertising
- guidelines for dealing with clients and customers

State license laws are administered in each state by a **real estate commission**. The commission is charged with administering and enforcing license laws. In addition, the commission may pass regulations that further refine or clarify state statutes.

1 The Real Estate Business Snapshot Review

REAL ESTATE PROFESSIONS

Real estate activities
- create, improve, manage, maintain, demolish, own, regulate, and transfer real properties

Property type specializations
- residential; residential income; office; retail; industrial; farm and ranch; special purpose; land

REAL ESTATE BROKERAGE
- procure a buyer or tenant for an owner or landlord, or vice versa

Forms of specialization
- by property type; geographical area; type of transaction; type of client; by form of business organization; or by form of client relationship

Skills and knowledge
- market conditions; law; financing; marketing; ethics; selling; communications; computer basics; and other skills

PROFESSIONAL ORGANIZATIONS
- promote interests of practitioners and enhance their professional standing

REGULATION AND LICENSING

Regulation of business practices
- all facets of the industry are regulated by federal, state, and local laws; agents must understand relevant laws and adapt business practices accordingly

Real estate license laws
- the primary body of laws and regulations governing the licensure and conduct of real estate brokers and agents

- license laws are administered and enforced under the jurisdiction of the state real estate commission

2 Rights in Real Estate

Real Estate as Property
Real Versus Personal Property
Regulation of Real Property Interests

REAL ESTATE AS PROPERTY

Land
Real estate
Property
Real property rights
Water rights

A simple definition of real estate is that it is air, water, land, and everything affixed to the land. Real estate in the United States may be owned privately by individuals and private entities or publicly by government entities. Private ownership rights in this country are not absolute. The government can impose taxes and restrictions on private ownership rights, and it can take private property away altogether. In addition, other private parties can exert their rights and interests on one's real property. A bank, for example, can take a property if the owner fails to pay a mortgage. A neighbor can claim the right to walk across one's property whether the owner likes it or not, provided he or she has done so for a certain number of years.

In attempting to define real estate, it is essential to understand *what rights and interests parties have in a parcel of real estate*. And to understand real estate rights and interests, one must first recognize the distinctions between:

> ▸ land and real estate
> ▸ real estate and property
> ▸ real property and personal property

Land

The legal concept of land encompasses

> ▸ the surface area of the earth
> ▸ everything beneath the surface of the earth extending downward to its center
> ▸ all *natural* things permanently attached to the earth
> ▸ the air above the surface of the earth extending outward to infinity.

Land, therefore, includes minerals beneath the earth's surface, water on or below the earth's surface, and the air above the surface. In addition, land includes all plants attached to the ground or in the ground, such as trees and grass. A **parcel**, or **tract**, of land is a portion of land delineated by boundaries.

Physical characteristics. Land has three unique physical characteristics: *immobility, indestructibility, and heterogeneity.*

Land is immobile, since a parcel of land cannot be moved from one site to another. In other words, the geographical location of a tract of land is fixed and cannot be changed. One can transport portions of the land such as mined coal, dirt, or cut plants. However, as soon as such elements are detached from the land, they are no longer considered land.

Land is indestructible in the sense that one would have to remove a segment of the planet all the way to the core in order to destroy it. Even then, the portion extending upward to infinity would remain. For the same reason, land is considered to be permanent.

Land is non-homogeneous, since no two parcels of land are exactly the same. Admittedly, two adjacent parcels may be very similar and have the same economic value. However, they are inherently different because each parcel has a unique location.

Real estate

The legal concept of real estate encompasses:

- land
- all *man-made structures* that are "permanently" attached to the land

Real estate therefore includes, in addition to land, such things as fences, streets, buildings, wells, sewers, sidewalks and piers. Such man-made structures attached to the land are called **improvements**. The phrase "permanently attached" refers primarily to one's intention in attaching the item. Obviously, very few if any manmade structures can be permanently attached to the land in the literal sense. But if a person constructs a house with the intention of creating a permanent dwelling, the house is considered real estate. By contrast, if a camper affixes a tent to the land with the intention of moving it to another camp in a week, the tent would not be considered real estate.

Exhibit 2.1 The Legal Concept of Land and Real Estate

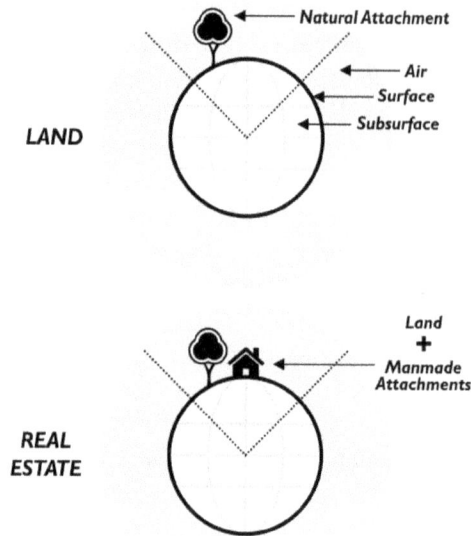

LAND

Natural Attachment

Air
Surface
Subsurface

REAL ESTATE

Land + Manmade Attachments

Property

In common understanding, property is something that is owned by someone. A car is the property of Bill Brown if Bill Brown owns the car. If the item is not owned, it is not property. For example, if a car is abandoned and left to rust in the desert, the car is no longer property, since no one claims ownership. Similarly, the planet Jupiter is not property, since no one owns it.

From a more technical standpoint, property is not only the item that is owned but also a *set of rights to the item enjoyed by the owner*. These rights are commonly known as the "bundle of rights."

Exhibit 2.2 The Bundle of Rights

Possess   Use   Exclude   Transfer   Encumber

In owning property, one has the right to possess and use it as the law allows. The owner has the right to transfer ownership of the item (sell, rent, donate, assign, or bequeath). The owner may also encumber the item by mortgaging it as collateral for debt. Finally, the owner has the right to exclude others from use of the item. In the example of the car, when Bill Brown bought the car, the car became his property: he owned the car itself. At the same time, he also acquired the legal rights to transfer, use, encumber, exclude, and possess the car.

Classifications of property. Our legal system recognizes two classifications of property: *real property* and *personal property*. **Real property** is ownership of real estate and the bundle of rights associated with owning the real estate. **Personal property** is ownership of anything which is not real estate, and the rights associated with owning the personal property item. Items of personal property are also called **chattels** or **personalty**.

Note: since all real estate in the United States is owned by some person, private organization, or government entity, all real estate in the country *is* real property. Given that fact, this text will follow the customary practice of using the two terms interchangeably and synonymously.

Tangible versus intangible property. Real and personal property may be further categorized as **tangible** or **intangible** property. Tangible property is physical, visible, and material. Intangible property is abstract, having no physical existence in itself, other than as evidence of one's ownership interest.

Exhibit 2.3 Tangible vs. Intangible Property

	Tangible	Intangible
Real Property	all types	
Personal Property	boat, car, jewelry	stock certificate, contract, patent

All real estate, by its physical nature, is tangible property. Personal property may be tangible or intangible. Boats, jewelry, coins, appliances, computers, and art work are examples of tangible personal property. Stocks, copyrights, bonds, trademarks, patents, franchises, and listing agreements are examples of intangible personal property.

Real property rights

Real property rights consist of the bundle of rights associated with owning a parcel of real estate. Foremost of these rights is the right of possession.

The *right to use* a property refers to the right to use it in certain ways, such as mining, cultivating, landscaping, razing, and building on the property. The right is subject to the limitations of local zoning and the legality of the use. One's right to use may not infringe on the rights of others to use and enjoy their property. For example, an owner may be restricted from constructing a large pond on her property if in fact the pond would pose flooding and drainage hazards to the next door neighbor.

The *right to transfer* interests in the property includes the right to sell, bequeath, lease, donate, or assign ownership interests. An owner may transfer certain individual rights to the property without transferring total ownership. Also, one may transfer ownership while retaining individual interests. For example, a person may sell mineral rights without selling the right of possession. On the other hand, the owner may convey all rights to the property except the mineral rights.

While all rights are transferrable, the owner can only transfer what the owner in fact possesses. A property seller, for example, cannot sell water rights if there are no water rights attached to the property.

The *right to encumber* the property essentially means the right to mortgage the property as collateral for debt. There may be restrictions to this right, such as a spouse's right to limit the degree to which a homestead may be mortgaged.

The *right to exclude* gives the property owner the legal right to keep others off the property and to prosecute trespassers.

The bundle of real property rights also applies separately to the individual components of real estate: the air, the surface, and the subsurface. An owner can, for example, transfer subsurface rights without transferring air rights. Similarly, an owner can rent air space without encumbering surface or subsurface rights. This might occur in a city where adjoining building owners want to construct a walkway over a third owner's lot. Such owners would have to acquire the air rights for the walkway. If the city wants to construct a subway through the owner's subsurface, the city has to obtain the subsurface rights to do so.

An ordinary lease is a common example of the transfer of a portion of one's bundle of rights. The owner relinquishes the right to possess portions of the surface, perhaps a building, in return for rent. The tenant enjoys the rights to possess and use the building over the term of the lease, after which these rights revert to the landlord. During the lease term, the tenant has no rights to the property's subsurface or airspace other than what the building occupies. Further, the tenant does not enjoy any of the other rights in the bundle of rights: he cannot encumber the property or transfer it. To a limited degree, the tenant may exclude persons from the property, but he may not exclude the legal owner.

Surface rights. Surface rights apply to the real estate contained within the surface boundaries of the parcel. This includes the ground, all natural things affixed to the ground, and all improvements. Surface rights also include water rights.

Air rights. Air rights apply to the space above the surface boundaries of the parcel, as delineated by imaginary vertical lines extended to infinity. Since the advent of aviation, air rights have been curtailed to allow aircraft to fly over one's property, provided the overflights do not interfere with the owner's use and enjoyment of the property. The issue of violation of air rights for the benefit of air transportation is an ongoing battle between airlines, airports, and nearby property owners.

Subsurface rights. Subsurface rights apply to land beneath the surface of the real estate parcel extending from its surface boundaries downward to the center of the earth. Notable subsurface rights are the rights to extract mineral and gas deposits and subsurface water from the water table.

Water rights

Water rights basically concern the rights to own and use water found in lakes, streams, rivers, and the ocean. In addition, they determine where parcel boundaries can be fixed with respect to adjoining bodies of water. What water rights does an owner of a property that contains or adjoins a body of water enjoy? The answer depends on three variables:

> ▸ whether the state controls the water
> ▸ whether the water is moving
> ▸ whether the water is navigable

Doctrine of Prior Appropriation. Since water is a resource necessary for survival, some states -- particularly those where water is scarce -- have taken the legal position that the state owns and controls all bodies of water. Called the Doctrine of Prior Appropriation, this position requires that property owners obtain permits for use of water. If a proposed usage is reasonable and beneficial, the state will grant a permit which, over time, can attach to the property of the permit holder. If a state does not operate under prior appropriation, it operates under the common law doctrines of *littoral rights* and *riparian rights.*

Littoral rights. Littoral rights concern properties abutting bodies of water that are not moving, such as lakes and seas. Owners of properties abutting a navigable, non-moving body of water enjoy the littoral right of use, but do not own the water nor the land beneath the water. Ownership extends to the high-water mark of the body of water.

Exhibit 2.4 Littoral Rights

Oceans, Seas and Lakes

The legal premise underlying the definition of littoral rights is that a lake or sea is a *navigable body of water, therefore, public property* owned by the state. By contrast, a body of water entirely contained within the boundaries of an owner's property is not navigable. In such a case, the owner would own the water as well as unrestricted rights of usage.

Littoral rights attach to the property. When the property is sold, the littoral rights transfer with the property to the new owner.

Riparian rights. Riparian rights concern properties abutting moving water such as streams and rivers. If a property abuts a stream or river, the owner's riparian rights are determined by whether the water *is navigable or not navigable.* If the property abuts a non-navigable stream, the owner enjoys unrestricted use of the water and *owns the land beneath the stream to the stream's midpoint.* If the waterway in question is navigable, the waterway is considered to be a public easement. In such a case, the owner's property extends *to the water's edge* as opposed to the midpoint of the waterway. The state owns the land beneath the water.

Exhibit 2.5 Riparian Rights

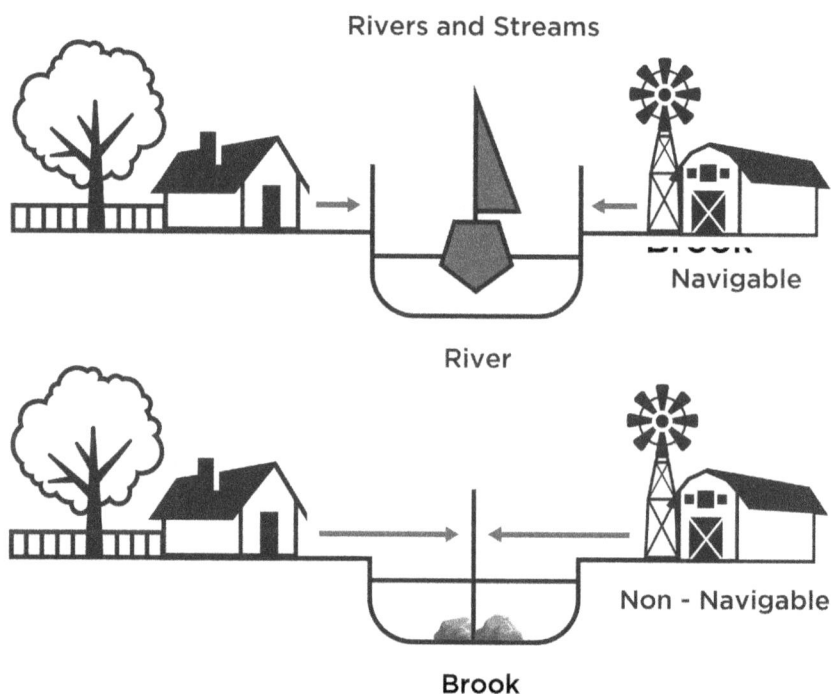

One's riparian rights to use flowing water are subject to the conditions that:

- ▸ the usage is reasonable and does not infringe on the riparian rights of other owners downstream
- ▸ the usage does not pollute the water
- ▸ the usage does not impede or alter the course of the water flow.

Like littoral rights, riparian rights attach to the property.

REAL VERSUS PERSONAL PROPERTY

Fixtures
Differentiation criteria
Trade fixtures
Emblements
Factory-built housing
Conversion

In conveying real property, it is vitally important to recognize the distinctions between personal property and the real property that is to be conveyed. Confusion can arise because items of property *may be either personal property or real property, depending on circumstances.*

The primary criterion for distinguishing real from personal property is whether the item is permanently attached to the land or to structures attached to the land. For example, a tree growing in one's yard is an item of real property. However, when the owner cuts the tree down, it becomes personal property. Similarly, a swimming pool pump on a shelf in the owner's garage is personal property. When it is installed with the rest of the pool, it becomes real property.

While the "attachment" criterion is pivotal in distinguishing between real and personal property, there are other tests to be applied. In addition, the attachment rule is subject to exceptions.

Fixtures

A personal property item that has been converted to real property by attachment to real estate is called a fixture. Typical examples are chandeliers, toilets, water pumps, septic tanks, and window shutters.

The owner of real property inherently owns all fixtures belonging to the real property. When the owner sells the real property, the buyer acquires rights to all fixtures. Fixtures not included in the sale must be itemized and excluded in the sale contract.

Differentiation criteria

In the event that the attachment criterion is insufficient to determine whether an article of property is real or personal, a court may apply one or more of the following additional criteria.

Intention. One's original intention can override the test of movability in determining whether an item is a fixture or not. If someone attached an item to real property, yet intended to remove it after a period of time, the article may be deemed personal property. If a person intended an article to be a fixture, even though the item is easily removable, the article may be deemed a fixture.

For example, an apartment renter installs an alarm system, fully intending to remove the system upon lease expiration. Here, the alarm system would be considered personal property.

Adaptation. If an item is uniquely adapted to the property, or the property is custom-designed to accommodate the item, it may be deemed real property whether the item is easily removable or not. House keys, a garbage compactor, and a removable door screen are examples.

Functionality. If an item is vital to the operation of the building, it may be deemed a fixture, even though perhaps easily removable. Window-unit air conditioners and detachable solar panels are possible examples.

Relationship of parties. If a tenant installs a fixture in order to conduct business, the fixture may be considered a trade fixture, which is the tenant's personal property.

Sale or lease contract provisions. In a sale or lease transaction, the listing of an item in the contract as a personal property item or a fixture overrides all other considerations. Unless otherwise stated as exceptions, all fixtures are included in the sale. For example, if a sale contract stipulates that the carpeting is not included in the sale, it becomes a personal property item. If the carpeting is not mentioned, it goes with the property, since it is attached to the floor of the building.

Trade fixtures

Trade fixtures, or **chattel fixtures,** are items of a tenant's *personal property* that the tenant has temporarily affixed to a landlord's real property in order to conduct business. Trade fixtures may be detached and removed before or upon surrender of the leased premises. Should the tenant fail to remove a trade fixture, it may become the property of the landlord through *accession*. Thereafter, the fixture is considered real property.

Examples of trade fixtures include a grocer's food freezers, a merchant's clothes racks, a tavern owner's bar, a dairy's milking machines, and a printer's printing press.

Emblements

Growing plants, including agricultural crops, may be either real property or personal property. Plants and crops that grow naturally without requiring anyone's labor or machinery are considered real property.

Plants and crops requiring human intervention and labor are called **emblements**. Emblements, despite their attachment to land, are considered personal property. If an emblement is owned by a tenant farmer, the tenant has the right to the harvested crop whether the tenant's lease is active or expired. If the tenant grew the crop, it is his or her personal property, and the landlord cannot take it.

Factory-built housing

Factory-built housing consists of dwelling units constructed off-site and transported to and assembled on a building site. The category also includes readily moveable housing of the type that can be relocated from place to place, once known by the term **mobile home.** The National Manufactured Housing Construction and Safety Standards Act of 1976 defined the types of factory-built housing and retired the mobile home designation. **Manufactured housing** is factory-built housing that conforms to HUD standards. Factory-built housing may be considered real property or personal property, depending on whether it is permanently affixed to the ground, and according to state law. Real estate practitioners should understand the local laws before selling any kind of factory-built housing.

Conversion
The classification of an item of property as real or personal is not necessarily fixed. The classification may be changed by the process of conversion. **Severance** is the conversion of real property to personal property by detaching it from the real estate, such as by cutting down a tree, detaching a door from a shed, or removing an antenna from a roof. **Affixing**, or attachment, is the act of converting personal property to real property by attaching it to the real estate, such as by assembling a pile of bricks into a barbecue pit, or constructing a boat dock from wood planks.

Exhibit 2.6 Real Property vs. Personal Property

Real Property	Personal Property
land fixtures attachments conversions by affixing	trade fixtures emblements conversions by severance

REGULATION OF REAL PROPERTY INTERESTS

Areas of regulation
Federal regulation
State regulation
Local regulation
Judicial regulation

Although the Constitution guarantees private ownership of real estate, laws and regulations at every level of government qualify and limit individual real property ownership and the bundle of rights associated with it.

Areas of regulation
Government entities regulate the following aspects of real property interests:

▶ the bundle of rights: possession, usage, transfer, encumbering and exclusion
▶ legal descriptions
▶ financing
▶ insurance
▶ inheritance
▶ taxation

Regulation takes the form of federal and state laws and regulations; county and local ordinances and codes; and court decisions in the judicial system.

Federal regulation
In regulating real property rights, the federal government is primarily concerned with broad standards of real property usage, natural disaster, land description, and discrimination.

Federal agencies such as the Federal Housing Administration promote and regulate home ownership. The Environmental Protection Agency establishes protective usage restrictions and guidelines for dealing with hazardous materials and other environmental concerns. Federal flood insurance legislation requires certain homeowners to obtain flood insurance policies. Federal laws such as the Federal Fair Housing Act of 1968 prohibit discrimination in housing based on race, religion, color, or national origin. Such laws as the Americans with Disabilities Act prescribe design and accessibility standards.

The federal government does not levy real estate taxes.

State regulation

State governments are the primary regulatory entities of the real estate business. State governments establish real estate license laws and qualifications. In addition, state governments have established real estate commissions to administer license laws and oversee activities of licensees.

State governments also exert regional influence in the usage and environmental control of real estate within the state. Relevant state laws might include laws relating to flood zones, waste disposal, drainage control, shore preservation, and pollution standards.

States also play a role in defining how real property may be owned, transferred, encumbered, and inherited. For example, in some states a mortgaged property becomes the legal property of the lender until the mortgage loan is paid.

States have the power to levy real estate taxes but generally pass this power to local government.

Local regulation

County and local government regulation focuses on land use control, control of improvements, and taxation. Land use regulations and ordinances control how all property within the jurisdiction may be developed, improved, demolished, and managed. County and local governments have the power to zone land, take over land for the public good, issue building permits, and establish the rules for all development projects.

County and local governments, along with school districts and other local jurisdictions, have the power to levy real estate taxes.

Judicial regulation

The judicial system exerts an influence on real estate ownership and use through decisions based on case law and common law, as distinguished from statutory law. Case law consists of decisions based on judicial precedent. Common law is the collective body of law deriving from custom and generally accepted practice in society.

Exhibit 2.7 Regulation of Real Property Interests

Federal	Constitution	Establishes absolute right of private ownership of real estate Prohibits federal government from levying real property taxes
	Laws	Create, regulate real estate-related agencies Prohibit discrimination Create standards for legal descriptions of real estate Establish environmental standards for all property Establish standards for protecting interests of handicapped people
	Agencies	Establish mortgage lending standards Establish housing construction standards Establish environmental standards
State	Constitution	May establish right to levy tax; or may delegate right to counties and municipalities
	Laws	Regulate real estate licensing Establish broad usage standards Define, qualify ownership rights
	Agencies	Regulate practitioners, administer real estate license laws
Local	Laws	Create and enforce real estate taxation Control land usage over specific parcels of land
Courts	Common law	Regulates real estate ownership and usage according to customary and accepted practices
	Case law	Regulates real estate ownership and usage according to prior court decisions

2 Rights and Interests in Real Estate
Snapshot Review

REAL ESTATE AS PROPERTY
- Constitution guarantees private ownership of real estate; ownership rights not absolute; others may exert claims against one's property

Land
- surface, all natural things attached to it, subsurface, and air above the surface; unique aspects: immobile, indestructible, heterogeneous

Real estate
- land plus all permanently attached man-made structures, called improvements

Property
- something that is owned by someone and the associated rights of ownership
- the bundle of rights: possession, use, transfer, exclusion, and encumbrance
- property is real or personal, tangible or intangible

Real property rights
- any of the bundle of rights, applied to airspace (air rights), surface (surface rights), and subsurface (subsurface rights)

Water rights
- Doctrine of Prior Appropriation: state controls water usage; grants usage permits
- littoral rights: abutting property owners own land to high water mark; may use, but state owns underlying land
- riparian rights: if navigable, abutting property owners own land to water's edge; may use, but state owns underlying land; if not navigable, owner owns land to midpoint of waterway

REAL VS PERSONAL PROPERTY
- an item may be real or personal property depending on the "attachment" criterion and other circumstances

Fixtures
- real property converted from personal property by attachment to real estate

Differentiation criteria
- intention; adaptation; functionality; relationship of parties; contract provisions

Trade fixtures
- personal property items temporarily attached to real estate in order to conduct business; to be removed at some point

Emblements
- plants or crops considered personal property since human intervention is necessary for planting, harvesting

Factory-built housing
- housing pre-built off-site; includes mobile homes; real or personal depending on attachment to land

Conversion
- transforming real to personal property through severance, or personal to real property through affixing

REGULATION OF REAL PROPERTY INTERESTS

Federal regulation
- grants overall rights of ownership; controls broad usage standards, discrimination

State regulation
- governs the real estate business; sets regional usage standards

Local regulation
- levies real estate taxes; controls specific usage

Judicial regulation
- applies case law and common law to disputes

3 Interests and Estates

Interests and Estates in Land
Freehold Estates
Leasehold Estates

INTERESTS AND ESTATES IN LAND

Interests
Estates in land

Interests

An interest in real estate is *ownership of any combination of the bundle of rights* to real property, including the rights to

- possess
- use
- transfer
- encumber
- exclude

Undivided interest. An undivided interest is an owner's interest in a property in which two or more parties share ownership. The terms "undivided" and "indivisible" signify that the owner's interest is in a fractional part of the entire estate, not in a physical portion of the real property itself. If two co-owners have an undivided equal interest, one owner may not lay claim to the northern half of the property for his or her exclusive use.

Examples of interests include:

- an owner who enjoys the complete bundle of rights
- a tenant who temporarily enjoys the right to use and exclude
- a lender who enjoys the right to encumber the property over the life of a mortgage loan
- a repairman who encumbers the property when the owner fails to pay for services
- a buyer who prevents an owner from selling the property to another party under the terms of the sale contract
- a mining company which temporarily owns the right to extract minerals from the property's subsurface
- a local municipality which has the right to control how an owner uses the property
- a utility company which claims access to the property in accordance with an easement

Interests differ according to

- how long a person may enjoy the interest
- what portion of the land, air, or subsurface the interest applies to
- whether the interest is public or private
- whether the interest includes legal ownership of the property

Exhibit 3.1 Interests in Real Estate

```
┌──────────────┐     ┌──────────────────────┐
│  Possession  │     │    Non-possession    │
└──────┬───────┘     └──────┬──────────┬────┘
       │                    │          │
┌──────┴───────┐     ┌──────┴──────┐ ┌─┴────────┐
│    Estate    │     │ Encumbrance │ │  Public  │
│              │     │             │ │ Interest │
└──────────────┘     └─────────────┘ └──────────┘
```

Interests are principally distinguished by whether they include possession. If the interest-holder enjoys the right of possession, the party is considered to have an **estate in land**, or, familiarly an estate. If a private interest-holder does not have the right to possess, the interest is an **encumbrance.** If the interest-holder is not private, such as a government entity, and does not have the right to possess, the interest is some form of *public interest*.

An encumbrance enables a non-owning party to restrict the owner's bundle of rights. Tax liens, mortgages, easements, and encroachments are examples.

Public entities may own or lease real estate, in which case they enjoy an estate in land. However, government entities also have non-possessory interests in real estate which act to control land use for the public good within the entity's jurisdiction. The prime example of public interest is **police power**, or the right of the local or county government to **zone**. Another example of public interest is the right to acquire ownership through the power of eminent domain.

Estates in land

An estate in land is an interest that includes the right of possession. Depending on the length of time one may enjoy the right to possess the estate, the relationships of the parties owning the estate, and specific interests held in the estate, an estate is a freehold or a leasehold estate.

Exhibit 3.2 Estates in Land

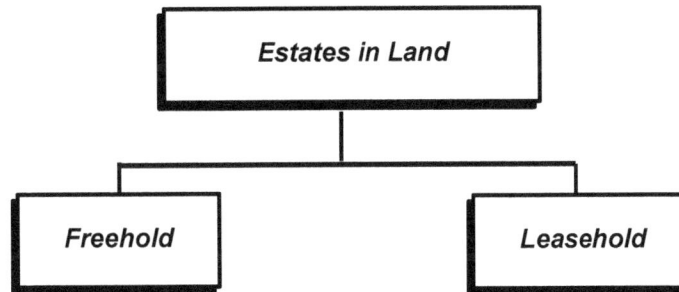

```
          ┌─────────────────────┐
          │   Estates in Land   │
          └──────────┬──────────┘
             ┌────────┴────────┐
     ┌───────────────┐  ┌───────────────┐
     │   Freehold    │  │   Leasehold   │
     └───────────────┘  └───────────────┘
```

In a **freehold estate**, the duration of the owner's rights cannot be determined: the rights may endure for a lifetime, for less than a lifetime, or for generations beyond the owner's lifetime.

A **leasehold estate** is distinguished by its specific duration, as represented by the lease term.

Ownership of a freehold estate is commonly equated with ownership of the property, whereas ownership of a leasehold estate is not so considered because the leaseholder's rights are temporary.

Both leasehold and freehold estates are referred to as **tenancies**. The owner of the freehold estate is the **freehold tenant**, and the renter, or lessee, is the **leasehold tenant**.

FREEHOLD ESTATES

Fee simple estate
Life estate
Conventional life estate
Legal life estate

Freehold estates differ primarily according to the duration of the estate and what happens to the estate when the owner dies. A freehold estate of potentially unlimited duration is a fee simple estate: an estate limited to the life of the owner is a life estate.

Exhibit 3.3 Freehold Estates

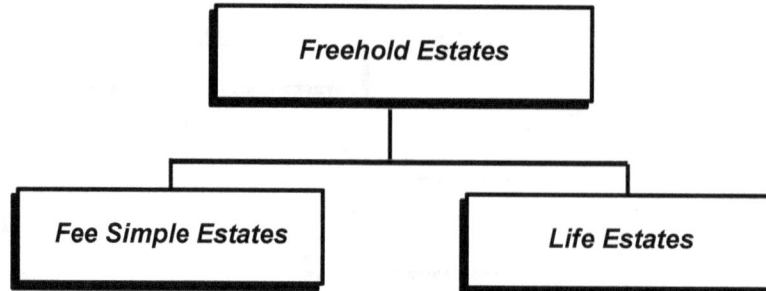

```
                    ┌─────────────────────┐
                    │  Freehold Estates   │
                    └──────────┬──────────┘
                    ┌──────────┴──────────┐
         ┌──────────────────┐   ┌──────────────────┐
         │ Fee Simple Estates│   │   Life Estates   │
         └──────────────────┘   └──────────────────┘
```

Fee simple estate

The **fee simple** freehold estate is the *highest form of ownership interest* one can acquire in real estate. It includes the complete bundle of rights, and the tenancy is unlimited, with certain exceptions indicated below. The fee simple interest is also called the "fee interest," or simply, the "fee." The owner of the fee simple interest is called the **fee tenan**t.

Fee simple estates, like all estates, remain subject to government restrictions and private interests.

There are two forms of fee simple estate: **absolute** and **defeasible**.

Exhibit 3.4 Fee Simple Estates

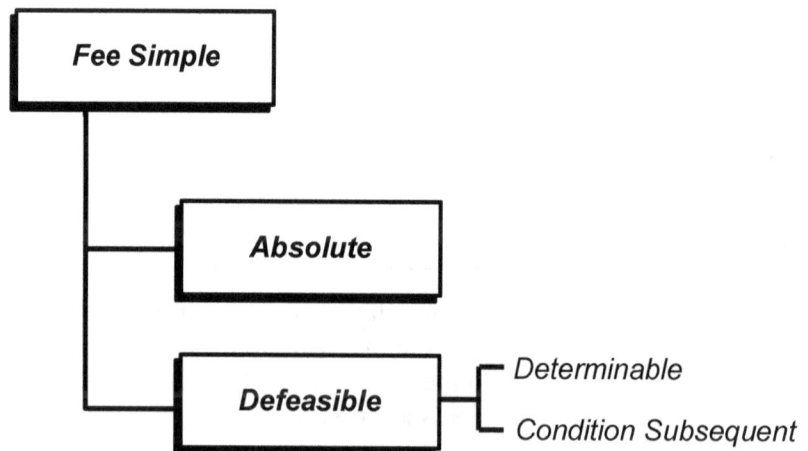

```
    ┌──────────────┐
    │ Fee Simple   │
    └──────┬───────┘
           │        ┌──────────────┐
           ├────────│   Absolute   │
           │        └──────────────┘
           │        ┌──────────────┐   ┌─ Determinable
           └────────│  Defeasible  │───┤
                    └──────────────┘   └─ Condition Subsequent
```

Fee Simple Absolute. The fee simple absolute estate is a perpetual estate that is *not conditioned by stipulated or restricted uses.* It may also be freely passed on to heirs. For these reasons, the fee simple absolute estate is the most desirable estate that can be obtained in residential real estate. It is also the most common.

Fee Simple Defeasible. The defeasible fee estate is perpetual, provided the usage *conforms to stated conditions.* Essential characteristics are:

▶ the property must be used for a certain purpose or under certain conditions

▶ if the use changes or if prohibited conditions are present, the estate reverts to the previous grantor of the estate.

The two types of fee simple defeasible are **determinable** and **condition subsequent**.

Determinable. The deed to the determinable estate states usage limitations. If the restrictions are violated, the estate automatically reverts to the grantor or heirs.

Condition subsequent. If any condition is violated, the previous owner may repossess the property. However, reversion of the estate is not automatic: the grantor must re-take physical possession within a certain time frame.

Life estate

A life estate is a freehold estate that is limited in duration to the life of the owner or other named person. Upon the death of the owner or other named individual, *the estate passes to the original owner or another named party.* The holder of a life estate is called the **life tenant**.

The distinguishing characteristics of the life estate are:

▶ the owner enjoys full ownership rights during the estate period

▶ holders of the future interest own either a reversionary or a remainder interest

▶ the estate may be created by agreement between private parties, or it may be created by law under prescribed circumstances.

Remainder. If a life estate names a third party to receive title to the property upon termination of the life estate, the party enjoys a future interest called a remainder interest or a remainder estate. The holder of a remainder interest is called a **remainderman**.

Reversion. If no remainder estate is established, the estate reverts to the original owner or the owner's heirs. In this situation, the original owner retains a reversionary interest or estate.

The two types of life estates are the **conventional** and the **legal** life estate.

Exhibit 3.5 Life Estates

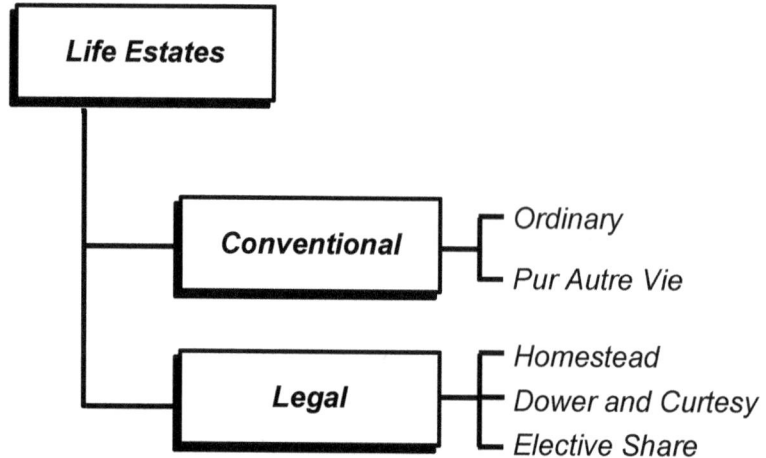

```
┌──────────────┐
│ Life Estates │
└──────┬───────┘
       │
       │        ┌──────────────┐      ┌─ Ordinary
       ├────────│ Conventional │──────┤
       │        └──────────────┘      └─ Pur Autre Vie
       │
       │        ┌──────────────┐      ┌─ Homestead
       └────────│    Legal     │──────┼─ Dower and Curtesy
                └──────────────┘      └─ Elective Share
```

Conventional life estate

A conventional life estate is created by grant from a fee simple property owner to the grantee, the life tenant. Following the termination of the estate, rights pass to a remainderman or revert to the previous owner.

During the life estate period, the owner enjoys all ownership rights, provided he or she does not infringe on the rights of the remainder or reversion interest holders, such as by damaging the property or jeopardizing its value. Should such actions occur, holders of the future interest may take legal action against the property owners.

The two types of conventional life estate are the **ordinary** and the **pur autre vie** life estate.

Exhibit 3.6 Conventional Life Estates

	Ordinary Life Estate	Pur Autre Vie
With reversion	duration: owner's life reverts to grantor	duration: another's life reverts to grantor
With remainder	duration: owner's life reverts to another	duration: another's life reverts to another

Ordinary life estate. An ordinary life estate *ends with the death of the life estate owner* and may pass back to the original owners or their heirs (reversion) or to a named third party (remainder).

For example, John King grants a life estate in a property to Mary Brown, to endure over Mary's lifetime. John establishes that when Mary dies, the property will revert to himself.

Pur autre vie. A pur autre vie life estate endures over the lifetime of a third person, after which the property passes from the tenant holder to the original grantor (reversion) or a third party (remainderman).

For example, Yvonne grants a life estate to Ryan, to endure over the lifetime of Yvonne's husband Steve. Upon Steve's death, Yvonne establishes that her mother, Rose, will receive the property.

Legal life estate

A legal life estate is *created by state law* as opposed to being created by a property owner's agreement. Provisions vary from state to state. The focus of a legal life estate is defining and protecting the property rights of surviving family members upon the death of the husband or wife.

The major forms of legal life estate are the **homestead**, **dower and curtesy**, and **elective share**.

Homestead. A homestead is one's principal residence. Homestead laws protect family members against losing their homes to general creditors attempting to collect on debts.

Homestead laws generally provide that:

- ▸ all or portions of one's homestead *are exempt* from a forced sale executed for the collection of general debts (judgment liens). The various states place different limits on this exemption.

- ▸ tax debts, seller financing debt, debts for home improvement, and mortgage debt are *not exempt*

- ▸ the family *must occupy* the homestead

- ▸ the homestead interest *cannot be conveyed by one spouse*; both spouses must sign the deed conveying homestead property

- ▸ the homestead exemption and restrictions *endure over the life* of the head of the household, and pass on to children under legal age. State laws define specifically how the interest transfers upon the death of the household head

- ▸ homestead interests in a property *are extinguished* if the property is sold or abandoned

- ▸ in some states the exemption is automatic; in others, homeowners must file for the exemption.

The homestead exemption from certain debts should not be confused with the *homestead tax* exemption, which exempts a portion of the property's value from taxation.

Dower and curtesy. Dower is a wife's life estate interest in the husband's property. When the husband dies, the wife can make a claim to portions of the decedent's property. Curtesy is the identical right enjoyed by the husband in a deceased wife's property. Property acquired under dower laws is owned by the surviving spouse for the duration of his or her lifetime.

To transfer property within dower and curtesy states, the husband (or wife) must obtain a release of the dower interest from the other spouse in order to convey clear title to another party. If both parties sign the conveyance, the dower right is automatically extinguished.

Dower and curtesy laws have been largely supplanted by community property laws and elective share laws.

Elective share. Elective share is a state-level statute enabling a surviving spouse to make a minimum claim to the deceased spouse's real and personal property in place of the provisions for such property in the decedent's will.

For example, if a husband's will excludes the wife from any property inheritance, the wife may, upon the husband's death make the elective share claim.

Elective share laws generally provide that:

> ▸ the surviving spouse is entitled to a percent of the deceased spouse's property, excepting homestead property and property the decedent owned exclusively
> ▸ the surviving spouse must file for the elective share within a limited time period
> ▸ if the spouse fails to file, the estate passes on according to the will or the state's laws of descent
> ▸ the elective share right pertains only to the surviving spouse and is not transferrable.

LEASEHOLD ESTATES

Estate for years
Estate from period-to-period
Estate at will
Estate at sufferance

A leasehold estate, or **leasehold**, arises from the execution of a lease by a fee owner- the **lessor,** or **landlord**-- to a **lessee**, or **tenant**. Since tenants do not own the fee interest, a leasehold estate is technically an item of personal property for the tenant.

Leasehold tenants are entitled to possess and use the leased premises during the lease term in the manner prescribed in the lease. They also have restricted rights to exclusion.

Estate for years

The estate for years is a leasehold estate for a definite period of time, with a beginning date and an ending date. The estate for years may endure for any length of term. At the end of the term, the estate automatically terminates, without any requirement of notice.

For example, a landlord grants a tenant a three-year lease. After the three years, the leasehold terminates, and the landlord may re-possess the premises, renew the lease, or lease to someone else.

Estate from period-to-period

In an estate from period-to-period, also called a **periodic tenancy**, the tenancy period automatically renews for an indefinite period of time, subject to timely payment of rent. At the end of a tenancy period, if the landlord accepts another regular payment of rent, the leasehold is considered to be renewed for another period.

For example, a two-year lease expires, and the landlord grants a six-month lease that is automatically renewable, provided the monthly rent is received on time. At the end of the six months, the tenant pays, and the landlord accepts another monthly rent payment. The acceptance of the rent automatically extends the leasehold for another six months.

The most common form of periodic tenancy is the month-to-month lease, which may exist without any written agreement.

Either party may terminate a periodic tenancy by giving proper notice to the other party. Proper notice is defined by state law.

Estate at will

The estate at will, also called a **tenancy at will**, has no definite expiration date and hence no "renewal" cycle. The landlord and tenant agree that the tenancy will have no specified termination date, provided rent is paid on time and other lease conditions are met.

For example, a son leases a house to his father and mother "forever," or until they want to move.

The estate at will is terminated by proper notice, or by the death of either party.

Estate at sufferance

In an estate at sufferance, a tenant occupies the premises without consent of the landlord or other legal agreement with the landlord. Usually such an estate involves a tenant who fails to vacate at the expiration of the lease, continuing occupancy without any right to do so.

For example, a tenant violates the provisions of a lease and is evicted. The tenant protests and refuses to leave despite the eviction order.

3   Interests and Estates
Snapshot Review

INTERESTS AND ESTATES IN LAND

Interests
- any combination of bundle of rights
- estates, encumbrances, police powers

Estates in land
- include right of possession; also called tenancies
- leaseholds: of limited duration
- freeholds: duration is not necessarily limited

FREEHOLD ESTATES
- implies "ownership" in contrast to leasehold

Fee simple estate
- also "fee"; most common form of estate; not limited by one's lifetime
- fee simple absolute: highest form of ownership interest
- defeasible: can revert to previous owner for violation of conditions

Life estate
- fee estate passes to another upon death of a named party
- remainder: interest of a named party to receive estate after holder's death
- reversion: interest of previous owner to receive estate after holder's death

Conventional life estate
- full ownership interest, limited to lifetime of life tenant or another named party
- created by agreements between parties
- ordinary: on death of life tenant, passes to remainderman or previous owner
- pur autre vie: on death of another; passes to remainderman or previous owner

Legal life estate
- automatic creation of estate through operation of law
- designed to protect family survivors
- homestead: rights to one's principal residence
- laws protect homestead from certain creditors
- dower and curtesy: a life estate interest of a widow(er) in the real property
- elective share: right to claim deceased spouse's property in lieu of will

LEASEHOLD ESTATES
- non-ownership possessory estates of limited duration

Estate for years
- specific, stated duration, per lease

Estate from period-to-period
- lease term renews automatically upon acceptance of monthly or periodic rent

Estate at will
- tenancy for indefinite period subject to rent payment; cancelable with notice

Estate at sufferance
- tenancy against landlord's will and without an agreement

4 Ownership

Sole Ownership
Co-Ownership
Estates in Trust
Ownership by Business Entities
Condominiums
Cooperatives
Time-Shares

There are numerous ways of holding ownership of a freehold estate according to how many parties share the ownership and how they share it. The primary distinction is between ownership by a single party, and ownership by multiple parties. Various trust structures enable an owner to employ a trustee to hold and manage an estate. Condominiums, cooperatives and time-shares are hybrids that combine several forms of ownership.

SOLE OWNERSHIP

Tenancy in severalty

Tenancy in severalty If *a single party owns* the fee or life estate, the ownership is a **tenancy in severalty**. Synonyms are **sole ownership**, **ownership in severalty**, and **estate in severalty**. When the would-be sole owner is a husband or wife, state laws may require homestead, dower or elective share rights to be released to allow ownership free and clear of any marriage-related claims.

The estate of a deceased tenant in severalty passes to heirs by probate.

CO-OWNERSHIP

Tenancy in common
Joint tenancy
Tenancy by the entireties
Community property
Tenancy in partnership

If more than one person, or a legal entity such as a corporation, owns an estate in land, the estate is held in some form of co-ownership. Co-owners are also called **cotenants**.

Tenancy in common

The tenancy in common, also known as the **estate in common,** is the most common form of co-ownership when the owners are not married. The defining characteristics are:

- two or more owners
- identical rights
- interests individually owned
- electable ownership shares
- no survivorship
- no unity of time

Two or more owners. Any number of people may be co-tenants in a single property.

Identical rights. Co-tenants share an indivisible interest in the estate, i.e., all have equal rights to possess and use the property subject to the rights of the other cotenants. No co-tenant may claim to own any physical portion of the property exclusively. They share what is called undivided possession or unity of possession.

Interests individually owned. All tenants in common have distinct and separable ownership of their respective interests. Co-tenants may sell, encumber, or transfer their interests without obstruction or consent from the other owners. (A co-tenant may not, however, encumber the entire property.)

Electable ownership shares. Tenants in common determine among themselves what share of the estate each party will own. For example, three co-tenants may own 40%, 35%, and 25% interests in a property, respectively. In the absence of stated ownership shares, it is assumed that each has a share equal to that of the others.

No survivorship. A deceased co-tenant's estate passes by probate to the decedent's heirs and devisees rather than to the other tenants in common. Any number of heirs can share in the ownership of the willed tenancy.

No unity of time. It is not necessary for tenants in common to acquire their interests at the same time. A new co-tenant may enter into a pre-existing tenancy in common.

The following exhibit illustrates how tenants in common may transfer ownership interests to other parties by sale or will.

Exhibit 4.1 Tenancy in Common

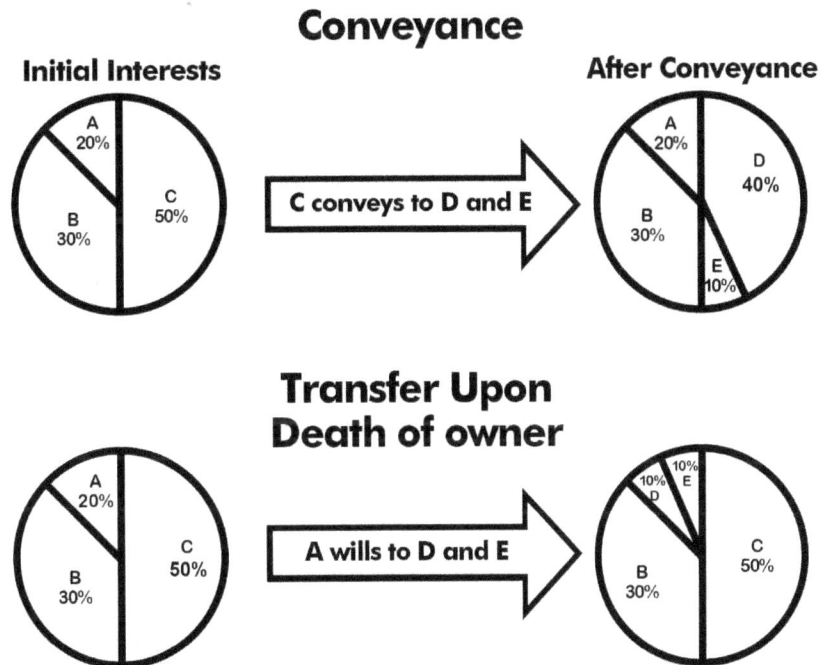

Conveyance

Initial Interests

After Conveyance

C conveys to D and E

Transfer Upon Death of owner

A wills to D and E

The exhibit shows three owners of a property as tenants in common: A owns 20%, B owns 30%, and C owns 50%. C decides to sell 4/5 of his interest to D and 1/5 to E. D's interest in the estate will be 40% (4/5 times 50%), and E's will be 10% (1/5 times 50%). Both new tenants are tenants in common with A and B. Note that any owner may sell any portion of his or her interest to other owners or outside parties.

The second part of the exhibit shows how, when co-owner A dies, she might bequeath her 20% share of the ownership to heirs D and E equally. In such a case, the heirs would each acquire a 10% share of ownership as tenants in common with B and C.

Joint tenancy

In a joint tenancy, two or more persons collectively own a property as if they were a single person. Rights and interests are indivisible and equal: each has a shared interest in the whole property which cannot be divided up. Joint tenants may only convey their interests to outside parties as tenant-in-common interests. One cannot convey a joint tenant interest.

The defining characteristics and requirements of joint tenancy are:

- unity of ownership
- equal ownership
- transfer of interest
- survivorship

Unity of ownership. Whereas tenants in common hold separate title to their individual interests, joint tenants together hold a single title to the property.

Equal ownership. Joint tenants own equal shares in the property, without exception. If there are four co-tenants, each owns 25% of the property. If there are ten co-tenants, each owns 10%.

Transfer of interest. A joint tenant may transfer his or her interest in the property to an outside party, but only as a tenancy in common interest. Whoever acquires the interest co-owns the property as a tenant in common with the other joint tenants. The remaining joint tenants continue to own an undivided interest in the property, less the new cotenant's share.

Survivorship. In most states, joint tenants enjoy rights of survivorship: if a joint tenant dies, all interests and rights pass to the surviving joint tenants free from any claims of creditors or heirs.

In other states, joint tenancy does not inherently include survivorship; survivorship must be expressly stated to be effected on transfer.

When only one joint tenant survives, the survivor's interest becomes an estate in severalty, and the joint tenancy is terminated. The estate will be then probated upon the severalty owner's death.

The survivorship feature of joint tenancy presents an advantage to tenancy in common, in that interests pass without probate proceedings. On the other hand, joint tenants relinquish any ability to will their interest to parties outside of the tenancy.

Exhibit 4.2 Joint Tenancy

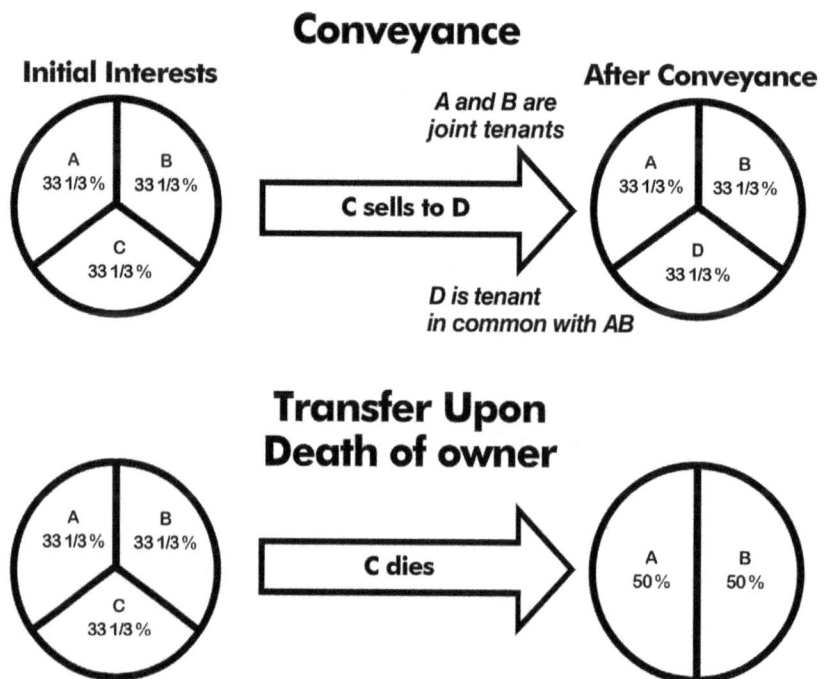

Conveyance

Initial Interests

A 33 1/3% B 33 1/3% C 33 1/3%

A and B are joint tenants

C sells to D

D is tenant in common with AB

After Conveyance

A 33 1/3% B 33 1/3% D 33 1/3%

Transfer Upon Death of owner

A 33 1/3% B 33 1/3% C 33 1/3%

C dies

A 50% B 50%

The exhibit shows three parties, A, B and C, who acquired a property as joint tenants. By definition, each owns a one-third share. If C sells to D, A and B automatically become joint tenants of two-thirds of the property. D becomes a tenant in common with A and B. D's interest will pass to her heirs upon her death.

If C dies, A and B receive equal shares of C's estate, making the remaining shares an equal 50%. If B then dies, A acquires the whole estate and becomes the sole owner. This event terminates the joint tenancy estate, and it becomes an estate in severalty.

Creation of joint tenancy. To create a joint tenancy, all owners must acquire the property at the same time, use the same deed, acquire equal interests, and share in equal rights of possession. These are referred to as the **four unities**.

> ▶ **Unity of time**
>
> all parties must acquire the joint interest at the same time
>
> ▶ **Unity of title**
>
> all parties must acquire the property in the same deed of conveyance
>
> ▶ **Unity of interest**
>
> all parties must receive equal undivided interests
>
> ▶ **Unity of possession**
>
> all parties must receive the same rights of possession

In most states, the conveyance must name the parties as joint tenants with rights of survivorship. Otherwise, and in the absence of clear intent of the parties, the estate will be considered a tenancy in common. In addition, a joint tenancy can only be created by agreement between parties, and not by operation of law.

In some states, a severalty owner may create a joint tenancy with other parties without the presence of the four unities by deeding the property to himself or herself and other parties as joint tenants.

Termination by partition suit. A partition suit can terminate a joint tenancy or a tenancy in common. Foreclosure and bankruptcy can also terminate these estates.

A partition suit is a legal avenue for an owner who wants to dispose of his or her interest against the wishes of other co-owners. The suit petitions the court to divide, or **partition**, the property physically, according to the owner's respective rights and interests. If this is not reasonably feasible, the court may order the property sold, whereupon the interests are liquidated and distributed proportionately.

Tenancy by the entireties

Tenancy by the entireties is a form of ownership traditionally reserved for **husband and wife,** though now available for same-sex spouses in some states. It features survivorship, equal interests, and limited exposure to foreclosure.

Survivorship. On the death of husband or wife, the decedent's interest passes automatically to the other spouse.

Equal, undivided interest. Each spouse owns the estate as if there were only one owner. Fractional interests cannot be transferred to outside parties. The entire interest may be conveyed, but only with the consent and signatures of both parties.

No foreclosure for individual debts. The estate is subject to foreclosure only for jointly incurred debts.

Termination. The estate may be terminated by divorce, death, mutual agreement, and judgments for joint debt.

Community property

Some states have established a community property form of ownership. This type of ownership defines property rights of legal spouses before, during, and after their marriage, as well as after the death of either spouse.

Community property law distinguishes real and personal property into categories of **separate** and **community** property. Separate property belongs to one spouse; community property belongs to both spouses equally.

Separate property consists of:

- ▸ property owned by either spouse at the time of the marriage
- ▸ property acquired by either spouse through inheritance or gift during the marriage
- ▸ property acquired with separate-property funds
- ▸ income from separate property

Community property consists of:

- ▸ all other property earned or acquired by either party during the marriage

For instance, John owns a car and a motorcycle, and Mary owns a car. They marry and buy a house. A year later, Mary's father dies and leaves her $10,000, which she uses to buy furniture. John, meanwhile, sells the motorcycle and buys a computer. John rents the computer to a programmer for $50 a month. The ownership of these properties is as follows:

	John	Mary	Community
	car 1	car 2	house
	motorcycle	$10,000	
	computer	furniture	
	$50 income		

A spouse owns separate property free and clear of claims by the other spouse. He or she can transfer it without the other spouse's signature. Upon the death of the separate property owner, the property passes to heirs by will or laws of descent. Community property cannot be transferred or encumbered without the signatures of both spouses. Upon the death of either spouse, half of the deceased's community property passes to the surviving spouse, and the other half passes to the decedent's heirs.

Tenancy in partnership

Tenancy in partnership is a form of ownership held by business partners, as provided by the **Uniform Partnership Act**. The partnership tenancy grants equal rights to all partners, but the property must be used in connection with the partnership's business. Individual rights are not assignable.

ESTATES IN TRUST

Living trust
Land trust

In an estate in trust, a fee owner-- the **grantor** or **trustor**-- transfers legal title to a fiduciary-- the **trustee**-- who holds and manages the estate for the benefit of another party, the **beneficiary**. The trust may be created by a deed, will, or trust agreement.

The trustee has fiduciary duties to the trustor and the beneficiary to maintain the condition and value of the property. The specific responsibilities and authorities are set forth in the trust agreement.

Exhibit 4.3 Estate in Trust

Trustor → Title, deed, agreement → Trustee → Ownership benefits, duties → Beneficiary

Duties ← (back to Trustor)

Living trust

A living trust allows the trustor, during his or her lifetime, to convey title to a trustee for the benefit of a third party. The trustor charges the trustee with all necessary responsibilities for managing the property, protecting its value, and securing whatever income it may produce. The trustee may also be ordered to sell the property at a given point. The beneficiary receives all income and sales proceeds, net of the trustee's fees.

Testamentary trust. A testamentary trust is structurally and mechanically the same as a living trust, except that it takes effect only when the trustor dies. Provisions of the decedent's will establish the trust.

Living and testamentary trusts may involve personal property as well as real property.

Land trust

A land trust allows the trustor to convey the fee estate to the trustee and *to name himself or herself the beneficiary*. The land trust applies only to real property, not to personal property. The agreement, or **deed in trust**, grants the beneficiary the rights to possess and use the property, and to exercise control over the actions of the trustee.

Conventional trust structure. The trustee holds legal title and has conventional fiduciary duties. The trustor must be a living person, but the beneficiary may be a corporation.

The distinguishing features of the land trust are:

> ▶ **beneficiary controls property**
>
> this includes occupancy and control of rents and sale proceeds

> ▶ **beneficiary controls trustee**
>
> the trustee is empowered to sell or encumber the property, but generally only with the beneficiary's approval

> ▶ **beneficiary identity not on record**
>
> public records do not identify the beneficiary; the beneficiary owns and enjoys the property in secrecy

> ▶ **limited term**
>
> the term of the land trust is limited and must be renewed or else the trustee is obligated to sell the property and distribute the proceeds

Beneficial interest. The beneficiary's interest in a land trust is *personal property*, not real property. This distinction offers certain advantages in transferring, encumbering, and probating the beneficiary's interest:

- ▸ **transferring**

  the beneficiary may transfer the interest by assignment instead of by deed

- ▸ **encumbering**

  the beneficiary may pledge the property as security for debt by collateral assignment rather than by recorded mortgage

- ▸ **probating**

  the property interests are probated in the state where the beneficiary resided at the time of death rather than the state where the property is located

---

OWNERSHIP BY BUSINESS ENTITIES

Corporation
Partnership
Limited liability company

Corporation

A corporation is a legal entity owned by stockholders. An elected board of directors oversees the business. Officers and managers conduct day-to-day activities. Officers and directors may be held fully liable for the corporation's actions, while shareholders are liable only to the extent of the value of their shares. Corporations, like individuals, may own real estate in severalty or as tenants in common.

Partnership

In a partnership, two or more persons agree to work together and share profits. A general partnership is not a distinct legal entity like a corporation. All the partners bear full liability for debts and obligations. A limited partnership has two or more partners, one or more being general partners and the others limited partners. The general partners run the business and are liable for debts and obligations. The limited partners are liable only to the extent of their investment in the partnership. Both general and limited partnerships may own real estate.

Limited liability company

A limited liability company (LLC) combines features of the corporation and the limited partnership. The LLC offers its members limited liability like a corporation, but income is passed directly to the members and is taxed to them as individual income. The management structure is flexible. Like a corporation or a partnership, an LLC may own real estate.

CONDOMINIUMS

Airspace and common elements
Interests and rights
Condominium creation
Organization and management
Owner responsibilities

A condominium is a hybrid form of ownership of multi-unit residential or commercial properties. It combines ownership of a fee simple interest in the **airspace** within a unit with ownership of an undivided share, as a tenant in common, of the entire property's **common elements,** such as lobbies, swimming pools, and hallways.

A condominium **unit** is one airspace unit together with the associated interest in the common elements.

Airspace and common elements

The unique aspect of the condominium is its fee simple interest in the airspace contained within the outer walls, floors, and ceiling of the building unit. This airspace may include internal walls which are not essential to the structural support of the building.

Common elements are all portions of the property that are necessary for the existence, operation, and maintenance of the condominium units. Common elements include:

- the land (if not leased)
- structural components of the building, such as exterior windows, roof, and foundation
- physical operating systems supporting all units, such as plumbing, power, communications installations, and central air conditioning
- recreational facilities
- building and ground areas used non-exclusively, such as stairways, elevators, hallways, and laundry rooms

Exhibit 4.4 The Condominium

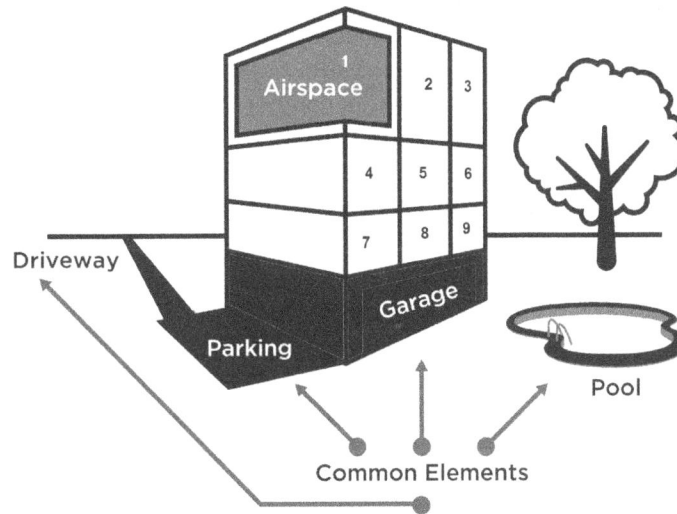

A buyer who purchases Unit #1 of the condominium illustrated obtains a fee simple interest in the airspace of apartment 1 and a tenancy in common interest in her pro rata share of the common elements. If all units in the building have the same ownership interest, the buyer would own an indivisible one-ninth interest in the common elements-- pool, parking lot, garage, pool, building structure, tree, etc.

Interests and rights   The condominium unit can be owned jointly, in severalty, in trust, or in any other manner allowed by state law. Unit owners hold an exclusive interest in their individual apartments, and co-own common elements with other unit owners as tenants in common.

Possession, use, and exclusion. Unit owners exclusively possess their apartment space, but must share common areas with other owners. The property's legal documents may create exceptions. For example, unit owners may be required to join and pay fees for use of a health club.

Unit owners as a group may exclude non-owners from portions of the common area, for instance, excluding uninvited parties from entering the building itself.

Transfer and encumbrance. Condominium units can be individually sold, mortgaged, or otherwise encumbered without interference from other unit owners. As a distinct entity, the condominium unit may also be foreclosed and liquidated. An owner may not sell interests in the apartment separately from the interest in the common elements.

Resale of a unit interest may entail limitations, such as the condominium association's prior approval of a buyer.

Condominium units are individually assessed and taxed. The assessment pertains to the value of the exclusive interest in the apartment as well as the unit's pro rata share of common elements.

Condominium creation

Condominium properties are created by executing and recording a condominium declaration and a **master deed**. The declaration must be legally correct in form and substance according to local laws. The party creating the declaration is referred to as the **developer**. The condominium may include ownership of the land or exclude it if the land is leased.

Declaration provisions. The condominium declaration may be required to include:

- a legal description and/or name of the property
- a survey of land, common elements, and all units
- plat maps of land and building, and floor plans with identifiers for all condominium units
- provisions for common area easements
- an identification of each unit's share of ownership in the overall property
- organization plans for creation of the condominium association, including its bylaws
- voting rights, membership status, and liability for expenses of individual owners
- covenants and restrictions regarding use and transfer of units

Organization and management

Organization. Condominium declarations typically provide for the creation of an **owner's association** to enforce the bylaws and manage the overall property. The association is often headed by a board of directors. The association board organizes how the property will be managed and by whom. It may appoint management agents, hire resident managers, and create supervisory committees. The board also oversees the property's finances and policy administration.

Management. Condominium properties have extensive management requirements, including maintenance, sales and leasing, accounting, owner services, sanitation, security, trash removal, etc. The association engages professional management companies, resident managers, sales and rental agents, specialized maintenance personnel, and outside service contractors to fulfill these functions.

Owner responsibilities

Individual units. Owner responsibilities relating to the apartment include:

- maintaining internal systems
- maintaining the property condition
- insuring contents of the unit

Common area assessments. Unit owners bear the costs of all other property expenses, such as maintenance, insurance, management fees, supplies, legal fees, and repairs. An annual operating budget totals these expenses and passes them through as **assessments** to unit owners, usually on a monthly basis.

Should an owner fail to pay periodic assessments, the condominium board can initiate court action to foreclose the property to pay the amounts owed.

The unit's pro rata share of the property's ownership as defined in the declaration determines the amount of a unit owner's assessment. For example, if a unit represents a 2% share of the property value, that unit owner's assessment will be 2% of the property's common area expenses.

COOPERATIVES

Interests, rights, and obligations
Organization and management

In a cooperative, or co-op, one owns **shares** in a non-profit corporation or cooperative association, which in turn acquires and owns an apartment building as its principal asset. Along with this stock, the shareholder acquires a **proprietary lease** to occupy one of the apartment units.

The number of shares purchased reflects the value of the apartment unit in relation to the property's total value. The ratio of the unit's value to total value also establishes what portions of the property's expenses the owner must pay.

Exhibit 4.5 The Cooperative

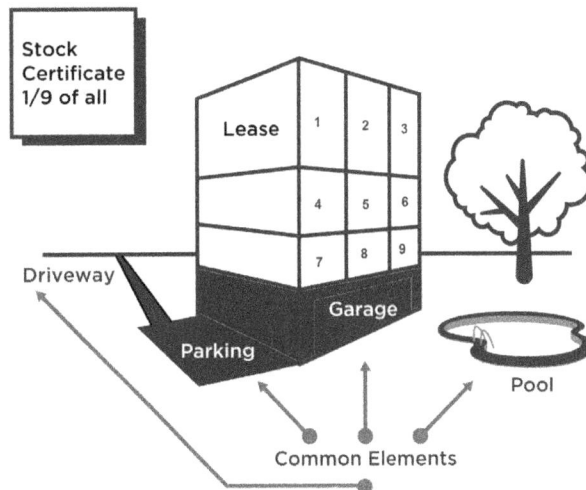

The exhibit shows a nine-unit apartment building. A cooperative corporation buys the building for $900,000. All nine units are of equal size, so the corporation decides that each apartment represents a value of $100,000, or 1/9 of the total. The co-op buyer pays the corporation $100,000 and receives 1/9 of the corporation's stock. The shareholder also receives a proprietary lease for apartment 1. The shareholder is now responsible for the apartment unit's pro rata share of the corporation's expenses, or 11.11%.

Interests, rights and obligations

Cooperative association's interest. The corporate entity of the cooperative association is the only party in the cooperative with a real property interest. The association's interest is an undivided interest in the entire property. There is no ownership interest in individual units, as with a condominium.

Shareholder's interest. In owning stock and a lease, a co-op unit owner's interest is *personal property* that is subject to control by the corporation. Unlike condominium ownership, the co-op owner owns neither a unit nor an undivided interest in the common elements.

Proprietary lease. The co-op lease is called a proprietary lease because the tenant is an owner (proprietor) of the corporation that owns the property. The lease has no stated or fixed rent. Instead, the proprietor-tenant is responsible for the unit's pro rata share of the corporation's expenses in supporting the cooperative. Unit owners pay monthly assessments. The proprietary lease has no stated term and remains in effect over the owner's period of ownership. When the unit is sold, the lease is assigned to the new owner.

Expense liability. The failure of individual shareholders to pay monthly expense assessments can destroy the investment of all the other co-op owners if the co-op cannot pay the bills by other means.

Since the corporation owns an undivided interest in the property, debts and financial obligations apply to the property as a whole, not to individual units. Should the corporation fail to meet its obligations, creditors and mortgagees may foreclose *on the entire property*. A completed foreclosure would terminate the shareholders' proprietary lease, and bankrupt the owning corporation. Compare this situation with that of a condominium, in which an individual's failure to pay endangers only that individual's unit, not the entire property.

Transfers. The co-op interest is transferred by assigning both the stock certificates and lease to the buyer.

Organization and management

A developer creates a cooperative by forming the cooperative association, which subsequently buys the cooperative property. The association's articles of incorporation, bylaws, and other legal documents establish operating policies, rules, and restrictions.

The shareholders elect a board of directors. The board assumes the responsibility for maintaining and operating the cooperative, much like a condominium board. Cooperative associations, however, also control the use and ownership of individual apartment units, since they are the legal owners. A shareholder's voting power is proportional to the number of shares owned.

TIME-SHARES

Time-share lease
Time-share freehold
Regulation

Time-share ownership is a fee or leasehold interest in a property whose owners or tenants agree to use the property on a periodic, non-overlapping basis. This type of ownership commonly concerns vacation and resort properties. Time-share arrangements provide for equal sharing of the property's expenses among the owners.

Time-share lease

In a leasehold time-share, the tenant agrees to rent the property on a scheduled basis or under any pre-arranged system of reservation, according to the terms of the lease. Generally, the scheduled use is denominated in weeks or months over the duration of the lease, a specified number of years.

Time-share freehold

In a freehold time-share, or **interval ownership estate**, tenants in common own undivided interests in the property. Expense prorations and rules governing interval usage are established by separate agreement when the estate is acquired.

For instance, the Blackburns want a monthly vacation in Colorado once a year. They find a time-share condominium that needs a twelfth buyer. The available month is May, which suits the Blackburns. The total price of the condominium is $240,000, and annual expenses are estimated to be $9,600. The Blackburns buy a one-twelfth interest with the other tenants in common by paying their share of the price, $20,000. They are also obligated to pay one-twelfth of the expenses every year, or $800. They have use of the property for one-twelfth of the year, in the month of May.

Interval owners must usually waive the right of partition, which would enable an owner to force the sale of the entire property.

Regulation

The development and sale of time-share properties has come under increased regulation in recent years. Developers and brokers in many states face more stringent disclosure requirements regarding ownership costs and risks. Other laws provide for a cooling-off period after the signing of a time-share sales contract, and require registration of advertising.

4 Ownership
Snapshot Review

SOLE OWNERSHIP

Tenancy in severalty
- sole ownership of a freehold estate

CO-OWNERSHIP
- ownership by two or more owners

Tenancy in common
- co-tenants enjoy an individually owned, undivided interest; any ownership share possible; no survivorship

Joint tenancy
- equal, undivided interest jointly owned, with survivorship
- requires four unities to create: time, title, interest, possession

Tenancy by the entireties
- equal, undivided interest jointly owned by husband and wife

Community property
- per state law, joint ownership of property by spouses as opposed to separate property
- separate: acquired before marriage or by gift or inheritance

Tenancy in partnership
- ownership by business partners

TRUSTS
- property granted by trustor to fiduciary trustee for benefit of beneficiary

Living trust
- personal and real property ownership created to take effect during one's lifetime (living trust) or after one's lifetime (testamentary)

Land trust
- real property ownership where grantor and beneficiary are same party; beneficiary uses, controls property, does not appear on public records

OWNERSHIP BY BUSINESS ENTITIES

Corporation
- owned by stockholders; board of directors, officers, directors run business; liability of shareholders limited to value of shares; may own real estate in severalty or tenant in common

Partnership
- two or more partners; in general partnership, all partners run business and share liability; in limited partnership, general partners run business and are liable, limited partners liable only to the extent of their investment; both types may own real estate

Limited liability company
- members liability limited like in corporation, management flexible, income passed through and taxed as personal income; may own real estate

CONDOMINIUMS
- freehold ownership of a unit of airspace plus an undivided interest in the common elements as tenant in common with other owners
- may be sold, encumbered or foreclosed without affecting other unit owners
- creation: by developer's declaration

COOPERATIVES
- ownership of shares in owning corporation, plus proprietary lease in a unit; corporation has sole, undivided ownership

TIME SHARES
- a lease or ownership interest in a property for the purpose of periodic use by the owners or tenants on a scheduled basis

5 Encumbrances and Liens

Encumbrances
Easements
Encroachments
Licenses
Deed Restrictions
Liens
Foreclosure

ENCUMBRANCES

An encumbrance is an interest in and right to real property that limits the legal owner's freehold interest. In effect, an encumbrance is another's right to use or take possession of a legal owner's property, or to prevent the legal owner from enjoying the full bundle of rights in the estate.

An encumbrance does not include the right of possession and is therefore a lesser interest than the owner's freehold interest. For that reason, encumbrances are not considered estates. However, an encumbrance can lead to the owner's loss of ownership of the property.

Easements and liens are the most common types of encumbrance. An easement, such as a utility easement, enables others to use the property, regardless of the owner's desires. A lien, such as a tax lien, can be placed on the property's title, thereby restricting the owner's ability to transfer clear title to another party.

The two general types of encumbrance are those that affect the property's use and those that affect legal ownership, value and transfer.

Exhibit 5.1 General Types of Encumbrance

Restrictions on Owner's Use by Others' Rights to Use	Restrictions on Ownership, Value and Transfer
easements encroachments licenses deed restrictions	liens deed conditions

EASEMENTS

Easement appurtenant
Easement in gross
Easement creation
Easement termination

An **easement** is an interest in real property that gives the holder the right to use portions of the legal owner's real property in a defined way. Easement rights may apply to a property's surface, subsurface, or airspace, but the affected area must be defined.

The receiver of the easement right is the **benefited party**; the giver of the easement right is the **burdened party**.

Essential characteristics of easements include the following:

> ▸ An easement must involve the owner of the land over which the easement runs, and another, non-owning party. *One cannot own an easement over one's own property.*

> ▸ an easement pertains to a specified physical area within the property boundaries

> ▸ an easement may be **affirmative**, allowing a use, such as a right-of-way, or **negative**, *prohibiting a use*, such as an airspace easement that prohibits one property owner from obstructing another's ocean view

The two basic types of easement are appurtenant and gross.

Easement appurtenant

An easement appurtenant gives a property owner a right of usage to portions of an *adjoining property* owned by another party. The property enjoying the usage right is called the **dominant tenement**, or **dominant estate**. The property containing the physical easement itself is the **servient tenement**, since it must serve the easement use.

The term appurtenant means "attaching to." An easement appurtenant attaches to the estate and transfers with it unless specifically stated otherwise in the transaction documents. More specifically, the easement attaches as a beneficial interest to the dominant estate, and as an encumbrance to the servient estate. The easement appurtenant then becomes part of the dominant estate's bundle of rights and the servient estate's obligation, or encumbrance.

Transfer. Easement appurtenant rights and obligations automatically transfer with the property upon transfer of either the dominant or servient estate, whether mentioned in the deed or not. For example, John grants Mary the right to share his driveway at any time over a five-year period, and the grant is duly recorded. If Mary sells her property in two years, the easement right transfers to the buyer as part of the estate.

Non-exclusive use. The servient tenement, as well as the dominant tenement, may use the easement area, provided the use does not unreasonably obstruct the dominant use.

Exhibit 5.2 Easements appurtenant

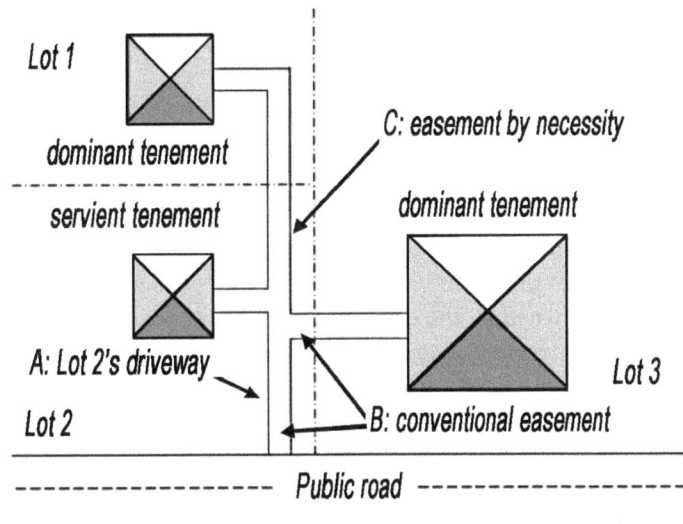

The exhibit shows a conventional easement appurtenant. The driveway marked A belongs to parcel #2. An easement appurtenant, marked B, allows parcel #3 to use #2's driveway. Parcel #3 is the dominant tenement, and #2 is the servient tenement.

Easement by necessity. An easement by necessity is an easement appurtenant granted by a court of law to a property owner because of a circumstance of necessity, most commonly the need for access to a property. Since property cannot be legally **landlocked**, or *without legal access to a public thoroughfare*, a court will grant an owner of a landlocked property an easement by necessity over an adjoining property that has access to a thoroughfare. The landlocked party becomes the dominant tenement, and the property containing the easement is the servient tenement.

In the exhibit, parcel #1, which is landlocked, owns an easement by necessity, marked C, across parcel #2.

Party wall easement. A party wall is a common wall shared by two separate structures along a property boundary.

Party wall agreements generally provide for severalty ownership of half of the wall by each owner, or at least some fraction of the width of the wall. In addition, the agreement grants a *negative* easement appurtenant to each owner in the other's wall. This is to prevent unlimited use of the wall, in particular a destructive use that would jeopardize the adjacent property owner's building. The agreement also establishes responsibilities and obligations for maintenance and repair of the wall.

For example, Helen and Troy are adjacent neighbors in an urban housing complex having party walls on property lines. They both agree that they separately own the portion of the party wall on their property. They also grant each other an easement appurtenant in their owned portion of the wall. The easement restricts any use of the wall that would impair its condition. They also agree to split any repairs or maintenance evenly.

Other structures that are subject to party agreements are common fences, driveways, and walkways.

Easement in gross   An easement in gross is a *personal right* that one party grants to another to use the grantor's real property. The right *does not attach* to the grantor's estate. It involves only one property, and, consequently, does not benefit any property owned by the easement owner. *There are no dominant or servient estates in an easement in gross.* An easement in gross may be personal or commercial.

Exhibit 5.3 Easements in Gross

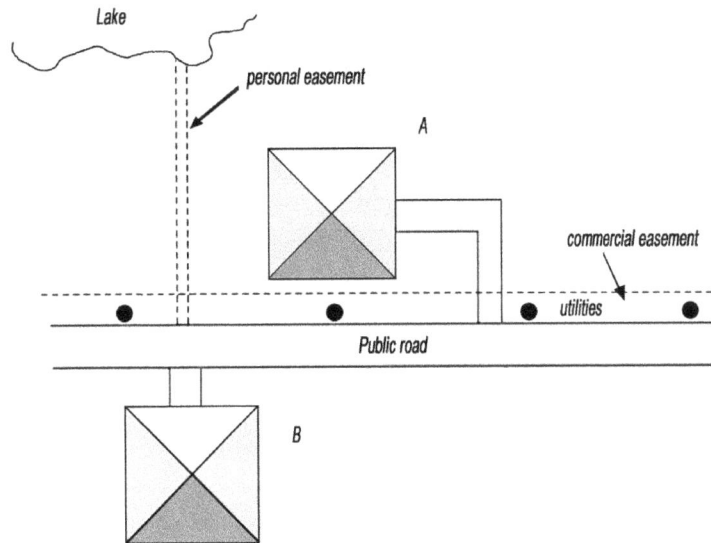

Personal. A personal easement in gross is granted for the grantee's lifetime. The right is irrevocable during this period, but terminates on the grantee's death. It may not be sold, assigned, transferred, or willed. A personal gross easement differs from a license in that the grantor of a license may revoke the usage right.

The exhibit shows that a beachfront property owner (A) has granted a neighbor (B) across the street the right to cross A's property to reach the beach.

Commercial. A commercial easement in gross is granted to a business entity rather than a private party. The duration of the commercial easement is not tied to anyone's
lifetime. The right may by assigned, transferred, or willed.

Examples of commercial gross easements include:

> ▶ a marina's right-of-way to a boat ramp
> ▶ a utility company's right-of-way across a lot owners' property to install and maintain telephone lines (as illustrated in the exhibit).

Easement creation

An easement may be created by *voluntary action, by necessary or prescriptive operation of law,* and *by government power of eminent domain.*

Voluntary. A property owner may create a voluntary easement by express grant in a sale contract, or as a reserved right expressed in a deed.

Necessity. A court decree creates an easement by necessity to provide access to a landlocked property. **Easement by prescription.** If someone uses another's property as an easement without permission for a statutory period of time and under certain conditions, a court order may give the user the easement right by **prescription**, *regardless of the owner's desires.*

For a prescriptive easement order to be granted, the following circumstances must be true:

> ▸ **Adverse and hostile use**
>
> the use has been occurring without permission or license

> ▸ **Open and notorious use**
>
> the owner knows or is presumed to have known of the use

> ▸ **Continuous use**
>
> the use has been generally uninterrupted over the statutory prescriptive period

For example, a subdivision owns an access road, which is also used by other neighborhoods to access a grocery store. One day, the subdivision blocks off the road, claiming it has never granted the neighbors permission to use the road. If the neighbors have been using the road for the prescribed period, they may sue for an easement by prescription, since the subdivision owners can be assumed to have known of the usage.

Eminent domain. Government entities can create easements through the exercise of eminent domain, wherein they condemn a portion of a property and cause it to be sold "for the greater good." A typical example is a town's condemnation of private land to create a new municipal sewer system.

Easement termination

Easements terminate by:

> ▸ *express release of the right* by the easement holder
> ▸ *merger*, as when a dominant tenement acquires the servient property, or vice versa
> ▸ *purposeful abandonment* by the dominant tenement
> ▸ *condemnation* through eminent domain
> ▸ *change or cessation of the purpose* for the easement
> ▸ *destruction* of an easement structure, such as a party fence
> ▸ *non-use* of an easement by prescription

ENCROACHMENTS

An encroachment is the unauthorized, physical intrusion of one owner's real property into that of another.

Examples of encroachments are:

  ▸   a tree limb extending into the neighbor's property, violating his or her airspace
  ▸   a driveway extending beyond the lot line onto the neighbor's land
  ▸   a fence built beyond the property line

Encroachments cause infringements on the rights of the trespassed owner, and may diminish the property's value, particularly when the property is to be sold.

Encroachments often do not appear on a property's title records. A survey may be required to detect or demonstrate the existence of an encroachment.

An owner may sue for removal of an encroachment or for compensation for damages. If an encroached owner takes no remedial action over a prescribed number of years, the encroachment may become an easement by prescription.

LICENSES

A license, much like a personal easement in gross, is a personal right that a property owner grants to another to use the property for a specific purpose. Licenses are not transferrable and do not attach to the land. They cease on the death of either party, or on the sale of the property.

Unlike a personal easement in gross, a license is revocable at any time. Licenses are often granted informally, as a verbal statement of permission.

A farmer granting a neighbor permission to cross his land to reach and fish in his pond is an example of a license.

DEED RESTRICTIONS

A deed restriction is a limitation imposed on a buyer's use of a property by stipulation in the deed of conveyance or recorded subdivision plat.

A deed restriction may apply to a single property or to an entire subdivision. A developer may place restrictions on all properties within a recorded **subdivision plat**. Subsequent re-sales of properties within the subdivision are thereby subject to the plat's covenants and conditions.

A private party who wants to control the quality and standards of a property can establish a deed restriction. Deed restrictions take precedence over zoning ordinances if they are more restrictive.

Deed restrictions typically apply to:

▸ the land use
▸ the size and type of structures that may be placed on the property
▸ minimum costs of structures
▸ engineering, architectural, and aesthetic standards, such as setbacks or specific standards of construction

Deed restrictions in a subdivision, for example, might include a minimum size for the residential structure, setback requirements for the home, and prohibitions against secondary structures such as sheds or cottages.

Deed restrictions are either covenants or conditions. A **condition** can only be created within a transfer of ownership. If a condition is later violated, a suit can force the owner to forfeit ownership to the previous owner. A **covenant** can be created by mutual agreement. If a covenant is breached, an injunction can force compliance or payment of compensatory damages.

LIENS

Lien types
Lien priority
Superior liens
Junior liens

A lien is a creditor's **claim** against personal or real property as security for a debt of the property owner. If the owner defaults, the lien gives the creditor the right to force the sale of the property to satisfy the debt.

For example, a homeowner borrows $5,000 to pay for a new roof. The lender funds the loan in exchange for the borrower's promissory note to repay the loan. At the same time, the lender places a lien on the property for $5,000 as security for the debt. If the borrower defaults, the lien allows the lender to force the sale of the house to satisfy the debt.

The example illustrates that a lien is an encumbrance that restricts free and clear ownership by securing the liened property as **collateral** for a debt. If the owner sells the property, the lienholder is entitled to that portion of the sales proceeds needed to pay off the debt. In addition, a defaulting owner may lose ownership altogether if the creditor forecloses.

In addition to restricting the owner's bundle of rights, a recorded lien effectively reduces the owner's equity in the property to the extent of the lien amount.

The creditor who places a lien on a property is called the **lienor**, and the debtor who owns the property is the **lienee**.

Liens have the following legal features:

▸ **A lien does not convey ownership, with one exception**

A lienor generally has an equitable interest in the property, but not legal ownership. The exception is a **mortgage lien** on a property in a title-theory state. In these states, the mortgage transaction conveys legal title to the lender, who holds it until the mortgage obligations are satisfied. During the mortgage loan period, the borrower has equitable title to the property.

▸ **A lien attaches to the property**

If the property is transferred, the *new owner acquires the lien securing the payment of the debt.* In addition, the creditor may take foreclosure action against the new owner for satisfaction of the debt.

▸ **A property may be subject to multiple liens**

There may be numerous liens against a particular property. The more liens there are recorded against property, the less secure the collateral is for a creditor, since the total value of all liens may approach or exceed the total value of the property.

▸ **A lien terminates on payment of the debt and recording of documents**

Payment of the debt and recording of the appropriate satisfaction documents ordinarily terminate a lien. If a default occurs, a suit for judgment or foreclosure enforces the lien. These actions force the sale of the property.

Lien types

Liens may be voluntary or involuntary, general or specific, and superior or inferior.

Voluntary and involuntary. A property owner may create a **voluntary** lien to borrow money or some other asset secured by a mortgage. An **involuntary** lien is one that a legal process places against a property regardless of the owner's desires.

If statutory law imposes an involuntary lien, the lien is a **statutory lien**. A real estate tax lien is a common example. If court action imposes an involuntary lien, the lien is an **equitable lien**. An example is a judgment lien placed on a property as security for a money judgment.

General and specific. A general lien is one *placed against any and all real and personal property* owned by a particular debtor. An example is an inheritance tax lien placed against all property owned by the heir. **A specific** lien *attaches to a single item* of real or personal property, and does not affect other property owned by the debtor. A conventional mortgage lien is an example, where the property is the only asset attached by the lien.

Superior and inferior lien. The category of superior, or **senior**, liens ranks above the category of inferior, or **junior**, liens, meaning that superior liens receive first payment from the proceeds of a foreclosure. The superior category includes liens for real estate tax, special assessments, and inheritance tax. Other liens, including income tax liens, are inferior.

Lien priority

Within the superior and inferior categories, a ranking of lien priority determines the order of the liens' claims on the security underlying the debt. The highest ranking lien is first to receive proceeds from the foreclosed and liquidated security. The lien with lowest priority is last in line. The owner receives any sale proceeds that remain after all lienors receive their due.

Lien priority is of paramount concern to the creditor, since it establishes the level of risk in recovering loaned assets in the event of default.

Establishment of priority. Two factors primarily determine lien priority:

- the lien's categorization as superior or junior
- the date of recordation of the lien

Exhibit 5.4 Priority of Real Estate Liens

Superior liens in rank order
1.   Real estate tax liens 2.   Special assessment liens 3.   Federal estate tax liens 4.   State inheritance tax liens

Junior liens: priority by date of recording
Federal income tax liens State corporate income tax liens State intangible tax liens Judgment liens Mortgage liens Vendor's liens Mechanic's liens (priority by date work was performed)

All superior liens take precedence over all junior liens regardless of recording date, since they are considered to be matters of public record not requiring further constructive notice. Thus, a real estate tax lien (senior) recorded on June 15 has priority over an income tax lien (junior) recorded on June 1.

A junior lien is automatically inferior, or **subordinate**, to a superior lien. Among junior liens, date of recording determines priority. The rule is: *the earlier the recording date of the lien, the higher its priority*. For example, if a judgment lien is recorded against a property on Friday, and a mortgage lien is recorded on the following Tuesday, the judgment lien has priority and must be satisfied in a foreclosure ahead of the mortgage lien.

The mechanic's lien is an exception to the recording rule. Its priority dates from the point in time when the work commenced or ended, as state law determines, rather than from when it was recorded.

The following example illustrates how lien priority works in paying off secured debts. A homeowner is foreclosed on a second mortgage taken out in 2018 for $25,000. The first mortgage, taken in 2016, has a balance of $150,000. Unpaid real estate taxes for the current year are $1,000. There is a $3,000 mechanic's lien on the property for work performed in 2017. The home sells for $183,000.

The proceeds are distributed in the following order:

1. $1,000 real estate taxes
2. $150,000 first mortgage
3. $3,000 mechanic's lien
4. $25,000 second mortgage
5. $4,000 balance to the homeowner

Note the risky position of the second mortgage holder: the property had to sell for at least $179,000 for the lender to recover the $25,000.

Subordination. A lienor can change the priority of a junior lien by voluntarily agreeing to subordinate, or lower, the lien's position in the hierarchy. This change is often necessary when working with a mortgage lender who will not originate a mortgage loan unless it is senior to all other junior liens on the property. The lender may require the borrower to obtain agreements from other lien holders to subordinate their liens to the new mortgage.

For example, interest rates fall from 8% to 6.5% on first mortgages for principal residences. A homeowner wants to refinance her mortgage, but she also has a separate home-equity loan on the house. Since the first-mortgage lender will not accept a lien priority inferior to a home equity loan, the homeowner must persuade the home equity lender to subordinate the home equity lien to the new first-mortgage lien.

Superior liens

Real estate tax lien. The local legal taxing authority annually places a real estate tax lien, also called an **ad valorem tax lien**, against properties as security for payment of the annual property tax. The amount of a particular lien is based on the taxed property's assessed value and the local tax rate.

Special assessment lien. Local government entities place assessment liens against certain properties to ensure payment for local improvement projects such as new roads, schools, sewers, or libraries. An assessment lien applies only to properties that are expected to benefit from the municipal improvement.

Federal and state inheritance tax liens. Inheritance tax liens arise from taxes owed by a decedent's estate. The lien amount is determined through probate and attaches to both real and personal property.

Junior liens

Tax liens. All tax liens other than those for ad valorem, assessment, and estate tax are junior liens. They include:

> **Federal income tax lien**
>
> placed on a taxpayer's real and personal property for failure to pay income taxes

> ▸ **State corporate income tax lien**
>
> filed against corporate property for failure to pay taxes

> ▸ **State intangible tax lien**
>
> filed for non-payment of taxes on intangible property

> ▸ **State corporation franchise tax lien**
>
> filed to ensure collection of fees to do business within a state

Judgment lien. A judgment lien attaches to real and personal property as a result of a money judgment issued by a court in favor of a creditor. The creditor may obtain a **writ of execution** to force the sale of attached property and collect the debt. After paying the debt from the sale proceeds, the debtor may obtain a **satisfaction of judgment** to clear the title records on other real property that remains unsold.

During the course of a lawsuit, the plaintiff creditor may secure a **writ of attachment** to prevent the debtor from selling or concealing property. In such a case, there must be a clear likelihood that the debt is valid and that the defendant has made attempts to sell or hide property.

Certain properties are exempt from judgment liens, such as homestead property and joint tenancy estates.

Mortgage and trust deed lien. In lien-theory states, mortgages and trust deeds secure loans made on real property. In these states, the lender records a lien as soon as possible after disbursing the funds in order to establish lien priority.

Vendor's lien. A vendor's lien, also called a **seller's lien**, secures a purchase money mortgage, a seller's loan to a buyer to finance the sale of a property.

Municipal utility lien. A municipality may place a utility lien against a resident's real property for failure to pay utility bills.

Mechanic's lien. A mechanic's lien secures the costs of labor, materials, and supplies incurred in the repair or construction of real property improvements. If a property owner fails to pay for work performed or materials supplied, a worker or supplier can file a lien to force the sale of the property and collect the debt.

Any individual who performs approved work may place a mechanic's lien on the property to the extent of the direct costs incurred. Note that unpaid subcontractors may record mechanic's liens *whether the general contractor has been paid or not.* Thus it is possible for an owner to have to double-pay a bill in order to eliminate the mechanic's lien if the general contractor neglects to pay the subcontractors. The mechanic's lienor must enforce the lien within a certain time period, or the lien expires.

In contrast to other junior liens, the priority of a mechanic's lien *dates from the time when the work was begun or completed*. For example, a carpenter finishes a job on May 15. The owner refuses to pay the carpenter in spite of the carpenter's two-month collection effort. Finally, on August 1, the carpenter places a mechanic's lien on the property. The effective date of the lien for purposes of lien priority is May 15, not August 1.

FORECLOSURE

Mortgage lien foreclosure
Judicial foreclosure
Non-judicial foreclosure
Strict foreclosure
Deed in lieu of foreclosure

All liens can be enforced by the sale or other transfer of title of the secured property, whether by court action, operation of law, or through powers granted in the original loan agreement. The enforcement proceedings are referred to as foreclosure.

State law governs the foreclosure process. Broadly, a statutory or court-ordered sale enforces a general lien, including a judgment lien. A lawsuit or loan provision authorizing the sale or direct transfer of the attached property enforces a specific lien, such as a mortgage. Real estate tax liens are enforced through **tax foreclosure sales**, or **tax sales**.

Mortgage lien foreclosure

Three types of foreclosure process enforce mortgage liens:

- ▸ judicial foreclosure
- ▸ non-judicial foreclosure
- ▸ strict foreclosure

Exhibit 5.5 Foreclosure Processes

Judicial	Non-judicial	Strict
Default	Default	Default
↓	↓	↓
Acceleration	Acceleration	Acceleration
↓	↓	↓
Foreclosure suit		Foreclosure suit
↓		↓
Notice	Notice	
↓	↓	
Sale	Sale	Title to lender
↓	↓	↓
Deficiency judgment	Deficiency suit	Deficiency suit

Judicial foreclosure   Judicial foreclosure occurs in states that use a two-party mortgage document (borrower and lender) that does not contain a "power of sale" provision. Lacking this provision, a lender must file a **foreclosure suit** and undertake a court proceeding to enforce the lien.

Acceleration and filing. If a borrower has failed to meet loan obligations in spite of proper notice and applicable grace periods, the lender can **accelerate** the loan, or declare that the loan balance and all other sums due on the loan are payable immediately.

If the borrower does not pay off the loan in full, the lender then files a foreclosure suit, naming the borrower as defendant. The suit asks the court to:

- ▸ terminate the defendant's interests in the property
- ▸ order the property sold publicly to the highest bidder
- ▸ order the proceeds applied to the debt

Lis Pendens. In the foreclosure suit, a **lis pendens** gives public notice that the mortgaged property may soon have a judgment issued against it. This notice enables other lienholders to join in the suit against the defendant.

Writ of execution. If the defendant fails to meet the demands of the suit during a prescribed period, the court orders the termination of interests of any and all parties in the property, and orders the property to be sold. The court's **writ of execution** authorizes an official, such as the county sheriff, to seize and sell the foreclosed property.

Public sale and sale proceeds. After public notice of the sale, the property is auctioned to the highest bidder. The new owner receives title free and clear of all previous liens, whether the lienholders have been paid or not. Proceeds of the sale are applied to payment of liens according to priority. After payment of real estate taxes, lienholders' claims and costs of the sale, any remaining funds go to the mortgagor (borrower).

Deficiency judgment. If the sale does not yield sufficient funds to cover the amounts owed, the mortgagee may ask the court for a deficiency judgment. This enables the lender to attach and foreclose a judgment lien on other real or personal property the borrower owns.

Right of redemption. The borrower's right of redemption, also called equity of redemption, is the right to *reclaim a property* that has been foreclosed by paying off amounts owed to creditors, including interest and costs. Redemption is possible within a **redemption period**. Some states allow redemption during the foreclosure proceeding at any time "until the gavel drops" at the sale. Other states have statutory periods of up to a year following the sale for the owner of a foreclosed property to redeem the estate.

Non-judicial foreclosure

When there is a "power of sale" provision in the mortgage or trust deed document, a non-judicial foreclosure can force the sale of the liened property *without a foreclosure suit*. The "power of sale" clause in effect enables the mortgagee to order a public sale without court decree.

Foreclosure process. On default, the foreclosing mortgagee records and delivers notice to the borrower and other lienholders. After the proper period, a "notice of sale" is published, the sale is conducted, and all liens are extinguished. The highest bidder then receives unencumbered title to the property.

Deficiency suit. The lender does not obtain a deficiency judgment or lien in a non-judicial foreclosure action. The lender instead must file a new deficiency suit against the borrower.

Re-instatement and redemption. During the notice of default and notice of sale periods, the borrower may pay the lender and terminate the proceedings. Exact re-instatement periods vary from state to state. There is no redemption right in non-judicial foreclosure.

Strict foreclosure

Strict foreclosure is a court proceeding that gives the lender title directly, by court order, instead of giving cash proceeds from a public sale.

On default, the lender gives the borrower official notice. After a prescribed period, the lender files suit in court, whereupon the court establishes a period within which the defaulting party must repay the amounts owed. If the defaulter does not repay the funds, the court orders transfer of full, legal title to the lender.

Deed in lieu of foreclosure

A defaulting borrower who faces foreclosure may avoid court actions and costs by voluntarily deeding the property to the mortgagee. This is accomplished with a deed in lieu of foreclosure , which transfers legal title to the lienholder. The transfer, however, does not terminate any existing liens on the property.

5 Encumbrances and Liens
Snapshot Review

ENCUMBRANCES	●	non-possessory interests limiting the legal owner's rights
EASEMENTS	●	a right to use portions of another's property
Easement appurtenant	●	dominant tenement's right to use or restrict adjacent servient tenement; attaches to the real estate
	●	easement by necessity: granted by necessity, e.g. to landlocked owners
	●	party wall: negative easement in a shared structure
Easement in gross	●	a right to use property that does not attach to the real estate
	●	personal: not revocable or transferrable; ends upon death of easement holder
	●	commercial: granted to businesses; transferrable
Easement creation	●	voluntary grant, court decree by necessity or prescription, eminent domain
	●	by prescription: obtainable through continuous, open, adverse use over a period
Easement termination	●	release; merger; abandonment; condemnation; change of purpose; destruction; non-use
ENCROACHMENTS	●	intrusions of real estate into adjoining property; can become easements
LICENSES	●	personal rights to use a property; do not attach; non-transferrable; revocable
DEED RESTRICTIONS	●	conditions and covenants imposed on a property by deed or subdivision plat
LIENS	●	claims attaching to real and personal property as security for debt
Lien types	●	voluntary and involuntary; general and specific; superior and junior
Lien priority	●	rank ordering of claims established by lien classification and date of recording; determines who gets paid first if lienee defaults
Superior liens	●	rank over junior liens; not ranked by recording date; real estate tax and assessment liens and inheritance taxes
Junior liens	●	rank by recording date: judgment; mortgage, vendor's, utility, mechanic's, other tax liens; mechanic's lien priority "dates back" to when work or sale transpired
FORECLOSURE	●	enforcement of liens through liquidation or transfer of encumbered property
Mortgage lien foreclosure	●	liquidation or transfer of collateral property by judicial, non-judicial, or strict foreclosure
Judicial foreclosure	●	lawsuit and court-ordered public sale; deficiency judgments, redemption rights
Non-judicial foreclosure	●	"power of sale" granted to lender; no suit; no deficiency judgment; no redemption period after sale
Strict foreclosure	●	court orders legal transfer of title directly to lender without public sale
Deed in lieu of foreclosure	●	defaulted borrower deeds property to lender to avoid foreclosure

6 Transferring & Recording Title To Real Estate

Title to Real Estate
Deeds of Conveyance
Wills
Involuntary Title Transfer
Title Records

TITLE TO REAL ESTATE

Legal and equitable title
Notice of title
Transferring title

Legal and equitable title

Owning title to real property commonly connotes owning the complete bundle of rights that attach to the property, including the right to possession. More accurately, someone who possesses all ownership interests owns **legal title** to the property. Legal title is distinct from **equitable title**, which is the interest or *right to obtain legal title* to a property in accordance with a sale or mortgage contract between the legal owner and a buyer or creditor. During the contractual period of time when ownership of legal title is contingent upon the contract, the buyer or lender owns equitable title to the property.

For example, a buyer enters into a contract for deed to purchase a house. The seller lends the bulk of the purchase price to the buyer for a term of three years. The buyer takes possession of the property, and makes payments on the loan. During this period, the seller retains legal title, and the buyer owns equitable title. If the buyer fulfills the terms of the agreement over the three year period, the buyer has an enforceable contract to obtain legal title.

Another common example is a mortgage loan transaction that gives the lender the right to execute a strict foreclosure, which transfers legal title to the lender in the event of a default. With this contractual right, the lender has equitable title to the property.

In practice, the terms "title" and "legal title" are often used interchangeably.

Notice of title

In any legal system that permits private ownership of real property, there will always be disputes as to who truly owns a particular parcel of real estate. For example, an owner might "sell" his property to three unrelated parties. The first party buys the property at the earliest date, the second party pays the highest price, and the third party receives the best deed, a warranty deed. Who owns legal title to the property?

Ownership of legal title is a function of evidence. A court will generally rule that the person who has the preponderance of evidence of ownership is the owner of the property. In the example, if the first two buyers did not receive a deed while the third party did, the third party may have the best evidence and be ruled the legal title-holder. However, what if the first buyer had moved into the house and occupied it for six months before the original owner sold the property to the second and third buyers? And what if the second buyer, after searching title records, reports that the seller never really owned the property and therefore could not legally sell it to anyone! Now who owns the property?

The illustration underscores the difficulty of proving title to real estate: there is no absolute and irrefutable proof that a party holds legal title. Our legal system has developed two forms of title evidence-- actual notice and constructive notice-- to assist in the determination.

Actual notice. The term "notice" is synonymous with "knowledge." A person who has received *actual* notice has *actual knowledge* of something. Receiving actual notice means learning of something through direct experience or communication. In proving real estate ownership, a person provides actual notice by producing direct evidence, such as by showing a valid will. Another party receives actual notice by seeing direct evidence, such as by reviewing the deed, reading title records, or physically visiting the property to see who is in possession. Thus if Mary Pierce drives to a property and sees directly that John Doe is in possession of the home, Mary then has received actual notice of John Doe's claim of ownership. Her knowledge is obtained through direct experience.

Constructive notice. Constructive notice, or **legal notice**, is knowledge of a fact that a person *could have or should have obtained*. The foremost method of imparting constructive notice is by recordation of ownership documents in public records, specifically, *title records*. Since public records are open to everyone, the law generally presumes that when evidence of ownership is recorded, the public at large *has received constructive notice* of ownership. By the same token, the law presumes that the owner of record is in fact the legal owner. Thus, if John Doe records the deed of conveyance, he has imparted, and Mary Pierce has received, constructive notice of ownership. Possession of the property can also be construed as constructive notice, since a court may rule that Mary *should have visited the property* to ascertain whether it was occupied.

A combination of actual and constructive notice generally provides the most indisputable evidence of real property ownership.

Transferring title

Transfer of title to real estate, also called **alienation**, occurs voluntarily and involuntarily. When the transfer uses a written instrument, the transfer is called a **conveyance.**

Exhibit 6.1 Transferring Title to Real Estate

Voluntary	Involuntary
public grant deed will	descent escheat foreclosure eminent domain adverse possession estoppel

Voluntary alienation. Voluntary alienation is an unforced transfer of title by sale or gift from an owner to another party. If the transferor is a government entity and the recipient is a private party, the conveyance is a **public grant**. If the transferor is a private party, the conveyance is a **private grant**.

A living owner makes a private grant by means of a **deed of conveyance**, or **deed**. A private grant that occurs when the owner dies is a **transfer by will**.

Involuntary alienation. Involuntary alienation is a transfer of title to real property without the owner's consent. Involuntary alienation occurs primarily by the processes of descent and distribution, escheat, foreclosure, eminent domain, adverse possession, and estoppel.

DEEDS OF CONVEYANCE

Delivery and acceptance
Validity
Deed clauses and covenants
Statutory deeds
Special purpose deeds
Transfer tax

Delivery and acceptance

A deed is a legal instrument used by an owner, the **grantor**, to transfer title to real estate voluntarily to another party, the **grantee**.

Execution of a valid deed in itself does not convey title. It is necessary for the deed to be *delivered to and accepted by the grantee* for title to pass. To be legally valid, delivery of the deed requires that the grantor

> ▸ be *competent* at the time of delivery
> ▸ *intend to deliver* the deed, beyond the act of making physical delivery

Validity of the grantee's acceptance requires only that the grantee have physical possession of the deed or record the deed.

Once accepted, title passes to the grantee. The deed has fulfilled its legal purpose and it cannot be used again to transfer the property. If the grantee loses the deed, there is no effect on the grantee's title to the estate. The grantor, for example, cannot reclaim the estate on the grounds that the grantee has lost the deed after it was delivered and accepted. Nor can the grantee return the property by returning the deed. To do so, the grantee would need to execute a new deed.

In states that use the Torrens system, title passes only when the *deed has been registered on the certificate of title and a transfer certificate has been issued to the new owner.*

Validity

Depending on state law, a deed must meet the following requirements for validity. The deed must:

> ▸ be delivered and accepted
>
> ▸ have a competent grantor and legitimate grantee
>
>   The grantor must be living, of legal age, and mentally competent. If grantor is a corporation, the signing party must be duly authorized. The grantee must be living or have legal existence, but need not be of legal age or mentally competent.
>
> ▸ be in writing
>
> ▸ contain a legal description
>
> ▸ contain a granting clause
>
>   The deed must express the grantor's present desire and intention to transfer legal title to the grantee.
>
> ▸ include consideration
>
>   The deed must be accompanied by valuable (monetary) or good (love and affection) consideration, but the amount need not reflect the actual price in most cases.
>
> ▸ be signed by the grantor
>
>   The deed must be signed by the grantor, but need not be signed by the grantee unless the deed contains special provisions requiring the grantee's acceptance. Grantors may give power of attorney to other parties, authorizing them to execute deeds on

their behalf. The power of attorney authorization should be recorded to ensure a valid conveyance.

> ▸ be acknowledged

> The grantor must declare before a notary or other authorized person that the grantor's identity and signature are genuine, and that the deed execution was a free, voluntary act. The grantor then receives a certificate of acknowledgment signed by the notary. Some states require acknowledgment to complete a valid conveyance. Most states require it before they will record the deed. A deed without an acknowledgement, therefore, tends to endanger one's claim to a property.

Recording. Recording is *not* necessary to make a deed valid. However, it is in the grantee's best interests to do so. Recording the deed gives the public constructive notice of the grantee's ownership.

Deed clauses and covenants

Conveyance clauses and *covenant,* or *warrant, clauses* set forth all the necessary provisions of the conveyance.

Conveyance clauses. Conveyance clauses describe the details of the transfer. The principal conveyance clauses are:

> ▸ **Granting clause, or premises clause**

> *the only required clause*; contains the conveyance intentions; names the parties; describes the property; indicates nominal consideration

> ▸ **Habendum clause**

> describes the type of estate being conveyed (fee simple, life, etc.)

> ▸ **Reddendum clause, or reserving clause**

> recites restrictions and limitations to the estate being conveyed, e.g., deed restrictions, liens, easements, encroachments, etc.

> ▸ **Tenendum clause**

> identifies property being conveyed in addition to land

Covenant, or warrant, clauses. Covenant clauses present the grantor's assurances to the grantee. A deed of conveyance usually contains one or more of the following covenants, depending on the type of deed.

> ▸ **Warrant of seisin**

> assures that the grantor owns the estate to be conveyed, and has the right to do so

> ▸ **Warrant of quiet enjoyment**

> assures that the grantee will not be disturbed by third party title disputes

> ▸ **Warrant of further assurance**

> assures that the grantor will assist in clearing any title problems discovered later

> ▸ **Warranty forever; warranty of title**

> assures that the grantee will receive good title, and that grantor will assist in defending any claims to the contrary

> ▸ **Warrant of encumbrances**

> assures that there are no encumbrances on the property except those expressly named

> ▸ **Warranty against grantor's acts**

> states the assurance of a trustee, acting as grantor on behalf of the owner, that nothing has been done to impair title during the fiduciary period

Statutory Deeds

A deed of conveyance can make a variety of warranties and convey a range of interests. The most common deeds are statutory deeds, in which the covenants are defined in law and do not need to be fully stated in the deed. The prominent types are the following.

Bargain and sale deed. In a bargain and sale deed, the grantor covenants that the title is valid but may or may not warrant against encumbrances or promise to defend against claims by other parties. If there *is* a warrant of defense, the deed is a full warranty bargain and sale deed.

The overall bargain and sale covenant is: *"I own, but won't defend."*

General warranty deed. The general warranty deed, or **warranty deed** for short, is the most commonly used deed. It contains the fullest possible assurances of good title and protection for the grantee. The deed is technically a bargain and sale deed in which the grantor promises to defend against any and all claims to the title.

The overall general warranty covenant is: *"I own and will defend."*

Special warranty deed. In a special warranty deed, the grantor warrants only against title defects or encumbrances not noted on the deed that may have occurred during the grantor's period of ownership or trusteeship. The deed does not protect the grantee against claims that predate the owner's period of ownership. Special warranty deeds are often used by trustees and grantors who acquired the property through a tax sale.

The overall special warranty covenant is: *"I own and will defend against my acts only."*

Quitclaim deed. A quitclaim deed transfers real and potential interests in a property, whether an interest is known to exist or not. The grantor makes no claim to any interest in the property being conveyed and offers no warrants to protect the grantee.

The quitclaim is typically used to clear title rather than convey it. Where there is a possibility that prior errors in deeds or other recorded documents might **cloud** (encumber) the title, the relevant parties execute a quitclaim deed to convey "any and all" interest to the grantee.

If a party responsible for encumbering title refuses to quitclaim the interest, the owner may file a **quiet title suit.** This requires the lienor to prove the validity of an interest. If the defendant is unable to do so, the court removes the cloud by decree.

The overall quit claim covenant is: *"I may or may not own, and I won't defend."*

Special purpose deeds

A special purpose deed is one tailored to the requirements of specific parties, properties, and purposes. The principal types are:

> ▸ **Personal representative's deed**
>
> used by an executor to convey a decedent's estate; also called an executor's deed

> ▸ **Guardian's deed**
>
> used by a court-appointed guardian to transfer property of minors or mentally incompetent persons

> ▸ **Sheriff's deed**
>
> used to convey foreclosed property sold at public auction

> ▸ **Deed *of* trust**
>
> used to convey property to a third party trustee as collateral for a loan; on satisfaction of the loan terms, the trustee uses a **reconveyance deed** to convey the property back to the borrower

> ▸ **Deed *in* trust**
>
> used to convey property to the trustee of a land trust. not to be confused with deed *of* trust

> ▸ **Master deed**
>
> used to convey land to a condominium developer; accompanied by the condominium declaration when recorded

▶ **Partition deed**

used to convey co-owned property in compliance with a court order resulting from a partition suit; a partition suit terminates an estate when one or more co-owners want to dissolve their relationship and are unable to do so without the assistance of a court.

▶ **Patent deed**

used to transfer government property to private parties

▶ **Tax deed**

used to convey property sold at a tax sale

Transfer tax

State law usually requires payment of a **documentary stamp tax** on a conveyance of real property. The tax is based on the actual price of the property conveyed, thus enabling taxing authorities to ascertain current market value for ad valorem tax purposes. Payment of the tax is evidenced on the deed.

Exemptions from transfer tax include:

- ▶ transfer within the immediate family
- ▶ consideration less than a certain amount
- ▶ transfer between government entities or non-profit organizations
- ▶ trust deed transfer and reconveyance
- ▶ tax deed

WILLS

Types of will
Validity
Probate

A will, or more properly, a **last will and testament**, is a legal instrument for the voluntary transfer of real and personal property after the owner's death. It describes how the maker of the will, called the **testator** or **devisor,** wants the property distributed. A beneficiary of a will is called an **heir** or **devisee**. The property transferred by the will is the **devise**.

A will takes effect only after the testator's death. It is an **amendatory** instrument, meaning that it can be changed at any time during the maker's lifetime.

Commonly, the testator names an **executor**, or **personal representative**, to oversee the settlement of the estate. If a minor is involved, the testator may identify a **guardian** to handle legal affairs on behalf of the minor.

Types of will   A will generally takes one of the following forms:

    ▶ **Witnessed**

      in writing and witnessed by two people

    ▶ **Holographic**

      in the testator's handwriting, dated and signed

    ▶ **Approved**

      on pre-printed forms meeting the requirements of state law

    ▶ **Nuncupative**

      made orally, and written down by a witness; generally *not valid* for the transfer of real property

Validity   State law establishes requirements for a valid will. The law generally requires that:

- ▶ the testator be of legal age and mentally competent
- ▶ the testator indicate that the will is the "last will and testament"
- ▶ the will be signed
- ▶ the completion of the will be witnessed and signed by the witnesses
- ▶ the will be completed voluntarily, without duress or coercion

Probate   A court proceeding called **probate** generally settles a decedent's estate, whether the person has died **testate** (having left a valid will) or **intestate** (having failed to do so). Real property may be exempted from probate if it is held in a land trust. Probate of real property occurs *under jurisdiction of courts in the state where the property is located, regardless of where the deceased resided.*

The probate court's objectives are to:

- ▶ validate the will, if one exists
- ▶ identify and settle all claims and outstanding debts against the estate
- ▶ distribute the remainder of the estate to the rightful heirs If the will does not name an executor, the court will appoint an **administrator** to fulfill this role.

Exhibit 6.2 Transfer of a Decedent's Estate by Probate

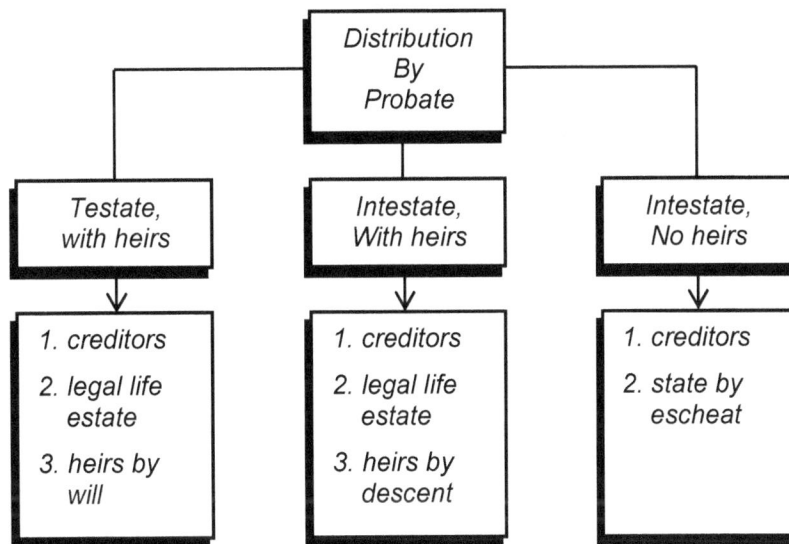

```
                        ┌─────────────┐
                        │ Distribution│
                        │     By      │
                        │   Probate   │
                        └──────┬──────┘
          ┌────────────────────┼────────────────────┐
   ┌──────┴──────┐      ┌───────┴──────┐      ┌───────┴──────┐
   │  Testate,   │      │  Intestate,  │      │  Intestate,  │
   │ with heirs  │      │  With heirs  │      │   No heirs   │
   └──────┬──────┘      └───────┬──────┘      └───────┬──────┘
          ▼                     ▼                     ▼
   ┌─────────────┐      ┌──────────────┐      ┌──────────────┐
   │ 1. creditors│      │ 1. creditors │      │ 1. creditors │
   │ 2. legal life│     │ 2. legal life│      │ 2. state by  │
   │    estate   │      │    estate    │      │    escheat   │
   │ 3. heirs by │      │ 3. heirs by  │      │              │
   │    will     │      │    descent   │      │              │
   └─────────────┘      └──────────────┘      └──────────────┘
```

The exhibit shows three possible channels of probate deliberation, depending on whether there is a will and heirs.

Testate proceeding. If the decedent died with a valid will, the court hears the claims of lienors and creditors and determines their validity. First in line are the superior liens: those for real estate taxes, assessment taxes, federal estate taxes, and state inheritance taxes. If the estate's liquid assets are insufficient to pay all obligations, the court may order the sale of personal or real property to satisfy the obligations.

The court must also hear and satisfy legal life estate claims, including those for dower, curtesy, homestead, and elective share. These interests may prevail even if the will does not provide for them.

Once all claims have been satisfied, the balance of the estate's assets passes to the rightful heirs *free and clear of all liens and debts*.

Intestate proceeding with heirs. If the decedent died without a valid will, the estate passes to lawful heirs according to the state's laws of **descent and distribution**, or **succession**. Laws of descent stipulate *who inherits and what share they receive,* without regard to the desires of the heirs or the intentions of the deceased.

For example, John Astor dies intestate, leaving a wife and four children. The laws of descent in his state provide that the surviving spouse receives one-third of the estate, and the four children receive equal shares of the remaining two thirds.

Intestate proceeding with no heirs. If an intestate decedent has no heirs, the estate **escheats**, or reverts, to the state or county after all claims and debts have been validated and settled.

INVOLUNTARY TITLE TRANSFER

Laws of descent
Abandonment
Foreclosure
Eminent domain
Adverse possession
Estoppel

State law regulates all forms of involuntary alienation, whether such transfer occurs by the laws of descent, abandonment, foreclosure, eminent domain, adverse possession, or estoppel.

Laws of descent

Involuntary alienation occurs when a title-holder dies without a valid will. The state's statutes of descent and distribution identify heirs and the respective shares of the estate they will receive. In the absence of heirs, title transfers to the state or county by escheat.

Abandonment

Property that has been abandoned for a statutory period may also escheat to the state or county.

Foreclosure

A property owner who fails to fulfill loan obligations or pay taxes may lose an estate through foreclosure.

Eminent domain

Various government and public entities can transfer private property to the public sphere by the power of eminent domain. The transfer is involuntary, even though the owner receives compensation. For example, a city government wants to widen a highway to accommodate growth. The government uses eminent domain to condemn and purchase all properties abutting the thoroughfare in order to complete the construction project.

Adverse possession

State laws may allow a real property owner to lose legal title to an **adverse possessor**. An adverse possessor is someone who enters, occupies, and uses another's property without the knowledge or consent of the owner, or with the knowledge of an owner who fails to take any action over a statutory period of time.

To claim legal title, the adverse possessor must:

- be able to show a **claim of right** or **color of title** as reason for the possession
- have **notorious possession**, which is possession without concealment
- maintain a consistent claim of **hostile possession**, which is a claim to ownership and possession regardless of the owner's claims or consent
- occupy the property continuously for a statutory period of time
- in some states, *pay taxes*

A **claim of right** is based on the adverse possessor's occupying and maintaining the property as if he or she were the legal owner. **Color of title** results when a grantee has obtained defective title, or received title by defective means, but occupies the property as if he or she were the legal owner. A court may hold that a claim of right or a claim of colored title is a valid reason for the possession.

Notorious possession and **hostile possession** give constructive notice to the public, including the legal owner, that a party other than the legal owner is occupying and claiming to own the property. It is possible for such notice to prevail over notice by recordation as the dominant evidence of legal ownership, provided the possessor has occupied the property continuously for the statutory period of time.

In some states, the possessor must have paid taxes over a prescribed period to obtain title. However, if the possessor has paid rent of any kind, the claim of ownership might be refuted.

Avoiding adverse possession. An owner can avert the danger of involuntary alienation by adverse possession by *periodically inspecting the property within statutory deadlines* and evicting any trespassers found. The owner may also sue to quiet title, which would eliminate the threat of the adverse possessor's claim to legal title.

A property registered in the Torrens system cannot be lost to adverse possession.

Estoppel

Estoppel prevents a person from claiming a right or interest that is inconsistent with the person's previous statements or acts. As a basis for involuntary alienation, the doctrine of estoppel can prevent an owner from re-claiming a property that was transferred under false pretenses. For example, an owner conveys a property with a defective title. The grantor is fully aware of the defect but makes no disclosure to the grantee. The grantor later cures the defect and then claims to be the rightful owner of the property on the basis of the effort and expense of clearing the title. Estoppel disallows the grantor's claim because of the prior conveyance action. The grantee remains legal owner and benefits from the cleared title as well.

TITLE RECORDS

Chain of title
Recording system
Title evidence

State laws require the recording of all documents that affect rights and interests in real estate in the public real estate records of the county where the property is located. These public records, or **title records**, contain a history of every parcel of real estate in the county, including names of previous owners, liens, easements, and other encumbrances that have been recorded.

Deeds, mortgages, liens, easements, and sale contracts are among the documents that must be recorded. Other public records that affect real estate title are marriage, probate, and tax records.

Generally, a County Recorder's Office or other similarly named office maintains the title records.

Title records serve a number of purposes, not the least of which is to avoid ownership disputes. Other important purposes are:

> **Public notice**
>
> Title records protect the public by giving all concerned parties **constructive notice** of the condition of a property's legal title: who owns the property, who maintains claims and encumbrances against the property.

> **Buyer protection**
>
> Title records protect the buyer by revealing whether a property has **marketable title**, one free of undesirable encumbrances. The buyer is legally responsible for knowing the condition of title, since it is a matter of public record. Recording a transaction also protects a buyer by replacing the deed as evidence of ownership.

> **Lienholder protection**
>
> Title records protect the lienholder by putting the public on notice that the lien exists, and that it may be the basis for a foreclosure action. Recording also establishes the lien's priority.

Chain of title

Chain of title refers to the succession of property owners *of record* dating back to the original grant of title from the state to a private party. If there is a missing link in the chronology of owners, or if there was a defective conveyance, the chain is said to be broken, resulting in a **clouded title** to the property. To remove the cloud, an owner may need to initiate a **suit to quiet title**, which clears the title record of any unrecorded claims.

Abstract of Title. An abstract of title is a written, chronological summary of the property's title records and other public records affecting rights and interests in the property. It includes the property's chain of title and all current recorded liens and encumbrances, by date of filing. A title abstractor or title company analyst conducts the search of public records, called a **title search**, needed to produce an abstract. Insurers and lenders generally require the search to identify title defects and ascertain the current status of encumbrances.

A **title plant** is a duplicate set of records of a property copied from public records and maintained by a private company, such as a title company.

Recording system

There are no federal recording standards. Each state prescribes procedures and requirements for recording in public title records: forms, proper execution, acknowledgment, and witnessing.

The Torrens system. Certain states and counties use the Torrens system of recording. The Torrens system differs from other title recording systems in that *title passes only when the conveyance has been duly registered on the title certificate itself*. Encumbrances likewise have no legal effect until they are recorded. In effect, the Torrens title record is the title itself. It is not necessary to search public records to ascertain the status of title; it is all reflected on the title certificate.

To enter a property in the Torrens system, a court action must first clear title by giving notice to all potential interest holders that they must express their claims. At the end of the proceeding, the court decrees that the title is accepted into Torrens registration. The Torrens registry retains the original registration documents and provides copies to the recorder or other appropriate office. All subsequent transactions affecting title must follow the proper Torrens recording procedures and requirements.

Title evidence

Since the value of a property is only as good as the marketability of its title, the evidence supporting the status of title is a significant issue. To demonstrate marketable title to a buyer, a seller must show that the title is free of

- ▶ doubts about the identity of the current owner
- ▶ defects, such as an erroneous legal description
- ▶ claims that could affect value
- ▶ undisclosed or unacceptable encumbrances

The four principal forms of evidence the owner can use to support these assurances are:

- ▶ a Torrens certificate
- ▶ a title insurance policy
- ▶ an attorney's opinion of the title abstract
- ▶ a title certificate

Torrens certificate. If available, the Torrens certificate is the best evidence, for the reasons given earlier-- it is not merely a record, but is the title itself.

Title insurance. In the absence of Torrens registration, a title insurance policy is commonly accepted as the best evidence of marketable title. A title insurance policy indemnifies the policy holder against losses arising from defects in the insured title.

The common policy types are the lender's policy and the owner's policy, which protect the respective policy holders' interests in the property. Thus, a lender who holds an $80,000 mortgage on a property will obtain protection worth $80,000 against the possibility that the lender's lien cannot be enforced. The owner's policy will insure against defective title to the extent of the property's initial or appreciated value.

An owner's policy may have *standard coverage* or *extended coverage*. Standard coverage protects against title defects such as incompetent grantors, invalid deeds, fraudulent transaction documents, and defects in the chain of title. Extended coverage protects against liabilities that may not be of public record, including fraud, unrecorded ownership claims, unintentional recording errors, and unrecorded liens. Extended coverage may also protect against adverse possessors, boundary disputes, and prescriptive easements. Neither standard nor extended coverage insures against defects expressly excluded by the policy or defects that the owner might have been aware of but did not disclose.

Before issuing a title insurance policy, a title company conducts a *title search* to uncover defects in title or unrecorded breaks in the chain of title. If the search fails to discover any uninsurable defects, the company issues a **binder**, or commitment to insure. The binder recapitulates the property description, interest to be insured, names of insured parties, and exceptions to coverage.

Attorney's opinion of abstract. An attorney's opinion of abstract states that the attorney has examined a title abstract, and gives the attorney's opinion of the condition and marketability of the title. Generally, an opinion is not a proof or guarantee of clear title. Further, it offers no protection in the event title turns out to be defective.

Title certificate. A title certificate is a summary of the condition of title as of the date of the certificate, based on a search of public records by an abstractor or title analyst. The certificate does not guarantee clear title against defects, unrecorded encumbrances or encroachments.

6 Transferring and Recording Title to Real Estate
Snapshot Review

TITLE TO REAL ESTATE

Legal and equitable title
- legal title: ownership of the bundle of rights
- equitable title: a conditional right to legal title subject to an owner's agreements with buyers and creditors

Notice of title
- how ownership is evidenced to the public
- actual notice: knowledge acquired or imparted directly through demonstrable evidence, e.g., presenting or inspecting a deed, visiting a party in possession
- constructive notice: knowledge one could or should have obtained, as presumed by law; imparted by recording in public records "for all to see"

Transferring title
- voluntary by grant, deed, or will
- involuntary by descent, escheat, eminent domain, foreclosure, adverse possession, estoppel

DEEDS OF CONVEYANCE
- instruments of voluntary conveyance by grantor to grantee

Delivery and acceptance
- legal title transfers upon competent grantor's intentional delivery and grantee's acceptance; in Torrens, title transfers upon registration

Validity
- grantor, grantee, in writing, legal description, granting clause, consideration, grantor's signature, acknowledgement, delivery and acceptance

Deed clauses and covenants
- premises clause: granting
- habendum clause: type of estate
- reddendum clause: restrictions
- tenendum clause: other property included
- warrants: seizen; quiet enjoyment; further assurance; forever; encumbrances; grantor's acts

Statutory deeds
- bargain and sale: "I own but won't defend"
- general warranty: "I own and will defend"
- special warranty: "I own and warrant myself only"
- quitclaim: "I may or may not own, and won't defend"

Special purpose deeds
- used for different purposes, to convey certain interests, or by certain parties

Transfer tax
- state tax on conveyances based on price

WILLS
- last will and testament: voluntary transfer to heirs after death
- maker: devisor or testator; heir: devisee; estate: devise

Types of will	• witnessed; holographic; approved; nuncupative
Validity	• adult; competent; indicates "last will and testament"; signed; witnessed; voluntary
Probate	• if testate, estate passes to heirs; if intestate, to successors by descent; if intestate with no heirs, estate escheats to state or county
	• process: validate will; validate, settle claims and pay taxes; transfer balance of estate to heirs
INVOLUNTARY TITLE TRANSFER	• descent and escheat: no will
	• foreclosure: lose title by forfeiture
	• eminent domain: lose title to public for the greater good
	• adverse possession: by claim of right or color of title; continuous, notorious, hostile possession; may have to pay taxes
	• estoppel: barred by prior acts or claims
TITLE RECORDS	• all instruments affecting title must be recorded
	• give public notice; protect owners; protect lienholders' claims
Chain of title	• successive property owners from original grant to present owner
	• abstract of title: chronology of recorded owners, transfers, encumbrances
Recording system	• local property recording system governed by state law
	• Torrens registry: requires court action initially: legal title does not pass until recordation occurs
Title evidence	• needed to prove marketable title as well as who owns
	• forms of evidence: Torrens; title insurance; attorney's opinion of abstract; title certificates

7 Leasing Essentials

The Lease Contract
Types of Lease
Default and Termination
Uniform Residential Landlord and Tenant Act

THE LEASE CONTRACT

Leasehold rights and obligations
Contract requirements
Lease clauses

A lease is both *an instrument of conveyance* and *a contract* between principal parties to uphold certain covenants and obligations. As a conveyance, a lease conveys an interest, called the leasehold estate, but does not convey legal title to the property. For this reason, a leasehold is also called a **less-than-freehold** estate.

The four principal types of leasehold estate are:

> ▶ **estate for years**: has a specific lease term

> ▶ **estate from period-to-period**: the lease term automatically renews

> ▶ **estate at will**: has no specified lease term

> ▶ **estate at sufferance**: a tenancy without consent

The legal essence of a valid lease is that *it conveys an exclusive right to use and occupy a property for a limited period of time in exchange for rent and the return of the property after the lease term is over.* Leasehold estates are distinguished from freeholds by their temporary nature. Every leasehold has a limited duration, whether the term is 99 years or not stated at all, as in an estate at will. While the lease conveys exclusive use, it may also *restrict such use* to conform to the landlord's desires. For example, an apartment lease may prohibit a tenant from using or storing hazardous materials within the premises.

Like other contracts, a lease becomes a binding agreement when the parties accept the terms of the agreement and communicate their agreement to the other party. Recording of a leasehold conveyance is not a requirement for validity, although it is usually good procedure to do so.

In a lease arrangement, the owner is the **landlord**, or **lessor**, and the renter is the **tenant**, or **lessee**.

Leasehold rights and obligations

Tenant's rights and obligations. A lease conveys a **leasehold interest** or **estate** that grants the tenant the following rights during the lease term:

> ▶ exclusive possession and occupancy
> ▶ exclusive use
> ▶ quiet enjoyment
> ▶ profits from use

A tenant has the sole right to occupy and use the premises without interference from outside parties, including the landlord. The landlord may enter the premises for specified purposes such as inspections, but the interference must be reasonable and limited. In addition, the landlord can do nothing outside of the lease's express provisions that would impair the tenant's enjoyment of income deriving from use of the premises. For example, the landlord can not place a kiosk in front of a retail tenant's entry in such a way as to prevent customers from entering the store.

The lease defines the tenant's obligations, which principally are to:

> ▶ pay the rent on time
> ▶ maintain the property's condition
> ▶ comply with the rules and regulations of the building

Landlord's rights and obligations. In conveying the leasehold estate, the landlord acquires a **leased fee estate,** which entails the rights to:

> ▶ receive rent
> ▶ re-possess the property following the lease term
> ▶ monitor the tenant's obligations to maintain the premises

The lease defines the landlord's obligations, which principally are to:

> ▶ provide the necessary building support and services
> ▶ maintain the condition of the property

Death of tenant or landlord. A valid lease creates obligations that survive the death of the landlord or tenant, with certain exceptions. A tenant's estate *remains liable for payment of rent if the tenant dies;* the landlord's estate *remains bound to provide occupancy despite the landlord's death.*

Conveyance of leased property. The landlord may sell, assign, or mortgage the leased fee interest. However, transferring and encumbering the leased property do not extinguish the obligations and covenants of a lease. Buyers and creditors, therefore, must take their respective interests subject to the terms of the lease.

Contract requirements

State contract laws determine the requirements for a valid lease. These laws generally require the following conditions.

Parties. The principal parties must be legally able to enter into the agreement; i.e., meet certain age, sanity, and other requirements.

Property description. The lease must identify the property by legal description or other locally accepted reference.

Exclusive possession. The landlord must provide an irrevocable right to exclusive possession during the lease term, provided the tenant meets all obligations.

Legal and permitted use. The intended use of the property must be legal. A use that is legal but not permitted does not invalidate the lease but constitutes grounds for default.

Consideration. The lease contract must be accompanied by consideration to the landlord for the rights conveyed. How the consideration is paid does not affect the lease's validity, so long as the parties comply with the terms of the lease.

Offer and acceptance. The parties must accept the lease, and communicate their acceptance to the other party, for the lease to take legal effect.

Signatures. The landlord must sign the lease to convey the leasehold interest. A tenant need not sign the lease, although it is prudent to do so in order to enforce the terms of the lease. Multiple tenants who sign a single lease are jointly and severally responsible for fulfilling lease obligations. Thus, if one renter abandons an apartment, the other renters remain liable for rent.

Oral versus written form. Generally, a *lease for a period exceeding one year cannot be oral but must be in writing to be enforceable* because of the Statute of Frauds. An oral lease or rental agreement is legally construed to be a tenancy at will, having no specified term. Further, an oral lease terminates on the death of either principal party.

Lease clauses

The clauses of a lease define the contractual relationship between landlord and tenant. The most important and basic clauses are the following.

Rent and security deposit. A rent clause stipulates the time, place, manner and amount of rent payment. It defines any grace period that is allowed, and states the penalties for delinquency.

The lease may also call for a security deposit to protect the landlord against losses from property damage or the tenant's default. State law regulates the handling of the security deposit: where it is deposited, and whether the tenant receives interest on the deposit. A landlord may require additional financial security from a tenant of dubious creditworthiness in the form of personal guarantees, third party guarantees, or pledges of other property as collateral.

Lease term. In the absence of an explicit term with beginning and ending date, a court will generally construe the lease to be a tenancy at will, cancelable upon proper notice.

Repairs and maintenance. Repairs and maintenance provisions define the landlord's and tenant's respective responsibilities for property repairs and maintenance. Generally, the tenant is responsible for routine maintenance of the premises while the landlord is responsible for general repairs. In residential leases, the landlord is responsible for major repairs and capital improvements. Payment of repairs and maintenance costs, however, is entirely negotiable between landlord and tenant.

Subletting and assignment. Subletting (subleasing) is the transfer by a tenant, the **sublessor**, of a *portion* of the leasehold interest to another party, the **sublessee**, through the execution of a **sublease**. The sublease spells out all of the rights and obligations of the sublessor and sublessee, including the payment of rent to the sublessor. The sublessor remains *primarily liable* for the original lease with the landlord. The subtenant is *liable* only to the sublessor.

For example, a sublessor subleases a portion of the occupied premises for a portion of the remaining term. The sublessee pays sublease rent to the sublessor, who in turn pays lease rent to the landlord.

An assignment of the lease is a transfer of the *entire leasehold interest* by a tenant, the **assignor**, to a third party, the **assignee**. There is no second lease, and the assignor retains no residual rights of occupancy or other leasehold rights unless expressly stated in the assignment agreement. The assignee becomes primarily liable for the lease and rent, and the assignor, the original tenant, remains secondarily liable. The assignee pays rent directly to the landlord.

All leases clarify the rights and restrictions of the tenant regarding subleasing and assigning the leasehold interest. Generally, the landlord cannot prohibit either act, but the tenant must obtain the landlord's written approval. The reason for this requirement is that the landlord has a financial stake in the creditworthiness of any prospective tenant.

Rules and regulations. A tenant must abide by all usage restrictions imposed by the lease's rules and regulations for the property. These rules aim to protect the property's condition as well as the rights of other tenants.

Improvements and alterations. A landlord typically wants to prevent a tenant from making alterations that later tenants may not desire. By the same token, a tenant who pays for an improvement wants to know who will own it at the end of the lease term. An improvements and alterations clause therefore identifies necessary permissions and procedures, and who owns improvements. Customarily, tenant improvements become the property of the landlord in the absence of an express agreement to the contrary.

Options. An option clause offers a tenant the opportunity to choose a course of action at some time in the future under certain terms. Typical options are the right to renew the lease, buy the property, and lease additional adjacent space. A tenant does not have to exercise an option, but the landlord must comply if the tenant does exercise it.

Damage and destruction. A damage and destruction provision defines the rights and obligations of the parties in the event the leased premises are damaged or destroyed. State laws regulate such provisions.

TYPES OF LEASE

Gross lease
Net lease
Percentage lease
Residential lease
Commercial lease
Ground lease
Proprietary lease
Leasing of rights

Gross lease

A gross lease, or **full service** lease, requires the landlord to pay the property's operating expenses, including utilities, repairs, and maintenance, while the tenant pays only rent. Rent levels under a gross lease are higher than under a net lease, since the landlord recoups expense outlays in the form of added rent.

Gross leases are common for office and industrial properties. Residential leases are usually gross leases with the exception that the tenants often pay utilities expenses.

Net lease

A net lease requires a tenant to pay for utilities, internal repairs, and a proportionate share of taxes, insurance, and operating expenses in addition to rent. In effect, the landlord "passes through" actual property expenses to the tenant rather than charging a higher rent level. Net leases vary as to exactly what expenses the tenant is responsible for. The extreme form of net lease requires tenants to cover all expenses, including major repairs and property taxes.

Net leases are common for office and industrial properties. They are sometimes also used for single family dwellings.

In practice, the terms net and gross lease can be misleading: some gross leases still require tenants to pay some expenses such as utilities and repairs. Similarly, some net leases require the landlord to pay certain expenses. Prudent tenants and landlords look at all expense obligations in relation to the level of rent to be charged.

Percentage lease

A percentage lease allows the landlord to share in the income generated from the use of the property. A tenant pays **percentage rent**, or an amount of rent equal to a percentage of the tenant's periodic gross sales. The percentage rent may be:

> ▸ a fixed percent of gross revenue without a minimum rent
> ▸ a fixed minimum rent plus an additional percent of gross sales
> ▸ a percentage rent or minimum rent, whichever is greater

Percentage leases are used only for retail properties.

Residential lease

A residential lease may be a net lease or a gross lease. Usually, it is a form of gross lease in which the landlord pays all property expenses except the tenant's utilities and water. Since residential leases tend to be short in term, tenants cannot be expected to pay for major repairs and improvements. The landlord, rather, absorbs these expenses and recoups the outlays through higher rent.

Residential leases differ from commercial and other types of lease in that:

- lease terms are shorter, typically one or two years

- lease clauses are fairly standard from one property to the next, in order to reflect compliance with local landlord-tenant relations laws

- lease clauses are generally not negotiable, particularly in larger apartment complexes where owners want uniform leases for all residents

Commercial lease

A commercial lease may be a net, gross, or percentage lease, if the tenant is a retail business. As a rule, a commercial lease is a significant and complex business proposition. It may involve hundreds of thousands of dollars for improving the property to the tenant's specifications. Since the lease terms are often long, total rent liabilities for the tenant can easily be millions of dollars.

Some important features of commercial leases are:

- long term, ranging up to 25 years
- require tenant improvements to meet particular usage needs
- virtually all lease clauses are negotiable due to the financial magnitude of the transaction
- default can have serious financial consequences; therefore, lease clauses must express all points of agreement and be very precise

Ground lease

A ground lease, or **land lease**, concerns the land portion of a real property. The owner grants the tenant a leasehold interest in the land only, in exchange for rent.

Ground leases are primarily used in three circumstances:

- an owner wishes to lease raw land to an agricultural or mining interest

- unimproved property is to be developed and either the owner wants to retain ownership of the land, or the developer or future users of the property do not want to own the land

- the owner of an improved property wishes to sell an interest in the improvements while retaining ownership of the underlying land

In the latter two instances, a ground lease offers owners, developers, and users various financing, appreciation, and tax advantages. For example, a ground lease lessor can take advantage of the increase in value of the land due to the new improvements developed on it, without incurring the risks of developing and owning the improvements. Land leases executed for the purpose of development or to segregate ownership of land from ownership of improvements are inherently long term leases, often ranging from thirty to fifty years.

Proprietary lease

A proprietary lease conveys a leasehold interest to an owner of a cooperative. The proprietary lease does not stipulate rent, as the rent is equal to the owner's share of the periodic expenses of the entire cooperative. The term of the lease is likewise unspecified, as it coincides with the ownership period of the cooperative tenant: when an interest is sold, the proprietary lease for the seller's unit is assigned to the new buyer.

Leasing of rights

The practice of leasing property rights other than the rights to exclusive occupancy and possession occurs most commonly in the leasing of water rights, air rights, and mineral rights.

For example, an owner of land that has deposits of coal might lease the mineral rights to a mining company, giving the mining company the limited right to extract the coal. The rights lease may be very specific, stating how much of a mineral or other resource may be extracted, how the rights may be exercised, for what period of time, and on what portions of the property. The lessee's rights do not include common leasehold interests such as occupancy, exclusion, quiet enjoyment, or possession of the leased premises.

Another example of a rights lease is where a railroad wants to erect a bridge over a thoroughfare owned by a municipality. The railroad must obtain an air rights agreement of some kind, whether it be an easement, a purchase, or a lease, before it can construct the bridge.

DEFAULT AND TERMINATION

Remedies for default
Default by tenant
Default by landlord
Causes for lease termination

Remedies for default

A landlord or tenant who violates any of the terms and covenants of the lease has breached the contract and is in default. In the event of a default, the damaged party may pursue court action, including suing for

> ▶ damages
> ▶ cancellation of the lease
> ▶ specific performance

A successful suit for **specific performance** compels the defaulting party to perform the contract obligation that was breached. For example, if a landlord fails to replace carpeting as promised in the lease, the tenant can sue to obtain the landlord's specific performance of installing a new carpet.

Default by tenant

Tenant default occurs most commonly from failure to pay rent or maintain the premises. If a tenant is in default, the landlord may file a **suit for possession**, also called a **suit for eviction**. If successful in this suit, the landlord can repossess the property and evict the tenant. The landlord also has the right to sue for damages.

Before filing a suit for possession, the landlord must give the tenant proper notice to pay monies due or otherwise cure the default before a deadline, or else vacate the premises. If the deadline passes without satisfaction, the landlord may file the suit and obtain a judgment for possession. The landlord may then obtain an order directing the sheriff to complete the eviction, forcibly if necessary.

Default by landlord

The most common form of landlord default is failure to provide services and maintain the property condition. When a landlord defaults on the terms of the lease, tenants may sue for damages. In an instance where the landlord's negligence or disruptive action has rendered the property unoccupiable, a tenant may vacate the premises and declare that the lease is cancelled by default. This action, called **constructive eviction**, can nullify the tenant's lease obligations if the claim succeeds in court. In order to obtain a constructive eviction judgment, the tenant *must vacate* the premises.

For example, a landlord will not repair a roof and will not allow an office tenant to make the repair and deduct the cost from the rent. A thunderstorm soaks the suite and ruins several pieces of office equipment. By refusing to act, the landlord has breached the lease covenant to maintain the premises. The tenant moves out, claiming the lease null and void. The tenant also sues the landlord for damages to the equipment and for recovery of relocation expenses.

Causes for lease termination

A lease may terminate for any of the following causes.

Breach or default. Breach of contract or default, as previously discussed, may terminate a lease.

Term expiration. In a tenancy for years, the lease automatically terminates at the end of the lease term.

Notice. Proper notice by either party may terminate a periodic leasehold, or a tenancy at will.

Voluntary agreement. Both parties can agree to terminate a lease at any time.

Property destruction. Destruction of the property is grounds for terminating lease obligations.

Condemnation. A taking by eminent domain proceedings generally terminates a lease.

Foreclosure. A foreclosure extinguishes all prior interests in a property, including a leasehold.

Death of tenant or landlord, with qualifications. A lease for tenancy at will terminates on the death of either landlord or tenant. A lease also terminates on the death of the landlord if the landlord held a life estate interest in the property, since the landlord could not have conveyed an interest that extended beyond his or her own interest.

Except in the circumstances mentioned, a lease *does not* terminate on the death of the landlord or tenant. Sale of the property also does not terminate a lease.

Abandonment. If a tenant abandons a leased property and demonstrates no intention of fulfilling the obligations of the lease, the landlord may re-take possession and pursue legal recourses for default. In such a case, the tenant remains liable for payment of rent. The landlord also has the option of terminating the lease, which releases the tenant from responsibility for rent.

However, the landlord may be able to sue for damages and at the same time re-let the property.

It is important to note that vacating leased premises does not in itself constitute abandonment, and certainly not if the tenant continues to abide by the lease obligations.

UNIFORM RESIDENTIAL LANDLORD AND TENANT ACT (URLTA)

Areas of regulation

The **Uniform Residential Landlord and Tenant Act (URLTA)** is a model law enacted as a blueprint for state laws to *regulate leasing and management practices of landlords with residential properties*. Numerous states have enacted tenant-landlord regulations in response to the law.

The act aims to:

> ▸ equalize and standardize rights of landlord and tenant
> ▸ protect tenants from unethical practices
> ▸ prevent unfair, complex leases and their enforceability

One important effect of URLTA is that it prompted legislation at the state level that empowered the courts to nullify residential leases that violated URLTA guidelines, particularly where a lease gave unfair advantage to the landlord.

Areas of regulation URLTA legislation primarily addresses the lease contract, deposits and advances, obligations of landlord and tenant, the landlord's rights of access, and standards for eviction.

Lease agreements. URLTA sets standards for improving oral, vague, or unbalanced lease agreements. The law's positions on these issues are:

> ▸ unclear lease term: becomes a periodic tenancy
> ▸ rent amount: fair market value or court's opinion
> ▸ waiving of rights: certain rights cannot be waived

The law intends to avoid irregularities and vagueness in the lease term and rent obligations, as these can cause exaggeration in a landlord's claim for the amount of rent due from a defaulting tenant. A vague lease term can also lead to a dispute about the duration of a tenant's possession rights. A landlord, for example, could claim that a lease has expired in order to acquire a higher-paying tenant. URLTA also discourages the landlord practice of persuading tenants to waive rights they do not understand or are unaware of.

Deposit and advance. URLTA requires leases to be clear about:

> ▸ maximum deposit amount
> ▸ the tenant's right to earn interest on the deposit

- ▶ commingling deposit or advance with other monies
- ▶ deadline for returning deposits
- ▶ procedures and criteria for return of the deposit to the tenant

Although URLTA applies to how landlords can handle deposits and advances, state laws also strictly regulate how brokers and agents may handle tenant monies.

Landlord's obligations. Under URLTA, a landlord must:

- ▶ bargain in good faith with the tenant
- ▶ provide required maintenance
- ▶ make repairs
- ▶ comply with local building codes
- ▶ provide access and safety services: elevator; fire escapes, etc.
- ▶ provide a procedure for delivery of official notices

Tenant's obligations. A tenant must:

- ▶ bargain in good faith
- ▶ maintain the condition of the leased premises
- ▶ abide by (legitimate) rules and regulations of the building
- ▶ refrain from abusing or causing destruction to the property
- ▶ limit uses to those approved
- ▶ avoid unduly disturbing other tenants

Access. URLTA attempts to balance the landlord's right to access the premises with the tenant's right of quiet enjoyment. The landlord has the right to enter the premises at any time when acting to prevent damage or destruction; to make repairs or show the property, on giving proper notice; if the purpose is not arbitrary and the time is reasonable The tenant may not refuse the landlord entry for acceptable reasons such as emergencies, repairs, inspections, and showings.

Default and eviction. URLTA attempts to establish equitable procedures for dealing with lease defaults. If the landlord defaults, a tenant may sue for damages, terminate the agreement, or negotiate a rent abatement. Tenants generally are not released of liability for rent during a dispute. Rents, however, may be paid to a court impound pending judgment. If a tenant defaults, the landlord may terminate and evict, provided proper notice is made and the landlord can justify the cause for the action.

Exemptions. State laws based on URLTA generally do not apply to transient occupancies, such as hotel and motel rentals, proprietary leases in cooperatives, or to occupancy in a residence that is under a contract for deed.

7 Leasing Essentials
Snapshot Review

THE LEASE CONTRACT
- instrument of leasehold conveyance; contract of covenants and obligations

Leasehold rights and obligations
- landlord grants temporary, exclusive use in trade for rent and reversion
- tenant rights: exclusive use and possession; quiet enjoyment; profits
- tenant obligations: pay rent; maintain premises; follow rules
- landlord rights: receive rent; repossess; monitor property condition
- landlord obligations: support and services; maintenance
- leasehold rights survive death and conveyance or encumbrance

Contract requirements
- parties; legal description; exclusive possession; legal use; lease term; consideration; offer and acceptance; signatures; written if over one year in term

Lease clauses
- rent; deposit; term; repairs and maintenance; subletting and assignment; rules and regulations; improvements; alterations; options; damage; destruction

TYPES OF LEASE
- based on expense responsibility; how rent is paid; property type; rights leased

Gross lease
- landlord pays expenses; tenant pays more rent

Net lease
- tenant pays some or all expenses; rent is less

Percentage lease
- landlord receives rent minimum plus percentage of retailer's sales

Residential lease
- gross lease hybrid; short term; uniform terms reflect landlord-tenant standards

Commercial lease
- longer term; entails tenant improvements; complex, negotiable lease terms

Ground lease
- landlord owns and leases ground but does not own improvements

Proprietary lease
- for cooperative unit owners; indefinite term; assigned to new unit owner on sale

Leasing of rights
- leasehold transfer of rights for limited use; examples: air, mineral, water rights

DEFAULT AND TERMINATION

Remedies for default
- sue for damages, lease cancellation, and/or specific performance

Default by tenant
- cancellation; damages; suit for possession; must give proper notice

Default by landlord
- suit for constructive eviction; must vacate premises to uphold

Causes for lease termination
- default; term expiration; notice; voluntary agreement; property destruction; condemnation; death, in some cases; abandonment

UNIFORM RESIDENTIAL LANDLORD AND TENANT ACT
- aims to balance landlord and tenant rights; to standardize leases and eviction procedures; to protect tenants; serve as model for state-level legislation

Areas of regulation
- contract language; waiver of rights; deposit; obligations of landlord and tenant; default and eviction

8 Land Use Planning And Control

Real Estate Planning
Public Land Use Control
Private Land Use Control
Environmental Controls

REAL ESTATE PLANNING

Goals of land use control
The master plan
Planning objectives
Plan development
Planning management

While the Constitution guarantees the right of individual ownership of real estate, it does not guarantee the uncontrolled sale, use, and development of real estate. As American history demonstrates, unregulated use of real estate has significant potential for eventual damage to property values as well as to the environment. Moreover, with the explosive urban growth in this century, it has become clear that regulation of land use is necessary to preserve the interests, safety, and welfare of the community.

Without a central authority to exert control, land use tends to be chaotic. For example, rapid growth can outpace the support capabilities of basic municipal services such as sewers, power, water, schools, roads and communications. On an aesthetic level, communities need controls to keep certain commercial and industrial land uses away from residential areas to avoid the undermining of property values by pollution, noise, and traffic congestion.

Goals of land use control

Over time, public and private control of land use has come to focus on certain core purposes. These are:

 ▸ preservation of property values
 ▸ promotion of the highest and best use of property
 ▸ balance between individual property rights and the public good, i.e., its health, safety and welfare
 ▸ control of growth to remain within infrastructure capabilities
 ▸ incorporation of community consensus into regulatory and planning activities

The optimum management of real property usage must take into account both the interests of the individual and the interests of the surrounding community. While maintaining the value of an individual estate is important, the owner of an estate must realize that unregulated use and development can jeopardize the value not only of the owner's estate but of neighboring properties. Similarly, the community must keep in mind the effect of government actions on individual property values, since local government is largely supported by taxes based on the value of property.

Exhibit 8.1 Public Land Use Control

| Develepmont | Administration | Implementation |

A community achieves its land usage goals through a three-phase process, as the exhibit illustrates:

> ▶ *development of a master plan* for the jurisdiction
> ▶ *administration of the plan* by a municipal, county, or regional planning commission
> ▶ *implementation of the plan* through public control of zoning, building codes, permits, and other measures

Municipal, county, and regional authorities develop comprehensive land use plans for a particular community with the input of property owners. A planning commission manages the master plan and enforces it by exercising its power to establish zones, control building permits, and create building codes.

In addition to public land use planning and control, some private entities, such as subdivision associations, can impose additional standards of land use on owners within the private entity's legal jurisdiction. Private controls are primarily implemented by deed restrictions.

The master plan
Public land use planning incorporates long-term usage strategies and growth policies in a **land use plan**, or **master plan**. In many states, the process of land use planning begins when the state legislature enacts laws *requiring all counties and municipalities to adopt a land use plan*. The land use plan must not only reflect the needs of the local area, but also conform to state and federal environmental laws and the plans of regional and state planning agencies. The state enforces its planning mandates by giving state agencies the power to approve county and local plans.

The master plan therefore fuses state and regional land use laws with local land use objectives that correspond to the municipality's social and economic conditions. The completed plan becomes the overall guideline for creating and enforcing zones, building codes, and development requirements.

Planning objectives The primary objectives of a master plan are generally to control and accommodate social and economic growth.

Amount of growth. A master plan *sets specific guidelines on how much growth the jurisdiction will allow*. While all communities desire a certain degree of growth, too much growth can overwhelm services and infrastructure.

To formulate a growth strategy, a plan initially forecasts growth trends, then estimates how well the municipality can keep pace with the growth forecast. The outcome is a policy position that limits building permits and development projects to desired growth parameters. A growth plan considers:

> ▶ nature, location and extent of permitted uses
> ▶ availability of sanitation facilities
> ▶ adequacy of drainage, waste collection, and potable water systems
> ▶ adequacy of utilities companies
> ▶ adequacy and patterns of thoroughfares
> ▶ housing availability
> ▶ conservation of natural resources
> ▶ adequacy of recreational facilities
> ▶ ability and willingness of the community to absorb new taxes, bond issues, and assessments

Growth patterns. In addition to the quantity of growth, a master plan also *defines what type of growth will occur, and where*. Major considerations are:

> ▶ the type of enterprises and developments to allow
> ▶ residential density and commercial intensity
> ▶ effects of industrial and commercial land uses on residential and public sectors, i.e., where to allow such uses
> ▶ effect of new developments on traffic patterns and thoroughfares
> ▶ effects on the environment and environmental quality (air, water, soil, noise, visual aspects)
> ▶ effect on natural resources that support the community
> ▶ code specifications for specific construction projects

Accommodating demand. As the master plan sets forth guidelines for how much growth will be allowed, it must also *make plans for accommodating expanding or contracting demand for services and infrastructure*. The plan must identify:

> ▶ facilities requirements for local government
> ▶ new construction requirements for streets, schools, and social services facilities such as libraries, civic centers, etc.
> ▶ new construction required to provide power, water and sewer services

Plan development   In response to land use objectives, community attitudes, and conclusions drawn from research, the planning personnel formulate their plan. In the course of planning, they analyze

> - population and demographic trends
> - economic trends
> - existing land use
> - existing support facilities
> - traffic patterns

Planning management   Public land use management takes place within county and municipal **planning departments**. These departments are responsible for:

> - long-term implementation of the master plan
> - creating rules and restrictions that support plans and policies
> - enforcing and administering land use regulation on an everyday basis

The planning commission. In most jurisdictions, a planning commission or board comprised of officials appointed by the government's legislative entity handles the planning function.

The commission oversees the operations of the department's professional planning staff and support personnel. In addition, the commission makes recommendations to elected officials concerning land use policy and policy administration.

The planning commission is responsible for:

> - approving site plans and subdivision plans
> - approving building permits
> - ruling on zoning issues

PUBLIC LAND USE CONTROL

Zoning
Zoning administration
Subdivision regulation
Building codes
Public acquisition and ownership
Environmental restrictions

At the state level, the legislature enacts laws that control and restrict land use, particularly from the environmental perspective. At the local level, county and city governments control land use through the authority known as **police power**. The most common expressions of police power are county and municipal **zoning**. Other examples of public land use control are:

- ► subdivision regulations
- ► building codes
- ► eminent domain
- ► environmental restrictions
- ► development requirements

Governments also have the right to **own** real property for public use and welfare. In exercising its ownership rights, a municipality may **annex** property adjacent to its existing property or purchase other tracts of land through conventional transfers. Where necessary, it may force property owners to sell their property through the power of **eminent domain**.

Zoning

Zoning is the primary tool by which cities and counties regulate land use and implement their respective master plans. The Constitution grants the states the legal authority to regulate, and the states delegate the authority to counties and municipalities through legislation called **enabling acts**.

The zoning ordinance. The vehicle for zoning a city or county is the **zoning ordinance**, a regulation enacted by the local government. The intent of zoning ordinances is to specify land usage for every parcel within the jurisdiction. In some areas, state laws permit zoning ordinances to apply to areas immediately beyond the legal boundaries of the city or county.

Zoning ordinances implement the master plan by regulating density, land use intensity, aesthetics, and highest and best use. Ordinances typically address:

- ► the nature of land use-- office, commercial, residential, etc.
- ► size and configuration of a building site, including setbacks, sidewalk requirements, parking requirements, and access
- ► site development procedures
- ► construction and design methods and materials, including height restrictions, building-to-site area ratios, and architectural styles
- ► use of space within the building
- ► signage

Ordinance validity. Local planners do not have unlimited authority to do whatever they want. Their zoning ordinances must be clear in import, apply to all parties equally, and promote health, safety, and welfare of the community in a reasonable manner.

Building permits. Local governments enforce zoning ordinances by issuing building permits to those who want to improve, repair, or refurbish a property. To receive a permit, the project must comply with all relevant ordinances and codes. Further zoning enforcement is achieved through periodic inspections.

Types of zones. One of the primary applications of zoning power is the separation of residential properties from commercial and industrial uses. Proper design of land use in this manner preserves the aesthetics and value of neighborhoods and promotes the success of commercial enterprises through intelligently located zones.

Six common types of zone are

  ▸ residential
  ▸ commercial
  ▸ industrial
  ▸ agricultural
  ▸ public
  ▸ planned unit development (PUD)

Residential. Residential zoning restricts land use to private, non-commercial dwellings. Sub-zones in this category further stipulate the types of residences allowed, whether single-family, multi-unit complexes, condominiums, publicly subsidized housing, or other form of housing.

Residential zoning regulates:

  ▸ *density,* by limiting the number and size of dwelling units and lots in an area
  ▸ values and aesthetics, by limiting the type of residences allowed. Some areas adopt **buffer zones** to separate residential areas from commercial and industrial zones.

Commercial. Commercial zoning regulates the location of office and retail land usage. Some commercial zones allow combinations of office and retail uses on a single site. Sub-zones in this category may limit the type of retail or office activity permitted, for example, a department store versus a strip center.

Commercial zoning regulates:

  ▸ intensity of usage, by limiting the area of store or office per site area. Intensity regulation is further achieved by minimum parking requirements, setbacks, and building height restrictions.

Industrial. Industrial zoning regulates:

  ▸ intensity of usage
  ▸ type of industrial activity
  ▸ environmental consequences

A municipality may not allow some industrial zones, such as heavy industrial, at all. The industrial park is a relatively recent concept in industrial zoning.

Agricultural. Agricultural zoning restricts land use to farming, ranching, and other agricultural enterprises.

Public. Public zoning restricts land use to public services and recreation. Parks, post offices, government buildings, schools, and libraries are examples of uses allowed in a public zone.

Planned Unit Development (PUD). planned unit development zoning restricts use to development of whole tracts that are designed to use space efficiently and maximize open space. A PUD zone may be for residential, commercial, or industrial uses, or combinations thereof.

Zoning administration

Zoning Board of Adjustment. A county or local board, usually called the zoning board of adjustment or zoning appeals board, administers zoning ordinances. The board rules on interpretations of zoning ordinances as they apply to specific land use cases presented by property owners in the jurisdiction. In effect, the zoning board is a court of appeals for owners and developers who desire to use land in a manner that is not entirely consistent with existing ordinances.

The board conducts hearings of specific cases and renders official decisions regarding the land use based on evidence presented.

A zoning board generally deals with such issues and appeals as:

> ▸ nonconforming use
> ▸ variance
> ▸ special exception or conditional use permit
> ▸ zoning amendment

If the board rejects an appeal, the party may appeal the ruling further in a court of law.

Exhibit 8.2 Zoning Appeals

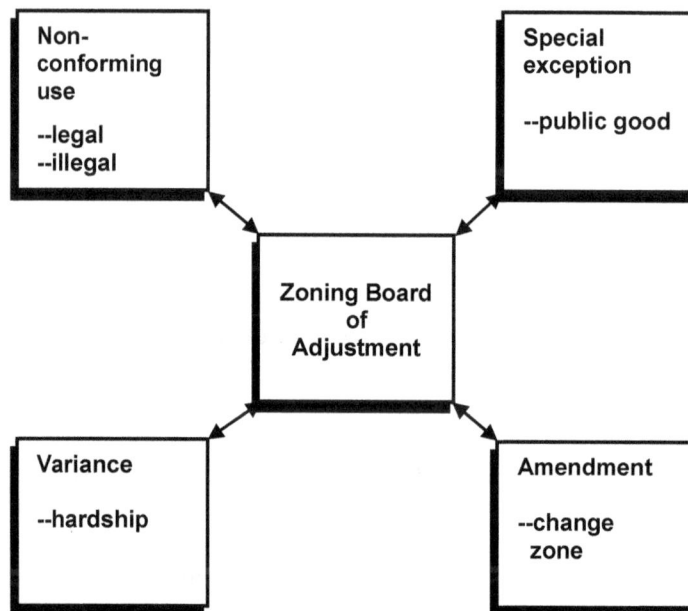

Nonconforming use. A nonconforming use is one *that clearly differs from current zoning.* Usually, nonconforming uses result when a zoning change leaves existing properties in violation of the new ordinance. This type of nonconforming use is a **legal** nonconforming use. A board usually treats this kind of situation by allowing it to continue either

- ▸ indefinitely
- ▸ until the structures are torn down
- ▸ only while the same use continues, or
- ▸ until the property is sold

For instance, a motel is situated in a residential area that no longer allows commercial activity. The zoning board rules that the motel may continue to operate until it is sold, destroyed or used for any other commercial purpose.

An **illegal nonconforming use** is one that conflicts with ordinances that were in place before the use commenced. For instance, if the motel in the previous example is sold, and the new owner continues to operate the property as a motel, the motel is now an illegal, nonconforming use.

Variance. A zoning variance allows a use that differs from the applicable ordinance for a variety of *justifiable* reasons, including that:

- ▸ compliance will cause unreasonable hardship
- ▸ the use will not change the essential character of the area
- ▸ the use does not conflict with the general intent of the ordinance

For example, an owner mistakenly violates a setback requirement by two feet. His house is already constructed, and complying with the full setback now would be extremely expensive, if not impossible. The zoning board grants a variance on the grounds that compliance would cause an unreasonable hardship.

A grant of a zoning variance may be unconditional, or it may require conditions to be fulfilled, such as removing the violation after a certain time.

Special exception. A special exception grant authorizes a use that is not consistent with the zoning ordinance in a literal sense, yet is clearly *beneficial or essential to the public welfare* and does not materially impair other uses in the zone.

A possible example is an old house in a residential zone adjacent to a retail zone. The zoning board might grant a special exception to a local group that proposes to renovate the house and convert it to a local museum, which is a retail use, since the community stands to benefit from the museum.

Amendment. A current or potential property owner may petition the zoning board for an outright change in the zoning of a particular property. For example, a property zoned for agricultural use has been idle for years. A major employer desires to develop the property for a local distribution facility, which would create numerous jobs, and petitions for an amendment. The board changes the zoning from agricultural to light industrial to permit the development. Since a change in zoning can have significant economic and social impact, an appeal for an amendment is a difficult process that often involves public hearings.

Subdivision regulation

In addition to complying with zoning ordinances, a developer of multiple properties in a subdivision must meet requirements for subdivisions.

Subdivision plat approval. The developer submits a plat of subdivision containing surveyed plat maps and comprehensive building specifications. The plat, as a minimum, shows that the plan complies with local zoning and building ordinances. The project can commence only after the relevant authority has approved the plat.

Subdivision requirements typically regulate:

- location, grading, alignment, surfacing, street width, highways
- sewers and water mains
- lot and block dimensions
- building and setback lines
- public use dedications
- utility easements
- ground percolation
- environmental impact report
- zoned density

Concurrency. Many states have adopted policies that require developers, especially of subdivisions, to take responsibility for the impact of their projects on the local infrastructure by taking corrective action. Concurrency is a policy that requires the developer to make accommodations *concurrently* with the development of the project itself, not afterwards. For example, if a project will create a traffic overload in an area, the developer may have to widen the road while constructing the project.

FHA requirements. In addition to local regulation, subdivisions must meet FHA (Federal Housing Authority) requirements to qualify for FHA financing insurance. The FHA sets standards similar to local ordinances to ensure an adequate level of construction quality, aesthetics, and infrastructure services.

Building codes

Building codes allow the county and municipality to protect the public against the hazards of unregulated construction. Building codes establish standards for virtually every aspect of a construction project, including offsite improvements such as streets, curbs, gutters, drainage systems, and onsite improvements such as the building itself.

Building codes typically address:

- architectural and engineering standards
- construction materials standards
- building support systems such as life safety, electrical, mechanical, and utility systems

Certificate of occupancy. Building inspectors inspect a new development or improvement for code compliance. If the work complies, the municipality or county issues a **certificate of occupancy** which officially clears the property for occupation and use.

Public acquisition and ownership

If efforts to regulate privately owned property are inadequate or impractical in a particular situation, or if there is a compelling public need, a county or local government may acquire property by means of direct purchase.

A government body might acquire land because of the public need for:

    ▸   thoroughfares and public rights-of-way
    ▸   recreational facilities
    ▸   schools
    ▸   essential public facilities
    ▸   urban renewal or redevelopment

In many cases, public acquisition of property is a voluntary transaction between the government entity and the private owner. However, if the private party is unwilling to sell, the government may purchase the property anyway. The power to do this is called **eminent domain**.

Eminent domain. Eminent domain allows a government entity to purchase a fee, leasehold, or easement interest in privately owned real property for the **public good** and for **public use**, regardless of the owner's desire to sell or otherwise transfer any interest. In exchange for the interest, the government must pay the owner "just compensation."

To acquire a property, the public entity initiates a condemnation suit. Transfer of title extinguishes all existing leases, liens, and other encumbrances on the property. Tenants affected by the condemnation sale may or may not receive compensation, depending on the terms of their agreement with the landlord.

Public entities that have the power of eminent domain include:

    ▸   all levels of government
    ▸   public districts (schools, etc.)
    ▸   public utilities
    ▸   public service corporations (power companies, etc.)
    ▸   public housing and redevelopment agencies
    ▸   other government agencies

To acquire a property, the public entity must first adopt a formal resolution to acquire the property, variously called a "resolution of necessity." The resolution must be adopted at a formal hearing where the owner may voice an opinion. Once adopted, the government agency may commence a condemnation suit in court. Subsequently, the property is purchased and the title is transferred in exchange for just compensation. Transfer of title extinguishes all existing leases, liens, and other encumbrances on the property. Tenants affected by the condemnation sale may or may not receive compensation, depending on the terms of their agreement with the landlord.

In order to proceed with condemnation, the government agency must demonstrate that the project is necessary, the property is necessary for the project, and that the location offers the greatest public benefit with the least detriment.

As an eminent domain proceeding is generally an involuntary acquisition, the condemnation proceeding must accord with due process of law to ensure that it does not violate individual property rights. Further, the public entity must justify its use of eminent domain in court by demonstrating the validity of the intended public use and the resulting "public good" or "public purpose" ultimately served.

The issue of eminent domain versus individual property rights has recently come under scrutiny in light of a 2005 Supreme Court ruling that affirmed the rights of state and local governments to use the power of eminent domain for urban re-development and revitalization. The ruling allowed that private parties could undertake a project for profit without any public guarantee that the project would be satisfactorily completed. The ruling brought the issue of "public use" into question, as the use of the re-development could well be private and even a private for-profit enterprise. The winning argument was that the "public purpose" is served when redevelopment creates much needed jobs in a depressed urban area. As a result of this decision, many see the power of eminent domain and the definition of public good as being in conflict with the constitutional rights of private property ownership. New and different interpretations of the public's right to pre-empt private property ownership by eminent domain may be expected.

PRIVATE LAND USE CONTROL

Deed restriction
Declaration restriction
Deed condition

Property owners in the private sector can regulate land use to some extent through deed restrictions and deed conditions.

Deed restriction

A restriction expressed in a conveyance (deed or lease) of a residential, commercial, or industrial property places limits on the use of the property. Such restrictions are also referred to as "covenants, conditions, and restrictions," or CCRs. A quitclaim deed can terminate a private deed restriction.

Typical restrictions concern:

> ▶ required minimum area of a residence
> ▶ setback
> ▶ prohibition against construction of sheds or secondary buildings
> ▶ prohibition against conducting certain commercial activities

Deed restrictions may not be discriminatory by restricting ownership or use on the basis of race, religion, marital status, or gender.

Restrictions on commercial property use may not violate fair trade and anti-trust laws.

Declaration restriction

The declaration of a subdivision, Planned Unit Development, condominium, and commercial or industrial park contains private use restrictions. These have the same legal effect as a deed restriction, as the declaration attaches to the rights in the property. A private party cannot, however, extinguish a declaration restriction by agreement or quitclaim deed.

The kinds of restrictions found in declarations are much the same as those found in deeds: construction restraints, aesthetics standards, etc.

The underlying purpose of restrictions is to preserve the value and quality of the neighborhood, commercial center, or industrial park.

Injunction. A private usage restriction can be enforced by filing for a court injunction. A court can order the violator to cease and desist, or to correct the infraction. If, however, owners in a subdivision or park allow a violation to continue for a sufficient length of time, they can lose their right to legal recourse.

Deed condition

A deed condition may restrict certain uses of a property, much like a deed restriction. However, violation of a deed condition gives the grantor the right to re- take possession of the property and file suit for legal title.

ENVIRONMENTAL CONTROLS

Areas of concern
Major legislation
Responsibilities and liabilities

In recent years, federal and state legislatures have enacted laws to conserve and protect the environment against the hazards of growth and development, particularly in terms of air, water, and soil quality.

Regional, county, and local planners must integrate environmental laws into their respective land use plans and regulations. Private property owners are responsible for complying with these laws.

Areas of concern

Air. Air quality, both indoor and outdoor, has been a matter of concern since the 1960's. With today's construction methods creating airtight, energy-efficient structures, attention to sources of indoor air pollution is more important than ever. Off-gassing from synthetic materials and lack of ventilation can lead to such consequences as Sick Building Syndrome (SBS) and Building-Related Illness (BRI) as well as other health problems. Among the significant threats are:

▸   *asbestos*, a powdery mineral once commonly used as a fireproof insulating material around pipes, in floor tiles and linoleum, in siding and roofing, in wallboard, joint compound, and many other applications.

    When airborne, it is a health hazard. Its use today is highly restricted, and removal can be expensive and dangerous. Inspection by a certified asbestos inspector is the best way to determine whether a building needs treatment.

▸   *carbon monoxide*, a colorless, odorless, poisonous gas that may result from faulty heating equipment. Home and commercial detection devices are available.

▸ *formaldehyde,* a chemical used in building materials and in other items such as fabrics and carpeting. As it ages, formaldehyde gives off a colorless, pungent gas.

Its use in urea-formaldehyde foam insulation (UFFI) was banned 1982 (ban later reduced to a warning) but the material is still present in many structures. *Other substances known in general as volatile organic compounds (VOCs) and* used in construction materials such as adhesives emit toxic fumes. Professional testing can identify levels and, in some cases, sources of formaldehyde gas and other VOCs.

▸ *lead,* a heavy metal once widely used in paints and plumbing materials. It has been banned in paint since 1978 and in new plumbing since 1988.

It continues to be a health threat, particularly to children, as it occurs in airborne paint particles, paint chips, and soil and groundwater polluted by various external sources of emission. Inspection should be performed by licensed lead inspectors.

▸ *mold,* a fungus that grows in the presence of moisture and oxygen on virtually any kind of organic surface.

It often destroys the material it grows on and emits toxic irritants into the air. Tightly sealed structures with inadequate ventilation are most susceptible. Roof leaks, improper venting of appliances, runoff from gutters and downspouts, and flood damage are common contributors. In recent years, mold- and mildew-related lawsuits and claims have become substantial.

▸ *radon*, a colorless, odorless, radioactive gas that occurs naturally in the soil throughout the United States.

It enters buildings through foundation and floor cracks, wall seams, sump pits, and windows, among other ways. At accumulations above certain levels, it is suspected of contributing to cancer. Excessive radon can be removed by special ventilation systems. Professional and home inspections are available.

Soil and water. Soil, groundwater, and drinking water supplies are vulnerable to pollution from leaking landfills; improper waste disposal; agricultural runoff; industrial dumping in waterways; highway and rail spills; industrial emissions; internal combustion emissions; and underground tanks leaking fuels and chemicals, to mention but a few sources. Some of the problems subject to controls are:

▸ dioxins, a family of compounds produced as a byproduct of manufacturing and incinerating materials that contain chlorine

▸ lead and *mercury*

▸ MTBE, Methyl Tertiary Butyl Ether, a gasoline additive

▸ PCB, Polychlorinated Biphenyl, a substance formerly widely used as an electrical insulation

▸ *Underground Storage Tanks* (USTs), regulated since 1984

▸ *Wetlands,* considered part of the natural water filtering system as well as special habitats, subject to restrictions on development and use.

Other ambient and natural conditions. Other regulated and controlled environmental conditions include:

▸ *Electromagnetic Fields* (EMFs) created by powerlines

▸ *noise* created by airports, air, rail and highway traffic

▸ *earthquake and flood hazards* that affect hazard insurance, lending practices, and construction requirements for buildings in designated flood and earthquake zones.

Exhibit 8.3 Environmental Concerns

	Indoors	**Outdoors**
Air	asbestos, BRI, carbon monoxide, formaldehyde, lead-based paint, mold, radon, SBS, VOCs	airborne lead, carbon dioxide, mercury, sulfur, dioxins
Soil		dioxins, lead, PCBs, waste, hazardous materials
Water	dioxins, lead plumbing, lead-paint, mercury, MTBE, PCBs	dioxins, lead, mercury, MTBE, PCBs, USTs, waste, hazardous materials
Ambience		EMFs, noise
Structure		flood, earthquake

BRI: Building-Related Illness SBS: Sick Building Syndrome VOC: Volatile Organic Compound MTBE: Methyl Tertiary Butyl Ether

PCB: Polychlorinated Biphenyl UST: Underground Storage Tank EMF: Electromagnetic Field UFFI: Urea-Formaldehyde Foam Insulation

Major legislation

National Environmental Policy Act (1969). This act created the Environmental Protection Agency (EPA) and the Council for Environmental Quality, giving them a mandate to establish environmental standards for land use planning. The act also required environmental impact surveys on large development projects.

Clean Air Amendment (1970). This act authorized the EPA to establish air quality standards for industrial land uses as well as for automobile and airplane emissions.

Water Quality Improvement Act (1970), the Water Pollution Control Act amendment (1972), the Clean Water Act Amendment (1977). These acts addressed standards to control water pollution and industrial wastes from the standpoints of future prevention as well as remediation of existing pollution.

Resource Recovery Act (1970), the Resource Conservation and Recovery Act (1976), the Comprehensive Environmental Response, Compensation and Liability Act (Superfund) (1980), the Superfund Amendment and Reauthorization Act (1986). These acts addressed disposal of solid and toxic wastes and measures for managing waste. In addition, the Superfund act provided money for hazardous waste disposal and the authority to charge cleanup costs to responsible parties.

Lead-based paint ban (1978) and Residential Lead-based Paint Hazard Reduction Act (1992, 1996). These regulations banned lead in the manufacture of paint and established disclosure requirements and guidelines for testing and remediation.

Exhibit 8.4 Landmarks in Environmental Control Legislation

Legislation	Date	Regulated
Solid Waste Disposal Act (later part of RCRA)	1965 (1976, 1999, 2002)	landfills
Air Quality Act, Clean Air Act	1967 (1970)	air quality standards
National Environmental Policy Act (NEPA)	1969 (1970)	created EPA
Flood Control Act	amended 1969	building in flood zones; flood insurance
Resource Recovery Act	1970	solid waste disposal
Water Quality Improvement Act	1970	dumping in navigable waters; wetlands
Water Pollution Control Act amendment	1972	dumping in navigable waters; wetlands
Marine Protection Research and Sanctuaries Act	1972	offshore waste dumping
Noise control legislation	1972	airport- and transportation-related noise
Coastal Zone Management Act	1972	beaches, marine habitats
Clean Water Act	1972 (1977)	dumping in navigable waters; wetlands
Safe Drinking Water Act	1974	public water supply, lead
Resource Conservation and Recovery Act (RCRA)	1976	hazardous waste, solid waste
Toxic Substances Control Act	1976	industrial chemicals
Lead-based paint ban (US Consumer Product Safety Commission rule)	1978	lead-based paint in residences
PCB ban (EPA rule)	1979	polychlorinated biphenyls
RCRA amendment	1984	underground storage tanks
Comprehensive Environmental Response, Compensation and Liability Act	1980	hazardous waste disposal
UFFI ban	1982	formaldehyde in insulation materials
Superfund Amendment and Reauthorization Act	1986	hazardous waste cleanup costs
Asbestos ban (EPA rule)	1989	asbestos in building materials
Residential Lead-based Paint Hazard Reduction Act (EPA and HUD rule)	1992 (1996)	lead-based paint disclosure and treatment
Flood Insurance Reform Act	1994	flood insurance in flood zones
Brownfields legislation	2002	industrial site cleanup

Responsibilities & liabilities

Licensees are expected to be aware of environmental issues and to know where to look for professional help. They are not expected to have expert knowledge of environmental law nor of physical conditions in a property. Rather, they must treat potential environmental hazards in the same way that they treat other material facts about a property: disclosure.

In sum, for their own protection, licensees should be careful to:

- be aware of potential hazards
- disclose known material facts
- distribute the HUD booklet (below)
- know where to seek professional help.

Lead. The Lead-based Paint Act of 1992 requires a seller or seller's agent to disclose known lead problems in properties built before 1978. The licensee must give the buyer or lessee a copy of the EPA-HUD-US Consumer Product Safety Commission booklet, "Protect Your Family from Lead in your home."

Further, the 1996 lead-based paint regulation requires sellers or lessors of almost all residential properties built before 1978 to disclose known lead-based paint hazards and provide any relevant records available. The seller is not required to test for lead but must allow the buyer a ten-day period for lead inspection. Only a licensed lead professional is permitted to deal with testing, removal or encapsulation. It is the real estate practitioner's responsibility to ensure compliance.

CERCLA/Superfund. Under CERCLA and the Superfund Amendment of 1986, current landowners as well as previous owners of a property may be held liable for environmental violations, even if "innocent" of a violation. Sellers often carry the greatest exposure, and real estate licensees may be held liable for improper disclosure.

A real property owner can be held liable for the entire cost of remediating soil, groundwater, or indoor air contamination. A tenant can be held liable for cleanup costs as an "operator" if tenant operations are linked to contamination

Sale of a contaminated property. Selling a property with an environmental problem does not avoid liability for the seller, although seller and buyer may agree to share or transfer some liability. If there is a concern, a Phase I audit or Environmental Site Assessment (ESA) should be conducted before proceeding with the transaction. A Phase I audit identifies

- prior uses
- presence of hazardous materials

The Phase I ESA reviews environmental documents; conducts a title search for environmental liens and restrictions; and includes a visual inspection of the site and surrounding properties. There is no sampling or testing. Fannie Mae, Freddie Mac, and HUD require special Phase I ESAs on certain properties.

A Phase II audit (ESA) is conducted if a site is considered contaminated. This is a more detailed investigation using chemical analysis to uncover hazardous substances and/or petroleum hydrocarbons in samples of soil, groundwater or building materials.

A Phase III audit (ESA) involves remediation. Intensive testing, sampling, monitoring, and modeling are applied to design plans for remediation, cleanup, and follow-up monitoring. Remediation may use a variety of techniques and technologies, such as excavation and removal, dredging, chemical treatment, pumping, and solidification. Major remediation efforts usually require extensive consultation with the surrounding community. Federal funding may be available.

See Chapter 20 for further discussion. For more information, also check these sources:

asbestos	https://www.epa.gov/indoor-air-quality-iaq
carbon monoxide	https://www.epa.gov/indoor-air-quality-iaq
formaldehyde	https://www.epa.gov/indoor-air-quality-iaq
lead	https://www.epa.gov/lead
	https://www.hud.gov/program_offices/healthy_homes/enforcement/disclosure
	https://www.epa.gov/lead/real-estate-disclosure
mold	https://www.epa.gov/mold/mold-and-your-home
radon	https://www.epa.gov/indoor-air-quality-iaq
	https://www.hud.gov/program_offices/healthy_homes/healthyhomes/radon
CERCLA	https://www.epa.gov/superfund

8 Land Use Planning and Control
Snapshot Review

REAL ESTATE PLANNING

Goals of land use control
- preserve property values; promote highest and best use; safeguard public health, safety and welfare; control growth; incorporate community consensus
- process: develop plan; create administration; authorize controls

The master plan
- long term growth and usage strategies; often required by state law
- local plans fuse municipal goals and needs with state and regional laws

Planning objectives
- control growth rates: how much growth will occur and at what rate
- control growth patterns: type of growth desired, where it should be located
- accommodate demand for services and infrastructure

Plan development
- research trends and conditions; blend local and state objectives into master plan

Planning management
- commission makes rules, approves permits, codes, and development plans

PUBLIC LAND USE CONTROL
- state laws; local regulations, zones, codes; public ownership; private restrictions

Zoning
- "police power" granted by state-level enabling acts; zoning ordinance: creates zones, usage restrictions, regulations, requirements

Types of zone
- residential, commercial, industrial, agricultural, public, PUD

Zoning administration
- Zoning Board of Adjustment oversees rule administration and appeals
- nonconforming use: legal if use prior to zone creation; variance: exception based on hardship; special exception: based on public interest; amendment: change of zones; rezoning

Subdivision regulation
- plat of subdivision and relevant requirements must be met and approved; must meet FHA requirements for insured financing

Building codes
- comprehensive onsite and offsite construction and materials standards; must be met to receive certificate of occupancy

Public acquisition and ownership
- eminent domain: public power to acquire property for public use

PRIVATE LAND USE CONTROL

Deed restriction
- single-property use restriction as stipulated in a deed; may not be discriminatory

Declaration restriction
- use restriction in multiple-property declarations; enforced by court injunction

Deed condition
- usage restriction that can trigger repossession by a previous owner if violated

ENVIRONMENTAL CONTROLS

Areas of concern
- air, soil, water quality; ambient health hazards; natural hazards

Major legislation
- limits damage to environment; standards for air, land, water, materials use

Responsibilities & liabilities
- disclosure and information for practitioners; remediation for owners; lead disclosure; CERCLA/Superfund exposure; Phase I, II, III Environmental Site Assessments to detect and mitigate contamination

9 Legal Descriptions

Methods of Legal Description
Metes and Bounds
The Rectangular Survey System
Recorded Plat Method
Describing Elevation

METHODS OF LEGAL DESCRIPTION

There are many common ways of describing properties: address (100 Main Street), name (Buckingham Palace), and general description ("the south forty acres"). Such informal descriptions are not acceptable for use in public recordation or, generally speaking, in a court of law because they lack both permanence and sufficient information for a surveyor to locate the property.

Even if a legal document or public record refers to an address, the reference is always supported by an accepted legal description.

A legal description of real property is one which *accurately locates and identifies the boundaries of the subject parcel to a degree acceptable by courts of law in the state where the property is located.*

The general criterion for a legal description is that it alone provides sufficient data for a surveyor to locate the parcel. A legal description identifies the property as unique and distinct from all other properties.

Legal description provides accuracy and consistency over time. Systems of legal description, in theory, facilitate transfers of ownership and prevent boundary disputes and problems with chain of title.

A legal description is required for:

> ▶   public recording
> ▶   creating a valid deed of conveyance or lease
> ▶   completing mortgage documents
> ▶   executing and recording other legal documents

In addition, a legal description provides a basis for court rulings on encroachments and easements.

The three accepted methods of legally describing parcels of real estate are:

- ▶ metes and bounds
- ▶ rectangular survey system, or government survey method
- ▶ recorded plat method, or lot and block method

Since the metes and bounds method preceded the inception of the rectangular survey system, the older East Coast states generally employ metes and bounds descriptions. States in the Midwest and West predominantly use the rectangular survey system. Some states combine methods.

METES AND BOUNDS

A metes and bounds description identifies the boundaries of a parcel of real estate using reference points, distances, and angles. The description always identifies an *enclosed* area by starting at an origination point, called **point of beginning**, or POB, and returning to the POB at the end of the description. A metes and bounds description *must return to the POB in order to be valid.*

The term "metes" refers to distance and direction, and the term "bounds" refers to fixed reference points, or **monuments** and **landmarks**, which may be natural and artificial. Natural landmarks include trees, rocks, rivers, and lakes. Artificial landmarks are typically surveyor stakes.

Many states use metes and bounds description to describe properties within the rectangular survey system.

A metes and bounds description begins with an identification of the city, county, and state where the property is located. Next, it identifies the POB and describes the distance and direction from the POB to the first monument, and then to subsequent monuments that *define the property's enclosed perimeter.*

Exhibit 9.1 Metes and Bounds Description

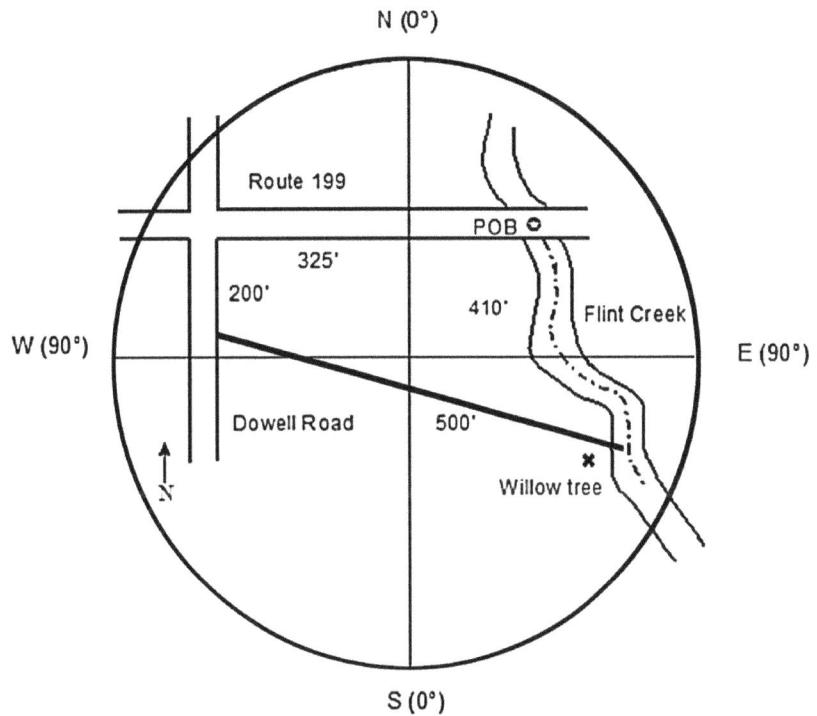

A parcel of land located in Bucks County, Pennsylvania, having the following description: commencing at the intersection of the south line of Route 199 and the middle of Flint Creek, thence southeasterly along the center thread of Flint Creek 410 feet, more or less, to the willow tree landmark, thence north 65 degrees west 500 feet, more or less to the east line of Dowell Road, thence north 2 degrees east 200 feet, more or less, along the east line of Dowell Road to the south line of Route 199, thence north 90 degrees east 325 feet, more or less, along the south line of Route 199 to the point of beginning.

THE RECTANGULAR SURVEY SYSTEM

The survey grid
Sections of township
Fractions of a section
Converting section fractions to acres

The federal government developed the **rectangular survey system**, or **government survey method**, to simplify and standardize property descriptions as a replacement for the cumbersome and often inaccurate metes and bounds method. The system was further modified to facilitate the transfer of large quantities of government-owned western lands to private parties.

To institute the system, all affected land was surveyed using latitude (east-west) and longitude (north-south) lines. The object was to create uniform grids of squares, called townships, which would have equal size and be given a numerical reference for identification.

The rectangular survey system works well for describing properties that are square or rectangular in shape, since these can be described as fractions of sections. However, for an irregular shape, such as a triangle, the rectangular system is inadequate as a method of legal description. The full description has to include a metes and bounds or lot and block description.

The survey grid The following exhibit shows a portion of the rectangular survey system.

Exhibit 9.2 A Sample Survey Grid: Florida

Meridian. The north-south, longitudinal lines on the survey grid are **meridians**. The **principal meridian** is the single designated meridian for identifying townships in the principal meridian's geographical "jurisdiction." There are 37 principal meridians in the national survey. In the exhibit, the principal meridian is the Tallahassee Principal Meridian.

Parallel. The east-west, latitudinal lines are called **parallels.** The **base parallel** or **base line** is the designated line for identifying townships. There is a base parallel for each principal meridian

Range. The north-south area between consecutive meridians is called a **range.** The area labeled "B" in the exhibit is a range. A range is identified by its relationship to the principal meridian. All ranges are six miles wide.

Tier. The east-west area between two parallels is called a **tier**, or a **township strip**. The area marked "C" in the exhibit is a tier. A tier is identified by its relationship to the base parallel. All tiers are six miles wide.

Township. A township is the area enclosed by the intersection of two consecutive meridians and two consecutive parallels, as the shaded square marked "A" in the exhibit illustrates. Since the parallels and meridians are six miles apart, a township is a square with six miles on each side. Its area is therefore 36 square miles.

Sections of a township

The rectangular survey system divides a township into thirty-six squares called **sections**. Each side of a section is one mile in length. Thus the area of a section is one square mile, or 640 acres. As the next exhibit illustrates, the sections in a township are numbered sequentially starting with Section 1 in the northeast corner, proceeding east to west across the top row, continuing from west to east across the next lower row, and so on, alternately, ending with Section 36 in the southeast corner.

Exhibit 9.3 Sections of a Township

**Fractions
of a section**

A section of a township can be divided into fractions as the next exhibit shows.

Exhibit 9.4 Fractions of Sections and Acreage

1 section = 640 acres

| 1/4 section 160 acres | 1/2 section 320 acres |

(diagram showing a section divided into:
1/4 section 160 acres,
1/2 section 320 acres,
1/16 section 40 acres,
1/8 section 80 acres,
1/32 sec 20 acres,
1/64 sec 10 acres)

**Converting section
fractions to acres**

The size in acres of a subsection of a township is a fraction of 640 acres, since there are 640 acres in a section.

For example, the SW 1/4 of a section is one quarter section. Thus, its acreage is one quarter of 640, or 160 acres. Going further, the E 1/2 of the SW 1/4 is one half of that one quarter, or 80 acres. The E 1/2 of the SW 1/4 of the SW ¼ is 20 acres.

A quick method of calculating the acreage of a parcel from its legal description is as follows:

(1) *Multiply the denominators* of the fractional descriptions together.

(2) Divide 640 by the resulting number.

Applying this method to the foregoing descriptions, we get:

SW 1/4 of a section:

$$\frac{640}{4} = 160 \; acres$$

E 1/2 of the SW 1/4 of a section:

$$\frac{640}{(2x4)} = 80 \; acres$$

E 1/2 of the SW 1/4 of the SW 1/4 of a section:

$$\frac{640}{(2x4x4)} = 20 \; acres$$

RECORDED PLAT METHOD

Subdivision plat map
Description format

Subdivision plat map The recorded plat method, also called the **lot and block system**, is used to describe properties in residential, commercial, and industrial *subdivisions*.

Under this system, tracts of land are subdivided into lots. The entire group of lots comprises the subdivision. In a large subdivision, lots may be grouped together into **blocks** for ease of reference. The entire subdivision is surveyed to specify the size and location of each lot and block. The surveyor then incorporates the survey data into a **plat of survey**, or **subdivision plat map**, which must comply with local surveying standards and ordinances.

If local authorities accept it, the subdivision plat map is recorded in the county where the subdivision is located. The recorded lot and block numbers of a subdivision parcel, along with its section, township and meridian reference, become the property's legal description. The exhibit shows a sample subdivision plat map.

Exhibit 9.5 Subdivision Plat Map

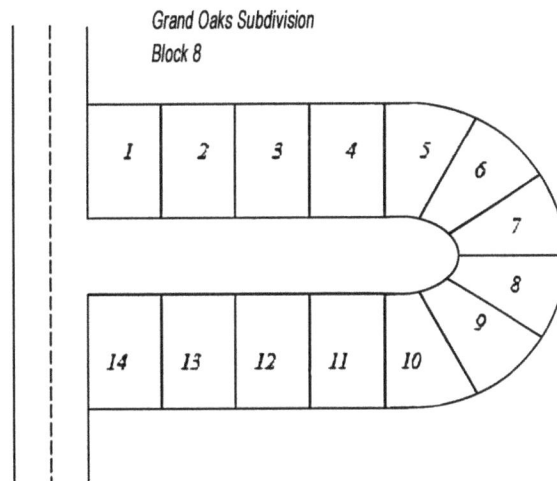

Grand Oaks Subdivision
Block 8

Description format The description of a recorded plat property first presents the property's lot number or letter, then the block identifier and the subdivision name. Note that this is only a portion of the full legal description, which must describe the subdivision's location within a section, a township, a county, and a state. For example, if the subdivision in the exhibit is situated in the southeast quarter of Section 35 of Township T28S, R19E, of the Tallahassee Principal Meridian, the legal description of the lot marked "7" would be:

> "Lot 7, Block 8 of the Grand Oaks Subdivision of the SE 1/4 of Section 35, Township T28S, R19E of the Tallahassee Principal Meridian in Pinellas County, Florida."

DESCRIBING ELEVATION

To describe property located above or below the earth's surface, such as the air rights of a condominium, a surveyor must know the property's elevation. Standard elevation reference points, called **datums**, have been established throughout the country. The original datum was defined by the U.S. Geological Survey as mean sea level at New York harbor. A surveyor uses a datum as an official elevation point to describe the height or depth of a property. If, for example, the datum for an area is a point 100 feet above sea level, all surveys in the area will indicate elevation as a distance above or below 100 feet above sea level.

In many cases it is impractical for a surveyor to rely on a single datum for an entire surveying area. To simplify matters, surveyors have identified local elevation markers, called **benchmarks,** to provide reference elevations for nearby properties. Once a benchmark is registered, it provides a valid reference point for surveying other elevations in the immediate area.

9 Legal Descriptions
Snapshot Review

METHODS OF LEGAL DESCRIPTION	• metes and bounds; rectangular survey system or government survey; recorded plat or lot and block
	• legal description is sufficiently accurate, acceptable in court of law; facilitates transfers; avoids disputes; used in legal contracts
METES AND BOUNDS	• describes property perimeter by landmarks, monuments, distances, angles
	• from point of beginning (POB), describes perimeter and returns to POB; usable within rectangular survey system
RECTANGULAR SURVEY SYSTEM	
The survey grid	• meridians: north-south lines six miles apart
	• parallels: east-west lines six miles apart
	• ranges: north-south strips of area between meridians; tiers: east-west strips of area between parallels; townships: the area representing the intersection of a range and a tier, consisting of six-mile by six-mile squares of land
Sections of a township	• 36 sections per township, each one-mile square (1 mile on each side)
Fractions of a section	• 1 section = 640 acres; fractions of sections described by size and location within progressively larger quarters of section
Converting section fractions to acres	• formula: multiply denominators of section fractions; divide product into 640
RECORDED PLAT METHOD	• or lot and block system; used in surveyed subdivisions
Subdivision plat map	• surveyed plat of subdivided tract; legal descriptor if approved and recorded
Description format	• lots within subdivision are identified by lot reference and block reference: "Lot 7 Block B of the Grand Oaks Subdivision"
DESCRIBING ELEVATION	• datum: a standard elevation reference point; benchmark: elevation marker officially surveyed and registered

10 Fundamentals of Contract Law

Contract Validity and Enforceability
Contract Creation
Classifications of Contracts
Contract Termination

Real estate contracts are the legal agreements that underlie the transfer and financing of real estate, as well as the real estate brokerage business. Sale and lease contracts and option agreements are used to transfer real estate interests from one party to another. Mortgage contracts and promissory agreements are part of financing real estate. Listing and representation contracts establish client relationships and provide for compensation.

In order to work with real estate contracts, it is imperative first to grasp basic concepts that apply to all contracts in general. These concepts provide a foundation for understanding the specifics of particular types of real estate contract.

CONTRACT VALIDITY AND ENFORCEABILITY

Legal status of contracts
Criteria for validity
Validity of a conveyance contract
Enforcement limitations
Electronic contracting

A **contract** is an agreement between two or more parties who, in a "meeting of the minds," have pledged to perform or refrain from performing some act. A *valid* contract is one that is *legally enforceable* by virtue of meeting certain requirements of contract law. If a contract does not meet the requirements, it is not valid and the parties to it cannot resort to a court of law to enforce its provisions.

Note that a contract is not a legal form or a prescribed set of words in a document, but rather the intangible agreement that was made in "the meeting of the minds" of the parties to the contract.

Legal status of contracts

In terms of validity and enforceability, a court may construe the legal status of a contract in one of four ways:

- ▶ valid
- ▶ valid but unenforceable
- ▶ void
- ▶ voidable

Valid. A valid contract is one which meets the legal requirements for validity. These requirements are explained in the next section.

A valid contract that is in writing is enforceable within a statutory time period. A valid contract that is made orally is also generally enforceable within a statutory period, with the exceptions noted below.

Valid but unenforceable. State laws declare that some contracts are enforceable only if they are in writing. These laws apply in particular to the transfer of interests in real estate. Thus, while an oral contract may meet the tests for validity, if it falls under the laws requiring a written contract, the parties will not have legal recourse to enforce performance. An oral long-term lease and an oral real estate sales contract are examples of contracts that may be valid but not enforceable.

Note that such contracts, if valid, remain so even though not enforceable. This means that if the parties fully execute and perform the contract, the outcome may not be altered.

Void. A void contract is an agreement that does not meet the tests for validity, and therefore is no contract at all. If a contract is void, neither party can enforce it.

For example, a contract that does not include consideration is void. Likewise, a contract to extort money from a business is void. Void contracts and instruments are also described as "null and void."

Voidable. A voidable contract is one which initially appears to be valid, but is subject to rescission by a party to the contract who is deemed to have acted under some kind of disability. Only the party who claims the disability may rescind the legal effect of the contract.

For example, a party who was the victim of duress, coercion, or fraud in creation of a contract, and can prove it, may disaffirm the contract. However, the disaffirmation must occur within a legal time frame for the act of rescission to be valid. Similarly, if the party who has cause to disaffirm the contract elects instead to perform it, the contract is no longer voidable but valid.

A voidable contract differs from a void contract in that the latter does not require an act of disaffirmation to render it unenforceable.

Criteria for validity   A contract is valid only if it meets all of the following criteria.

Exhibit 10.1 Contract Validity Requirements

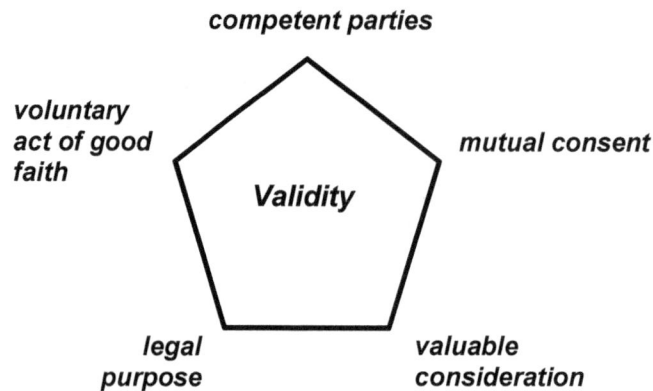

competent parties

voluntary
act of good
faith

mutual consent

Validity

legal
purpose

valuable
consideration

Competent parties. The parties to a contract must have the capacity to contract, and there must be at least two such parties. Thus, the owner of a tenancy for life cannot deed his interest to himself in the form of a fee simple, as this would involve only one party. Capacity to contract is determined by three factors:

▸   legal age
▸   mental competency
▸   legitimate authority

Depending on state law, a contract involving a minor as a party may be either void or voidable. If the law allows a minor to contract, the contract will generally be voidable and the minor can disaffirm the contract.

To be mentally competent, a party must have sufficient understanding of the import and consequences of a contract. Competency in this context is separate and distinct from sanity. Incompetent parties, or parties of "unsound mind," may not enter into enforceable contracts. The incompetency of a party may be ruled by a court of law or by other means. In some areas, convicted felons may be deemed incompetent, depending on the nature of the crime.

During the period of one's incompetency, a court may appoint a guardian who may act on the incompetent party's behalf with court approval.

If the contracting party is representing another person or business entity, the representative must have the *legal authority* to contract. If representing another person, the party must have a bona fide power of attorney. If the contracting party is representing a corporation, the person must have the appropriate power and approval to act, such as would be conferred in a duly executed resolution of the Board of Directors. If the contracting entity is a general partnership, any partner may validly contract for the partnership. In a limited partnership, only general partners may be parties to a contract.

Mutual consent. Mutual consent, also known as *offer and acceptance* and *meeting of the minds,* requires that a contract involve a clear and definite offer and an intentional, unqualified acceptance of the offer. In effect, the parties must agree to the terms without equivocation. A court may nullify a contract where the acceptance of terms by either party was partial, accidental, or vague.

Valuable consideration. A contract must contain a two-way exchange of valuable consideration as compensation for performance by the other party. The exchange of considerations must be two-way. The contract is not valid or enforceable if just one party provides consideration.

Valuable consideration can be something of tangible value, such as money or something a party promises to do or not do. For example, a home builder may promise to build a house for a party as consideration for receiving money from the home buyer. Or, a landowner may agree not to sell a property as consideration for a developer's option money. Also, valuable consideration can be something intangible that a party must give up, such as a homeowner's occupancy of the house in exchange for rent. In effect, consideration is the price one party must pay to obtain performance from the other party.

Valuable consideration may be contrasted with good consideration, or "love and affection," which does not qualify as consideration in a valid contract. Good consideration is something of questionable value, such as a child's love for her mother. Good consideration disqualifies a contract because, while one's love or affection is certainly valuable to the other party, it is not something that is specifically offered in exchange for something else. Good consideration can, however, serve as a nominal consideration in transferring a real property interest as a gift.

In some cases, what is promised as valuable consideration must also be deemed to be *sufficient* consideration. Grossly insufficient consideration, such as $50,000 for a $2 million property, may invalidate a contract on the grounds that the agreement is a gift rather than a contract. In other cases where there is an extreme imbalance in the considerations exchanged, a contract may be invalidated as a violation of good faith bargaining.

Exhibit 10.2 Consideration

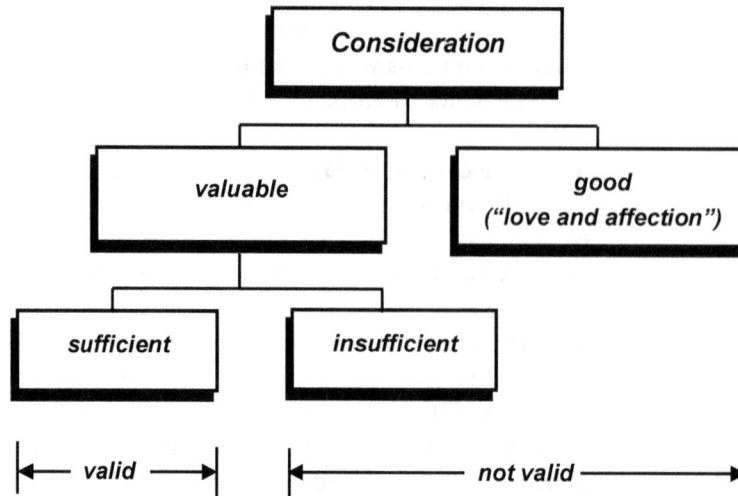

```
                    ┌─────────────────────┐
                    │    Consideration    │
                    └──────────┬──────────┘
                   ┌───────────┴────────────┐
         ┌─────────┴─────────┐   ┌──────────┴──────────┐
         │     valuable      │   │        good         │
         └─────────┬─────────┘   │ ("love and affection")│
            ┌──────┴──────┐      └─────────────────────┘
    ┌───────┴──────┐ ┌─────┴────────┐
    │  sufficient  │ │ insufficient │
    └──────────────┘ └──────────────┘
```

|←— valid —→| |←———————— not valid ————————→|

Legal purpose. The content, promise, or intent of a contract must be lawful. A contract that proposes an illegal act is void.

Voluntary, good faith act. The parties must create the contract in good faith as a free and voluntary act. A contract is thus voidable if one party acted under duress, coercion, fraud, or misrepresentation.

For example, if a property seller induces a buyer to purchase a house based on assurances that the roof is new, the buyer may rescind the agreement if the roof turns out to be twenty years old and leaky.

Validity of a conveyance contract

In addition to satisfying the foregoing requirements, a contract that conveys an interest in real estate must:

▶ be in writing
▶ contain a legal description of the property
▶ be signed by one or more of the parties

A lease contract that has a term of one year or less is an exception. Such leases do not have to be in writing to be enforceable.

Enforcement limitations

Certain contracts that fail to meet the validity requirements are voidable if a damaged party takes appropriate action. The enforcement of voidable contracts, however, is limited by **statutes of limitation.** Certain other contracts which are valid may not be enforceable due to the **statute of frauds.**

Statute of limitations. The statute of limitations restricts the time period for which an injured party in a contract has the right to rescind or disaffirm the contract. A party to a voidable contract must act within the statutory period.

Statute of frauds. The statute of frauds requires that certain contracts *must be in writing* to be enforceable. Real estate contracts that convey an interest in real property fall in this category, with the exception that a lease of one year's duration or less may be oral. All other contracts to buy, sell, exchange, or lease interests in real property must be in writing to be enforceable. In addition, *listing agreements* in most states must be in writing.

The statute of frauds concerns the enforceability of a contract, not its validity. Once the parties to a valid oral contract have executed and performed it, even if the contract was unenforceable, a party cannot use the Statute of Frauds to rescind the contract.

For example, a broker and a seller have an oral agreement. Following the terms of the agreement, the broker finds a buyer, and the seller pays the commission. They have now executed the contract, and the seller cannot later force the broker to return the commission based on the statute of frauds.

Electronic contracting
Contracting electronically through email and fax greatly facilitates the completion of transactions. Clients, lenders, title agents, inspectors, brokers, and other participants in a transaction can quickly share documentation and information. Electronic contracting is made possible by the Uniform Electronic Transactions Act (UETA) and the Electronic Signatures in Global and National Commerce Act (E-Sign), which are federal laws. UETA, which has been accepted in most states, provides that electronic records and signatures are legal and must be accepted. E-Sign makes contracts, records, and signatures legally enforceable, regardless of medium, even where UETA is not accepted.

CONTRACT CREATION

Offer and acceptance
Counteroffer
Revocation of an offer
Termination of an offer
Assignment of a contract
Contract preparation

Offer and acceptance The mutual consent required for a valid contract is reached through the process of offer and acceptance: The **offeror** proposes contract terms in an **offer** to the **offeree**. If the offeree accepts all terms without amendment, the offer becomes a contract. The exact point at which the offer becomes a contract is when the offeree gives the offeror notice of the acceptance.

Exhibit 10.3 Offer, Counteroffer and Acceptance

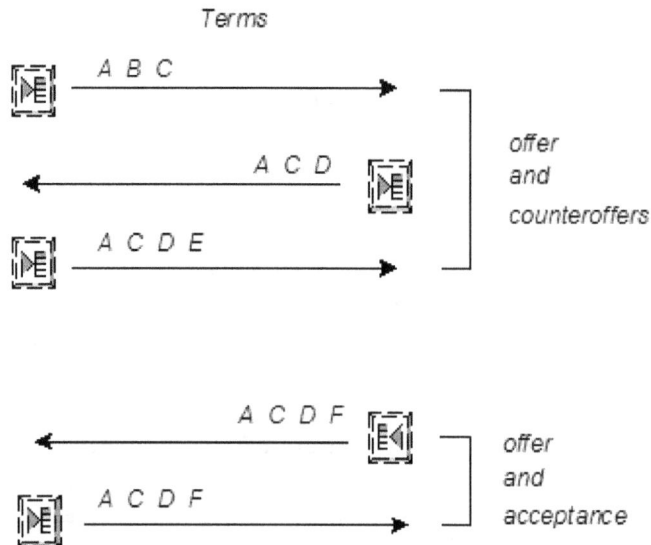

Offer. An offer expresses the offeror's intention to enter into a contract with an offeree to perform the terms of the agreement in exchange for the offeree's performance. In a real estate sale or lease contract, the offer must clearly contain all intended terms of the contract in writing and be communicated to the offeree.

If an offer contains an expiration date and the phrase "time is of the essence," the offer expires at exactly the time specified. In the absence of a stated time period, the offeree has a "reasonable" time to accept an offer.

Acceptance. An offer gives the offeree the power of accepting. For an acceptance to be valid, the offeree must manifestly and unequivocally accept all terms of the offer without change, and so indicate by signing the offer, preferably with a date of signing. The acceptance must then be communicated to the offeror. If the communication of acceptance is by mail, the offer is considered to be communicated as soon as it is placed in the mail.

Counteroffer

By changing any of the terms of an offer, the offeree creates a counteroffer, and the original offer is void. At this point, the offeree becomes the offeror, and the new offeree gains the right of acceptance. If accepted, the counteroffer becomes a valid contract provided all other requirements are met.

For example, a seller changes the expiration date of a buyer's offer by one day, signs the offer and returns it to the buyer. The single amendment extinguishes the buyer's offer, and the buyer is no longer bound by any agreement. The seller's amended offer is a counteroffer which now gives the buyer the right of acceptance. If the buyer accepts the counteroffer, the counteroffer becomes a binding contract.

Revocation of an offer

An offer may be revoked, or withdrawn, at any time before the offeree has communicated acceptance. The revocation extinguishes the offer and the offeree's right to accept it.

For example, a buyer has offered to purchase a house for the listed price. Three hours later, a family death radically changes the buyer's plans. She immediately calls the seller and revokes the offer, stating she is no longer interested in the house. Since the seller had not communicated acceptance of the offer to the buyer, the offer is legally cancelled.

If the offeree has paid consideration to the offeror to leave an offer open, and the offeror accepts, an option has been created which cancels the offeror's right to revoke the offer over the period of the option.

Termination of an offer

Any of the following actions or circumstances can terminate an offer:

- acceptance: the offeree accepts the offer, converting it to a contract
- rejection: the offeree rejects the offer
- revocation: the offeror withdraws the offer before acceptance
- lapse of time: the offer expires
- counteroffer: the offeree changes the offer
- death or insanity of either party

Assignment of a contract

A real estate contract that is not a personal contract for services can be assigned to another party unless the terms of the agreement specifically prohibit assignment.

Listing agreements, for example, are not assignable, since they are personal service agreements between agent and principal. Sales contracts, however, are assignable, because they involve the purchase of real property rather than a personal service.

Contract preparation

State laws define the extent to which real estate brokers and agents may legally prepare real estate contracts. Such laws, referred to as "broker-lawyer accords," also define what types of contracts brokers and agents may prepare. In some states, brokers and agents may not draft contracts, but they may use standard promulgated forms and complete the blanks in the form.

As a rule, a broker or agent who completes real estate contracts is engaging in the unauthorized practice of law unless the broker is a party to the agreement, such as a in a listing agreement or sales contract. Brokers and agents may not complete leases, mortgages, contracts for deed, or promissory notes to which they are not a party.

Agents must be fully aware of what they are legally allowed to do and not do in preparing and interpreting contracts for clients. In addition to practicing law without a license, agents expose themselves to lawsuits from clients who relied on a contract as being legally acceptable.

CLASSIFICATIONS OF CONTRACTS

Oral vs. written
Express vs. implied
Unilateral vs. bilateral
Executed vs. executory

Oral vs. written

A contract may be in writing or it may be an oral, or **parol**, contract. Certain oral contracts are valid and enforceable, others are not enforceable, even if valid. For example, most states require listing agreements, sales contracts, and leases exceeding one year to be in writing to be enforceable.

Express vs. implied

An **express contract** is one in which all the terms and covenants of the agreement have been manifestly stated and agreed to by all parties, whether verbally or in writing.

An **implied contract** is an unstated or unintentional agreement that may be deemed to exist when the *actions of any of the parties* suggest the existence of an agreement.

A common example of an implied contract is an implied agency agreement. In implied agency, an agent who does not have a contract with a buyer performs acts on the buyer's behalf, such as negotiating a price that is less than the listing price. In so doing, the agent has possibly created an implied contract with the buyer, albeit unintended. If the buyer compensates the agent for the negotiating efforts, the existence of an implied agency agreement becomes even less disputable.

Bilateral vs. unilateral

A **bilateral contract** is one in which both parties promise to perform their respective parts of an agreement in exchange for performance by the other party.

An example of a bilateral contract is an exclusive listing: the broker promises to exercise due diligence in the efforts to sell a property, and the seller promises to compensate the broker when and if the property sells.

In a **unilateral contract**, only one party promises to do something, provided the other party does something. The latter party is not obligated to perform any act, but the promising party must fulfill the promise if the other party chooses to perform.

An option is an example of a unilateral contract: in an option-to-buy, the party offering the option (optionor) promises to sell a property if the optionee decides to exercise the option. While the potential buyer does not have to buy, the owner must sell if the option is exercised.

Executed vs. executory

An **executed contract** is one that has been fully performed and fulfilled: neither party bears any further obligation. A completed and expired lease contract is an executed contract: the landlord may re-possess the premises and the tenant has no further obligation to pay rent.

An **executory contract** is one in which performance is yet to be completed. A sales contract prior to closing is executory: while the parties have agreed to buy and sell, the buyer has yet to pay the seller and the seller has yet to deed the property to the buyer.

CONTRACT TERMINATION

Forms of contract termination
Breach of contract

Forms of contract termination

Termination of a contract, also called **cancellation** and **discharge**, may occur for any of the following causes.

Performance. A contract terminates when fully performed by the parties. It may also terminate for:

> ▸ partial performance, if the parties agree
> ▸ sufficient performance, if a court determines a party has sufficiently performed the contract, even though not to the full extent of every provision

Infeasibility. An otherwise valid contract can be canceled if it is not possible to perform. Certain personal services contracts, for example, depend on the unique capabilities of one person which cannot be substituted by someone else. If such a person dies or is sufficiently disabled, the contract is cancelable.

Mutual agreement. Parties to a contract can agree to terminate, or renounce, the contract. If the parties wish to create a new contract to replace the cancelled contract, they must comply with the validity requirements for the new contract. Such substitution is called **novation**.

Cooling-period rescission. Rescission is the act of nullifying a contract. In many states, parties to certain contracts are allowed a statutory amount of time after entering into a contract, or "cooling period", to rescind the contract without cause. No reason need be stated for the cancellation, and the cancelling party incurs no liability for performance.

For example, consider the unsuspecting buyer of a lot in a new resort development. Such buyers are often the targets of hard-sell tactics which lead to a completed sales contract and a deposit. The statutory cooling period gives the buyer an opportunity to reconsider the investment in the absence of the persistent salesperson.

Revocation. Revocation is cancellation of the contract by one party without the consent of the other. For example, a seller may revoke a listing to take the property off the market. While all parties have the *power* to revoke, they may not have a defensible *right*. In the absence of justifiable grounds, a revocation may not relieve the revoking party of contract obligations.

For example, a seller who revokes a listing without grounds may be required to pay a commission if the broker found a buyer, or reimburse the broker's marketing expenses if no buyer was found.

Abandonment. Abandonment occurs when parties fail to perform contract obligations. This situation may allow the parties to cancel the contract.

Lapse of time. If a contract contains an expiration provision and date, the contract automatically expires on the deadline.

Invalidity of contract. If a contract is void, it terminates without the need for disaffirmation. A voidable contract can be cancelled by operation of law or by rescission.

Breach of contract

A breach of contract is a failure to perform according to the terms of the agreement. Also called **default**, a breach of contract gives the damaged party the right to take legal action.

The damaged party may elect the following legal remedies:

- rescission
- forfeiture
- suit for damages
- suit for specific performance

Rescission. A damaged party may rescind the contract. This cancels the contract and returns the parties to their pre-contract condition, including the refunding of any monies already transferred.

Forfeiture. A forfeiture requires the breaching party to give up something, according to the terms of the contract. For example, a buyer who defaults on a sales contract may have to forfeit the earnest money deposit.

Suit for damages. A damaged party may sue for money damages in civil court. The suit must be initiated within the time period allowed by the statute of limitations. When a contract states the total amount due to a damaged party in the event of a breach, the compensation is known as **liquidated damages**. If the contract does not specify the amount, the damaged party may sue in court for **unliquidated damages**.

Suit for specific performance. A suit for specific performance is an attempt to force the defaulting party to comply with the terms of the contract. Specific performance suits occur when it is difficult to identify damages because of the unique circumstances of the real property in question. The most common instance is a defaulted sale or lease contract where the buyer or seller wants the court to compel the defaulting party to go through with the transaction, even when the defaulter would prefer to pay a damage award.

10 Fundamentals of Contract Law
Snapshot Review

CONTRACT VALIDITY AND ENFORCEABILITY

- contract: mutual promises based on "meeting of the minds" to do or refrain from doing something; potentially enforceable if created validly

Legal status of contracts

- valid: meets criteria

- void: does not meet criteria

- voidable: invalid if disaffirmed

- valid yet unenforceable: certain oral contracts

Criteria for validity

- competent parties; mutual consent; valuable consideration; legal purpose; voluntary, good faith act

Validity of a conveyance contract

- must be in writing; contain a legal description; be signed by one or more parties

Enforcement limitations

- statute of frauds: must be written to be enforceable

- statute of limitations: must act within time frame

Electronic contracting

- federal law: electronic records and signatures are legal and must be accepted; enforceable regardless of medium

CONTRACT CREATION

Offer and acceptance

- valid offer and valid acceptance creates contract

- offer becomes contract on communication of acceptance by offeree to offeror

Counteroffer

- any offer in response to an offer or any altered original offer; nullifies original offer

Revocation of an offer

- offeror may revoke offer prior to communication of acceptance by offeree

Termination of an offer

- acceptance; rejection; revocation; expiration; counteroffer; death or insanity

Assignment of a contract

- assignable unless expressly prohibited or a personal service

Contract preparation

- restricted unless licensed as attorney or a party to the contract

CLASSIFICATIONS OF CONTRACTS

- oral or written; express or implied; unilateral or bilateral; executed or executory

CONTRACT TERMINATION

Forms of contract termination

- performance; infeasibility; mutual agreement; cooling-period rescission; revocation; abandonment; lapse of time; invalidity of contract; breach of contract

Breach of contract

- default without cause

- legal remedies: rescission; forfeiture; suit for damages; specific performance

11 National Agency

The Agency Relationship
Fiduciary Duties
Forms of Real Estate Agency
Agency Disclosure Rules

THE AGENCY RELATIONSHIP

Basic roles
Types of agency
Creating an agency relationship
Terminating an agency relationship

The most primary of relationships in real estate brokerage is that between broker and client, the relationship known in law as the **agency relationship**. In every state, a body of law, generally called the **law of agency,** defines and regulates the legal roles of this relationship. The parties to the relationship are the **principal** (a client), the **agent** (a broker), and the **customer** (a third party).

The laws of agency are distinct from laws of contracts, although the two groups of laws interact with each other. For example, the listing agreement -- a contract -establishes an agency relationship. Thus the relationship is subject to contract law. However, agency law dictates how the relationship will achieve its purposes, regardless of what the listing contract states.

The essence of the agency relationship is *trust, confidence, and mutual good faith*. The principal trusts the agent to exercise the utmost skill and care in fulfilling the authorized activity, and to promote the principal's best interests. The agent undertakes to strive in good faith to achieve the desired objective, and to fulfill the fiduciary duties.

It is important to understand that the agency relationship does *not* require compensation or any form of consideration. Nor does compensation define an agency relationship: a party other than the principal may compensate the agent.

Basic roles

In an agency relationship, a principal hires an agent as a *fiduciary* to perform a desired service on the principal's behalf. As a fiduciary, the agent has a legal obligation to fulfill specific *fiduciary duties* throughout the term of the relationship.

The **principal,** or **client**, is the party who hires the agent. The agent works *for* the client. The principal may be a seller, a buyer, a landlord, or a tenant.

The **agent** is the fiduciary of the principal, hired to perform the authorized work and bound to fulfill fiduciary duties. In real estate brokerage the agent *must* be a licensed broker.

The **customer** or **prospect** is a third party in the transaction whom the agent does not represent. The agent works *with* a customer in fulfilling the client's objectives. A seller, buyer, landlord, or tenant may be a customer. A third party who is a potential customer is a **prospect**.

Types of agency

According to the level of authority delegated to the agent, there are three types of agency: *universal, general, and special.*

Universal agency. In a universal agency relationship, the principal empowers the agent to perform any and all actions that may be legally delegated to an agency representative. The instrument of authorization is the power of attorney.

General agency. In a general agency, the principal delegates to the agent ongoing tasks and duties within a particular business or enterprise. Such delegation may include the authority to enter into contracts.

Special, or **limited, agency.** Under a special agency agreement, the principal delegates authority to conduct a specific activity, after which the agency relationship terminates. In most cases, the special agent *may not* bind the principal to a contract.

In most instances, real estate brokerage is based on a special agency. The principal hires a licensed broker to procure a ready, willing, and able buyer or seller. When the objective is achieved, the relationship terminates, although certain fiduciary duties survive the relationship.

Creating an agency relationship

An agency relationship may arise from an express oral or written agreement between the principal and the agent, or from the actions of the parties by implication.

Written or oral listing agreement. The most common way of creating an agency relationship is by listing agreement, which may be oral or written. The agreement sets forth the various authorizations and duties, as well as requirements for compensation. A listing agreement establishes an agency for a specified transaction and has a stated expiration.

Implied agency. An agency relationship can arise by implication, intentionally or unintentionally. Implication means that the parties act *as if* there were an agreement. For example, if an agent promises a buyer to do everything possible to find a property at the lowest possible price, and the buyer accepts the proposition, there may be an implied agency relationship even though there is no specific agreement. Even if the agent does not wish to establish an agency relationship, the agent's actions may be construed to imply a relationship.

Whether intended or accidental, the creation of implied agency obligates the agent to fiduciary duties and professional standards of care. If these are not fulfilled, the agent may be held liable

Terminating an agency relationship

Full performance of all obligations by the parties terminates an agency relationship. In addition, the parties may terminate the relationship at any time by *mutual agreement*. Thirdly, the agency relationship automatically terminates on the *expiration* date, whether the obligations were performed or not.

Involuntary termination. An agency relationship may terminate contrary to the wishes of the parties by reason of:

- death or incapacity of either party
- abandonment by the agent
- condemnation or destruction of the property
- renunciation
- breach
- bankruptcy
- revocation of the agent's license

Involuntary termination of the relationship may create legal and financial liability for a party who defaults or cancels. For example, a client may renounce an agreement but then be held liable for the agent's expenses or commission.

FIDUCIARY DUTIES

Agent's duties to the client
Agent's duties to the customer
Principal's duties
Breach of duty

The agency relationship imposes fiduciary duties on the client and agent, but particularly on the agent. An agent must also observe certain standards of conduct in dealing with customers and other outside parties.

Agent's duties to the client

Skill, care, and diligence. The agent is hired to do a job, and is therefore expected to do it with diligence and reasonable competence. Competence is generally defined as a level of real estate marketing skills and knowledge comparable to those of other practitioners in the area.

The notion of care extends to observing the limited scope of authority granted to the agent. A conventional listing agreement does not authorize an agent to obligate the client to contracts, and it does not allow the agent to conceal offers to buy, sell, or lease coming from a customer or another agent. Further, since a client relies on a broker's representations, a broker must exercise care not to offer advice outside of his or her field of expertise. Violations of this standard may expose the agent to liability for the unlicensed practice of a profession such as law, engineering, or accounting.

Exhibit 11.1 Fiduciary Duties

```
┌─────────────────────┐            ┌─────────────────────┐
│       Agent         │            │      Client         │
│ skill               │   ──────▶  │                     │
│ care                │            │  availability       │
│ diligence           │            │                     │
│ loyalty             │            │  information        │
│ obedience           │   ◀──────  │                     │
│ confidentiality     │            │  compensation       │
│ accounting          │            │                     │
│ full disclosure     │            │                     │
└─────────────────────┘            └─────────────────────┘

┌─────────────────────┐            ┌─────────────────────┐
│       Agent         │            │     Customer        │
│ honesty             │            │                     │
│ fairness            │   ──────▶  │                     │
│ reasonable          │            │                     │
│   care and skill    │            │                     │
│ disclosures         │            │                     │
└─────────────────────┘            └─────────────────────┘
```

Loyalty. The duty of loyalty requires the agent to place the interests of the client above those of all others, particularly the agent's own. This standard is particularly relevant whenever an agent discusses transaction terms with a prospect.

Obedience. An agent must comply with the client's directions and instructions, *provided they are legal.* An agent who cannot obey a legal directive, for whatever reason, must withdraw from the relationship. If the directive is illegal, the agent must also immediately withdraw.

Confidentiality. An agent must hold in confidence any personal or business information received from the client during the term of employment. An agent may not disclose any information that would harm the client's interests or bargaining position, or anything else the client wishes to keep secret.

The confidentiality standard is one of the duties that extends *beyond the termination of the listing*: at *no time* in the future may the agent disclose confidential information.

An agent must exercise care in fulfilling this duty: if confidentiality conflicts with the agent's legal requirements to disclose material facts, the agent must inform the client of this obligation and make the required disclosures. If such a conflict cannot be resolved, the agent must withdraw from the relationship.

Accounting. An agent must safeguard and account for all monies, documents, and other property received from a client or customer. State license laws regulate the broker's accounting obligations and escrow practices.

Full disclosure. An agent has the duty to inform the client of all material facts, reports, and rumors that might affect the client's interests in the property transaction.

In recent years, the disclosure standard has been raised to require an agent to disclose items that a practicing agent *should know,* whether the agent actually had the knowledge or not, and regardless of whether the disclosure furthers or impedes the progress of the transaction.

The most obvious example of a "should have known" disclosure is a property defect, such as an inoperative central air conditioner, that the agent failed to notice. If the air conditioner becomes a problem, the agent may be held liable for failing to disclose a material fact if a court rules that the typical agent in that area would detect and recognize a faulty air conditioner.

There is no obligation to obtain or disclose information related to a customer's race, creed, color, religion, sex or national origin: anti-discrimination laws hold such information to be immaterial to the transaction.

Some states have recently enacted laws requiring a seller to make a written disclosure about property condition to a prospective buyer. This seller disclosure may or may not relieve the agent of some liabilities for disclosure.

Exhibit 11.2 Disclosure of Material Facts

Critical material facts for disclosure include:

- the agent's opinion of the property's condition

- information about the buyer's motivations and financial qualifications

- discussions between agent and buyer regarding the possibility of the agent's representing the buyer in another transaction.

- adverse material facts, including property condition, title defects, environmental hazards, and property defects

Agent's duties to the customer

The traditional notion of *caveat emptor*-- let the buyer beware-- no longer applies unequivocally to real estate transactions. Agents *do* have certain obligations to customers, even though they do not represent them. In general, they owe a third party:

- ▶ honesty and fair dealing
- ▶ reasonable care and skill
- ▶ proper disclosure

An agent has a duty to deal fairly and honestly with a customer. Thus, an agent may not deceive, defraud, or otherwise take advantage of a customer.

"Reasonable care and skill" means that an agent will be held to the standards of knowledge, expertise, and ethics that are commonly maintained by other agents in the area.

Proper disclosure primarily concerns disclosure of agency, property condition, and environmental hazards.

An agent who fails to live up to prevailing standards may be held liable for negligence, fraud, or violation of state real estate license laws and regulations. Agents should be particularly careful about misrepresenting and offering inappropriate expert advice when working with customers.

Intentional misrepresentation. An agent may intentionally or unintentionally defraud a buyer by misrepresenting or concealing facts. While it is acceptable to promote the features of a property to a buyer or the virtues of a buyer to a seller, it is a fine line that divides promotion from misrepresentation. Silent misrepresentation, which is intentionally failing to reveal a material fact, is just as fraudulent as a false statement.

Negligent misrepresentation. An agent can be held liable for failure to disclose facts the agent was not aware of if it can be demonstrated that the agent *should have known* such facts. For example, if it is a common standard that agents inspect property, then an agent can be held liable for failing to disclose a leaky roof that was not inspected.

Misrepresentation of expertise. An agent should not act or speak outside the agent's area of expertise. A customer may rely on anything an agent says, and the agent will be held accountable. For example, an agent represents that a property will appreciate. The buyer interprets this as expert investment advice and buys the property. If the property does not appreciate, the buyer may hold the agent liable.

Principal's duties

The obligations of a principal in an agency relationship concern the following:

Availability. In a special agency, the power and decision-making authority of the agent are limited. Therefore, the principal must be available for consultation, direction, and decision-making. Otherwise the agent cannot complete the job.

Information. The principal must provide the agent with a sufficient amount of information to complete the desired activity. This may include property data, financial data, and the client's timing requirements.

Compensation. If an agreement includes a provision for compensating the agent and the agent performs in accordance with the agreement, the client is obligated to compensate the agent. As indicated earlier, however, the agency relationship does not necessarily include compensation.

Breach of duty

An agent is liable for a breach of duty to client or customer. Since clients and customers rely on the expertise and actions of agents performing within the scope of their authority, regulatory agencies and courts aggressively enforce agency laws, standards, and regulations.

A breach of duty may result in:

- ▸ rescission of the listing agreement (causing a loss of a potential commission)
- ▸ forfeiture of any compensation that may have already been earned
- ▸ disciplinary action by state license law authorities, including license suspension or revocation
- ▸ suit for damages in court

FORMS OF REAL ESTATE AGENCY

Single agency
Subagency
Dual agency
No agency
No subagency

The primary forms of agency relationship between brokers and principals are: *single agency, dual agency, and subagency*. In a fourth kind of relationship, referred to as *transaction brokerage*, no agency relationship exists in the transaction. Finally, some states are beginning to disallow subagency altogether. Students are advised to ascertain which agency relationships are allowed and practiced in their particular state.

Exhibit 11.3   Forms of Agency and No Agency in Real Estate Brokerage

Single Agency: Agent → Client

- -

Sub Agency: Agent → Client; Subagent ↑ Agent

- -

Dual Agency: Buyer ← Agent → Seller

- -

No Agency: Buyer ←-- Agent --→ Seller

- -

No Sub Agency: Agent → Client

Single agency

The agent represents one party in a transaction. The client may be either seller or buyer.

Seller agency. In the traditional situation, a seller or landlord is the agent's client. A buyer or tenant is the customer.

Buyer agency. Recently, it has become common for an agent to represent a buyer or tenant. In this relationship, the property buyer or tenant is the client and the property owner is the customer.

Real estate vernacular calls an agent of the seller or owner the **listing broker**. An agent who works for the listing broker and who obtained the listing is the **listing agent**. A broker who represents a buyer is the **buyer's broker.** One who does this as a specialization is a **buyer broker**. A broker or salesperson who represents tenants is a **tenant representative**.

Subagency

In a subagency, a broker or licensed salesperson works as the agent of a broker who is the agent of a client. Subagents might include a cooperating licensed broker, that broker's licensed salespeople, and the listing broker's licensed salespeople, all of whom agree to work for the listing broker on behalf of the client. In effect, a subagent is an agent of the broker who is agent of the client. The subagent owes the same duties to the agent as the agent owes to the client. By extension, a subagent owes all the fiduciary duties to the client.

Outside "co-brokers" and agents. It is common practice for brokers and salespersons to "cooperate" with a listing broker in finding buyers or tenants. A listing broker, in return, agrees to share the commission with a cooperating broker.

It is cooperating brokers who form multiple listing services to facilitate the process of bringing together buyers and sellers.

The broker's salespersons. All of the listing broker's salespeople who have agreed to work for the broker to find a customer are subagents of the listing broker and owe the fiduciary duties to the broker and, by extension, to the broker's client.

Dual agency

Dual agency means representing both principal parties to a transaction. The agent represents both buyer and seller or tenant and owner. For instance, if a salesperson completes a buyer agency agreement with a party on behalf of a broker, and the party then becomes interested in a property listed by the broker, the broker becomes a dual agent.

Dual agency has become increasingly prevalent with the advent of buyer and tenant representation. Dual agency may arise from voluntary, specific agreement between the principal parties or from the parties' actions, much like implied single agency.

Conflict of interest. Dual agency contains an inherent conflict of interest. Since many of an agent's fiduciary duties can only be rendered to one party, dual agency is, by definition, difficult, if not impossible.

Written, informed consent. In states that permit dual agency, the agent must meet strict disclosure requirements, and principals must agree *in writing* to proceed with the dual agency relationship.

Disclosed (voluntary) dual agency. The parties to a transaction may create a dual agency by giving written consent in disclosure forms, confirmation forms, and sale contract forms. For example, an agent represents a buyer who becomes interested in a property that the agent has listed with the seller. The agent then discloses the relationship with the principals to both principals, and the principals agree in writing to move ahead. A disclosed dual agency is thus voluntarily created.

Implied and undisclosed dual agency. If a broker or agent acts in any way that leads a customer to believe that the agent is representing the customer, a dual agency has potentially been created. For example, a buyer makes confidential disclosures to the agent who works for the seller and exhorts the agent to keep them confidential. The buyer wants the house but knows he is going to lose his job in a month and probably will not qualify for financing. If the agent agrees to keep the information confidential, the agent has not only created an agency relationship with the buyer, but is now in a dual agency situation. Moreover, if the agent fails to disclose the buyer's confidence to the seller, the agent has violated fiduciary duty to the seller.

Duties of a disclosed dual agent. A dual agent's first duty is to disclose the agency relationship to both principal parties or to withdraw from one side of the duality. After disclosing, the agent must obtain the written consent of both parties.

If both parties accept the dual agency, the agent owes all the fiduciary duties to both parties except full disclosure, undivided loyalty, and exclusive representation of one principal's interests.

No agency

In recent years, the brokerage industry has striven to clear up the question of who works for whom, and who owes fiduciary duties to whom. A recent solution allows a broker to represent *no one* in a transaction. That is, the broker acts as a **transaction broker**, or **facilitator**, and is not an agent of either the buyer or seller. In this relationship, the facilitator does not advocate the interests of either party.

Duties of the transaction broker, or facilitator. In the role of transaction broker, the broker's duties and standards of conduct are to

- account for all money and property received or handled
- exercise reasonable skill and care
- provide honesty and fair dealing
- present all offers in a timely fashion
- assist the parties in closing the transaction
- keep the parties fully informed
- advise the parties to obtain expert advice or counsel
- disclose to both parties in residential sale transactions all material facts affecting the property's value
- protect the confidences of both parties in matters that would materially disadvantage one party over the other.

Duties not imposed on the transaction broker. Since there are no fiduciary duties binding the transaction broker, the broker is held to standards for dealing with customers as opposed to clients. These include honesty, fair dealing, and reasonable care. The transaction broker is under no obligation to inspect the property for the benefit of a party or verify the accuracy of statements made by a party.

As state regulatory authorities formalize the facilitator role, it is expected that brokers will have to obtain written consent from the principal parties, just as in the case of dual agency.

No subagency

As another response to the problem of 'who works for whom,' some states have recently moved in the direction of disallowing subagency. In this scenario, subagency is replaced by buyer agency and seller agency *only*. In other words, an agent either represents the buyer directly, or the seller directly. An agent who shows a buyer a property either represents the buyer, or is in fact the listing agent. Note that this arrangement need not change traditional compensation structures: an agent may represent a buyer and still receive a portion of the commission paid by the seller.

AGENCY DISCLOSURE RULES

Objectives of disclosure
Seller agent disclosures
Buyer agent disclosures
Dual agent disclosures
Facilitator disclosures

Traditionally, brokers and agents have disclosed to customers whose interests it is that they are serving. This traditional ethic is now, in many states, required by law. Agents must know what agency disclosures they have to make, to whom, and when in the business relationship they must make them.

Objectives of disclosure

Disclosure removes confusion about who an agent is working for. It may obviate complaints arising from customers and clients who feel they have been deceived.

Specifically, the requirement to disclose aims to:

> ▶ notify clients and customers about whom the agent represents

> ▶ inform clients and customers of the fiduciary duties and standards of care the agent owes them

> ▶ inform prospective clients and customers that they have a choice in how they are represented

> ▶ obtain acknowledgement and acceptance of the disclosure from the principal parties

Recent legislation requires an agent to disclose to all parties the fact that the agent represents one party and does not represent the other. In other words, an agent must inform client and customer that the agent represents the client and does not represent the customer (unless it is a dual agency). An agent must disclose agency relationships whenever there is a transfer of a real estate interest, whether the interest is a fee, partial fee, exchange, leasehold, sublease, assignment, air right or subsurface right.

Seller agent disclosures

Client disclosure. Depending on state regulations, an agent who intends to represent a seller or owner must disclose the import of the proposed agency relationship in writing before the listing agreement is executed. The agent must inform the seller or landlord in writing that the agent will be representing the client's interests as a fiduciary, and will not be representing the interests of any potential buyer. Any subsequent sale or lease contract with a customer should confirm this disclosure.

Customer disclosure. A listing agent must disclose in writing to a buyer or tenant that the agent represents the owner in the transaction. This disclosure must occur before or at the first "substantive contact" with the customer prospect. The disclosure must also be confirmed in any subsequent sale or lease contract.

Substantive contact. Subject to variations in state regulation, "substantive contact" between listing agent and customer occurs whenever the agent is:

- showing the prospect a property
- eliciting confidential information from a prospect regarding needs, motivation, or financial qualification
- executing a contractual offer to sell or lease

Exclusions. Interaction between a seller's agent and a customer is not always substantive. Possible instances that might be excluded from the requirement of disclosure are:

- attendance at, or supervision of, an open house, providing the agent does not engage in any of the contacts described above
- preliminary "small talk" concerning price ranges, locations, and architectural styles
- responding to questions of fact regarding advertised properties

Oral disclosure. If an agent becomes involved in a substantive contact over the phone or in a such way that it is not feasible to make written disclosure, the agent must make the disclosure orally and follow up with a written disclosure at the first face-to-face meeting.

Buyer agent disclosures

Client disclosure. An agent who plans to represent a buyer or tenant must disclose the import of the proposed agency relationship in writing before the representation agreement is executed.

Customer disclosure. A buyer agent must disclose the agency relationship to the seller or seller's agent on first contact. Substantive contact is assumed.

Dual agent disclosures

Informed written consent. An agent who desires to operate in a dual agency capacity must obtain the informed written consent of all parties. Subsequent contracts should confirm the disclosure. "Informed written consent" means both parties have read, understood, and signed an acceptable disclosure form.

Prohibited disclosures. State regulations prohibit a dual agent from making certain disclosures. For instance, a dual agent, unless expressly instructed by the relevant party, usually cannot disclose:

- to the buyer that the seller will accept less than the listed price
- to the seller that the buyer will pay more than the price submitted in a written offer to the seller
- the motivation of any party concerning the transaction
- that a seller or buyer will agree to financing terms other than those offered

Facilitator disclosures

Rules for disclosing a transaction broker's status of non-agency are similar to those of dual agency. The agent must provide written notice to all parties or their agents on first becoming a transaction broker or on the first substantive contact, whichever comes first.

11 National Agency Snapshot Review

THE AGENCY RELATIONSHIP

Basic roles
- principal, or client, hires agent (broker) to find a ready, willing, and able customer (buyer, seller, tenant); client-agent fiduciary foundations: trust, confidence, good faith

Types of agency
- universal: represent in business and personal matters; can contract for principal
- general: represent in business matters; agent can contract for principal
- special: represent in single business transaction; normally agent cannot contract for principal; the brokerage relationship is usually special agency

Creating an agency relationship
- created by express written or oral agreement or as an implied agreement by actions of either party

Terminating an agency relationship
- causes: fulfillment; expiration; mutual agreement; incapacity; abandonment; or destruction of property; renunciation; breach; bankruptcy; revocation of license

FIDUCIARY DUTIES

Agent's duties to the client
- skill, care, diligence; loyalty; obedience; confidentiality; disclosure; accounting

Agent's duties to the customer
- honesty and fair dealing; exercise of reasonable care and skill; proper disclosures; danger areas: misrepresentation; advising beyond expertise

Principal's duties
- availability; provide information; compensation

Breach of duty
- liabilities: loss of listing, compensation, license; suit for damages

FORMS OF REAL ESTATE AGENCY

Single agency
- seller agency; buyer agency; tenant representation

Subagency
- outside brokers and agents who help listing agent; listing broker's own agents

Dual agency
- representing both sides; potential conflict of interest; must disclose, obtain written consent; types: voluntary by consent; involuntary by actions of parties (implied agency); duties: all but full disclosure and loyalty

No agency
- "facilitator" or "transaction broker"; representing neither party in the transaction; duties to both parties: accounting; skill, care and diligence; honesty and fair dealing; disclosures affecting property value

AGENCY DISCLOSURE

Objectives of disclosure
- declare; explain; offer choice; obtain documented consent

Seller agent disclosures
- to client: in writing on or before listing is executed; to customer: prior to substantive contact, in writing; oral permitted but must have written follow-up

Buyer agent disclosures
- in writing; upon first contact with listing agent or seller

Dual agent disclosures
- "informed, written consent"; may not disclose: price or financing positions or motivations unless authorized

Facilitator disclosures
- on becoming transaction broker or on substantive contact whichever is first

12 Listing Agreements: an Overview

Review of Legal Foundations
Types of Listing Agreement
Fulfillment and Termination
Agreement Clauses

REVIEW OF LEGAL FOUNDATIONS

Agency law
Contract law

A listing agreement, the document that puts an agent or broker in business, is a legally enforceable real estate agency agreement between a real estate broker and a client, authorizing the broker to perform a stated service for compensation. The unique characteristic of a listing agreement is that it is governed both by agency law and by contract law.

Agency law

The cornerstones of agency law in the context of a listing agreement are:

▸ definition of the roles of parties involved
▸ fiduciary duties of the agent
▸ agent's scope of authority

Parties. The principal parties to the contract are the **listing broker** and the **client**. The client may be buyer, seller, landlord or tenant in the proposed transaction. Legally, the broker is the client's **agent**. The principal party on the other side of the transaction is a **customer** or a potential customer, called a **prospect**. A broker or salesperson who assists the listing broker in finding a customer is an **agent** of the listing broker and a **subagent** of the client. A broker who represents the party on the other side of the transaction is an agent of that party, and not an agent of the listing broker, unless a dual agency arrangement is specifically allowed.

Fiduciary duties. A listing agreement establishes an agency relationship between agent and client that commits the agent to the full complement of fiduciary duties to the client in fulfilling the agreement.

Scope of authority. Customarily, a listing is a *special agency,* or *limited agency,* agreement. Special agency *limits* the scope of the broker's authority to specific activities, generally those which generate customers and catalyze the transaction. A special agency agreement usually *does not* authorize a broker to obligate the client to a contract as a principal party, unless the agreement expressly grants such authorization or the client has granted power of attorney to the broker. For example, a listing broker may not tell a buyer that the seller will accept an offer regardless of its terms. Telling the offeror that the offer *is* accepted would be an even more serious breach of the agreement.

Under agency law, a client is liable for actions the broker performs that are within the scope of authority granted by the listing agreement. A client is *not liable* for acts of the broker which go beyond the stated or implied scope of authority.

Thus, in the previous example, the seller would not be liable for the broker's statements that the offer would be accepted or was accepted, since the broker did not have the authority to make such statements. A broker who exceeds the scope of authority in the listing agreement risks forfeiting compensation and perhaps even greater liabilities.

Contract law

Bilateral or unilateral agreement. Listings may be bilateral or unilateral, depending on the type of listing and the wording of the agreement. An open listing is a unilateral agreement in that the seller promises to pay a commission to any agent who produces a buyer but no agent promises or is obligated to take any action. On the other hand, most exclusive listings are bilateral agreements because of wording that promises the due diligence of the agent to procure a buyer in return for the seller's promise to pay a commission if a buyer is produced.

Validity. A listing agreement must meet the requirements for a valid contract to be enforceable.

Termination. A listing, like any contract, may terminate for any of the following causes: performance, infeasibility, mutual agreement, rescission, revocation, abandonment, lapse of time, invalidity, and breach.

Legal form. A valid listing may be oral or written. However, many states consider only a written listing to be enforceable, particularly an exclusive right-to-sell listing. In practice, a broker should get every listing in writing and make sure it clearly states what the broker is authorized to do and how the broker will be paid. An oral listing, even if enforceable, limits a broker's ability to remedy problems:

- a contested oral listing must be supported by considerable evidence to be enforced

- a broker may not be able to sue a principal for damages incurred under an oral lease

- if the client dies, the broker may not be able to obtain compensation for a successfully performed oral listing

An express listing, verbal or written, manifestly authorizes the broker to pursue certain actions for the client. Clients and agents may also create an *implied agency listing* based on substantive actions rather than on an express agreement. For example, if a seller allows a broker to undertake certain activities toward effecting a transaction without a specific authorization, but with full knowledge and consent, an implied agency may have been created. Consequently, if the principal proceeds with a customer procured in this manner, he or she may be liable to the broker for compensation. Conversely, the agent may be held responsible for fulfilling fiduciary duties imposed by the implied agency.

Assignment. Since a listing agreement is a personal service contract, it is *not assignable*. In particular, a broker cannot assign a listing to another broker.

TYPES OF LISTING AGREEMENT

Exclusive right-to-sell (or lease)
Exclusive agency
Open listing
Net listing
Buyer and tenant agency agreement
Transaction broker agreement
Multiple listing

A broker may represent any principal party of a transaction: seller, landlord, buyer, tenant. An **owner listing** authorizes a broker to represent an owner or landlord. There are three main types of owner listing agreement: *exclusive right-to-sell (or lease)*; *exclusive agency*; and *open listing*. Another type of listing, rarely used today and illegal in many states, is a *net listing*. The first three forms differ in their statement of conditions under which the broker will be paid. The net listing is a variation on how much the broker will be paid.

A **buyer agency** or **tenant representation agreement** authorizes a broker to represent a buyer or tenant. The most commonly used form is an *exclusive right-to-represent* agreement, the equivalent of an exclusive right-to-sell. However, exclusive agency and open types of agreement may be also used to secure a relationship on this side of a transaction.

Though not a distinct type of listing agreement, *multiple listing* is a significant feature of brokerage practice. Multiple listing is an authorization to enter a listing in a multiple listing service.

Exclusive right-to-sell (or lease)

The exclusive right-to-sell, also called **exclusive authorization-to-sell** and, simply,
the **exclusive**, is the most widely used owner agreement. Under the terms of this listing, a seller contracts exclusively with a single broker to procure a buyer or effect a sale transaction. If a buyer is procured during the listing period, the broker is entitled to a commission, *regardless of who is procuring cause*. Thus, if anyone-the owner, another broker-- sells the property, the owner must pay the listing broker the contracted commission.

The exclusive right-to-lease is a similar contract for a leasing transaction. Under the terms of this listing, the owner or landlord must pay the listing broker a commission if anyone procures a tenant for the named premises.

The exclusive listing gives the listing broker the greatest assurance of receiving compensation for marketing efforts.

In some states, an exclusive right-to-sell listing is enforceable only if it is in writing and has an expiration date. Some states do not require the agreement to be in writing, but if it is in writing, it must have an expiration date.

Exclusive agency

An exclusive agency listing authorizes a single broker to sell the property and earn a commission, but *leaves the owner the right to sell the property without the broker's assistance*, in which case no commission is owed. Thus, if any party other than the owner is procuring cause in a completed sale of the property, including another broker, the contracted broker has earned the commission. This arrangement may also be used in a leasing transaction: if any party other than the owner procures the tenant, the owner must compensate the listing broker.

An exclusive agency listing generally must have an expiration date. Most states allow either an oral or written agreement.

Open listing

An open listing, or, simply, **open**, is a *non-exclusive* authorization to sell or lease a property. The owner may offer such agreements to any number of brokers in the marketplace. With an open listing, the broker who is the first to perform under the terms of the listing is the sole party entitled to a commission. Performance usually consists of being the procuring cause in the finding of a ready, willing, and able customer. If the transaction occurs without a procuring broker, no commissions are payable.

Open listings are rare in residential brokerage. Brokers generally shy away from them because they offer no assurance of compensation for marketing efforts. In addition, open listings cause commission disputes. To avoid such disputes, a broker has to register prospects with the owner to provide evidence of procuring cause in case a transaction results.

An open listing may be oral or written.

Net listing

A net listing is one in which an owner sets a minimum acceptable amount to be received from the transaction and allows the broker to have any amount received in excess as a commission, assuming the broker has earned a commission according to the other terms of the agreement. The owner's "net" may or may not account for closing costs.

For example, a seller requires $75,000 for a property. A broker sells the property for $83,000 and receives the difference, $8,000, as commission.

Net listings are generally regarded as unprofessional today, and many states have outlawed them. The argument against the net listing is that it creates a conflict of interest for the broker. It is in the broker's interest to encourage the owner to put the lowest possible acceptable price in the listing, regardless of market value. Thus the agent violates fiduciary duty by failing to place the client's interests above those of the agent.

Exhibit 12.1 Types of Listing

Exclusive Right	$ ➡ Broker	**IF customer is procured**
Exclusive Agency	$ ➡ Broker	**IF customer is procured and client does not procure**
Open	$ ➡ Broker	**IF broker procures customer**
Net	$ ➡ Broker	**IF customer is due commission, receives proceeds over seller's minimum**
"Multiple Listing"	$ ➡ Broker	**Authority to enter listing in multiple listing service**

Buyer and tenant agency agreements

Buyer and tenant agency agreements create a fiduciary relationship with the buyer or tenant just as seller listings create a fiduciary relationship with the seller. Generally, buyer and tenant representation agreements are subject to the same laws and regulations as those applying to owner listings. Thus:

▸ a representation agreement may be an exclusive, exclusive agency, or open listing. As with owner listings, the most widely used agreement is the exclusive. In this arrangement, the buyer agrees to only work with the buyer representative in procuring a property.

▸ an exclusive listing generally must have an expiration date along with other requirements of a valid listing.

▸ state laws require an exclusive authorization to be in writing

Duties of the Agent. At the formation of the relationship, the buyer agent has the duty to explain how buyer or tenant agency relationships work. This is culminated by a signed agreement where the principal understands and accepts these circumstances. During the listing term, the buyer or tenant agent's principal duties are to diligently locate a property that meets the principal's requirements. In addition, the agent must comply with his or her state agency-disclosure laws which may differ from those of traditional listing agents. This involves timely disclosures to prospective sellers and their agents, usually upon initial contact.

Transaction broker agreement

In terms of agency, a transaction broker is in a non-agency relationship with the seller or buyer. The agent is not bound by fiduciary duties to either party. Nevertheless, transaction brokers enter into binding agreements with buyers and sellers to complete transactions. Such agreements may be exclusive or non-exclusive. Like conventional listings, the transaction brokerage agreement binds the principal to a compensation agreement in the event the broker procures a property or a buyer. Typical agreements affirm the nature of the relationship, contain expiration dates, and describe the terms of the agreement, such as the type of property desired or the price a seller deems acceptable.

Like other listing agreements, transaction broker agreements vary among the states where this form of relationship is practiced.

Multiple listing A multiple listing is not a distinct listing contract but rather a provision in an exclusive listing authorizing the broker to place the listing into a multiple listing service.

A multiple listing service is an organization of member brokers who agree to cooperate in the sale of properties listed by other brokers in exchange for a share of the broker's resulting commission.

The authorization enables and requires the broker to disseminate the listing information in a timely fashion so that members in the organization can participate in the sale of the property as subagents.

FULFILLMENT AND TERMINATION

Agent's performance
Compensation
Causes for termination
Revoking a listing

A listing agreement may terminate in many ways. The only desirable and favorable way is by fulfillment of the contract. Fulfillment results when both parties have performed the actions they have promised to perform.

Agent's performance An agent performs a listing agreement by achieving the result specified in the agreement. When and if the result is achieved, the agent's performance is complete.

Find a customer or effect a transaction. A listing generally specifies the result to be either finding a customer or effecting a completed transaction.

Finding a customer means locating a party who is *ready, willing, and able* to transact under the client's terms. Effecting a completed transaction means finding a customer who is not only ready, willing, and able, but one who makes an acceptable offer.

A ready, willing, and able customer is one who is:

> ▸ amenable to the terms of the transaction (ready and willing)
> ▸ financially capable of paying the price and legally capable of completing the transaction (able)

Specific responsibilities. A listing agreement authorizes a broker to undertake actions relevant to achieving the performance objective. Authorized activities usually include the following:

- ▸ show or seek property
- ▸ locate buyer, seller, tenant, or landlord
- ▸ communicate the client's transaction terms
- ▸ promote features and advantages of the terms to customers
- ▸ assist in negotiating a meeting of the minds between parties

Due diligence. Due diligence in the listing context refers to verifying the accuracy of the statements in the listing regarding the property, the owner, and the owner's representations. Especially important facts for a broker or agent to verify are:

- ▸ the property condition
- ▸ ownership status
- ▸ the client's authority to act

Failure to perform a reasonable degree of due diligence may increase an agent's exposure to liability in the event that the property is not as represented or that the client cannot perform as promised.

Delegation of responsibilities. In the normal course of business, a listing broker *delegates* marketing responsibilities to salespeople. A salesperson may not, however, seek compensation directly from a client. Only the broker can obtain and disburse the compensation.

Compensation

The main item of performance for the client is payment of compensation, if the agreement calls for it. A broker's compensation is earned and payable when the broker has performed according to the agreement. The amount and structure of the compensation, potential disputes over who has earned compensation, and the client's liability for multiple commissions are other matters that a listing agreement should address.

Negotiated compensation. The amount of a broker's commission is whatever amount the client and broker have agreed to. Compensation may be in the form of a percentage of the sale or lease price, or a flat fee. In practice, commissions vary for different geographical areas, types of property and transaction, and services performed.

Procuring cause. Disputes often arise as to whether an agent is owed a commission. Many such disputes involve open listings where numerous agents are working to find customers for the principal, and none has a clear claim on a commission. In other cases, a client may claim to have found the customer alone and therefore to have no responsibility for paying a commission. There are also situations where cooperating brokers and subagents working under an exclusive listing dispute about which one(s) deserve a share of the listing broker's commission.

The concept that decides such disputes is that the party who was the "procuring cause" in finding the customer is entitled to the commission or commission share. The two principal determinants of procuring cause are:

- ▸ being first to find the customer
- ▸ being the one who induces the customer to complete the transaction

For example, Broker A and Broker B each have an open listing with a property owner. Broker A shows Joe the property on Monday. Broker B shows Joe the same property on Friday, and then Joe buys the property. Broker A will probably be deemed to be the procuring cause by virtue of having first introduced Joe to the property.

Compensation for buyer brokers. Buyer agency agreements stipulate how the agent will be compensated in the relationship. The compensation may be a client-paid retainer fee or a commission contingent upon a completed transaction or procured seller. It is common practice for the agent to be paid by the customer to the transaction, the seller, as opposed to the fiduciary principal, the buyer or tenant. In addition, the agent may be paid by the buyer in the event that the seller or listing agent refuses to offer any compensation to the buyer broker. This might occur, for example, in the case of a for-sale-by-owner transaction.

In addition to the form of compensation and the parties responsible for paying the agent, the buyer agency agreement defines when the compensation is in fact earned and will be paid. Customarily, the commission is earned when a sales contract is completed by the transacting parties. The agent may be entitled to compensation even if the buyer defaults on the terms of the sales contract. Normally, agents are paid at closing or upon the buyer's default.

Causes for termination

A listing may terminate on grounds of:

- *performance*: all parties perform; the intended outcome
- *infeasibility*: it is not possible to perform under the terms of the agreement
- *mutual agreement*: both parties agree to cancel the listing
- *revocation*: either party cancels the listing, with or without the right
- *abandonment*: the broker does not attempt to perform
- *breach*: the terms of the listing are violated
- *lapse of time*: the listing expires
- *invalidity of contract*: the listing does not meet the criteria for validity
- *incapacitation or death of either party*
- *involuntary title transfer*: condemnation, bankruptcy, foreclosure
- *destruction of the property*

Listing expiration regulations. In most states, open listings do not require a stated expiration date. Rather, they expire after a "reasonable" period of time as locally defined.

The other types of listing generally must specify a termination date and may not have an automatic renewal mechanism. Courts in many states construe any listing that has no expiration as an open listing. However, some states make these requirements only of written listings, and may not require exclusives to be in writing.

Revoking a listing

Power vs. right. Both principals to the listing agreement have the power to revoke the contract at any time. They do not, however, always have the right. That is, client or broker may cancel a listing but remain liable for damages to the other party.

Revocation by the client. If the client revokes the listing after the broker has already earned a commission, the client must pay the commission, no matter what type of listing it was.

If the broker has not fully performed prior to the revocation, the following guidelines apply:

- exclusive right-to-sell: if the property sells during the term of the revoked listing, the client is liable for the commission. If the property does not sell, the client is liable for the broker's actual costs.
- exclusive agency: if the property sells during the term of the revoked listing, the client is liable at least for the broker's costs and possibly for the commission. If the property does not sell during the term, the client is liable for the broker's costs.
- open: if revoked prior to performance, the client is generally not liable for any payment

Revocation by the broker. If the broker cancels the listing or otherwise defaults, the client may sue the broker for money damages.

LISTING AGREEMENT CLAUSES

Exclusive right-to-sell clauses
Exclusive buyer agency clauses
Transaction brokerage clauses

A written listing, particularly an exclusive, is a formal contract which contains the entirety of all agreements between the parties. If an agreement is left out, it is assumed not to exist. An agreement that is included is assumed to exist and is generally enforceable. If a written agreement contains mistakes, it is probably not valid or enforceable. For these reasons, it is extremely important for a listing agreement to be accurate, error-free, and complete.

Students are cautioned to note that listing agreements vary in language and form from state to state. For that reason it is important to ascertain the legal requirements and required clauses for certain types of listings, particularly exclusive listings, in your state. In addition, some states require that if agents use pre-printed forms, such forms must contain certain provisions.

Exclusive right-to-sell clauses

Requirements for exclusive listing agreements vary from state to state. Generally, a written listing agreement requires as a minimum:

- names of all owners
- address or legal description of the listed property
- listing price
- expiration date
- commission terms
- authority granted

The following clause descriptions are found in a typical exclusive right-to-sell listing agreement.

Parties and authorization. The agreement should name all legal owners of the property, or duly authorized representatives of the owners, as the client party. It must also name the broker.

An authorization clause sets forth the nature of what the broker is allowed to do, i.e., the type of listing. Note that the phrase "right-to-sell" is a misnomer. A broker cannot legally sell the property without proper power of attorney. The usual right is to effect a sale or find a buyer.

Real Property. The real property description may include an address, but in some states it must include the *legal description*.

It is critical to identify both the real property and any personal property that are for sale and included in the listing price.

Fixtures. Typical agreements list what fixtures are included in the sale specifically, and "all other things attached or affixed to the property" generally. The seller must then enter which items are excluded from the sale.

Personal Property. The listing agreement should include all personal property that is to be included in the transaction and listing price.

Listing price. A clause usually sets forth the gross price for the property and possibly the financing terms the owner will accept, particularly if seller financing or assumption of the seller's loan is involved.

The listing price is the seller's asking price for the property. This may or may not be the price the seller ultimately accepts. The full listing price does not have to be obtained for the broker to earn a commission. The listing price clause may also state the seller's agreement to pay customary closing costs.

Listing term. In most states, exclusive listings must have a specific beginning and ending date of the listing agreement. In many states, failure to name a termination date in a written listing is grounds for revocation of the real estate license. Any provision for renewal of the listing term should be very specific. Automatic renewals are illegal in many states.

To protect the broker, some listings contain a provision to extend the listing period in the event an expiration occurs during the period in which a sale contract is pending.

Agent's duties. This clause specifies the broker's responsibilities and authorization to carry out certain activities. These typically include marketing activities, multiple listing service activities, property access and showings, authority to allow other parties access, permission to inspect existing mortgage financing documents, and authority to accept deposits. Commonly, the clause specifically bars the broker from executing any contract on behalf of the owner.

Agent's compensation. A clause will identify the broker's fee and the necessary conditions for the fee to be earned. For instance, it may state that a commission is earned if a buyer is procured, a contract is executed, or the seller voluntarily transfers the property for any price during the listing period.

A fee clause usually provides for remedies in the event of default by the buyer or seller. In effect, if the seller breaches the listing without grounds after a buyer has been procured, the commission is payable. If the owner cannot sell the property for reasons beyond the owner's control, the owner is not liable for a commission. If the buyer breaches a sale contract, the owner and broker may split the buyer's earnest money deposit as liquidated damages, depending on state law.

Protection period. Many listings include a protection clause stating that, for a certain period after expiration, the owner is liable for the commission if the property sells to a party that the broker procured, unless the seller has since listed the property with another broker.

Multiple listing. This provision obtains the seller's consent to placing the listing in a multiple listing service and authorization to disseminate information about the listing to members.

Cooperation with other agents. This clause requires the seller to agree or refuse to cooperate with subagents or buyer agents in selling the property, under what terms, and whether the seller agrees to compensate these parties. Recent agreements stipulate that subagents and buyer agents must disclose their relationships to the buyer upon initial contact and subsequently in writing. There may also be a warning to the seller not to disclose confidential information to a buyer broker insofar as this agent is required to disclose all relevant information to the buyer.

Non-discrimination. Most exclusive listings contain an affirmation that the agent will conduct all affairs in compliance with state and federal fair housing and nondiscrimination laws.

Dual agency. In the absence of disclosure and consent, dual agency represents a conflict of interest for the broker. A good agreement specifically asks the owner to consent to or refuse to allow the broker's representation of both parties.

If the clause states that the owner refuses to accept dual agency, the broker agrees not to show the property to any buyers the broker represents.

If the seller accepts dual agency, the broker may represent both parties under the restrictions set forth in the listing. The restrictions are generally to protect the confidentialities of either party, particularly those relating to price and terms. Additionally, the broker covenants to deal honestly and impartially with the parties.

Other disclosures by agent. In addition to agency, other disclosures might be included to cover any direct or indirect interest the broker has in the transaction and special compensation the broker might be receiving from other parties connected with the transaction.

Seller's representations and promises. In this clause, the owner represents that he or she in fact owns the property in the manner stated in the listing, and is legally capable of delivering fee simple, marketable title.

The clause may further require the owner to warrant that he or she

- is not represented by another party and will not list the property elsewhere during the listing period
- will not lease the property during the listing period without approval
- agrees to provide necessary information
- will refer all prospects directly to the broker without prior direct negotiation
- has reviewed a sample "Offer to Purchase and Sell" contract
- will make the property presentable and available for showing at reasonable times upon notice by agent.

Seller's property condition disclosure. Most current listing forms require the seller to disclose the condition of the property to prospective buyers. New laws in most states allow buyers to cancel a sale contract if they have not received the seller's property condition disclosure before closing or occupancy or other deadline. In addition, the listing may include among the seller's duties the requirement to complete and provide the agent with a Lead Paint Hazard addendum. A copy of the required notice to buyers may be attached to the listing agreement as part of the agreement.

Seller's title and deed. A provision usually requires the owner to promise to deliver good and marketable title, title insurance, and to convey the property using a general warranty deed to a buyer. Without this covenant, the broker has no assurance that a transaction will occur, and in turn that he or she will be paid for procuring a buyer.

Flood hazard insurance. This clause requires the seller to disclose whether he or she is required to or presently maintains flood insurance on the property.

Limitation of liability. There is often a clause requiring the owner to indemnify the broker against liability resulting from casualty, loss, and owner misrepresentation during the listing period.

In practice, liability and indemnification clauses do not necessarily absolve a broker from liability.

Escrow authorization. The seller authorizes escrow officers to disburse earned commission funds to the broker upon the broker's instructions to do so.

IRS requirements; alien seller withholding. A clause may state that the seller will comply with IRS requirements for providing tax-related information. This ensures that a seller who is an alien understands that a buyer will be required to withhold a percentage of the sale price for the IRS.

Other listing provisions. An exclusive listing might also provide for:

> ▸ *mediation*: in the event of a dispute, the owner agrees to arbitrate differences before filing a lawsuit
> ▸ *attorney fees*: the losing party in a lawsuit must pay court costs and attorney fees
> ▸ *acknowledgment*: the owner acknowledges reading and understanding the agreement
> ▸ *entire agreement*: the listing cannot be changed without written agreement; the listing sets forth all agreements made
> ▸ *binding effect*: listing is binding and enforceable
> ▸ *saving clause*: if a portion of the agreement is invalid or unenforceable, the balance of the agreement remains valid as permitted by law

Notices to owner. Some listing agreements include notices to the seller concerning:

> ▸ *fee negotiability*: the broker's fee is the result of negotiations with the seller
> ▸ *fair housing laws*: the broker and seller must comply with discrimination laws
> ▸ *keyboxes; security*: the seller should take prudent measures to protect personal property and remove dangerous items that could cause injury
> ▸ *legal advice disclaimer*: the broker cannot give legal advice

Signatures. All owners and the broker must sign the listing and indicate the date of signing.

Exclusive buyer agency clauses

The exclusive buyer agency agreement is very similar to the exclusive right-to-sell agreement, the only significant differences being the agent's objectives and the fact that the principal is the buyer instead of the seller. The notable exception is how the agent is paid, as previously discussed.

The clauses which are virtually identical to the exclusive right-to-sell are:

> ▸ the identity of the principal and the agent's authorized activity
> ▸ the description of the property desired in terms of location, price, size, etc.
> ▸ the term of the agreement and its automatic termination
> ▸ the buyer's agreement to work exclusively through the agent
> ▸ the agent's duties to locate a suitable property according to the buyer's specifications
> ▸ the non-discrimination clause
> ▸ signatures of the parties

The following clauses distinguish the buyer agency agreement from the exclusive right-to sell agreement.

Buyer's representation of exclusivity. Here the buyer affirms that he or she is not represented by another agent. In addition the buyer acknowledges an understanding of the agency relationship.

Agent compensation. This clause sets forth how the agent is to be paid, whether by retainer or commission, who is to pay the commission, and what the buyer owes the agent in the event the seller does not participate in the agent's compensation. Second, the clause establishes the circumstances under which the agent has earned the commission. This includes finding a property during the agreement term or the buyer contracting to buy a property shown by the agent within a stipulated period of time following expiration. In addition, the clause provides that the agent will be paid in the event the buyer defaults on a sale contract.

Other buyers acknowledged. In this provision, the buyer acknowledges that the agent is working with other buyers who may be in competition for any property the buyer is shown by the agent.

Transaction brokerage clauses

Transaction brokerage agreements vary greatly among the states where this brokerage relationship is practiced. The agreement may be exclusive or non-exclusive. Despite the lack of standardization and uniformity, these agreements contain the following principal provisions.

Parties and property identification. The agreement identifies the principals and if a seller, the description of the property to be sold, or if a buyer a description of the property desired.

Agent's authorized activity. This clause gives the agent the exclusive right and authority to sell or locate property for the principal.

Non-agency declaration. The agreement clearly sets forth that it is a non-agency personal services contract with a legally binding effect. This provision expressly states that the broker is not an agent of the buyer or seller and is not acting in a fiduciary capacity. In addition, the principal agrees that the agent is not working for the benefit of either party nor advocating the interests of either party. Usually this clause requires the principal's acknowledgment that he or she has read a state-level approved document describing and explaining the forms of agency or non-agency relationships practiced in that state.

Transaction broker duties. Like other listings, this clause defines what activities the agent will undertake to earn compensation. Key words are 'assist,' or 'offer information' or 'facilitate' as opposed to 'represent.' Activities include web searches, showings, advertising, etc.

Other buyers acknowledged. If a buyer agreement, the buyer will acknowledge that the agent is working with other buyers who may be in competition for any property the buyer is shown by the agent.

Compensation. This clause stipulates what the agent will be paid, by whom, and upon what circumstances, much like the buyer agency agreement. The clause will likely include that the compensation may be partially or wholly provided by the seller. In addition, the clause provides that, if the buyer purchases a property that was previously shown by the agent within a certain amount of time following the listing's expiration date, then the agent is owed the commission.

Buyer or seller duties. Here the agreement states what the buyer or seller commits to do during the listing term, most notably to compensate the agent for fulfilling the agreement. In addition, the seller typically agrees to show the property, and provide property condition disclosures. The buyer agrees to work exclusively with the agent (if an exclusive agreement) and provide information regarding the desired property and certain financial information.

Agreement term. Like other listings, the transaction agreement contains a beginning and ending date for the listing term. The term is extendable to closing if the principal buys or sells a property for which the settlement date is beyond the original expiration date.

Non-discrimination. The agreement affirms that the agent will conduct all affairs in compliance with state and federal fair housing and non-discrimination laws.

Signatures of parties. The signatures of the principal and agent affirm the agreement as well as acknowledge that the principal has received a copy of the agreement.

12 Listing Agreements: an Overview
Snapshot Review

**REVIEW OF LEGAL
FOUNDATIONS**

- listing: broker's enforceable contract of employment with client establishing special agency relationship to procure a customer

Agency law

- parties: listing broker and client; broker's subagents; customers and prospects

- fiduciary duties: loyalty; obedience; disclosure; care; diligence; accounting

- scope of authority: listings are special or limited agency, not general agency agreements; broker may not contract for client unless specifically authorized; clients liable only for broker's acts within scope of authority

Contract law

- listings are unilateral contracts; listing must be valid to be enforceable; legal form: oral listings are valid and enforceable except, in many states, exclusive right-to-sell listings which must be written to be enforceable

- listings are not assignable since they are personal service contracts

**TYPES OF LISTING
AGREEMENT**

- owner listing: authorization to sell or lease; buyer or tenant listing: authorization to represent buyer or tenant

**Exclusive right-to-sell
(or lease)**

- most prevalent; given to one broker; must usually be written; must expire; broker gets commission if property transfers during period

Exclusive agency

- exclusive excepting owner; oral or written; must expire; broker gets commission unless owner sells

Open listing

- non-exclusive; oral or written; no stated expiration; procuring cause gets commission; no commission if client procures customer

Net listing

- all sale proceeds above a seller's minimum price go to the broker; discouraged, if not illegal

**Buyer and tenant
agency agreements**

- open or exclusive listings with buyers or tenants to represent their interests compensation in form stipulated by agreement; may be paid by seller or landlord at closing; payable if buyer defaults; agent has fiduciary and disclosure duties

**Transaction broker
agreements**

- non-agency; no fiduciary duties; agent does not work in the interests of or for the benefit of either party

Multiple listing

- listing placed in MLS; owners consent to rules and provisions of MLS

**FULFILLMENT AND
TERMINATION**

Agent's performance

- based on results: find ready willing and able customer or effect a sale; may perform only authorized tasks to achieve result; must verify owner and property data; may delegate duties to salespeople and other brokers

Compensation

- negotiated; where disputed, procuring cause is owed commission

Causes for termination

- performance; infeasibility; mutual agreement; revocation; abandonment; breach; expiration; invalidity; incapacitation or death; involuntary transfer; destruction of property

Revoking a listing

- clients always have power to revoke during period, but may incur liability for commission or damages

LISTING AGREEMENT CLAUSES

Exclusive right-to-sell clauses

- minimal requirements: broker's and owners' names; address and/or legal description; listing price; expiration date; agent's duties; compensation terms; authority granted; agency and non-agency disclosures: seller's representations and condition disclosures

Exclusive buyer agency clauses

- minimal requirements virtually identical to exclusive right-to-sell; distinguishing features: buyer's representation of exclusivity; agent compensation; buyer's acknowledgment of other buyers

Transaction broker clauses

- may be exclusive or non-exclusive; typical principle provisions: identification of parties and property; agent's authorized activity; declaration of non-agency; broker's duties; buyer's acknowledgment of other buyers; compensation; buyer or seller duties; expiration date

13 General Brokerage Practices

Function and Organization
The Broker-Salesperson Relationship
Operating a Real Estate Brokerage
Business Brokerage
Syndications and Securities Brokerage

FUNCTION AND ORGANIZATION

The core activity of brokerage
Who may legally broker real estate?
Types of brokerage organization
Trade organizations

The core activity of brokerage

Effecting a transaction. The core activity of real estate brokerage is the business of procuring a buyer, seller, tenant, or property on behalf of a client for the purpose of completing a transaction. If successful, the broker receives a commission according to the provisions of a listing agreement. A broker's compensation for effecting a transaction is usually a negotiated percentage of the purchase price.

Broker cooperation. In most cases, transactions require the assistance of a cooperating broker from another brokerage company acting as a subagent. Most listing agreements provide for brokerage cooperation in the multiple listing clause. A transaction involving a cooperating subagent is called **co-brokerage**. In a co-brokered transaction, the listing broker splits the commission with the "co-broker," typically on a 50-50 basis. A broker may cooperate with other brokers on either side of a transaction, either assisting a listing agent to locate a buyer or tenant, or assisting a buyer or tenant representative in locating a seller or landlord.

In the most common form of broker cooperation, an outside broker locates a buyer for the listing broker's seller. In such cases, the listing broker shares the commission with the cooperating "selling" broker on a pre-determined basis.

Multiple listing service (MLS). The second prevalent form of broker cooperation is the multiple listing service, or MLS. A multiple listing service is an organization of brokers who have agreed to cooperate with member brokers in marketing listings. Members of the service also agree to enter all exclusive listings into the listing distribution network so that every member is promptly informed of new listings as they come on the market.

The listing agreement used by members of a multiple listing service discloses relevant procedures and policies so that all principal parties to the agreement are aware of the pooling of the listing. A broker who works on a transaction listed in the MLS has all the duties and responsibilities inherent in the laws of agency as the client's fiduciary agent. The listing agreement sets forth specific duties.

Critical brokerage skills. To generate business, as well as achieve the transactional objectives of clients, a broker must be proficient in four skill areas:

> ▸ obtaining a client listing
> ▸ marketing a listing
> ▸ facilitating the closing of a transaction
> ▸ managing market information

A client hires a broker by executing a listing agreement. Once hired, the broker or agent implements a marketing plan to procure the other principal party for the transaction. The broker then plays an important role in pre-closing activities to ensure successful closing of the transaction.

To serve clients and locate customers, a broker must become expert in local real estate market conditions. A fundamental part of maintaining market expertise is organizing and managing an information system.

Types of transactions and properties brokered. Brokers and salespeople are licensed to broker all types of real property for clients in any form of transaction. In practice, it is common for brokers and agents to specialize in a type of property, a type of transaction, or a geographical area.

Brokerage vs. trading. The distinction between brokerage and trading for one's own account is important for determining whether one must be licensed to perform the real estate activity in question. To be considered brokerage, an agent's activity must generally be conducted on behalf of a person or business entity other than the agent. Buying, selling, and leasing real estate for one's own account or for one's company are generally not considered brokerage.

Brokerage vs. advisory services. Technically, brokerage is distinct from the practice of rendering real estate advisory services. A licensed broker acting as a consultant for a fee usually is not working to effect a particular transaction. Since the objective is not purely transaction-oriented, the activity is not really brokerage. Examples of advisory services include:

> ▸ providing an estimate of value
> ▸ performing market analysis
> ▸ managing property

Even though fee consulting is not brokerage in the strict sense, real estate consultants who offer advisory services to the public must have a real estate license in most states.

Exhibit 13.1 Common Brokerage Specialties

Transaction type	
sales rentals assignments	exchanges subleases options
Property type	
Residential single family condominiums cooperatives mobile homes apartments	**Commercial** retail office industrial
Land undeveloped developed agricultural	**Special purpose** government religious recreational
Businesses	**Real estate securities**

Who may legally broker real estate?

Real estate license laws. All fifty states (and Canada) impose legal licensing requirements on any person or business entity desiring to broker real estate. To obtain a broker's license, an applicant must complete required education, meet experience requirements as a salesperson, and pass a state examination. There may be additional requirements concerning age, criminal record, and professional background. Practicing real estate brokerage without a valid license is illegal. Anyone who plans to obtain a real estate license should become familiar with the real estate license law of the relevant state.

Range of business entities. Some business entities may legally broker real estate, and others may not. The principal types of business organization and the legal restrictions on their ability to broker real estate are described below. Note that all the business entities may own, buy, and sell *their own* real estate in varying degrees without violating license laws.

Sole proprietorship. A sole proprietorship is a business owned by a single individual. When the proprietor dies, the business terminates. Sole proprietorships must follow state licensing and registration laws to conduct business, such as fictitious name laws. Other distinguishing characteristics of sole proprietorships are:

> ▶ liability: sole proprietors are personally liable for their own debts and actions and those of employees while performing business duties; proprietors may be sued personally

➤ taxation: business profits are taxed once as the proprietor's personal income

A sole proprietorship *may broker* real estate if properly licensed.

Corporation for profit. A corporation is a legal entity owned by stockholders. A corporation for profit consists of one or more persons authorized to conduct business for profit. A board of directors elected by stockholders oversees the business. Officers (president, vice president, secretary, treasurer) and managers conduct day-to-day affairs. Other distinguishing characteristics are:

➤ "perpetual" existence: the corporation survives the death of any of the stockholders, directors, or officers

➤ formation: to incorporate, principal parties must complete and file articles of incorporation in accordance with state law; a corporation is domestic if it is headquartered in the state where the articles of incorporation were filed. Otherwise, the corporation is a foreign corporation

➤ liability: shareholders of the corporation are only liable to the extent of the value of one's shares; officers and directors may be held personally liable for the corporation's actions under the Sarbanes-Oxley Act of 2002

➤ taxation: owners are double-taxed on business profits; corporate profits are taxed and after-tax dividends distributed to shareholders are taxed again as personal income

A corporation *may broker* real estate if it is legally authorized to do business in a state and licensed to broker there. State license laws may require one or more officers to hold active or inactive broker's licenses. Generally, shareholders may not broker real estate for the corporation.

Non-profit corporation. A non-profit corporation is a corporate entity which is not legally entitled to generate profit. A board of directors and officers manage operations. Non-profit organizations are not subject to taxation.

A non-profit organization *may not* broker real estate.

General partnership. A general partnership is a for-profit business consisting of two or more co-owners who have agreed to share business profits. Unlike a corporation, the general partnership is not a distinct, legal entity, although a corporation may be a partner in a general partnership. Additional distinguishing features are:

➤ formation: the partnership is formed by a written or oral partnership agreement with or without a financial investment by either partner

➤ dissolution: the partnership may be terminated through mutual agreement, withdrawal or death of a partner, or by legal action

➤ liability: all partners bear full liability for debts and obligations jointly and severally

➤ taxation: partners are taxed once on their respective partnership profits; partnerships do not have double-taxation

A general partnership *may* broker real estate if properly licensed. State law may require one or all partners to hold active or inactive broker's licenses.

Limited partnership. A limited partnership consists of general partners and limited partners. General partners are wholly responsible for business operations, while limited partners are investors who participate only in business profits. The general partners typically receive compensation for their management responsibilities. Other defining features are:

> ▸   limited partners: a limited partner must make an investment, which subsequently comprises the extent of the partner's liability. Limited partners are taxed once, on profits distributed by the partnership.
>
> ▸   general partners: bear sole liability for debts and obligations

A limited partnership *may* broker real estate. However, limited partners may not broker real estate for the partnership. State laws may require the general partners to have active or inactive broker's licenses. Limited partners need not be licensed for the partnership to broker real estate.

Joint venture. A joint venture is a partnership formed to complete a specific business endeavor, such as a real estate development. Individuals, general and limited partnerships, and corporations may participate. In forming the entity, the partners identify how they will conduct business and share profits. Principal parties in the joint venture share liability, but may not obligate the other co-venturers to agreements outside of the joint venture project.

A joint venture *may* broker real estate, provided the co-venturers are duly licensed.

Business trust and real estate investment trust. A business trust is a group of investors who invest in a pooled trust fund managed by their elected trustee. The trustee purchases investment assets and distributes profits and gains to the trustors. A business trust that invests primarily in real estate and meets certain other requirements is a real estate investment trust (REIT) and receives special tax treatment.

A business trust may *not* broker real estate, but it may buy and sell its own real estate assets.

Cooperative association. A cooperative association is a non-profit, tax-exempt alliance of individuals or companies formed to promote common goods or services.

A cooperative association *may not* broker real estate.

Exhibit 13.2 Who may broker real estate

May broker	May not broker
individual sole proprietor for-profit corporation general partnership limited partnership joint venture	non-profit corporation business trust co-operative association

Types of brokerage organization

In addition to being organized as a sole proprietorship, partnership, corporation or joint venture, a brokerage may be:

> ▶ independent or affiliated
> ▶ specialized in a type of property
> ▶ specialized in a type of transaction
> ▶ specialized in a type of client

These variations in brokerage organization are usually a response to competitive conditions in the local real estate market.

Independent brokerage. A brokerage that is not affiliated with a franchise is an independent agency. Many independent agencies participate in networks on a local, regional, or national basis. Such networks expose the independent broker to a larger market without compromising individual identity.

Franchise. A franchised brokerage is an independently-owned company that enters into a licensing arrangement with a franchisor to participate in various benefits offered in exchange for compensation. Franchisors generally offer local franchisees:

> ▶ the use of a recognized trade name
> ▶ national and regional advertising
> ▶ training programs
> ▶ standardized operating procedures
> ▶ a national referral system

In exchange, a franchisee pays the franchisor start-up fees and a portion of gross income.

Commercial and residential brokerages. Many brokerages deal primarily with limited types of property: residential, commercial, industrial, undeveloped land, etc. In practice, most residential companies conduct a small amount of commercial brokerage, while commercial brokerages tend to deal strictly with retail, office, industrial, or land properties. A large company may handle all types of properties but will probably have a separate organizational division for each property type.

Transaction-specialized brokerages. Brokerages often organize around a particular type of transaction. Thus, there are companies that specialize in apartment rentals, office rentals, exchanges, business brokerage, and, most commonly, residential sales.

Buyer- and seller-oriented brokerages. Companies sometimes specialize even further by choosing to represent only one side in a transaction. Thus a brokerage may represent only commercial tenants, or only residential buyers, or some other limited type of client.

Trade organizations

Numerous trade organizations serve the real estate brokerage industry and all of its areas of specialization. The largest is the National Association of Realtors® (NAR). NAR is comprised of a national headquarters, a state association in each state, and within each state, local Realtor® boards.

One should note that the term Realtor® is a protected trade name of NAR. *Only members of the organization may use the term to refer to themselves.* More specifically, there are two identities within NAR: Realtor, and Realtor-Associate. By definition, a Realtor® is a member broker and a Realtor-Associate® is a member sales agent. (In some states, Realtor applies to both broker and sales agent.) Membership in the local board automatically includes membership in the local MLS, the state association, and NAR.

THE BROKER-SALESPERSON RELATIONSHIP

Legal relationships
Salesperson's employment status
Obligations and responsibilities
Agent compensation

Legal relationships

Only a broker with an active broker's license can hire and employ a licensed salesperson. A licensed salesperson may work only for the employing broker and may not work for or receive direct compensation from any other broker.

Agent's scope of authority. State real estate license laws provide for two distinct licenses to conduct real estate brokerage: the broker license and the salesperson or sales agent license.

A licensed real estate broker is duly authorized to represent clients directly in brokering real estate. A sales agent, on the other hand, is only authorized to represent a broker and carry out such duties as the broker may legitimately delegate. In other words, a sales agent does not directly represent the client in a transaction but is rather the agent of the broker and subagent of the client. A sales agent is therefore a fiduciary of the employing broker.

As agent of a broker, a salesperson may offer properties for sale or lease, procure buyers, negotiate transaction terms, and otherwise conduct the business of brokerage. The agent, however, must act entirely on the broker's behalf.

A salesperson *may not*:

▸ bind a client to any contract
▸ receive compensation directly from a client
▸ accept a listing or deposit that is not in the name of the broker

Salesperson's employment status

A sales agent may be an independent contractor (IC) or an employee. In either case, the broker is responsible and liable for the sales agent's actions. Brokers are subject to guidelines of the U.S. Equal Employment Opportunity Commission (EEOC), a federal agency that enforces laws against workplace discrimination.

Independent contractor / broker relationship. Generally, a broker has limited control over the actions of a contractor. Specifically:

▸ a broker can require performance results, but is limited in demanding *how* a contractor performs the work. For example, a broker may not prescribe selling methods, meeting attendance, or office hours.

▸ an IC is responsible for income and social security taxes; the broker does not withhold taxes

▸ a broker cannot provide an IC with employee benefits such as health insurance or pension plans

Employee / broker relationship. A broker has greater control over the actions of an employee. Specifically:

▸ a broker can impose a sales methodology. In addition, a broker can enforce all office policies, including hours, meeting attendance, and telephone coverage.

▸ a broker must withhold income taxes and pay unemployment compensation tax on behalf of an employee

▸ an employee may receive the benefits enjoyed by the broker's non-selling employees

A written agreement between broker and employee or independent contractor should clearly state each party's duties and responsibilities to the other. In addition, the agreement should clarify the agent's compensation program as well as who is to pay for incidental business expenses.

Real estate assistant or personal assistant. Brokers and salespersons may hire licensed or unlicensed employees to assist them with a variety of tasks. Unlicensed assistants may perform clerical or ministerial acts, but nothing requiring a license. Licensed assistants may perform tasks requiring a license. Unlicensed assistants usually may be compensated directly by the sales associate they work for, but licensed assistants must be compensated by the employing broker and are subject to that broker's supervision.

Obligations and responsibilities

Sales agent's duties and responsibilities. In accepting employment from a broker, a salesperson generally makes a commitment to:

▸ work diligently to sell the broker's listings
▸ work diligently to procure new listings

- ▸ promote the business reputation of the broker
- ▸ abide by the broker's established policies
- ▸ fulfill the fiduciary duties owed clients as their subagent
- ▸ maintain insurance policies as required by the broker
- ▸ have transportation for conducting business, as required by the broker
- ▸ conform to ethical standards imposed by broker and trade organization
- ▸ uphold all covenants and provisions of the employment agreement

Broker's obligations to the sales agent. In employing a salesperson, a broker generally makes a commitment to:

- ▸ make the brokerage's listings available
- ▸ make the brokerage's market and property data available
- ▸ provide whatever training was promised at the time of hiring
- ▸ provide whatever office support was promised at the time of hiring
- ▸ uphold the commission structure and expense reimbursement policy
- ▸ conform to ethical standards imposed by the broker's trade organization
- ▸ uphold all covenants and provisions of the employment agreement

Agent compensation An agent employee of a broker may receive wages, salary, additional commissions, expense reimbursements, and benefit plans. An independent contractor's compensation is a normally a combination of commissions and free office support. Most sales agents work as independent contractors who earn a commission.

Commission splits. A sales agent earns compensation for procuring listings and for procuring buyers or tenants, whenever a transaction results. In the jargon of brokerage, these are the two "sides" to a commission: the listing side and the selling side. An agent who procures a listing receives a share of the broker's listing side commission, according to the agent's commission schedule. An agent who sells a listing, i.e., finds the customer, receives a share of the broker's selling side of the commission, according to the commission schedule. An agent who procures both listing and customer receives a share of the broker's listing side commission and selling side commission.

Commission schedules. An agent's commission schedule is a comprehensive summary of commission splits under various circumstances, including:

- ▸ listing and selling side
- ▸ salesperson's level of sales performance
- ▸ broker's level of expense reimbursement to agent
- ▸ the particular policies or organization of the agency
- ▸ prevailing commission splits in the market

In view of these circumstances, an agent's commission schedule can vary widely. For example, an agent who is the highest sales producer in the market may be able to secure a 70% or 80% commission split with the broker, regardless of side. If the broker is paying an inordinate amount of selling expenses, an agent's commission split may only be 40%. Some brokerages have a policy of not paying any expenses except the rent. In such cases, agents may receive an 80% or 90%

commission split. In almost all cases, broker and agent negotiate the schedule of commissions in the environment of competitive market conditions.

Calculating commissions. The following exhibit illustrates how commissions might be split in a hypothetical transaction.

Exhibit 13.3 Calculating Commissions

Sale price: $500,000   Co-brokerage splits: 50%
Commission: 6%, or $30,000   Agent splits: 50% on both sides

Situation A: a cooperating broker is involved

	Commission $	Commission %
Listing broker	7,500	1.5%
Listing agent	7,500	1.5%
Selling broker	7,500	1.5%
Selling agent	7,500	1.5%

Situation B: no cooperating broker; listing agent finds buyer

Listing broker	15,000	3.0%
Listing agent	15,000	3.0%

Situation C: no cooperating broker; another agent *in the same agency* finds buyer

Listing broker	15,000	3.0%
Listing agent	7,500	1.5%
Selling agent	7,500	1.5%

OPERATING A REAL ESTATE BROKERAGE

Obtaining listings
Marketing listings
Pre-closing activities
Managing information
Policy manual
Advertisement regulations
Anti-trust laws

Obtaining listings
Listings are the traditional source of a broker's income. By obtaining a listing, a broker obtains a share of the commission generated whenever a cooperating broker finds a buyer. It is not so certain that working with a buyer will provide income. In the absence of an exclusive buyer representation agreement, a buyer may move from one agent to another without making any commitment. Agents can spend considerable time with a buyer and earn nothing. Hence the special value of a listing: it is likely to generate revenue.

Listing procedures. The marketing and self-promotional efforts of agents generate listings. New agents usually focus on becoming well known in a small geographical area and hope to encounter clients there who are willing to list with them. More experienced and better-known agents are able to rely to a greater extent on referrals in obtaining listings.

New or experienced, an agent needs certain skills at each step in the process of obtaining a listing.

Exhibit 13.4 Listing Steps

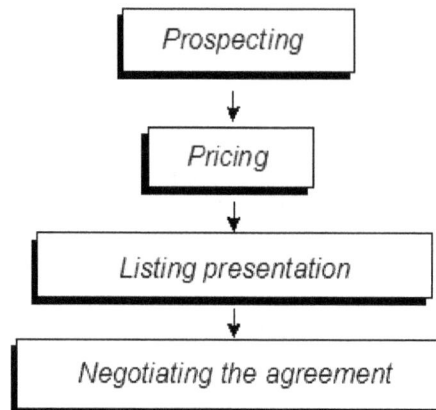

```
┌─────────────────────────┐
│      Prospecting        │
└─────────────────────────┘
            │
            ▼
┌─────────────────────────┐
│        Pricing          │
└─────────────────────────┘
            │
            ▼
┌─────────────────────────────────┐
│      Listing presentation       │
└─────────────────────────────────┘
            │
            ▼
┌───────────────────────────────────────┐
│      Negotiating the agreement         │
└───────────────────────────────────────┘
```

Prospecting. Prospecting is any activity designed to generate listing prospects: parties who intend to sell or lease property and who have not yet committed to a broker. Prospecting activities include mailing newsletters and flyers, selling directly and person-to-person, advertising, and selling indirectly via community involvement.

The goal of prospecting is to reach a potential seller or landlord, make that person aware of the agent's and brokerage's services, and obtain permission to discuss the benefits of listing, often in the form of a formal selling presentation.

Pricing. It is almost always necessary for an agent seeking a listing to suggest a listing price or price range for the property. It is important to make a careful estimate, because underpricing a property is not in the best interests of the seller, and overpricing it often prevents a transaction altogether.

The "Appraisal" chapter describes methods of estimating value. In brief, an agent usually relies on an analysis of comparable properties which have recently sold in the same neighborhood. By making adjustments for the differences between the subject property and the comparables, the agent arrives at a general price range.

Agents must be careful to caution sellers that they are not appraisers, and that the suggested price range is not an expert opinion of market value. If a more precise estimate of market value is desired, the seller should hire a licensed appraiser.

Listing presentation and negotiation of agreement. A listing presentation is an agent's opportunity to meet with a seller and present the merits of the agent's marketing plan, personal expertise, and company strengths. At the same time, an agent can explain the many phases and details of a real estate transaction and point out how the provisions of the listing agreement and the agent-principal relationship work to ensure a smooth transaction.

Ultimately, the agent's aim in a presentation meeting is to have the principal execute a listing agreement. The agent must then submit the listing to the broker for approval and signing. This result will set in motion the process of marketing the property. In practice, it may take an agent many meetings with a prospect before the prospect signs an agreement.

Marketing listings The process of marketing a listed property occurs in three broad steps, leading to the desired end of a completed sale contract. At each of these steps, there are critical skills an agent must master.

Exhibit 13.5 Marketing Steps

```
┌─────────────────────────┐
│     Marketing Plan       │
└─────────────────────────┘
            │
            ▼
┌─────────────────────────┐
│   Selling the Prospect   │
└─────────────────────────┘
            │
            ▼
┌─────────────────────────┐
│     Obtaining Offers     │
└─────────────────────────┘
```

Marketing plan. After the broker formalizes the listing agreement, the sales agent initiates a marketing plan for the property. An ideal marketing plan is a cohesive combination of promotional and selling activities directed at potential customers. The best combination is one that aims to have maximum impact on the marketplace in relation to the time and money expended.

Selling the prospect. When marketing activities produce prospects, the agent's marketing role becomes more interpersonal. An agent must now:

▸ qualify prospects' plans, preferences, and financial capabilities
▸ show properties that meet the customer's needs
▸ elicit the buyer's reactions to properties
▸ report material results to the seller or listing agent

At the earliest appropriate time, an agent must make certain disclosures to a prospective customer. Depending on state laws, an agent may have to disclose the relevant agency relationship, the property's physical condition, and the possible presence of hazardous materials.

Obtaining offers. If a buyer is interested in purchasing a property, an agent obtains the buyer's offer of transaction terms, including price, down payment, desired closing date, and financing requirements.

An agent must be extremely careful at this point to abide by fiduciary obligations to the client, whoever that party may be. Discussions of price are particularly delicate: whether the client is buyer or seller, the agent's duty is to uphold the client's best interests. Thus it is not acceptable to suggest to a customer what price the client will or will not accept. With pricing and other issues, it is always a good practice to understand what role the client wants the agent to assume in the offering phase of the transaction; in other words, exactly how far the agent may go in developing terms on the client's behalf.

When a buyer or tenant makes an offer, the agent *must* present it to the seller or landlord at the earliest possible moment. If the terms of the offer are unacceptable, the agent may assist the seller in developing a counteroffer, which the agent would subsequently submit to the customer or customer's agent. The offering and counteroffering process continues until a meeting of the minds results in a sale contract.

Pre-closing activities Between the execution of the sale contract and the closing of the transaction, the property is "under contract" or "contract pending." During this period, buyer and seller have certain things to do to achieve a successful closing. The buyer often needs to arrange financing and dispose of other property; the seller may need to clear up title encumbrances and make certain property repairs. The sale contract should specify all such required tasks.

The time period between contracting and closing is referred to as the **contingency period**, or **pre-closing period**.

Agent's responsibilities. As dictated by custom and the circumstances of a transaction, an agent has a range of duties and responsibilities during the pre-closing period.

An agent's foremost duty following acceptance of an offer is to submit the contract and the earnest money to the employing broker without delay. Most states impose deadlines for this requirement, usually within twenty-four hours from the agent's receipt of the deposit.

Other possible responsibilities are:

- ▶ assisting the buyer in obtaining financing
- ▶ assisting the seller in clearing title
- ▶ assisting the seller in completing property repairs
- ▶ recommending inspectors, appraisers, attorneys, and title companies
- ▶ assisting in communications between principals
- ▶ assisting in the exchange of transaction documents

Broker's responsibilities. The listing broker has the primary responsibility for handling deposit monies and for overseeing the agent's pre-closing activities. State license laws require that earnest money deposits be placed in an account which is separate from the broker's operating accounts. They also require the broker to keep accurate records and follow accepted accounting procedures.

These precautions protect the buyer and seller and safeguard the deposited funds. A broker must be careful to avoid two common violations of escrow regulations: commingling and conversion.

Commingling. Commingling is the act of mixing the broker's personal or business funds with escrow funds. A broader definition of commingling includes the failure to deposit earnest money into escrow in a timely manner. In most states, commingling funds constitutes grounds for license suspension or revocation.

Conversion. Conversion is the act of misappropriating escrow funds for the broker's business or personal use. More serious than mere commingling, conversion is effectively an act of theft: using monies which do not belong to the broker. Conversion carries serious consequences, including license revocation.

Communications and technology

Multiple listing services and websites. The posting and sharing of property listings and data among broker websites, firm websites, and multiple listing services (MLS) is one of the most effective marketing tools available to today's licensees. Broker cooperation assures sellers of maximum exposure for their properties, just as it assures buyers of seeing the widest possible range of listed properties.

To ensure fair use of MLS facilities, the National Association of REALTORS® has developed an Internet Data Exchange (IDX) policy that enables MLS members to display and use MLS data while respecting the rights of property owners and brokers to market their properties however they want.

Basically, persons who want to make use of MLS data have to share their own data as well. They can opt out of the sharing policy so that competitors cannot post their properties on competing websites, but then they cannot post competitors' properties on their own sites.

There are a number of websites that provide consumers with the capability to search through listings all over the country and even the world. Of course, it is always wise to recognize that information posted on the internet is not necessarily reliable and that the source of the information should be considered carefully.

Email and texting. Frequent and virtually instantaneous contact between real estate practitioners and consumers is possible via email and texting. As both these forms of communication fall under the category of advertising, practitioners need to carefully observe their state's advertising regulations. In brief, be truthful, direct, and concise. Provide the information required by law, and do not violate prohibitions against unsolicited emails and messages.

Social media. Social media websites allow rapid exchange of information, documents, photos, messages and data with a select group of contacts. They also represent another form of advertising and so are subject to real estate commission advertising regulations in most states.

Smartphones. Smartphones facilitate the use, not only of email, texting, and social media, but also of immediate internet access, document review, photo and document sharing, data storage, and video conferencing. They offer, in fact, an almost complete mobile office.

Managing information

The ability to satisfy the needs of clients and customers is largely dependent on a broker's ability to obtain, organize, and manage information. Information is a cornerstone of the broker's perceived value in the marketplace and a major reason why buyers and sellers seek a broker out. Systematic collection and updating of relevant information is therefore a business priority.

Property data. Most brokerages maintain two categories of property data: available properties, and all properties in the market area. In residential brokerage, available property basically consists of the listings in the MLS and for-sale-by-owner properties. Records for all properties in an area are accessible in tax records. Commercial brokerages usually keep track of available and occupied commercial properties in a proprietary database.

Buyer data. Buyer information is usually compiled and maintained, often informally, by each agent in a brokerage. An agency's base of prospects who are looking for property at any given time is valuable for marketing new listings.

Tenant data. In residential and commercial leasing companies, information is compiled and maintained on all tenants in an area, by property type used. Such files contain a tenant's lease expiration, property size, and rent.

Client data. It is important to keep track of both current and former clients. Former clients are likely prospects to become clients again or customers. They are also a source of referrals. Current clients, of course, should be the broker's primary concern.

Market data. Today's clients and customers expect a broker to know the market intimately. It is often the broker or agent with the best market knowledge who dominates business in the market. Knowing a market includes keeping up to date on:

> ▶ pricing and appreciation trends
> ▶ financing rates and terms
> ▶ demographic patterns and trends
> ▶ construction trends
> ▶ general economic trends

Policy manual

A well-managed brokerage relies on a written policy manual to keep the business running smoothly and professionally. A policy manual sets forth company rules, regulations, and policies.

Advertisement regulations

Advertising is an important tool in marketing properties and procuring buyers. It is, however, subject to regulation and restrictions. In general, state laws and regulations require that:

> ▶ advertising must not be misleading
> ▶ the broker is responsible for the content of advertising done by agents

- all advertising must reveal the identity of the broker; licensed brokers and agents may not use blind ads that conceal their identities

- brokers selling their own property through the brokerage must disclose the brokerage identity

- salespersons must include the broker's business identity in any advertising; they may not advertise in their own name solely (unless selling their own property through channels other than the agency)

Telephone Consumer Protection Act. The TCPA (Telephone Consumer Protection Act) addresses the regulation of unsolicited telemarketing phone calls. Rules include the following:

- telephone solicitors must identify themselves, on whose behalf they are calling, and how they can be contacted

- telemarketers must comply with any do-not-call request made during the solicitation call

- consumers can place their home and wireless phone numbers on a national Do-Not-Call list which prohibits future solicitations from telemarketers.

CAN-SPAM Act. The CAN-SPAM Act (Controlling the Assault of Non-Solicited Pornography and Marketing Act of 2003) supplements the Telephone Consumer Protection Act (TCPA). It

- bans sending unwanted email 'commercial messages' to wireless devices
- requires express prior authorization
- requires giving an 'opt out' choice to terminate the sender's messages

Anti-trust laws

Brokerage companies, like other businesses, are subject to anti-trust laws designed to prevent monopolies and unfair trade practices.

Sherman Antitrust Act. Enacted in 1890, the Sherman Antitrust Act prohibits restraint of interstate and foreign trade by conspiracy, monopolistic practice, and certain forms of business combinations, or mergers. The Sherman Act empowers the federal government to proceed against antitrust violators.

Clayton Antitrust Act. The Clayton Antitrust Act of 1914 reinforces and broadens the provisions of the Sherman Act. Among its prohibitions are certain exclusive contracts, predatory price cutting to eliminate competitors, and inter-related boards of directors and stock holdings between same-industry corporations. The Clayton Act also legalizes certain labor strikes, picketing, and boycotts.

Anti-competitive behavior. The effect of antitrust legislation is to prohibit trade practice and trade restraints that unfairly disadvantage open competition. Business practices and behaviors which violate antitrust laws include collusion, price fixing, market allocation, bid rigging, restricting market entry, exclusive dealing, and predatory pricing.

Collusion. Collusion is the illegal practice of two or more businesses joining forces or making joint decisions which have the effect of putting another business at a competitive disadvantage. Businesses may not collude to fix prices, allocate markets, create monopolies, or otherwise interfere with free market operations.

Price fixing. Price fixing is the practice of two or more brokers agreeing to charge certain commission rates or fees for their services, regardless of market conditions or competitors. In essence, such pricing avoids and disturbs the dynamics of a free, open market.

For instance, the two largest brokerages in a market jointly decide to cut commission rates by 50% in order to draw clients away from competitors. The cut-rate pricing could destroy smaller agencies that lack the staying power of the large companies.

Market allocation. Market allocation is the practice of colluding to restrict competitive activity in portions of a market in exchange for a reciprocal restriction from a competitor: "we won't compete against you here if you won't compete against us there."

For example, Broker A agrees to trade only in single family re-sales, provided that Broker B agrees to focus exclusively on apartment rentals and condominium sales. The net effect is an illegally restricted market where collusion and monopoly supplant market forces.

Tie-in agreements. In a tie-in agreement, the sale of one product or performance of a service is tied to the sale of another, less desirable product or service. For instance, "I will sell you this car, but you have to hire my brother-in-law to drive it." Or, more likely, "I will list and sell your old home if you hire me to find you a new home to purchase." Tie-ins restrict competition and limit the freedom of the consumer.

Violations of fair trade and anti-trust laws may be treated as felonies, and penalties can be substantial. Loss of one's license is also at stake. Brokers are well-advised to understand and recognize these laws.

BUSINESS BROKERAGE

Business brokerage vs. real property brokerage
Transaction knowledge
Accounting
Determining a price
Business brokerage regulation

Business brokerage is *effecting a sale or exchange of an existing business*. In most cases, the sale of a business entails the simultaneous transfer of an estate in land, whether a leasehold or a fee. Thus to sell businesses, a broker must generally hold a real estate license.

In some states, business brokerage is classified into *opportunity brokerage* and *enterprise brokerage* in accordance with the size of the business being sold. **Opportunity brokerage** concerns a small business, usually a proprietorship or partnership, where the transaction consists of a sale of assets and an assignment of a lease. **Enterprise brokerage** concerns a larger company, usually a corporation, where the transaction involves the sale of stock and multiple real estate parcels leased or owned by the seller.

The process of business brokerage is similar to real estate brokerage: a broker secures a listing, procures a purchaser, and facilitates the closing. Once a ready, willing, and able buyer is found, the broker earns a commission.

Business brokerage vs real property brokerage

The critical difference between selling a business and selling real estate is that selling a business includes the transfer of *business income, personal property assets*, and, possibly, *liabilities*, in addition to real property. To be competent in this brokerage specialty, a business broker must have specialized skills concerning transactions, accounting, and pricing. A business broker must also rely on a professional team to complete the transaction. Members of this team would include the client's legal counsel, accountant, and, preferably, a professional appraiser.

Transaction knowledge

Types of sale. There are generally two types of business sale transaction for a business broker to be aware of: the *asset sale* and the *stock sale*. In an **asset sale**, the purchaser takes possession of some or all of the assets of the business, as well as the real estate, in exchange for the sale price. The purchase usually does not include acquiring the existing business entity or its liabilities. An asset sale is preferred by buyers who want to buy only portions of a business, or to avoid liabilities inherent in a stock purchase.

In a **stock sale**, a purchaser acquires complete ownership of a business, including the legal corporate entity, all assets, all financial liabilities, and any current or future legal liabilities arising from incidents that have occurred prior to the sale. A purchaser may prefer a stock sale to avoid creating a new business entity or to benefit from a possible tax advantage. In addition, a stock sale keeps a business identity intact, which can be very valuable.

Transaction documents. The most common transaction documents in business brokerage are a *sale contract,* an *assignment* or *real estate sale contract,* a *no-compete agreement,* and a *consulting agreement.*

A **sale contract** sets forth all terms and conditions of the agreement, including exactly what is being sold. An **assignment** or **real estate sale agreement** is an agreement for transferring any and all real property involved in the transaction. A **no-compete agreement** is a seller's covenant, for compensation, not to compete with the buyer under prescribed conditions and time periods. A **consulting agreement** is an employment agreement that hires the seller to assist the buyer in taking over business operations.

For the most part, transaction documents in business brokerage are not fully standardized. For that reason, a business broker must exercise caution in dealing with document language so as to avoid the unauthorized practice of law.

Accounting

A broker or agent who wants to undertake business brokerage needs basic proficiency in accounting. In particular, one must know how to read and interpret:

> ▶ income, expenses, and profit on an income statement
> ▶ assets, liabilities, and net worth on a balance sheet

Income, expenses, and profit. A business's profit is the revenue remaining from gross income after all expenses have been paid. A business broker must evaluate an owner's income and expenses in order to determine what the business may be worth to a buyer. This often involves interpreting which income and expense items will change after the business is sold. For example, a seller owns a grocery store and uses family members to perform clerical work without pay. If a buyer is a bachelor without children, much of the clerical work will have to be hired out. The additional payroll suddenly changes the store's profitability significantly. Neglecting to consider how income and expenses might change is likely to lead to serious problems in working with buyers.

Business assets. The assets of a business include **tangible** assets and **intangible** assets. Tangible assets include:

> ▶ cash and marketable securities
> ▶ inventory
> ▶ trade fixtures and equipment
> ▶ real property
> ▶ accounts receivable

Intangible assets include:

> ▶ the company name
> ▶ trademarks
> ▶ copyrights
> ▶ licenses
> ▶ contracts for future sales of goods or services
> ▶ goodwill

In valuing a business, both tangible and intangible assets must be taken into account, even though intangible assets may be very difficult to appraise.

Business liabilities. Business liabilities acquired in a corporate stock sale include short-term debt, such as accounts payable, and long-term liabilities, such as mortgages and leases.

Goodwill. Goodwill is a business brokerage term with two meanings. In one sense, goodwill is an intangible asset consisting of any factor that an owner values in the business, apart from any other specific asset. For example, goodwill might include reputation, a long history of success in a market, name recognition, a dominant market share, and an excellent business location. In the second sense, which is more familiar to accountants, goodwill is the difference in value between an owner's price and the value of all other business assets. For example, if an owner wants $400,000 for a business, and the totality of tangible and intangible assets is valued at $320,000, the goodwill is an $80,000 asset.

Determining a price

The most difficult task for a business broker is often finding the proper price range for a business. An owner of a smaller business has probably built the business from scratch and tends to overvalue it. Moreover, such an owner may have incomplete and disorganized accounting records, making the valuation of assets quite difficult. Finally, a business's true income may be different for one owner than it would be for another because of variations in management style and ability.

In any case, the value of the business is a function of the following:

- past, present, and future net profits, and capitalized value of these
- amount of risk and certainty associated with realizing future profits
- value of all assets as reflected in the books of account
- impact of goodwill on the value of the business
- prices paid for similar businesses
- all other risks associated with the business

Business brokerage regulation

Licensing. A business broker generally must have an active real estate license. In addition, the broker may need to have a valid securities license since a transaction may entail the sale of securities.

Uniform Commercial Code (UCC). The Uniform Commercial Code regulates the sale of personal property on a state-by-state basis, and forms the basis for standardized sale documents. Standard documents include promissory notes, security agreements, and bills of sale.

Bulk Sales Act. The Bulk Sales Act protects creditors against loss of collateral in an indebted business through the undisclosed sale of the business's inventory. If a business sells over half of its inventory to a buyer, the act declares that the sale is a bulk sale, and, as such, is potentially an asset sale. Since a creditor could lose security in such a sale, the seller must disclose the names of creditors to the buyer in a Bulk Sales Affidavit. The buyer must notify the creditors of the sale, who may then take appropriate action to secure their loans.

SYNDICATIONS AND SECURITIES BROKERAGE

Syndicating real estate
Securities licensing
Securities registration

Syndicating real estate

A real estate syndication is a form of investment in which two or more investors contribute capital to a pool for the purpose of acquiring, managing, and selling an investment property for a profit.

There are two groups of parties in a syndication: the *syndicator* and the *investors*. The syndicator is the organizer and usually the party who provides the expertise to undertake the acquisition, management, and sale of the property. The investors' role is to provide funds. Investors in a syndication have little or no role in managing the investment.

Participants in a syndication may be any legal entity, for example, corporations, partnerships, individuals, and joint ventures. Most often, a syndication is structured as a limited partnership.

Benefits. The primary benefit of a syndication is that investors can participate and profit in a venture that would otherwise be beyond their individual financial and managerial capabilities. Financial benefits include income, appreciation, and possible passive loss tax deductions resulting from depreciation.

Securities licensing

The **Federal Securities Act of 1933** defined participation in a limited partnership as a *security*, since investors expect to make a profit from a common enterprise without direct control over the marketing and managing of the investment.

Since the sale of shares in a syndication represents a sale of securities, syndicators and real estate brokers *must comply with federal and state securities licensing and registration laws*. The primary federal law outlining securities registration and licensing is the **Federal Securities Exchange Act of 1934.** This law requires that any person selling securities must be registered, or licensed, with the Securities and Exchange Commission (SEC). Subsequently, the **Maloney Act of 1938** revised the requirement that securities sellers register with the SEC. Instead, it authorized self-regulation of the securities industry through any national association which would itself register with the SEC. This precipitated the formation of the only such association ever to register with the SEC: the National Association of Securities Dealers, or NASD. NASD later merged with the regulation committee of the New York Stock Exchange to form the Financial Industry Regulatory Agency (FINRA).

At present, all securities dealers must register with FINRA, including real estate brokers wishing to sell syndication participations. Depending on the type of security in question, FINRA issues a variety of licenses authorizing a dealer to market and sell the security.

The Direct Participation Program license. In 1980, FINRA (NASD) created a limited securities license exclusively for persons selling real estate syndications and other similar investment programs. The license is called the direct participation program license (DPP license).

There are two levels of DPP license, one for principals of a syndication, the DPP Limited Principal License (the "Series 39" license), and one for salespersons who work for the principal, the DPP Limited Representative License (the "Series 22" license). Both licenses are awarded upon completion of the appropriate examination and FINRA application forms.

Securities registration

Disclosure and registration. Real estate syndications are subject to strict disclosure requirements imposed by the Securities and Exchange Commission. Disclosure is in the form of a *prospectus* for the investment program. A prospectus is a comprehensive summary of all facts relating to the investment. The prospectus also expressly warns investors that there are risks and uncertainties associated with the investment.

Certain syndications must be registered with the SEC. Full-scale registration discloses all aspects of the prospective program.

Exemptions. Certain SEC rules allow for exemption from securities registration. Generally, there are two forms of exemption, the *Intrastate Exemption*, and the *Private Offering Exemption*.

> ▸ **The Intrastate Exemption**
>
> if the syndicator, the property, and all investors are located within a single state, the syndication is exempt from registration

> ▸ **The Private Offering Exemption**
>
> if the syndication is limited to 35 investors or fewer, and the syndication is not advertised in any way, the program is exempt

Whether the syndication is exempt or not, a syndicator must give investors a prospectus of the syndication.

State regulation. All states have securities licensing and registration laws in addition to federal laws. As a rule, these laws recognize FINRA licensing and self-regulation practices. However, real estate licensees wishing to engage in syndications should be familiar with applicable securities laws in their state.

13 General Brokerage Practices
Snapshot Review

FUNCTION AND ORGANIZATION

The core activity of brokerage

- procuring buyer, seller, tenant, or leased property for a client, often with the help of other brokers and a multiple listing service
- skills: listing, marketing, facilitating, managing information
- Multiple Listing Service: network of brokers who share listings

Who may legally broker real estate?

- yes: sole proprietorship, for-profit corp., general or limited partnership, joint venture. no: non-profit corp., business trust, cooperative association

Types of brokerage organization

- independents; franchises; agencies by property type, by transaction type, and by client type; limited and full service agencies

THE BROKER-SALESPERSON RELATIONSHIP

Legal relationships

- salesperson is agent, fiduciary of broker; acts in broker's name; subagent of client
- **may not:** have two employers; be paid by other parties; bind clients contractually

Salesperson's employment status

- may be employee or contractor; relationship defined by agreement; assistant may be licensed or unlicensed; if licensed, supervised and paid by employing broker

Obligations and responsibilities

- agent to broker: obtain & sell listings; follow policies and employment provisions; promote ethics and broker's reputation
- broker to agent: provide data, office support, compensation, training; uphold ethics, policies, and employment agreement

Agent compensation

- commissions per schedule after splits with cooperating brokers

OPERATING A REAL ESTATE BROKERAGE

Obtaining listings

- generate prospects; develop price range; complete listing presentation; negotiate execute and agreement

Marketing listings

- develop marketing plan; sell and qualify prospective buyers; complete necessary disclosures; obtain offers

Pre-closing activities

- facilitate fulfillment of contract contingencies and provisions
- no commingling or conversion of escrow funds

Communications and technology

- marketing techniques using technology: broker cooperation via MLS and competitors' websites; email and texting; social media websites; smartphone communication capabilities; all must be used carefully and in conformity with advertising rules and other laws

Managing information

- property data; buyer and tenant files; market data files

Policy manual	• written procedures **and** policies on all aspects of the business to ensure smooth, consistent operations
Advertisement regulations	• no misleading ads; must contain broker's ID; broker responsible for content; no blind ads
Anti-trust laws	• Sherman Act and Clayton Act pioneered antitrust laws to prohibit unfair trade practices, trade restraints, and monopolies
	• illegal to collude, disadvantage competitors; fix prices; allocate markets; force tie-ins
BUSINESS BROKERAGE	• sale of existing business and its real estate; opportunity and enterprise brokerage
Business brokerage vs. real estate brokerage	• special skills: transaction knowledge; accounting; determining the price
Transaction knowledge	• types of sale: asset sale and stock sale
	• documents: sale contract; real estate sale contract or assignment; no-compete agreement; consulting agreement
Accounting	• income, expenses, and profit
	• balance sheet: assets, liabilities, net worth
	• assets: tangible and intangible
	• goodwill: intangible asset--difference between price & other assets
Determining a price	• reconciliation of income, cost, and market data approaches; influenced by risk and stability of future income
Business brokerage regulation	• may need securities license; must comply with Bulk Sales law
SYNDICATIONS AND SECURITIES BROKERAGE	
Syndicating real estate	• pooling capital and expertise to profit from property investment
	• syndication is a security; investor may profit without management
Securities licensing	• must be FINRA-licensed to sell DPP's (syndications); Limited Principal License to own; Limited Representative License to sell
Securities registration	• must disclose; must register with SEC if not exempt; DPP exempt if within state or offered unadvertised and limited to 35 investors

14 Overview of Conveyance Contracts

Contract for Sale
Sale Contract Provisions
Option-To-Buy Contract
Contract for Deed

CONTRACT FOR SALE

Legal characteristics
Contract creation
Earnest money escrow
Contract contingencies
Default

A real estate sale contract is a binding and enforceable agreement wherein a buyer, the **vendee**, agrees to buy an identified parcel of real estate, and a seller, the **vendor**, agrees to sell it under certain terms and conditions. It is the document that is at the center of the transaction.

The conventional transfer of real estate ownership takes place in three stages. First, there is the negotiating period where buyers and sellers exchange offers in an effort to agree to all transfer terms that will appear in the sale contract. Second, when both parties have accepted all terms, the offer becomes a binding sale contract and the transaction enters the pre-closing stage, during which each party makes arrangements to complete the sale according to the sale contract's terms. Third is the closing of the transaction, when the seller deeds title to the buyer, the buyer pays the purchase price, and all necessary documents are completed. At this stage, the sale contract has served its purpose and terminates.

Other names for the sale contract are *agreement of sale, contract for purchase, contract of purchase and sale*, and *earnest money contract*.

Legal characteristics   **Executory contract.** A sale contract is *executory:* the signatories have yet to perform their respective obligations and promises. Upon closing, the sale contract is fully performed and no longer exists as a binding agreement.

Signatures. All owners of the property should sign the sale contract. If the sellers are married, both spouses should sign to ensure that both spouses release homestead, dower, and curtesy rights to the buyer at closing. Failure to do so does not invalidate the contract but can lead to encumbered title and legal disputes.

Enforceability criteria. To be enforceable, a sale contract must:

- be validly created (mutual consent, consideration, legal purpose, competent parties, voluntary act)
- be in writing
- identify the principal parties
- clearly identify the property, preferably by legal description
- contain a purchase price
- be signed by the principal parties

Written vs. oral form. A contract for the sale of real estate is enforceable only if it is in writing. A buyer or seller cannot sue to force the other to comply with an oral contract for sale, even if the contract is valid.

Assignment. Either party to a sale transaction can assign the sale contract to another party, subject to the provisions and conditions contained in the agreement.

Who may complete. A broker or agent may assist buyer and seller in completing an offer to purchase, provided the broker represents the client faithfully and does not charge a separate fee for the assistance. It is advisable, and legally required in most states, for a broker to use a standard contract form promulgated by state agencies or real estate boards, as such forms contain generally accepted language. This relieves the broker of the dangers of creating new contract language, which can be construed as a practice of law for which the broker is not licensed.

Contract creation

Offer and acceptance. A contract of sale is created by full and unequivocal acceptance of an offer. Offer and acceptance may come from either buyer or seller. The offeree must accept the offer without making any changes whatsoever. A change terminates the offer and creates a new offer, or counteroffer. An offeror may revoke an offer for any reason prior to communication of acceptance by the offeree.

Equitable title. A sale contract gives the buyer an interest in the property that is called equitable title, or *ownership in equity*. If the seller defaults and the buyer can show good faith performance, the buyer can sue for specific performance, that is, to compel the seller to transfer legal title upon payment of the contract price.

Earnest money escrow

The buyer's earnest money deposit fulfills the consideration requirements for a valid sale contract. In addition, it provides potential compensation for damages to the seller if the buyer fails to perform. The amount of the deposit varies according to local custom. It should be noted that the earnest money deposit is not the only form of consideration that satisfies the requirement.

The sale contract provides the *escrow instructions* for handling and disbursing escrow funds. The earnest money is placed in a third party trust account or escrow. A licensed escrow agent employed by a title company, financial institution, or brokerage company usually manages the escrow. An individual broker may also serve as the escrow agent.

The escrow holder acts as an impartial fiduciary for buyer and seller. If the buyer performs under the sale contract, the deposit is applied to the purchase price.

Strict rules govern the handling of earnest money deposits, particularly if a broker is the escrow agent. For example, state laws direct the broker when to deposit the funds, how to account for them, and how to keep them separate from the broker's own funds.

Contract contingencies

A sale contract often contains contingencies. A contingency is a condition that must be met before the contract is enforceable.

The most common contingency concerns financing. A buyer makes an offer contingent upon securing financing for the property under certain terms on or before a certain date. If unable to secure the specified loan commitment by the deadline, the buyer may cancel the contract and recover the deposit. An appropriate and timely loan commitment eliminates the contingency, and the buyer must proceed with the purchase.

It is possible for both buyers and sellers to abuse contingencies in order to leave themselves a convenient way to cancel without defaulting. To avoid problems, the statement of a contingency should:

- ▶ be explicit and clear
- ▶ have an expiration date
- ▶ expressly require diligence in the effort to fulfill the requirement

A contingency that is too broad, vague, or excessive in duration may invalidate the entire contract on the grounds of insufficiency of mutual agreement.

Default

A sale contract is bilateral, since both parties promise to perform. As a result, either party may default by failing to perform. Note that a party's failure to meet a contingency does not constitute default, but rather entitles the parties to cancel the contract.

Buyer default. If a buyer fails to perform under the terms of a sale contract, the breach entitles the seller to legal recourse for damages. In most cases, the contract itself stipulates the seller's remedies. The usual remedy is forfeiture of the buyer's deposit as **liquidated damages**, provided the deposit is not grossly in excess of the seller's actual damages. It is also customary to provide for the seller and broker to share the liquidated damages. The broker may not, however, receive liquidated damages in excess of what the commission would have been on the full listing price.

If the contract does not provide for liquidated damages, the seller may sue for damages, cancellation, or specific performance.

Seller default. If a seller defaults, the buyer may sue for specific performance, damages, or cancellation.

SALE CONTRACT PROVISIONS

Primary provisions
Secondary provisions

Sale contracts can vary significantly in length and thoroughness. They also vary according to the type of sale transaction they describe. Some of the varieties are:

- ▸ Residential Contract of Sale
- ▸ Commercial Contract of Sale
- ▸ Foreclosure Contract of Sale
- ▸ Contract of Sale for New Construction
- ▸ Contract of Sale for Land
- ▸ Exchange Agreement

As the most common sale transaction is a residential sale, a Residential Contract of Sale is the type with which a licensee should first become familiar.

Primary provisions   A typical residential sale contract contains provisions of the following kind.

Parties, consideration, and property. One or more clauses will identify the parties, the property, and the basic consideration, which is the sale of the property in return for a purchase price.

There must be at least two parties to a sale contract: one cannot convey property to oneself. All parties must be identified, be of legal age, and have the capacity to contract.

The property clause also identifies fixtures and personal property included in the sale. Unless expressly excluded, items commonly construed as fixtures are *included* in the sale. Similarly, items commonly considered personal property are *not included* unless expressly included.

Legal description. A legal description must be sufficient for a competent surveyor to identify the property.

Price and terms. A clause states the final price and details how the purchase will occur. Of particular interest to the seller is the buyer's down payment, since the greater the buyer's equity, the more likely the buyer will be able to secure financing. In addition, a large deposit represents a buyer's commitment to complete the sale.

If seller financing is involved, the sale contract sets forth the terms of the arrangement: the amount and type of loan, the rate and term, and how the loan will be paid off.

It is important for all parties to verify that the buyer's earnest money deposit, down payment, loan proceeds, and other promised funds together equal the purchase price stated in the contract.

Loan approval. A financing contingency clause states under what conditions the buyer can cancel the contract without default and receive a refund of the earnest money. If the buyer cannot secure the stated financing by the deadline, the parties may agree to extend the contingency by signing next to the changed dates.

Earnest money deposit. A clause specifies how the buyer will pay the earnest money. It may allow the buyer to pay it in installments. Such an option enables a buyer to hold on to the property briefly while obtaining the additional deposit funds. For example, a buyer who wants to buy a house makes an initial deposit of $200, to be followed in twenty-four hours with an additional $2,000. The sale contract includes the seller's acknowledgment of receipt of the deposit.

Escrow. An escrow clause provides for the custody and disbursement of the earnest money deposit, and releases the escrow agent from certain liabilities in the performance of escrow duties.

Closing and possession dates. The contract states when title will transfer, as well as when the buyer will take physical possession. Customarily, possession occurs on the date when the deed is recorded, unless the buyer has agreed to other arrangements.

The closing clause generally describes what must take place at closing to avoid default. A seller must provide clear and marketable title. A buyer must produce purchase funds. Failure to complete any pre-closing requirements stated in the sale contract is default and grounds for the aggrieved party to seek recourse.

Conveyed interest; type of deed. One or more provisions will state what type of deed the seller will use to convey the property, and what conditions the deed will be subject to. Among common "subject to" conditions are easements, association memberships, encumbrances, mortgages, liens, and special assessments. Typically, the seller conveys a fee simple interest by means of a general warranty deed.

Title evidence. The seller covenants to produce the best possible evidence of property ownership. This is commonly in the form of title insurance.

Closing costs. The contract identifies which closing costs each party will pay. Customarily, the seller pays title and property-related costs, and the buyer pays financing-related costs. Annual costs such as taxes and insurance are prorated between the parties. Note that who pays any particular closing cost is an item for negotiation.

Damage and destruction. A clause stipulates the obligations of the parties in case the property is damaged or destroyed. The parties may negotiate alternatives, including seller's obligation to repair, buyer's obligation to buy if repairs are made, and the option for either party to cancel.

Default. A default clause identifies remedies for default. Generally, a buyer may sue for damages, specific performance, or cancellation. A seller may do likewise or claim the earnest money as liquidated damages.

Broker's representation and commission. The broker discloses the applicable agency relationships in the transaction and names the party who must pay the brokerage commission.

Seller's representations. The seller warrants that there will be no liens on the property that cannot be settled and extinguished at closing. In addition, the seller warrants that all representations are true, and if found otherwise, the buyer may cancel the contract and reclaim the deposit.

Secondary provisions

A sale contract may contain numerous additional clauses, depending on the complexity of the transaction. The following are some of the common provisions.

Inspections. The parties agree to inspections and remedial action based on findings.

Owner's association disclosure. The seller discloses existence of an association and the obligations it imposes.

Survey. The parties agree to a survey to satisfy financing requirements.

Environmental hazards. The seller notifies the buyer that there may be hazards that could affect the use and value of the property.

Compliance with laws. The seller warrants that there are no undisclosed building code or zoning violations.

Due-on-sale clause. The parties state their understanding that loans that survive the closing may be called due by the lender. Both parties agree to hold the other party harmless for the consequences of an acceleration.

Seller financing disclosure. The parties agree to comply with applicable state and local disclosure laws concerning seller financing.

Rental property; tenants rights. The buyer acknowledges the rights of tenants following closing.

FHA or VA financing condition. A contingency allows the buyer to cancel the contract if the price exceeds FHA or VA estimates of the property's value.

Flood plain; flood insurance. Seller discloses that the property is in a flood plain and that it must carry flood insurance if the buyer uses certain lenders for financing.

Condominium assessments. Seller discloses assessments the owner must pay.

Foreign seller withholding. The seller acknowledges that the buyer must withhold 15% of the purchase price at closing if the seller is a foreign person or entity and forward the withheld amount to the Internal Revenue Service. Certain limitations and exemptions apply.

Tax deferred exchange. For income properties only, buyer and seller disclose their intentions to participate in an exchange and agree to cooperate in completing necessary procedures.

Merger of agreements. Buyer and seller state that there are no other agreements between the parties that are not expressed in the contract.

Notices. The parties agree on how they will give notice to each other and what they will consider to be delivery of notice.

Time is of the essence. The parties agree that they can amend dates and deadlines only if they both give written approval.

Fax transmission. The parties agree to accept facsimile transmission of the offer, provided receipt is acknowledged and original copies of the contract are subsequently delivered.

Survival. The parties continue to be liable for the truthfulness of representations and warranties after the closing.

Dispute resolution. The parties agree to resolve disputes through arbitration as opposed to court proceedings.

C.L.U.E. Report. CLUE (Comprehensive Loss Underwriting Exchange) is a claims history database used by insurance companies in underwriting or rating insurance policies. A CLUE Home Seller's Disclosure Report shows a five-year insurance loss history for a specific property. Among other things, it describes the types of any losses and the amounts paid. Many home buyers now require sellers to provide a CLUE Report (which only the property owner or an insurer can order) as a contingency appended to the purchase offer. A report showing a loss due to water damage and mold, for instance, might lead a buyer to decide against making an offer because of the potential difficulty of getting insurance. A report showing no insurance loss within the previous five years, on the other hand, is an indication that the availability and pricing of homeowner's insurance will not present an obstacle to the purchase transaction, and also that the property has not experienced significant damage or repair during that time period.

Addenda. Addenda to the sale contract become binding components of the overall agreement. The most common addendum is the seller's property condition disclosure. Examples of other addenda are:

agency disclosure	asbestos / hazardous materials
liquidated damages	radon disclosure
flood plain disclosure	tenant's lease

OPTION-TO-BUY CONTRACT

Contract requirements
Common provisions
Legal aspects

An option-to-buy is an enforceable contract in which a potential seller, the **optionor**, grants a potential buyer, the **optionee**, the right to purchase a property before a stated time for a stated price and terms. In exchange for the right of option, the optionee pays the optionor valuable consideration.

For example, a buyer wants to purchase a property for $150,000, but needs to sell a boat to raise the down payment. The boat will take two or three months to sell. To accommodate the buyer, the seller offers the buyer an option to purchase the property at any time before midnight on the day that is ninety days from the date of signing the option. The buyer pays the seller $1,000 for the option. If buyer exercises the option, the seller will apply the $1,000 toward the earnest money deposit and subsequent down payment. If the optionee lets the option expire, the seller keeps the $1,000. Both parties agree to the arrangement by completing a sale contract as an addendum to the option, then executing the option agreement itself.

An option-to-buy places the optionee *under no obligation* to purchase the property. However, the seller must perform under the terms of the contract if the buyer exercises the option. An option is thus a *unilateral* agreement. Exercise of the option creates a bilateral sale contract where both parties are bound to perform. An unused option terminates at the expiration date.

An optionee can use an option to prevent the sale of a property to another party while seeking to raise funds for the purchase. A renter with a **lease option-to-buy** can accumulate down payment funds while paying rent to the landlord. For example, an owner may lease a condominium to a tenant with an option to buy. If the tenant takes the option, the landlord agrees to apply $100 of the monthly rent paid prior to the option date toward the purchase price. The tenant pays the landlord the nominal sum of $200 for the option.

Options can also facilitate commercial property acquisition. The option period gives a buyer time to investigate zoning, space planning, building permits, environmental impacts, and other feasibility issues prior to the purchase without losing the property to another party in the meantime.

Contract requirements

To be valid and enforceable, an option-to-buy must:

▸ include actual, non-refundable consideration

The option must require the optionee to pay a specific consideration *that is separate from the purchase price*. The consideration cannot be refunded if the option is not exercised. If the option is exercised, the consideration may be applied to the purchase price. If the option is a lease option, portions of the rent may qualify as separate consideration.

- ▶ include price and terms of the sale

  The price and terms of the potential transaction must be clearly expressed and cannot change over the option period. It is customary practice for the parties to complete and attach a sale contract to the option as satisfaction of this requirement.

- ▶ have an expiration date

  The option must automatically expire at the end of a specific period.

- ▶ be in writing

  Since a potential transfer of real estate is involved, most state statutes of fraud require an option to be in writing.

- ▶ include a legal description

- ▶ meet general contract validity requirements

  The basics include competent parties, the optionor's promise to perform, and the optionor's signature. Note that it is not necessary for the optionee to sign the option.

Common provisions   Beyond the required elements, it is common for an option to include provisions covering:

- ▶ how to deliver notice of election

  A clause clarifies how to make the option election, exactly when the election must be completed, and any additional terms required such as an earnest money deposit.

- ▶ forfeiture terms

  A clause provides that the optionor is entitled to the consideration if the option term expires.

- ▶ property and title condition warranties

  The optionor warrants that the property will be maintained in a certain condition, and that title will be marketable and insurable.

▸ how option consideration will be credited

A clause states how the optionor will apply the option consideration toward the purchase price.

Legal aspects

Equitable interest. The optionee enjoys an equitable interest in the property because the option creates the right to obtain legal title. However, the option does not in itself convey an interest in real property, only a right to do something governed by contract law.

Recording. An option should be recorded, because the equitable interest it creates can affect the marketability of title.

Assignment. An option-to-buy is assignable unless the contract expressly prohibits assignment.

CONTRACT FOR DEED

Interests and rights
Legal form
Default and recourse
Usage guidelines

A contract for deed is also called a *land contract*, an *installment sale*, a *conditional sales contract,* and an *agreement for deed*. It is a bilateral agreement between a seller, the **vendor,** and a buyer, the **vendee**, in which the vendor defers receipt of some or all of the purchase price of a property over a specified period of time. During the period, the *vendor retains legal title* and the vendee acquires equitable title. The vendee takes possession of the property, makes stipulated payments of principal and interest to the vendor, and otherwise fulfills obligations as the contract requires. At the end of the period, the buyer pays the vendor the full purchase price and the vendor deeds legal title to the vendee.

Like an option, a contract for deed offers a means for a marginally qualified buyer to acquire property. In essence, the seller acts as lender, allowing the buyer to take possession and pay off the purchase price over time. A buyer may thus avoid conventional down payment and income requirements imposed by institutional lenders. During the contract period, the buyer can work to raise the necessary cash to complete the purchase or to qualify for a conventional mortgage.

A contract for deed serves two primary purposes for a seller. First, it facilitates a sale that might otherwise be impossible. Second, it may give the seller certain tax benefits. Since the seller is not liable for capital gains tax until the purchase price is received, the installment sale lowers the seller's tax liability in the year of the sale.

Interests and rights   **Vendor's rights and obligations.** During the contract period, the seller may:

> ▸ mortgage the property
> ▸ sell or assign whatever interests he or she owns in the property to another party
> ▸ incur judgment liens against the property

The vendor, however, is bound to the obligations imposed by the contract for deed. In particular, the vendor may not breach the obligation to convey legal title to the vendee upon receipt of the total purchase price. In addition, the vendor remains liable for underlying mortgage loans.

Vendee's rights and obligations. During the contract period, the buyer may occupy, use, enjoy, and profit from the property, subject to the provisions of the written agreement. The vendee must make periodic payments of principal and interest and maintain the property. In addition, a vendee may have to pay property taxes and hazard insurance.

Legal form   Like other conveyance contracts, a contract for deed instrument identifies:

> ▸ the principal parties
> ▸ the property's legal description
> ▸ consideration: specifically what the parties promise to do
> ▸ the terms of the sale
> ▸ obligations for property maintenance
> ▸ default and remedies
> ▸ signatures and acknowledgment

The contract specifies the vendee's payments, payment deadlines, when the balance of the purchase price is due, and how the property may be used.

Default and recourse   **Seller default.** If the seller defaults, such as by failing to deliver the deed, the buyer may sue for specific performance, or for cancellation of the agreement and damages.

Buyer default. States differ in the remedies they prescribe for the seller in case of buyer default. Some states consider the default a breach of contract that may be remedied by cancellation, retention of monies received, and eviction. Others provide foreclosure proceedings as a remedy.

Usage guidelines   Many areas have no standardized contract for deed or any form sanctioned by associations and agencies. Therefore, this kind of conveyance presents certain pitfalls for buyer and seller.

In some states, a breach of the contract for deed is remedied under *local contract law* rather than foreclosure law. The buyer may not have the protections of a redemption period or other buyer-protection laws which accompany formal foreclosure proceedings. The vendor might sue the vendee for breach of contract for the slightest infraction of the contract terms.

A second danger for the vendee is that the vendor has the power and the right to encumber the property in ways that may not be desirable for the buyer. For example, the seller could place a home equity loan on the property, then fail to make periodic payments. The bank could then foreclose on the vendor, thus jeopardizing the vendee's eventual purchase.

For the seller, the principal danger is that the buyer acquires possession in exchange for a minimal down payment. A buyer might damage or even vacate the property, leaving the seller to make repairs and retake possession. Further, since the contract is recorded, the seller must also bear the time and expense of clearing the title.

To minimize risk, principal parties in a contract for deed should observe the following guidelines:

- ▶ use an attorney to draft the agreement
- ▶ adopt the standard forms, if available
- ▶ become familiar with how the contract will be enforced
- ▶ utilize professional escrow and title services
- ▶ record the transaction properly
- ▶ be prepared for the possible effect on existing financing

14 Overview of Conveyance Contracts
Snapshot Review

CONTRACT FOR SALE

Legal characteristics
- binding, bilateral contract for purchase and sale; enforceable; executory, or to be fulfilled; expires upon closing; must be in writing; contain valuable consideration; identify property; be signed by all; be a valid contract

Contract creation
- by unqualified acceptance of an offer; gives buyer equitable title, power to force specific performance

Earnest money escrow
- secures contract validity and buyer's equitable interest; varies in amount; deposit controlled by disinterested party who must act according to escrow instructions

Contract contingencies
- conditions that must be met for the contract to be enforceable

Default
- buyer may sue for cancellation and damages or for specific performance; seller may claim deposit as liquidated damages, or may sue for cancellation, other damages, or for specific performance

SALE CONTRACT PROVISIONS

Primary provisions
- parties, consideration, legal description, price and terms, loan approval, earnest money, escrow, closing and possession dates, conveyed interest, type of deed, title evidence, property condition warranty, closing costs, damage and destruction, default, broker's representation, commission, seller's representations

Secondary provisions
- inspections, owner's association disclosure, survey, environmental hazards, compliance with laws, due-on-sale, seller financing disclosure, rental property tenant's rights, FHA or VA financing condition, flood plain and flood insurance, condominium assessments, foreign seller withholding, tax-deferred exchange, merger of agreements, notices, time of the essence, fax transmission, survival, dispute resolution, addenda

THE OPTION-TO-BUY CONTRACT
- optionor gives option to optionee; unilateral contract: seller must perform; buyer need not; if option exercised, option becomes bilateral sale contract

Contract requirements
- must include: non-refundable consideration for the option right; price and terms of the sale; option period expiration date; legal description; must be in writing and meet contract validity requirements

Common clause provisions
- special provisions: how to exercise option; terms of option money forfeiture; how option money will be applied to purchase price

Legal aspects
- creates equitable interest; is assignable; should be recorded

CONTRACT FOR DEED
- purchase price is paid over time in installments; seller retains title; buyer takes possession; at end of period, buyer pays balance of price, gets legal title

Interests and rights
- seller may encumber or assign interest; remains liable for underlying mortgage
- buyer may use, possess, profit; must make periodic payments, maintain the property, and purchase at end of term

Default and recourse
- if seller defaults, buyer may sue for cancellation and damages or specific performance; seller's default remedies vary by area; may sue for specific performance or damages, or may need to foreclose

15 Real Estate Market Economics

The Market System
Real Estate Market Dynamics

Real estate is an economic product that is subject to economic laws and influences, much like all of the other goods and services in our economic system.

Real estate professionals do not have to be economists; in fact, they are better off leaving complex economic theories to those professing expertise in that often confusing field. However, brokers and agents do need a basic understanding of how our economy works, and particularly, how real estate as an economic product fits into the real estate marketplace.

Understanding the fundamentals of real estate economics enables one to:

> ▸ recognize the effect of current economic conditions in the real estate market on transactions, prices, and values
> ▸ apply economic principles to estimates of future conditions in the real estate market
> ▸ apply economic principles to specific geographical areas and property types in order to assess economic conditions for a particular property and site

These are abilities that will benefit the clients of any real estate professional.

THE MARKET SYSTEM

Supply and demand
Price and value
Productivity and costs
Market interaction
Market equilibrium

Supply and demand

The goal of an economic system is to produce and distribute a *supply* of goods and services to satisfy the *demand* of its constituents. Economic activity therefore centers on the production, distribution and sale of goods and services to meet consumer demand.

Supply is *the quantity of a product or service available for sale, lease, or trade at any given time.*

Demand is *the quantity of a product or service that is desired for purchase, lease, or trade at any given time.*

The interplay of supply and demand is what makes an economy work: consumers demand goods and services; suppliers and sellers produce and distribute the goods and services for a negotiated price.

Price and value

The price mechanism. In addition to supply and demand, the other critical component of an economic system is the price mechanism, or simply, price. A **price** is the amount of money or other asset that a buyer has agreed to pay and a seller has agreed to accept to complete the exchange of a good or service. It is a quantification of the value of an item traded.

Price in this context means the final trading price; it is not the preliminary asking price of the seller nor the initial bidding price of the purchaser. Asking and bidding prices are pricing positions in a negotiation between the parties prior to the exchange. The true price of an item or service is the final number the parties agree to.

Value and value determinants. Price is not something of value in itself. It is only a number that *quantifies value.* The economic issue underlying the interplay of supply and demand is, how do trading parties arrive at the value of a good or service as indicated by the price?

Consider consumer demand for air conditioners. Why do air conditioners have value? How do they command the price they do?

The value of something is based on the answers to four questions:

- How much do I desire it?
- How useful is it?
- How scarce is it?
- Am I able to pay for it?

Desire. One determinant of value is how dear the item is to the purchaser. Returning to the air conditioner example, the question becomes "how much do I desire to be cool, dry, and comfortable?" To a person who lives in the tropics, it is safe to say that air conditioning is *more valuable* than a heating system. It is also safe to say the opposite is true for residents of northern Alaska.

Utility. The second determinant of value is the product's *ability to do the job.* Can the air conditioner satisfy my need to stay cool? How cool does it make my house? Does it even work properly? Of course, I won't pay as much if it is old or ineffectual.

Scarcity. The third critical element of value is a product's *availability in relation to demand.* The air conditioner is quite valuable if there are only five units in the entire city and everyone is hot. On the other hand, the value of an air conditioner goes down if there are ten thousand units for sale in a 500-person market.

Purchasing power. A fourth component of value is the *consumer's ability to pay* for the item. If one cannot afford to buy the air conditioner, the value of the air conditioner is diminished, since it is financially out of reach. If all air conditioners are too expensive, consumers are forced to consider alternatives such as ceiling fans.

In the marketplace, the relative presence or absence of the four elements of value is constantly changing due to innumerable factors. Since price is a reflection of the total of all value factors at any time, changes in the underlying factors of value trigger changes in price.

Productivity and costs

To produce a good or service, a supplier incurs **costs**, or those expenses necessary to generate and deliver the item to the market. The essential production costs are the costs of capital, materials, and supplies; labor; management; and overhead.

Costs play an important role in the dynamics of supply, demand, and value. Since a producer has limited resources, it is imperative to maximize the efficiency of the production process and minimize its costs. Moreover, since consumers will pay the lowest possible price for comparable goods and services, the producer must be price-competitive to stay in business. A competitor who can produce an item of similar quality for less will eventually force higher-priced items out of the market.

Cost and price. Consider a producer who is efficient and produces the product or service in demand at the lowest possible cost. Adding to the cost a required profit margin, the producer establishes a minimum price for the item. In this scenario, cost essentially equals price. To the efficient producer, costs and sufficient profit are paramount, since a lower price puts the producer out of business. At that point, the elements of value-- desire, utility, scarcity, and purchasing power-- do not matter: if the consumer wants the item at all, he or she must cover the producer's costs and profit.

In summary, supply, demand, and price interact continuously in a market. Underlying and influencing these forces are the dynamics of value and the costs of producing goods and services.

Market interaction

What is a market? A market is a place where supply and demand encounter one another: suppliers sell or trade their goods and services to demanders, who are consumers and buyers. It is a *transaction arena* where the price mechanism is constantly defining and quantifying the value produced by the relative elements of supply and demand.

Supply, demand and price interrelationships. In a market economy, the primary interactions between supply, demand and price are:

> ▸ if supply increases relative to demand, price decreases
> ▸ if supply decreases relative to demand, price increases
> ▸ if demand increases relative to supply, price increases
> ▸ if demand decreases relative to supply, price decreases

These relationships reflect simple common sense: if a valued product becomes increasingly scarce, its value and price go up as consumers compete for the limited supply. If there is an overabundance of a product, the price falls, as demand is largely met. On the other side, if demand for a product or service increases in relation to supply, prices will go up as consumers compete for the popular item. If demand diminishes, the price drops with it.

The inverse of these principles also applies. By tracking a price trend, one can draw conclusions about supply and demand trends:

> ▸ if price decreases, demand is declining in relation to supply
> ▸ if price increases, demand is increasing in relation to supply

To assess price movements, the supply and demand of a product or service must always be considered together. It is always possible for demand and supply to rise and fall together at the same rate, with no detectable price change resulting.

For example, if demand for bicycles jumps a million units, and manufacturers easily produce the necessary new supply, there may be no increase in price. The price may even go down as manufacturers obtain better prices on the larger quantities of raw materials they now use.

Market equilibrium

Another significant principle of supply/demand/price interaction is **market equilibrium**:

> ▸ a market tends toward a state of equilibrium in which supply equals demand, and price, cost, and value are identical

According to this principle, market demand moves to meet supply, and supply moves to meet demand. If there is an extreme shortage of an item for which there is normally a strong demand, suppliers will rush to increase production to close the gap. If inventories of an item are very high, suppliers will stop production until the oversupply has been depleted.

Similarly, if the price of an item far exceeds its cost, new suppliers will enter the market with lower prices. If the price of an item is far less than its perceived value, either consumers will bid up the price or the perceived value will decline.

For example, a new convenience store opens on the edge of a rapidly growing town. The owners know demand will increase, so they anticipate the demand with their increment of supply. Initially, the store creates excess supply, so business is slow. However, as people move in, demand increases, and the store begins to make substantial profits. After some time, other retailers hear that the store is profitable: demand now significantly exceeds supply, and the operator's costs are out of line with values and prices. A second retailer opens a store to equalize the imbalance. The new competitor, an addition of supply, now forces prices, costs, and profits into closer proximity.

The equilibrium time lag. In theory, markets strive for equilibrium, but in reality there is always a time lag between a recognized imbalance and the completion of the market adjustment. Since the underlying determinants of supply and demand (scarcity, desire, utility, purchasing power and costs) are constantly changing, a market is usually in some condition of imbalance.

REAL ESTATE MARKET DYNAMICS

Economic characteristics of real estate
Real estate supply and demand
Market influences on supply and demand

Economic characteristics of real estate

As an economic commodity, real estate is bought, sold, traded, and leased as a product within a real estate market.

Real estate, like other products and services, is:

> ▶ subject to the laws of supply and demand
> ▶ governed in the market by the price mechanism
> ▶ influenced by the producer's costs to bring the product to market
> ▶ influenced by the determinants of value: utility, scarcity, desire, and purchasing power

Distinguishing features. In comparison with other economic products and services, real estate has certain unique traits. These include:

> ▶ **Inherent product value**
>
> Land is a scarce resource as well as a required factor of production. Like gold and silver, it has both inherent value and utility value.

> ▶ **Unique appeal of product**
>
> Since no two parcels of real estate can be alike (each has a different location), every parcel of real property has its own appeal. Likewise, no two parcels of real estate can have exactly the same value, except by coincidence.

> ▶ **Demand must come to the supply**
>
> Since real property cannot be moved, real property investors and users must come to the supply. This creates risk, because if demand drops, the supply cannot be transported to a higher demand market.

> ▶ **Illiquid**
>
> Real estate is a relatively illiquid economic product, meaning it cannot always be readily sold for cash. Since it is a large, long-term investment that has no exact duplicate, buyers must go through a complex process to evaluate and purchase the right parcel of real estate.

> ▸ **Slow to respond to changes**
>
> Real estate is relatively slow to respond to market imbalances. Because new construction is a large-scale, time-consuming process, the market is slow to respond to increases in demand. The market is similarly slow to respond to sharp declines in demand, since the product cannot be moved and sold elsewhere. Instead, owners must wait out slow periods and simply hope for the best.
>
> ▸ **Decentralized, local market**
>
> A real property cannot be shipped to a large, central real estate marketplace. Real estate markets are thus local in nature and highly susceptible to swings in the local economy.

Real estate supply and demand

Supply. In real estate, supply is the *amount of property available* for sale or lease at any given time. Note that supply is generally not the number of properties available, except in the case of residential real estate. The units of supply used to quantify the amount of property available differ for different categories of property. These supply units, by property type, are:

- ▸ residential: dwelling units
- ▸ commercial and industrial: square feet
- ▸ agricultural: acreage

Factors influencing supply. In addition to the influences of demand and the underlying determinants of value, real estate supply responds to

- ▸ development costs, particularly labor
- ▸ availability of financing
- ▸ investment returns
- ▸ a community's master plan
- ▸ government police powers and regulation

Demand. Real estate demand is the amount of property buyers and tenants wish to acquire by purchase, lease or trade at any given time. Units of demand, by property classification, are:

- ▸ residential: households
- ▸ commercial and industrial: square feet
- ▸ agricultural: acreage

The unit of residential demand is the household, which is an individual or family who would occupy a dwelling unit. Residential demand can be further broken down into demand to lease versus buy, and demand for single family homes versus apartments.

Residential demand can be very difficult to quantify. One measure is the number of buyers employing agents to locate property. Another measure is the net population change in an area, plus families that attempted to move in but could not.

The unit of commercial (retail and office) and industrial real estate demand is the square foot, further broken down into demand for leased space versus purchased space. In most instances, the area demanded refers to the improved area rather than the total lot area.

Demand for office and industrial real estate is calculated by identifying employment growth or shrinkage in a market, then multiplying the employment change times the average area of floor space a typical employee uses. For example, consider an office property market where employment in the community increases by 500 employees. If each employee uses an average of 120 square feet, the increased demand for space is 60,000 square feet.

Factors affecting demand. The demand for particular types of real estate relates to the specific concerns of users. These concerns revolve around the components of value: desire, utility, scarcity, and purchasing power.

Residential users are concerned with:

- quality of life
- neighborhood quality
- convenience and access to services and other facilities
- dwelling amenities in relation to household size, lifestyle, and costs

Retail users are concerned with:

- sufficient trade area population and income
- the level of trade area competition
- sales volume per square foot of rented area
- consumer spending patterns
- growth patterns in the trade area

Office users are concerned with:

- costs of occupancy to the business
- efficiency of the building and the suite in accommodating the business's functions
- accessibility by employees and suppliers
- matching building quality to the image and function of the business

Industrial users are concerned with:

- functionality
- the availability and proximity of the labor pool
- compliance with environmental regulations
- permissible zoning
- health and safety of the workers
- access to suppliers and distribution channels

Base employment and total employment. The engine that drives demand for real estate of all types in a market is employment-- *base* employment and *total* employment.

Exhibit 15.1 Basis of Real Estate Demand

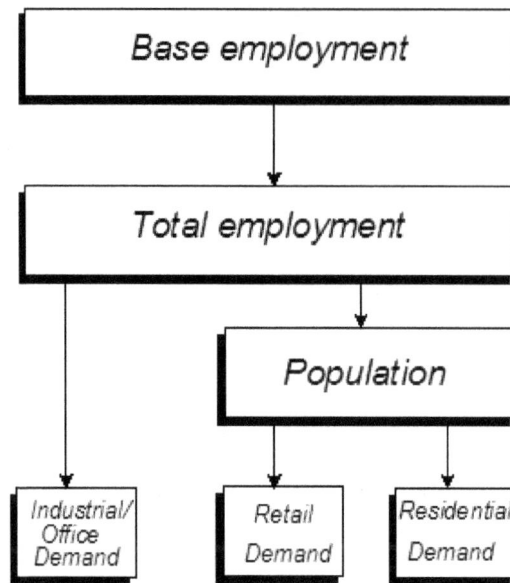

```
                    ┌──────────────────────────────┐
                    │      Base employment         │
                    └──────────────────────────────┘
                                   │
                                   ▼
                    ┌──────────────────────────────┐
                    │      Total employment        │
                    └──────────────────────────────┘
                         │                │
                         │          ┌──────────────────┐
                         │          │   Population     │
                         │          └──────────────────┘
                         │           │       │       │
                         ▼           ▼       ▼       ▼
                  ┌──────────┐  ┌────────┐  ┌────────────┐
                  │Industrial/│  │ Retail │  │Residential │
                  │  Office   │  │        │  │            │
                  │  Demand   │  │ Demand │  │  Demand    │
                  └──────────┘  └────────┘  └────────────┘
```

Base employment is the number of persons employed in the businesses that represent the economic foundation of the area. For example, the auto industry has traditionally been the primary base employer of the Detroit metropolitan area.

Base industries lead to the rise of supporting and secondary industries in the market. If the auto industry is the base, auto parts manufacturers and assembly industries will develop to support the auto manufacturing plants. In addition, service businesses emerge to support the many needs of the local population engaged in primary and secondary employment.

Thus, base employment feeds total employment. Total employment in a market includes base, secondary, and support industries. Total employment creates a demand for a labor force. From total employment derives demand for industrial and office space on the one hand; on the other hand, as employment grows, so grows the population, leading to the demand for housing and for retail support. In addition to creating demand for real estate, employment creates the purchasing power necessary for households to acquire dwellings and retail products.

Without employment, a real estate market evaporates, as there is no demand for commercial or industrial facilities, nor is there demand for retail services or housing. The best example of this phenomenon is a gold rush boom town: as soon as the gold runs out, there is no more mining. Without mining employment, everyone moves away and the town becomes a ghost town.

Supply and demand interaction. Real estate supply and demand, like supply and demand for other economic products, interact in the marketplace to produce *price movements.*

Exhibit 15.2 Real Estate Supply-Demand Cycle

Undersupply
High Prices
Low Vacancy

Construction
Up

Falling Vacancy
Rising Prices

Rising Vacancy
Falling Prices

Supply - Demand
Equilibrium

Supply - Demand
Equilibrium

Falling Vacancy
Rising Prices

Rising Vacancy
Falling Prices

Construction
Down

Oversupply
Low Prices
High Vacancy

As the exhibit illustrates, prices, construction, and vacancy move up and down in the cycle. Construction represents the addition of new supply. **Vacancy** is the amount of total real estate inventory of a certain type that is unoccupied at a given time. **Absorption** is the amount of available property that becomes occupied over a period of time.

Taking the point of undersupply, or high demand, as a starting point in the cycle, vacancy is low and prices are high. This situation stimulates suppliers to construct additional housing or commercial space. New construction, by adding supply, causes vacancy to rise and prices to fall until supply-demand equilibrium results. As more new space is added, supply begins to outstrip demand, vacancy continues to rise, and prices continue to fall. At the bottom of the cycle, prices and vacancy are at unacceptable levels, and construction ceases. The market "dies" until excess supply can be absorbed. The absorption process continues through the equilibrium point until price and vacancy conditions are sufficiently attractive to encourage renewed construction. Then the cycle repeats.

Market influences on supply and demand

Numerous factors in a market influence the real estate cycle to speed up or slow down. These influences can be local or national, and from the public or private economic sector.

Local market influences. Since the real estate market is local by definition, local factors weigh heavily in local real estate market conditions. Among these are:

> ▸ cost of financing
> ▸ availability of developable land
> ▸ construction costs
> ▸ capacity of the municipality's infrastructure to handle growth

- ▶ governmental regulation and police powers
- ▶ changes in the economic base
- ▶ in- and out-migrations of major employers

National trends. Regional and national economic forces influence the local real estate market in the form of:

- ▶ changes in money supply
- ▶ inflation
- ▶ national economic cycles

In recent years international economic trends have increasingly influenced local real estate markets, particularly in border states, large metropolitan areas, and in markets where the economic base is tied to foreign trade. In these instances, currency fluctuations have significant impact on the local economy.

Governmental influences. Governments at every level exert significant influence over local real estate markets. The primary forms of government influence are:

- ▶ local zoning power
- ▶ local control and permitting of new development
- ▶ local taxing power
- ▶ federal influence on interest rates
- ▶ environmental legislation and regulations

A good example of government influence over the local real estate market is a city government's power to declare a moratorium on new construction, regardless of demand. Such officially declared stoppages may occur because of water or power shortages, insufficiency of thoroughfares, or incompatibility with the master plan.

15 Real Estate Market Economics Snapshot Review

THE MARKET SYSTEM

Supply and demand
- supply: goods or services available for sale, lease, or trade
- demand: goods or services desired for purchase, lease, or trade

Price and value
- price mechanism: quantified value of an exchange
- value components: desire; utility; scarcity; purchasing power

Productivity and costs
- cost plus profit equals minimum price; production cost possible component of value

Market interaction
- market: transaction arena where suppliers and demanders define value through the price mechanism
- if supply increases relative to demand, price decreases; if demand increases relative to supply, price increases

Market equilibrium
- supply and demand tend toward balance where they are equal
- market equilibrium: price, cost, value theoretically the same; market imbalances are caused by changes in supply or demand

REAL ESTATE MARKET DYNAMICS

Economic characteristics of real estate
- governed by supply, demand, price, costs, value components, government influence
- inherent value; unique appeal; immovable supply; illiquid; slow response to cycles; decentralized market

Real estate supply and demand
- supply: property available for sale or lease; measured in dwelling units, square feet, acres; influenced by costs, finance, returns, government regulation
- demand: property buyers and tenants wish to acquire; measured in households, square feet, acres; influences: residential-- quality, amenities, price convenience; retail-trade area, sales, competition, site access, visibility; growth patterns; office-efficiency, costs, functionality; industrial-- functionality, labor, regulatory compliance, access to labor, supplies, distribution channels
- base employment, total employment, population determine overall demand
- if employment and population increase, demand and prices increase; if they decrease, the opposite occurs
- supply-demand indicators are price, vacancy, and absorption; vacancy is existing, unoccupied supply; absorption is the "filling up" of vacancy
- real estate supply-demand cycle: undersupply > accelerated construction adds supply > equilibrium > construction adds more supply > oversupply > construction stops > equilibrium > demand absorbs supply

Market influences on supply and demand
- local economic factors; national economic trends in money supply, inflation; government regulation at all levels

16 Appraising and Estimating Market Value

Real Estate Value
Appraising Market Value
The Sales Comparison Approach
The Cost Approach
The Income Capitalization Approach
Regulation of Appraisal Practice

REAL ESTATE VALUE

Foundations of real estate value
Types of value

The valuation of real property is one of the most fundamental activities in the real estate business. Its role is particularly critical in the transfer of real property, since the value of a parcel establishes the general price range for the principal parties to negotiate.

Real estate value in general is *the present monetary worth of benefits arising from the ownership of real estate*. The primary benefits that contribute to real estate value are:

> ▶ income
> ▶ appreciation
> ▶ use
> ▶ tax benefits

Ownership of real estate produces income when there are leases on the land, the improvements, or on air, surface, or subsurface rights. Such income is part of real estate value because an investor will pay money to buy the income stream generated by ownership of the property.

Appreciation is an increase in the market value of a parcel of land over time, usually resulting from a general rise in sale prices of real estate throughout a market area. Such an increase, whether actual or projected, is another investment benefit that contributes to real estate value.

The way a property is used -- whether residential, commercial, agricultural, recreational, etc. -- in large part determines the property's value. Each kind of use has its own benefits.

Depending on current tax law, tax benefits from ownership of a property may take the form of preferred treatment of capital gain, tax losses, depreciation, and deferrals of tax liability. These tax benefits contribute to the income and potential sale price of a property.

Foundations of real estate value

A number of economic forces interact in the marketplace to contribute to real estate value. Among the most recognized of these principles are those listed below.

Exhibit 16.1 Economic Principles Underlying Real Estate Value

supply and demand	change
utility transferability	highest and best use
anticipation substitution	conformity
contribution	progression and regression
	assemblage
	subdivision

Supply and demand. The availability of certain properties interacts with the strength of the demand for those properties to establish prices. When demand for properties exceeds supply, a condition of scarcity exists, and real estate values rise. When supply exceeds demand, a condition of surplus exists, and real estate values decline. When supply and demand are generally equivalent, the market is considered to be in balance, and real estate values stabilize.

Utility. The fact that a property has a use in a certain marketplace contributes to the demand for it. Use is not the same as function. For instance, a swampy area may have an ecological function as a wetland, but it may have no economic utility if it cannot be put to some use that people in the marketplace are willing to pay for.

Transferability. How readily or easily title or rights to real estate can be transferred affects the property's value. Property that is encumbered has a value impairment since buyers do not want unmarketable title. Similarly, property that cannot be transferred due to disputes among owners may cause the value to decline, because the investment is wholly illiquid until the disputes are resolved.

Anticipation. The benefits a buyer *expects to derive from a property over a holding period* influence what the buyer is willing to pay for it. For example, if an investor anticipates an annual rental income from a leased property to be one million dollars, this expected sum has a direct bearing on what the investor will pay for the property.

Substitution. According to the principle of substitution, a buyer will *pay no more for a property than the buyer would have to pay for an equally desirable and available substitute property*. For example, if three houses for sale are essentially similar in size, quality and location, a potential buyer is unlikely to choose the one that is priced significantly higher than the other two.

Contribution. The principal of contribution focuses on the degree to which a particular improvement affects market value of the overall property. In essence, the contribution of the improvement is *equal to the change in market value that the addition of the improvement causes*. For example, adding a bathroom to a house may contribute an additional $15,000 to the appraised value. Thus the contribution of the bathroom is $15,000. Note that an improvement's contribution to value has little to do with the improvement's cost. The foregoing bathroom may have cost $5,000 or $20,000. Contribution is what the market recognizes as the change in value, not what an item cost. If continuous improvements are added to a property, it is possible that, at some point, the cost of adding improvements to a property no longer contributes a corresponding increase in the value of the property. When this occurs, the property suffers from *diminishing marginal return,* where the costs to improve exceed contribution.

Change. Market conditions are in a state of flux over time, just as the condition of a property itself changes. These fluctuations and changes will affect the benefits that can arise from the property, and should be reflected in an estimate of the property's value. For example, the construction of a neighborhood shopping center in the vicinity of a certain house may increase the desirability of the house's location, and hence, its value.

Highest and best use. This principle holds that there is, theoretically, a single use for a property that produces the greatest income and return. A property achieves its maximum value when it is put to this use. If the actual use is not the highest and best use, the value of the property is correspondingly less than optimal. Technically, highest and best use must be legally permissible, physically possible, financially feasible, and maximally productive.

For example, a property with an old house on it may not be in its highest and best use if it is surrounded by retail properties. If zoning permits the property to be converted to a retail use, its highest and best use may well be retail rather than residential.

Conformity. This principle holds that a property's maximal value is attained when its form and use are in tune with surrounding properties and uses. For example, a two-bedroom, one-bathroom house surrounded by four-bedroom, three-bathroom homes may derive maximal value from a room addition.

Progression and regression. The value of a property influences, and is influenced by, the values of neighboring properties. If a property is surrounded by properties with higher values, its value will tend to rise (progression); if it is surrounded by properties with lower values, its value will tend to fall (regression).

Assemblage. Assemblage, or the conjoining of adjacent properties, sometimes creates a combined value that is greater than the values of the unassembled properties. The excess value created by assemblage is called **plottage value.**

Subdivision. The division of a single property into smaller properties can also result in a higher total value. For instance, a one-acre suburban site appraised at $50,000 may be subdivided into four quarter-acre lots worth $30,000 each. This principle contributes significantly to the financial feasibility of subdivision development.

Types of value

The purpose of an appraisal influences an estimate of the value of a parcel of real estate. This is because there are different types of value related to different appraisal purposes. Some of the possibilities are listed below.

Exhibit 16.2 Types of Real Estate Value

market	reversionary
reproduction	appraised
replacement	rental
salvage	leasehold
plottage	insured
assessed	book
condemned	mortgage

Market value. Market value is an estimate of the price at which a property will sell at a particular time. This type of value is the one generally sought in appraisals and used in brokers' estimates of value.

Reproduction value. Reproduction value is the value based on the cost of constructing a precise duplicate of the subject property's improvements, assuming current construction costs.

Replacement value. Replacement value is the value based on the cost of constructing a functional equivalent of the subject property's improvements, assuming current construction costs.

Salvage value. Salvage value refers to the nominal value of a property that has reached the end of its economic life. Salvage value is also an estimate of the price at which a structure will sell if it is dismantled and moved.

Plottage value. Plottage value is an estimate of the value that the process of assemblage adds to the combined values of the assembled properties.

Assessed value. Assessed value is the value of a property as estimated by a taxing authority as the basis for ad valorem taxation.

Condemned value. Condemned value is the value set by a county or municipal authority for a property which may be taken by eminent domain.

Depreciated value. Depreciated value is a value established by subtracting accumulated depreciation from the purchase price of a property.

Reversionary value. Reversionary value is the estimated selling price of a property at some time in the future. This value is used most commonly in a proforma investment analysis where, at the end of a holding period, the property is sold and the investor's capital reverts to the investor.

Appraised value. Appraised value is an appraiser's opinion of a property's value.

Rental value. Rental value is an estimate of the rental rate a property can command for a specific period of time.

Leasehold value. Leasehold value is an estimate of the market value of a lessee's interest in a property.

Insured value. Insured value is the face amount a casualty or hazard insurance policy will pay in case a property is rendered unusable.

Book value. Book value is the value of the property as carried on the accounts of the owner. The value is generally equal to the acquisition price plus capital improvements minus accumulated depreciation.

Mortgage value. Mortgage value is the value of the property as collateral for a loan.

APPRAISING MARKET VALUE

Market value
The appraisal and its uses
Steps in the appraisal process

Market value

Market value is an opinion of the price that a willing seller and willing buyer would probably agree on for a property at a given time if:

▸ the transaction is a cash transaction
▸ the property is exposed on the open market for a reasonable period
▸ buyer and seller have full information about market conditions and about potential uses
▸ there is no abnormal pressure on either party to complete the transaction
▸ buyer and seller are not related (it is an "arm's length" transaction)
▸ title is marketable and conveyable by the seller
▸ the price is a "normal consideration," that is, it does not include hidden influences such as special financing deals, concessions, terms, services, fees, credits, costs, or other types of consideration.

Another way of describing market value is that it is the highest price that a buyer would pay and the lowest price that the seller would accept for the property.

The market price, as opposed to market value, is what a property actually sells for. Market price should theoretically be the same as market value if all the conditions essential for market value were present. Market price, however, may not reflect the analysis of comparables and of investment value that an estimate of market value includes.

The appraisal and its uses

While most appraisals seek to estimate market value, any of the types of value described earlier may be the objective of an appraisal. An appraisal is distinguished from other estimates of value in that it is an opinion of value supported by data and performed by a professional, disinterested third party.

Appraisers acting in a professional capacity are also regulated by state laws and bound to standards set by the appraisal industry.

Broker's opinion of value. A broker's opinion of value may resemble an appraisal, but it differs from an appraisal in that it is not necessarily performed by a disinterested third party or licensed professional and it generally uses only a limited form of one of the three appraisal approaches. In addition, the opinion is not subject to regulation, nor does it follow any particular professional standards.

Uses. The appraisal itself is used in real estate decision-making to estimate one or more types of value, depending on the kind of decision to be made. Appraisals may be ordered and used by mortgage lenders, government agencies, investors, utilities companies, and real estate buyers and sellers.

An appraisal helps in setting selling prices and rental rates, determining the level of insurance coverage, establishing investment values, and establishing the value of the real estate as collateral for a loan.

Appraisals may be developed and reported in a narrative format or on a prescribed form with attachments. The most commonly used form for residential appraisals is the "Uniform Residential Appraisal Report" (URAR) promoted by the Federal National Mortgage Association (FNMA) and Federal Home Loan Mortgage Corporation (FHLMC) (known as Fannie Mae and Freddie Mac, respectively).

Steps in the appraisal process

A systematic procedure enables an appraiser to collect, organize and analyze the necessary data to produce an appraisal report.

Exhibit 16.3 Steps in the Appraisal Process

1.	Identify the purpose
2.	Assimilate relevant data
3.	Assess the highest and best use
4.	Estimate the value of the land
5.	Apply the three approaches to estimating value
6.	Reconcile the values from the approaches
7.	Compile the report

Purpose. The first step in the process is to define the appraisal problem and the purpose of the appraisal. This involves

▶ identifying the subject property by legal description
▶ specifying the interest to be appraised
▶ specifying the purpose of the appraisal, for example, to identify market value for a purchase, identify rental levels, or establish a value as collateral for a loan

> ▸ specifying the date for which the appraisal is valid
> ▸ identifying the type of value to be estimated

Data. The second step is to collect, organize and analyze relevant data about the subject property. Information relevant to the property includes notes and drawings from physical inspection of the subject, public tax and title records, and reproduction costs. Relevant information about the market includes environmental, demographic, and economic reports concerning the neighborhood, community, and region.

Highest and best use. The third step is to analyze market conditions to identify the most profitable use for the subject property. This use may or may not be the existing use.

Land value. The fourth step is to estimate the land value of the subject. An appraiser does this by comparing the subject site, but not its buildings, with similar sites in the area, and making adjustments for significant differences.

Three approaches. The fifth step is to apply the three basic approaches to value to the subject: *the sales comparison approach, the cost approach, and the income capitalization approach*. Using multiple methods serves to guard against errors and to set a range of values for the final estimate.

Reconciliation. The sixth step is to reconcile the value estimates produced by the three approaches to value into a final value estimate. To do this, an appraiser must

> ▸ weigh the appropriateness of a particular approach to the type of property being appraised

> ▸ take into account the quality and quantity of data obtained in each method

Report. The final step is to present the estimate of value in the format requested by the client.

THE SALES COMPARISON APPROACH

Steps in the approach
Identifying comparables
Adjusting comparables
Weighting comparables
Broker's comparative market analysis

The sales comparison approach, also known as the *market data approach*, is used for almost all properties. It also serves as the basis for a broker's opinion of value. It is based on the principle of substitution-- that a buyer will pay no more for the subject property than would be sufficient to purchase a comparable property-- and contribution-- that specific characteristics add value to a property.

The sales comparison approach is widely used because it takes into account the subject property's specific amenities in relation to competing properties. In addition, because of the currency of its data, the approach incorporates present market realities.

The sales comparison approach is limited in that every property is unique. As a result, it is difficult to find good comparables, especially for special-purpose properties. In addition, the market must be active; otherwise, sale prices lack currency and reliability.

Steps in the approach

The sales comparison approach consists of comparing sale prices of recently sold properties that are comparable with the subject, and making dollar adjustments to the price of each comparable to account for competitive differences with the subject. After identifying the adjusted value of each comparable, the appraiser weights the reliability of each comparable and the factors underlying how the adjustments were made. The weighting yields a final value range based on the most reliable factors in the analysis.

Exhibit 16.4 Steps in the Sales Comparison Approach

1. Identify comparable sales.
2. Compare comparables to the subject and make adjustments to comparables.
3. Weight values indicated by adjusted comparables for the final value estimate of the subject.

Identifying comparables

To qualify as a comparable, a property must:

▶ resemble the subject in size, shape, design, utility and location
▶ have sold recently, generally within six months of the appraisal
▶ have sold in an arm's-length transaction

An appraiser considers three to six comparables, and usually includes at least three in the appraisal report.

Appraisers have specific guidelines within the foregoing criteria for selecting comparables, many of which are set by secondary market organizations such as FNMA. For example, to qualify as a comparable for a mortgage loan appraisal, a property might have to be located within one mile of the subject. Or perhaps the size of the comparable must be within a certain percentage of improved area in relation to the subject.

The time-of-sale criterion is important because transactions that occurred too far in the past will not reflect appreciation or recent changes in market conditions.

An arm's length sale involves objective, disinterested parties who are presumed to have negotiated a market price for the property. If the sale of a house occurred between a father and a daughter, for example, one might assume that the transaction did not reflect market value.

Principal sources of data for generating the sales comparison are tax records, title records, and the local multiple listing service.

Adjusting comparables

The appraiser adjusts the sale prices of the comparables to account for competitive differences with the subject property. Note that the sale prices of the comparables are known, while the value and price of the subject are not. Therefore, adjustments can be made *only to the comparables' prices, not to the subject's*. Adjustments are made to the comparables in the form of a value deduction or a value addition.

Adding or deducting value. If the comparable is *better* than the subject in some characteristic, an amount is *deducted* from the sale price of the comparable. This neutralizes the comparable's competitive advantage in an adjustment category.

For example, a comparable has a swimming pool and the subject does not. To equalize the difference, the appraiser deducts an amount, say $6,000, from the sale price of the comparable. Note that the adjustment reflects the contribution of the swimming pool to market value. The adjustment amount is not the cost of the pool or its depreciated value.

If the comparable is *inferior* to the subject in some characteristic, an amount is *added* to the price of the comparable. This adjustment equalizes the subject's competitive advantage in this area.

Adjustment criteria. The principal factors for comparison and adjustment are *time of sale, location, physical characteristics, and transaction characteristics*.

> ▶ **time of sale**
>
> An adjustment may be made if market conditions, market prices, or financing availability have changed significantly since the date of the comparable's sale. Most often, this adjustment is to account for appreciation.

> ▶ **location**
>
> An adjustment may be made if there are differences between the comparable's location and the subject's, including neighborhood desirability and appearance, zoning restrictions, and general price levels.

> ▶ **physical characteristics**
>
> Adjustments may be made for marketable differences between the comparable's and subject's lot size, square feet of livable area (or other appropriate measure for the property type), number of

rooms, layout, age, condition, construction type and quality, landscaping, and special amenities.

> ▶ **transaction characteristics**

An adjustment may be made for such differences as mortgage loan terms, mortgage assumability, and owner financing.

Weighting comparables

Adding and subtracting the appropriate adjustments to the sale price of each comparable results in an adjusted price for the comparables that indicates the value of the subject. The last step in the approach is to perform a weighted analysis of the indicated values of each comparable. The appraiser, in other words, must identify which comparable values are more indicative of the subject and which are less indicative.

An appraiser primarily relies on experience and judgment to weight comparables. There is no formula for selecting a value from within the range of all comparables analyzed. However, there are three quantitative guidelines: the total number of adjustments; the amount of a single adjustment; and the net value change of all adjustments.

As a rule, *the fewer the total number of adjustments, the smaller the adjustment amounts, and the less the total adjustment amount, the more reliable the comparable.*

Number of adjustments. In terms of total adjustments, the comparable with the fewest adjustments tends to be most similar to the subject, hence the best indicator of value. If a comparable requires excessive adjustments, it is increasingly less reliable as an indicator of value. The underlying rationale is that there is a margin of error involved in making any adjustment. Whenever a number of adjustments must be made, the margin of error compounds. By the time six or seven adjustments are made, the margin becomes significant, and the reliability of the final value estimate is greatly reduced.

Single adjustment amounts. The dollar amount of an adjustment represents the variance between the subject and the comparable for a given item. If a large adjustment is called for, the comparable becomes less of an indicator of value. The smaller the adjustment, the better the comparable is as an indicator of value. If an appraisal is performed for mortgage qualification, the appraiser may be restricted from making adjustments in excess of a certain amount, for example, anything in excess of 10-15% of the sale price of the comparable. If such an adjustment would be necessary, the property is no longer considered comparable.

Total net adjustment amount. The third reliability factor in weighting comparables is the total net value change of all adjustments added together. If a comparable's total adjustments alter the indicated value only slightly, the comparable is a good indicator of value. If total adjustments create a large dollar amount between the sale price and the adjusted value, the comparable is a poorer indicator of value. Fannie Mae, for instance, will not accept the use of a comparable where total net adjustments are in excess of 15% of the sale price.

For example, an appraiser is considering a property that sold for $100,000 as a comparable. After all adjustments are made, the indicated value of the comparable is $121,000, a 21% difference in the comparable's sale price. This property, if allowed at all, would be a weak indicator of value.

Broker's comparative market analysis

A broker or salesperson who is attempting to establish a listing price or range of prices for a property uses a scaled-down version of the appraiser's sales comparison approach called a comparative market analysis, or CMA (also called a competitive market analysis). While the CMA serves a useful purpose in setting general price ranges, brokers and agents need to exercise caution in presenting a CMA as an appraisal, which it is not. Two important distinctions between the two are objectivity and comprehensiveness.

First, the broker is not unbiased: he or she is motivated by the desire to obtain a listing, which can lead one to distort the estimated price. Secondly, the broker's CMA is not comprehensive: the broker does not usually consider the full range of data about market conditions and comparable sales that the appraiser must consider and document. Therefore, the broker's opinion will be less reliable than the appraiser's.

The following exhibit illustrates the sales comparison approach. An appraiser is estimating market value for a certain house. Four comparables are adjusted to find an indicated value for the subject. The grid which follows the property and market data shows the appraiser's adjustments for the differences between the four comparables and the subject.

Exhibit 16.5 Sales Comparison Approach Illustration

Data

Subject property:
8 rooms-- 3 bedrooms, two baths, kitchen, living room, family room; 2,000 square feet of gross living area; 2-car attached garage; landscaping is good. Construction is frame with aluminum siding.

Comparable A:
Sold for 1,000,000 within previous month; conventional financing at current rates; located in subject's neighborhood with similar locational advantages; house approximately same age as subject; lot size smaller than subject; view similar to subject; design less appealing than subject's; construction similar to subject; condition similar to subject; 7 rooms-- two bedrooms, one bath; 1,900 square feet of gross living area; 2-car attached garage; landscaping similar to subject.

Comparable B:
Sold for 1,200,000 within previous month; conventional financing at current rates; located in subject's neighborhood with similar locational advantages; house six years newer than subject; lot size smaller than subject; view is better than the subject's; design is more appealing than subject's; construction (brick and frame) better than subject's; better condition than subject; 10 rooms-four bedrooms, three baths; 2,300 square feet of gross living area; 2-car attached garage; landscaping similar to subject.

Comparable C:
Sold for 1,150,000 within previous month; conventional financing at current rates; located in subject's neighborhood with similar locational advantages; house five years older than subject; lot size larger than subject; view similar to subject; design and appeal similar to subject's; construction similar to subject; condition similar to subject; 8 rooms-- three bedrooms, two baths; 2,000 square feet of gross living area; 2-car attached garage; landscaping similar to subject.

Comparable D:
Sold for 1,090,000 within previous month; conventional financing at current rates; located in a neighborhood close to subject's, but more desirable than subject's; house approximately same age as subject; lot size same as subject; view similar to subject; design less appealing than subject's; construction (frame) poorer than subject's; poorer condition than subject; 7 rooms-- two bedrooms, one and one half baths; 1,900 square feet of gross living area; 2-car attached garage; landscaping similar to subject.

Exhibit 16.5, cont. Sales Comparison Approach Illustration

Adjustments

	Subject	A	B	C	D
Sale price		1,000,000	1,200,000	1,150,000	1,090,000
Financing terms		standard	standard	standard	standard
Sale date	NOW	equal	equal	equal	equal
Location		equal	equal	equal	-20,000
Age		equal	-12,000	+10,000	equal
Lot size		+10,000	+10,000	-10,000	equal
Site/view		equal	-10,000	equal	equal
Design/appeal		+10,000	-12,000	equal	+5,000
Construction quality	good	equal	-30,000	equal	+10,000
Condition	good	equal	-50,000	equal	+20,000
No. of rooms	8				
No. of bedrooms	3	+5,000	-5,000	equal	+5,000
No. of baths	2	+10,000	-15,000	equal	+5,000
Gross living area	2,000	+10,000	-20,000	equal	+10,000
Other space					
Garage	2 car/attd.	equal	equal	equal	equal
Other improvements					
Landscaping	good	equal	equal	equal	equal
Net adjustments		+45,000	-144,000	0	+35,000
Indicated value	1,120,000	1,045,000	1,056,000	1,150,000	1,125,000

For comparable A, the appraiser has made additions to the lot value, design, number of bedrooms and baths, and for gross living area. This accounts for the comparable's *deficiencies* in these areas relative to the subject. A total of five adjustments amount to $45,000, or 4.5% of the purchase price.

For comparable B, the appraiser has deducted values for age, site, design, construction quality, condition, bedrooms, baths, and living area. This accounts for the comparable's superior qualities relative to the subject. The only addition is the lot size, since the subject's is larger. A total of nine adjustments amount to $144,000, or 12% of the sale price.

For comparable C, the appraiser has added value for the age and deducted value for the lot size. The two adjustments offset one another for a net adjustment of zero.

For comparable D, one deduction has been made for the comparable's superior location. This is offset by six additions reflecting the various areas where the comparable is inferior to the subject. A total of seven adjustments amount to $35,000, or 3.2% of the sale price.

In view of all adjusted comparables, the appraiser developed a final indication of value of $1,120,000 for the subject. Underlying this conclusion is the fact that Comparable C, since it only has two minor adjustments which offset each other, it is by far the best indicator of value. Comparable D might be the second best indicator, since the net adjustments are very close to the sale price. Comparable A might be the third best indicator, since it has the second fewest number of total adjustments. Comparable B is the least reliable indicator, since there are numerous adjustments, three of which are of a significant amount. In addition, Comparable B is questionable altogether as a comparable, since total adjustments alter the sale price by12%.

THE COST APPROACH

Types of cost appraised
Depreciation
Steps in the approach

The cost approach is most often used for recently built properties where the actual costs of development and construction are known. It is also used for special-purpose buildings which cannot be valued by the other methods because of lack of comparable sales or income data.

The strengths of the cost approach are that it:

> ▸ provides an upper limit for the subject's value based on the undepreciated cost of reproducing the improvements

> ▸ is very accurate for a property with new improvements which are the highest and best use of the property.

The limitations of the cost approach are that:

> ▸ the cost to create improvements is not necessarily the same as market value

> ▸ depreciation is difficult to measure, especially for older buildings

Types of cost appraised

The cost approach generally aims to estimate either the *reproduction cost* or the *replacement cost* of the subject property.

Reproduction cost is the cost of constructing, at current prices, a *precise duplicate* of the subject improvements. **Replacement cost** is the cost of constructing, at current prices and using current materials and methods, a *functional equivalent* of the subject improvements.

Replacement cost is used primarily for appraising older structures, since it is impractical to consider reproducing outmoded features and materials. However, reproduction cost is preferable whenever possible because it facilitates the calculation of depreciation on a structure.

Depreciation

A cornerstone of the cost approach is the concept of depreciation. Depreciation is the *loss of value in an improvement over time*. Since land is assumed to retain its value indefinitely, depreciation only applies to the improved portion of real property. The loss of an improvement's value can come from any cause, such as deterioration, obsolescence, or changes in the neighborhood. The sum of depreciation from all causes is accrued depreciation.

An appraiser considers depreciation as having three causes: physical deterioration, functional obsolescence, and economic obsolescence.

Physical deterioration. Physical deterioration is wear and tear from use, decay, and structural deterioration. Such deterioration may be either *curable or incurable*.

Curable deterioration occurs when the costs of repair of the item are less than or equal to the resulting increase in the property's value. For example, if a paint job costs $6,000, and the resulting value increase is $8,000, the deterioration is considered curable. Incurable deterioration is the opposite: the repair will cost more than can be recovered by its contribution to the value of the building. For example, if the foregoing paint job cost $10,000, the deterioration would be considered incurable.

Functional obsolescence. Functional obsolescence occurs when a property has outmoded physical or design features which are no longer desirable to current users. If the obsolescence is curable, the cost of replacing or redesigning the outmoded feature would be offset by the contribution to overall value, for example, a lack of central air conditioning. If the functional obsolescence is incurable, the cost of the cure would exceed the contribution to overall value, for example, a floor layout with a bad traffic pattern that would cost three times as much as the ending contribution to value.

Economic obsolescence. Economic (or **external**) obsolescence is the loss of value due to adverse changes in the surroundings of the subject property that make the subject less desirable. Since such changes are usually beyond the control of the property owner, economic obsolescence is considered *an incurable value loss*. Examples of economic obsolescence include a deteriorating neighborhood, a rezoning of adjacent properties, or the bankruptcy of a large employer.

Steps in the approach   The cost approach consists of estimating the value of the land "as if vacant;" estimating the cost of improvements; estimating and deducting accrued depreciation; and adding the estimated land value to the estimated depreciated cost of the improvements.

Exhibit 16.6 Steps in the Cost Approach

1.	Estimate land value.
2.	Estimate reproduction or replacement cost of improvements.
3.	Estimate accrued depreciation.
4.	Subtract accrued depreciation from reproduction or replacement cost.
5.	Add land value to depreciated reproduction or replacement cost.

Estimate land value. To estimate land value, the appraiser uses the sales comparison method: find properties which are comparable to the subject property in terms of land and adjust the sale prices of the comparables to account for competitive differences with the subject property. Common adjustments concern location, physical characteristics, and time of sale. The indicated values of the comparable properties are used to estimate the land value of the subject. The implicit assumption is that the subject land is vacant (unimproved) and available for the highest and best use.

Estimate reproduction or replacement cost of improvements. There are several methods for estimating the reproduction or replacement cost of improvements. These are as follows.

▶ **Unit comparison method (square-foot method)**

The appraiser examines one or more new structures that are similar to the subject's improvements, determines a cost per unit for the benchmark structures, and multiplies this cost per unit times the number of units in the subject. The unit of measurement is most commonly denominated in square feet.

▶ **Unit-in-place method**

The appraiser uses materials cost manuals and estimates of labor costs, overhead, and builder's profit to estimate the cost of constructing separate components of the subject. The overall cost estimate is the sum of the estimated costs of individual components.

▶ **Quantity survey method**

The appraiser considers in detail all materials, labor, supplies, overhead and profit to get an accurate estimate of the actual cost to build the improvement. More thorough than the unit-in-place method, this method is used less by appraisers than it is by engineers and architects.

> **Cost indexing method**

The original cost of constructing the improvement is updated by applying a percentage increase factor to account for increases in nominal costs over time.

Estimate accrued depreciation. Accrued depreciation is often estimated by the **straight-line** method, also called the **economic age-life method**. This method assumes that depreciation occurs at a steady rate over the economic life of the structure. Therefore, a property suffers the same incremental loss of value each year.

The **economic life** is the period during which the structure is expected to remain useful in its original use. The cost of the structure is divided by the number of years of economic life to determine an annual amount for depreciation. The straight-line method is primarily relevant to depreciation from physical deterioration.

Subtract accrued depreciation from reproduction or replacement cost. The sum of accrued depreciation from all sources is subtracted from the estimated cost of reproducing or replacing the structure. This produces an estimate of the current value of the improvements.

Add land value to depreciated reproduction or replacement cost. To complete the cost approach, the estimated value of the land "as if vacant" is added to the estimated value of the depreciated reproduction or replacement cost of the improvements. This yields the final value estimate for the property by the cost approach.

Exhibit 16.7 Cost Approach Illustration

I. LAND VALUE

Land value, by direct sales comparison	80,000

II. IMPROVEMENTS COST

Main building (by one or more of the four methods)	260,000
Plus: other structures	16,000
Total cost new	276,000

III. ACCRUED DEPRECIATION

Physical depreciation	
Curable	10,000
Incurable	14,000
Functional obsolescence	6,000
External obsolescence	
Total depreciation	30,000

IV. IMPROVEMENTS COST MINUS DEPRECIATION

Total cost new	276,000
Less: total depreciation	30,000
Depreciated value of improvements	246,000

V. OVERALL ESTIMATED VALUE

Total land value	80,000
Depreciated value of improvements	246,000
Indicated value by cost approach	326,000

THE INCOME CAPITALIZATION APPROACH

Steps in the approach
Gross rent and gross income multiplier approach

The income capitalization approach, or income approach, is used for income properties and sometimes for other properties in a rental market where the appraiser can find rental data. The approach is based on the principle of anticipation: the expected future income stream of a property underlies what an investor will pay for the property. It is also based on the principle of substitution: that an investor will pay no more for a subject property with a certain income stream than the investor would have to pay for another property with a similar income stream.

The strength of the income approach is that it is used by investors themselves to determine how much they should pay for a property. Thus, in the right circumstances, it provides a good basis for estimating market value.

The income capitalization approach is limited in two ways. First, it is difficult to determine an appropriate capitalization rate. This is often a matter of judgment and experience on the part of the appraiser. Secondly, the income approach relies on market information about income and expenses, and it can be difficult to find such information.

Steps in the approach   The income capitalization method consists of estimating annual net operating income from the subject property, then applying a capitalization rate to the income. This produces a principal amount that the investor would pay for the property.

Exhibit 16.8 Steps in the Income Capitalization Approach

1.	Estimate potential gross income.
2.	Estimate effective gross income.
3.	Estimate net operating income.
4.	Select a capitalization rate.
5.	Apply the capitalization rate.

Estimate potential gross income. Potential gross income is the scheduled rent of the subject plus income from miscellaneous sources such as vending machines and telephones. Scheduled rent is the total rent a property will produce if fully leased at the established rental rates.

$$
\begin{array}{r}
\text{Scheduled rent} \\
+ \quad \text{Other income} \\
\hline
\text{Potential gross income}
\end{array}
$$

An appraiser may estimate potential gross rental income using current market rental rates (market rent), the rent specified by leases in effect on the property (contract rent), or a combination of both. Market rent is determined by market studies in a process similar to the sales comparison method. Contract rent is used primarily if the existing leases are not due to expire in the short term and the tenants are unlikely to fail or leave the lease.

Estimate effective gross income. Effective gross income is potential gross income minus an allowance for vacancy and credit losses.

$$
\begin{array}{r}
\text{Potential gross income} \\
- \quad \text{Vacancy \& credit losses} \\
\hline
\text{Effective gross income}
\end{array}
$$

Vacancy loss refers to an amount of potential income lost because of unrented space. Credit loss refers to an amount lost because of tenants' failure to pay rent for any reason. Both are estimated on the basis of the subject property's history, comparable properties in the market, and assuming typical management quality. The allowance for vacancy and credit loss is usually estimated as a percentage of potential gross income.

Estimate net operating income. Net operating income is effective gross income minus total operating expenses.

$$
\begin{array}{l}
\text{Effective gross income} \\
\text{- Total operating expenses} \\
\hline
\text{Net operating income}
\end{array}
$$

Operating expenses include fixed expenses and variable expenses. Fixed expenses are those that are incurred whether the property is occupied or vacant, for example, real estate taxes and hazard insurance. Variable expenses are those that relate to actual operation of the building, for example, utilities, janitorial service, management, and repairs.

Operating expenses typically include an annual reserve fund for replacement of equipment and other items that wear out periodically, such as carpets and heating systems. Operating expenses do not include debt service, expenditures for capital improvements, or expenses not related to operation of the property.

Select a capitalization rate. The capitalization rate is an estimate of the *rate of return* an investor will demand on the investment of capital in a property such as the subject. The judgment and market knowledge of the appraiser play an essential role in the selection of an appropriate rate for the subject property. In most cases, the appraiser will research capitalization rates used on similar properties in the market.

Apply the capitalization rate. An appraiser now obtains an indication of value from the income capitalization method by dividing the estimated net operating income for the subject by the selected capitalization rate

$$
\frac{NOI}{capitalization\ rate} = value
$$

Using traditional symbols for income (I), rate (R) and value (V), the formula for value is

$$
\frac{I}{R} = V
$$

Exhibit 16.9 Income Capitalization Method Illustration

I. ESTIMATE POTENTIAL GROSS INCOME

Potential gross rental income	192,000
Plus: other income	2,000
Potential gross income	194,000

II. ESTIMATE EFFECTIVE GROSS INCOME

Less: vacancy and collection losses	9,600
Effective gross income	184,400

III. ESTIMATE NET OPERATING INCOME

Operating expenses	
Real estate taxes	32,000
Insurance	4,400
Utilities	12,000
Repairs	4,000
Maintenance	16,000
Management	12,000
Reserves	1,600
Legal and accounting	2,000
Total expenses	84,000

Effective gross income	184,400
Less: total expenses	84,000
Net operating income	100,400

IV. SELECT CAPITALIZATION RATE

Capitalization rate: 7%

V. APPLY CAPITALIZATION RATE

$$\frac{I}{R} = V = \frac{100,400}{.07} = 1,434,300 \text{ (rounded)}$$

Indicated value by income approach: 1,434,300

Gross rent and gross income multiplier approach

The gross rent multiplier (GRM) and gross income multiplier (GIM) approaches are simplified income-based methods used primarily for properties that produce or might produce income but are not primarily income properties. Examples are single-family homes and duplexes.

The methods consist of applying a multiplier to the estimated gross income or gross rent of the subject. The multiplier is derived from market data on sale prices and gross income or gross rent.

The advantage of the income multiplier is that it offers a relatively quick indication of value using an informal methodology. However, the approach leaves many variables out of consideration such as vacancies, credit losses, and operating expenses. In addition, the appraiser must have market rental data to establish multipliers.

Steps in the gross rent multiplier approach. There are two steps in the gross rent multiplier approach.

First, select a gross rent multiplier by examining the sale prices and monthly rents of comparable properties which have sold recently. The appraiser's judgment and market knowledge are critical in determining an appropriate gross rent multiplier for the subject. The gross rent multiplier for a property is:

$$\frac{Price}{Monthly\ rent} = GRM$$

Second, estimate the value of the subject by multiplying the selected GRM by the subject's monthly income.

$$GRM\ x\ Subject\ monthly\ rent = estimated\ value$$

Exhibit 16.10 Gross Rent Multiplier Illustration

Property	Sale price	Monthly rent	GRM
Comparable A	500,000	1660	151
Comparable B	248,000	1500	165
Comparable C	324,000	2,200	147
Comparable D	304,000	1,800	169
Subject	320,000	2,000	160

In the illustration, the indicated GRM for the subject is 160, based on the appraiser's research and judgment. Applying the GRM to a rental rate of $2,000, the indicated value for the subject is $320,000.

Steps in the gross income multiplier approach. The GIM approach is identical to the GRM approach, except that a different denominator is used in the formula. Step one is to select a gross income multiplier by examining the sale prices and gross annual incomes of comparable properties which have sold recently. The gross income multiplier for a property is:

$$\frac{Price}{Gross\ annual\ income} = GIM$$

Step two is to estimate the value of the subject by multiplying the selected GIM by the subject's gross annual income:

GIM x Subject gross annual income = estimated value

Exhibit 16.11 Gross Income Multiplier Illustration

Property	Sale price	Gross income	GIM
Comparable A	250,000	19,920	12.55
Comparable B	248,000	18,000	13.78
Comparable C	324,000	26,400	12.27
Comparable D	304,000	21,600	14.07
Subject	324,000	24,000	13.50

In the illustration, the indicated GIM for the subject is 13.5 , based on the appraiser's research and judgment. Applying the GIM to the property's gross annual income gives an indicated value for the subject of $324,000.

REGULATION OF APPRAISAL PRACTICE

Licensure
Professional standards
Professional associations and designations

Licensure

In 1989, Congress passed the Financial Institutions Reform, Recovery and Enforcement Act (FIRREA) in response to the savings and loan crisis. This act included provisions to regulate appraisal.

Title XI of FIRREA requires that competent individuals whose professional conduct is properly supervised perform all appraisals used in federally-related transactions. Such federally-related appraisals must be performed only by state-certified appraisers. A state-certified appraiser is one who has passed the necessary examinations and competency standards as established by each state in conformance with the federal standards stated in FIRREA and USPAP (Uniform Standards of Professional Appraisal Practice). The criteria for certification as a minimum must follow those established by the Appraiser Qualifications Board of the Appraisal Foundation.

Professional standards

The Uniform Standards of Professional Appraisal Practice (USPAP) is a set of standards, guidelines and provisions for the appraisal industry. It resulted from the cooperation of nine national appraisal organizations in 1985.

The "competence" provision requires appraisers to assess whether they have the necessary knowledge and competence to perform a specific assignment. If they do not, they must disclose this fact.

The "departure" provision permits appraisers to perform an appraisal that does not meet all the USPAP guidelines provided they have informed the client of the limitations of the incomplete appraisal and if the partial appraisal will not be misleading.

The "standards" concern:

- recognized appraisal methods
- definition of due diligence
- how appraisal results are reported
- disclosures and assumptions
- appraisal review
- real estate analysis
- mass appraisals
- personal property appraisals
- business appraisals
- compliance with USPAP
- compliance with the Code of Professional Ethics and Standards of Professional Practice

Professional associations and designations

Prior to the establishment of state certification programs, the only indication of professional competence for an appraiser was membership in and designation by one of the national appraisal associations. These associations continue to provide education and recognition of professional accomplishment for appraisers.

The appraisal organizations who jointly formed the Appraisal Foundation in 1987 are:

- American Institute of Real Estate Appraisers
- American Society of Appraisers
- American Society of Farm Managers and Rural Appraisers
- International Association of Assessing Officers
- International Right of Way Association
- National Association of Independent Fee Appraisers
- National Society of Real Estate Appraisers
- Society of Real Estate Appraisers

The American Institute of Real Estate Appraisers and the Society of Real Estate Appraisers have since joined to become the Appraisal Institute.

16 Appraising and Estimating Market Value
Snapshot Review

REAL ESTATE VALUE

- present monetary worth of benefits arising from ownership, including: income, appreciation, use, tax benefits

Foundations of real estate value

- anticipation, substitution, contribution, change, highest and best use, conformity, supply, demand, progression, regression, assemblage, subdivision, utility, transferability

Types of value

- market, reproduction, replacement, salvage, plottage, assessed, condemned, depreciated, reversionary, appraised, rental, leasehold, insured, book, mortgage

APPRAISING MARKET VALUE

Market value

- price willing buyer and seller would agree on given: cash transaction, exposure, information, no pressure, arm's length, marketable title, no hidden influences

The appraisal and its uses

- a professional's opinion of value, supported by data, regulated, following professional standards; used in real estate decision-making

Steps in the appraisal process

- define purpose, collect and analyze data, identify highest and best use, estimate land value, apply basic appraisal approaches, reconcile, compile report

SALES COMPARISON APPROACH

- most commonly used; relies on principles of substitution and contribution

Steps in the approach

- compare sale prices, adjust comparables to account for differences with subject

Identifying comparables

- must be physically similar, in subject's vicinity, recently sold in arm's length sale

Adjusting comparables

- deduct from comp if better than subject; add to comp if worse than subject

Weighting adjustments

- best indicator has fewest and smallest adjustments, least net adjustment from the sale price

Broker's comparative market analysis

- abridged sales comparison approach by brokers and agents to find a price range

COST APPROACH

- most often used for recently built properties and special-purpose buildings

Types of cost appraised

- reproduction: precise duplicate; replacement: functional equivalent

Depreciation

- loss of value from deterioration, or functional or economic obsolescence

Steps in the approach

- land value plus depreciated reproduction or replacement cost of improvements

INCOME APPROACH

- used for income properties and in a rental market with available rental data

Steps in the approach

- value = NOI divided by the capitalization rate

GRM and GIM approach

- GRM: price divided by monthly rent; value: GRM times monthly rent; GIM: price divided by gross annual income; value: GIM times annual income

REGULATION OF APPRAISAL

Licensure

- state-licensed or -certified per FIRREA/USPAP for federally-related appraisals

Professional standards

- USPAP establishes appraisal standards, guidelines and provisions

Professional associations and designations

- founders of Appraisal Foundation offer education and professional designations

17 Real Estate Finance

Anatomy of Mortgage Lending
Initiating a Mortgage Loan
Qualifying for a Mortgage Loan
Closing a Loan
Laws Affecting Mortgage Lending
The Mortgage Market
Types of Real Estate Loans

ANATOMY OF MORTGAGE LENDING

Mechanics of a loan transaction
Financial components of a loan
Promissory note
Mortgage document and trust deed

Mechanics of a loan transaction

It is common to use borrowed money to purchase real estate. When a borrower gives a note promising to repay the borrowed money and executes a mortgage on the real estate for which the money is being borrowed as security, the financing method is called mortgage financing. The term "mortgage financing" also applies to real estate loans secured by a deed of trust. The process of securing a loan by pledging a property without giving up ownership of the property is called **hypothecation**.

States differ in their interpretation of who owns mortgaged property. Those that regard the mortgage as a lien held by the mortgagee (lender) against the property owned by the mortgagor (borrower) are called **lien-theory** states. Those that regard the mortgage document as a conveyance of ownership from the mortgagor to the mortgagee are called **title-theory** states. Some states interpret ownership of mortgaged property from a point of view that combines aspects of both title and lien theory.

A valid mortgage or trust deed financing arrangement requires

> ▸ a *note* as evidence of the debt
> ▸ the *mortgage or trust deed* as evidence of the collateral pledge

Note. In addition to executing a mortgage or trust deed, the borrower signs a promissory note for the amount borrowed. The amount of the loan is typically the difference between the purchase price and the down payment. A promissory note creates a personal liability for the borrower to repay the loan.

Mortgage. A mortgage is a legal document stating the pledge of the borrower (the **mortgagor**) to the lender (the **mortgagee**). The mortgage document pledges the borrower's ownership interest in the real estate in question as collateral against performance of the debt obligation.

The flow of funds and obligations in a mortgage transaction is as follows:

Exhibit 17.1 Flow of a Mortgage Transaction

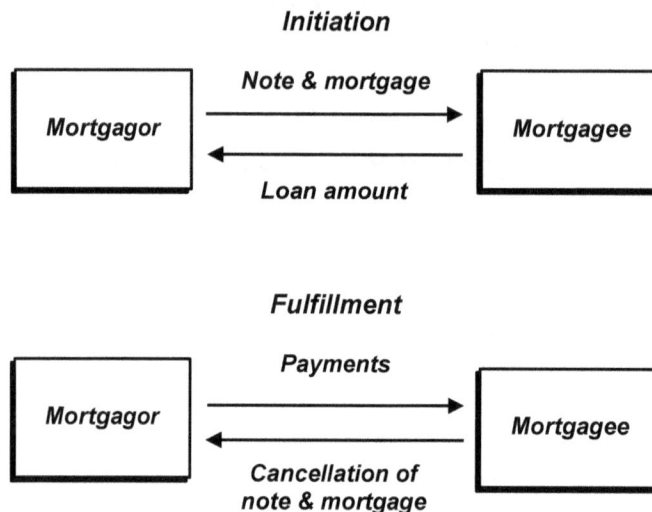

Initiation

Mortgagor	→ *Note & mortgage* →	Mortgagee
	← *Loan amount*	

Fulfillment

Mortgagor	→ *Payments* →	Mortgagee
	← *Cancellation of note & mortgage*	

The deed of trust. A deed of trust conveys title to the property in question from the borrower (**trustor**) to a **trustee** as security for the loan. The trustee is a third party fiduciary to the trust. While the loan is in place, the trustee holds the title on behalf of the lender, who is the **beneficiary** of the trust. On repayment of the loan, the borrower receives the title from the trustee in the form of a deed of reconveyance.

The flow of funds and obligations in a trust deed transaction is as follows:

Exhibit 17.2 Flow of a Trust Deed Transaction

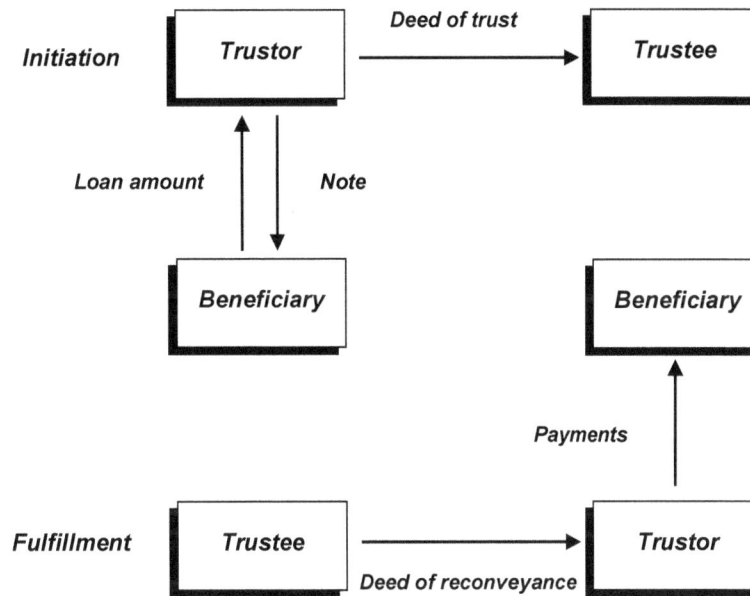

Financial components of a loan

The financial components of a mortgage loan include:

- ▶ principal
- ▶ interest and interest rate
- ▶ points
- ▶ term
- ▶ payments

Principal. The capital amount borrowed, on which interest payments are calculated, is the original loan **principal**. In an amortizing loan, part of the principal is repaid periodically along with interest, so that the principal balance decreases over the life of the loan. At any point during the life of a mortgage loan, the remaining unpaid principal is called the **loan balance**, or **remaining balance**.

Interest and interest rate. Interest is a charge for the use of the lender's money. Interest may be paid in *advance* at the beginning of the payment period, or in *arrears* at the end of the payment period, according to the terms of the note. Mortgage interest is most commonly paid in arrears. The **interest rate** is a percentage applied to the principal to determine the amount of interest due. The rate may be *fixed* for the term of the loan, or it may be *variable*, according to the terms of the note. A loan with a fixed interest rate is called a fixed-rate loan; a loan with a variable interest rate is commonly called an adjustable rate loan.

Because the interest rate on a mortgage loan does not reflect the full cost of the loan to the borrower, federal law requires a lender on a residential property to compute and disclose an **Annual Percentage Rate (APR)** that includes other finance charges in addition to the basic interest rate in the calculation.

Many states have laws against **usury**, which is the charging of excessive interest rates on loans. Such states have a maximum rate that is either a flat rate or a variable rate tied to an index such as the prime lending rate.

Points. From the point of view of a lender or investor, the amount loaned in a mortgage loan is the lender's capital investment, and the interest paid by the borrower is the return earned by the invested capital. It is often the case that a lender needs to earn a greater return than the interest rate alone provides. For example, a lender may require additional yield on a low-interest VA loan which has an interest rate maximum. In such a case, the lender charges up-front **discount points** to make up the difference between the interest rate on the loan and the required return. This effectively raises the yield of the loan to the lender.

A discount point is *one percent of the loan amount*. Thus, one point on a $100,000 loan equals $1,000. The lender charges this as *pre-paid interest* at closing by funding only the face amount of the loan minus the discount points. The borrower, however, must repay the full loan amount, along with interest calculated on the full amount.

The value of one discount point to a lender is usually estimated to be equivalent to raising the interest rate on the loan by 1/8%. Thus, a lender has to charge eight points to raise the yield by 1%. If a lender needs to earn 7% on a loan offered at 6.5%, the number of points necessary would be figured as follows:

$$7.0\% - 6.5\% = .5\%$$
$$.5\% \times 8 \text{ (points per } 1\%) = 4 \text{ points}$$

On a loan of $100,000, the 4 points would cost the borrower:

$$100,000 \times .04 = \$4,000.$$

The borrower would effectively receive from the lender $96,000, and owe principal and interest based on $100,000. For tax reasons, it is usually advisable for the borrower to receive the full loan amount from the lender and pay the points in a check which is separate from that used for other closing costs. As pre-paid interest, points paid in this way may be deductible on the borrower's income tax return for the year of the purchase. The borrower should seek the advice of a tax consultant concerning this matter.

Term. The loan term is the period of time over which the loan must be repaid. A "30-year loan" is a loan whose balance must be fully paid off at the end of thirty years. A "five-year balloon loan" is a loan whose balance must be paid off at the end of five years, although its payments may be calculated on a term of another length, such as fifteen or thirty years. Such a loan is also sometimes described as a 30-year loan with a five-year "call."

Payments. The loan term, loan amount, and interest rate combine to determine the periodic payment amount. When these three quantities are known, it is possible to identify the periodic payment from a mortgage table or with a financial calculator. Mortgage payments are usually made on a monthly basis. On an amortizing loan, a portion of the payment goes to repay the loan balance in advance, and a portion goes to payment of interest in arrears.

For example, Mary and Jerry King borrow $400,000 to finance the purchase of a home. The loan has a term of thirty years at an interest rate of 5% and is amortizing. The monthly payment for this loan will be $2,147. For the first payment at the end of the month, the Kings owe interest on $400,000 for the monthly period. At 5%, this amounts to $1,666.67. Since their payment is $2,147 and the interest charge is $1,666.67, the difference, which is $480.33, is applied to an advance payment of principal. The following month, the Kings will pay interest on the new, smaller loan balance of $399,519.67 ($400,000.00 – 480.33).

If a borrower pays more than the scheduled payment amount, the excess is credited to repayment of the principal, which is reduced by the amount of the excess payment. The required minimum payment amount remains constant for the life of the loan, but the loan term can be reduced by this means, thereby also reducing the total amount of interest paid over the life of the loan.

Promissory note

A borrower who executes a promissory note is the **maker** or **payer** of the note. The lender is the **payee**. To be properly executed, all parties who have an interest in the property should sign the note. The note sets forth:

- the loan amount
- the term of the loan
- the method and timing of repayment
- the interest rate to be paid
- the borrower's promise to pay

The note may also state that it is payable to the bearer, if used with a deed of trust, or to the mortgagee, if used with a mortgage. Other items in the mortgage document or deed of trust may be repeated in the promissory note, especially:

- the right to prepay the loan balance
- charges for late payment
- conditions for default
- notifications and cures for default
- other charges

A promissory note is a **negotiable instrument**, which means the payee may *assign* it to a third party. The assignee would then have the right to receive the borrower's periodic payments.

Mortgage document and trust deed

A borrower who executes a mortgage is a **mortgagor**. The lender named in the mortgage is the **mortgagee**. In a trust deed, the borrower is the **trustor** and the lender is **beneficiary**. The mortgage or trust document identifies the property being given as security, giving both its legal description and mailing address. The document contains much of the same information as the note, including:

- the debt amount
- the term of the loan
- method and timing of payments

The document does not usually provide details about the payment amount, interest rate, or charges.

Among the major clauses of a typical mortgage are the following.

Payment of Principal and Interest: Prepayment and Late Charges. The borrower must make timely payments according to the terms of the note.

Funds for Taxes and Insurance. Unless waived by the lender or prohibited by law, the borrower must make monthly payments to cover taxes and hazard insurance. If applicable, the borrower must also pay flood insurance and mortgage insurance installments.

Periodic payments of taxes and insurance are held in a reserve fund called the **escrow account**. The Real Estate Settlement Procedures Act (RESPA) limits the amount of funds that the lender can require and hold for this purpose.

The borrower's monthly payment to the lender for principal and interest is called the **P&I** payment (principal and interest). The amount which also includes the escrow payment is called **PITI** (principal, interest, taxes, insurance).

Application of Payments. The amount of each payment is applied to various items in order of priority. Unless local law provides otherwise, this order is: 1) prepayment charges; 2) escrow; 3) interest; 4) principal; 5) late charges.

Charges and Liens. The borrower is liable for paying any charges, liens, or other expenses that may have priority over the mortgage or trust instrument.

Hazard or Property Insurance. The borrower must keep the property insured as the lender requires. Insurance proceeds, in case of a claim, are applied first to restoring the property, or, if that is not feasible, to payment of the debt.

Occupancy, Preservation, Maintenance and Protection of the Property. The borrower must take and maintain occupancy of the property as the borrower's principal residence according to the lender's requirements. The borrower must not use or neglect the property in such a way as to impair the lender's lien on the property. This could include using the property for illegal purposes, creating hazardous waste on the property, or destroying the improvements.

Protection of Lender's Rights in the Property. The lender may take actions it believes are necessary to protect its rights in the property if the borrower's actions threaten them. The costs of these actions would be charged to the borrower, and become part of the monthly payment.

Mortgage Insurance. The lender may require the borrower to obtain *private mortgage insurance, or PMI*. Mortgage insurance protects the lender against loss of a portion of the loan (typically 20-25%) in case of borrower default. Private mortgage insurance generally applies to loans that are not backed by the Federal Housing Administration (FHA) or Veterans Administration (VA) and that have a down payment of less than 20% of the property value.

Inspection. With proper notice, the lender may inspect the property if there is reasonable cause to fear damage to its lien.

Condemnation. If the property is condemned or taken by eminent domain, the lender declares a claim on any resulting proceeds.

Borrower Not Released; Forbearance by Lender Not a Waiver. The lender reserves the right to take future action against the borrower for default, even if the lender decides not to take immediate action. If the lender agrees to change the terms of the loan, it does not release the borrower from the original liability.

Transfer of the Property or a Beneficial Interest in Borrower. If the borrower sells or transfers its interest in the property without the lender's approval, the lender may demand immediate and full repayment of the loan balance. This is an **alienation** clause, also known as a **due-on-sale** clause and a **call** clause. It allows the lender to prevent the assumption of the mortgage by a buyer if the borrower sells the property. The requirement to repay the loan before the scheduled date is called **acceleration**.

Borrower's Right to Reinstate. If the lender holds the borrower in default under the terms of the mortgage and proceeds to enforce its rights under the document, such as by foreclosing, the borrower has the right to reinstate his or her interest by performing certain actions. This usually means paying overdue mortgage payments and any other expenses the lender may have incurred in protecting its rights. The clause, also known as a **redemption** clause, gives the borrower a period of time to satisfy obligations and prevent the lender from forcing a sale of the property.

Release. The lender agrees to release the mortgage or trust document to the borrower when the borrower has paid off the loan and all other sums secured by the document. The release clause, also known as a **defeasance** clause, may specify that the mortgagee will execute a **satisfaction of mortgage** (also known as **release of mortgage** and **mortgage discharge**) to the mortgagor. In the case of a deed of trust, the lender as beneficiary requests the trustee to execute a **release deed** or **deed of reconveyance** to the borrower as trustor. The release deed or satisfaction should be recorded as necessary in county records to show that the mortgagee/trustee has extinguished all liens against the property.

INITIATING A MORTGAGE LOAN

The loan application
Mortgage loan underwriting

The process of initiating a mortgage loan begins when a borrower completes a loan application and submits it to a lender for evaluation by the lender's underwriters.

The loan application   **Forms**. Most lenders use some version of the "Uniform Residential Loan Application" promulgated by Fannie Mae. This form requests the borrower to provide information about the property and the borrower. In addition, the application must include supporting documentation, as indicated in the following exhibit.

Exhibit 17.3 Property and Borrower Information

Property information	age & year built original cost	year acquired current loan balance
Borrower information	age employment history assets	education monthly income & expenses debts
Supporting documentation	appraisal report purchase contract	credit report income and employment verification

The standard form includes the loan amount requested, based on an estimate of the purchase, refinance, or other underlying transaction.

Completion. The application must be complete for the lender to consider it. The form must be signed and dated by the applicant(s) and delivered to the lending institution. The **initiation** of the application process occurs when the lender receives the completed application package from the applicant. Federal law requires the lender to accept all applications and to give applicants notice concerning the disposition of the application. If the lender denies the loan application because of fraudulent information on the application form, the borrower has no claim to a refund of the application fee.

Mortgage loan underwriting

Loan underwriting is the process of assessing the lender's risk in giving a loan. Mortgage underwriting includes:

  ▶ evaluating the borrower's ability to repay the loan
  ▶ appraising the value of the property offered as security
  ▶ determining the terms of the loan

Risk. A lender undertakes a number of risks in lending money. The principal risks are that the borrower will default on repayment of the loan, and that the borrower will damage the value of the property as security. In addition, the lender runs the risk that, in the event of a foreclosure, the sales proceeds from the property will be insufficient to cover the lender's loss.

Qualification. A lender assesses risks by examining, or *qualifying*, both borrower and property. In qualifying a borrower, an underwriter weighs the ability of the borrower to repay the loan. This requires an analysis of whether the borrower's income, cash resources, creditworthiness, net worth, and employment stability meet the lender's standards.

In qualifying a property, an underwriter assesses the ability of the property value to cover potential losses. In this evaluation, a lender requires that the appraised value of the property be more than adequate to cover the contemplated loan and costs. To protect further against loss, a lender will usually lend only a portion of the property's value. The relationship of the loan amount to the property value, expressed as a percentage, is called the **loan-to-value ratio, or LTV**. If the lender's loan to value ratio is 80%, the lender will lend only $80,000 on a home appraised at $100,000. The difference between what the lender will lend and what the borrower must pay for the property is the amount the borrower must provide in cash as a down payment.

Even if borrower and property qualify, a lender may, under certain circumstances, seek further protection against risk by requiring the borrower to obtain private mortgage insurance. This is frequently the case with loans requiring a relatively small down payment, leading to a high loan-to-value ratio.

QUALIFYING FOR A MORTGAGE LOAN

Equal Credit Opportunity Act
Income qualification
Cash qualification
Net worth
Credit evaluation
Loan commitment

To qualify for a mortgage loan, a borrower must meet the lender's qualifications in terms of *income, debt, cash, and net worth*. In addition, a borrower must demonstrate sufficient *creditworthiness* to be an acceptable risk.

Equal Credit Opportunity Act

The Equal Credit Opportunity Act (ECOA) requires a lender to evaluate a loan applicant on the basis of that applicant's own income and credit rating, unless the applicant requests the inclusion of another's income and credit rating in the application. In addition, ECOA has prohibited a number of practices in mortgage loan underwriting. Accordingly, a lender may not:

> ▶ discount or disregard income from part-time work, a spouse, child support, alimony, or separate maintenance. Further, the loan officer may not ask whether any of the applicant's income is derived from these sources.

> ▶ assume that income for a certain type of person will be reduced because of an employment interruption due to child-bearing or child-raising. The loan officer may not ask about the applicant's plans or behavior concerning child-bearing or birth control.

> ▶ refuse a loan solely on the basis that the security is located in a certain geographical area.

> ▶ ask applicants any question about their age, sex, religion, race or national origin, except as the law may require.

> ▸ require a spouse to sign any document unless the spouse's income is to be included in the qualifying income, or unless the spouse agrees to become contractually obligated, or the state requires the signature for some purpose such as clearing clouded title.

If a lender denies a request for a loan, or offers a loan under different terms than those requested by an applicant, the lender must give the applicant written notice providing specific reasons for the action.

Qualifying the borrower. The lender must rely on eight types of information to determine that the borrower has the ability to repay the loan:

1. current income or assets (excluding the value of the mortgaged property)
2. current employment status
3. credit history
4. monthly payment for the mortgage
5. monthly payments being made on other loans on the same property
6. monthly payments for other mortgage-related expenses
7. other debts
8. monthly debt payments compared to monthly income (debt-to-income ratio)

The lender cannot use a temporarily low rate (introductory or "teaser" rate) to determine qualification. For an adjustable rate mortgage (ARM), the highest rate the borrower might have to pay is generally to be used.

The "ability to repay" requirements are relaxed in certain circumstances where the borrower is attempting to refinance from a riskier loan (such as an interest-only loan) to a less risky one (such as a fixed-rate mortgage loan.

Qualified Mortgage. A Qualified Mortgage is one that meets the "ability-to-repay" requirements, has certain required features and is not allowed to have others. There are exceptions to these rules for certain kinds of small lenders. Issuing a Qualified Mortgage gives the lender certain legal protections in case the borrower fails to repay the loan.

Generally not allowed:

> ▸ an "interest-only" period--when interest, but not principal, is being repaid
>
> ▸ negative amortization–when principal increases over time
>
> ▸ balloon payment–larger than normal payment at the end of the loan term
>
> ▸ loan term longer than 30 years
>
> ▸ excessive upfront fees and points

Generally required:

▸ monthly debt no more than 43 % of monthly pre-tax income
▸ limits on points

Qualified Mortgages include loans that can be bought by Fannie Mae or Freddie Mac or insured by certain government agencies, such as the Department of Agriculture, even if the debt ratio is higher than 43 percent. Also, loans that are insured or guaranteed by the Department of Housing and Urban Development, including through the Federal Housing Administration, are qualified mortgages under rules issued by that agency.

Valuations. Before issuing a first mortgage loan, a lender must

▸ notify the borrower within three days of the loan application that a copy of any appraisal will be promptly provided
▸ provide the borrower with a free copy of any valuation used, including appraisal reports, automated valuation model reports, and broker's price opinions, promptly when completed and no later than three days before closing
▸ provide these copies even if the loan does not close

The lender may ask for the deadline to be waived so that the copies may be delivered at closing, and may charge a reasonable fee for obtaining the valuation.

Discovery and disclosure requirements. Creditors are required to provide applicants with free copies of all appraisals and other written valuations developed in connection with an application for a loan to be secured by a first lien on a dwelling and must notify applicants in writing that copies of appraisals will be provided to them promptly.

High cost loans. When the annual percentage rate (APR) or points and fees on a home loan, home equity loan, or home equity line of credit (HELOC) exceed certain limits, special consumer protections apply. The lender must provide information in advance that explains the costs, terms, and associated fees, and get a housing counselor to certify that the borrower has received counseling about the high-cost mortgage.

With high-cost mortgages, lenders are not allowed to add many kinds of fees and charges to the loan amount, namely:

▸ prepayment penalties for early loan payoff
▸ balloon payments
▸ late fees larger than 4 percent of the regular payment
▸ fees for payoff statements (statements of loan balance)
▸ loan modification fees

Income qualification   Lenders want to be assured that the borrower has adequate means to make all necessary periodic payments on the loan in addition to other housing expenses and debts such as credit card payments and car payments. Most lenders use two ratios to estimate an applicant's ability to fulfill a loan obligation: an *income ratio*, or *housing ratio*, and a *debt ratio*, or *housing plus debt ratio*. They also consider the stability of an applicant's income. Please note that the income and debt ratios in the discussion below do not necessarily reflect the latest ratios used by FHA, VA, or other lenders. Check for updates on the websites of those agencies.

Income ratio. The income ratio, or housing expense ratio, establishes borrowing capacity by limiting the percent of gross income a borrower may spend on housing costs. Housing costs include principal, interest, taxes, and homeowner's insurance, and may include monthly assessments, mortgage insurance, and utilities. The income ratio formula is:

Income Ratio

$$\frac{monthly\ housing\ expense}{monthly\ GROSS\ income} = income\ ratio$$

To identify the maximum monthly housing expense an income ratio allows, modify the formula as follows:

$$monthly\ gross\ income\ x\ income\ ratio = monthly\ housing\ expense$$

Most conventional lenders require that this ratio be *no greater than 25-28%*. In other words, a borrower's total housing expenses cannot exceed 28% of gross income. For an FHA-backed loan, the ratio is 31%. VA-guaranteed loans do not use this qualifying ratio.

For example, if a couple has combined monthly gross income of $12,000, and a lender's maximum income ratio is 28%, the couple's monthly housing expense cannot exceed $3,360:

$$\$12,000\ x\ 28\% = \$3,360$$

Debt ratio. The debt ratio considers all of the monthly obligations of the income ratio *plus any additional monthly payments the applicant must make for other debts*. The lender will look specifically at minimum monthly payments due on revolving credit debts and other consumer loans. The debt ratio formula is:

Debt Ratio

$$\frac{monthly\ housing\ expense + monthly\ debt\ obligations}{monthly\ GROSS\ income} = debt\ ratio$$

To identify the housing expenses plus debt a debt ratio allows, modify the formula as follows:

monthly gross income x debt ratio = monthly housing expense + monthly debt obligations

Most conventional lenders require that this debt ratio be *no greater than 36%*. For an FHA-backed loan, the debt ratio may not exceed 43%. The VA uses 41% and a variable "residual income" calculation. The FHA and VA include in the debt figure any obligation costing more than $100 per month and any debt with a remaining term exceeding six months.

Using the 36% debt ratio, the couple whose monthly income is $12,000 will be allowed to have monthly housing and debt obligations of $4,320:

$12,000 gross income x 36% = $4,320 expenses and debt

VA-guaranteed loans also require a borrower to meet certain qualifications based on net income after paying federal, state, and social security taxes, housing maintenance and utilities expenses. Such **residual income requirements** vary by family size, loan amount, and geographical region.

Income stability. A lender looks beyond income and debt ratios to assess an applicant's income stability. Important factors are:

> ▸ how long the applicant has been employed at the present job
>
> ▸ how frequently and for what reasons the applicant has changed jobs in the past
>
> ▸ how likely secondary income such as bonuses and overtime is to continue on a regular basis
>
> ▸ how educational level, training and skills, age, and type of occupation may affect the continuation of the present income level in the future.

Cash qualification

Since a lender lends only part of the purchase price of a property according to the lender's loan-to-value ratio, a lender will verify that a borrower has the cash resources to make the required down payment. If some of a borrower's cash for the down payment comes as a gift from a relative or friend, a lender may require a **gift letter** from the donor stating the amount of the gift and lack of any requirement to repay the gift. On the other hand, if someone is lending an applicant a portion of the down payment with a provision for repayment, a lender will consider this another debt obligation and adjust the debt ratio accordingly. This can lower the amount a lender is willing to lend.

Net worth

An applicant's **net worth** shows a lender the depth of the applicant's cash reserves, the value and liquidity of assets, and the extent to which assets exceed liabilities. These facts are important to a lender as an indication of the applicant's ability to sustain debt payment in the event of loss of employment.

Credit evaluation

Credit report and credit score. A lender must obtain a written credit report on any applicant who submits a completed loan application. The credit report will contain the applicant's history regarding:

- outstanding debts
- payment behavior (timeliness, collection problems)
- legal information of public record (lawsuits, judgments, bankruptcies, divorces, foreclosures, garnishments, repossessions, defaults)

Problems with payment behavior and legal actions are likely to cause a lender to deny the application, unless the applicant can provide an acceptable explanation of mitigating and temporary circumstances that caused the problem.

If a lender denies a loan on the basis of a credit report, the lender must disclose in writing that the applicant is entitled to a statement of reason from any creditor responsible for the negative report.

Since 1995, the Federal Home Loan Mortgage Corporation and the Federal National Mortgage Association have been encouraging lenders to use *credit scoring* to evaluate loan applicants. **Credit scoring** is a computer-based method of assigning a numerical value to an applicant's credit. The credit score is a statistical prediction of a borrower's likelihood of defaulting on a loan.

Loan commitment

When a lender's underwriters have qualified an applicant and the lender has decided to offer the loan, the lender gives the applicant a written notice of the agreement to lend under specific terms. This written promise is the **loan commitment**. The commitment may take a number of common forms, including *a firm commitment, a lock-in commitment, a conditional commitment, and a take-out commitment.*

A **firm commitment** is a straight forward offer to make a specific loan at a specific interest rate for a specific term. This kind of commitment is the one most commonly offered to home buyers.

A **"lock-in" commitment** is an offer to lend a specific amount for a specific term at a specific interest rate, *but the interest rate is subject to an expiration date*, for instance, sixty days. This guarantees that the lender will not raise the interest rate during the application and closing periods. The borrower may have to pay points or some other charge for the lock-in.

A **conditional commitment** offers to make a loan if certain provisions are met. This kind of commitment generally applies to construction loans. A typical condition for funding the loan is completion of a development phase.

A **take-out commitment** offers to make a loan that will "take out" another lender's loan, i.e., pay it off and replace it. The take-out loan is most often used to retire a construction loan. The take-out lender agrees to pay off the short-term construction loan by issuing a long-term permanent loan.

CLOSING A LOAN

Closing of a mortgage loan normally occurs with the closing of the real estate transaction. At the real estate closing, the lender typically has deposited the funded amount with an escrow agent, along with instructions for disbursing the funds.

The borrower deposits necessary funds with the escrow agent, executes final documents, and receives signed copies of all relevant documents.

Title to the mortgaged property is transferred and recorded according to legal procedures in effect at the time of closing. The borrower receives a package containing copies of all documents relevant to the transaction.

LAWS AFFECTING MORTGAGE LENDING

Truth-in-Lending and Regulation Z
Equal Credit Opportunity Act
Real Estate Settlement Procedures Act
National Flood Insurance Act

Truth-in-Lending and Regulation Z

The Consumer Credit Protection Act, enacted in 1969 and since amended by the Truth-in-Lending Simplification and Reform Act, is implemented by the Federal Reserve's **Regulation Z**. Regulation Z applies to all loans secured by a residence. It does not apply to commercial loans or to agricultural loans over $25,000. Its provisions cover *the disclosure of costs, the right to rescind the credit transaction, advertising credit offers, and penalties for non-compliance with the act.*

The Dodd-Frank Wall Street Reform and Consumer Protection Act of 2010 (Dodd-Frank Act) established the Consumer Financial Protection Bureau (CFPB.) to protect consumers by carrying out federal consumer financial laws. The CFPB consolidates most Federal consumer financial protection authority in one place, including enforcement of RESPA, ECOA, and Truth in Lending.

Disclosure of costs. Under Regulation Z, a lender must disclose all finance charges as well as the true Annualized Percentage Rate (APR) in advance of closing. A lender does not have to show the total interest payable over the loan term or include in finance charges such settlement costs as fees for appraisal, title, credit report, survey, or legal work. Disclosure must be distinctly presented in writing.

Rescission. A borrower has a limited right to cancel the credit transaction, usually within three days of completion of the transaction. The right of rescission does not apply to "residential mortgage transactions," that is, to mortgage loans used to finance the purchase or construction of the borrower's primary residence. However, state law may require a rescission period and notice on these transactions as well.

Advertising. Any type of advertising to offer credit is subject to requirements of full disclosure if it includes:

- a down payment percentage or amount
- an installment payment amount
- a specific amount for a finance charge
- a specific number of payments
- a specific repayment period
- a statement that there is no charge for credit

If any of these items appears in the advertising, the lender must disclose the down payment amount or percentage, repayment terms, the APR, and whether the rate can be increased after consummation of the loan.

Noncompliance. Willful violation of Regulation Z is punishable by imprisonment of up to a year and/or a fine of up to $5,000. Other violations may be punished by requiring payment of court costs, attorneys' fees, damages, and a fine of up to $1,000.

Equal Credit Opportunity Act

ECOA prohibits discrimination in extending credit based on race, color, religion, national origin, sex, marital status, age, or dependency upon public assistance. A creditor may not make any statements to discourage an applicant on the basis of such discrimination or ask any questions of an applicant concerning these discriminatory items. A real estate licensee who assists a seller in qualifying a potential buyer may fall within the reach of this prohibition. A lender must also inform a rejected applicant in writing of reasons for denial within 30 days. A creditor who fails to comply is liable for punitive and actual damages.

Real Estate Settlement Procedures Act

RESPA is a federal law which aims to *standardize settlement practices and ensure that buyers understand settlement costs*. RESPA applies to purchases of residential real estate (one- to four-family homes) to be financed by "federally related" first mortgage loans. Federally related loans include:

> ‣ VA- and FHA-backed loans
> ‣ other government-backed or -assisted loans
> ‣ loans that are intended to be sold to FNMA, FHLMC, GNMA, or other government-controlled secondary market institutions
> ‣ loans made by lenders who originate more than one million dollars per year in residential loans.

In addition to imposing settlement procedures, RESPA provisions prohibit lenders from paying kickbacks and unearned fees to parties who may have helped the lender obtain the borrower's business. This would include, for example, a fee paid to a real estate agent for referring a borrower to the lender.

To assist in informing and educating borrowers, RESPA requires that lenders provide a loan applicant with a **loan information booklet** and a **loan estimate**. The booklet, produced by the Consumer Financial Protection Bureau, explains RESPA provisions, general settlement costs, and the required **Closing Disclosure** form. The lender must provide the estimate of closing costs within three days following the borrower's application. RESPA is discussed further in the chapter on "Closings."

Disclosures. The Consumer Financial Protection Bureau (CFPB) requires lenders to use two specific forms to disclose settlement costs to the buyer. A lender must provide a Loan Estimate (H-24) within three days of receiving the loan application and allow the buyer to see the Closing Disclosure (H-25) three days before loan consummation. A lender must also provide a buyer with a copy of the information booklet, "Your Home Loan Toolkit," concerning mortgage loan, closing costs and closing procedures. The disclosures specify:

- ▸ settlement charges
- ▸ title charges
- ▸ recording and transfer fees
- ▸ reserve deposits required
- ▸ tax and insurance escrow deposits required
- ▸ any other fees or charges
- ▸ total closing costs

The disclosure forms vary, depending on loan type. The costs in the Closing Disclosure must match those in the Loan Estimate within certain standards. A sample of the H-25 Closing Disclosure is provided in Chapter 21.

National Flood Insurance Act

Federal law requires that borrowers seeking to finance real estate through federally related loans obtain flood insurance if the property is located in a designated flood-hazard area. The Department of Housing and Urban Development administers a program to subsidize flood insurance for borrowers in communities that have entered the program and complied with its construction standards. The Army Corps of Engineers has prepared flood-zone maps for the entire country.

THE MORTGAGE MARKET

Supply and demand for money
The primary mortgage market
The secondary mortgage market
Role of FNMA, GNMA, and FHLMC

Mortgage loans provide borrowers with funds to purchase real estate. Money for mortgages primarily comes from cash savings of individuals, government, and businesses. This money may become available through the process of **intermediation**, in which funds on deposit with financial institutions are loaned out to borrowers, or **disintermediation**, in which the owners of the savings invest their money directly by making loans or other investments. Government actions and investor activities affect the supply of money for mortgage loans and encourage or discourage the market for mortgage loans as an investment.

Supply and demand for money

Money is a limited commodity subject to the effects of supply and demand. The federal government's monetary policy *controls the supply of money* in order to achieve the country's economic goals. An excessive supply of money usually causes interest rates to fall and consumer prices to rise. Conversely, an excessive demand for money, such as for mortgage loans, causes interest rates to rise and prices to fall. Regulation of the money supply addresses these fluctuations with the aim to control and limit wide swings in the supply and demand cycle. These efforts, in turn, help to buffer the economy from severe inflationary or recessionary trends.

Regulating the money supply. The Federal Reserve System regulates the money supply by means of three methods:

> - *selling or re-purchasing government securities*, primarily Treasury bills
> - changing the *reserve requirement* for member banks. The reserve is a percentage of depositors' funds that banks and other regulated financial institutions may not lend out.
> - changing the interest rate, or *discount rate,* the system charges member institutions for borrowing funds from the Federal Reserve System central banks

When the Federal Reserve sells Treasury bills, the money paid for the securities is removed from the economy's money supply. Conversely, when it repurchases Treasury bills, the cash paid out to investors puts money back into the economy.

The second control, regulating reserve requirements, effectively restricts how much money banks can put into the economy through the disbursement of loans. When the Federal Reserve *raises* reserve requirements, banks have less money to lend, decreasing the money supply. When the Fed *lowers* reserve requirements, banks have more money to lend, increasing the money supply.

The third control, and perhaps the most effective, is regulation of the discount rate which member banks must pay to borrow money. If the discount rate goes up, it becomes more cost-prohibitive to borrow. Therefore the money supply tightens. If the discount rate is lowered, banks have an incentive to borrow more money to lend to customers.

The primary mortgage market

The **primary mortgage market** consists of lenders who originate mortgage loans directly to borrowers. Primary mortgage market lenders include:

- savings and loans
- commercial banks
- mutual savings banks
- life insurance companies
- mortgage bankers
- credit unions

Mortgage brokers are also part of the primary mortgage market, even though they do not lend to customers directly. Rather, they are instrumental in procuring borrowers for primary mortgage lenders.

The primary lender assumes the initial risk of the long-term investment in the mortgage loan. Primary lenders sometimes also **service** the loan until it is paid off. Servicing loans entails collecting the borrower's periodic payments, maintaining and disbursing funds in escrow accounts for taxes and insurance, supervising the borrower's performance, and releasing the mortgage on repayment. In many cases, primary lenders employ mortgage servicing companies, which service loans for a fee.

Portfolio lenders. A primary mortgage market lender may or may not sell its loans into the secondary market. Many lenders originate loans for the purpose of retaining the investments in their own loan *portfolio.* These loans are referred to as *portfolio loans*, and lenders originating loans for their own portfolio are called *portfolio lenders.* Portfolio lenders are less restricted by the standards and forms imposed on other lenders by secondary market organizations. In retaining their portfolio loans, portfolio lenders may vary underwriting criteria and hold independent standards for down payment requirements and the condition of the collateral.

The secondary mortgage market

Lenders, investors and government agencies that buy loans already originated by someone else, or originate loans indirectly through someone else, constitute the **secondary mortgage market**.

Secondary mortgage market organizations include:

- ▸ Federal National Mortgage Association (FNMA, or Fannie Mae)
- ▸ Federal Home Loan Mortgage Corporation (FHLMC, or Freddie Mac)
- ▸ Government National Mortgage Association (GNMA, or Ginnie Mae)
- ▸ investment firms that assemble loans into packages and sell securities based on the pooled mortgages
- ▸ life insurance companies
- ▸ pension funds
- ▸ primary market institutions who also invest as secondary lenders

Secondary mortgage market organizations buy pools of mortgages from primary lenders and sell securities backed by these pooled mortgages to investors. By selling securities, the secondary market brings investor money into the mortgage market. By purchasing loans from primary lenders, the secondary market returns funds to the primary lenders, thereby enabling the primary lender to originate more mortgage loans.

Exhibit 17.4 The Mortgage Money Flow

Primary lenders make a profit on the sale of loans to the secondary market. The secondary market acquires a profitable long-term investment without having to underwrite, originate, and service the loans. Secondary market organizations customarily hire primary lenders or loan servicing companies to service mortgage pools.

Secondary market loan requirements. The secondary market only buys loans that meet established requirements for quality of collateral, borrower and documentation. Since many primary lenders intend to sell their loans to the secondary market, the qualification standards of the secondary market limit and effectively regulate the kind of loans the primary lender will originate.

Role of FNMA GNMA, and FHLMC

As major players in the secondary market, the Federal National Mortgage Association (FNMA, "Fannie Mae"), Government National Mortgage Association (GNMA, "Ginnie Mae), and Federal Home Loan Mortgage

Corporation (FHLMC, "Freddie Mac") tend to set the standards for the primary market.

Federal National Mortgage Association, or Fannie Mae. Fannie Mae is a government-sponsored enterprise, originally organized as a privately-owned corporation. As a secondary market player, it:

> ▸ buys conventional, FHA-backed and VA-backed loans
>
> ▸ gives banks mortgage-backed securities in exchange for blocks of mortgages
>
> ▸ offers lenders firm loan purchase commitments, provided they conform to Fannie Mae's lending standards
>
> ▸ sells bonds and mortgage-backed securities
>
> ▸ guarantees payment of interest and principal on mortgage-backed securities

Government National Mortgage Association, or Ginnie Mae. Ginnie Mae is a division of the Department of Housing and Urban Development. Its purpose is to administer special assistance programs and to help Fannie Mae in its secondary market activities. Specifically, GNMA

> ▸ guarantees payment on FNMA high-risk, low-yield mortgages and absorbs the difference in yield between the mortgages and market rates
>
> ▸ guarantees privately generated securities backed by pools of VA-and FHA-guaranteed loans

Federal Home Loan Mortgage Corporation, or Freddie Mac. Freddie Mac is a government-sponsored enterprise, originally chartered as an corporation in 1970. As a secondary market player, FHLMC buys mortgages and pools them, selling bonds backed by the mortgages in the open market. Freddie Mac guarantees performance on FHLMC mortgages.

A federal conservator, the Federal Housing Finance Authority (FHFA), now operates Fannie Mae and Freddie Mac as conservator with the U.S. Treasury a majority owner of both organizations.

TYPES OF REAL ESTATE LOANS

Conventional loans
FHA-insured loans
VA-guaranteed loans
Common loan structures
Seller financing
Special-purpose loans

Conventional loans

A **conventional mortgage** loan is a permanent long-term loan that is not FHA-insured or VA-guaranteed. Market rates usually determine the interest rate on the loan. Because of the lack of insurance or guarantee by a government agency, the risk to a lender is greater for a conventional loan than for a non-conventional loan. This risk is usually reflected in higher interest rates and stricter requirements for the down payment and the borrower's income qualification. At the same time, conventional loans allow greater flexibility in fees, rates, and terms than do insured and guaranteed loans.

The primary sources of conventional loans are banks and savings and loan associations. Other conventional lenders include credit unions, life insurance companies, pension funds, mortgage bankers, and private individuals. Various types of lenders specialize in mortgage lending for specific purposes and type of borrower, such as commercial, construction, or single-family residential loans.

FHA-insured loans

The Federal Housing Administration (FHA) is an agency of the Department of Housing and Urban Development (HUD). It does not lend money, but *insures* permanent long-term loans made by others. The lender must be approved by the FHA, and the borrower must meet certain FHA qualifications. In addition, the property used to secure the loan must meet FHA standards. The FHA insures that the lender will not suffer significant loss in the case of borrower default. To provide this security, FHA provides insurance and charges the borrower an insurance premium. FHA loans typically have a higher loan-to-value ratio than conventional loans, enabling a borrower to make a smaller down payment. The basic FHA-insured loan program is the **Title II, Section 203(b)** program for loans on one- to four-family residential properties. Among the features of this program are the following.

FHA mortgage insurance. The FHA determines how much mortgage insurance must be provided and charges the borrower an appropriate mortgage insurance premium (MIP). The initial premium is payable at closing or is added to the borrower's loan balance and financed. Further annual premiums are charged monthly. The amount of the premium varies according to the loan term and the applicable loan-to-value ratio.

Borrower default. The FHA reimburses the lender for losses due to default by the borrower, including costs of foreclosure.

Appraisal. The property must be appraised by an FHA-approved appraiser. The property must also meet the FHA's standards for type and quality of construction, neighborhood quality, and other features.

Maximum loan amount. The FHA has set maximum loan amounts for over 80 regions. Borrowers within a region are limited to the loan ceiling amount in effect for the region. In addition, the maximum loan amount is restricted by the loan-to-value ratios in effect. The maximum FHA-backed loan a borrower can obtain will be the lesser of the regional ceiling amount or the amount dictated by the loan-to-value standard. Calculations are based on the lesser of sale price or appraised value.

Down payment requirement. The minimum down payment for an FHA-backed loan is based on the lower of the appraised value or the sales price. The present requirement for single-family residential loans is 3.5%.

Maximum loan term. Thirty years is the maximum length of the repayment period.

Prepayment privilege. The borrower has the right to pay off the loan at any time without penalty, provided the lender is given prior notice. The lender may charge up to 30 days' interest if the borrower provides less than 30 days' notice.

Assumability. FHA-backed loans on owner-occupied properties are assumable if the buyer is qualified. Lenders and borrowers should check with FHA for current requirements.

Interest rate. The lender and borrower negotiate the interest rate on an FHA-backed loan without any involvement by FHA.

Points, fees and costs. The lender may charge discount points, a loan origination fee, and other such charges. These may be paid by buyer or seller. However, if the seller pays more than a specified percentage of the costs normally paid by a buyer, the FHA may regard these as sales concessions and lower the sales price on which the loan insurance amount is based.

In addition to Section 203(b) loan programs, FHA offers insurance coverage for other loan products. These include:

- home improvement loans
- subsidized loans for low- and middle-income families
- loans for condominiums
- loans for multi-family projects
- graduated-payment loans
- adjustable-rate loans

VA-guaranteed loans

The Veterans Administration (Department of Veterans Affairs) offers *loan guarantees to qualified veterans*. The VA, like the FHA, does not lend money except in certain areas where other financing is not generally available. Instead, the VA partially guarantees permanent long-term loans originated by VA-approved lenders on properties that meet VA standards. The VA's guarantee enables lenders to issue loans with higher loan-to-value ratios than would otherwise be possible. The interest rate on a VA-guaranteed loan is usually lower than one on a conventional loan. The borrower does not pay any premium for the loan guarantee, but does pay a VA funding fee at closing.

Borrower default. The VA reimburses the lender for losses up to the guaranteed amount if foreclosure sale proceeds fail to cover the loan balance.

Appraisal. The property must be appraised by a VA-approved appraiser. The VA issues a *Certificate of Reasonable Value* which creates a maximum value on which the VA-guaranteed portion of the loan will be based. The property must meet certain VA specifications.

Down payment requirement. The VA usually requires no down payment, although the lender may require one.

Maximum loan amount. The VA does not cap the loan amount, but it does limit the liability it can assume, which usually influences the amount an institution will lend. The amount a qualified veteran with full entitlement can borrow without making a downpayment determines the practical loan limits. This amount varies by county. The basic entitlement available to each eligible veteran is $36,000. Lenders will generally lend a maximum of 4 times that amount without a down payment if the veteran is fully qualified and the property appraises for the asking price.

A veteran must apply for a *Certificate of Eligibility* to find out how much the VA will guarantee in a particular situation.

Maximum loan term. The maximum loan term for one- to four-family residences is 30 years. For loans secured by farms, the maximum loan term is 40 years.

Prepayment privilege. The loan may be paid off early without penalty.

Assumability. VA loans are assumable with lender approval. Usually, the person assuming the loan must have VA eligibility, and the assumption may have to be approved by the VA.

Interest rate. Lender and borrower negotiate the interest rate for all VA-insured loans.

Points, fees and costs. The lender may charge discount points, origination fees, and other reasonable costs. These may be paid by seller (with some limits) or buyer, but may not be financed. The VA funding fee, however, may be included in the loan amount. The funding fee is a percentage of the loan amount which varies based on the type of loan, military category, whether the loan is a first-time loan, and whether there is a down payment.

Other VA programs. In addition to insuring loans to veterans, the VA may insure loans for lenders who set up a special account with the VA. The VA may also actually lend money directly when an eligible veteran cannot find other mortgage money locally.

Common loan structures

Variations in the structure of interest rate, term, payments, and principal payback produce a number of commonly recognized loan types. Among these are the following.

Amortizing loan. Amortization provides for gradual repayment of principal and payment of interest over the term of the loan. The borrower's periodic payments to the lender include a portion for interest and a portion for principal. In a fully amortizing mortgage, the principal balance is zero at the end of the term. In a partially amortizing loan, the payments are not sufficient to retire the debt. At the end of the loan term, there is still a principal balance to be paid off.

Negatively amortized loan. Negative amortization causes the loan balance to increase over the term. This occurs if the borrower's periodic payment is insufficient to cover the interest owed for the period. The lender adds the amount of unpaid interest to the borrower's loan balance. Temporary negative amortization occurs on graduated payment loans, and may occur on an adjustable rate mortgage.

Adjustable and fixed rate loans. Loans may have fixed or variable rates of interest over the loan term. Adjustable rate mortgages (ARMs) allow the lender to change the interest rate at specified intervals and by a specified amount. Federal regulations place limits on incremental interest rate increases and on the total amount by which the rate may be increased over the loan term.

Senior and junior loans. When there are multiple loans on a single property, there is an order of priority in the liens which the mortgages create. The first, or senior, loan generally has priority over any subsequent loans. Second loans are riskier than first loans because the senior lender will be satisfied first in case of default. Therefore, interest rates on second mortgages are generally higher than on first mortgages.

Fixed and graduated payment loans. Loans may have variable payment amounts over the term of the loan, or a single fixed payment amount. With a graduated payment mortgage, the payments at the beginning of the loan term are not sufficient to amortize the loan fully, and unpaid interest is added to the principal balance. Payments are later adjusted to a level that will fully amortize the loan's increased balance over the remaining loan term.

Interest-only loan. In an interest-only loan, periodic payments over the loan term apply only to interest owed, not to principal. At the end of the term, the full balance must be paid off in a lump-sum, "balloon" payment. Since these loans have no periodic principal payback, their monthly payments are smaller than amortizing loans for the same amount at the same rate of interest.

Buydown loan. A buydown loan entails a prepayment of interest on a loan. The prepayment effectively lowers the interest rate and the periodic payments for the borrower. Buydowns typically occur in a circumstance where a builder wants to market a new development to a buyer who cannot quite qualify for the necessary loan at market rates. By "buying down" a borrower's mortgage, a builder enables the borrower to obtain the loan. The builder may then pass the costs of the buydown through to the buyer in the form of a higher purchase price.

Seller financing

The seller may provide some or all of the financing for the buyer's purchase. Some of the most common methods of seller financing are purchase money mortgages, including the wraparound, and the contract for deed.

Purchase money mortgage. With a purchase money mortgage, the borrower gives a mortgage and note to the seller to finance some or all of the purchase price of the property. The seller in this case is said to "take back" a note, or to "carry paper," on the property. Purchase money mortgages may be either senior or junior liens.

Wraparound. In a wraparound loan arrangement, the seller receives a junior mortgage from the buyer, and uses the buyer's payments to make the payments on the original first mortgage. A wraparound enables the buyer to obtain financing with a minimum cash investment. It also potentially enables the seller to profit from any difference between a lower interest rate on the senior loan and a higher rate on the wraparound loan. A wraparound is possible only if the senior mortgagee allows it.

Contract for deed. Under a contract for deed arrangement, the seller retains title and the buyer receives possession and equitable title while making payments under the terms of the contract. The seller conveys title when the contract has been fully performed.

Special-purpose loans

Home equity loan. The ostensible purpose of this type of loan is to obtain funds for home improvement. Structurally, the home equity loan is a junior mortgage secured by the homeowner's equity. For some lenders, the maximum home equity loan amount is based on the difference between the property's appraised value and the maximum loan-to-value ratio the lender allows on the property, inclusive of all existing mortgage loans. Thus if a home is appraised at $500,000 and the lender's maximum LTV is 80%, the lender will lend a total of $400,000. If the owner's existing mortgage balance is $325,000, the owner would qualify for a $75,000 home equity loan.

Package loan. A package loan finances the purchase of real estate and personal property. For example, a package loan might finance a furnished condominium, complete with all fixtures and decor.

Construction loan. A construction loan finances construction of improvements. This type of loan is paid out by the lender in installments linked to stages of the construction process. The loan is usually interest-only, and the borrower makes periodic payments based on the amount disbursed so far. As short-term, high-risk financing, the interest rates are usually higher than those for long-term financing. The borrower is expected to find permanent ("take out") financing elsewhere to pay off the temporary loan when construction is complete.

Bridge loan. A bridge, or gap, loan is used to cover a gap in financing between short-term construction financing and long-term permanent financing. For instance, a developer may have difficulty finding a long-term lender to take out the construction lender. However, as the construction loan is expensive and must be paid off as soon as possible, the developer may find an interim lender who will pay off the construction loan but not agree to a long-term loan.

Participation loan. In a participation loan, the lender participates in the income and/or equity of the property, in return for giving the borrower more favorable loan terms than would otherwise be justified. For instance, the borrower makes smaller periodic payments than the interest rate and loan amount require, and the lender makes up the difference by receiving some of the property's income. This type of loan usually involves an income property.

Permanent (take-out) loan. A permanent loan is a long-term loan that "takes out" a construction or short-term lender. The long-term lender pays off the balance on the construction loan when the project is completed, leaving the borrower with a long-term loan under more favorable terms than the construction loan offered.

Reverse annuity. In a reverse annuity mortgage, a homeowner pledges the equity in the home as security for a loan which is paid out in regular monthly amounts over the term of the loan. The homeowner, in effect, is able to convert the equity to cash without losing ownership and possession.

Blanket. A blanket mortgage is secured by more than one property, such as multiple parcels of real estate in a development.

For more information:

FHA loans:	https://entp.hud.gov/idapp/html/hicostlook.cfm
VA loans:	https://www.va.gov/housing-assistance/
HUD:	https://www.hud.gov/resources
FNMA:	http://www.fanniemae.com/portal/index.html
FHLMC:	www.freddiemac.com
GNMA:	https://www.ginniemae.gov/pages/default.aspx
ECOA:	https://www.consumer.ftc.gov/articles/0347-your-equal-credit-opportunity-rights
CFPB:	https://www.consumerfinance.gov/policy-compliance/guidance/tila-respa-disclosure-rule/

17 Real Estate Finance Snapshot Review

ANATOMY OF MORTGAGE LENDING

Mechanics of a loan transaction

- mortgage financing: using borrowed money secured by a mortgage to finance the purchase of real estate

- instruments: note and mortgage or trust deed

- mortgage mechanics: borrower gives lender note and mortgage; lender gives borrower funds and records a lien

- trust deed mechanics: trust deed conveys title from the borrower/trustor to a third-party trustee who holds title on behalf of the lender/beneficiary until the debt is repaid

Financial components of a loan

- original principal: capital amount borrowed on which interest payments are calculated

- loan balance: remaining unpaid principal at any point in the life of the loan

- interest: charge for the use of money; rate fixed or variable

- Annual Percentage Rate (APR) includes interest and all other finance charges; lender must disclose on residential properties

- point: one percent of the loan amount, charged by lender at origination to obtain required return

- term: period of time for repayment of interest and principal

- payment: the periodic payment of interest and/or principal

Promissory note

- legal instrument executed by borrower stating debt amount, loan term, method and timing of repayment, interest rate, promise to pay; may repeat other provisions from mortgage document or deed of trust; negotiable instrument assignable to a third party

Mortgage document and trust deed

- the legal documents which pledge the property as collateral for the loan

- may include clauses covering payment of principal and interest, prepayment, late charges, escrow for taxes and insurance, liens, insurance requirements, occupancy and maintenance, lender's rights, private mortgage insurance, inspection, and other conditions of performance

INITIATING A MORTGAGE LOAN

The loan application

- borrower provides personal and property data; supporting documentation: appraisal report, credit report, purchase contract, income and/or employment verification

- lenders must accept all completed applications and notify applicants about disposition of application

Mortgage loan underwriting

- process of evaluating borrower's ability to repay and value of the property

- loan-to-value ratio: relationship of loan amount to property value, expressed as a percentage

QUALIFYING FOR A MORTGAGE LOAN

Equal Credit Opportunity Act

- lender must evaluate applicant according to applicant's own income and credit information

Income qualification

- income ratio and debt ratio qualify borrower's income; income ratio applied to gross income determines housing expense maximum; debt ratio takes revolving debt into account

Cash qualification

- lender verifies applicant's sources of cash for down payment; extra cash enhances income qualification evaluation

Net worth

- extent to which applicant's assets exceed liabilities as a further source of reserves

Credit evaluation

- lender obtains credit reports to evaluate applicant's payment behavior

Loan commitment

- written pledge by lender to grant loan under specific terms; firm, lock-in, conditional, take-out

CLOSING A LOAN

- usually simultaneous with closing of real estate transaction; transfer of funds, signing of documents, escrow deposits

LAWS AFFECTING MORTGAGE LENDING

Truth-in-Lending and Regulation Z

- Reg Z implements Truth-in-Lending Simplification and Reform Act and Consumer Credit Protection Act

- provisions: lender must disclose finance charges and APR prior to closing; borrower has limited right of rescission; lender must follow disclosure requirements in advertising

Equal Credit Opportunity Act

- ECOA prohibits discrimination in lending

Real Estate Settlements and Procedures Act

- RESPA standardizes settlement practices

- provisions: lender must provide CFPB booklet explaining loans, settlement costs and procedures; lender must provide CFPB Loan Estimate of settlement costs within three days of application; lender must provide CFPB Closing Disclosure three days before loan consummation

National Flood Insurance Act

- borrowers of "federally-related loans" must obtain flood insurance if property is in designated flood-hazard area

THE MORTGAGE MARKET

Supply and demand for money

- relationship between money supply and demand affects interest rates, consumer prices, availability of mortgage money

- Federal Reserve controls: T-bills; reserve requirement, discount rate

The primary mortgage market

- originates mortgage loans directly to borrowers; savings and loans, commercial banks, mutual savings banks, life insurance companies, mortgage bankers, credit unions

The secondary mortgage market

- buys existing loans to provide liquidity to primary lenders; Fannie Mae, Ginnie Mae, Freddie Mac, investment firms, life insurance companies, pension funds

Role of FNMA, GNMA, and FHLMC

- FNMA buys conventional, FHA- and VA-backed loans and pooled mortgages; guarantees payment on mortgage-backed securities; GNMA guarantees payment on certain types of loans; FHLMC buys and pools mortgages; sells mortgage-backed securities

TYPES OF REAL ESTATE LOANS

Conventional loans

- permanent, long-term loans not insured by FHA or guaranteed by VA

FHA-insured loans

- insured loans granted by FHA-approved lenders to borrowers who meet FHA qualifications

VA-guaranteed loans

- guaranteed loans granted by VA-approved lenders to qualified veterans

Common loan structures

- amortizing, negative amortizing, interest only, fixed rate, adjustable rate, senior, junior, fixed or graduated payment, balloon, buydown

Seller financing

- purchase money mortgages: loans by the seller to the property buyer for all or part of the purchase price; contract for deed: installment sale where seller finances buyer and retains title until contract terms are met

Special- purpose loans

- home equity, package, construction, bridge, equity participation, take-out, reverse annuity, and blanket

18 Real Estate Investment

Investment Fundamentals
Real Estate as an Investment
Real Estate Investment Entities
Taxation of Real Estate Investments
Investment Analysis of a Residence
Investment Analysis of an Income Property

INVESTMENT FUNDAMENTALS

Investment characteristics
Rewards
Risks
Types of investments

Investment characteristics

The idea of investment is simple: take something of value and put it to work in some way to increase its value over time. With any investment, one wants the original investment to grow, without losing it. This idea is called **conservation of capital**. Unfortunately, no investment is truly secure. External conditions change, and the investment itself can change. Even if you do nothing with it, its value does not remain constant.

Risk versus return. The general rule in investments is that the safer the investment, the more slowly it gains in value. The more you want it to gain, and the more quickly, the more you must risk losing it. How much do you want to earn, and how much are you willing to risk to earn it? Reward in investing corresponds directly to the degree of risk.

Management. Another aspect of investment is the amount of attention you must pay to it to make it work. You can deposit cash in a passbook account and forget about it. You can use your cash to buy a business and then run the business yourself to make your asset grow and earn. How much do you want to be involved in managing your investment?

Liquidity. The issue of exchangeability is an important one in investment. How easy is it to recover your invested resource, without loss, and exchange it for another one that you want? If there is a **market** for the type of resource you have-- other people want to buy and sell it for themselves-- your investment is **liquid**. The most liquid form of financial investment is generally cash, since cash is itself a medium of exchange and people always want it. A more illiquid investment is one which takes a long time to exchange for something you prefer to own. How long are you willing to wait to recover your invested resource and its earnings?

Rewards

The basic aim of financial investment is to increase one's wealth, to add value to what you have. This can occur in several ways.

Income. An investment can generate income in some way on a periodic basis. You may consume this cash, spending it for goods and services that, when used up, have no further value. Or, you may use the cash to put into another investment.

Appreciation. Your invested asset itself may gain value over time because of an increase in market demand for it. When you sell or exchange it for something else you prefer to have, you get more than you originally put into the investment.

Leverage. You may pledge the value of your resource to borrow funds in order to make an investment that is larger than your own resource permits you to do directly. The small resource is used as a lever to make a larger investment, and thus increases your opportunity to benefit from income, appreciation, and the other rewards of investment.

Tax benefits. Some investments receive treatment under tax laws that enables the investor to reduce or defer the amount of tax owed. Tax dollars you don't have to pay are dollars you have available for some other use, such as consuming or further investing.

Risks

Investment risks come from a variety of general sources, including the market, business operations, the value of money, and changes in the interest rate.

Market risk. Changes in the demand for your invested resource may cause your investment to lose value and to become illiquid.

Business risk. Changes in the operation of a business with which your investment is connected may reduce or eliminate the income- and appreciation-earning capacity of your investment.

Purchasing power risk. Changes in the value of money as an exchange medium, such as through inflation, may decrease the practical value of your invested resource.

Financial risk. Changes in financial markets, particularly in interest rates, may reduce the value of your investment by making it less desirable to others and by making it more expensive for you to maintain.

An investment may fail to produce any or all of the desired investment rewards listed earlier. The expected income may not be realized. The invested asset may fail to appreciate as expected. It may even decline in value. Perhaps even worse, you may be called on to **add** to the investment just to keep it in place. Your leverage may turn against you, becoming **negative leverage**. This is the situation when your cost of borrowing funds to make the investment becomes greater than the income the investment returns to you. Finally, your expectation of a tax advantage may be disappointed. Tax laws are constantly changing.

Types of investments

Four of the most important types of investment are investments in money, equity, debt, and real estate.

Money investments. A money investment is one in which the basic form of the investment remains money. Examples are: deposit accounts, certificates of deposit, money funds, and annuities. The basic reward from a money investment comes in the form of interest. Money investments are relatively safe, with correspondingly conservative rates of return.

Debt investments. A debt investment is one in which an investor buys a debt instrument. Examples are bonds, notes, mortgages, and bond mutual funds. The basic reward comes in the form of interest. Debt investments are usually riskier than money investments and less risky than stocks or real estate.

Equity investments. An equity investment is one in which an investor buys an ownership interest in a business concern. Examples are stocks and stock mutual funds. The basic rewards come in the form of dividends and appreciation of share value. Equity investments are generally riskier than money and debt investments.

Real estate investments. A real estate investment is one in which an investor *buys real estate for its investment benefits rather than primarily for its utility*. It may have the features of both an equity and debt investment, depending on the type of real estate involved and numerous other factors, such as the type of interest one owns. A real estate investor may invest in an income-producing property or a non-income producing property.

> ▶ **Non-income property**
>
> a residential property used as the investor's primary residence. The basic reward, beyond the enjoyment of use, comes in the form of appreciation. There may also be tax benefits, depending on how the purchase is financed.

> ▶ **Income property**
>
> a property owned specifically for the investment rewards it offers. Examples are multi-family residential properties, retail stores, industrial properties, and office buildings. Rewards come in any or all of the forms mentioned earlier: income, appreciation, leverage and tax advantages.

REAL ESTATE AS AN INVESTMENT

Risk and reward
Illiquidity
Management requirements

Real estate investments participate in the general risks and rewards of all investments. However, real estate investments are often complex. They are also distinguished by their lack of liquidity and by the amount of management they require. In addition, each investor has specific aims and circumstances that affect the viability of any particular real estate investment for that individual. Licensees who lack expertise in the area of real estate investment analysis should refer potential investors to a competent advisor. Nevertheless, a licensee should be familiar with the basics of real estate as an investment.

Risk and reward

Capital put into real estate is always subject to the full range of risk factors: market changes, income shortfalls, negative leverage, tax law changes, and poor overall return.

Market demand for a specific type of property can decline. For example, a business district's retailers may vacate stores in an area in order to obtain better space in a new shopping center. Market downturns leave the income property investor with an unmarketable property or one which can only be re-leased at a loss of some portion of the original investment. Thus the expected reward from income or appreciation may never be obtained.

Another risk of the investment property is the cost of development or operation. If start-up costs or ongoing operating costs exceed rental income, the owner must dip into additional capital resources to maintain the investment until its income increases. If income does not rise, or if costs do not decline, the investor can simply run out of money.

Leverage is a constant risk in real estate investment. If the property fails to generate sufficient revenue, the costs of borrowed money can bankrupt the owner, just as development and operating costs can. Investors often overlook the fact that leverage only works when the yield on the investment exceeds the costs of borrowed funds.

Tax law is an ongoing risk in long-term real estate investment. If the investor's tax circumstances change, or if the tax laws do, the investor may end up paying more capital gains and income taxes than planned, undermining the return on the investment. An investor needs to consider carefully the value of such potential tax benefits as deductions for mortgage interest, tax losses, deferred gains, exemptions, and tax credits for certain types of real estate investment.

Another consideration is *opportunity cost*. Opportunity cost is the return that an investor could earn on capital invested with minimal risk. If the real estate investment, with all its attendant risk, cannot yield a greater return than an investment elsewhere involving less risk, then the opportunity cost is too high for the real estate investment. Despite all the risks, real estate remains a popular investment, because, historically, the rewards have outweighed the risks. Real estate has proven to be relatively resistant to adverse inflationary trends that have hurt money, debt, and stock investments. In addition, real estate has proven to be a viable investment in view of the economy's continued expansion over the last fifty years.

Illiquidity

Compared with other classes of investment, real estate is relatively illiquid. Even in the case of liquidating a single-family residence, one can expect a marketing period of at least several months in most markets. In addition, it takes time for the buyer to obtain financing and to complete all the other phases of closing the transaction. Commercial and investment properties can take much longer, depending on market conditions, leases, construction, permitting, and a host of other factors. The investor who is in a hurry to dispose of such an investment can expect to receive a lower sales price than may be ideal. Compare this with the ease of drawing money out of a bank account or selling a stock.

Management requirements

Real estate tends to require a high degree of investor involvement in management of the investment. Even raw land requires some degree of maintenance to preserve its value: drainage, fencing, payment of taxes, and periodic inspection, to name a few tasks. Improved properties often require extensive management, including repairs, maintenance, onsite leasing, tenant relations, security, and fiscal management.

REAL ESTATE INVESTMENT ENTITIES

Direct
Syndicate and partnership
Real Estate Investment Trust
Real Estate Mortgage Investment Conduit

Direct

Individuals, corporations or other investor entities may invest as **active investors** in a property by buying it directly and taking responsibility for managing and operating the property.

Syndicate and partnership

A real estate **syndicate** is a group of investors who combine resources to buy, develop, and/or operate a property.

A **general partnership** is a syndicate in which all members participate equally in managing the investment and in the profits or losses it generates. The group designates a trustee to hold title in the name of the syndicate.

A **limited partnership** is a syndicate in which a **general partner** organizes, operates and is generally responsible for the partnership's interests in the property. **Limited partners** invest money in the partnership but do not participate in operating the property. These limited partners are **passive investors**.

Real Estate Investment Trust (REIT)

In a Real Estate Investment Trust, investors buy certificates in the trust, and the trust in turn invests in mortgages or real estate. Investors receive income according to the number of shares they own. A trust must receive at least 75% of its income from real estate to qualify as a REIT, and if certain other conditions are met, the trust does not have to pay any corporate income tax.

Real Estate Mortgage Investment Conduit (REMIC)

A REMIC is a kind of partnership entity formed to hold a fixed pool of mortgages that are secured by real property. The entity issues two kinds of interest. Holders of residual interests are treated, for tax purposes, as partners. Holders of regular interests are regarded as owning debt instruments. Income (or loss) received by regular or residual interest holders is treated as **portfolio** income or loss, and is not included in determining losses from **passive** activities.

TAXATION OF REAL ESTATE INVESTMENTS

Taxable income
Cost recovery
Gain on sale
Interest
Passive activities

Real estate investments are taxed on the income they produce and on the increase in value, or gain, when the investment is sold. These forms of taxation are distinct from the ad valorem taxation of real estate.

Taxable Income

Taxable income from investment real estate is *the gross income received minus any expenses, deductions or exclusions that current tax law allows*. Taxable income from real estate is added to the investor's other income and taxed at the investor's marginal tax rate. The "Investment Analysis of an Income Property" section below gives details.

Cost recovery

Cost recovery, or **depreciation**, allows the owner of income property to deduct a portion of the property's value from gross income each year over the life of the asset. The "life of the asset" and the deductible portion are defined by law. In theory, the owner recovers the full cost of the investment if it is held to the end of the asset's economic life as defined by the Internal Revenue Service. At the time of selling the asset, the accumulated cost recovery is subtracted from the investment's original value as part of determining the taxable capital gain.

Cost recovery is allowed only for income properties and that portion of a non-income property which is used to produce income. It applies only to improvements. Land cannot be depreciated. The part of a property which can be depreciated is called the **depreciable basis**.

Depreciation schedules. Residential rental properties are depreciated over a period of 27.5 years. The basic annual deduction for such property is 3.636%, with adjustments for the month of the taxable year in which the property was placed in service. Non-residential income properties placed in service after 1994 are depreciated over a period of 39 years (basic annual percentage is 2.564%). The proper method of depreciation should be determined in consultation with a qualified tax advisor.

Gain on sale

When real estate, whether non-income or income, is sold, a *taxable event* occurs. If the sale proceeds *exceed* the original cost of the investment, subject to some adjustments, there is a **capital gain** that is subject to tax. If the sales proceeds are less than the original cost with adjustments, there is a **capital loss**.

An investor can sometimes defer the reporting of gain or loss, and, hence, taxation of gain, by participating in an exchange of like-kind assets. The legislation that deals with like-kind exchanges is contained in Section 1031 of the IRS code. These tax-deferred exchanges are sometimes called **Section 1031 exchanges** and **Starker exchanges**, named for an investor who won a case against the IRS.

To qualify under Section 1031, there must have been a legitimate exchange of the assets involved. The property being transferred must have been held for productive use in a trade or business or held as an investment and must be exchanged for property that will also be used in a trade or business or be held as an investment. Tax on gain is deferred until the investment or business property is sold and not exchanged.

Interest

Mortgage interest incurred by loans to buy, build, or materially improve a primary or secondary residence is deductible from gross income. The interest on a home equity loan may be deducted only if the loan is used to "buy, build or substantially improve" the home that secures the loan. Principal payments on a loan are *not* deductible.

For income properties that are held as investments, interest on debts incurred to finance the investment is deductible as **investment interest** up to the amount of net income received from the property.

Passive activities

Passive activities are business activities in which the taxpayer does not materially participate. Included are interests in **limited partnerships** and **rental** activities. Losses from such activities may be used to offset income from other passive activities. Passive losses, with certain limitations, may be carried forward to future years or accumulated and deducted from capital gain at the time of sale.

INVESTMENT ANALYSIS OF A RESIDENCE

Appreciation
Deductibles
Tax liability
Gains tax exclusion

Investment analysis examines the economic performance of an investment. The analysis includes costs, income, taxation, appreciation, and return.

A property acquired and used as a primary residence is an example of a non-income property. If a portion of a residence is used for business (i.e., a home office), this portion only may be treated as an income property for tax purposes. Since, by definition, a non-income property does not generate income, its value as an investment must come from one or more of the other sources: appreciation, leverage, or tax benefits.

Appreciation

Appreciation is the increase in value of an asset over time. A simple way to estimate appreciation on a primary residence is to subtract the price originally paid from the estimated current market value:

Current value - original price = total appreciation

For example, if a house was bought for $300,000 and its estimated market value now is $400,000, it has appreciated by $100,000.

Original price:	$300,000
Current market value:	$400,000
Total appreciation:	$100,000

Total appreciation can be stated as a percentage increase over the original price by dividing the estimated total appreciation by the original price.

The house in the last example has appreciated by 33%:

$$\frac{(Total\ appreciation)}{Original\ price} = \%\ appreciated$$

$$\frac{100,000}{300,000} = 33\%$$

To estimate the percentage of *annual appreciation*, divide the percent appreciated by the number of years the house has been owned:

$$\frac{\%\ total\ appreciation}{years\ owned} = \%\ appreciation\ per\ year$$

If the house in the previous example has been owned for three years, the annual appreciation has been 11%.

$$\frac{33\%}{3 \ years} = 11\% \ appreciation \ per \ year$$

Deductibles

The primary tax benefit available to the owner of a non-income property is the *annual deduction for mortgage interest*. The portion of annual mortgage payments that goes to repay principal must be subtracted to determine the amount paid for interest. Principal repayment is not deductible. Furthermore, depreciation is not allowed for non-income properties.

Tax liability

The seller of a principal residence may owe tax on capital gain that results from the sale. The IRS defines gain on the sale of a home as **amount realized** from the sale minus the **adjusted basis** of the home sold.

Amount realized. The amount realized, also known as **net proceeds from sale**, is expressed by the formula:

```
    sale price
-   costs of sale
    ----------
    amount realized
```

The sale price is the total amount the seller receives for the home. This includes money, notes, mortgages or other debts the buyer assumes as part of the sale.

Costs of sale include brokerage commissions, relevant advertising, legal fees, seller-paid points and other closing costs. Certain *fixing-up expenses*, as discussed further below, can be deducted from the amount realized to derive an **adjusted sale price** for the purpose of postponing taxation on gain.

For example, Larry and Mary sold their home for $350,000. Their selling costs, including the commission they paid Broker Betty and amounts paid to inspectors, a surveyor, and the title company, amounted to ten percent of the selling price, or $35,000. The amount they realized from the sale was therefore $315,000.

Adjusted basis. Basis is a measurement of how much is invested in the property for tax purposes. Assuming that the property was acquired through purchase, the **beginning basis** is the cost of acquiring the property. Cost includes cash and debt obligations, and such other settlement costs as legal and recording fees, abstract fees, surveys, charges for installing utilities, transfer taxes, title insurance, and any other amounts the buyer pays for the seller.

The beginning basis is increased or decreased by certain types of expenditures made while the property is owned. Basis is increased by the cost of **capital improvements** made to the property. Assessments for local improvements such as roads and sidewalks also increase the basis. Examples of capital improvements are: putting on an addition, paving a driveway, replacing a roof, adding central air conditioning, and rewiring the home.

Basis is decreased by any amounts the owner received for such things as easements.

The basic formula for **adjusted basis** is:

	Beginning basis
+	capital improvements
-	exclusions, credits or other amounts received
	------------------------------
	adjusted basis

For example, Mary and Larry originally paid $200,000 for their home. They spent an additional $10,000 on a new central heating and cooling unit. Their adjusted basis at the time of selling it is therefore $210,000.

Gain on sale. The gain on sale of a primary residence is represented by the basic formula:

	amount realized (net sales proceeds)
-	adjusted basis
	------------
	gain on sale

Gain on sale, if it does not qualify for an exclusion under current tax law, is taxable.

Exhibit 18.1 Gain on Sale

	Selling price of old home	$350,000
-	Selling costs	35,000
=	Amount realized	315,000
	Beginning basis of old home	200,000
+	Capital improvements	10,000
=	Adjusted basis of old home	210,000
	Amount realized	315,000
-	Adjusted basis	210,000
=	Gain on sale	105,000

In the case of Mary and Larry, their capital gain was $315,000 - $210,000, or $105,000. They will owe tax on this amount in the year of the sale unless they qualify for the exclusion described below.

Gains tax exclusion   Tax law provides an exclusion of $250,000 for an individual taxpayer and $500,000 for married taxpayers filing jointly. The exclusion of gain from sale of a residence can be claimed *every two years*, provided the taxpayer

1. owned the property for at least two years during the five
    years preceding the date of sale;

2. used the property as principal residence for a total of two
    years during that five-year period;

3. has waited two years since the last use of the exclusion for any
    sale.

Losses are not deductible, and there is no carry-over of any unused portion of the exclusion. Postponed gains from a previous home sale under the earlier rollover rules reduce the basis of the current home if that home was a qualifying replacement home under the old rule.

INVESTMENT ANALYSIS OF AN INCOME PROPERTY

Pre-tax cash flow
Tax liability
After-tax cash flow
Investment performance

Income properties are those which are held primarily for the generation of income. In addition to commercial and investment properties such as office buildings, this category includes residential rental properties. An important difference between income and non-income properties is that deductions for depreciation are allowed on income properties. Income properties, like non-income properties, generate a gain (or loss) on sale, and they also create an annual income stream. The annual income streams are determined on both a pre-tax and after-tax basis in order to determine the productivity of the investment.

Pre-tax cash flow

Cash flow is the difference between the amount of actual cash flowing into the investment as revenue and out of the investment for expenses, debt service, and all other items. Cash flow concerns cash items only, and therefore excludes depreciation, which is not a cash expense **Pre-tax cash flow**, or cash flow before taxation, is calculated as follows:

	potential rental income	
-	vacancy and collection loss	
=	effective rental income	
+	other income	
=	gross operating income (GOI)	
-	operating expenses	
-	reserves	
=	net operating income (NOI)	
-	debt service	
=	pre-tax cash flow	

Potential rental income is the annual amount that would be realized if the property is fully leased or rented at the scheduled rate. **Vacancy and collection loss** is rental income lost because of vacancies or tenants' failure to pay rent. **Effective rental income** is the potential income adjusted for these losses. To that is added any **other income** the property generates, such as from laundry or parking charges, to obtain **gross operating income**. **Operating expenses** paid by the landlord include such items as utilities and maintenance. These are deducted from gross operating income. Some owners also set aside a cash **reserve** each year to build up a fund for capital replacements in the future, for example, to replace a roof or a furnace. Cash reserves are <u>not</u> deductible for tax purposes until spent as deductible repairs or maintenance. The remainder is **net operating income (NOI)**. When the annual amount paid for **debt service**, including principal and interest, is subtracted, the remainder is the **pre-tax cash flow**.

For instance, a small office building of 3,500 square feet rents at $20 per square foot. If fully rented, the annual rental income would be $70,000. Historically, the property averages $4,200 in vacancy and collection losses. Equipment rental will provide an additional $2,000 per year in income. The owner will have to pay operating expenses amounting to ten dollars per square foot, or $35,000 per year. The owner sets aside one dollar per square foot, or $3,500 per year, for reserves. The owner financed the purchase of the building with a loan that requires annual debt service in the amount of $20,000. The pre-tax cash flow for the building is illustrated in the following exhibit.

Exhibit 18.2 Pre-tax Cash Flow

	potential rental income	$70,000
-	vacancy and collection loss	4,200
=	effective rental income	65,800
+	other income	2,000
=	gross operating income (GOI)	67,800
-	operating expenses	35,000
-	reserves	3,500
=	net operating income (NOI)	29,300
-	debt service	20,000
=	pre-tax cash flow	9,300

Tax liability   The owner's tax liability on taxable income from the property is based on *taxable income* rather than cash flow. Taxable income and tax liability are calculated as follows:

	net operating income (NOI)
+	reserves
-	interest expense
-	cost recovery expense
=	taxable income
x	tax rate
=	tax liability

Taxable income is net operating income minus all allowable deductions. Cost recovery expense is allowed as a deduction, while allowances for reserves and payments on loan principal payback are not allowed. Thus, since reserves were deducted from gross operating income to determine NOI, this amount must be added back in. As only the interest portion of debt service is deductible, the principal amount must be removed from the debt service payments and the *interest expense* deducted from NOI. Taxable income, multiplied by the owner's marginal tax bracket, gives the **tax liability**.

Note on tax rate: when a rental property is owned as an individual or by way of a pass-through entity (partnership, LLC treated as a partnership for tax purposes, or S corporation), its net income is taxed at the individual's personal marginal income tax rate. The next exhibit shows the tax liability for the previous example using an individual rate of 24%.

Exhibit 18.3 Tax Liability

	net operating income (NOI)	29,300
+	reserves	3,500
-	interest expense	10,000
-	cost recovery expense	22,000
=	taxable income	800
x	tax rate (24%)	
=	tax liability	192

After-tax cash flow   After-tax cash flow is the amount of income from the property that actually goes into the owner's pocket *after income tax is paid*. It is figured as:

	pre-tax cash flow
-	tax liability
=	after-tax cash flow

The after-tax cash flow for the sample property is illustrated in the following exhibit.

Exhibit 18.4 After-tax Cash Flow

	pre-tax cash flow	9,300
-	tax liability	224
=	after-tax cash flow	9,076

Investment performance

Investors measure the investment performance of an income property in many different ways, depending on their needs. A few of the common measures are:

$$\frac{Net\ operating\ income}{price} = return\ on\ investment\ (ROI)$$

$$\frac{cash\ flow}{cash\ invested} = cash\text{-}on\text{-}cash\ return\ (C\ on\ C)$$

$$\frac{cash\ flow}{equity} = return\ on\ equity\ (ROE)$$

Other measures of return use the process of **discounted cash flow analysis**. These methods, chief of which is probably **internal rate of return (IRR)**, require an estimate of projected after-tax proceeds from sale of the property. A licensee who does not have the expertise necessary for these more complicated measures should refer clients to a qualified investment expert.

18 Real Estate Investment Snapshot Review

INVESTMENT FUNDAMENTALS

Investment characteristics
- the greater the risk, the higher the expected return
- some investments require more investor involvement than others
- some investments are more liquid (convertible to cash) than others

Rewards
- investors seek to increase wealth through income, appreciation, leverage and tax benefits

Risks
- risks: changes in supply and demand for the investment (market risk), changes in businesses with which the investment is connected (business risk), changes in the value of money (purchasing power risk), and changes in interest rates (financial risk)

Types of investments
- among the investor's choices are investments in money (e.g., certificates of deposit), equity (e.g., stocks), debt (e.g., bonds and mortgages), and real estate (income and non-income properties)

REAL ESTATE AS AN INVESTMENT

Risk and reward
- the real estate investor must weigh the potential risks and returns inherent in market variability, expected vs. real income, use of borrowing leverage, changes in tax treatment of capital gains and income, and the cost of capital

Illiquidity
- real estate is generally less liquid than other investment types: it takes time to market a property

Management requirements
- real estate tends to require more investor involvement than other investments do: maintenance, management, operation

REAL ESTATE INVESTMENT ENTITIES

Direct
- buying a property and taking responsibility for management and operation

Syndicate and partnership
- a group of investors pool resources to buy, develop and/or operate a property

Real Estate Investment Trust
- REIT: investors buy certificates in a trust that invests in mortgages or real estate and receive income according to shares owned

Real Estate Mortgage Investment Conduit
- REMIC: investors hold residual or regular interests in an entity that holds a pool of mortgages secured by real property

TAXATION OF REAL ESTATE INVESTMENTS

Taxable income
- gross income received minus allowable expenses, deductions and exclusions

Cost recovery
- deduction of a portion of a property's value from gross income each year over the

Gain on sale
- an excess of proceeds from sale of a property over the original cost of the property, subject to adjustments

Interest
- mortgage interest is deductible from annual gross income from a property, subject to limitations

Passive activities
- business activities in which the taxpayer does not materially participate, including interests in limited partnerships and rental activities; losses from such activities can be used to offset income from other passive activities

INVESTMENT ANALYSIS OF A RESIDENTIAL PROPERTY

Appreciation
- increase in the value of an asset over time; may be stated as a difference between the original price and current market value, or as a percentage increase over the original price; not a true measure of investment return

Deductibles
- for non-income properties, primary tax benefit is annual deduction for mortgage

Tax liability
- the seller of a principle residence owes tax on any capital gain that results from the sale unless excluded; capital gain is defined as the amount realized minus the adjusted basis

Gains tax exclusion
- up to $250,000 for a single seller and $500,000 for a married couple can be excluded from gains tax every two years

INVESTMENT ANALYSIS OF AN INCOME PROPERTY

Pre-tax cash flow
- annual pre-tax cash flow is net operating income minus debt service

Tax liability
- tax liability on income from a property is based on taxable income: net operating income minus interest expense and cost recovery

After-tax cash flow
- annual after-tax cash flow is pre-tax cash flow minus tax liability

Investment performance
- a few common measures of investment performance are:
  - return on investment (net operating income divided by price)
  - cash-on-cash return (cash flow divided by cash invested)
  - return on equity (cash flow divided by equity)
  - discounted cash flow analysis
  - internal rate of return

19 Real Estate Taxation

Taxing Entities
Ad Valorem Taxation
Special Assessments
Tax Lien Enforcement

TAXING ENTITIES

State government
County and local government
Tax districts

Real estate taxation refers to the taxation of real estate as property. Real estate property taxes are imposed by "taxing entities" or "taxing districts" at county and local levels of government.

There are *no federal taxes on real property*. The Constitution of the United States specifically prohibits such taxes. The federal government does, however, tax income derived from real property and gains realized on the sale of real property. The federal government can impose a tax lien against property for failure to pay any tax due the Internal Revenue Service.

State government

States may legally levy taxes on real property, but most delegate this power to counties, cities, townships and local taxing districts. Some states place limits on how local governments may levy such taxes. States may impose a tax lien against property for failure to pay any real property taxes which the state has levied or delegated to local taxing bodies.

County and local government

Counties, cities and municipalities, townships and special tax districts levy taxes on real property to raise funds for providing local services. It is common for the county to collect all real property taxes and distribute it among the other taxing bodies.

Tax districts

County and local governments establish **tax districts** to collect funds for providing specific services. The boundaries of such districts typically do not coincide with municipal boundaries. The major tax district in most areas is the school district. Other important tax districts are those for fire protection, community colleges, and parks.

A property tax bill might include tax levies from such districts as the following.

- bridge and highway	- health services
- nursing home	- historical museum
- storm water management	- sanitorium
- township	- forest preserve/land management
- fire district	- public library district
- school district	- park district
- retirement fund	- community college district

In addition to generally established tax districts, a local government authority may establish a **special tax district** to pay for the cost of a specific improvement or service that benefits that area. For instance, a special tax district might be created to fund extension of municipal water service to a newly incorporated area. Unlike a permanent tax district such as the school district, a special tax district is temporary, ceasing to exist once the costs of the specific project have been paid for.

AD VALOREM TAXATION

Tax base totalling
Homestead exemption
Other exemptions
Tax rate derivation
Tax billing and collection

General property taxes are levied on an ad valorem basis, meaning that they are based on the **assessed value** of the property. Assessed value is determined according to state law, usually by a county or township assessor or appraiser. The actual tax, though based on assessed value, may be derived as a legislated percentage of the assessed value. Land and improvements may be assessed separately. Ad valorem taxes are paid annually.

Tax base totalling   The **tax base** of an area is the total of the appraised or assessed values of all real property within the area's boundaries, excluding partially or totally exempt properties:

tax base = assessed values - exemptions

Taxing entities generate the annual revenues they require by levying taxes on the tax base. The **tax rate**, or **millage rate**, determines how much of a tax levy the tax base will receive. The tax rate for each taxing entity is calculated by dividing the amount of revenue required by the tax base. This rate is then applied to the taxable value of each individual real property to determine its tax levy.

Value assessment. County or township officers, called assessors or appraisers, value the real property within their jurisdiction for purposes of levying taxes. This valuation process results in an **assessed value**. Assessment practices differ from state to state. In many states, assessed value does not reflect the market value that an appraisal for other purposes might aim to estimate. For instance, in some areas, assessors use a sales comparison approach to assess the value of land and a cost approach to value improvements.

The role of the assessor in the taxing process is limited to making the valuation and notifying the owner of the assessed value; other tax officials determine the tax rate and the tax levy.

Equalization. Some taxing bodies recognize that local assessments can lead to unfairly high or low values for properties in certain areas. Therefore the jurisdiction may establish **equalization factors** to level out the unevenness of valuations. For instance, if assessed values of properties in one county are consistently ten percent below the average for other counties, an **equalization board** may multiply each assessed value in that county by a factor of 110% to raise them to the average level for the state.

Appeals. Property owners may object to the assessed value of their property, but not to the tax rate. An owner usually has a certain period to protest after receiving notice of the assessed value. According to local law, a property owner must present evidence that the assessor made an error to a review board or appeal board. Typical evidence would include market data on comparable properties that sold recently, or evidence that neighboring properties had less appreciation or even declined in assessed value in comparison with the protestor's property. An owner who is dissatisfied with the actions of the appeals or review board can take the protest to court.

Homestead exemption

A homestead is a parcel of real property that is owned and occupied as a family home. Some states exempt a portion of the value of the homestead from judgments to protect families against eviction by creditors. States and counties may *exempt a portion of the assessed value of the principal residence from property taxation.*

A property owner generally qualifies for a homestead exemption by meeting two criteria:

> ▶ is head of a family
> ▶ resides on the property for a required length of time

Some states also allow a single person to claim the homestead exemption.

Depending on state law, home owners may have to apply every year for the exemption, or they may receive it automatically without filing.

Other exemptions

Properties. Most states exempt certain types of property from property taxes. Certain classes of property owner may also be exempted or have a reduced liability. Exempted are:

> ▶ **Government-owned properties**
>
>   real properties owned by federal, state, and local governments are **immune** from real property taxation

▶   **Properties owned by non-profit organizations**

real properties owned by churches and non-profit organizations are **exempt** from real property taxation

Owner classes. Miscellaneous exemptions may be granted to classes of property owner, such as: senior citizens, widows, and disabled individuals.

States and municipalities may also offer property tax reductions or exemptions to certain industries to encourage economic growth.

Tax rate derivation

Tax district budgeting. The derivation of a tax rate, or millage rate, begins with the taxing body determining its funding requirements to provide services for the year. This requirement is formalized in the annual budget. Then the county or district looks at its sources of revenue, such as sales taxes, business taxes, income taxes, state and federal grants, fees, and so forth. The part of the budgeted expenditures that cannot be funded from other income sources *must come from real property taxes*. This budgetary shortfall becomes the ad valorem **tax levy**. The tax levy is derived every year, since budget requirements and revenue tallies are performed on an annual cycle.

Tax rate. Each individual taxing body has its own tax rate. The tax rate is determined by dividing the taxing body's budgeted amount to be collected from real estate taxes by the tax base:

$$\frac{\text{tax requirement}}{\text{tax base}} = \text{tax rate (millage rate)}$$

If, for example, a taxing body needs $500,000 from property taxes, and the tax base for the district is $15,000,000, the tax rate for this body is:

$$\frac{500,000}{15,000,000} = .03$$

This tax rate of .03 or 3% may be expressed in a number of ways, depending on local practice: as **mills**, as dollars per $100 of assessed value, or as dollars per $1,000 of assessed value. A mill is one one-thousandth of a dollar ($.001). A tax rate of one mill means that the owner pays one dollar for every thousand dollars of assessed value. Thus the rate of .03 above could be expressed as:

30 mills
$3 per $100
$30 per $1,000
3 percent

Tax rate limitations. Some states, counties or other taxing districts place limitations or **caps** on the absolute millage rate or the annual increase in millage for property taxes. In such situations, taxing bodies are *forced to limit their budget requirements*, unless there has been a sufficient increase in tax base to produce the required funds without raising the millage rate.

Tax billing and collection

Individual owner billings. Each property owner's tax bill is determined by multiplying the tax rate for each taxing district times the **taxable value** of the property. Taxable value is *the assessed value after all exemptions and adjustments have been taken into account.*

For example, a certain property is owned and occupied as a primary residence and qualifies for a homestead exemption. The assessed value of the property is $240,000, and the exemption is $75,000. The property is taxed by the school district at a rate of 5 mills, and by the county at a rate of 2 mills. The property tax bill for these items would be calculated as follows.

Exhibit 19.1 Tax Bill Calculation

I. Taxable Value

	assessed value	$ 240,000
-	homestead exemption	$ 75,000
	taxable value	$ 165,000

II. Tax Calculations

	taxable value	$ 165,000
x	5 mills—school dist.	.005
	school tax	$ 825

	taxable value	$ 165,000
x	2 mills—county	.002
	county tax	$ 330

III. Totaling

	school tax	$ 825
+	county tax	$ 330
	total tax bill	$ 1,155

Payment deadlines are usually set by law and differ from region to region. Different taxing bodies may have different fiscal years, and as a result may issue tax bills at different times of the year. It is more common for a county to issue a bill that consolidates the bills of all the lesser taxing bodies. The consolidated bill may be payable annually, semi-annually, quarterly, or on some other schedule as prescribed by law. In many cases where the owner has a mortgage and a required escrow account, the escrow officer will pay the tax bill. The owner will only receive notice of the assessed value and the tax statement.

SPECIAL ASSESSMENTS

A special assessment is a tax levied against specific properties that will benefit from a public improvement. Common examples are assessments for sidewalks, water service and sewers. Special assessments are based on the cost of the improvement and apportioned on a pro rata basis among benefiting properties according to the value that each parcel will receive from the improvement.

For example, a dredging project is approved to deepen the canals for a canal-front subdivision. The project cost is $200,000. Although there are 100 properties in the subdivision, only the 50 that are directly on the canal stand to benefit. Therefore, assuming each canal-front lot receives equal benefit, the 50 properties are each assessed $4,000 as a special assessment tax. Note that once the work is completed and paid, the assessment is discontinued.

If a taxing entity initiates an assessment, the assessment creates an **involuntary tax lien**. If property owners initiate the assessment by requesting the local government to provide the improvement, the assessment creates a **voluntary tax lien.**

Special assessments are usually paid in installments over a number of years. However, taxpayers generally have the option of paying the tax in one lump sum or otherwise accelerating payment.

TAX LIEN ENFORCEMENT

Sale of tax certificates
Tax deed
Tax sale

If taxes remain unpaid for a period of time specified by state law, the tax collecting agency may enforce the tax lien in several ways, depending on what the law prescribes.

Sale of tax certificates

Some states sell **tax certificates**. The buyer of a tax certificate agrees to pay the taxes due. After a period of time specified by law, the holder of the tax certificate on a property may then apply for a **tax deed**.

Tax deed

A tax deed is a legal instrument for conveying title when a property is sold for non-payment of taxes. The application for a tax deed causes the taxing agency to institute a **tax sale** or **tax foreclosure**.

Tax sale

A tax sale is frequently some type of auction. If the tax has not already been paid through the tax certificate process, the buyer of the property must pay the taxes due. There is usually a legally-prescribed **redemption period** during which the defaulted taxpayer has the right to buy back the property and reclaim title. If the taxpayer can redeem the property by paying the delinquent taxes and any other charges before the tax sale occurs, this right is known as an **equitable right of redemption**. If the taxpayer can redeem the property after the tax sale, this right is known as a **statutory right of redemption**. In this case, the taxpayer must pay the amount paid by the winning bidder at the tax sale, plus any charges, additional taxes, or interest that may have accumulated. If the defaulted taxpayer does not redeem the property within the allotted time, the state issues the tax deed to convey title.

Exhibit 19.2 Tax Lien Enforcement

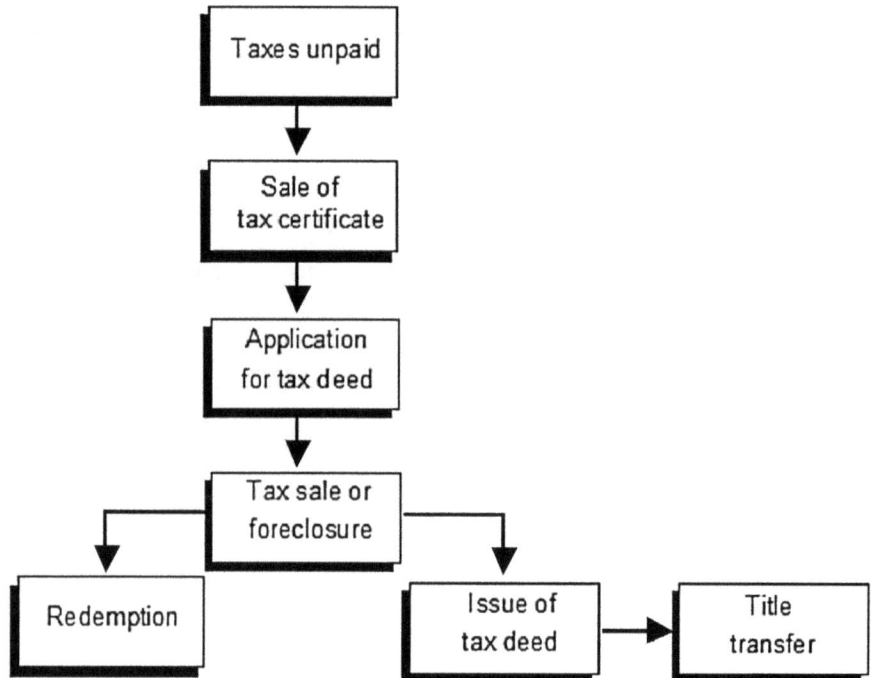

```
                    ┌──────────────┐
                    │ Taxes unpaid │
                    └──────┬───────┘
                           │
                           ▼
                    ┌──────────────┐
                    │   Sale of    │
                    │tax certificate│
                    └──────┬───────┘
                           │
                           ▼
                    ┌──────────────┐
                    │ Application  │
                    │ for tax deed │
                    └──────┬───────┘
                           │
                           ▼
                    ┌──────────────┐
            ┌───────┤ Tax sale or  ├───────┐
            │       │ foreclosure  │       │
            ▼       └──────────────┘       ▼
     ┌─────────────┐              ┌──────────────┐     ┌──────────────┐
     │ Redemption  │              │   Issue of   │────▶│    Title     │
     │             │              │   tax deed   │     │   transfer   │
     └─────────────┘              └──────────────┘     └──────────────┘
```

19   Real Estate Taxation Snapshot Review

TAXING ENTITIES	• no federal ad valorem taxes, only federal tax on income and gain; federal government can impose a tax lien against real property
State government	• states may levy property taxes but many delegate this power to county and local government; states can impose a tax lien against real property
County and local government	• counties, cities, municipalities, townships and special tax districts levy taxes on real property
Tax districts	• established to collect funds for providing specific services, e.g., schools, fire protection, parks, community colleges, libraries, road maintenance
AD VALOREM TAXATION	• property tax levied annually on the taxable value of a property in order to help fund government and public services
Tax base totalling	• tax base equals the total of assessed values of all real property within the area, excluding exemptions
Homestead exemption	• a tax exemption of a portion of the assessed value of a property owned and occupied as a family home
Other exemptions	• immune from tax: government-owned properties; exempt from taxes: properties owned by non-profit-organizations
Tax rate derivation	• (1) taxing entity determines what budget requirements must be met by ad valorem tax; (2) divide tax requirement by the tax base
	• tax rate stated as mills ($.001), or dollars per $100 of assessed value, or dollars per $1,000 of assessed value, or as a percentage of assessed value
Tax billing and collection	• individual tax bill: tax rate times taxable value
	• taxable value: assessed value minus exemptions and adjustments
SPECIAL ASSESSMENTS	• tax levied against specific properties that will benefit from a public improvement; amount is based on a pro rata share of the cost of the improvement and the value each parcel will receive from the improvement
TAX LIEN ENFORCEMENT	
Sale of tax certificates	• the buyer of a tax certificate agrees to pay the taxes due and after a period of time may apply for a tax deed on the property
Tax deed	• conveys title in the tax sale
Tax sale	• the buyer must pay the taxes due, if still unpaid; the defaulted taxpayer may be able to redeem the property and reclaim title; if not redeemed, the state issues the tax deed to convey title to the buyer

20 Professional Practices

Fair Housing Laws
Property Disclosures
Other Professional Practices

FAIR HOUSING LAWS

Civil Rights Act of 1866
Civil Rights Act of 1968
Forms of illegal discrimination
Title VIII exemptions
Jones v. Mayer
Equal Opportunity in Housing poster
Fair Housing Amendments Act of 1988
Discrimination by the client
Violations and enforcement
Fair financing laws
Americans with Disabilities Act

Federal and state governments have enacted laws prohibiting discrimination in the national housing market. The aim of these **fair housing laws,** or **equal opportunity housing laws,** is to give all people in the country an equal opportunity to live wherever they wish, provided they can afford to do so, without impediments of discrimination in the purchase, sale, rental, or financing of property.

State Fair Housing Laws. While states have enacted fair housing laws that generally reflect the provisions of national law, each state may have slight modifications of national law. For that reason, it is incumbent upon real estate students to learn their state laws and, in particular, note where these laws differ from national fair housing laws.

Fair Housing and Local Zoning. The Fair Housing Act prohibits a broad range of practices that discriminate against individuals on the basis of race, color, religion, sex, national origin, familial status, and disability. The Act does not pre-empt local zoning laws. However, the Act applies to municipalities and other local government entities and prohibits them from making zoning or land use decisions or implementing land use policies that exclude or otherwise discriminate against protected persons, including individuals with disabilities.

Civil Rights Act of 1866

The original fair housing statute, the Civil Rights Act of 1866, prohibits discrimination in housing *based on race.* The prohibition relates to selling, renting, inheriting, and conveying real estate.

Executive Order 11063. While the Civil Rights Act of 1866 prohibited discrimination, it was only marginally enforced. In 1962, the President issued Executive Order 11063 to *prevent discrimination in residential properties financed by FHA and VA loans.* The order facilitated enforcement of fair housing where federal funding was involved.

Civil Rights Act of 1968

Title VIII (Fair Housing Act). Title VIII of the Civil Rights Act of 1968, known today as the Fair Housing Act, prohibits discrimination in housing *based on race, color, religion, or national origin.* The Office of Fair Housing and Equal Opportunity (FHEO) administers and enforces Title VIII under the supervision of the Department of Housing and Urban Development (HUD).

Forms of illegal discrimination

The Fair Housing Act specifically prohibits such activities in residential brokerage and financing as the following.

Discriminatory misrepresentation. An agent may not conceal available properties, represent that they are not for sale or rent, or change the sale terms for the purpose of discriminating. For example, an agent may not inform a minority buyer that the seller has recently decided not to carry back second mortgage financing when in fact the owner has made no such decision.

Discriminatory advertising. An agent may not advertise residential properties in such a way as to restrict their availability to any prospective buyer or tenant.

Providing unequal services. An agent may not alter the nature or quality of brokerage services to any party based on race, color, sex, national origin, or religion. For example, if it is customary for an agent to show a customer the latest MLS publication, the agent may not refuse to show it to any party. Similarly, if it is customary to show qualified buyers prospective properties immediately, an agent may not alter that practice for purposes of discrimination.

Steering. Steering is the practice of directly or indirectly channeling customers toward or away from homes and neighborhoods. Broadly interpreted, steering occurs if an agent describes an area in a subjective way for the purpose of encouraging or discouraging a buyer about the suitability of the area.

For example, an agent tells Buyer A that a neighborhood is extremely attractive, and that desirable families are moving in every week. The next day, the agent tells Buyer B that the same neighborhood is deteriorating, and that values are starting to fall. The agent has blatantly steered Buyer B *away* from the area and Buyer A *into* it.

Blockbusting. Blockbusting is the practice of inducing owners in an area to sell or rent to avoid an impending change in the ethnic or social makeup of the neighborhood that will cause values to go down.

For example, Agent Smith tells neighborhood owners that several minority families are moving in, and that they will be bringing their relatives next year. Smith informs homeowners that, in anticipation of a value decline, several families have already made plans to move.

Restricting MLS participation. It is discriminatory to restrict participation in any multiple listing service based on one's race, religion, national origin, color, or sex.

Redlining. Redlining is the residential financing practice of refusing to make loans on properties in a certain neighborhood regardless of a mortgagor's qualifications. In effect, the lender draws a red line around an area on the map and denies all financing to applicants within the encircled area.

Title VIII exemptions The Fair Housing Act allows for exemptions under a few specific circumstances. These are:

> ▸ a privately owned single-family home where no broker is used and no discriminatory advertising is used, with certain additional conditions
> ▸ rental of an apartment in a 1-4 unit building where the owner is also an occupant, provided the advertising is not discriminatory
> ▸ facilities owned by private clubs and leased non-commercially to members
> ▸ facilities owned by religious organizations and leased non-commercially to members, provided membership requirements are not discriminatory

Jones v. Mayer In 1968, the Supreme Court ruled in *Jones v. Mayer* that all discrimination in selling or renting residential property based on race is prohibited under the provisions of the Civil Rights Act of 1866. Thus, while the Federal Fair Housing Act exempts certain kinds of discrimination, anyone who feels victimized by discrimination *based on race* may seek legal recourse under the 1866 law.

Equal Opportunity in Housing poster In 1972, HUD instituted a requirement that brokers display a standard HUD poster. The poster affirms the broker's compliance with fair housing laws in selling, renting, advertising, and financing residential properties. Failure to display the poster may be construed as discrimination.

Fair Housing Amendments Act of 1988 Amendments to federal fair housing laws prohibit discrimination based on sex and discrimination against handicapped persons and families with children.

Exemptions. Federal fair housing laws do not prohibit age and family status discrimination under the following circumstances:

> ▸ in government-designated retirement housing
> ▸ in a retirement community if all residents are 62 years of age or older
> ▸ in a retirement community if 80 % of the dwellings have one person who is 55 years of age or older, provided there are amenities for elderly residents

	▸ in residential dwellings of four units or less, and single family houses if sold or rented by owners who have no more than three houses

Discrimination by the client

Fair housing laws apply to home sellers as well as to agents, with the exception of the exemptions previously cited. If an agent goes along with a client's discriminatory act, the agent is equally liable for violation of fair housing laws. It is thus imperative to avoid complicity with client discrimination. Further, an agent should withdraw from any relationship where client discrimination occurs.

Examples of potential client discrimination are:

- refusing a full-price offer from a party
- removing the property from the market to sidestep a potential purchase by a party
- accepting an offer from one party that is lower than one from another party

Violations and enforcement

Persons who feel they have been discriminated against under federal fair housing laws may file a complaint with the Office of Fair Housing and Equal Opportunity (FHEO) within HUD, or they may file suit in a federal or state court.

Filing an FHEO complaint. Complaints alleging fair housing violations must be filed with the Office of Fair Housing and Equal Opportunity within one year of the violation. HUD then initiates an investigation in conjunction with federal or local enforcement authorities.

If HUD decides that the complaint merits further action, it will attempt to resolve the matter out of court. If efforts to resolve the problem fail, the aggrieved party may file suit in state or federal court.

Filing suit. In addition to or instead of filing a complaint with HUD, a party may file suit in state or federal court within two years of the alleged violation.

Penalties. If discrimination is confirmed in court, the respondent may be enjoined to cease practicing his or her business. For example, a discriminating home builder may be restrained from selling available properties to buyers. Also, the plaintiff may be compensated for damages including humiliation, suffering, and pain. In addition, the injured party may seek equitable relief, including forcing the guilty party to complete a denied action such as selling or renting the property. Finally, the courts may impose civil penalties for first-time or repeat offenders.

Fair financing laws

Parallel anti-discrimination and consumer protection laws have been enacted in the mortgage financing field to promote equal opportunity in housing.

Equal Credit Opportunity Act (ECOA). Enacted in 1974, the Equal Credit Opportunity Act requires lenders to be fair and impartial in determining who qualifies for a loan. A lender may not discriminate on the basis of race, color, religion, national origin, sex, marital status, or age. The act also requires lenders to inform prospective borrowers who are being denied credit of the reasons for the denial.

Home Mortgage Disclosure Act. This statute requires lenders involved with federally guaranteed or insured loans to exercise impartiality and non-discrimination in the geographical distribution of their loan portfolio. In other words, the act is designed to prohibit redlining. It is enforced in part by requiring lenders to report to authorities where they have placed their loans.

Exhibit 20.1 Equal Opportunity in Housing Poster

U. S. Department of Housing and Urban Development

EQUAL HOUSING OPPORTUNITY

We Do Business in Accordance With the Federal Fair Housing Law

(The Fair Housing Amendments Act of 1988)

It is illegal to Discriminate Against Any Person Because of Race, Color, Religion, Sex, Handicap, Familial Status, or National Origin

- In the sale or rental of housing or residential lots
- In advertising the sale or rental of housing
- In the financing of housing
- In the provision of real estate brokerage services
- In the appraisal of housing
- Blockbusting is also illegal

Anyone who feels he or she has been discriminated against may file a complaint of housing discrimination:
1-800-669-9777 (Toll Free)
1-800-927-9275 (TTY)
www.hud.gov/fairhousing

U.S. Department of Housing and Urban Development
Assistant Secretary for Fair Housing and Equal Opportunity
Washington, D.C. 20410

Previous editions are obsolete

form HUD-928.1 (6/2011)

Americans with Disabilities Act (ADA)

Purpose. The ADA, which became law in 1990, is a civil rights law that prohibits discrimination against individuals with disabilities in all areas of public life, including employment, education, transportation, and facilities that are open to the general public. The purpose of the law is to make sure that people with disabilities have the same rights and opportunities as everyone else.

The Americans with Disabilities Act Amendments Act (ADAAA) became effective on January 1, 2009. Among other things, the ADAAA clarified that a disability is "a physical or mental impairment that substantially limits one or more major life activities." This definition applies to all titles of the ADA and covers private employers with 15 or more employees, state and local governments, employment agencies, labor unions, agents of the employer, joint management labor committees, and private entities considered places of public accommodation. Examples of the latter include hotels, restaurants, retail stores, doctor's offices, golf courses, private schools, day care centers, health clubs, sports stadiums, and movie theaters.

Components. The law consists of five parts.

- Title I (Employment) concerns equal employment opportunity. It is enforced by the U.S. Equal Employment Opportunity Commission.

- Title II (State and Local government) concerns nondiscrimination in state and local government services. It is enforced by the U.S. Department of Justice.

- Title III (Public Accommodations) concerns nondiscrimination in public accommodations and commercial facilities. It is enforced by the U.S. Department of Justice.

- Title IV (Telecommunications) concerns accommodations in telecommunications and public service messaging. It is enforced by the Federal Communications Commission.

- Title V (Miscellaneous) concerns a variety of general situations including how the ADA affects other laws, insurance providers, and lawyers.

Real estate practitioners are most likely to encounter Titles I and III and should acquire familiarity with these. In advising clients, licensees are well-advised to seek qualified legal counsel.

Requirements. As noted in Chapter 24 under "Management Functions," the act requires landlords in certain circumstances to modify housing and facilities so that disabled persons can access them without hindrance.

The ADA also requires that disabled employees and members of the public be provided access that is equivalent to that provided to those who are not disabled.

- Employers with at least fifteen employees must follow nondiscriminatory employment and hiring practices.

- Reasonable accommodations must be made to enable disabled employees to perform essential functions of their jobs.

- Modifications to the physical components of a building may be necessary to provide the required access to tenants and their customers, such as widening doorways, changing door hardware, changing how doors open, installing ramps, lowering wall-mounted telephones and keypads, supplying Braille signage, and providing auditory signals.

  ▸ Existing barriers must be removed when the removal is "readily achievable," that is, when cost is not prohibitive. New construction and remodeling must meet a higher standard.

  ▸ If a building or facility does not meet requirements, the landlord must determine whether restructuring or retrofitting or some other kind of accommodation is most practical.

Penalties. Violations of ADA requirements can result in citations, business license restrictions, fines, and injunctions requiring remediation of the offending conditions. Business owners may also be held liable for personal injury damages to an injured plaintiff.

PROPERTY DISCLOSURES

Residential property condition
Environmental issues
Warranties
Inspections
Homeowners' associations

Residential property condition

Seller's disclosure form. Many states require sellers to make a written disclosure about property condition to a prospective buyer. This seller disclosure may or may not relieve the agent of some liabilities for disclosure. The residential property condition disclosure is the seller's written summary of the property's condition at the time of contracting for sale. The disclosure is entered on state-approved forms.

Owner's role. State legislation requires owners of previously occupied single family homes and buildings containing 1-4 dwelling units to provide the disclosure to prospective buyers if they are selling, exchanging, or optioning their property. Some exceptions and exemptions apply. When required, the disclosure must be transmitted to the prospective buyer no later than when the buyer makes an offer.

A typical form requires the seller to affirm whether or not problems exist in any of the listed features and systems of the property. In denying that a problem exists, the seller claims to have no knowledge of a defect. If a defect does in fact exist, the seller can be held liable for intentional misrepresentation. A third possible response to a property condition question is that of "no representation." Here, the seller makes no claim of knowledge as to whether a problem exists. With this answer, the seller is no longer held liable for a disclosure of any kind relating to a particular feature, whether a defect is known or otherwise.

Once the seller has signed the form and delivered it to the buyer, the buyer must acknowledge receipt and knowledge of the property condition disclosures, along with other provisions set forth on the form.

Licensee's role. The residential property re-seller must comply with the property condition disclosure requirement whether an agent is employed in the transaction or not. If an agent is involved in the transaction, the agent must disclose any and all material facts he or she knows or should reasonably know about the property, regardless of what the seller may have disclosed on the form.

Right of rescission. Sellers who fail to complete and deliver the property condition disclosure statement to buyers in a timely fashion effectively give the buyer a subsequent right under certain conditions to rescind the sale contract and re-claim their deposits. The buyer must follow certain procedures and meet certain deadlines in order to legitimately effect the cancellation. The buyer's right to cancel persists until closing or occupancy, whichever comes first.

Property condition and material facts. As explained in the chapter on agency, an agent has the duty to inform the client of all material facts, reports, and rumors that might affect the client's interests in the property transaction. A material fact is one that might affect the value or desirability of the property to a buyer if the buyer knew it. Material facts include

- ▸ the agent's opinion of the property's condition
- ▸ adverse facts about property condition, title defects, environmental hazards, and property defects

In recent years, the disclosure standard has been raised to require an agent to disclose items that a practicing agent *should know,* whether the agent actually had the knowledge or not, and regardless of whether the disclosure furthers or impedes the progress of the transaction.

Facts not considered to be material, and therefore not usually subject to required disclosure, include such items as property stigmatization (e.g., that a crime or death occurred on the property) and the presence of registered sex offenders in the neighborhood (in accordance with Megan's Law, federal legislation that requires convicted offenders to register with the state of residence; in some states, agents must provide registry information to buyers).

The agent may be held liable for failing to disclose a material fact if a court rules that the typical agent in that area would detect and recognize the adverse condition. There is no obligation to obtain or disclose information that is immaterial to the transaction, such as property stigmas.

An agent who sees a "red flag" issue such as a potential structural or mechanical problem should advise the seller to seek expert advice. Red flags can seriously impact the value of the property and/or the cost of remediation. In addition to property condition per se, they may include such things as

- ▸ environmental concerns
- ▸ property anomalies, such as over-sized or peculiarly shaped lot
- ▸ neighborhood issues

- ▶ poor construction
- ▶ signs of flooding
- ▶ poor floorplan
- ▶ adjacent property features

The following exhibit is part of a typical property condition disclosure form showing the level of detail that is expected in a seller's disclosure.

Exhibit 20.2 Property Condition Disclosure Form

Buyers and seller should be aware that any agreement executed between the parties will supercede this form as to any abligations on the part of the seller to repair items identified below and/or the obligation of the buyer to accept such items "as is".

INSTRUCTIONS TO THE SELLER

Complete this form yourself and answer each question to the best of your knowledge. If an answer is an estimate, clearly label it as such. The Seller hereby authorizes any agent(s) representing any party in this transaction to provide a copy of this statement to any person or entity in connection with any actual or anticipated sale of the subject property.

PROPERTY ADDRESS _____ CITY _____

SELLER'S NAMES(S) _____ PROPERTY AGE _____

DATE SELLER ACQUIRED THE PROPERTY_____ DO YOU OCCUPY THE PROPERTY? _____

IF NOT OWNER–OCCUPIED. HOW LONG HAS IT BEEN SINCE THE SELLER OCCUPIED THE PROPERTY? _____

(Check the one that applies) THIS PROPERTY IS A ☐ SITE BUILT HOME ☐ NONSITE BUILT HOME

☐ Range	☐ Central Air Conditioning	☐ Garage Door Opener(s)
☐ Oven	☐ Wall/Window Air Conditioning	☐ (Number of openers _____)
☐ Microwave	☐ Window Screens	☐ Intercom
☐ Dishwasher	☐ Rain Gutters	☐ TV Antenna/Satellite Dish
☐ Garbage Disposal	☐ Fireplace(s) (Number _____)	☐ Pool
☐ Trash Compactor	☐ Gas Starter for Fireplace	☐ Spa/Whirlpool Tub
☐ Water Softener Alarm	☐ Smoke Detector/Fire	☐ Hot Tub
☐ 220 Volt Wiring	☐ Burglar Alarm	☐ Sauna
☐ Washer/Dryer Hookups	☐ Patio/Decking/Gazebo	☐ Current Termite Contract
☐ Central Heating	☐ Irrigation System	☐ Access to Public Streets
☐ Heat Pump	☐ Sump Pump	☐ Other_____
		☐ Other_____

Garage:	☐ Attached	☐ Not Attached	☐ Carport	
Water Heater:	☐ Gas	☐ Solar	☐ Electric	
Water Supply:	☐ City	☐ Well	☐ Private Utility	Other_____
Waste Disposal:	☐ City Sewer	☐ Septic Tank	☐ Other _____	
Gas Supply:	☐ Utility	☐ Bottled	☐ Other _____	

Roof(s): Type _____ Age(approx) _____

Other Items: _____

To the best of your knowledge, are any of the above NOT in operating condition?   ☐ YES ☐ NO

If YES, then describe (Attach additional sheets if necessary);

ARE YOU (SELLER) AWARE OF ANY DEFECTS/AMLFUNCTIONS IN ANY OF THE FOLLOWING?

	YES	NO	UNKNOWN		YES	NO	UNKNOWN
Interior Walls	☐	☐	☐	Central Heating	☐	☐	☐
Ceilings	☐	☐	☐	Central Air Conditioning	☐	☐	☐
Floors	☐	☐	☐	Electrical System	☐	☐	☐
Windows	☐	☐	☐	Exterior Walls	☐	☐	☐
Doors	☐	☐	☐	Roof	☐	☐	☐
Insulation	☐	☐	☐	Basement	☐	☐	☐
Plumbing	☐	☐	☐	Foundation	☐	☐	☐
Sewer/Septic	☐	☐	☐	Slab	☐	☐	☐
Heat Pump	☐	☐	☐	Driveway	☐	☐	☐
				Sidewalks	☐	☐	☐

If any of the above is/are marked YES, Please explain:

_____
_____
_____

This Form Compliments of Kirkland, Rothman-Branning & Associates, PLLC
901-758-558

ww. kr-ba.com
jtk10-02

Exhibit 20.2 Property Condition Disclosure Form, page 2

C. ARE YOU (SELLER) AWARE OF ANY OF THE FOLLOWING?

	YES	NO	UNKNOWN
1. Substances, materials, or products which may be an environmental hazard such as, but not limited to: asbestos, radon gas, lead-based paint, fuel or chemical storage tanks, and/or contaminated water on the subject property	☐	☐	☐
2. Features shared in common with adjoining landowners, such as, but not limited to, walls, fences, and driveways, whose use or responsibility for maintenance may have an effect on the subject property	☐	☐	☐
3. Any authorized changes in roads, drainage, or utilities affecting the property, or contiguous to the property	☐	☐	☐
4. Any changes since the most recent survey of this property was done	☐	☐	☐
Most recent survey of the property: _____ [check here ☐ if unknown]			
5. Any encroachments, easements, or similar items that may affect your ownership interest in the property	☐	☐	☐
6. Room additions, structural modifications, or other alterations or repairs made without necessary permits	☐	☐	☐
7. Room additions, structural modifications, or other alterations or repairs not in compliance with building codes	☐	☐	☐
8. Is heating and air conditioning supplied to all finished rooms?	☐	☐	☐
If the same type of system is not used for all finished rooms, please explain _____			
9. Landfill (compacted or otherwise) on the property or any portion thereof	☐	☐	☐
10. Any settling from any cause, or slippage, sliding, or other soil problems	☐	☐	☐
11. Flooding, drainage, or grading problems	☐	☐	☐
12. Any requirement that flood insurance be maintained on the property	☐	☐	☐
13. Property or structural damage from fire, water, wind, storm, earthquake/tremor, landslide or wood destroying organisms	☐	☐	☐
14. Any zoning violations, nonconforming uses, and/or violations of "setback" requirements	☐	☐	☐
15. Neighborhood noise problems or other nuisances	☐	☐	☐
16. Subdivisions and/or deed restrictions or obligations	☐	☐	☐
17. A Homeowners Association (HOA) which has any authority over the subject property	☐	☐	☐
Name of HOA: _____			
HOA Address: _____			
Monthly Dues: _____ Special Assessments: _____			
18. Any "common area" (facilities such as, but not limited to, pools, tennis courts, walkways, or other areas co-owned in undivided interest with others)	☐	☐	☐
19. Any notices of abatement or citations against the property	☐	☐	☐
20. Any lawsuit(s) or proposed lawsuit(s) by or against the seller which affect or will affect the property	☐	☐	☐
21. Is any system, equipment or part of the property being leased	☐	☐	☐
If yes, please explain, and include a written statement regarding payment information.			
22. Any exterior wall covering of the structure covered with exterior insulation and finishing systems (EIFS), also known as "synthetic stucco"	☐	☐	☐
If yes, has there been a recent inspection to determine whether the structure has excessive moisture accumulation and/or moisture related damage? (The Tennessee Real Estate Commission urges any buyer or seller who encounters this product to have a qualified professional inspect the structure in question for the preceding concern and provide a written report of their finding.)	☐	☐	☐
If yes, please explain. If necessary, please attach an additional sheet.			

_____

_____

D. CERTIFICATION:
I/we certify that the information herein, concerning the real property located at _____, is true and correct to the best of my/our knowledge as of the date signed. Should any of these conditions change prior to conveyance of title to this property, these changes will be disclosed in addendum(a) to this document.

_____   _____
Transferor (Seller)   Date

_____   _____
Transferor (Seller)   Date

> **Parties may wish to obtain professional advice and/or inspections of the property and to negotiate appropriate provisions in the purchase agreement regarding advice, inspections, or defects.**

TRANSFEREE/BUYER'S ACKNOWLEDGMENT: I/we understand that this disclosure statement is not intended as a substitute for any inspection, and that I/we have a responsibility to pay diligent attention to and inquire about those material defects which are evident by careful observation.

I/we acknowledge receipt of a copy of this disclosure.

_____   _____
Transferee (Buyer)   Date

_____   _____
Transferee (Buyer)   Date

This Form Compliments of Kirkland, Rothman-Branning & Associates, PLLC 901-758-5588	www.kr-ba.com jtk10-02

Environmental issues

Health hazards occur within structures, on real estate parcels, and in the area surrounding real estate. They may occur naturally or as a result of human activity. Environmental laws regulate some, but not all, health hazards that affect real estate. Real estate agents, owners, and sellers have various responsibilities for detecting, disclosing, and remediating regulated hazards. Some important issues are reviewed below. There is further information in the "Environmental Controls" section of Chapter 8.

Lead-based paint. This hazard cannot be absorbed through the skin, but it becomes dangerous when it is ingested or inhaled. It can be found in most homes built before 1978 and can be present in the air, drinking water, food, contaminated soil, deteriorating paint, and dust from the paint. Children are particularly susceptible because young children are known to eat chips of the paint, allowing the lead to enter their bloodstreams. Homebuyers and renters are required to be given the EPA-HUD-US Consumer Product Safety Commission's booklet, "Protect Your Family from Lead in Your Home" and must be informed if lead-based paint is present in the home. Buyers may have a risk assessment performed prior to purchasing the home.

Mold. This is a fungus that grows under moist conditions and causes allergic reaction for some people. The presence of mold in the home must be disclosed as a latent defect. Flooding and water damage must also be disclosed as both of those can lead to mold growth. Inspections do not always find mold because it often grows inside walls and ductwork. Most molds require removal by a professional.

Asbestos. While harmless in its original condition, it can cause lung cancer if its dust filters into the air. If it is found in a home during remodeling, it must be removed by professionals to prevent contamination. It can be found in roofing and siding, older insulation, textured paint, artificial ashes sold for gas fireplaces, some vinyl floor tiles, coatings for older hot water and steam pipes.

Air quality. The quality of air in a home can be adversely impacted by the presence of carbon monoxide, radon, deteriorating asbestos and lead-based paint, methamphetamine production, formaldehyde, and other toxic chemicals. Homes can and should be tested for many of these contaminants prior to purchase.

Water quality. Ground water is easily contaminated from septic tanks, agricultural runoff, highway de-icing, landfills, pesticides, animal waste, etc. Many people rely on ground water for drinking so must be aware that contaminated water can cause problems from mild stomach problems to cancer and death. The Environmental Protection Agency (EPA) sets standards for protecting ground water from contamination. It also offers advice and resources to facilitate the rehabilitation of contaminated ground water sources. One such means of protection is to advise private well users to have the water tested at least once a year.

Carbon monoxide. This is an odorless, colorless, toxic gas that can kill a person before its presence is known. It can be caused by unvented kerosene and gas space heaters; leaking chimneys; back-drafting from furnaces, gas water heaters, wood stoves, and fireplaces; gas stoves, gasoline powered equipment, vehicle exhaust in garages, tobacco smoke. Carbon monoxide can be detected in a structure by a unit similar to a smoke alarm which should be included in every home, especially those with gas equipment and fireplaces or furnaces.

Faulty septic systems. Inspections of septic systems are important because these systems take wastewater from the property, remove most of the contaminants, and then put the water into the soil. If the system is faulty, it can be releasing contaminated water into the soil, thereby contaminating the soil. Potential buyers and septic system users should have the county health department conduct an inspection of the system.

Illegal drug manufacturing. Manufacturing illegal drugs such as methamphetamine produces highly toxic fumes that last a long time. Continued exposure to the fumes can cause fatal burns to the lungs, can damage the liver and spleen, and can lead to learning disabilities. Any property suspected as having been a place for drug manufacturing should be investigated prior to being sold or leased, and the possible health hazards must be disclosed to the potential buyer or renter.

Radon. This is the easiest hazard to detect and mitigate. It is an odorless, colorless, tasteless, and radioactive gas that is created in the ground where uranium and radium exist. Prolonged exposure to radon can cause lung cancer. It can enter the home through any cracks, gaps, or cavities, including crawl spaces and openings around pipes. It can be easily detected by a radon test, so home inspections should include this test.

Urea formaldehyde. This type of hazard is found in foam thermal insulation in homes built before 1980. The formaldehyde gas emissions from the insulation decrease over time, so most homes with the insulation no longer pose a threat. The most common sources of formaldehyde in a home are pressed wood products such as particleboard, hardwood plywood paneling, and medium density fiberboard. Plastic furniture, new carpeting, and other vinyl materials also emit formaldehyde gases during the first few months after installation. Formaldehyde can cause eye problems, nausea, breathing problems, and allergic reactions.

Leaking underground storage tanks. USTs have at least 10 percent of their volume underground and are used to store fuel oil, gasoline, and other toxic fluids. Tanks made of steel can corrode over time and leak their contents into the surrounding soil, contaminating groundwater. They also provide a potential for fire and explosion. Tank removal is expensive, so removal is not common. Therefore, potential buyers must be informed of the presence of a UST on the property and of the health and financial risks of purchasing a property that contains a UST.

Clean Air and Clean Water Acts. The Clean Air Act of 1963, since amended a number of times, was designed to control air pollution on a national level. Among other things, the act authorizes the setting of standards for controlling the emission of pollutants and monitoring air quality. It identifies hazardous air pollutants such as formaldehyde and regulates their use. Importantly, the act allows private citizens to sue other citizens to enforce the law.

The Clean Water Act, officially known as the Federal Water Pollution Control Act Amendments of 1972, together with revisions contained in the Clean Water

Act of 1977 and the Water Quality Act of 1987, is the primary federal law governing water pollution. It applies to all waters connected with navigable waters, but the interpretation of exactly which waters are covered remains open to dispute. The Clean Water Act does not directly deal with groundwater contamination, which is addressed in the Safe Drinking Water Act, Resource Conservation and Recovery Act, and the Superfund act.

Safe Drinking Water Act. Congress passed the Safe Drinking Water Act (SDWA) in 1974 (amended 1986 and 1996) to regulate and protect the public supply of drinking water. The act authorizes the setting of standards, protection of water sources, training of operators, funding of improvements, and dissemination of information. Under the act, water suppliers must report health risks to the EPA within 24 hours of discovery. Hydraulic fracturing (fracking) oil and gas production poses one of the greatest current threats to groundwater.

Property sellers generally must disclose the source of drinking water for the property and the presence, type and location of any septic system on the property. A water supply other than a municipal one and any septic system other than a standard one should be tested.

Brownfields Law. Brownfields are abandoned commercial or industrial sites that are likely to contain toxic material. The Small Business Liability Relief and Brownfields Revitalization Act (known as the Brownfields Law), passed in 2002 provides clean-up funds, liability protections, and tax incentives to reclaim contaminated properties. Under this law, owners who neither caused nor contributed to the contamination are released from liability for the clean up.

Environmental Protection Agency. The EPA was established on December 2, 1970 to bring together federal research, monitoring, standard-setting and enforcement activities into one agency dedicated to environmental protection. The EPA, working with state, local, and tribal governments, enforces the Clean Air and Clean Water Acts along with other environmental laws.

Disclosure obligations and liabilities. As discussed in an earlier chapter, licensees are expected to be aware of environmental issues and to know where to look for professional help. They are not expected to have expert knowledge of environmental law nor of physical conditions in a property. Rather, they must treat potential environmental hazards in the same way that they treat other material facts about a property: disclosure. It is advisable to have an attorney draft the appropriate disclosures to lessen the broker's liability should problems occur in the future.

The Lead-based Paint Act of 1992 requires a seller or seller's agent to disclose known lead problems in properties built before 1978. The licensee must give the buyer or lessee a copy of the EPA-HUD-US Consumer Product Safety Commission booklet, "Protect Your Family from Lead in your home."

Further, the 1996 lead-based paint regulation requires sellers or lessors of almost all residential properties built before 1978 to disclose known lead-based paint hazards and provide any relevant records available. The seller is not required to test for lead but must allow the buyer a ten-day period for lead inspection. Only a licensed lead professional is permitted to deal with testing, removal or encapsulation. It is the real estate practitioner's responsibility to ensure compliance.

Under CERCLA and the Superfund Amendment of 1986, current landowners as well as previous owners of a property may be held liable for environmental violations, even if "innocent" of a violation. Sellers often carry the greatest exposure, and real estate licensees may be held liable for improper disclosure.

In sum, for their own protection, licensees should be careful to:

> ▸ be aware of potential hazards
> ▸ disclose known material facts
> ▸ distribute the HUD booklet
> ▸ know where to seek professional help.

Warranties

Purpose and scope. Home warranties, or home service contracts, cover service, repair, or replacement of a home's major systems and appliances. Warranties are usually purchased for one year at a time with the annual cost determined by the following:

> ▸ the location of the property – prices vary from state to state due to cost of living and property regulations in the specific area
> ▸ the type of property – single family homes have different price points than mobile homes or multifamily properties
> ▸ the size of the property – smaller homes have cheaper coverage options than large homes. often, the home's square footage determines the cost of the warranty
> ▸ the amount of coverage – standard coverage plans may exclude certain parts of the property, resulting in a lower price for the plan. The excluded items can be covered with a more extensive plan at a higher cost

Home warranties are often included in the purchase price of a home or are purchased by the buyer at the time of the home purchase.

Limitations. Purchasers of home warranties need to fully understand their coverage limitations in order to have realistic expectations of the warranty. Similarly, it is important for a homeowner to understand what may not be covered in the warranty. These items may include

> ▸ conditions that existed prior to the effective coverage of the warranty
> ▸ failures caused by something other than normal wear and tear
> ▸ improperly installed or modified items
> ▸ damages caused by failure of another system or appliance, such as kitchen cabinets being damaged from a plumbing leak in the pipes under the sink, called consequential damages
> ▸ outdoor items such as sprinklers or swimming pool
> ▸ repairs to faucets
> ▸ refrigerators, washers and dryers, or garage door openers are often not covered

Basically, unless an item is specifically listed in the warranty contract, it will not be covered.

With a home warranty, the homeowner must go through the warranty company to have the service performed. The company usually has established relationships with specific service providers and may use only those providers for service under the warranty. The homeowner is typically charged a service fee on top of the annual fee for each repair job.

Inspections

Process. Property inspections may identify builder oversights or the need for major repairs. They may also identify the need for regular maintenance to keep the property in good condition. In addition to looking for structural issues, plumbing and electrical problems, and roof and foundation issues, inspections can uncover termites or other pests that are damaging the structure. Inspections can also uncover environmental issues that have a detrimental impact on the property.

Termite inspections. Termites are destructive pests that exist in all states except Alaska. They cause an estimated $50 billion in damage to buildings each year. They often cause extensive damage to the property before the owner even realizes there is a problem. Termites eat wood from the inside out, so they are not easily discovered except by professional inspectors. Having homes inspected annually for termites can prevent substantial damage and cost.

The most common type of termite is the subterranean termite. They are often confused with winged ants, but they are much more destructive. Termite inspectors look for the following indications that termites are present in the structure:

- ▶ swarms of termites inside the home
- ▶ termite excrement
- ▶ termite bodies found in spider webs near the structure
- ▶ the presence of termite mud tubes by which termites traverse open spaces between sources of wood; the tubes protect the termites from dehydration and predators; their diameter is similar to that of a drinking straws
- ▶ areas on the property that serve to harbor termites, such as wood fencing, mulch, piles of firewood, dead tree limbs, etc.
- ▶ a hollow sound when a wood beam is tapped
- ▶ long, deep grooves in wood

Because termites cause such extensive damage and can live inside the structure of a home for years, a termite inspection should be part of any home buying transaction as well as a periodic event.

Exhibit 20.3 For Your Protection...

U.S. Department of
Housing and Urban
Development
Federal Housing Administration (FHA)

OMB Approval No: 2502-
0538 (exp. 04/30/2018)

For Your Protection:
Get a Home Inspection

Why a Buyer Needs a Home Inspection

A home inspection gives the buyer more detailed information about the overall condition of the home prior to purchase. In a home inspection, a qualified inspector takes an in-depth, unbiased look at your potential new home to:

Evaluate the physical condition: structure, construction, and mechanical systems; Identify items that need to be repaired or replaced; and
Estimate the remaining useful life of the major systems, equipment, structure, and finishes.

You Must Ask for a Home Inspection

A home inspection will only occur if you arrange for one. FHA does not perform a home inspection.

Decide early. You may be able to make your contract contingent on the results of the inspection.

Appraisals are Different from Home Inspections

An appraisal is different from a home inspection and does not replace a home inspection. Appraisals estimate the value of the property for lenders. An appraisal is required to ensure the property is marketable. Home inspections evaluate the condition of the home for buyers.

FHA Does Not Guarantee the Value or Condition of your Potential New Home

If you find problems with your new home after closing, FHA cannot give or lend you money for repairs, and FHA cannot buy the home back from you. Ask a qualified home inspector to inspect your potential new home and give you the information you need to make a wise decision.

Radon Gas Testing and other safety/health issues

The United States Environmental Protection Agency and the Surgeon General of the United States have recommended that all houses should be tested for radon. For more information on radon testing, call the toll-free National Radon Information Line at 1-800-SOS-Radon or 1-800-767-7236.

Ask your home inspector about additional health and safety tests that may be relevant for your home.

Be an Informed Buyer

It is your responsibility to be an informed buyer. You have the right to carefully examine your potential new home with a qualified home inspector. To find a qualified home inspector ask for references from friends, realtors, local licensing authorities and organizations that qualify and test home inspectors.

HUD-92564-CN (6/14)

Environmental inspections. Home inspections should include looking for common environmental issues that can affect the property and the residents of the property. Environmental hazards can have a significant impact on the sale of a property. An environmental site assessment (ESA) may be conducted to identify environmental impairments and protect parties against becoming involved in contamination issues. Such assessments are performed in three phases. A Phase 1 ESA identifies potential problems on or near the subject property. A Phase 2 ESA involves active testing of soil, water, and other components of the subject property.

Environmental impact statements. When a project is federally funded, the responsible parties must provide an environmental impact statement (EIS) detailing how the project will affect the environment. Privately funded projects are also often required to prepare an EIS before any permits are issued. An EIS is expected to address air and water quality issues, noise, health and safety, wildlife, vegetation, water and sewer requirements, traffic, population density, and other issues as appropriate.

Agent disclosure duties. Most states require disclosure of known material facts regarding residential properties of one to four units. If a licensee knows the result of an inspection, this is a material fact to be disclosed. Disclosure of environmental issues on commercial and industrial properties is often not mandated. Where disclosure is not required, real estate licensees should suggest the use of a professional environmental audit.

Homeowners' associations

States have various requirements for a seller's property condition disclosure statement to be completed by the seller and furnished to the buyer. Any such disclosure is likely to include whether the property is subject to a common interest property plan (e.g. condominium), whether the plan imposes any restrictions, whether membership in a Homeowners' Association (HOA) is obligatory, and the identity of the HOA, if any.

State law will typically require the association or management company to provide association documents to the buyer to satisfy the seller disclosure requirements. These documents may be attached to or delivered in conjunction with the sale contract. The contract itself usually specifies the timing of the disclosures. There may be a place on the contract for the buyer to acknowledge receipt and knowledge of the HOA disclosures. In some states, the seller's agent gathers and provides the documents to a buyer or buyer's agent before the writing of an offer.

A typical HOA disclosure package includes

- declarations
- articles of incorporation
- bylaws
- articles of organization
- operating agreements
- rules and regulations
- party wall agreements
- minutes of annual owners' meeting

- minutes of directors' or managers' meetings
- financial documents: balance sheet, income and expenditures, budget, reserve study, unpaid assessments, audit report, list of fees and charges
- list of insurance policies
- list of assessments by unit type

The seller is responsible for making the disclosures, but the buyer must exercise due diligence in the reading and understanding of them. The agent's responsibility is to make sure the disclosures are made.

OTHER PROFESSIONAL PRACTICES

Codes of ethics
Job performance
Duties to clients
Duties to customers
Disclosure
Professional relationships

Codes of ethics

The real estate industry has developed a code of professional standards and ethics as a guideline in serving the real estate needs of consumers. This professional code has emerged from three primary sources:

- federal and state legislation
- state real estate licensing regulation
- industry self-regulation through trade associations and institutes

Federal legislation focuses primarily on anti-discrimination laws and fair trade practices. State laws and licensing regulations focus on agency and disclosure requirements and regulating certain brokerage practices within the state jurisdiction. Real estate trade groups focus on professional standards of conduct in every facet of the business.

By observing professional ethics and standards, licensees will serve clients and customers better, foster a professional image in the community, and avoid regulatory sanctions and lawsuits.

Today's professional ethics are not only important for one's career; they are also legal imperatives.

Trade associations representing the real estate industry have instituted their own codes of ethics and professional practices covering every facet of brokerage activity. For the latest Code of Ethics of the National Association of REALTORS®, see https://www.nar.realtor/about-nar/governing-documents/code-of-ethics/2019-code-of-ethics-standards-of-practice .

The standards of most codes for real estate licensees concern the following general areas of practice.

Job performance

A professional real estate agent must understand the skills and knowledge the profession requires and make a commitment to maintain and improve expertise in these areas. Of particular importance are:

- market knowledge
- real estate laws
- evolving standards of practice

Other aspects of professional performance that are usually supported include:

- promoting exclusive listings
- promoting the professionalism of the real estate industry
- promoting arbitration of disagreements rather than litigation
- obtaining transactional agreements between parties in writing
- submitting offers and counteroffers in a timely and objective manner
- keeping the funds of others separate from broker and personal funds
- providing equal professional services to all persons
- providing services only within the agent's area of competence or with the assistance of a specialist
- observing the highest standards of truthfulness in advertising
- cooperating with real estate boards and commissions in their enforcement of standards

A real estate professional must recognize the limits of the agent's role and avoid practicing other professions beyond the agent's qualifications, such as law, investment counseling, securities brokerage, and tax advising.

Duties to clients

Most codes of ethics uphold the commitment to fulfill fiduciary duties. Specific applications include:

- honestly representing market value and property condition
- respecting rights and duties of other client-agent relationships
- submitting all offers
- avoiding commingling and conversion
- keeping transaction documents current
- maintaining confidentiality
- managing client property competently

Duties to customers

Some of the guidelines for working with customers are:

- honestly representing market value and property condition
- avoiding calling a service "free" that in fact is contingent on receiving a commission
- advertising truthfully

Disclosure

In compliance with applicable laws and to promote respect for the real estate profession, licensees should be careful to disclose

- that the agent is going to receive compensation from more than one party in a transaction
- property defects if they are reasonably apparent; however there is no duty to disclose a defect which it would require technical expertise to discover
- any interest the agent has in a listed property if the agent is representing a party concerning the property
- any profits made on a client's money
- the agent's identity in advertisements
- the agent's representation of both parties in a transaction
- the existence of accepted offers
- identity of broker and firm in advertising as required by state law

Professional relationships

Professional conduct excludes disparagement of competitors. Real estate professionals also

- forgo pursuit of unfair advantage
- arbitrate rather than litigate disputes
- respect the agency relationships of others
- conform to accepted standards of co-brokerage practices

For more Fair Housing information:

HUD's central fair housing site:
    www.hud.gov/program_offices/fair_housing_equal_opp

Fair housing laws:
    www.hud.gov/program_offices/fair_housing_equal_opp/fair_housing_and_related_law
    www.hud.gov/program_offices/fair_housing_equal_opp/fair_housing_act_overview

Complaint procedures, with state links:
    www.hud.gov/program_offices/fair_housing_equal_opp/online-complaint

Advertising guidelines vis a vis fair housing:
    www.hud.gov/program_offices/fair_housing_equal_opp/advertising_and_marketing

20 Professional Practices
Snapshot Review

FAIR HOUSING LAWS
- enacted to create equal opportunity and access to housing and housing finance
- state laws generally reflect federal fair housing laws; federal laws do not pre-empt local zoning laws but prohibit them from discriminating

Civil Rights Act of 1866
- no discrimination in selling or leasing housing *based on race*
- Executive Order 11063: no race discrimination involving FHA- or VA-backed loans

Civil Rights Act of 1968
- Title VIII (Fair Housing Act): no housing discrimination *based on race, color, religion, national origin*
- certain exceptions permitted

Forms of illegal discrimination
- discriminatory misrepresentation, advertising, and financing; unequal services; steering; blockbusting; restricting access to market; redlining

Title VIII exemptions
- privately-owned single-family with no broker and no discriminatory advertising; 1-4 unit apartment building where owner is resident and no discriminatory advertising; private club facilities leased to members; religious organization-owned facilities for members and no discrimination

Jones v. Mayer
- no race discrimination, without exception

Equal Opportunity in Housing Poster
- must be displayed by brokers

Fair Housing Amendments Act of 1988
- no discrimination *based on sex or against the handicapped or families with children*

Discrimination by the client
- agent liable for complying with client's discriminatory acts

Violations and enforcement
- file HUD complaint, sue in court, or both; may obtain injunction, damages; violators subject to prosecution

Fair financing laws
- Equal Credit Opportunity Act: no discrimination in housing finance based on race, color, religion, sex, marital status, age; Home Mortgage Disclosure Act: no redlining

Americans with Disabilities Act
- no discrimination against those with disabilities; applies to employment, education, transportation, public facilities; equivalent access
- Titles I (employment) and III (public accommodation) most common for real estate agents

PROPERTY DISCLOSURES

Residential property condition
- written seller disclosure may be required; may or may not relieve agent of some liabilities
- seller discloses known problems; agent discloses known material facts known or should have known; failure to disclose grants right of rescission to buyer
- agent should advise seller of red flag issues detected; may include environmental concerns, property size and shape, neighborhood, construction quality, flooding, floorplan, adjacent property

Environmental issues	•	duties of detecting, disclosing, remediating for owner and agent vary; typically include: lead-based paint, mold, asbestos, air quality, water quality, carbon monoxide, septic system, drug manufacturing, radon, formaldehyde, underground tanks
	•	agents need to be familiar with requirements of EPA, CERCLA/Superfund Act, Clean Air and Water Acts, Lead-based Paint Act, among others
	•	licensees must be aware of issues, know where to find professional help, disclose
Warranties	•	agents should inform clients of limitations of home warranties; not a substitute for inspection
Inspections	•	inspections can reveal structural, electrical, plumbing, roof, foundation, pest, environmental issues; agent must disclose inspection results if known
Homeowners' Associations	•	agent must make sure existence, requirements, mandates, costs of homeowners' association are disclosed
OTHER PROFESSIONAL PRACTICES	•	codes of ethics provide self-regulating standards of conduct covering all facets of the profession; serve clients, customers, and the public; avoid sanctions and liability; cover practices such as job performance, duties to clients and customers, disclosures, non-discrimination, professional relationships
Job performance	•	maintain knowledge of market, laws, practices; recognize limits of agent's role
Duties to clients	•	fiduciary duties; truthful representation of facts; respect client relationships; submit offers; avoid illegal practices; document transaction
Duties to customers	•	truthful representation of facts; truthful advertising
Disclosure	•	compensating parties; property defects; agent's interest in property; use of client funds; agent's identity in advertising
Non-discrimination	•	compliance with fair housing laws
Professional relationships	•	no disparagement of competitors; no unfair advantage; respect for others; arbitration of disputes
Residential property condition disclosure	•	where required, re-seller of residential property must complete and deliver to buyer on or before offering; failure gives buyer right to rescind prior to closing or occupancy; agents must disclose material facts; buyers must acknowledge receipt

21 Closings

THE CLOSING EVENT

The setting
The closing process
Transfer of title
Transfer of purchase funds
Escrow procedures
Lender closing requirements
Broker's role

The setting

The closing event is the culmination of the real estate transaction. During this event, the buyer pays the purchase price and receives title to the purchased real estate. At the same time, the buyer completes financing arrangements, and buyer and seller pay all required taxes, fees, and charges.

Customary Practices. Procedures and customary practices for conducting real estate closings vary from state to state. For example, it is common in some states for sellers to pay title insurance, while in other states the buyer and seller might share this expense. Students should refer to supplemental state materials to ascertain prevailing practices in their state.

Time. The sale contract sets the date of the closing, usually within sixty days of signing. The time period between signing and closing is expected to be sufficient for the removal of any contingencies, such as the buyer's obtaining of financing, the performance of inspections, and the correction of identified physical defects. Failure of either buyer or seller to perform pre-closing actions specified in the contract can delay or terminate the transaction. If the contract includes a statement that "time is of the essence," all parties agree to meet the time limitations exactly as stated. If both parties consent, however, they can re-schedule the closing date.

Location. Closings occur at various locations, such as the office of the title company, the lender, the escrow agent, one of the attorneys, the broker, or the county recorder. The sale contract specifies the location.

Parties at closing. The primary parties at the closing are normally buyer, seller, and a closing agent or escrow officer. Other parties who might be present include the title officer, attorneys, brokers or agents, and the lender's representative. It is not actually necessary for any of these parties to attend the meeting. The closing agent can complete the transaction, provided all documents have been duly executed in advance.

The closing process
The closing process consists of buyer and seller verifying that each has fulfilled the terms of the sale contract. If they have, then the mortgage loan, if any, is closed, all expenses are apportioned and paid, the consideration is exchanged for the title, final documents are signed, and arrangements are made to record the transaction according to local laws.

Exhibit 21.1 The Closing Process

```
┌─────────────────────────┐
│   Confirm performance   │
└─────────────────────────┘
            │
            ▼
┌─────────────────────────┐
│       Close loan        │
└─────────────────────────┘
            │
            ▼
┌─────────────────────────┐
│      Pay expenses       │
└─────────────────────────┘
            │
            ▼
┌─────────────────────────┐
│  Exchange funds & title │
└─────────────────────────┘
            │
            ▼
┌─────────────────────────┐
│    Complete documents   │
└─────────────────────────┘
            │
            ▼
┌─────────────────────────┐
│    Record transaction   │
└─────────────────────────┘
```

Transfer of title
The seller must produce evidence of marketable title, such as a commitment for title insurance by a title insurer. Before making a title commitment, a title company performs a title search to discover any liens, encumbrances, restrictions, conditions, or easements attaching to the title.

If there are any encumbrances or liens that damage the title, the seller is expected to remove these prior to the date specified in the contract. The most common title cloud is an unpaid lien.

The seller may also be asked to execute an affidavit of title stating that, since the date of the original title search, the seller has incurred no new liens, judgments, unpaid bills for repairs or improvements, no unrecorded deeds or contracts, no bankruptcies or divorces that would affect title, or any other defects the seller is aware of.

The purchaser, purchaser's lender, or title company may require a survey to verify the location and size of the property. The survey also identifies any easements, encroachments, or flood plain hazard.

The buyer should inspect the property to make certain that the property is in the condition in which the seller states that it is, and that any repairs or other required actions have been performed. A final inspection, called a **buyer's walk-through**, should be conducted as close to the closing date as possible.

If the seller's mortgage lien(s) are to be satisfied at closing, the lender will provide a **payoff statement**, also called an **offset statement**, specifying the amount of unpaid principal and any interest due as of the closing date, plus fees that will be due the lender and any credits or penalties that may apply. The holder of a note secured by a trust deed will provide a similar statement, called a **beneficiary statement**, to show any unpaid balance. Even if the buyer is assuming the seller's mortgage loan, the buyer will want to know the exact amount of the unpaid balance as of the closing date.

Finally, the seller produces and/or deposits with the escrow agent the deed that conveys the property to the buyer.

Transfer of purchase funds

The buyer usually produces and/or deposits with the escrow agent the following:

> ▸ earnest money
> ▸ loan funds and documents
> ▸ any other cash needed to complete the purchase

Escrow procedures

If the closing occurs "in escrow" rather than face-to-face, the principal parties deposit funds and documents with the appointed escrow agent, and the escrow agent disburses funds and releases documents to the appropriate parties when all the conditions of the escrow have been met. If for any reason the transaction cannot be completed, for instance if the buyer refuses the title as it is offered, or the buyer fails to produce the necessary cash, the escrow instructions usually provide a mechanism for reconveying title to the seller and funds to the buyer. In such a case, both parties return to their original status as if no sale had occurred.

Lender closing requirements

A lender is concerned about the quality of the collateral a borrower is providing in return for the mortgage loan. The collateral would be endangered by defects in the title, by liens that would take precedence over the mortgage lien, such as a tax lien, and by physical damage to the property which is not repaired. Consequently, the lender typically requires a survey; a property inspection; hazard insurance; a title insurance policy; a reserve account for taxes and insurance; and possibly, private mortgage insurance. In some cases the lender may also require a *certificate of occupancy* verifying that any new construction performed complies with local building codes.

Broker's role

A broker usually continues to provide service between the signing of the sale contract and the closing by helping to make arrangements for pre-closing activities such as inspections, surveys, appraisals and repairs and generally taking steps to ensure that the closing can proceed as scheduled.

A broker may conduct proceedings at the closing meeting, or may have no further role in the transaction after the sale contract is signed, depending on local practices and the transaction in question. In many states, the broker is charged with the responsibility for accuracy and timely delivery of the closing documents to the principal parties. A broker may also have the responsibility for reporting the transaction to the Internal Revenue Service.

Finally, if the seller of the property is a non-resident alien, U.S. law may require the broker to withhold and transmit to the Internal Revenue Service a portion of the sale proceeds to cover the alien seller's income tax liability. There are also special reporting requirements when the transaction involves a non-resident alien.

REAL ESTATE SETTLEMENT PROCEDURES ACT (RESPA)

TRID
Information booklet
Loan Estimate
Mortgage servicing disclosure
Closing Disclosure
Disclosures after settlement
Limits on escrow accounts
Referral fees and kickbacks

The **Real Estate Settlement Procedures Act** (RESPA) is a consumer protection statute enacted in 1974. Its purpose is to clarify settlement costs and to eliminate kickbacks and fees that increase settlement costs. RESPA specifies certain closing procedures when a purchase:

▶   involves a residential property, including one- to four-family residences, cooperatives and condominiums;

▶   involves a first or second mortgage lien; and

▶   is being financed by a "federally-related" mortgage loan, which includes loans made by a federally-insured lender; loans insured or guaranteed by the VA or FHA, loans administered by HUD, and loans intended to be sold to FNMA, FHLMC, or GNMA.

RESPA regulations do not apply to transactions being otherwise financed except in the case of an assumption in which the terms of the assumed loan are modified or the lender's charges for the assumption are greater than $50.

RESPA is directed at lenders and settlement companies, but licensees should be familiar with requirements and changes implemented as of January, 2014. The Dodd-Frank Act of 2010 granted rule-making authority under RESPA to the Consumer Financial Protection Bureau (CFPB) and generally granted the CFPB authority to supervise and enforce compliance with RESPA and its implementing regulations. In 2013, the CFPB made substantive and technical changes to the existing regulations. Substantive changes included modifying the servicing transfer notice requirements and implementing new procedures and notice requirements related to borrowers' error resolution requests and information requests. The amendments also included new provisions related to escrow payments, force-placed insurance, general servicing policies, procedures, and requirements, early intervention, continuity of contact, loss mitigation and the relation of RESPA's servicing provisions to State law. These RESPA amendments went into effect on January 10, 2014.

TRID

Effective October 3, 2015, a TILA/RESPA Integrated Disclosure Rule (TRID) integrates the disclosure requirements of RESPA and Truth-in-Lending, replacing the old Good Faith Estimate form and HUD-1 Uniform Settlement Statement a new Loan Estimate form and Closing Disclosure form, respectively.

Information booklet

A lender subject to RESPA must give loan applicants the CFPB booklet, "Your Home Loan Toolkit," within three days of receiving a loan application. This booklet describes loans, closing costs, and the Closing Disclosure form.

Loan Estimate

A lender must give the applicant, at the time of application or within three business days of application, a Loan Estimate (H-24) of likely settlement costs. This estimate is usually based on comparable transactions completed in the area. The terms stated in the Closing Disclosure must agree with those of the Loan Estimate within certain limits.

Mortgage servicing disclosure

The lender must disclose to the buyer whether the lender intends to service the loan or convey it to another lender for servicing. This disclosure must also be accompanied by information as to how the buyer can resolve complaints.

Closing Disclosure

Under CFPB rules, a lender must use the Closing Disclosure (H-25) to disclose settlement costs to the buyer. This form covers all costs that the buyer will have to pay at closing, whether to the lender or to other parties. Use of this form enforces RESPA's prohibitions against a lender's requiring a buyer to deposit an excessive amount in the tax and insurance escrow account or to use a particular title company for title insurance. The consumer must receive the completed form not later than three business days before closing and has the right to inspect a revised form one business day before closing. A description and example of this form are provided later in this chapter.

Disclosures after settlement

Loan servicers must provide borrowers with an annual escrow statement which summarizes all inflows and outflows in the prior 12-month period. The statement must also disclose shortfalls or overages in the account, and how the discrepancies will be resolved.

Limits on escrow accounts

Section 10 of RESPA limits the amounts lenders can require borrowers to place in escrow for purposes of paying taxes, hazard insurance, and other property-related expenses. The limitation applies to the initial deposits as well as deposits made over the course of the loan's term.

**Referral fees
and kickbacks**   RESPA prohibits the payment of fees as part of a real estate settlement when no services are actually rendered. This prohibition includes referral fees for such services as title searches, title insurance, mortgage loans, appraisals, credit reports, inspections, surveys, and legal services.

Business relationships and affiliations among real estate firms, mortgage brokers, title insurance firms and other such companies that are involved in a transaction are permitted, provided the relationships are disclosed in writing to the consumer, the consumer is free to go elsewhere for the relevant service, and the companies do not exchange fees for referrals.

FINANCIAL SETTLEMENT OF THE TRANSACTION

**Settlement process
Selling terms and closing costs
Debits and credits
Non-prorated items
Prorated items**

Settlement process   The process of settlement consists of five basic steps:

1. Identify selling terms and closing costs.
2. Determine non-prorated debits and credits.
3. Determine prorated debits and credits.
4. Complete the closing statement.
5. Disburse funds.

**Selling terms and
closing costs**   Selling terms are the price of the property, the buyer's deposit and downpayment, and the terms and amounts of the buyer's financing arrangements. Closing costs are final expenses that buyer or seller must pay at closing to complete the transaction. The sale contract identifies all selling terms and who pays which costs. The apportionment of expenses is subject to negotiation, and in the absence of a specific agreement, is determined by custom. Closing costs include such items as brokerage fees, mortgage-related fees, title-related expenses, and real estate taxes.

Debits and credits   The closing statement accounts for the debits and credits of the buyer and seller to settle and complete the transaction. A debit is an amount that one party must pay at closing or has already paid prior to closing. A credit is an amount that a party must receive at closing or that has already been received prior to closing.

Exhibit 21.2 Debit and Credit

$ Received or Receivable **Credit** »» **Buyer or Seller** »» Paid or Payable **Debit**

The excess of the buyer's debits over the buyer's credits is the amount the buyer must bring to the closing. The excess of the seller's credits over the seller's debits is the amount the seller will receive at closing.

An individual expense item that one party owes to a party unrelated to the transaction, such as an attorney or the state, is treated as *a debit to that party only*. An income or expense item that affects both parties is apportioned, or **prorated**, to each party to reflect the proper amount that each owes or should receive. A prorated item is treated as *a debit to one party and a credit to the other party for the same amount*.

Buyer's debits and credits. To determine how much money the buyer owes at closing, the buyer's debits are totaled and compared with the total of the buyer's credits. The excess of debits over credits is the amount the buyer must bring to the closing, usually in the form of a cashier's check or certified check. The items typically debited and credited to the buyer are illustrated in the following exhibit.

Exhibit 21.3 Buyer's Credits and Debits

Buyer's Credits
earnest money
loan amount (borrowed or assumed)
seller's share of prorated items the buyer will pay

Buyer's Debits
purchase price
expenses (per agreement or custom)
buyer's share of prorated items prepaid by seller

Seller's credits and debits. To determine how much the seller will receive at closing, the same procedure is followed for the seller's debits and credits. The excess of credits over debits is what the seller will receive. The items typically debited and credited to the seller are illustrated in the following exhibit.

Exhibit 21.4 Seller's Debits and Credits

> **Seller's Debits**
>
> expenses (per agreement or custom)
> seller's share of prorated items the buyer will pay
> loan balance or other lien to be paid off

> **Seller's Credits**
>
> purchase price
> buyer's share of prorated items prepaid by seller

Non-prorated items   Non-prorated items are costs *incurred by one party only.* Items not prorated include those listed in the next exhibit.

Exhibit 21.5 Non-Prorated Items

Buyer usually pays	Seller usually pays
Mortgage recording fees Documentary stamp tax Intangible tax on mortgage Mortgage-related fees: appraisal, credit, survey, loan Impound reserves: insurance, taxes Attorney fees	Stamp tax on deed Title insurance Brokerage fee Inspection fees Title-related expenses Attorney fees

Prorated items   Many of the items to be settled at the closing are partly the responsibility of the buyer and partly of the seller. Some are expense items that the seller has *paid in advance*, where the buyer owes the seller part of the expense. Some are income items that the seller received in advance, and the seller owes the buyer a part of the income. Others are items the buyer will have to pay *in arrears*, and the seller owes the buyer part of the expense. The method of dividing financial responsibility for such items is **proration**. With a prorated item, there is always a debit to one party and a corresponding credit for the same amount to the other party.

Items paid in advance. At the time of closing, the seller has paid some items in advance that cover a period of time that goes beyond the closing date. In effect, the seller has prepaid some of the buyer's expenses, and the buyer must reimburse the seller. Heating oil and natural gas are typical items. By the same token, the seller of a rental property may have received rent or rental deposits in advance, and must reimburse the buyer for the part that belongs to the buyer.

For an expense the seller paid in advance, *the buyer receives a debit and the seller receives a credit.*

For income the seller received in advance, *the buyer receives a credit and the seller receives a debit.*

Items paid in arrears. At the time of closing, the seller has incurred certain expenses that have not been billed or paid at the time of closing and that the buyer will have to pay later. A typical item is real estate taxes.

For an item the buyer will pay in arrears, *the buyer receives a credit and the seller receives a debit.*

Exhibit 21.6   Items Paid in Arrears and Advance

	arrears	advance
real estate taxes	x	
mortgage interest	x	
rents received by seller		x
utilities	x	

Charging shares. If the seller has paid the buyer's share of an item, *charge the buyer for the buyer's share of the period.* If the buyer will pay the seller's share of an item, *charge the seller for the seller's share of the period.* If the seller has received the buyer's share of an income item, *charge the seller for the buyer's share of the period.*

Exhibit 21.7 Who Gets Charged

Seller paid for the year: charge buyer for buyer's share

Annual expense – closing August 7

Jan	Feb	Mar	Apr	May	Jun	Jul	Aug	Sep	Oct	Nov	Dec
						7	8				

Seller's share   Buyer's share

Buyer will pay for the month: charge seller for seller's share

Monthly expense – closing August 7

August

1	2	3	4	5	6	7	8-31

Seller's share   Buyer's share

COMPUTING PRORATIONS

12-month/30-day method
365-day method

The primary methods of calculating prorations are the 360/30-day method, which computes prorations on the basis of a 360-day year and 30-day month, and the 365-day method, which computes prorations on the basis of a 365-day year. The 360/30-day method is commonly used for prorating mortgage interest. Either method may be used for real estate taxes, depending on local practice.

It is customary in most states that the seller owns the property up to and including the day of closing unless stated otherwise in the contract. Thus the closing day is apportioned to the seller in computing prorations. The method of prorating, if not specified in the contract, will follow local custom.

12-month / 30 day method

The 12-month/30-day method determines an average daily rate of payment for an item to be prorated *based on a 30-day month and a 360-day year*. The method consists of the following steps for annual and monthly items.

Annual items

1. Identify the total amount to be prorated.
2. Divide this amount by 12 to obtain an average monthly rate.
3. Divide the monthly rate by 30 to obtain an average daily rate.
4. Multiply the monthly amount times the seller's number of months of ownership in the year of the sale up to the month of closing. For the month of closing, multiply the seller's number of days of ownership times the daily amount and add the result to the previous result. The final result is the seller's pro rata share of this item.
5. The buyer's pro rata share of an item is the total amount less the seller's pro rata share.

Monthly items

1. Identify the total amount to be prorated.
2. Divide this amount by 30 to obtain the average daily amount.
3. Multiply the daily amount times the seller's number of days of ownership. The result is the seller's pro rata share of this item.
4. The buyer's pro rata share of an item is the total amount less the seller's pro rata share.

Exhibit 21.8 Prorating Annual Item: Real Estate Tax
12-month/30-day Method

A sale transaction on a single-family house closes on March 2. County taxes for the previous year, to be paid in arrears, amount to $1,730. The seller owns the house through the day of closing. What are the seller's and buyer's prorated shares of this item?

Total amount due:		=	$	1,730.00
Monthly amount:	1,730 ÷ 12	=	$	144.17
Daily amount:	144.17 ÷ 30	=	$	4.81
Seller's share:	144.17 x 2 mo.	=	$	288.34
	4.81 x 2 days	=	$	9.62
	288.34 + 9.62	=	$	297.96
Buyer's share	1,730 - 297.96	=	$	1,432.04

Closing statement entries. The seller will be charged for the seller's share of the proration; an amount of $297.96 will be entered as a debit to the seller and a credit to the buyer because the buyer will have to pay the seller's share when the tax bill is received.

Exhibit 21.9 Prorating Monthly Item: Rent Received
12-month/30-day Method

The house in the previous example has been rented during the listing and selling period at a rate of $1800 per month. Rent for the month of March was paid to the seller on March 1. What is the buyer's prorated share of this rent? The day of closing, March 2, belongs to the seller.

Total received:		=	$	1,800.00
Daily amount:	1800 ÷ 30	=	$	60.00
Seller's share:	60.00 x 2 days	=	$	120.00
Buyer's share	1800.00 – 120.00	=	$	1,680.00

Closing statement entries. The seller will be charged for the buyer's share of the proration; an amount of $1,680.00 will be debited to the seller's account and credited to the buyer's account because the seller has received rent that belongs to the new owner after closing.

365-day method

The 365-day method uses the actual number of days in the calendar. The steps in the calculation are the same for annual and monthly prorations. The steps are:

1. Identify the total annual or monthly amount to be prorated.
2. For an annual proration, divide the total amount by 365 to obtain a daily amount (366 in a Leap Year). For a monthly proration, divide the total amount by the actual number of days in the month to obtain the daily amount.
3. Multiply the daily amount times the seller's number of days of ownership. The result is the seller's pro rata share of the item.
4. The buyer's pro rata share of an item is the total amount less the seller's pro rata share.

Exhibit 21.10 Prorating an Annual Tax Bill, 365-day Method

The seller in the previous example has a $1,730 tax bill, paid annually in arrears on December 31. Closing is on March 2, and the seller owns the day of closing. What is the seller's prorated share of this item?

Total amount due:		=	$ 1.730.00
Daily amount:	1730 ÷ 365	=	$ 4.74
Seller's share:	61 days x 4.75	=	$ 289.14
Buyer's share:	1730 - 289.14	=	$ 1,440.86

Closing statement entries. The seller will be charged for the seller's share of the proration; an amount of $289.14 will be debited to the seller's account and credited to the buyer's account because the buyer will have paid the seller's share of the tax bill in arrears.

TAXES DUE AT CLOSING

State taxes on the deed
State taxes on the mortgage

Certain transfer taxes that are due in connection with the closing appear and are accounted for on the closing statement. These include state taxes relating to the deed and to the buyer's mortgage. In addition to state-imposed taxes, counties and municipalities may also impose a tax on the real estate transfer.

State taxes
on the deed

Most states impose a **transfer tax** when real estate is conveyed. The tax is usually paid when the deed is recorded, often in the form of **documentary stamps** purchased from the recorder where the deed is recorded. The stamps must be attached to deeds and conveyances before they are recorded.

Tax rates are specific to each state. Methods of stating the transfer tax due include quoting the tax as a percentage of the taxable consideration and as a dollar rate per $100.00 of total selling price. If the number of 100's is not a whole number, it must be rounded up to the next 100. For instance, if a property sells for $350,120 and the tax rate is $.55 per $100.00 "or any fraction thereof," the tax stamps will cost:

350,120 ÷ 100.00	=	3,501.20
3,501.20 *rounded up*	=	3,502
3,502 x $.55	=	$1,926.10

State taxes
on the mortgage

Some states also impose a tax on instruments that contain promises to pay money, such as mortgages, notes, and contracts. Such taxes may be paid by the purchase of documentary stamps from the agency which will record the instrument. In addition, some states impose a further tax on the mortgage as an item of intangible personal property.

Taxes on the mortgage are typically paid by the buyer/borrower.

CLOSING COST ITEMIZATION:
CASE ILLUSTRATION

Selling terms and closing costs
Prorations and charges

The Closing Disclosure summarizes the financial settlement of a transaction. At closing, the closing agent also generally provides a statement to the buyer and/or seller detailing receipts and disbursements from relevant escrow accounts to which the buyer and seller have contributed funds as part of the transaction. The following illustration shows how some of these cost components are calculated and allocated in a sample transaction.

Selling terms and
closing costs

Lawrence and Sandy Binder have accepted an offer on their house located at 928 Elm Street, Littleburg. The buyers, Bill and Dillis Waite, offered $450,000, with earnest money of $70,000 and the remaining $380,000 of the purchase price to come from a new conventional loan from Scepter Mortgage Company. The loan is for 30 years at 5.5% interest, with a monthly principal plus interest payment of $2,158. The lender is charging 1.5 points and a 1% origination fee. Closing is set to occur at Alta Title Company at 4 p.m. on May 10 of the current (non-leap) year.

The Binders have an agreement to pay a broker's commission of 6% to Littleburg Realty. Their unpaid mortgage loan balance as of May 1 will be $184,000. Their monthly interest payments are $613.00. The annual interest rate is 4%. The previous year's county taxes, amounting to $2,572, have been paid by the seller in arrears. The current year's taxes, not yet billed or paid, are assumed to be the same as the previous year's. The parties agree to prorate using the 365-day method, and that the day of closing belongs to the seller. The relevant facts and costs, and who pays them according to the terms of the sale contract, are summarized below.

Selling terms

Sale price:	$450,000
Deposit/downpayment	$70,000
Loan amount	$380,000

Seller-paid Costs

Commissions:	6% of sale price (.06)
Real estate taxes:	$2,572, to be prorated
Title insurance:	$900 owner's coverage
Seller's attorney:	$1,500
Record Release Deed:	$25
Survey:	$550
Transfer stamps	
state:	$162
county:	$162
Seller's loan payoff:	$184,000 + 10 days' prorated May interest @ $613/month

Buyer- paid Costs

Sale price:	$450,000 ($70,000 earnest money already deposited by buyer)
Appraisal fee:	$400 already paid by buyer
Credit report:	$50 already paid by buyer
Closing fee:	$350
Recording fees:	$55
Title insurance:	$250 for lender's coverage
Buyer's attorney:	$1200
Pest inspection:	$100
Buyer's loan:	$380,000; 30-year fixed @ 5.5% (.055) points: 1.5% of loan amount (.015) origination fee: 1.0% of loan amount (.01)
Hazard insurance:	$2,400/year
Real estate taxes:	$2,572.00, to be prorated
Tax and insurance escrow:	8 months' taxes, 4 months' insurance
Prepaid interest:	from day after closing to end of month

Prorations and charges

According to the summarized sale contract, the only cost to be prorated and shared between seller and buyer is the real estate tax. Other costs to be computed are the broker's commission, the seller's unpaid mortgage interest, the buyer's loan fees and points, the buyer's tax and insurance escrows, and the buyer's prepaid mortgage interest.

Commission. The commission paid by the seller is:

$$\$450,000 \times 6\% \qquad = \qquad \$27,000.00$$

At closing this amount will be charged, or debited, to the seller.

Real estate taxes. Using the 365-day method, the daily amount is $2,572 ÷ 365, or $7.05 (rounded). The total number of days is the number of days in January, February, March and April, plus 10 days in May, or (31+28+31+30+10), or 130 days. At closing, the seller's share of $916.50 is charged to the seller and the buyer is credited with the same amount.

Total amount due:		=	$	2,572.00
Daily amount:	2,572 ÷ 365	=	$	7.05
Seller's share	7.051 x 130	=	$	916.50
Buyer's share:	2,572 – 560.30	=	$	1,655.50

Seller's unpaid mortgage interest. Since mortgage interest is paid in arrears, the seller owes the lender for interest not yet charged for the ten days of the month of closing. This amount is therefore debited to the seller.

Daily amount:	613 ÷ 31 days	=	$	19.77
Seller's charge:	19.77 x 10 days	=	$	197.70

Buyer's loan origination and points. The buyer's debits for loan fees and points are:

Fee:	380,000 x 1%	=	$	3,800
Points:	380,000 x 1.5%	=	$	5,700

Buyer's escrow. The lender requires the buyer to establish an escrow account to cover eight months of real estate taxes and four months of hazard insurance. The debits charged to the buyer are therefore:

Taxes:

Annual amount:		=	$	2,572.00
Monthly amount:	2,572 ÷ 12	=	$	214.33
Amount due:	214.33 x 8 mo.	=	$	1,714.64

Insurance:

Annual amount:		=	$	2400.00
Monthly amount:	2400 ÷ 12	=	$	200.00
Amount due:	200 x 4 mo.	=	$	800.00

Prepaid interest. The lender requires the buyer (borrower) to pay, in advance, the interest on the loan amount disbursed at closing to cover the 21 days of the closing month that would be due in arrears later. Note that the lender is not charging the borrower for interest for the day of closing. The buyer's first mortgage payment, which will cover the month of June, will not be due until July 1. Charged to buyer:

Monthly amount:	380K x 5.5% ÷ 12	=	$	1741.67
Daily amount:	1,741.67 ÷ 31	=	$	56.18
Total prepaid interest	56.18 x 21 days	=	$	1179.78

TILA/RESPA INTEGRATED DISCLOSURE RULE

Forms and procedures
Good faith
Types of charges
Applicable transactions
The H-25 Closing Disclosure form

Forms and procedures

As mentioned earlier, the TILA/RESPA Integrated Disclosures (TRID) rule is in effect as of October 3, 2015. These changes introduce new mandatory forms and procedures to replace the old ones, as follows.

> ▸ Lenders must give the consumer a copy of the **booklet**, "Your Home Loan Toolkit" **at the time** of loan application.

> ▸ Lenders must deliver or mail the **Loan Estimate** (Form H-24) to the consumer **no later than the third business day** after receiving a loan application. (A "business day" in this context is any day on which the lender's offices are open for business. An "application" exists when the consumer has given the lender or mortgage broker six pieces of information: name; income; Social Security number; property address; estimated value of property; loan amount sought).

> ▸ Lenders must provide the **Closing Disclosure** (Form H-25) to the consumer **at least three business days** before consummation of the loan. (A "business day" in this context is any calendar day except a Sunday or the day on which a legal public holiday is observed. "Consummation" refers to the day on which the borrower becomes indebted to the creditor; this may or may not correspond to the day of closing the transaction.)

Good faith

Creditors are responsible for ensuring that the figures stated in the Loan Estimate are made in good faith and consistent with the best information reasonably available to the creditor at the time they are disclosed.

Good faith is measured by calculating the difference between the estimated charges originally provided in the Loan Estimate and the actual charges paid by or imposed on the consumer in the Closing Disclosure.

Generally, if the charge paid by or imposed on the consumer exceeds the amount originally disclosed on the Loan Estimate it is not in good faith, regardless of whether the creditor later discovers a technical error, miscalculation, or underestimation of a charge, although there are exceptions.

Types of charges

For certain costs or terms, creditors are permitted to charge consumers more than the amount disclosed on the Loan Estimate without any tolerance limitation.

These charges are:

- prepaid interest; property insurance premiums; amounts placed into an escrow, impound, reserve or similar account

- charges for services required by the creditor if the creditor permits the consumer to shop and the consumer selects a third-party service provider not on the creditor's written list of service providers

- charges paid to third-party service providers for services not required by the creditor (may be paid to affiliates of the creditor)

However, creditors may only charge consumers more than the amount disclosed when the original estimated charge, or lack of an estimated charge for a particular service, was based on the best information reasonably available to the creditor at the time the disclosure was provided.

Charges for third-party services and recording fees paid by or imposed on the consumer are grouped together and subject to a 10% cumulative tolerance ("10% tolerance" charges). This means the creditor may charge the consumer more than the amount disclosed on the Loan Estimate for any of these charges so long as the total sum of the charges added together does not exceed the sum of all such charges disclosed on the Loan Estimate by more than 10%.

For all other charges ("zero tolerance" charges), creditors are not permitted to charge consumers more than the amount disclosed on the Loan Estimate under any circumstances other than changed circumstances that permit a revised Loan Estimate.

If the amounts paid by the consumer at closing exceed the amounts disclosed on the Loan Estimate beyond the applicable tolerance threshold, the creditor must refund the excess to the consumer no later than 60 calendar days after consummation.

Applicable transactions

The Integrated Disclosures rule applies to most closed-end consumer mortgages. It does not apply to:

- home equity lines of credit (HELOCs)
- reverse mortgages
- mortgages secured by a mobile home or by a dwelling that is not attached to real property (i.e., land)
- loans made by persons who are not considered "creditors" by virtue of the fact they make five or fewer mortgages in a year.

However, certain types of loans that used to be subject to TILA but not RESPA are now subject to the TILA-RESPA rule's integrated disclosure requirements, including:

- construction-only loans
- loans secured by vacant land or by 25 or more acres
- credit extended to certain trusts for tax or estate planning

Guides and detailed information about the current TILA-RESPA rule can be found on the Consumer Financial Protection Bureau (CFPB) website at

https://www.consumerfinance.gov/policy-compliance/guidance/tila-respa-disclosure-rule/

The H-25 Closing Disclosure form

The H-25 Closing Disclosure form consists of five pages. Pages 1, 4, and 5 vary, depending on the loan type. To illustrate the form, we use a sample disclosure for a *30-year fixed rate* loan that is presented on the CFPB website.

Page 1 has four sections: general information, Loan Terms, Projected Payments, and Costs at Closing.

General information. This section has three columns:

- ▶ Closing information –issue date, closing date, disbursement date, settlement agent, file number, property address, and sale price
- ▶ Transaction information – names and addresses for borrower, seller and lender
- ▶ Loan information – loan term, loan purpose, product type, loan type and loan ID number

Loan Terms. This section states the loan amount, interest rate, and monthly principal and interest payment, and indicates whether any of those amounts can increase after closing. It also gives specifics of any prepayment penalty or balloon payment.

Projected Payment. This section displays the borrower's payment for principal and interest and mortgage insurance, an estimated escrow payment, and the total estimated monthly mortgage payment for years 1-7 and 8-30 of the loan term. It also provides an estimate of monthly tax, insurance, and assessment payments and indicates whether the payments will be held in escrow.

Costs at Closing. The last section of page 1 shows the borrowers' total closing costs (brought forward from page 2) and the total amount of cash the buyer needs to close (brought forward from page 3).

Page 2 details the closing costs. There are two sections divided into four columns:

- ▶ Description of the costs—loan costs and other costs
- ▶ Costs paid by the borrower – "at closing" or "before closing"
- ▶ Costs paid by the seller – "at closing" or "before closing"
- ▶ Costs paid by others (in the example, someone other than buyer or seller pays for the appraisal)

Loan Costs. The first section deals with the loan costs:

- A. Origination charges, such as points, application fee, and underwriting fee
- B. Charges for services the borrower did not shop for - items the lender requires, such as appraisals and credit reports

C. Services the borrower did shop for - items the borrower orders on his own, such as pest inspections, survey fees, and title insurance

D. The total of A, B, and C above

Other Costs. The second section deals with additional transaction-related costs:

E. Taxes and other government fees, such as recording fees and transfer taxes

F. Prepaid items, such as homeowner's insurance, mortgage insurance, prepaid interest, and property taxes to be paid before the first scheduled loan payment

G. Initial escrow payment at closing – an amount the borrower will pay the lender each month to be held in escrow until due, typically for insurance premiums and tax instalments

H. Other costs not covered elsewhere on the disclosure, such as items as association fees, home warranty fees, home inspection fees, real estate commission, and prorated items

I. The total of the costs of E, F, G, and H above

J. The total borrower-paid closing costs from D + I above. This total is carried to the bottom of page 1 as "Costs at Closing – Closing Costs."

Page 3 has two sections, one for calculating cash to close, the other for summarizing the transactions of borrower and seller.

Calculating Cash to Close. The first section compares the final costs of the loan with the lender's original Loan Estimate. This calculation considers costs paid before closing, down payment, deposits, seller credits, adjustments, and other credits. The last line of the calculation is "Cash to close," the amount the borrower needs to produce at closing.

When an amount has changed, the creditor must indicate where the consumer can find the amounts that have changed on the Loan Estimate. For example, if the Seller Credit amount changed, the creditor can indicate that the consumer should "See Seller Credits in Section L." When the increase in Total Closing Costs exceeds the legal limits, the creditor must disclose this fact and the dollar amount of the excess in the "Did this change?" column. A statement directing the consumer to the Lender Credit on page 2 must also be included if the creditor owes a credit to the consumer at closing for the excess amount.

Summaries of Transactions. The second section of page 3 is divided into two columns (or subsections), one to summarize the borrower's transaction and the other for the seller's transaction. The borrower's column includes:

K. amounts due from the borrower at closing, including the sale price and adjustments for items paid by the seller in advance.

L. amounts already paid by or on behalf of the borrower at closing, such as deposit, loan amount, loan assumptions, seller credits, other credits, and adjustments for items unpaid by the seller, such as taxes and assessments.

The calculation at the bottom of the left column subtracts the totals already paid by the borrower (line L) from the total due from the borrower (line K) to derive the Cash to Close due from the borrower at closing. This figure is the same as that at the bottom of page 1 under "Costs at Closing – Cash to Close."

The seller's column of the Summaries section includes:

M.   amounts due to the seller at closing, including the sale price of the property and adjustments for items paid by the seller in advance.

N.   amounts due from the seller at closing, such as closing costs the seller will pay, payoff of first or second mortgages, seller credit, and adjustments for items unpaid by the seller, such as taxes and assessments.

The calculation at the bottom of the right column subtracts the total due <u>from</u> the seller (line N) from the total due to the seller (line M) to derive the Cash to Seller, which is the amount the seller will receive at closing.

Page 4 provides additional Loan Disclosures:

- Assumption –whether the lender will allow a loan assumption on a future transfer
- Demand feature –whether the lender can require early repayment
- Late payment – the fee the lender will charge for a late payment
- Negative amortization –whether the loan is negatively amortized, which increases loan amount and diminishes the borrower's equity over the term
- Partial payments –whether the lender accepts partial payments and applies them to the loan
- Security interest –identifies the property securing the loan
- Escrow account – itemizes what is included in the escrow account and states the monthly escrow payment

Page 5 provides additional calculations, disclosures, and contact information:

- Loan Calculations –the total amount of all payments on the loan, the dollar amount of the finance charges over the life of the loan, the amount financed, the annual percentage rate (APR), and the total interest percentage (TIP)
- Other Disclosures –other important information for the borrower, including the right to a copy of the appraisal report and an indication of whether the borrower is protected against liability for the unpaid balance in the event of a foreclosure
- Contact Information –names, addresses, license numbers, contact names, email addresses, and phone numbers for persons involved in the transaction.
- Confirm Receipt –the borrowers' signatures confirming receipt of the Closing Disclosure document. **Signing the document does not indicate acceptance of the loan.**

Exhibit 21.11 Sample H-25 Closing Disclosure, Page 1

Closing Disclosure

This form is a statement of final loan terms and closing costs. Compare this document with your Loan Estimate.

Closing Information
Date Issued	4/15/2013
Closing Date	4/15/2013
Disbursement Date	4/15/2013
Settlement Agent	Epsilon Title Co.
File #	12-3456
Property	456 Somewhere Ave
	Anytown, ST 12345
Sale Price	$180,000

Transaction Information
Borrower	Michael Jones and Mary Stone
	123 Anywhere Street
	Anytown, ST 12345
Seller	Steve Cole and Amy Doe
	321 Somewhere Drive
	Anytown, ST 12345
Lender	Ficus Bank

Loan Information
Loan Term	30 years
Purpose	Purchase
Product	Fixed Rate
Loan Type	☒ Conventional ☐ FHA ☐ VA ☐ _____
Loan ID #	123456789
MIC #	000654321

Loan Terms

		Can this amount increase after closing?
Loan Amount	$162,000	NO
Interest Rate	3.875%	NO
Monthly Principal & Interest *See Projected Payments below for your Estimated Total Monthly Payment*	$761.78	NO
		Does the loan have these features?
Prepayment Penalty		YES • As high as $3,240 if you pay off the loan during the first 2 years
Balloon Payment		NO

Projected Payments

Payment Calculation	Years 1-7	Years 8-30
Principal & Interest	$761.78	$761.78
Mortgage Insurance	+ 82.35	+ —
Estimated Escrow *Amount can increase over time*	+ 206.13	+ 206.13
Estimated Total Monthly Payment	$1,050.26	$967.91

Estimated Taxes, Insurance & Assessments *Amount can increase over time* *See page 4 for details*	$356.13 a month	**This estimate includes** ☒ Property Taxes ☒ Homeowner's Insurance ☒ Other: Homeowner's Association Dues *See Escrow Account on page 4 for details. You must pay for other property costs separately.*	**In escrow?** YES YES NO

Costs at Closing

Closing Costs	$9,712.10	Includes $4,694.05 in Loan Costs + $5,018.05 in Other Costs – $0 in Lender Credits. *See page 2 for details.*
Cash to Close	$14,147.26	Includes Closing Costs. *See Calculating Cash to Close on page 3 for details.*

CLOSING DISCLOSURE

PAGE 1 OF 5 • LOAN ID # 123456789

Exhibit 21.12 Sample H-25 Closing Disclosure, Page 2

Closing Cost Details

Loan Costs		Borrower-Paid		Seller-Paid		Paid by Others
		At Closing	Before Closing	At Closing	Before Closing	
A. Origination Charges		**$1,802.00**				
01 0.25 % of Loan Amount (Points)		$405.00				
02 Application Fee		$300.00				
03 Underwriting Fee		$1,097.00				
04						
05						
06						
07						
08						
B. Services Borrower Did Not Shop For		**$236.55**				
01 Appraisal Fee	to John Smith Appraisers Inc.					$405.00
02 Credit Report Fee	to Information Inc.		$29.80			
03 Flood Determination Fee	to Info Co.	$20.00				
04 Flood Monitoring Fee	to Info Co.	$31.75				
05 Tax Monitoring Fee	to Info Co.	$75.00				
06 Tax Status Research Fee	to Info Co.	$80.00				
07						
08						
09						
10						
C. Services Borrower Did Shop For		**$2,655.50**				
01 Pest Inspection Fee	to Pests Co.	$120.50				
02 Survey Fee	to Surveys Co.	$85.00				
03 Title – Insurance Binder	to Epsilon Title Co.	$650.00				
04 Title – Lender's Title Insurance	to Epsilon Title Co.	$500.00				
05 Title – Settlement Agent Fee	to Epsilon Title Co.	$500.00				
06 Title – Title Search	to Epsilon Title Co.	$800.00				
07						
08						
D. TOTAL LOAN COSTS (Borrower-Paid)		**$4,694.05**				
Loan Costs Subtotals (A + B + C)		$4,664.25	$29.80			

Other Costs		Borrower-Paid		Seller-Paid		Paid by Others
E. Taxes and Other Government Fees		**$85.00**				
01 Recording Fees	Deed: $40.00 Mortgage: $45.00	$85.00				
02 Transfer Tax	to Any State			$950.00		
F. Prepaids		**$2,120.80**				
01 Homeowner's Insurance Premium (12 mo.) to Insurance Co.		$1,209.96				
02 Mortgage Insurance Premium (mo.)						
03 Prepaid Interest ($17.44 per day from 4/15/13 to 5/1/13)		$279.04				
04 Property Taxes (6 mo.) to Any County USA		$631.80				
05						
G. Initial Escrow Payment at Closing		**$412.25**				
01 Homeowner's Insurance $100.83 per month for 2 mo.		$201.66				
02 Mortgage Insurance per month for mo.						
03 Property Taxes $105.30 per month for 2 mo.		$210.60				
04						
05						
06						
07						
08 Aggregate Adjustment		– 0.01				
H. Other		**$2,400.00**				
01 HOA Capital Contribution	to HOA Acre Inc.	$500.00				
02 HOA Processing Fee	to HOA Acre Inc.	$150.00				
03 Home Inspection Fee	to Engineers Inc.	$750.00			$750.00	
04 Home Warranty Fee	to XYZ Warranty Inc.			$450.00		
05 Real Estate Commission	to Alpha Real Estate Broker			$5,700.00		
06 Real Estate Commission	to Omega Real Estate Broker			$5,700.00		
07 Title – Owner's Title Insurance (optional) to Epsilon Title Co.		$1,000.00				
08						
I. TOTAL OTHER COSTS (Borrower-Paid)		**$5,018.05**				
Other Costs Subtotals (E + F + G + H)		$5,018.05				

		Borrower-Paid		Seller-Paid		Paid by Others
J. TOTAL CLOSING COSTS (Borrower-Paid)		**$9,712.10**				
Closing Costs Subtotals (D + I)		$9,682.30	$29.80	$12,800.00	$750.00	$405.00
Lender Credits						

CLOSING DISCLOSURE

Exhibit 21.13 Sample H-25 Closing Disclosure, Page 3

Calculating Cash to Close

Use this table to see what has changed from your Loan Estimate.

	Loan Estimate	Final	Did this change?
Total Closing Costs (J)	$8,054.00	$9,712.10	YES • See Total Loan Costs (D) and Total Other Costs (I)
Closing Costs Paid Before Closing	$0	– $29.80	YES • You paid these Closing Costs before closing
Closing Costs Financed (Paid from your Loan Amount)	$0	$0	NO
Down Payment/Funds from Borrower	$18,000.00	$18,000.00	NO
Deposit	– $10,000.00	– $10,000.00	NO
Funds for Borrower	$0	$0	NO
Seller Credits	$0	– $2,500.00	YES • See Seller Credits in Section L
Adjustments and Other Credits	$0	– $1,035.04	YES • See details in Sections K and L
Cash to Close	$16,054.00	$14,147.26	

Summaries of Transactions

Use this table to see a summary of your transaction.

BORROWER'S TRANSACTION

K. Due from Borrower at Closing		$189,762.30
01	Sale Price of Property	$180,000.00
02	Sale Price of Any Personal Property Included in Sale	
03	Closing Costs Paid at Closing (J)	$9,682.30
04		
Adjustments		
05		
06		
07		
Adjustments for Items Paid by Seller in Advance		
08	City/Town Taxes to	
09	County Taxes to	
10	Assessments to	
11	HOA Dues 4/15/13 to 4/30/13	$80.00
12		
13		
14		
15		

L. Paid Already by or on Behalf of Borrower at Closing		$175,615.04
01	Deposit	$10,000.00
02	Loan Amount	$162,000.00
03	Existing Loan(s) Assumed or Taken Subject to	
04		
05	Seller Credit	$2,500.00
Other Credits		
06	Rebate from Epsilon Title Co.	$750.00
07		
Adjustments		
08		
09		
10		
11		
Adjustments for Items Unpaid by Seller		
12	City/Town Taxes 1/1/13 to 4/14/13	$365.04
13	County Taxes to	
14	Assessments to	
15		
16		
17		

CALCULATION	
Total Due from Borrower at Closing (K)	$189,762.30
Total Paid Already by or on Behalf of Borrower at Closing (L)	– $175,615.04
Cash to Close ☒ From ☐ To Borrower	**$14,147.26**

SELLER'S TRANSACTION

M. Due to Seller at Closing		$180,080.00
01	Sale Price of Property	$180,000.00
02	Sale Price of Any Personal Property Included in Sale	
03		
04		
05		
06		
07		
08		
Adjustments for Items Paid by Seller in Advance		
09	City/Town Taxes to	
10	County Taxes to	
11	Assessments to	
12	HOA Dues 4/15/13 to 4/30/13	$80.00
13		
14		
15		
16		

N. Due from Seller at Closing		$115,665.04
01	Excess Deposit	
02	Closing Costs Paid at Closing (J)	$12,800.00
03	Existing Loan(s) Assumed or Taken Subject to	
04	Payoff of First Mortgage Loan	$100,000.00
05	Payoff of Second Mortgage Loan	
06		
07		
08	Seller Credit	$2,500.00
09		
10		
11		
12		
13		
Adjustments for Items Unpaid by Seller		
14	City/Town Taxes 1/1/13 to 4/14/13	$365.04
15	County Taxes to	
16	Assessments to	
17		
18		
19		

CALCULATION	
Total Due to Seller at Closing (M)	$180,080.00
Total Due from Seller at Closing (N)	– $115,665.04
Cash ☐ From ☒ To Seller	**$64,414.96**

Exhibit 21.14 Sample H-25 Closing Disclosure, Page 4

Additional Information About This Loan

Loan Disclosures

Assumption

If you sell or transfer this property to another person, your lender

☐ will allow, under certain conditions, this person to assume this loan on the original terms.

☒ will not allow assumption of this loan on the original terms.

Demand Feature

Your loan

☐ has a demand feature, which permits your lender to require early repayment of the loan. You should review your note for details.

☒ does not have a demand feature.

Late Payment

If your payment is more than 15 days late, your lender will charge a late fee of 5% of the monthly principal and interest payment.

Negative Amortization (Increase in Loan Amount)

Under your loan terms, you

☐ are scheduled to make monthly payments that do not pay all of the interest due that month. As a result, your loan amount will increase (negatively amortize), and your loan amount will likely become larger than your original loan amount. Increases in your loan amount lower the equity you have in this property.

☐ may have monthly payments that do not pay all of the interest due that month. If you do, your loan amount will increase (negatively amortize), and, as a result, your loan amount may become larger than your original loan amount. Increases in your loan amount lower the equity you have in this property.

☒ do not have a negative amortization feature.

Partial Payments

Your lender

☒ may accept payments that are less than the full amount due (partial payments) and apply them to your loan.

☐ may hold them in a separate account until you pay the rest of the payment, and then apply the full payment to your loan.

☐ does not accept any partial payments.

If this loan is sold, your new lender may have a different policy.

Security Interest

You are granting a security interest in

456 Somewhere Ave., Anytown, ST 12345

You may lose this property if you do not make your payments or satisfy other obligations for this loan.

Escrow Account

For now, your loan

☒ will have an escrow account (also called an "impound" or "trust" account) to pay the property costs listed below. Without an escrow account, you would pay them directly, possibly in one or two large payments a year. Your lender may be liable for penalties and interest for failing to make a payment.

Escrow		
Escrowed Property Costs over Year 1	$2,473.56	Estimated total amount over year 1 for your escrowed property costs: Homeowner's Insurance Property Taxes
Non-Escrowed Property Costs over Year 1	$1,800.00	Estimated total amount over year 1 for your non-escrowed property costs: Homeowner's Association Dues. You may have other property costs.
Initial Escrow Payment	$412.25	A cushion for the escrow account you pay at closing. See Section G on page 2.
Monthly Escrow Payment	$206.13	The amount included in your total monthly payment.

☐ will not have an escrow account because ☐ you declined it ☐ your lender does not offer one. You must directly pay your property costs, such as taxes and homeowner's insurance. Contact your lender to ask if your loan can have an escrow account.

No Escrow		
Estimated Property Costs over Year 1		Estimated total amount over year 1. You must pay these costs directly, possibly in one or two large payments a year.
Escrow Waiver Fee		

In the future,

Your property costs may change and, as a result, your escrow payment may change. You may be able to cancel your escrow account, but if you do, you must pay your property costs directly. If you fail to pay your property taxes, your state or local government may (1) impose fines and penalties or (2) place a tax lien on this property. If you fail to pay any of your property costs, your lender may (1) add the amounts to your loan balance, (2) add an escrow account to your loan, or (3) require you to pay for property insurance that the lender buys on your behalf, which likely would cost more and provide fewer benefits than what you could buy on your own.

Exhibit 21.15   Sample H-25 Closing Disclosure, Page 5

Loan Calculations

Total of Payments. Total you will have paid after you make all payments of principal, interest, mortgage insurance, and loan costs, as scheduled.	$285,803.36
Finance Charge. The dollar amount the loan will cost you.	$118,830.27
Amount Financed. The loan amount available after paying your upfront finance charge.	$162,000.00
Annual Percentage Rate (APR). Your costs over the loan term expressed as a rate. This is not your interest rate.	4.174%
Total Interest Percentage (TIP). The total amount of interest that you will pay over the loan term as a percentage of your loan amount.	69.46%

Questions? If you have questions about the loan terms or costs on this form, use the contact information below. To get more information or make a complaint, contact the Consumer Financial Protection Bureau at **www.consumerfinance.gov/mortgage-closing**

Other Disclosures

Appraisal
If the property was appraised for your loan, your lender is required to give you a copy at no additional cost at least 3 days before closing. If you have not yet received it, please contact your lender at the information listed below.

Contract Details
See your note and security instrument for information about
 • what happens if you fail to make your payments,
 • what is a default on the loan,
 • situations in which your lender can require early repayment of the loan, and
 • the rules for making payments before they are due.

Liability after Foreclosure
If your lender forecloses on this property and the foreclosure does not cover the amount of unpaid balance on this loan,

☒ state law may protect you from liability for the unpaid balance. If you refinance or take on any additional debt on this property, you may lose this protection and have to pay any debt remaining even after foreclosure. You may want to consult a lawyer for more information.

☐ state law does not protect you from liability for the unpaid balance.

Refinance
Refinancing this loan will depend on your future financial situation, the property value, and market conditions. You may not be able to refinance this loan.

Tax Deductions
If you borrow more than this property is worth, the interest on the loan amount above this property's fair market value is not deductible from your federal income taxes. You should consult a tax advisor for more information.

Contact Information

	Lender	Mortgage Broker	Real Estate Broker (B)	Real Estate Broker (S)	Settlement Agent
Name	Ficus Bank		Omega Real Estate Broker Inc.	Alpha Real Estate Broker Co.	Epsilon Title Co.
Address	4321 Random Blvd. Somecity, ST 12340		789 Local Lane Sometown, ST 12345	987 Suburb Ct. Someplace, ST 12340	123 Commerce Pl. Somecity, ST 12344
NMLS ID					
ST License ID			Z765416	Z61456	Z61616
Contact	Joe Smith		Samuel Green	Joseph Cain	Sarah Arnold
Contact NMLS ID	12345				
Contact ST License ID			P16415	P51461	PT1234
Email	joesmith@ ficusbank.com		sam@omegare.biz	joe@alphare.biz	sarah@ epsilontitle.com
Phone	123-456-7890		123-555-1717	321-555-7171	987-555-4321

Confirm Receipt

By signing, you are only confirming that you have received this form. You do not have to accept this loan because you have signed or received this form.

_____   _____
Applicant Signature   Date

_____   _____
Co-Applicant Signature   Date

CLOSING DISCLOSURE   PAGE 5 OF 5 • LOAN ID # 123456789

REPORTING REQUIREMENTS

Who must report
What must be filed

Who must report

The Tax Reform Act of 1986 requires that persons designated by the act as "real estate brokers" must report a closed real estate transaction to the Internal Revenue Service and provide the information contained in the report to each party to the transaction. The act defines "real estate broker" as any of the following:

> ▶ the seller's broker
> ▶ the buyer's broker
> ▶ the settlement agent, escrow agent, attorney, title company or other party responsible for closing the transaction
> ▶ the mortgage lender
> ▶ anyone so designated by the Internal Revenue Service

What must be filed

The person reporting files a Form 1099-S information return with the Internal Revenue Service. This form includes the names and addresses of the parties to the transaction and information about the sale proceeds.

The reporting person also provides each party to the transaction with a written statement showing the name and address of the reporting party as well as the information reported in the 1099.

If the transaction involves a non-resident alien, the reporting person may also have tax reporting and withholding responsibilities under the Foreign Investment and Real Property Tax Act of 1980 (FIRPTA), the Deficit Reduction Act of 1984 (DEFRA), and/or the Branch Profits Tax and Technical and Miscellaneous Revenue Act of 1988 (TAMRA).

21 Closings
Snapshot Review

THE CLOSING EVENT

The setting
- sale contract sets date, location, and who participates

The closing process
- verify contract fulfillment; exchange consideration and title; pay expenses; sign final documents; arrange for recording the transaction

Transfer of title
- seller gives evidence of marketability-- title abstract or title insurance commitment; may also need affidavit stating no new encumbrances incurred; seller must remove encumbrances or liens prior to the specified date; if seller is paying off mortgage lien, lender provides a payoff statement

Transfer of purchase funds
- buyer produces funds and documents needed to complete the transaction

Escrow procedures
- if closing "in escrow," escrow agent holds and disburses funds and releases documents when escrow conditions have been met

Lender closing requirements
- common: survey, inspections, hazard insurance, title insurance, certificate of occupancy, reserves for taxes and insurance, private mortgage insurance

Broker's role
- broker's role ranges from nil to conducting the proceedings to reporting the transaction

REAL ESTATE SETTLEMENT PROCEDURES ACT
- for residential property, first or second mortgage, federally-related mortgage, assumption modifying loan terms, lender charging over $50 for assumption

Information booklet
- lender must provide borrower with CFPB booklet, "Your Home Loan Toolkit"

Loan Estimate
- lender must provide CFPB's H-24 Loan Estimate of settlement costs

Mortgage servicing disclosure
- lender must disclose who will be servicing loan

Closing Disclosure
- lender must use CFPB's H-25 Closing disclosure

Disclosures after settlement
- loan servicers must provide annual escrow statements to borrowers

Limits on escrow accounts
- places ceiling on amounts lenders may compel borrowers to place in escrow

Referral fees and kickbacks
- RESPA prohibits payment of referral fees and kickbacks; business relationships between firms involved in the transaction must be disclosed

FINANCIAL SETTLEMENT OF THE TRANSACTION

Settlement process
- identify closing costs; determine who pays what; do prorations; assign debits and credits; complete closing statement; disburse funds

Selling terms and closing costs
- price, deposits, downpayment, financing, final expenses to be paid at closing; apportionment of expenses determined by sale contract or custom

Debits and credits
- excess of buyer's debits over credits is amount buyer must produce at closing; excess of seller's credits over debits is amount seller must receive

Non-prorated items
- incurred by one party only; not shared

Prorated items	• incurred by buyer or seller in advance or arrears; shared by buyer and seller; typical: real estate taxes, insurance premiums, mortgage interest, rents
COMPUTING PRORATIONS	• sale contract or local custom establishes methods of proration to be used for particular items
12-month/30-day method	• determines average daily amount based on 12-month year and 30-day month
365-day method	• determines an amount using the actual number of calendar days
TAXES DUE AT CLOSING	
State taxes on deed	• state, counties and municipalities may impose taxes on transfer
State taxes on mortgage	• state may impose taxes on mortgages, notes and contracts
TILA/RESPA INTEGRATED DISCLOSURES RULE	
Forms and procedures	• effective October 3, 2015
	• mandatory: Your Home Loan Toolkit booklet at loan application; Loan Estimate form 3 business days after loan application; Closing disclosure 3 business days before consummation
Good faith	• Loan Estimate costs based an best information available
	• Closing Disclosure costs equal estimate costs within certain tolerances
Types of charges	• no limitation on increase over estimate
	• 10% tolerance charges
	• 0 tolerance charges
Applicable transactions	• most closed-end consumer mortgages, including: construction loans, loans secured by vacant land, loans to trusts
	• not covered: home equity loans, reverse mortgages, loans on mobile homes, loans by small lenders (no more than 5 loans per year)
The H-25 form	• 5 pages, variable by loan type
REPORTING REQUIREMENTS	
Who must report	• "real estate broker" defined by the Tax Reform Act of 1986; buyer's or seller's broker, settlement agent, mortgage lender, other IRS-designated party
What must be filed	• Form 1099-S Information Return
	• statements to each party
	• tax reporting and withholding if FIRPTA applies (non-resident alien)

22 Overview of Licensing and Regulation

State License Law
Obtaining a Real Estate License
License Regulation

STATE LICENSE LAW

Virtually every real estate practitioner in the United States is subject to license requirements according to the laws of the state in which the practitioner resides and does business.

States have enacted real estate license laws to ensure a minimal level of competence in real estate professionals. State license laws also protect the public by requiring licensees to adhere to standards of ethical conduct and professionalism. A licensee who violates ethical and professional standards faces the temporary or permanent loss of the legal right to practice real estate.

The general thrust of state real estate legislation is to:

- establish personal, educational, and professional requirements for obtaining a license
- establish statutory guidelines of professional conduct and continuing education to maintain a license
- establish a regulatory entity to administer and enforce licensing
- authorize the regulatory body to create regulations and procedures that will enable it to discharge its legal responsibilities

For all students of real estate who are planning to enter a field of practice, it is vitally important to understand state real estate license laws and their effect on one's envisioned career in real estate. Since real estate is a large and complex industry, students must investigate local licensing requirements for specific activities. For example, it is likely that a state has special license requirements for appraisers. On the other hand, a state may require no license at all for one who works in corporate real estate. All fifty states have licensing requirements for practicing brokers and agents.

Where state license laws and regulations conflict with federal laws, the state's laws prevail.

OBTAINING A REAL ESTATE LICENSE

Services requiring licensure
Types of license
Licensing requirements and procedures

Services requiring licensure

Generally, any person who performs a real estate service *on behalf of another party for consideration* must be duly licensed under state law. For example, a person who receives payment for helping a buyer locate a house must be licensed. However, an investor searching for a property to buy does not need to be licensed because the investor is not acting on behalf of another party.

Consideration includes money compensation, exchange of free services, or any other valuable good or service that a person expects to be paid.

The following services generally fall into the license-required category:

> ▶ brokering of sale, lease and exchange transactions
> ▶ managing property, including rental activities
> ▶ appraising
> ▶ counseling
> ▶ syndicating
> ▶ auctioning

Within these service areas, states may have more specific requirements or exemptions, depending on the nature of the activity. For example, some states include business brokerage in the brokerage category while other states do not. Similarly, some states allow certain forms of counseling while others do not. The point is to find out what kind of license, if any, your state requires for the real estate activity you will be pursuing.

Exemptions. Real estate license laws commonly exempt the following from licensing requirements:

> ▶ employees of a property owner who are not paid on a per-transaction basis, such as an onsite rental agent in an apartment complex
> ▶ employees of transient lodging facilities such as motels and hotels
> ▶ managers of residential condominiums or cooperatives
> ▶ dealers in cemetery lots
> ▶ attorneys performing regular legal duties for a principal
> ▶ persons acting in a court-appointed capacity

Types of license

State licensing agencies issue two principal types of license: a broker's license and a salesperson's license. Within these types are variations based on the active or inactive status of the license and on the business identity and professional capacity of the licensee.

Exhibit 22.1 Types of Real Estate License

Broker's license	Salesperson's license
individual: active or inactive corporation limited liability company partnership non-resident	individual: active or inactive broker-salesperson: active or inactive

Broker's license. An active broker's license authorizes a licensee to represent clients by performing real estate services. A broker whose license has expired or is inactive may not perform brokerage services. Broker's licenses are typically valid for a one- or two-year period, after which they must be renewed. Inactive status typically occurs at the option of a licensee who wants to leave the real estate business temporarily. A broker who is acting under another name must register the name as a fictitious business identity.

The most common brokerage identity is the sole proprietorship. Other business entities, however, may broker real estate. These include corporations, general partnerships, and limited partnerships. In order for these entities to perform real estate services, certain individuals within the organization generally must maintain an active broker's license.

A broker who does business at locations other than the principal office requires a branch office license. While the branch office must be licensed, state laws vary as to whether the branch manager requires a broker's license.

A broker's license authorizes a broker to perform services anywhere within the state's borders. This allows a broker to arrange the sale of an out-of-state property as long as the services are conducted within the state. It also allows a broker from one state to co-broker a transaction with a broker in another state, provided neither broker performs services in the other's state. A *non-resident license* empowers a broker to practice in another state. This type of license is commonly issued in areas near state lines where residents of the two states are frequently principals in transactions.

In the absence of a non-resident license, a broker's license from one state usually does not confer the authority to operate in another state since there is no *reciprocity* in licensing between states. A broker who holds a Maryland real estate license has no authority to operate in Wyoming. However, a licensed broker desiring a license in another state may be excused from some of the licensing requirements that an unlicensed applicant has to meet.

Salesperson's license. A salesperson may hold an active or inactive license, depending on whether the agent is currently employed and performing services. As in the case of a broker's license, a salesperson who wishes to leave the business temporarily can voluntarily de-activate the license.

A broker-salesperson's license is a salesperson's license held by a duly licensed broker who prefers to act as a salesperson on behalf of an employing broker instead of performing services as a broker. Since a salesperson can only act in one capacity -- as agent of an employing broker -- an individual may not be an active broker while holding an active broker-salesperson license.

Voided license. Licensees may not practice real estate with a voided license. The three causes for voiding of a license are:

- ▸ expiration
- ▸ suspension
- ▸ revocation

In addition, it is important to note that if an employing broker's license expires, is suspended, or is revoked, then the licenses of all of the broker's salespeople are likewise voided.

Licensing requirements and procedures

To obtain a real estate license, an applicant must fulfill certain requirements. While license requirements vary from state to state, they commonly focus on personal background, education, real estate experience, and a licensing examination.

Personal requirements. To qualify for a broker's or salesperson's license, an applicant must be of legal age and mentally competent. In addition, an applicant may be required to have a high school diploma or its equivalent.

Moral character. The application process in most states also evaluates an applicant's character and reputation in terms of honesty, trustworthiness, and possible criminal record. Direct questioning, reference checking, and fingerprinting are part of the process.

Educational prerequisites. Most states now require successful completion of a certain number of hours of classroom or self-study instruction for licensing. Other states may allow for testing or conditional licensure provided that the licensee or licensee-candidate has completed portions of the requirement, or commits to completion within a certain time-frame following issuance of the license.

For salespeople, the pre-license education requirement may range from 24-180 contact hours of instruction. In most cases, an applicant must first enroll in a number of required courses and then a number of elective courses to complete the hour requirement. In certain states, prior college courses may be counted toward the education requirement.

Educational prerequisites for a broker's license usually consist of additional required real estate courses and other advanced courses, including college business courses. Whenever a real estate course is required, a student must demonstrate successful completion by passing a course examination.

Required brokerage experience. Most states require an applicant for a broker's license to have experience as an actively licensed salesperson within a certain period preceding the date of the application. For example, an applicant may need to have completed one year of service for a broker within the previous four years prior to the application.

Agency affiliation. Generally, an applicant for a salesperson's license does not need to have a commitment from an employing broker to obtain a license. In the absence of an employer, the state will issue an inactive license which can be activated when the licensee is hired. Similarly, a broker may obtain an inactive license without any pre-existing commitment to begin practice immediately.

Application. All aspects of the license application, including background data, references, prior experience in real estate, fingerprinting, and required fees must be complete for an application to be processed. An application is usually completed and processed before an applicant takes the state license examination.

The state license examination. All states require license applicants to pass a comprehensive license examination. Generally, the examination consists of multiple-choice questions. If an applicant passes the exam, the state issues a broker's or salesperson's license, provided all other licensing requirements are met.

Continuing education. Most states now require licensees to complete continuing education courses in order to *renew* a license. Failure to complete continuing education requirements can cause a licensee to lose the license to practice real estate.

LICENSE REGULATION

The Real Estate Commission
Regulation focus
Bonds and recovery funds

The Real Estate Commission

In addition to establishing real estate license requirements, state license laws provide for the establishment of a real estate regulatory entity to administer and enforce licensing legislation. This entity is most often known as the state's *real estate commission*. In some states, it is a *real estate department* or similarly-named entity within the state's department of license regulation.

A state real estate commission has the authority to:

> ▸ oversee the licensing process
> ▸ administer all aspects of the license laws
> ▸ receive and deliberate on consumer complaints
> ▸ handle problems between licensees

To enable it to discharge its responsibilities, a state empowers its real estate commission to institute binding regulations for licensees.

Structure. Most real estate commissions are comprised of a group of commissioners appointed by the executive branch of state government, commonly the governor. Commissioners serve a term of office which may be renewable, depending on state law. A real estate commission usually employs a support staff to manage the day-to-day affairs of the agency. It is common for the support staff to be headed by a salaried executive director.

Authority. A real estate commission's authority is generally

- ▶ regulatory
- ▶ judicial
- ▶ administrative

Regulatory powers enable the agency to pass specific regulations and rules to support the administration of the license law. Judicial powers enable it to conduct hearings and investigations into the activities of licensees and to rule on license suspensions or revocations. Administrative powers enable it to establish the staff organization, records, and facilities to manage the licensing process and the licensees themselves.

Education and research foundation. In addition to administering the licensing process and the conduct of licensees, most real estate commissions establish and maintain an education and research foundation. The foundation serves the real estate industry and the public by carrying out various real estate research projects.

Regulation focus

License status. As primary tasks, a real estate commission manages the initial licensing and then the maintenance of license status of practitioners. Managing the status of licenses entails establishing rules and procedures for changes of status: activation, deactivation, renewal, re-issue, suspension, revocation. Among other things, the commission validates education certificates, sets rules for changing employers, and keeps track of licensee's address changes.

Real estate schools. As part of managing the licensing process, real estate commissions approve and regulate the practices of real estate schools and the pre-license curricula of colleges and universities. This regulatory activity extends to the approval or certification of courses, materials, instructors, and administrative policies of any organization or institution offering courses that apply toward the state's education requirements for licensure.

Regulated standards of practice and conduct. A second mission of a real estate commission is to enact enforceable guidelines defining the ethical and professional behavior of licensees. These guidelines may include specific sanctions against

- ▶ fraud, including misrepresentation, concealment, and collusion
- ▶ violations of fiduciary duty
- ▶ negligence
- ▶ failure to make required disclosures
- ▶ practicing law in completing or interpreting contracts
- ▶ mismanaging escrow funds, earnest money deposits, advance fees, and rental deposits
- ▶ making improper commission arrangements with clients, customers, or other licensees
- ▶ accepting or paying illegal kickbacks and referral fees
- ▶ false or misleading advertising

> ▸ noncompliance with office identity requirements
> ▸ exceeding one's authority as a broker or salesperson

Handling complaints against licensees. Real estate commissions must enforce license laws and regulations. Enforcement commonly takes the form of acting on complaints received from consumers and other licensees. A real estate commission typically establishes a formal procedure to handle complaints and disputes in an orderly fashion. When a complaint comes into the commission, the complainant generally must file a formal complaint detailing all relevant circumstances of the dispute. Delegated officials then investigate the complaint. If they find the complaint has substance, the commission conducts hearings and further investigation. If necessary, the commission then issues an official order of disciplinary action. The licensee may appeal the commission's ruling in the appropriate state court.

Violation of any license law provision or regulation is punishable by suspension or revocation of license. If the infraction is a violation of criminal law, the commission may report the case to the proper judicial authority.

Bonds and recovery funds

The outcome of many cases of license law violation is a negotiated financial settlement or a court-ordered money judgment against the violator. If the licensee lacks financial resources, the settlement or judgment may be to some extent uncollectible. To avoid this situation, many states require licensees to obtain a bond at the cost of a nominal annual fee. The bond covers the difference between a potential settlement amount and the licensee's financial resources for satisfying the judgment or settlement.

Other states, rather than requiring a bond, establish a real estate recovery fund. The recovery fund is a reserve account funded through license fees and collected fines. The fund pays portions of a money judgment on behalf of a licensee, up to a prescribed amount. A licensee must repay all amounts so withdrawn, during which time the person's license is suspended.

22 Licensing And Regulation Overview
Snapshot Review

STATE LICENSE LAW

- most real estate practitioners must be licensed

- protects public, ensures professional competency of licensees

- establishes: requirements for licensure, guidelines of conduct for maintaining license, commission to administer the law

- applicants need a sound understanding of local license law

OBTAINING A REAL ESTATE LICENSE

Services requiring licensure

- license required to perform a real estate service for another for consideration, specifically: brokerage; property management; appraising; counseling; syndicating; auctioning

- exemptions: wage-paid employees of property owners, transient facility employees, condo or coop managers, cemetery lot merchants, attorneys; court-appointed representatives

Types of license

- broker's: individual, corporation, partnership, branch office, non-resident; salesperson's: individual, broker-salesperson

- active if practicing; inactive if not practicing; inactive or expired if renewal requirements not met

- voided: by suspension, revocation, expiration

Licensing requirements

- personal: age, mental competence, general education, character

- specific education: completion of required real estate courses

- experience: salesperson experience may be required if applying for a broker's license

- agency affiliation: not necessary

- other: complete application; pass state license examination; complete continuing education if applicable

LICENSE REGULATION

The Real Estate Commission

- state-level government entity that regulates and administers the license law

- oversees licensing process; enforces license law provisions; handles consumer and licensee complaints; consists of appointed commissioners and permanent support staff; maintains education and research foundation

Regulation focus

- management of licensing and license status; regulation of real estate schools and programs; regulation of practices of licensees; enactment of professional guidelines to protect public; resolution of disputes and complaints; suspension or revocation of licenses

Bonds and recovery funds

- ensure that the public will be able to collect on settlements for damages and money judgments against licensees

23 Risk Management

Risk Management Strategies
Risk Management Procedures
Primary Areas of Risk

Risk is the chance of losing something. Its two dimensions are the probability of occurrence and the extent of exposure to monetary or non-monetary consequences. Since most risks are related to judgments and decisions, the real estate licensee, who makes numerous complex decisions every day, faces a high degree of *risk potential*.

Risk management is a structured approach to dealing with the uncertainties and consequences of risk. In real estate practice, the aim is to reduce risk to an acceptable level through anticipation and planning.

RISK MANAGEMENT STRATEGIES

Avoidance
Reduction
Transference
Retention

Four well-established strategies for managing risk are:

- ▶ Avoidance (elimination)
- ▶ Reduction (mitigation, sharing)
- ▶ Transference (outsourcing, insuring)
- ▶ Retention (acceptance and budgeting)

Not all of these strategies are always possible or available, but a real estate firm or licensee who fails to make a conscious effort to employ one or more of them increases the likelihood of loss from the many potential risks that are always present in the real estate business.

Avoidance   Avoidance includes refraining from an activity that carries risk. One can avoid the risks of being in an automobile accident by not riding in automobiles. Avoiding risks also means missing the opportunity to benefit from the avoided activity. By avoiding automobile travel, one is confined to modes of transportation, such as buses and walking, that do not offer the same high degree of personal freedom and efficiency. Complete avoidance of risk in real estate practice is almost impossible. A broker, for instance, may believe that hiring only experienced affiliates eliminates the risk that affiliates will commit license law violations. However, even experienced practitioners may not know the law, and, sometimes, people break the law deliberately. The risk may be reduced, but it remains.

Reduction

Reduction involves taking steps to reduce the probability or the severity of a potential loss. However, this strategy may result in reducing risk in one area only to increase it in another. A familiar example is a sprinkler system that dispenses water to reduce the risk of fire but at the same time increases the risk of water damage.

In real estate practice, one risk reduction tactic is to share responsibility for making a decision. The agent provides the consumer with expertise, and perhaps some advice, but lets the consumer decide how much to offer. In this way, the agent gets some relief from the risks inherent in the buyer's decision to purchase.

Transference

Transference means passing the risk to another party, by contract or other means. An insurance policy is the common example, but sometimes the wording of a sales or personal services contract can transfer risk without resorting to insurance.

In the real estate business, transference is typically and most successfully accomplished by means of an errors and omissions (E&O) insurance policy, either on the individuals in a firm or on the firm itself. State law may require such insurance.

Retention

Retention of risk means entering into an activity in spite of known risks and taking full responsibility for the consequences. This is, in effect, self-insurance, the only strategy left when risk cannot be reduced or transferred and one has decided not to avoid it because of the desirability of the potential benefits.

RISK MANAGEMENT PROCEDURES

Education
Disclosure
Documentation and record keeping
Insurance

Experience shows that the most practical strategies for risk management in real estate practice are reduction and transference, with procedures focusing on:

- ▶ Education
- ▶ Disclosure
- ▶ Documentation
- ▶ Insurance

Education

Education is the first line of defense against risk. When agents are familiar with the forms provided by the office, how and when to complete them and where to send them, the likelihood of errors is reduced. Likewise, agents need to be able to identify and understand common contract elements, complete contract forms developed by attorneys, and evaluate offers received from co-op agents on their listings without committing a license violation or breach of law.

In most states, brokers have a legal obligation to provide training to affiliated licensees. Licensees also have the obligation to seek out appropriate education and training outside the brokerage to ensure that they know how to comply with the law. In addition, licensees must satisfy legal requirements for continuing education, while those who care about personal excellence will seek further education and training to enhance their professional skills.

Disclosure

By ensuring that all parties have the information they are entitled to, proper disclosure reduces the risk that clients and customers will accuse a licensee of misleading or inducing them to make a decision with incomplete information. Further, laws in every state require disclosures of one kind or another.

Disclosure may be made in writing or verbally and may or may not require written acknowledgment from the receiving party.

Required disclosures usually include:

- agency relationships
- property condition
- duties and obligations
- personal interest in the transaction
- personal interest in referrals

Documentation and Record keeping

Documentation provides evidence of compliance with laws and regulations. It proves what clients and customers and licensees said and did in a transaction. Some documentation is required by law.

The components of a thoroughly documented paper trail include:

- Policy and procedure manuals
- Standard forms
- Communication records
- Transaction records
- Contracts
- Accounting
- Other important documents

Policy manual. A written and uniformly enforced company policy lets everyone in the firm know what to expect before problems arise. The policy manual should cover the company's rules in such areas as floor duty privileges, assignment of relocation properties to agents, referrals between agents within the company, and requirements for continuing education, sales meeting participation, and property tours.

Procedures manual. A company procedures manual should spell out how to handle every aspect of the company's business that agents and brokers need to know—from handling consumers' funds and documents, conducting consumer transactions, dealing with MLS-related matters, and placing signage, to all procedures prescribed by state or federal law, especially license, banking and fair housing laws. Adherence to a procedures manual reduces the risk that an individual will inadvertently commit an unlawful act. Whenever changes are made to the policy or procedures manual, each agent should sign the revised manual as evidence that the agent has examined it.

Standard forms. Standard forms save time and protect against the unauthorized practice of law. Since they are most often prepared by lawyers familiar with the market area, they can address contingencies that are common in the area in a manner that reflects the real estate laws of the state. On the other hand, a licensee often needs to adapt a standardized form for a client by assisting with filling in blanks, modifying terms, and attaching addenda. The licensee must always remain aware of the limitations the state has placed on such activities.

Here are a few of the standard forms a brokerage should provide for its agents and affiliates:

- buyer and seller representation agreements, exclusive and non-exclusive
- agreement to show property
- purchase and sale agreement
- agency disclosure form
- property condition disclosure, disclaimer, and exemption form
- lease agreement
- personal interest disclosure form
- referral for service disclosure form
- lead-based paint disclosure form
- special disclosure forms (mold, radon, subsurface sewage system, impact fees/adequate facilities taxes, etc.)
- referral agreement
- independent contractor agreement
- closing checklist

Communication records. Some communications with transaction parties are good and necessary for business. Others are required by law, such as certain disclosures. A transaction checklist is a good tool for managing risk associated with the failure to make required communications to all principals and for keeping track of required communications from co-op agents.

Retaining evidence that information has been communicated is a necessary procedure. Electronic communications should be archived on suitable electronic media. Copies of mailed or faxed communications should be maintained in the transaction folder.

It is always difficult to document telephone or face-to-face conversations, especially with the constant use of cell phones from a variety of locations. It is a good practice to make brief notes at the time and then write them up later for mailing or faxing to the other party. Be sure, however, that you can produce these notes on demand, lest you be accused later of withholding documentation that has been promised.

Maintaining a good record of communications is useful for resolving disagreements where parties dispute what has been said because it allows the agent to produce a dated document that resolves the issue definitively.

Transaction records. State laws require licensees to document transactions. Firms are required to keep written records of all real estate transactions for a number of years (usually three to five) after closing or termination. Required records typically include:

- listing agreements
- offers
- contracts
- closing statements
- agency agreements
- disclosure documents
- correspondence and other communication records
- notes and any other relevant information

Accounting. In addition to other accounting records, there is the requirement to maintain written accounting of escrow funds. For each transaction, property, and principal, escrow records will include:

- depositor
- date of deposit
- date of withdrawal
- payee
- other information deemed pertinent by the real estate commission

Other documents. Additional documents may be required by law or regulation, or should be kept simply as protection in case of disputes and lawsuits. These would include copies of advertising materials, materials used in training agents, records of compliance with continuing education requirements, safety manuals, and anything else that shows how the firm conducts its business and safeguards its staff as well as the rights of consumers.

Insurance

Many forms of insurance are available for property owners and managers. Some of these types are also used to manage certain risks of brokers and licensees.

General Liability. General liability insurance provides coverage for risks incurred by a property owner when the public or a licensee enters the owned property (**public liability**). The insurer pays the covered claim and legal fees, costs, and expenses, including medical expenses, resulting from owner negligence or other causes. This type of insurance does not cover **professional liability,** for which an Errors & Omissions policy is necessary.

Errors and Omissions. Professional liability is of two general types:

1. Unprofessional conduct – a claim that one has failed to carry out fiduciary duties and provide an acceptable standard of care

2. Breach of contract – a claim that one has failed to perform services under the terms of a contract in a timely manner

The primary method for transferring the professional liability risks of brokers, managers, and licensees is Errors & Omissions (E&O) insurance. A standard E&O policy provides coverage for "damages resulting from any negligent act, error or omission arising out of Professional Services." A standard policy does NOT cover:

- violations of law
- fraudulent, dishonest, criminal or malicious acts
- mishandling of escrow moneys, earnest money deposits, or security deposits
- antitrust violations
- sexual harassment
- Fair Housing violations
- agent-owned properties
- environmental violations
- failure to detect or disclose environmental conditions, including mold
- acts committed prior to licensure or after termination of active status
- activities as an appraiser if licensing other than a real estate license is required

E&O insurance, in short, covers "mistakes" but not crimes.

Fire and hazard. The risks of property damage caused by fire, wind, hail, smoke, civil disturbance, and other such causes are covered by fire and hazard insurance.

Flood. The risks of property damage caused by floods, heavy rains, snow, drainage failures, and failed public infrastructures such as dams and levies are covered by a specialized flood policy. Regular hazard policies do not include flood coverage.

Other insurance. Other common types of insurance coverage for income and commercial properties include:

- **casualty**—coverage for specific risks, such as theft, vandalism, burglary, illness and accident, machinery damage

- **workers' compensation**—hospital and medical coverage for employees injured in the course of employment, mandated by state laws

- **contents and personal property**—coverage for building contents and personal property when they are not actually on the building premises

- **consequential loss, use, and occupancy**—coverage for the business losses resulting from a disaster, such as loss of rent and other revenue, when the property cannot be used for business

- **surety bond**—coverage against losses resulting from criminal or negligent acts of an employee

PRIMARY AREAS OF RISK

Agency
Property disclosures
Listing and selling process
Contracting process
Fair Housing
Antitrust
Rules and regulations
Misrepresentation
Recommending providers
Financing and closing
Trust fund handling
Safety And security

Risks for licensees are present every day in business transactions. Many of these risks carry legal implications as well as possible financial and professional consequences.

Agency

The risks of agency will occur in one of two areas:

> ▶ the requirement to inform and disclose
> ▶ the requirement to carry out an agency duty.

Most states require agency relationships to be in writing and to be disclosed to all parties to a transaction. State law may spell out agency duties, or the duties may be a part of general agency law. In states that do not use agency, there is still the obligation to explain and disclose the nature of the relationship.

Disclosure requirements. A licensee may be acting in a transaction as facilitator, agent, subagent, designated agent, single agent, dual agent, non-agent or in some capacity. Regardless of status, the licensee must follow state disclosure requirements. These are, typically, to:

> ▶ disclose status *verbally* to other licensees on initial contact
> ▶ disclose status *verbally* to buyer and seller before providing real estate services
> ▶ confirm the disclosure *in writing* before signing a listing agreement or presenting a purchase offer (to an unrepresented seller) or before preparing a purchase offer (to an unrepresented buyer)
> ▶ get a *signed receipt* indicating the written disclosure has been made

Carrying out the duties of agency also require disclosures of :

> ▶ personal interest the agent has in a transaction (such as owner or buyer)
> ▶ personal benefit the agent will derive from a service referral
> ▶ required property and market information
> ▶ information about customers a client is entitled to have

Duties. A licensee who acts for a principal in a real estate transaction is required by law to assume certain responsibilities toward the parties to the transaction. Whether a state applies the fiduciary duties of agency law or specifies its own duties toward clients and consumers, the basic duties remain:

To all parties

- honesty
- fairness
- reasonable care and skill
- disclosures

To clients

- skill
- care
- diligence
- loyalty
- obedience
- confidentiality
- accounting
- full disclosure

The duty to exercise **skill, care and diligence** means that licensees may not be casual or negligent in their actions. Licensee negligence is actionable when principals are harmed by the licensee's failure.

The duty of **loyalty** requires the agent to *put the client's interests above those of everyone else*, including his or her own.

The duty of **obedience** requires the agent to act on the principal's wishes regarding the transaction as long as they do not result in any illegal action. The duty of obedience never overrides the legal obligation of agents to deal fairly and honestly with all parties.

The duty of **confidentiality** requires the agent to hold in confidence any information that would harm the client's interests or bargaining position or anything else the client wishes to keep secret, unless the law requires disclosure. The duty of confidentiality survives the termination of the listing contract.

The duty of **accounting** applies to all funds involved in a real estate transaction. Accounts must be maintained as required by law, and escrow funds are to be handled strictly in accordance with the law.

The duty of **disclosure** applies to both parties to a transaction, although usually with some differences. Proper disclosure to customers primarily concerns agency, property condition, and environmental hazards. To the client, it generally concerns all known facts regarding the property and the transaction, including information about the other transaction party. State laws prescribe what may, must, and must not be disclosed. Licensees must be vigilant to avoid oversights and conflicts of interest that can lead to a disclosure to the wrong party or disclosure of information that is confidential.

Conflicts of interest. Conflicts of interest arise when an agent forgets to put the best interests of a client ahead of those of everyone else. This can happen in situations involving undisclosed dual agencies, broker-owned listings, licensees buying for their own account, vendor referrals, and property management subcontracting of services, among many others. Even ordinary, everyday transactions carry a built-in risk of conflict of interest. Consider the fact that a licensee usually receives no compensation for a failed transaction. Therefore, it is in the licensee's interest to see the transaction completed, even if it may not be in the client's best interest. A negative result from a home inspection or other test has the potential to cause a buyer to back out of a contract. A licensee who has forgotten whose best interest should be primary might be tempted to recommend inspectors who will overlook problems in exchange for receiving referrals. Licensees must always disclose any self-interest they have in a transaction, and always remember their duties to clients and consumers.

Confidentiality. Licensees have a responsibility to maintain the confidentiality of certain kinds of information they obtain concerning clients and customers. The duty to maintain confidentiality generally survives the termination of a listing agreement into perpetuity. If it seems that revealing confidential information might benefit the client, the licensee should obtain the client's written permission to proceed.

Confidential information generally includes information about a client's motivations in a transaction, financial and personal details, and information specifically designated as confidential by the client. Public information, such as that contained in public records, information that becomes known without the licensee's participation, or that the client reveals to another, is not considered confidential.

State laws often require businesses to provide security for the personal information they obtain about consumers. Security procedures should protect personal information from unauthorized access, destruction, use, modification, or disclosure. Confidential information, when it is not to be retained, must be disposed of in a secure manner.

Penalties. Possible penalties for breach of agency relationships include:

- rescission of transaction
- loss of compensation
- fees and costs
- punitive damages
- ethics discipline
- license discipline

Property disclosures

Property condition. Most states require the seller of a residential property to deliver to the buyer a written disclosure or disclaimer about the property's condition, including any material defects the owner knows about. The disclosure is usually required before any purchase contract is accepted.. A second disclosure may be required at closing. The licensee should always obtain the parties' signatures acknowledging receipt of these disclosures.

Depending on the state, the licensee may have no further duty to disclose property condition after properly informing parties of their rights and obligations. However, the licensee may still be subject to legal action for

- deliberately distorting the facts (intentional misrepresentation)
- cheating any party (fraud)
- concealing or failing to disclose adverse facts which the licensee knew about or should have known about (intentional or unintentional misrepresentation)

Lead-based paint and other disclosures. Federal law requires sellers of houses built before 1978 to make a lead-based paint disclosure before accepting an offer to purchase. The licensee must tell the seller about this requirement, give the seller the proper disclosure form, and make sure that the buyer receives it.

The licensee must also make sure the seller discloses any other circumstances the situation and the law require, which may include:

- wood infestation inspection report
- soil test report
- subsurface sewage disposal system permit disclosure
- impact fees or adequate facilities taxes disclosure
- mold and radon reports or treatments

Listing and selling process

Nature and accuracy of the listing agreement. In most states, a listing agreement is enforceable only if it is in writing. Most states forbid net listings, because they violate the requirement that a valid listing agreement must specify a selling price and the agent's compensation. The licensee, in accordance with the duty of due diligence, must verify the accuracy of the statements in the listing regarding the property, the owner, and the owner's representations. Especially important facts for a broker or agent to verify are:

- the property condition
- ownership status
- the client's authority to act

An agent who does not to act with a reasonable degree of due diligence in these matters may be exposed to liability if it turns out that the property is not as represented or the client cannot perform the contract as promised.

Comparative Market Analysis (CMA). In preparing a Comparative Market Analysis, licensees should guard against using the terms "appraisal" and "value," which are reserved for the use of certified appraisers. Misuse of these terms could lead to a charge of misrepresenting oneself as an appraiser. In discussing listed properties with clients or customers, real estate licensees should be careful to use guarded terms such as "recommended listing price," "recommended purchase price,' and "recommended listing price range."

Agents should make every effort to help the sellers find a reasonable listing price based on the current market. If the CMA leads the seller to list at a price that is too high, the seller may blame the agent when the transaction fails because of an appraisal that comes in below the selling price. To minimize this risk, it is best to be conservative in the CMA and retain documentation that the seller went above the recommended price in spite of the agent's advice.

Estimate of Closing Costs. In preparing an estimate of closing costs for a seller or buyer, there is the risk of forgetting something, leading to an unpleasant surprise when the consumer suddenly faces unexpected costs or conditions. Licensees should use their broker's form, if there is one, and make it clear to the consumer that it is only an estimate of likely costs, not a statement of actual costs. In some states, brokers and agents do not prepare closing cost estimates, leaving that task to the lender.

Advertising. State and federal laws regulate advertising, including the federal Fair Housing laws as they pertain to discriminatory advertising and providing of services. Advertising includes electronic communication, social media/networking, and internet marketing. Usage must be consistent with company image and legal requirements. The license laws of most states list illegal advertising actions subject to discipline such as:

> ▸ making any substantial and intentional misrepresentation
>
> ▸ making any promise that might cause a person to enter into a contract or agreement when the promise is one the licensee cannot or will not abide by
>
> ▸ making continued and blatant misrepresentations or false promises through affiliate brokers, other persons, or any advertising medium
>
> ▸ making misleading or untruthful statements in any advertising, including using the term "Realtor" when not authorized to do so and using any other trade name, insignia or membership in a real estate organization when the licensee is not a member.

Committing such acts may result in license suspension or revocation.

Authorizations and Permissions. Licensees should stay within the bounds of the authority granted by the agency agreement or must not do anything requiring permission without first getting that permission in writing. For instance, permission should be obtained before doing any of the following unless the listing agreement specifically grants the authority:

> ▸ post a sign on the property
> ▸ remove other signs
> ▸ show the property
> ▸ hand out the property condition disclosure
> ▸ distribute marketing materials
> ▸ advertise in various media
> ▸ use a multiple listing service
> ▸ cooperate with other licensees
> ▸ divide the commission or negotiate a commission split
> ▸ share final sales data with the MLS
> ▸ place a lock box on the property

> ▸ appoint subagents
> ▸ appoint a designated agent
> ▸ change agency status

Scope of expertise. Real estate licensees are not, by nature, financial consultants, accountants, appraisers, soil scientists, well diggers, lawyers, decorators, contractors, builders, plumbers, carpenters, inspectors, prognosticators, and a number of other kinds of expert. However, in today's competitive environment, consumers often demand much more from a licensee than the traditional basic services. An agent who fails to live up to prevailing standards may be held liable for negligence, fraud, or violation of state real estate license laws and regulations. At the same time, agents must be particularly careful about the temptation to misrepresent themselves as experts and offer inappropriate expert advice. Disclaimer and referral are always the best risk control procedures to forestall an accusation of misrepresentation from a consumer who claims to have been harmed by reliance on the licensee's non-existent expertise. The exact nature of the services to be provided should be stated as clearly as possible in the listing agreement.

Contracting process   According to the Statute of Frauds, all contacts for real estate must be in writing to be enforceable. Contracts that contain incorrect information or are inadequately prepared can pose a serious liability for a licensee. To avoid such a situation, it is imperative for the contract to reflect the terms that the parties have agreed upon in the most accurate and honest manner. The agent must also be careful to comply with the letter of the real estate law. Violations can jeopardize the enforceability of a listing or sales contract, in addition to resulting in criminal prosecution.

Common risks and errors in the contracting process include:

> ▸ using an illegal form
>
> A licensee may be punished for using any real estate listing agreement form, sales contract form, or offer to purchase form that lacks a *definite termination date*.
>
> ▸ failing to state inclusions and exclusions
>
> The parties should identify as included in or excluded from the transfer any ambiguous items. Unwritten agreements between the parties are a source of later dispute and trouble.
>
> ▸ failing to track the progress of contingency satisfaction
>
> The time period for completing contingencies such as inspections is specific and limited. Failure to meet or waive a condition may terminate the contract. A "time is of the essence" clause in the standard agreement makes the time period for contingencies critical.
>
> ▸ mistakes in entering data in a form
>
> All data should be checked and verified: dates, times, amounts,

warranties, descriptions, names, representations, promises, procedures, authority, etc. One way to reduce risk in the contracting process is to use a checklist that covers all the contract items.

Unauthorized practice of law. The unintentional practice of law without a license is a great risk in the contracting process, as well as in the representation process. It is illegal for real estate professionals who are not attorneys to draw up contracts for transactions they are not involved in or to charge a separate fee for preparing a contract.

Such licensees may fill in blanks or make deletions on a preprinted contract form prepared by a lawyer. While a licensee may make deletions, additions to a form should be drafted by an attorney. The principals themselves can make changes as long as each change is signed or initialed by all signers. Preprinted riders can often be attached as addenda to a contract without an attorney.

It is also illegal for real estate licensees who are not lawyers to give legal advice or interpret contract language. Licensees, however, may express opinions. For instance, if a licensee believes that a party has grasped the meaning of a contract, it is permissible to say something like, "Though I am not an attorney, in my opinion your understanding of this contract is correct." It would be questionable to make a definitive statement like, "That's correct."

Fair Housing

The risk of violating fair housing laws can be minimized through ongoing education that addresses both the content and the intent of the laws. It is especially necessary for paperwork and documentation to be accurate and concise in a situation where a fair housing issue could arise.

Advertising. The Fair Housing Act forbids real estate advertising that mentions race, color, religion, national origin, sex, handicap, or familial status in any way that suggests preference or discrimination. State laws may add other protected categories, such as creed and age.

Risk can be reduced by the use of street names or other non-biased geographical references when stating where the property is located, and by describing the property rather than the type of persons who might live in or around it. Even if a home appears "ideal for a young family," it is best not to advertise it as such. Such advertising would exclude other groups such as singles, the elderly, and older families.

In advertising the sale or rental of housing covered by the Fair Housing Act, HUD recommends using the Fair Housing Logo or phrase "Equal Housing Opportunity."

Answering questions. When faced with questions that might lead to a *steering* charge or other violation of fair housing laws, it is best for the licensee to limit the response to features of the home and to the process of selling, buying, and listing properties, and refer the questioner to someone else to answer questions about such matters as the demographic make-up of the neighborhood. It is illegal for the licensee to voice an opinion based on race, religion, color, creed, national origin, sex, handicap, elderliness, or familial status. The agent should explain this fact to the buyer and be wary of any situation where the agent's behavior might be construed as discriminatory.

Listing agreements. Before entering into a listing agreement, a licensee should explain that it is necessary to comply with fair housing laws and obtain the potential client's acknowledgment and agreement. The agent should make it clear that the agent will

- ▶ reject the use of terms indicating race, religion, creed, color, national origin, sex, handicap, age or familial status to describe prospective buyers.

- ▶ terminate the listing if the seller uses race, religion, creed, color, national origin, sex, handicap, age, or familial status in the consideration of an offer.

- ▶ inform the broker if the seller makes any attempt to discriminate illegally.

Offers. A seller cannot refuse to sell a property to an individual based on the individual's belonging to a protected class, and if this is attempted, the real estate professional must not be involved. If the seller asks about the color, religion, creed, national origin, ethnicity, age, or familial status of a buyer, the agent must explain that it is illegal to give out such information. The best risk reduction procedure is to treat all buyers and sellers equally, showing no preference for one over another.

Antitrust

Antitrust laws forbid brokers to band together to set a price on their services in listing and selling property. Even being overheard discussing commission rates or being present at such a conversation can lead to charges of *price fixing*.

The law recognizes that some cooperative arrangements between firms – such as joint development projects – may help consumers by allowing these firms to compete more effectively against each other. Even so the government does not prosecute all agreements between companies, but only those that will raise prices for the public or deny the public new and better products.

Sherman Antitrust Act. The *Sherman Antitrust Act* makes illegal all contracts, agreements, and conspiracies among competitors that would unfairly restrict interstate trade by fixing prices, rigging bids, or other means. An unlawful monopoly is created when one company becomes the only supplier of a product or service by getting rid of competition via secret agreements with other companies.

Clayton Act. The *Clayton Act* prohibits mergers or acquisitions that are likely to lessen competition and increase prices to consumers. The Act also prohibits certain other business practices that under certain circumstances may harm competition. Private parties injured by an antitrust violation may sue in federal court for three times their actual damages, plus court costs and attorneys' fees.

Federal Trade Commission Act. The *Federal Trade Commission Act* forbids unfair competition in interstate commerce but establishes no criminal penalties.

Enforcement. Federal antitrust laws are enforced in three main ways:

> ▸ the Antitrust Division of the Department of Justice (DOJ) brings criminal and civil enforcement actions

> ▸ the FTC brings civil enforcement actions

> ▸ private parties bring lawsuits claiming damages

To collect evidence, Department of Justice lawyers often work with the Federal Bureau of Investigation (FBI) on court-authorized searches of a business, monitoring phone calls and employing informants equipped with secret listening devices.

State attorneys general may sue under the Clayton Act on behalf of injured consumers in their states, and groups of consumers often bring lawsuits on their own.

Anyone associated with an organization found guilty of an antitrust violation and determined to have had knowledge of that violation may also suffer legal consequences.

Penalties. Penalties for Violation of Antitrust Laws include:

> ▸ fines for individuals and corporations, as well as possible imprisonment.

> ▸ Under the Clayton Antitrust Act, parties can sue antitrust violators and recover three times the damages they incurred plus court costs and attorneys' fees.

Rules and regulations

State real estate laws and commissioners' rules and regulations attempt to cover every possible risky situation. Non-compliance poses a direct threat to the legal and financial status of licensee and license in the following general ways:

> ▸ license expiration
> ▸ license revocation or suspension
> ▸ licensee discipline
> ▸ suit for damages

License expiration. Licenses expire because licensees neglect to:

> ▸ maintain E & O insurance when required
> ▸ meet education requirements
> ▸ observe correct renewal procedures

License revocation or suspension. Licenses are typically revoked or suspended when a licensee is found guilty of:

- obtaining a license under false pretenses
- committing a "prohibited act"
- neglecting to present every written offer as required
- neglecting to deliver signed copies of accepted offers to transaction parties as required
- failing to make sure that all required terms and conditions are present in a contract to purchase
- handling earnest money and other escrow funds improperly

Licensee discipline. A state real estate commission may assess a civil penalty for violations of a statute, rule, or order. Licensees are disciplined for:

- acting without a license when a license is required
- demanding a referral fee without reasonable cause
- entering into a net listing
- trying to induce another licensee's client to end or change an existing agency contract
- paying a commission to an unlicensed individual or company
- receiving an illegal referral fee, rebate or kickback
- practicing with an expired license

Licensee lawsuits. A licensee may be sued by the Department of Justice, Federal Trade Commission, a state real estate commission, a human rights commission, another licensee or firm, or an individual consumer. Licensees are mainly sued for:

- fair housing violations
- antitrust violations
- license law and other state law violations
- breach of contract
- agency duty violations
- illegal practice of law
- failures to disclose
- customer or client dissatisfaction
- fraud
- theft

Misrepresentation   Misrepresentation may be unintentional or intentional.

Unintentional misrepresentation. This type of misrepresentation occurs when a licensee *unknowingly* conveys inaccurate information to a consumer concerning a property, financing or agency service. False or inaccurate information that the licensee, as a professional, should have known to be false or inaccurate may be included in the definition. Those found guilty generally have to pay fines and may be disciplined by state real estate regulators and professional organizations.

Risky areas for unintentional misrepresentation include:

- making and reporting measurements
- describing property
- offering opinions about future growth and development of a neighborhood or neighboring property
- making declarative statements about the presence or absence of hazardous materials

The risks of unintentional misrepresentation are reduced if an agent

- learns to measure and calculate areas accurately
- relies on measurements reported by others only with extreme caution and specific disclaimers
- refrains from exaggeration
- avoids stating opinions a consumer might take for expertise

Intentional misrepresentation. Also known as fraud, this kind of misrepresentation occurs when a licensee _knowingly_ conveys false information about a property, financing or service. Fraud is a criminal act that may result in fines and incarceration, in addition to discipline from state regulators and professional organizations.

Recommending providers

There are several risks attending the recommendation of vendors and service providers to a consumer. First, the consumer may not be satisfied with the performance of the recommended party and blame the licensee. Second, in cases where a recommended provider performs illegal acts, there may be legal consequences for the licensee. Third, if a licensee has a business relationship with a recommended vendor or provider and neglects to disclose the fact, there are license violation consequences.

The major risk management technique is to shift the responsibility for choosing a vendor to the consumer. This can be done by refusing to recommend vendors at all; by presenting a broad range of choices and allowing the consumer to select; or by presenting a short list of thoroughly vetted vendors and allowing the consumer to make the decision, always with the disclaimer that *to the best of the licensee's knowledge*, the vendors on the list are competent and honest, but that the consumer is responsible for investigating and making his or her own judgment before hiring or buying.

Financing and closing

In the financing and closing phases of a transaction, a consumer may feel that a licensee has been incompetent or misleading. Licensees have an obligation to inform and educate their clients throughout the transaction process. Surprises and accusations of incompetence or misrepresentation are among possible results of failing to keep the party informed.

Discrimination. Of course, it is important to comply with relevant laws. Licensees must be mindful of the requirements of ECOA and refrain from participating in any manner of discriminatory lending. It is illegal to:

> threaten, coerce, intimidate or interfere with a person who is exercising a fair housing right or assisting another other to exercise that right.

> indicate a limitation or preference based on race, color, national origin, religion, sex, familial status, or handicap in any advertisement or communication. Single-family and owner-occupied housing that is otherwise exempt from the Fair Housing Act is subject to this prohibition against discriminatory advertising.

Progress reporting. All inspections and tests must comply with local and state laws and with the purchase contract. Progress reports should be accurate, timely, in writing, and free of speculation. If a consumer has a question about the meaning of something in an inspection report, the licensee should refer the consumer to the person who wrote the report rather than trying to explain it. This method transfers some of the risk inherent in interpreting the report.

Qualifying buyers. Many transactions fail because a buyer has been improperly qualified before the offer is presented. Using a lender to qualify the buyer saves time and protects the agent against leading a seller to believe a purchaser is fully qualified when this may not be the case. Also, lenders and loan agents are better able to look into the buyer's qualifications than a real estate licensee is. If it becomes necessary to show a property to a potential buyer who has not been qualified by a lender, the licensee can gain some protection by performing an informal qualification and documenting the fact that it was based on the information provided by the buyer. The buyer's signature on this documentation indicates the buyer's acceptance of at least partial responsibility for the qualification.

Lending fees disclosure. The licensee should explain loan fees, charges,

amounts, timing, and responsibilities. Agents can assist in the loan decision by explaining how to compare loans with differing charges and interest rates. The fact that a high origination fee and points may make a loan with a low interest rate unattractive to a borrower is important information for the agent to provide, and providing it may protect the agent against a later complaint that the buyer suffered a loss because of the agent's failure to inform.

Appraisal problems. Delays and appraised value are the typical problem areas. Failure to inform parties about delays can compromise the transaction. An under-appraisal will require the buyer to make a larger down payment or the seller to lower the price. If the property appraises for more than the purchase price, the seller may blame the agent for suggesting the lower price. In such a case, the seller's agent's defense is that the seller agreed to the listing price and that the price was a factor in attracting the buyer to the property.

RESPA Violations. The **Real Estate Settlement Procedures Act (RESPA)** stipulates that the parties to certain purchase transactions must be given accurate information reflecting their closing costs. It also prohibits certain business practices that are not considered to be in the consumer's best interest.

The licensee's risks regarding RESPA primarily relate to

- failing to ensure that the consumer is informed about his or her rights under the law

- giving or receiving an illegal kickback.

RESPA currently requires lenders to:

- give a copy of a Consumer Financial Protection Bureau loan information booklet to the applicant. The booklet explains RESPA provisions, general settlement costs, and the required **Closing Disclosure** form. The lender must provide the estimate of closing costs within three business days following the borrower's application.

- give the applicant a Loan Estimate (Form H-24) of expected closing costs within three business days of receiving the application. Actual closing costs may not vary from the estimate beyond certain limits.

- give the buyer the Closing Disclosure (Form H-25) specifying costs to be paid by buyer and seller at closing three business days before consummation.

- give the *buyer* the opportunity to review the final settlement statement *one business day prior to closing*.

RESPA specifically *prohibits* any fee or kickback paid to a party for a service when the party has not actually rendered the service. For example, it is prohibited for an insurance company to pay a real estate agent or a lender for referring a client.

Fees for referring clients to the following services are strictly forbidden:

- title services (search, insurance)
- appraisals
- inspections
- surveys
- loan issue
- credit report
- attorney services

The sharing of commissions and the payment of referral fees among cooperating brokers and multiple-listing services are not RESPA violations.

Trust fund handling   State laws prescribe how licensees must handle any escrow or earnest money deposits they receive. Those laws usually state that a broker must hold money received in connection with the purchase or lease of real property in a trust fund account. The type of account and financial depository are specified. The broker must record receipt of the money and place that money in the trust account within a specified time period. Usually, the law allows the broker to hold an earnest money check uncashed until the offer is accepted, provided the buyer gives written permission and the seller is informed.

Typical trust fund handling requirements include:

▶ the broker named as trustee of the account
▶ a federally-insured bank or recognized depository located in the state
▶ an account that is not interest-bearing if the financial institution ever requires prior written notice for withdrawals
▶ maintenance of records in a particular accounting format
▶ separate records kept for each beneficiary, property, or transaction
▶ records of funds received and paid out regularly reconciled with bank statements
▶ withdrawals only by the broker-trustee or other specifically authorized person

Commingling and conversion. Mixing of personal or company funds with client funds is grounds for the revocation or suspension of a real estate license. Depositing client funds in a personal or business account, or using them for any purpose other than the client's business, is also grounds for suspension or revocation of a license. It is important for the broker to remove commissions, fees or other income earned by the broker from a trust account within the period specified by law to avoid committing an act of commingling.

23 Risk Management Snapshot Review

RISK MANAGEMENT STRATEGIES

- two dimensions of risk: size, probability; risk management: structured approach to uncertainty

Avoidance
- refrain from risky activity

Reduction
- reduce probability; share responsibility

Transference
- pass risk by contract; insurance

Retention
- accept risk; self-insurance

RISK MANAGEMENT PROCEDURES

Education
- train in laws, forms and procedures, job performance

Disclosure
- provide information to reduce misunderstanding & lawsuits; agency, property condition, duties, personal interest

Documentation and record keeping
- maintain evidence of compliance; manuals, forms, records, contracts, accounting, other documents

Insurance
- general liability, E & O, fire and hazard, flood, casualty, workers, personal property, consequential loss, surety bond

PRIMARY AREAS OF RISK

Agency
- main failures: to inform and disclose, to fulfill duties

- disclosures: verbal, written, signed receipt; agency relationship and duties; personal interest in transaction; required information

- duties: to all– honesty, fairness, care, skill, required disclosures; additional to clients– diligence, loyalty, obedience, confidentiality, accounting, full disclosure

- conflicts of interest arise from failing to put client's interest first

- confidentiality duty lasts forever; laws define what is confidential, how to treat and dispose of information

- penalties include loss of transaction, compensation, fees and costs, damages, license

Property disclosures
- property condition, lead-based paint, other conditions; disclosure may discharge liability; failure to disclose may be construed as misrepresentation

Listing and selling process
- areas of risk include listing agreement accuracy, Comparative Market Analysis results, closing cost estimates, advertising, authorizations and permissions, exceeding expertise

Contracting process
- contracts for real estate must be in writing; inaccuracy endangers contract; other risks: illegal form, omitted elements, lapsed contingencies, wrong data

- unauthorized practice of law: non-lawyers may fill in blanks and delete words on standard contract forms; no legal advice to public allowed

Fair Housing
- advertising may not state preference, limitation or discrimination based on race, color, religion, national origin, sex, handicap, familial status

- agent must not be involved with discriminatory actions of a client or customer

Antitrust
- government prosecutes cooperative arrangements that raise prices or reduce consumer choices: Sherman Antitrust Act outlaws restraint of trade; Clayton Act outlaws practices that harm competition; Federal Trade Commission Act outlaws unfair methods of competition

- violations punishable by government criminal and civil actions as well as by private lawsuits; fines, damages, and imprisonment possible

Rules and regulations
- violators of state rules and regulations risk license expiration, revocation, suspension, and other discipline

- prime causes of discipline include commission of prohibited acts, practicing with an expired license, disclosure failures, earnest money mishandling

Misrepresentation
- unintentional: inaccurate information conveyed unknowingly; subject to fines and license discipline; occurs most often in measurements, property descriptions

- intentional: fraud, knowingly conveying false information; criminal act subject to fines, license discipline, and incarceration

Recommending providers
- risks include consumer dissatisfaction, possible vicarious liability for illegal acts committed by a recommended provider, undisclosed business relationship (RESPA violation as well as license violation)

- best practice: do not recommend any vendors, or provide a list of trusted vendors with no recommendation and a disclaimer

Financing and closing
- risk areas include fair housing and ECOA violations; failed transactions because of agent failure to monitor contingency period; failure to ensure proper disclosure of closing costs; RESPA violations

Trust fund handling
- risk areas include mishandling of earnest money deposits; commingling and conversion of trust funds; errors in use of trust accounts

24 Property Management

Management Functions
The Management Agreement
Leasing Considerations
The Management Business

MANAGEMENT FUNCTIONS

Reporting
Budgeting
Renting
Property maintenance
Construction
Risk management

Property management is a specialty within the real estate profession. Many states require persons who manage real estate on behalf of other persons or entities to be licensed as real estate brokers. Other states license such persons specifically as property managers. Real estate firms that handle the sale of commercial and investment properties are in a natural position to manage those properties for their owners. Some property managers work for firms that manage multiple properties under blanket management contracts. Others are independent agents. Some are employees of the owner. They generally fall into one of the following categories:

▶   **individual property manager**-- usually a real estate broker who manages properties for one for one or more owners; may belong to a small property management firm devoted to full-time property management, be self-employed, or be one of several managers in a large real estate firm.

▶   **individual building manager**-- usually manages a single large property; may be employed by a property manager or directly by an owner; may or may not have a real estate license.

▶   **resident manager** (residential properties only)-- lives on the property and may be employed by a real estate broker, a managing agent or an owner to manage a property on a part-time or full-time basis; may be required by state law for properties of certain types and sizes.

A manager has a fiduciary relationship with the principal and, in general, is charged with producing the greatest possible net return on the owner's investment while safeguarding the value of the investment for the owner/investor. At the same time, the manager has some responsibilities to tenants, who want the best value and the best space for their money. Professional managers are therefore much more than rent collectors. They need technical expertise in marketing, accounting, finance, and construction. Property managers often specialize in one type of property - apartment, office, retail, industrial, farm, single-family-and acquire specialized knowledge of that property type. Whatever the property type and management arrangement, the manager's work involves leasing, managing, marketing, and maintaining the property. The services a manager provides thus can be seen to fall into three areas: financial, physical, and administrative. Specific functions, duties, and responsibilities are determined by the management agreement, although most agreements will include at least the following functions.

Reporting

Financial reporting to the principal is a fundamental responsibility of the property manager. Reports may be required monthly, quarterly, and annually. Required reports typically include an annual operating budget (see below); monthly cash flow reports indicating income, expenses, net operating income, and net cash flow; profit and loss statements based on the cash flow reports and showing net profit; and budget comparison statements showing how actual results match the original budget.

Budgeting

An operating budget based on expected expenses and revenues is a necessity for management. The budget will determine rental rates, amounts available for capital expenditures, required reserve funds, salaries and wages of employees, amounts to be paid for property taxes and insurance premiums and mortgage or debt service. It will indicate the expected return, based on the previous year's performance. A typical budget will contain a projection, also based on past performance and on current market information, of income from all sources, such as rents and other services, and of expenses for all purposes, such as operating expenses, maintenance services, utilities, taxes, and capital expenditures. Operating statements itemizing income and expenses are then presented to the owner on a regular basis so that the owner can evaluate the manager's performance against the budget.

Income. The total of scheduled rents plus revenues from such sources as vending services, storage charges, late fees, utilities, and contracts is the *potential gross income*. Subtracting losses caused by uncollected rents, vacancies and evictions gives *effective gross income*. Operating expenses are subtracted from this total to show *net operating income*. When debt service and reserves (which are not counted as operating expenses) are subtracted, the result is *cash flow*.

Expenses. Expenses may be fixed or variable. Fixed expenses are those that remain constant and may include operating expenses, regular maintenance costs, and administration. Variable expenses are those that may change from month to month or occur sporadically, such as specific repairs or capital expenditures.

Capital expenditures. Expected expenditures for major items such as renovation or expansion should be included as a budgeting item. Large-scale projects are typically budgeted over a period of years.

Cash reserve. A cash reserve is a fund set aside from operating revenues for variable expenses, such as supplies, redecorating, and repairs. The amount of the reserve is based on experience with variable expenses in previous years.

Renting

The property manager, whose full responsibilities include maintaining and managing the property in accordance with the owner's financial goals, include seeing that the property is properly rented and tenanted. The manager may use the services of a leasing agent, whose concern is solely to rent the space. In such a situation, some of the manager's tasks may be performed by the leasing agent. Renting the property includes the following tasks, regardless of which party is actually performing them.

Controlling vacancies. There are many possible reasons for vacancies in a building:

- rent too high or too low
- ineffective marketing
- management quality
- poor tenant-retention program
- image and appearance problems
- high market vacancy rate

Successful managers look for these factors and take steps to limit or counteract their effects.

Marketing. Finding and attracting the right kind of tenants for a property is the aim of a marketing program. A marketing plan based on the property's features and the relationship between supply and demand in the market area, and consonant with the money available, will determine the best mix of advertising and promotional activities. Marketing methods include:

- billboard advertising
- brochures and fliers
- meetings and presentations
- networking
- newspaper ads
- radio and television advertising
- signs
- tenant referrals
- websites and online services

The efficiency of marketing activities can be judged in terms of how many prospects per completed lease they generate. The lower the cost per prospect per lease, the more effective and efficient the program.

Setting rents. Rental income must be sufficient to cover fixed expenses, operating expenses, and desired return on investment. But rental rates must also be realistic, taking into account what is happening in the market. The manager must consider prevailing rents in comparable properties as well as vacancy rates in the market and in the property. The manager makes a detailed survey of competitive space and makes adjustments for differences between the subject property and competing properties before setting the rental rates for the property. Residential apartment rates are stated in monthly amounts per unit, while commercial rates are usually stated as an annual or monthly amount per square foot. If vacancy rates in the managed property are too high, the manager may have to lower rates or identify problems in the property or its management that are contributing to vacancy level. On the other hand, if the property's vacancy rate is significantly lower than market rates, the manager may conclude that higher rental rates are called for.

Selecting tenants. To ensure that the property produces the desired level of income from rent, it is essential to find the most suitable tenants. For commercial space, the manager must determine that:

- the space meets the tenant's needs for size, configuration, location, and quality.
- the tenant will be able to pay for the space.
- the tenant's business is compatible with that of other tenants.
- there is room for expansion if the tenant's need for space is likely to grow.

For residential space, in addition to ascertaining the tenant's creditworthiness, the manager must be careful to comply with all federal and local fair housing laws. A manager should collect the same type of information on all prospective tenants. However, even though the law prohibits discrimination on the basis of race, sex, age and other protected classes, a manager may discriminate in certain other ways. For example, a manager has the right to refuse to rent to a person who has a history paying rent late, damaging property, fighting with other tenants, or spotty employment.

Collecting rents. The lease agreement should clearly specify the terms of rental payment. The manager must establish a system of notices and records as well as a method of collecting rents on schedule. Compliance with all state laws and regulations concerning collecting and accounting for rents is a necessity to avoid unwanted legal complications. As for monies received, the manager must follow trust fund handling procedures established by law and laid out in the rental and management agreements. If authorized by the management agreement, the manager may also collect security deposits and handle them as required by law.

Maintaining tenant relations. Happy tenants remain in a rented space longer than unhappy tenants. High tenant turnover adds to increased advertising and redecorating expenses. For these reasons, it is incumbent on the manager to

- communicate regularly with tenants
- respond promptly and satisfactorily to maintenance and service requests
- enforce rules and lease terms consistently and fairly
- comply with all relevant laws, such as fair housing and ADA (Americans with Disabilities Act) regulations

Legal issues (Fair Housing, ADA, and ECOA). Fair housing laws govern landlords and tenants just as they do sellers and buyers. They ensure that persons receive fair treatment regardless of race, color, religion, national origin, sex, handicap, or familial status. Families with children must receive equal treatment with those who do not have children. Landlords cannot charge higher rents or security deposits because of the presence of children. Managers must make sure that their marketing and leasing practices are in accordance with fair housing laws.

The Americans with Disabilities Act similarly requires landlords in certain circumstances to make housing and facilities available to disabled persons without hindrance. Familiarity with this law and with the latest state, federal, and local fair housing laws is essential.

The Equal Credit Opportunity Act, which prohibits discrimination in lending, applies to how property managers evaluate potential tenants. The manager must be consistent in evaluating the creditworthiness of applicants. The same application forms and the same credit requirements should be used with all applicants.

Property maintenance

Physical maintenance of the property is one of the property manager's primary functions. The costs of services provided must always be balanced with financial objectives and the need to satisfy tenant needs. The manager will also be concerned with staffing and scheduling requirements, in accordance with maintenance objectives.

Maintenance objectives. The foremost maintenance objective is generally to preserve the value of the physical asset for the owner over the long term. Although not every property is best served by vast expenditures on top-level maintenance, it is almost always important to maintain the viability of the property as a rental. Three general types of maintenance are required to keep a property in serviceable condition: routine, preventive, and corrective.

Routine maintenance. Routine maintenance activities are those necessary for the day-to-day functioning of the property. Regular performance of these activities helps to keep tenants satisfied as well as forestall serious problems requiring repair or correction. Routine activities are such things as:

- regular inspections
- scheduled upkeep of mechanical systems-heating, air-conditioning, rest rooms, lighting, landscaping
- regular cleaning of common areas
- minor repairs
- supervision of purchasing

Preventive maintenance. Preventive maintenance goes beyond the routine in attempting to deal with situations that can become serious problems if ignored. Seasonal or scheduled replacement of appliances and equipment, regular painting of exterior and interior areas, and planned replacement of a roof are a few examples.

Corrective maintenance. When routine and preventive maintenance fail, repairs and replacements become mandatory to keep the property operational. A boiler may develop a leak, an air-conditioning unit may break down, an elevator may cease to function properly.

Maintenance contracting. Depending on building type and size, tenant needs, and budgetary constraints, a manager may decide to hire an outside firm to handle maintenance services rather than hiring on-site employees. Efficiency, competence, responsiveness, and effective cost will be major deciding factors.

Construction

Commercial and industrial property managers are regularly called upon to make alterations to existing space to accommodate a tenant's needs. They may also have to undertake or oversee construction that alters or expands common areas or the entire building itself. Again, such work may be contracted out or done by in-house employees.

Tenant improvements. Alterations made specifically for certain tenants are called build-outs or tenant improvements. The work may involve merely painting and re-carpeting a rental space, or erecting new walls and installing special electrical or other systems. In new buildings, spaces are often left incomplete so that they can be finished to an individual tenant's specifications. In such cases, it is important to clarify which improvements will be considered tenant property (trade fixtures) and which will belong to the building.

Renovations. When buildings lose functionality (become functionally obsolescent), they generally also lose tenants, drop in class, and suffer declining rental rates. Maintenance becomes more expensive because of the difficulties of servicing out-of-date building components. Renovation may solve some of these problems, but the manager will have to help the owner determine whether the costs of renovation can be recovered by increased revenues resulting from the renovation.

Environmental concerns. A variety of environmental concerns confronts a property manager, ranging from air quality to waste disposal, tenant concerns, and federal, state and local environmental regulations. The managed property may contain asbestos, radon, mold, lead, and other problematic substances. Tenants may produce hazardous waste. The manager must be aware of the issues and see that proper procedures are in place to deal with them, including providing means for proper disposal of hazardous materials, arranging for environmental audits and undertaking possible remediation. For instance, an audit may show that a building is causing tenants to become sick because of off-gassing from construction materials combined with a lack of ventilation. Remediation may consist of nothing more than replacing carpets and improving ventilation, and the manager, if empowered to do so, should take the necessary steps.

Legal concerns (ADA). The Americans with Disabilities Act requires managers to ensure that disabled employees and members of the public have the same level of access to facilities as is provided for those who are not disabled. Employers with at least fifteen employees must follow nondiscriminatory employment and hiring practices. Reasonable accommodations must be made to enable disabled employees to perform essential functions of their jobs. Modifications to the physical components of the building may be necessary to provide the required access to tenants and their customers, such as widening doorways, changing door hardware, changing how doors open, installing ramps, lowering wall-mounted telephones and keypads, supplying Braille signage, and providing auditory signals. Existing barriers must be removed when the removal is "readily achievable," that is, when cost is not prohibitive. New construction and remodeling must meet a higher standard, Managers must be aware of the laws and determine whether their buildings meet requirements. If not, the manager must determine whether restructuring or retrofitting or some other kind of accommodation is most practical.

Risk management

Many things can go wrong in a rented property, from natural disaster to personal injury to terrorism to malfeasance by employees. Huge monetary losses for the owner, in the form of civil and criminal penalties, legal costs, fines, damages, and costs of remediation can be the result. A manager must consider the possibility of such events and have a plan for dealing with them.

Risk management strategies. Depending on the nature of the risk, the size of the potential losses, the likelihood of its happening, and the costs of doing something about it, a manager and owner will generally choose one or more of the following risk management strategies:

> ▸ avoidance-removing the source of the risk, such as by closing off a dangerous area of the building

> ▸ reduction-taking action to forestall the event before it happens, such as by installing fire alarms, sprinklers, and security systems

> ▸ transference-shifting the risk to someone else by buying an insurance policy

> ▸ retention-taking the chance that the event is not likely enough to occur to justify the expense of one of the other strategies; self-insurance

Security and safety. A court may hold a manager and owner responsible for the physical safety of employees, tenants, and customers in leased premises. In addition to standard life safety and security systems such as sprinklers, fire doors, smoke alarms, fire escapes, and door locks, a manager may have to provide electronic and human monitoring systems (security cameras, security guards) and be prepared to take action against tenants who allow, conduct or contribute to dangerous criminal activities such as assault and drug use.

Insurance. Many types of insurance are available to allow for the shifting of liability away from the owner. An insurance audit by a competent insurance agent will indicate what kind of and how much coverage is advisable. Common types of insurance coverage for income and commercial properties include:

> ▸ casualty-coverage for specific risks, such as theft, vandalism, burglary, illness and accident, machinery damage

- liability-coverage for risks incurred by the owner when the public enters the building; medical expenses resulting from owner negligence or other causes

- workers' compensation-hospital and medical coverage for employees injured in the course of employment, mandated by state laws

- fire and hazard-coverage for damage to the property by fire, wind, hail, smoke, civil disturbance, and other causes

- flood-coverage for damages caused by heavy rains, snow, drainage failures, and failed public infrastructures such as dams and levies; flood insurance is not included in regular hazard policies

- contents and personal property-coverage for building contents and personal property when they are not actually on the building premises

- consequential loss, use, and occupancy-coverage for the business losses resulting from a disaster, such as loss of rent and other revenue, when the property cannot be used for business

- surety bond-coverage against losses resulting from criminal or negligent acts of an employee

The owner may opt for a multi-peril policy which combines standard types of commercial policies and may allow special coverage for floods, earthquakes, and terrorism.

The amount of coverage provided by certain types of policies may be based on whether the property is insured at depreciated value or current replacement value. Depreciated value is its original value minus the loss in value over time. Current replacement value, which is more expensive, is the amount it would cost to rebuild or replace the property at current rates.

Commercial policies include coinsurance clauses requiring the insured to bear a portion of the loss. Fire and hazard policies usually require the coverage to be in an amount equal to at least 80 percent of the replacement value.

Owner's policies do not cover what is owned by the tenant. Tenants should obtain their own renter's or tenant's insurance to cover personal belongings. Residential and commercial or business variants are available. The question of who owns tenant improvements is not only important when it is time for the tenant to leave the premises. It is also likely to determine whether the tenant's or the landlord's insurance company will be paying if the improvements are damaged or destroyed.

Handling of trust funds. Managers are responsible for proper handling of monies belonging to other parties that come into the manager's hands in the course of doing business. For property managers, such funds include rents collected from tenants, security deposits, and capital contributions from the property owner. State laws, usually incorporated into real estate commission rules and the state's real estate law, specify how a property manager is to manage trust funds. In general, the agent is to maintain a separate bank account for these funds, with special accounting, in a qualified depository institution. The rules for how long an agent may hold trust funds before depositing them, and how the funds are to be disbursed, are spelled out. The fundamental requirements are that the owners of all funds must be identified, and there must be no commingling or conversion of client funds and agent funds. Mishandling carries heavy penalties.

THE MANAGEMENT AGREEMENT

Components
Rights, Duties, and Liabilities

Components

The management agreement establishes an agency agreement between manager and owner as well as specifying such essentials as the manager's scope of authority, responsibilities, objectives, compensation, and the term of the agreement. Property managers are usually considered to be general agents empowered to perform some or all of the ongoing tasks and duties of operating the property, including the authority to enter into contracts. The agency relationship creates the fiduciary duties of obedience, care, loyalty, accounting, and disclosure. The contractual relationship ensures that the manager will strive to realize the highest return for the owner consistent with the owner's objectives and instructions. The agreement should be in writing and include at least the basics of any real estate contract, as follows.

▶ **Names of the parties**--owner, landlord, manager, tenant or other party to be bound by the contract

▶ **Property description**--street address, unit number and location, square footage, and other information that specifies the leased premises

▶ **Term**--time period (**months**, years) covered by the contract; termination conditions and provisions

▶ **Owner's purpose--maximize** net income, maximize asset value, maximize return, minimize expenditure, maintain property quality, etc.; long-term goals for the property

▶ **Owner's responsibilities--management** fees, plus any management expenses such as payroll, advertising and insurance that the manager will not be expected to pay

▶ **Manager's authority**--the **scope** of powers being conveyed to the manager: hiring and staffing, setting rents, contracting with vendors, ordering repairs, limits on expenditures without seeking owner permission

> ‣ **Manager's responsibilities--specification** of duties, such as marketing, leasing, maintenance, budgeting, reporting, collecting and handling rents; the manager should be included as an additional insured on the liability policy for the property

> ‣ **Budget**--amounts, or percentages of revenues, allotted for operations, taxes, insurance, capital expenditures, etc.

> ‣ **Allocation of costs**--who is to pay certain expenses, that is, which will be treated as expenses of the manager vs. which will be paid directly by the owner

> ‣ **Reporting**--how often and what kind of reports are to be made

> ‣ **Compensation**--the management fee or other means of compensation to the manager; there may be a flat fee based on square footage, a rental commission based on a percentage of annual rent, a combination of these, or some other arrangement; in compliance with anti-trust laws, management fees are not standardized but must be negotiated by agent and principal

> ‣ **Equal opportunity statement**--the HUD statement or equivalent concerning availability to all persons and classes protected by law, incorporated into the agreement in the case of a residential property

Rights, duties, liabilities

Both the manager and the landlord have rights, duties and liabilities under the terms of the management contract. How these are apportioned should be clearly stated in the agreement.

Landlord. The landlord has the right to receive rent according to the agreement, and to receive the premises in the specified condition at the end of the agreement term. The landlord and his or her agents may have the right to enter and inspect the premises, examine the books, hire and fire staff, and choose vendors. The landlord may retain or grant the power to enter into contracts, to set rents, and to select tenants. The landlord will have the right to terminate the management contract according to the terms of the contract. The landlord will have the duty to pay the agreed management fee, and to make other such payments as detailed in the agreement. State law will determine to what extent a principal is liable for the acts of the manager and the manager's employees. As owner, the landlord is liable for failures to comply with certain local, state, and federal laws, particularly the Environmental Protection Act and fair housing laws.

Manager. Depending on the degree of authority granted by the agreement, the manager may have the right to hire and fire, enter into contracts, and perform routine management tasks without interference from the owner. The manager has the duties described earlier: to maintain financial records and make reports; to budget; to find, retain, and collect from tenants; to maintain and secure the property; to meet the owner's objectives. The manager's liabilities include the consequences of mishandling trust funds, violating fiduciary responsibilities, and violating fair housing laws, credit laws, and employment laws.

Exhibit 24.1 Abbreviated Sample Management Agreement

MANAGEMENT AGREEMENT

Agreement made_____[date], between_____, a corporation organized under the laws of the State of _____, having its principal office at_____[address],_____[city],_____[state], here referred to as owner, and_____, a corporation organized under the laws of the State of_____, having its principal office at address],_____[city],_____[state], here referred to as agent.

RECITALS

1. Owner holds title to the following-described real property:_____[insert legal or other appropriate description], here referred to as the property.
2. Agent is experienced in the business of operating and managing real estate similar to the above-described property.
3. Owner desires to engage the services of agent to manage and operate the property, and agent desires to provide such services on the following terms and conditions.

In consideration of the mutual covenants contained herein, the parties agree:

EMPLOYMENT OF AGENT. Agent shall act as the exclusive agent of owner to manage, operate, and maintain the property.

BEST EFFORTS OF AGENT. On assuming the management and operation of the property, agent shall thoroughly inspect the property and submit a written report to owner concerning the present efficiency under which the property is being managed and operated, and recommended changes, if necessary.

LEASING OF PROPERTY. Agent shall make reasonable efforts to lease available space of the property, and shall be responsible for all negotiations with prospective tenants. Agent shall also have the right to execute and enter into, on behalf of owner, month-to-month tenancies of units of the property.

ADVERTISING AND PROMOTION. Agent shall advertise vacancies by all reasonable and proper means; provided, agent shall not incur expenses for advertising in excess of____Dollars ($_____) during any calendar quarter without the prior written consent of owner.

MAINTENANCE, REPAIRS, AND OPERATIONS. Agent shall use its best efforts to insure that the property is maintained in an attractive condition and in a good state of repair. Expenditures for repairs, alterations, decorations or furnishings in excess of_____Dollars ($____) shall not be made without prior written consent of owner.

EMPLOYEES. Agent shall employ, discharge, and supervise all on-site employees or contractors required for the efficient operation and maintenance of the property. All on-site personnel, except independent contractors and employees of independent contractors, shall be the employees of agent.

INSURANCE. Agent shall obtain the following insurance at the expense of owner, and such insurance shall be maintained in force during the full term of this agreement:

1. Comprehensive public liability property insurance of_____Dollars ($_____) single limit for bodily injury, death, and property damage;

2. Comprehensive automobile insurance of_____ Dollars ($____) single limit for bodily injury, death, and property damage;

3. Fire and extended coverage hazard insurance in an amount equal to the full replacement cost of the structure and other improvements situated on the property; and

4. A fidelity bond in the amount of_____ Dollars ($_____) on each employee who handles cash, and workers' compensation and employer liability insurance to cover the agents and employees of both employer and agent.

Exhibit 24.1 Abbreviated Sample Management Agreement, continued

COLLECTION OF INCOME. Agent shall use its best efforts to collect promptly all rents and other income issuing from the property when such amounts become due. It is understood that agent does not guarantee the collection of rents.

BANK ACCOUNTS. Agent shall deposit (either directly or in a depositary bank for transmittal) all revenues from the property into the general property management trust fund of agent, here referred to as the trust account. From the revenues deposited in the trust account, agent shall pay all items with respect to the property for which payment is provided in this agreement, including the compensation of agent and deposits to the reserve accounts as provided for. Agent shall remit any balance of monthly revenues to owner concurrently with the delivery of the monthly report.

RESERVE ACCOUNT. Agent shall establish a reserve account for the following items: taxes, assessments, debt service, insurance premiums, repairs (other than normal maintenance), replacement of personal property, and refundable deposits.

RECORDS AND REPORTS. Agent shall furnish owner, no later than the end of the next succeeding month, a detailed statement of all revenues and expenditures for each preceding month. Within   days after the end of each calendar year, agent shall prepare and deliver to owner a detailed statement of revenues received and expenditures incurred and paid during the calendar year that result from operations of the property.

COMPENSATION OF AGENT. Agent shall receive a management fee equal to___percent (__ %) of the gross receipts collected from the operation of the property. Any management fee due agent hereunder shall be paid to agent within _____days after the end of each month.

TERMINATION AND RENEWAL. This agreement shall be for a term commencing on_____[date], and ending on _____[date].

MODIFICATION. This agreement may not be modified unless such modification is in writing and signed by both parties to this agreement.

IN WITNESS WHEREOF, the parties have executed this agreement at [designate place of execution] the day and year first above written.

_____

_____

LEASING CONSIDERATIONS

Lease types
Owned and leased inclusions
Reversionary rights of owners
Landlord rights and responsibilities
Tenant rights and responsibilities
Evictions
Tenant improvements
Termination of a lease
Security deposit procedures
Universal Residential Landlord-Tenant Act

Lease types

Recall from the chapter on leases that a leasehold estate may grant tenancy for years, from period-to-period, at will, and at sufferance.

For years. An estate for years may be for any definite period—years, months, weeks, days. When the estate expires, the lessee must return the premises to the lessor and vacate the premises. Most commercial leases grant this type of estate.

Periodic. An estate from period-to-period does not have any definite period. Such an estate begins as a lease for a definite period but continues after the expiration of the lease, as long as the lessee continues to pay rent at the regular interval, the lessor accepts it, and no one gives notice to terminate the lease. This type of leasehold is common with residential properties.

At will. A tenancy at will is similar to the periodic tenancy, except that it does not begin with a definite period. It continues, with the consent of the lessor, as long as the tenant pays rent at regular intervals. It is terminated by the death of either party. The tenancy at will is rarely, if ever, used in a written lease.

At sufferance. A tenancy or estate at sufferance comes into existence when a tenant stays beyond the expiration of another type of lease without the lessor's permission. This type of tenancy is never intentionally used in a written lease.

Leases, depending on how rent is determined, are also defined as gross, net, percentage leases, and graduated leases.

Gross. In a gross lease, the tenant pays an established, fixed rent, and the landlord pays all property operating expenses, such as taxes, insurance, utilities, and other services. This is the arrangement commonly used in residential leases.

Net. Net leases have the tenant paying rent plus some or all of the operating expenses attributable to the rented space. This arrangement is commonly used in office and industrial leases.

Percentage. A percentage lease may be gross or net, but the rent is not fixed, but depends on the income generated by the tenant in the leased property. A common arrangement is to set a fixed base rent plus a percentage of the tenant's gross income or sales at the site. The percentage calculation may take effect only when the income reaches a certain level. This arrangement is commonly used in retail leases.

Graduated. Either a gross or a net lease may also be a graduated lease, in which the rental rate increases at specified times over the lease term.

Owned and leased inclusions

The lease should set forth items that are excluded or included in the leased property. For instance, a residential lease may include built-in appliances such as dishwashers but exclude freestanding ones, such as refrigerators. Furniture may be included or excluded. At issue for the landlord is the cost of maintenance. If a refrigerator is not included, it does not have to be maintained by the property manager.

Ownership also relates to insurance policies: one can only insure what one owns, so if a property item is destroyed by fire, the owner's policy will not provide any coverage for an item that is not included in the lease as belonging to the property. This may be of critical importance in a commercial lease where certain improvements might be owned by either the landlord or the tenant, according to the lease.

The lease should also have clear rules about making alterations. If the tenant is not satisfied with an item that is part of the property, the lease may provide for the tenant to make changes only with permission or with the obligation to return the premises to their original condition on termination, or that any alterations made to fixtures become the property of the landlord. Trade fixtures, by definition, belong to the tenant and can be removed when the tenant leaves.

Inclusions may also be of a financial nature-what is included in the rent. Principal and interest on a mortgage loan, homeowner's association dues, common area maintenance charges, liability and hazard insurance, and various operating expenses are items that might be included in the lease as the owner's or the tenant's responsibilities.

Reversionary rights of owners

Like the grantor of a life estate, the grantor of a leasehold estate retains a future interest in the estate. The lease grants a number of rights to the property, including, primarily, the rights to enter, possess, and use the property for the term of the lease. The lessee does not enjoy the full bundle of rights to the property. For instance, the lessee may not encumber or sell the property. When the lease expires (a condition subsequent), all rights revert to the original owner. A common example is the leasing of an apartment for a one-year period. When the lease expires, the lessee has no further rights in the property and full ownership reverts to the lessor. Another condition subsequent that may cause reversion of rights is tenant default.

Landlord rights and responsibilities

State law, often incorporating or modeling the Universal Residential Landlord Tenant Act (see below) prescribes rights and responsibilities for residential landlords and tenants.

Rights. Commonly, the landlord retains a right of entry into the premises in order to perform needed repairs and maintenance on a property. The lease and/or the law may specify that a landlord may enter the tenant's property only under one or more of the following conditions:

- ▸ An emergency requires the landlord to enter.

- ▸ The tenant gives consent to enter.

- ▸ The landlord enters during normal business hours and only after giving notice to either make repairs or to show the property to prospective tenants, purchasers or contractors.

- ▸ The tenant has abandoned or surrendered the property.

- ▸ The landlord has a court order allowing the entry.

Likewise, the landlord has the right to expect prompt payment of rent and adherence to building rules. At the end of the lease term, the landlord has the right to retake possession of the premises. In case of tenant breach or default, the landlord has the right to pursue the remedies provided by law, such as eviction, to take possession.

Responsibilities. The landlord (by way of the property manager), is expected to deliver a property that is habitable. This means that the landlord at the very least must:

- ▸ keep the heating, cooling, electrical, and plumbing systems in good working condition

- ▸ keep floors, stairways and railings safe and in good repair

- ▸ provide pest control as needed

- ▸ repair roof leaks and broken windows promptly.

Tenant rights and responsibilities

Rights. Beyond the right to quiet enjoyment (privacy) of a property received and maintained in a habitable condition, the tenant has other rights, depending on state law. For instance, a tenant may be able to take any of the following actions if a landlord fails to correct a problem that is the landlord's responsibility:

- ▸ move out without liability for back rent or the unexpired portion of the lease

- ▸ refer the problem to mediation, arbitration or small claims court

- ▸ after giving the owner written notification of an emergency situation, call a professional repair person and deduct the cost from the next month's rent.

Responsibilities. Depending on state law, a tenant generally must:

- ▸ pay rent on time
- ▸ follow the rules and regulations set out by the landlord
- ▸ give a 30-day notice when terminating a month-to-month lease
- ▸ return all door and mailbox keys when leaving the property

- ▸ leave the unit in as clean a condition as it was at the start of the lease
- ▸ keep the unit clean and sanitary
- ▸ dispose of all rubbish, garbage and other waste in a sanitary manner
- ▸ use and operate all electrical, gas and plumbing fixtures properly
- ▸ refrain from destroying or damaging the property
- ▸ prevent others from destroying or damaging the property
- ▸ use the property and the rooms only for their intended purposes

Evictions

An *actual eviction* follows a procedure prescribed in state law and stated in the lease contract. The landlord must serve notice on the tenant a specified number of days before beginning the eviction suit. A court issues a judgment for possession, which requires the tenant to vacate. A court officer, such as a sheriff, may forcibly remove the tenant and possessions if the tenant refuses to vacate. The landlord can then enter and take possession.

A *constructive eviction* occurs when a tenant vacates the leased premises and declares the lease void, claiming that the landlord's actions have made the premises unfit for the purpose described in the lease. The tenant must prove that it was the landlord's actions that were responsible and may be able to recover damages.

Tenant improvements

As discussed earlier, leased spaces are often modified to a tenant's specifications. Such alternations may be made by the landlord on the tenant's behalf or by the tenant. Buildings usually have "standard" improvements, which any tenant improvements must equal or improve on. Many leases have a clause that requires the tenant to return the premises to the condition in which they were received at the end of the lease term. Who pays for improvements and who owns them are major matters for negotiation.

Termination of a lease

Like contracts in general, leases may terminate in a number of ways. Principal among these are the following. See the chapters on leases and contract law for more information.

Expiration. A lease with a term (estate for years) automatically expires at the end of the term.

Performance. Any contract terminates when all parties have performed their obligations.

Agreement. The parties may agree to terminate the lease before the end of the term.

Abandonment. The landlord may retake possession and pursue the tenant for default if the tenant abandons the premises and fails to fulfill lease obligations. The tenant's obligation to pay rent continues.

Default or Breach. A default occurs when either the tenant or landlord violates any of the terms or covenants of the lease. The damaged party may sue for damages, specific performance (of the breached obligation), or cancellation of the lease. When the default arises from the tenant's failure to pay rent or maintain the premises, the landlord may sue for possession and for eviction. Before filing suit, the landlord must give proper notice and allow the tenant to remedy the breach. The most common form of landlord default is failure to maintain the property and provide services. The tenant may vacate the premises and declare the lease cancelled if the landlord's default has made the premises unoccupiable. This action is called constructive eviction.

Notice. A periodic leasehold or tenancy at will may be terminated by proper notice given by either party.

Destruction. Property destruction is grounds for termination of the lease.

Condemnation. Eminent domain proceedings terminate leases.

Foreclosure. Foreclosure actions terminate lease obligations.

Death. A tenancy at will terminates on the death of either party. The landlord's death terminates any lease if the landlord held the leased property under a life estate, since the landlord cannot convey an interest that extends beyond the landlord's life.

Security deposit Procedures

As previously mentioned in the context of handling trust funds, state laws, real estate commission rules, and the state's real estate law, usually specify how a property manager is to manage security deposits. Such funds are normally held in a special trust account and may not be used for any purpose other than the intended one. Whether the deposit can earn interest, and to whom that interest belongs, are likewise prescribed by law. The law also prescribes when the deposit must be returned to the tenant, and under what circumstances any of it may be withheld. The contract language should clearly state the rules, among other things, governing what happens to the deposit when the lease terminates.

Uniform Residential Landlord-Tenant Act

The Uniform Residential Landlord-Tenant Act is model legislation that has been adopted to a greater or lessor extent in many states. In addition to addressing fair and equitable remedies for breaches by both landlord and tenant, the act aims to clarify imprecise language in residential leases that can lead to confusion or exploitation in such areas as:

> ▸ lease term
> ▸ rental amount
> ▸ security deposit
> ▸ landlord access
> ▸ procedures for default and eviction
> ▸ general obligations of landlord and tenant.

See the chapter on "Real Estate Leases" for more detail.

THE MANAGEMENT BUSINESS

Sources of business
Securing business
Professional development

Sources of business
Property management is increasingly a specialization within real estate. There is a growing need for skilled managers because of the increasing number and complexity of properties.

Specialist opportunities. Property managers with specialized training are in demand in a wide variety of property types, including shopping centers, commercial buildings, residential properties, and industrial parks. Within these property specialties are opportunities to specialize even further in such areas as:

- leasing
- asset management
- corporate property management
- resort management
- association management
- housing program management
- mobile home park management
- office building management

Owners and investors in these various property types are among the consumers of management services who represent potential clients for a professional property manager. Such owners and investors may be individuals, corporations, developers, landlords, banks, trusts, homeowners' associations, condominium associations, or investment syndicates

Securing business
Reputation, demonstrated competence, professional training, and smart advertising are keys to finding management business. Before entering into a management agreement, the manager should make sure that the owner's management objectives are clear and that they are realistic.

Management plan. Developing a management plan is a necessary step in beginning a management project, and it may also be part of obtaining a management contract. The manager must consider the owner's objectives, including financial goals; the competitive market for the property, both local and regional, depending on the property type; and the features of the particular property. The plan will take into account market indicators such as vacancy rates, occupancy rates, absorption rates, and new supply coming onto the market. It will also include a budgetary component that considers sources of revenue and anticipated expenses. Finally, the plan will indicate what the manager intends to do with the property, given these considerations, to manage the property in a way that will meet the owner's objectives.

Professional development
A number of organizations provide valuable information and training in subjects related to property management. The certifications and designations provided by

these organizations are often viewed as valuable signs of competence and can be a significant factor in getting hired as a manager. Important associations include:

- ▶ IREM-The Institute of Real Estate Management, offering the CPM (Certified Property Manager) designation

- ▶ BOMA and BOMI-The Building Owners and Managers Association International and the affiliated Building Managers and Owners Institute International, offering the RPA (Real Property Administrator), SMA (Systems Maintenance Administrator), and FMA (Facilities Management Administrator) designations

- ▶ NAA-The National Apartment Association, offering designations in apartment building management, maintenance, leasing, portfolio supervision and other related areas

- ▶ NARPM-The National Association of Residential Property Managers, offering the RPM (Residential Property Manager), MPM (Master Property Manager) and other related designations

- ▶ ICSC-The International Council of Shopping Centers, offering designations in retail property leadership, management, marketing, leasing, and development

- ▶ NACM-The National Association of Condominium Managers, offering the RCM (Registered Condominium Manager) designation

24 Property Management Snapshot Review

MANAGEMENT FUNCTIONS

- main manager types: individual broker or firm managing for multiple owners; building manager, employed by owner or other manager to manage a single property; resident manager, employed by owner, broker, or management firm to live and manage on site.

- manager is a fiduciary of the principal; duty to act in principle's best interests; may specialize in a property type

- needed skills: marketing, accounting, finance, construction; financial, physical, administrative services; specific functions determined by management agreement

Reporting

- monthly, quarterly, or annually; annual operating budget, cash flow reports, profit and loss statements, budget comparison statements

Budgeting

- operating budget based on expected expenses and revenues; determines rental rates, capital expenditures, reserves, salaries and wages; projects income based on past performance and current market

- potential gross income: total of scheduled rents plus revenues from other sources; effective gross income: total gross minus losses from vacancies, evictions, uncollected rents; net operating income: effective gross minus operating expenses; cash flow: net operating income minus debt service and reserves

- expenses are variable and fixed; capital expenditures are outlays for major renovations and construction; cash reserves set aside for variable expenses

Renting

- manager must keep property properly rented and tenanted; vacancies managed by rent setting, marketing, tenant relations, good service

- selecting compatible tenants and collecting scheduled rents are top priorities

- legal issues concern compliance with fair housing laws, Americans with Disabilities Act, and ECOA

Property maintenance

- main consideration: balance between costs of services, owner financial objectives, and tenant needs

- may be routine, preventive, or corrective; staffed in-house or contracted out

Construction

- tenant alterations, renovations, and expansion; also environmental remediation

- legal concerns: Americans with Disabilities Act; applies to employers with fifteen or more employees; manager to determine feasibility of restructuring, retrofitting, new construction, or other alternatives to comply

Risk management

- risk ranges from natural disaster to personal injury, terrorism, and employee malfeasance; handled by avoiding or removing the source, installing protective systems, buying insurance, self-insuring (risk retention)

- life safety systems include sprinklers, fire doors, smoke alarms, fire escapes, monitoring systems

- insurance includes casualty, liability, workers' comp, fire and hazard, flood, contents, consequential loss, surety bonds, multi-peril; tenants need their own insurance

- handling of trust funds is a major risk area; mishandling carries heavy penalties

MANAGEMENT AGREEMENT

Components	• names of parties; property description; lease term; owner's purpose; responsibilities; authority; budget; allocation of costs; reporting; compensation; Equal Opportunity statement
Rights, duties and liabilities	• landlord: receive rent; receive premises in specified condition; enter and inspect; examine books; enter into contracts, hire vendors, set rents; pay management; comply with laws
	• manager: hire and fire; enter into contracts; perform management tasks; maintain records, make reports, budget, collect rent, find tenants, maintain the property, meet owner goals; handle trust funds; comply with laws

LEASING CONSIDERATIONS

Lease types	• for years, periodic, at will, at sufferance, gross, net, percentage, graduated
Owned and leased inclusions	• items included or excluded in the lease; owner's insurance covers only what is included; alterations to inclusions only with owner's permission
	• "inclusion" also refers to financial items included as lessee's responsibility, such as operating expenses
Reversionary rights of owners	• all rights of ownership revert to owner at end of lease term
Landlord rights and responsibilities	• rights: enter premises, receive payment, retake on termination, pursue remedies; responsibilities: provide habitable conditions; maintain heating, cooling, electrical, plumbing; keep clean and in repair
Tenant rights and responsibilities	• rights: quiet enjoyment, habitable conditions, right to take action for default; responsibilities: pay rent, obey rules, give proper notice, return property in prescribed condition, use only for intended purpose
Evictions	• actual: prescribed legal procedure; notice, suit, judgment, taking of premises; constructive: tenant vacates for landlord failure to maintain premises
Tenant improvements	• ownership of and payment for improvements according to agreement
Termination of a lease	• causes: expiration, performance, agreement, abandonment, breach, notice, destruction of premises, condemnation, foreclosure, death of either party (tenancy at will), death of landlord (life estate)
Security deposit procedures	• determined by state law, commission rules, agreement
Universal Residential Landlord-Tenant Act	• model law regulating lease language and lease terms; adopted by many states

MANAGEMENT BUSINESS

Sources of business	• leasing, asset management, corporate properties, resorts, association management, housing programs, mobile home parks, office buildings; owners, investors, corporations, developers, landlords, condo and homeowners' associations, banks, trusts, syndicates
Securing business	• develop reputation and competence; obtain training; use effective advertising; make management plan in accordance with owner objectives
Professional development	• training, designations, certifications to increase and demonstrate competence

25 The Maryland Regulatory Environment

Maryland Real Estate Commission
Definitions
Complaints and Disciplinary Process
Guaranty Fund
Examination of Records (Broker Only)

MARYLAND REAL ESTATE COMMISSION

Governing laws
Commission establishment
Membership
Powers and duties

Governing laws

The business of real estate in Maryland is regulated by state statutes under the 2010 Maryland Code of Business Occupations and Professions, Title 17, known as the Real Estate Brokers Act. Real estate practice is also governed by administrative law under the Code of Maryland Regulations (COMAR), Title 09 Department of Labor, Licensing, and Regulation, Subtitle 11 Real Estate Commission. These laws can be found on the Maryland Real Estate Commission website at **www.dllr.state.md.us/license/law/mreclaw.shtml**.

Commission establishment

The Maryland Real Estate Commission (MREC) was established by Title 17, Subtitle 2, Section 17-201 and is overseen by the Maryland Division of Occupational and Professional Licensing.

Purpose. The MREC's purpose is to protect the health, safety, and welfare of the public by licensing and regulating real estate activities, by upholding real estate laws, by providing professional assistance, and by conducting disciplinary actions.

Membership

The MREC consists of nine members who are appointed by the Governor with the advice of the Secretary and the advice and consent of the State Senate. All nine must be citizens of Maryland. Five of the members must be licensed real estate brokers, associate brokers, or salespersons. Those five must have been residents of specifically designated counties for at least 5 years. They must also have held their real estate licenses for at least 10 years immediately before appointment to the Commission.

The remaining four members must be consumer members of the general public who are not licensees and are not subject to regulation by the Commission. Further, these consumer members may not be required to meet the qualifications for the professional members. During the year prior to appointment to the Commission and while a member of the Commission, consumer members may not have had a financial interest in or received compensation from any person regulated by the Commission. Nor may consumer members grade any examination given by or for the Commission.

Members serve staggered 4-year terms and elect a chairman from the membership who serves 1-year terms. Members continue to serve at the end of their terms until successors are appointed. The Secretary appoints an executive director from three nominees submitted by the membership. The executive director is not a member of the Commission and must not hold a real estate license from any state. Any member may be removed from the Commission by the Governor for incompetence or misconduct.

Powers and duties   The Commission regulates approximately 48,000 licensed real estate brokers and associates. To accomplish its purpose of protecting the public, the Commission has the power to adopt and enforce regulations to administer the Brokers Act. The MREC also has the power and responsibility to perform the following:

- meet at least once a month and allow members of the public to be heard at such meetings when requested
- employ a staff and/or an investigative staff
- develop procedures for and administer the licensing examination
- develop and impose requirements for obtaining a real estate license
- adopt reasonable regulations to govern license applications
- approve educational courses
- adopt a code of ethics for real estate licensees
- issue, renew, suspend, or revoke licenses
- adopt reasonable bylaws and regulations for conducting its proceedings and hearings
- adopt guidelines for the timely processing and resolution of complaints
- investigate alleged violations of Title 17 by holding hearings, administering oaths, issuing subpoenas for witness testimony or evidence, and taking depositions
- impose discipline and penalties for proven violations of laws or regulations
- sue to enforce a provision of Title 17 by ex parte, interlocutory, or final injunction in cases where the violation may result in irreparable harm to a person
- seek an injunction without posting bond for an unlicensed violator or without proving an adequate remedy does not exist
- investigate complaints alleging an unauthorized person has provided real estate brokerage services
- adopt a seal to be used to authenticate the Commission's proceedings
- set reasonable fees for its services and publish the fee schedule (the current fee schedule can be found online at

updated as appropriate with public notice provided)

- ▸ collect fees and fines and make payment of fees to the Comptroller who deposits the monies into the Real Estate Commission Fund
- ▸ maintain and administer the guarantee fund for reimbursing members of the public for actual losses caused by licensees
- ▸ submit an annual report of Commission activities to the Secretary
- ▸ certify the license status and qualifications of any person upon request and payment of fee (https://www.dllr.state.md.us/cgi-bin/ElectronicLicensing/RE/certification/RECertification1.cgi)
- ▸ may NOT adopt a regulation that would allow issuance of a conditional or temporary license

The Commission is required to provide a copy of adopted regulations and the code of ethics to each licensee at least every 2 years and make a copy available upon request.

DEFINITIONS

Under Title 17, certain terms have specific meanings when used within the statutes.

Affiliate – to establish an employment or other contractual relationship between an individual and a real estate broker under which the individual is authorized to provide real estate brokerage services on behalf of the real estate broker

Associate broker – an individual who meets the requirements for a broker license but chooses to obtain an associate broker license instead and who provides brokerage services on behalf of and under the supervision of an affiliate licensed broker

Brokerage services –any of the listed services provided to another person for consideration: selling, buying, exchanging, leasing real estate; collecting rent for the use of any real estate; assisting in locating or obtaining residential real estate for purchase or lease; engaging or dealing in real estate, leases, or options on real estate; promoting the sale of real estate; engaging in subdividing land and selling the divided lots; serving as a consultant for any of these activities

Commission – the Maryland Real Estate Commission (MREC).

Consideration – compensation or payment for brokerage services.

Guaranty Fund – a fund established by the Commission to reimburse victims for monetary or property losses resulting from a licensee's fraud, misrepresentation, theft, embezzlement, false pretenses, or forgery

Hearing board or panel – three appointed members of the MREC who hear complaints and claims and determine appropriate action

License – a real estate broker, associate broker, or salesperson license issued by the Commission which allows the individual to provide real estate brokerage services

License revocation – a penalty whereby the real estate license is terminated as a result of the licensee's act or omission, thus severing the individual's right to perform any function that requires a license

License summary suspension – a penalty whereby the license is immediately suspended when the licensee's act or omission constitutes imminent danger or threats to the health, safety, or welfare of the public

License suspension – a penalty whereby the licensee may not perform any function that requires a license for a specified length of time

Real estate – an interest in real property, including condominiums and time-shares

---

COMPLAINTS AND DISCIPLINARY PROCESS

Complaints
Investigations
Hearings
Appeals
Penalties

Complaints

Who may file. An individual who is represented by a licensed broker in a real estate transaction may file a complaint with the Commission based on the broker or licensee's actions or omissions during the transaction. The Commission does not handle complaints against homebuilders, inspectors, sellers, or mortgage brokers. The most common complaints are for fraud, breach of duty, and breach of contract. Based on the complaint itself, the entire complaint process can take up to two years.

Requirements. Complaints must be in writing and filed with the Commission using the complaint form provided on the Maryland Department of Labor's website at **https://www.dllr.state.md.us/cgi-bin/ElectronicLicensing/CIPS/complaintform1.cgi?board=11&lib=DLLR**.

The complaint must state the facts of the alleged violation. All supporting documentation must be submitted to the Commission within 30 days of the complaint submission. If the complainant is not a member of the Commission, the complaint must be made under oath.

The Commission may summarily dismiss any complaint filed after 3 years from the date of a written listing contract, contract of sale, lease agreement, option, or actions resulting in the complaint. However, if the Commission finds the delay in filing the complaint is justified or that the delay does not cause undue burden to the licensee, the complaint will be accepted and processed as any timely complaint.

Acknowledgement and notice. When the complaint is received and determined to fall under the jurisdiction of the MREC, the Commission sends a letter to the complainant to acknowledge receipt of the complaint and sends a copy of the complaint to the accused licensee and to the licensee's affiliated broker. The licensee and broker are asked to respond to the complaint in writing within 10 days.

Investigations

After receiving the responses to the complaint, the Commission determines whether a violation has occurred. If the answer is no, the Commission may dismiss the complaint. Any member of the Commission who disagrees with the dismissal may file an exception and have the Commission hold a hearing to determine if an investigation is warranted. The exception must be filed within 30 days of the dismissal. If no hearing request or exception is filed, the order becomes the final order.

If the Commission's review indicates that a violation may have occurred, the Commission will investigate the complaint. Depending on the results of the investigation, the Commission may

> ‣ order the licensee to pay an amount not to exceed $5,000; the licensee may, within 30 days, file an exception or request a hearing
> ‣ set the matter for a hearing
> ‣ dismiss an insufficient or frivolous claim

Hearings

Notice. At least 10 days prior to the hearing date, the Commission must provide notice of the hearing to the complainant and other relevant parties, including the accused licensee's affiliated broker. Notices must be served personally or sent by certified mail to the individual's business address.

Hearing board. With the Secretary's approval, the Commission may establish one or more hearing boards. Each board is made up of at least three members of the Commission, at least one of whom must be a consumer member and at least one of whom must be a licensed professional member. The Commission also designates a chairperson for the board from among the members of the hearing board.

Hearing. The Commission refers complaints, claims, and other matters requiring a hearing to the hearing board. The hearing board determines whether there is reason to take punitive action. If the board does not find a reasonable basis for disciplinary action, it must dismiss the complaint.

During a hearing, the burden of proof is on the complainant. The accused licensee may be accompanied and represented at the hearing by an attorney. If the accused licensee fails to appear at the hearing, the hearing may proceed and the matter be determined without the licensee in attendance.

Final decision. When the hearing is completed, the board reports its findings to the Commission. The report includes any action taken against a licensee for involvement in monetary loss, misappropriation of funds, and fraud. The board's decision is the final decision of the Commission.

Appeals

Judicial review. The hearing board's final decision may be appealed. The aggrieved party must file a petition for judicial review with the circuit court for the county where the party resides or has a principal place of business. The court may order a stay provided the licensee files a bond of up to $50,000 to be held as indemnity against financial losses resulting from the accused licensee's future violations.

Appeal hearing. The court may allow additional evidence, oral arguments and written briefs at the appeal hearing. The court may order further proceedings, affirm the final decision, or reverse or modify the final decision.

Complaint dismissals at any point may also be appealed in the circuit court within 30 days of the dismissal.

Penalties

Summary actions. Before a hearing is held, the Commission may take summary, or immediate, action to stop an individual who is causing or engaging in an activity that constitutes a threat to the health, safety, or welfare of the public.

Suspensions. The Commission may summarily suspend the licensee's license if the licensee

- fails to account for money held in trust
- fails to show the Commission records, books, and accounts of money held in trust
- has been convicted of a felony under federal or state laws
- fails to notify the Commission within 10 days of the felony conviction or within 10 days of the licensee's release from incarceration for the felony conviction, whichever is later

The Commission must provide written notice of the suspension to the licensee. If the licensee is an associate broker or a salesperson, notice will also be sent to the affiliated broker, the Maryland Association of Realtors, and the local board of Realtors.

The Commission must also provide the licensee an opportunity to be heard before the Commission or a hearing board regarding the suspension. The summary suspension begins when ordered and continues until the licensee complies with the order's conditions or until the Commission changes the order after holding a hearing.

Revocations. The Commission may summarily revoke a license if

- the licensee is convicted of a violation
- the conviction is final, and
- the period for an appeal has expired

The Commission must send written notice of the revocation to the licensee and, if the licensee is an associate broker or a salesperson, to the affiliated broker, the Maryland Association of Realtors, and the local board of Realtors.

The Commission must allow the licensee an opportunity to appear before the Commission or a hearing board regarding the revocation. The Commission may delay the revocation until after the hearing.

Nonresident license suspension or revocation. If the Maryland license of a nonresident licensee is suspended or revoked, the Commission will notify the real estate commission or other licensing authority in the licensee's resident state. The notice must include the cause for the revocation or suspension. If the nonresident's license is revoked in the resident state, it will also be revoked in Maryland once the MREC is notified by the other state.

GUARANTY FUND

Purpose
Fund maintenance
Claims
Payments

Purpose	The Maryland Real Estate Fund was established by Title 17-402 of the Brokers Act to reimburse persons who have suffered actual monetary or property losses resulting from an act of fraud, misrepresentation, theft, embezzlement, false pretenses, or forgery committed by a real estate licensee or unlicensed employee in relation to the provision of real estate services..
Fund maintenance	**Source of funds.** All applicants for a real estate license must pay a one-time $20 Guaranty Fund fee before receiving their licenses. The Commission deposits these fees with the State Treasurer to be placed into an account for the Fund. The Treasurer may invest Fund money and place the investment earnings into the Fund.
	Minimum balance. The Commission is required to maintain the Fund at a minimum of $250,000. If the Fund's balance falls below $250,000, the Commission must assess each licensee an additional fee in an amount that will restore the Fund to its required balance. If the Fund's balance falls below $300,000, the Commission may transfer $500,000 from its current year's operating surplus to the Guaranty Fund.
Claims	**Filing a claim.** An individual may file a claim to recover a financial or property loss suffered because of a licensee's or a broker's unlicensed employee's act of fraud, misrepresentation, theft, embezzlement, false pretenses, or forgery. The individual must file the claim on the combined Complaint form and Guaranty Fund claim form found on the Maryland Department of Labor's website at https://www.dllr.state.md.us/cgi-bin/ElectronicLicensing/CIPS/complaintform1.cgi?board=11&lib=DLLR.

Ineligible claims. Losses related to the following transactions are not eligible for a recovery payment from the Fund:

> ▸ the purchase of any interest in a limited partnership formed for investing in real estate
> ▸ a joint venture promoted by a licensee for two or more individuals to invest in real estate
> ▸ the purchase of commercial paper secured by real estate

The following individuals may not file claims:

> ▸ the spouse of the licensee or of the unlicensed employee who was accused of the act or omission leading to the claim
> ▸ the personal representative of either of these spouses

Claim requirements. A claim must be filed within 3 years after the claimant discovered the loss or should have discovered the loss using ordinary diligence. Any sales contract provided by a broker must include a statement that the buyer is protected by the Guaranty Fund for losses up to $50,000.

Guaranty Fund claims must meet the following requirements:

> ▸ be in writing
> ▸ be made under oath
> ▸ state the loss amount being claimed
> ▸ state the facts on which the claim is based
> ▸ include any documentation or other evidence that supports the claim

Claim process. When the Commission receives a claim for payment from the Guaranty Fund, it must forward a copy of the claim to each licensee and unlicensed employee allegedly responsible for the act or omission leading to the claim and to each affiliated broker. The Commission requires these individuals to respond to the allegations in writing within 10 days.

The Commission then reviews the claim and responses and may conduct an investigation. Depending on the findings of the review and investigation, the Commission will either issue a proposed award to the claimant, set the matter for a hearing, or dismiss the claim if it appears frivolous, in bad faith, or legally insufficient.

The licensee or the claimant may, within 30 days of receiving a proposed order, request a Commission hearing or file an exception to the proposed order. If no hearing is requested and no exception filed, the proposed order becomes the final order.

Hearings. The Commission must give notice of the hearing to the parties involved and provide them an opportunity to participate in the hearing.

During a claim hearing, the burden of proof is on the claimant. Knowingly making a false statement or material misstatement of fact about a Guaranty Fund matter is a misdemeanor with a penalty of a fine and/or imprisonment imposed by a criminal court, not by the Commission, which does not have the legal power to impose a prison sentence.

To be awarded a reimbursement payment from the Fund, the claimant must prove the claim is valid and show the claimant is not the licensee's spouse or unlicensed employee's spouse or personal representative.

Payments

The maximum claim payout from the Fund is $50,000 per claim. The actual amount that is recoverable is restricted to the claimant's monetary loss from the original transaction and not to losses related to any other transactions.

Actual losses do not include commissions owed to a licensee who is either a principal or agent in a real estate transaction. Losses also may not include attorney's fees incurred by the claimant in pursuing the claim.

Payments may only be made after the deadline for seeking a judicial review has expired and after the expiration of any judicial stay of the Commission's order. If more than one claim is awarded, payment from the Fund will be made in the order the awards were granted.

Penalties

License suspension. When the Commission finds a licensee at fault for an act leading to a claim and then orders payment from the Fund, the Commission will immediately suspend the licensee's license. The license will not be reinstated until the former licensee repays the amount the Fund paid plus interest and applies to the Commission for reinstatement. If the former licensee also had sanctions imposed under the disciplinary proceedings, repaying the Fund will not lift those sanctions.

Repayment to the Fund. A licensee responsible for the payment of a claim on the Fund must reimburse the Guaranty Fund for the amount paid, plus interest.

The Commission or the State Central Collection Unit may bring action and receive a judgment against any former licensee who fails to reimburse the Fund within 30 days of the Fund making the payment.

Lien on real property. If, after receiving a demand for payment, the former licensee still fails to reimburse the Fund, the amount becomes a lien on the former licensee's real property. The lien must be recorded and indexed. When the lien amount is paid in full, the clerk will record the release of lien.

EXAMINATION OF RECORDS (BROKERS ONLY)

The Commission may request an inspection of a broker's records at any time the Commission chooses. Upon receiving reasonable notice, the broker must make the records, books, and accounts available, providing, at. the broker's expense, a paper copy of any document or record the Commission requests. Accounts for any money the broker is holding in trust must also be made available to the Commission for inspection. Under Title 17-328, a licensee's failure to provide all records, books, and accounts to the Commission when requested may result in a summary suspension of the licensee's license.

25 The Maryland Regulatory Environment
Snapshot Review

MARYLAND REAL ESTATE COMMISSION

Governing laws
- Real Estate Brokers Act, Code of Maryland Regulations

Commission establishment
- Code of Business Occupations and Professions, Title 17, Subtitle 2, Section 17-201; governed by Division of Occupation and Professional licensing
- to protect public health, safety, welfare; uphold real estate law

Membership
- 9 members approved by Governor with advice of Secretary and advice and consent of State Senate; all 9 to be citizens of Maryland; 5 to be licensees, residents of specific counties for 5 years, licensees for 10 years
- 4 to be consumer members, not licensees, not subject to MREC regulations, not required to meet professional qualifications, no financial interest in or receipt of compensation from anyone regulated by MREC; may not grade exams
- staggered 4-year terms; chairman serves 1-year term; nonmember and non-licensee executive director appointed by Secretary
- Governor may remove members removed for incompetence or misconduct

Powers and duties
- include adopting and enforcing regulations to administer the Brokers Act; developing procedures and requirements for licensure, education, application, examinations, and code of ethics; issue, renew, suspend, or revoke licenses; resolve complaints through investigations, hearings, appeals, and penalties; set and collect fees and fines; administer the Guaranty Fund; and more
- may not allow conditional or temporary license

COMPLAINTS AND DISCIPLINARY PROCESS

Complaints
- filed by client of licensed broker or Commission member based on licensee's acts or omissions during a transaction
- must be in writing, state facts of the complaint, be filed with the Commission with supporting documents filed within 30 days; made under oath if complainant is not a Commission member
- may be dismissed if filed after 3 years unless delay is justified
- acknowledgement letter sent to complainant and complaint sent to accused licensee and affiliated broker with response requested within 10 days

Investigations
- complaint may be dismissed if review shows no violation; an exception may be filed within 30 days if Commission member disagrees with dismissal; hearing then held to determine if investigation is warranted; if no exception, dismissal order is final
- investigation may result in up-to-$5,000 payment ordered, referral to hearing, dismissal for insufficient or frivolous claim

Hearings
- Commission to provide notice to all involved parties within 10 days of hearing date; provided via personal service or certified mail
- hearing board of 1 consumer Commission member, 1 professional member, and 1 chairman to hear complaint and determine if penalties are warranted; hearing board has same powers as Commission; if no penalties are warranted, complaint is dismissed
- burden of proof is on complainant; if licensee does not attend and or send attorney, matter determined without licensee

	• board reports findings and actions taken to Commission; board's decision is final
Appeals	• aggrieved party may appeal hearing board's decision by petitioning circuit court for judicial review; court may order a stay if the licensee files a bond up to $50,000
	• court may allow additional evidence; remand the case for further proceedings, affirm, reverse, or modify the final decision
	• dismissals may be appealed within 30 days
Penalties	• include summary action to stop dangerous behaviors, suspensions with opportunity to be heard, or revocation with opportunity to be heard
	• nonresident suspensions or revocations reported to state of residency; if revoked is in resident state, also revoked in Maryland

GUARANTY FUND

Purpose	• to reimburse monetary or property losses resulting from licensee or unlicensed employee's act or omission related to brokerage services within Maryland
Fund maintenance	• license applicants pay $20 fee to be deposited into the Fund; Fund needs minimum balance of $250,000; lower balance results in licensee assessment to restore the balance; Commission may transfer $500,000 to the Fund if balance falls below $300,000
Claims	• eligible: loss due to licensee fraud, misrepresentation, theft, embezzlement, false pretenses, or forgery; ineligible: loss incurred in limited partnership for real estate investments, joint ventures to invest in real estate, purchase of commercial paper secured by real estate; spouse of licensee or unlicensed employee or the personal representative of those spouses may not file
	• **claim requirements** – filed within 3 years of loss discovery, be in writing, made under oath, state loss amount and facts of claim, include supporting documents or evidence; sales contracts must state buyer is protected for losses up to $50,000
	• **claim process** – Commission to forward copy of claim to all involved parties and request response within 10 days; Commission reviews and investigates, then issues proposed award, refers for hearing, or dismisses; licensee or claimant may file exceptions or request hearing within 30 days of proposed order; otherwise, proposed order becomes final
	• **hearings** – Commission notifies involved parties; burden of proof is on claimant; making false statement or material misstatement of fact about Fund claims is misdemeanor punishable by fine and/or imprisonment
Payments	• maximum payout is $50,000 and restricted to claimant's loss from original transaction; payments are made in the order the awards were granted
Penalties	• immediate license suspension; cannot be reinstated until licensee fully reimburses Fund
	• licensee must repay Fund within 30 days or Commission may bring action for judgment; unpaid amount may become lien placed against licensee's real property, released upon full repayment
EXAMINATION OF RECORDS	• licensees must provide records for Commission inspection whenever the Commission gives reasonable notice; must provide paper copies at licensee's expense; failure to do so may result in summary suspension of license

26 Maryland Licensing Requirements

Activities Requiring a License
License Requirements
Changes in License Status
License Renewal
Continuing Education Requirements
Business Entities
Place of Business Requirements

ACTIVITIES REQUIRING A LICENSE

Licensed brokerage services
Exceptions

Licensed brokerage services

Under Title 17-301, an individual must be licensed by the Maryland Real Estate Commission as a real estate broker, associate broker, or salesperson before providing real estate brokerage services in Maryland.

Brokerage services that require a license include the following when performed for consideration or compensation:

> ▸ selling, buying, exchanging, or leasing any real estate;
> ▸ collecting rent for the use of any real estate
> ▸ assisting another person to locate or obtain any residential real estate to purchase or lease
> ▸ engaging regularly in a business of dealing in real estate or leases or options on real estate
> ▸ engaging in a business with the primary purpose of promoting the sale of real estate through a listing in a publication issued primarily for the promotion of real estate sales
> ▸ engaging in a business that subdivides land that is located in any state and sells the divided lots
> ▸ serving as a consultant regarding any activity set forth in the above listed items

Exceptions

Exempt services. Property management is not a real estate brokerage service and does not require licensure.

Exempt persons. Under the Brokers Act, no real estate license is required for the following when performing brokerage services:

- ▶ an individual acting under a court order or judgment
- ▶ a public officer performing duties of office
- ▶ an individual acting under a power of attorney to sell or lease real estate in a single transaction
- ▶ a licensed auctioneer selling real estate at public auction
- ▶ an owner or lessor managing, leasing, or selling the subject real estate, unless the individual is in the real estate brokerage business
- ▶ an individual acting as a receiver, trustee, personal representative, or guardian
- ▶ a financial institution, subsidiary of a financial institution, or incorporated mortgage loan institution managing, selling, or leasing property acquired through foreclosure or deed in lieu of foreclosure
- ▶ an attorney who does not regularly provide real estate services, who does not advertise that he or she is in the business of providing brokerage services, and who does provide brokerage services while representing another person in the course of the attorney's regular law practice
- ▶ a home builder initially renting or selling the home
- ▶ a broker or owner's agent managing or leasing the broker's or owner's real estate
- ▶ a person negotiating the sale, lease, or other transfer of a business enterprise as long as the transfer does not include an interest in real property other than the lease under which the business enterprise operates
- ▶ a person subdividing and selling his the person's own unimproved property
- ▶ an individual who sells 6 or fewer of his or her own unimproved lots in a calendar year
- ▶ an individual subdividing and selling unimproved property owned by the individual for at least 10 years (the 10 years may include ownership by successive individuals if the property has passed by inheritance to those individuals)

LICENSE REQUIREMENTS

License types
General requirements
Salesperson license
Associate broker license
Broker license
Reciprocal license
Expedited licensing for military

License types   In Maryland, there are three types of real estate licenses: broker, associate broker, and salesperson. The MREC also issues branch office certificates and reciprocal licenses for out-of-state licensees seeking to provide brokerage services within Maryland.

When all general and specific requirements for licensure have been met, the license applicant will be issued a license certificate and a pocket card that show the licensee's name, license expiration date, and the licensee's registration number.

Each associate broker or salesperson license certificate will also include the affiliated brokerage firm name. Salespersons and associate brokers may provide brokerage services on behalf of the licensed broker listed on their license certificate but may not provide brokerage services on their own behalf or on behalf of any other person.

Maryland licensees may obtain additional licenses and affiliate with more than one broker.

General requirements

To qualify for any of the three Maryland real estate license types, the applicant must meet the following general requirements:

- ▸ be of good character and reputation
- ▸ be at least 18 years old
- ▸ successfully complete the educational course based on the type of license being sought
- ▸ pay a fee and pass the license examination
- ▸ submit an application for licensure using the appropriate form provided by the Commission (https://www.dllr.state.md.us/cgi-bin/ElectronicLicensing/RE/original/REOriginal1.cgi); the application must be submitted within 1 year of passing the examination.
- ▸ submit a copy of the license examination results to the Commission
- ▸ pay the Guaranty Fund fee
- ▸ pay the application fee to the Commission
- ▸ submit any additional information required by the Commission

Felony or misdemeanor convictions. An applicant with a felony or misdemeanor conviction will not automatically be denied licensure. If the applicant submits True Test copies of the conviction proceedings with the application, the Commission will review convictions on a case by case basis. If the application is denied, the applicant has the right to appeal the denial.

Examinations. Applicants who meet all requirements, general and specific to license type, for licensure must pass the license examination which is given by either the Commission or a testing service selected by the Commission. The Commission or testing service will provide each qualified applicant with notice of the time and place of the examination. The Commission determines the subjects, scope, form, and passing score for the examination and requires it to be written. To avoid discrimination, each examination given on a specific day for a specific license type will contain the same questions which may, however, be in a different order.

The examinations consist of a national portion and a state portion. Each portion must be passed with a score of 70% or higher. Individuals who pass both portions have 1 year to apply for licensure. Individuals who pass only one portion must retake and pass the second portion within 1 year. Licensure applicants must take and pass both portions of the appropriate examination within 1 year of completing prelicensing education. Individuals are given 2 hours to complete the examination.

Broker license examinations are structured to test the applicant's ability to perform authorized services and the applicant's knowledge of the general practice of handling real estate transactions.

Salesperson license

In addition to the general licensure requirements, to qualify for a Maryland salesperson license, the applicant must meet the following specific requirements:

> ▸ successfully complete a Commission-approved basic course in real estate to include not more than 60 hours of classroom, remote access, video, internet, or home study instruction
> ▸ complete 3 clock hours of real estate ethics as part of the basic course; applicant may obtain approval from Commission to substitute college real estate and ethics courses
> ▸ pass the salesperson licensure examination
> ▸ obtain a commitment from a licensed broker to have the salesperson become the broker's affiliate once the salesperson's license is granted; the commitment must be obtained within 3 years from the date the salesperson license was issued on inactive status. The salesperson must be affiliated with a broker prior to providing brokerage services.
> ▸ meet any additional requirements established by the Commission

Associate broker license

Applicants wishing to obtain licensure as an associate broker must meet the general licensure requirements and the broker licensure requirements. The applicant must also obtain a licensed broker's commitment to allow the newly licensed associate broker to work as an affiliate of the broker.

Broker license

To qualify for a real estate broker license in Maryland, the applicant must meet the general licensure requirements as well as the following broker-specific requirements:

> ▸ successfully complete the required 135-hour commission-approved coursework for brokers that includes 3 clock hours of real estate ethics
> ▸ have been an active and lawful licensed real estate salesperson for at least 3 years with no breaks such as becoming inactive, renewing late, or being suspended
> ▸ pass the broker licensure examination

- ▸ meet any additional requirements established by the Commission
- ▸ submit a credit report completed by a Commission-approved credit reporting agency or pay the credit report fee for the Commission to obtain the credit report
- ▸ notify the applicant's current affiliated broker of his or her plan to obtain a broker license or affiliate with an additional broker

The Commission will waive the broker license education and experience requirements for any applicant who is qualified to practice law in Maryland. These applicants must still pass the licensure examination.

Branch office certificate. Brokers who wish to maintain one or more branch offices in addition to the principal place of business must apply for a branch office certificate and pay the certificate fee. The broker must submit a separate application for each branch office and indicate who will manage each office. The application can be found online at https://www.dllr.state.md.us/license/mrec/mreclic.shtml.

Branch office certificates are issued for 2-year terms and expire on the first April 30 after the effective date of the certificate and in an even-numbered year. They may be renewed for additional 2-year terms by the broker submitting a renewal application and fee to the Commission prior to the certificate expiration date.

Reciprocal license

Reciprocity agreements. A reciprocal license is one that allows individuals who are real estate licensees in another state to provide real estate services within Maryland. Typically, the two states have a signed reciprocity agreement that includes the requirements for issuing a reciprocal license to licensees in the other state. The complete provisions for a reciprocal licensure agreement between Maryland and another state are found in Title 17-3A of the Brokers Act.

Currently, Maryland has signed reciprocity agreements only with Pennsylvania and Oklahoma. However, Maryland also allows licensees in all other states to apply for an out-of-state license recognition, or waiver, if they qualify.

- ▸ licensees who hold reciprocal licenses under the Maryland-Pennsylvania agreement are not required to take the Maryland exam or complete continuing education

- ▸ licensees who hold reciprocal licenses under the Maryland-Oklahoma agreement are not required to complete continuing education, but they must pass the Maryland state portion of the exam

With some states, the Commission may determine that a Maryland licensee is not offered reciprocal licensure opportunities that are substantially comparable to those Maryland offers to licensees of the other state. In such cases, applicants from that other state who are seeking a Maryland reciprocal license will be required to meet education, experience, and examination requirements that are substantially comparable to those required of Maryland licensees who seek a reciprocal license in that other state.

Requirements. To qualify for a reciprocal license in Maryland, the applicant must meet the following requirements:

- submit a licensure application, pay a fee, and include a full and complete certified license history which is dated within 30 days of the submission date; the certificate must indicate whether the applicant has been the subject of any disciplinary proceeding or criminal conviction

- submit a statement that there is no proceeding alleging the applicant's misconduct under licensing or criminal law; the applicant has not been convicted of a crime and agrees to be bound by Maryland regulations and code of ethics and permits disclosure of any disciplinary proceedings involving the applicant

- hold a current and active license; if the license in the other state becomes inactive or expires, the Maryland reciprocal license becomes void; the type of reciprocal license to be issued will be the same as the license held in the other state.

Applicants must agree to any additional provisions included in §17-3A. The MREC will review each applicant's education and experience from the home state for transferability.

Out of state license. Under § 17-308, the Commission may choose to waive any particular licensure requirement for an applicant who holds a comparable or equivalent license in another state if the applicant does all three of the following:

- pays the application fee, provides evidence of his or her qualifications that meet Maryland's requirements

- submits a certified copy of the comparable license from the other state

- provides evidence that the broker applicant actively maintains an office in the other state

Education and experience from a home state are reviewed for transferability, individually for each applicant. Waivers may be offered only to active licensees.

Licensed broker. If an out-of-state licensed broker has practiced real estate for at least 3 of the 5 years immediately preceding application for a Maryland reciprocal broker license, the applicant is exempt from completing Maryland's broker education requirements.

Brokers must obtain a Maryland reciprocal license before any affiliated associate brokers or salespersons may apply.

Brokers may not have a principal place of business located in Maryland. If the principal place of business moves to Maryland after the broker obtains a reciprocal license, reciprocal licensees who have not previously taken a Maryland exam must then do so. The licensees must also obtain a standard Maryland license within 90 days of the move.

Associate broker and salesperson. Associate brokers and salespersons must submit a letter from the sponsoring broker stating the broker is currently licensed and will supervise the affiliated licensees who obtain reciprocal licensure.

Consent to service and jurisdiction. Nonresident applicants must submit an irrevocable consent, signed by the applicant, to the Commission that specifies that service of process on the Commission's executive director will bind the applicant in any action, suit, or proceeding brought against the applicant.

When a nonresident licensee participates in any real estate transaction in Maryland or divides fees or holds deposits from any transaction in the State, the act constitutes an irrevocable consent with the same effect as one that has been submitted to the Commission as required for licensure.

Holding a reciprocal license constitutes sufficient contact with the State of Maryland to allow the Commission and the state's courts to have personal jurisdiction over the licensee in any action taken as a result of the licensee's acts or omissions.

Issue and renewal. A reciprocal license is issued for 2 years and is renewable. To renew the reciprocal license, the licensee must continue to hold a current license in the other state and must not be the subject of a disciplinary action or investigation.

Expedited licensing for military

Maryland law requires the Division of Occupational and Professional Licensing to help veterans and active members of the United States armed forces, including their spouses, obtain occupational and professional licenses in Maryland. Service members include active duty reservists and members of the National Guard.

Eligibility. Under the Veterans Full Employment Act of 2013 (amended 2019), qualifying parties include:

- current service members-- upon being assigned to a duty station in Maryland
- veterans-- former service members discharged under any circumstances other than dishonorable, regardless of when the discharge occurred
- spouses-- of current members and veterans and of deceased service members regardless of when the service member died

Applicants must hold a valid license in good standing in another state and submit the following documents as appropriate based on military status:

- DD FORM 214
- military orders
- marriage certificate
- death certificate
- proof of residence

The law requires applications for expedited licensing to be processed immediately and licenses issued within 60 days of receipt of the application and supporting documentation.

CHANGES IN LICENSE STATUS

Affiliated broker
Contact information
Inactive and active status
Reinstatement
Upgrading and downgrading
Death of broker

Where to file. License status changes can be made on the MREC's website at https://www.dllr.state.md.us/license/mrec/mrecchange.shtml.

Dishonored checks. If a check offered in payment of a fee is dishonored, the licensee will be charged a collection cost in addition to the original fee. The fee is not considered paid until both the fee and the collection cost are paid in full.

Affiliated broker

Transfer of affiliation. A licensed salesperson or associate broker may transfer affiliation from one broker to another by submitting the following to the Commission:

- ▶ license certificate and pocket card
- ▶ transfer application on the Commission-provided form
- ▶ statement from either the current affiliated broker or from the licensee that the affiliation with the current broker is terminated
- ▶ evidence from a licensed broker that said broker will accept the licensee as an affiliate when the licensee is issued a new license certificate and pocket card
- ▶ transfer fee

Termination of affiliation. To terminate affiliation with a licensee, a broker must send the licensee a letter on company letterhead, signed by the broker. The letter must state the broker's intent to terminate the licensee. The broker must also complete the appropriate termination sections of the Commission's License Change form and send it to the Commission for processing. Along with the form, the broker must send a copy of the termination letter and the terminated licensee's license certificate.

The form can be found online at https://www.dllr.state.md.us/cgi-bin/ElectronicLicensing/RE/termination/RETermination1.cgi.

Contact information

Name/Address changes. To change the name of a licensee or brokerage firm, the licensee or broker must submit the appropriate application to the Commission along with the license certificate and pocket card and appropriate fee. The

Commission will then issue a new license certificate and pocket card with the new information.

Inactive and active status

Deactivation. A licensee may request a change to inactive status by surrendering the license certificate and pocket card to the Commission. The license of an associate broker or salesperson also becomes inactive status when the licensee is no longer affiliated with the licensed broker whose name appears on the licensee's license certificate.

If the licensee on inactive status does not reactivate the license within 3 years of becoming inactive, the license will expire. During the period of inactive status, the licensee must continue to renew the license.

Inactive licensees remain subject to disciplinary action, license suspension, and license revocation. Any licensee who is on inactive status is prohibited from performing or offering brokerage services. Violating this prohibition constitutes a misdemeanor punishable by a fine, imprisonment, or both.

Reactivation. To reactivate a license that is on inactive status, the licensee must request reactivation, pay the reissuance fee to the Commission, and meet any continuing education requirements that would have been due at the time of license renewal. Associate brokers and salespersons must also submit evidence of a licensed broker's commitment to affiliate with the licensee upon reactivation of the license.

Reinstatement

A licensee may have an expired license reinstated by applying to the Commission for reinstatement within 3 years of the expiration date. The Commission must receive the application at least 30 days prior to the expiration of the 3-year period. The licensee must also meet good character and reputation requirements, complete required continuing education, and pay all past due renewal fees and the reinstatement fee.

Licenses that have been expired longer than 3 years cannot be reinstated without meeting education and examination requirements. Licensees who misrepresent their completion of continuing education will be fined, charged a reinstatement fee, and given 1 month to actually complete the continuing education.

Upgrading and downgrading

Application procedure. Whether upgrading or downgrading a license for another license type, ae licensee must

  ▸ surrender the current license to the Commission
  ▸ submit the appropriate application
  ▸ if appropriate, submit acknowledgment from affiliated broker and licensee that the affiliation is terminated
  ▸ pay the application fee
  ▸ submit additional information as required

Upgrade from salesperson to associate broker. Salespersons who wish to upgrade to associate broker status must have previously held an associate broker or broker license, have been continually licensed since initial licensure, have and obtained a commitment from a broker to work as an affiliate of that broker.

Upgrade from salesperson to broker. Salespersons who wish to upgrade to broker status must have previously held an associate broker or broker license and have been continually licensed since initial licensure. A salesperson who has not previously held a broker or associate broker license must complete all requirements for broker licensure.

Upgrade from associate broker to broker. Associate brokers who wish to upgrade to broker status submit a broker license application along with the following:

> ▶ an original credit report no older than 6 months
> ▶ an escrow account number and name of the Maryland bank where the account is held
> ▶ a breakdown of the brokerage ownership structure to include each owner and percentage of ownership
> ▶ the approved trade name registration and articles of incorporation, if applicable, acknowledging real estate brokerage services will be provided
> ▶ a statement of sole proprietorship and nonregistration, if applicable, along with the name and address to appear on the license
> ▶ a franchise agreement, if applicable

Unless operating as an unregistered sole proprietor, the applicant must contact the Commission to confirm that the brokerage name being registered is not similar to or the same as that of another registered licensee. Then the brokerage must be registered with the Maryland Department of Assessments and Taxation.

Downgrade to associate broker license or salesperson license. Current licensees who wish to exchange their license for a lower level license must obtain a commitment from a licensed broker to work as an affiliate of that broker and comply with all application procedures.

Death of broker

Six-month reissue. If a licensed broker dies or becomes totally and permanently disabled, an adult member of the broker's family may continue the broker's business for up to 6 months to close and terminate the brokerage.

The family member must surrender the broker's license to the Commission along with any other required documentation. The Commission will then reissue the broker's license to the family member for a 6-month term.

Four-year issue. A member of the broker's immediate family may qualify for the broker's license for a term of 4 years if the individual

> ▶ has been continuously licensed as a salesperson for the previous 3 years,
> ▶ passes the broker's examination whether or not he or she has met broker prelicensure educational requirements

> ▸ surrenders his or her own salesperson license certificate and pocket card
>
> ▸ complies with requirements to surrender the broker's license

The individual must complete the broker prelicense education requirements within the 4 years, or the license will automatically expire at the end of the term. If the education requirements are met, the individual may continue to hold the license and renew it when appropriate.

LICENSE RENEWAL

Expiration
Renewal procedure

Expiration

License term. Maryland Statute 17-314 mandates that licenses are issued for 2-year terms beginning and ending in even-numbered years. The statute specifies March 1 and April 30 dates for the first renewal of broker, associate broker, and salesperson licenses.

However, Section (c) of the statute provides the Secretary with authority to determine staggered renewal dates, which has now been the practice for several years. Under the staggered renewals, licenses expire every 2 years on the month and day the license was originally issued, for both first renewals or subsequent renewals.

For example, if Mike's broker license was issued on September 1, 2021, his first renewal must take place by September 1, 2023. All subsequent renewals of his license must take place by September 1 every 2 years.

Renewal requirement. Failure to renew a license before the expiration date will result in the license expiring, at which point the individual may no longer provide brokerage services that require licensure until the license has been reinstated.

Renewal procedure

Notice. At least 1 month prior to the license expiration date, the Commission sends a renewal application and notice that states the license expiration date, the date by which the application must be received by the Commission, and the renewal fee. Both documents are emailed or mailed to the broker's principal office or the affiliated broker's principal office.

Application. Licensees may renew online or submit a paper renewal application. Prior to the expiration date, licensees may renew their licenses for the next 2-year term if they

> ▸ are entitled to be licensed
>
> ▸ pay the renewal fee
>
> ▸ submit the renewal application
>
> ▸ submit the original certificate of completion of continuing education requirements

Associate brokers and salespersons must also notify the Commission of the names of their affiliated brokers.

Brokers must also submit a credit report from a Commission-approved agency or pay the required fee for the Commission to obtain the credit report.

CONTINUING EDUCATION REQUIREMENTS

Course hours
Exceptions
Subject matter
Instruction

Course hours

Instruction time. The purpose of continuing education (CE) is to keep licensees up to date on current facts and laws so their real estate transactions can continue in a legal and professional manner. Consequently, brokers, associate brokers, and salespersons are required to complete at least 15 clock hours of CE coursework within the 2 years preceding license renewal. Clock hours are defined as 50 minutes of instruction per 60 minutes of clock time. Clock hours over the required 15 may not be rolled over for credit in the next licensing term.

Exceptions

Continuing education requirements are sometimes modified based on the licensees' education or practice of real estate:

- ▶ licensees who possess a graduate degree in law or real estate from an accredited school and are not acting as a designated branch office manager or team leader may meet CE requirements by completing at least 7.5 clock hours of coursework
- ▶ licensees who provide nonresidential brokerage services may satisfy 1.5 clock hours with coursework on the federal Americans with Disabilities Act or coursework in fair housing laws
- ▶ licensees possessing graduate degrees in law or real estate may satisfy 3 of the required 15 clock hours with a course that outlines relevant changes in federal, state, or local laws and regulations
- ▶ out-of-state licensees must complete at least 15 hours of CE but may substitute CE clock hours earned in the other state if the coursework is approved in the other state and meets the distribution requirements of Maryland required CE; the MREC will allow such substitution of coursework only if the other state allows Maryland CE coursework to be substituted for Maryland licensees meeting required CE in the other state

Subject matter

The Commission must approve form, substance, and subject matter of all CE courses. Currently approved coursework includes at least

- ▶ 3 clock hours of changes in federal, state, or local law, court cases, and industry trends relevant to real estate

- 1.5 clock hours on federal, state, and local fair housing laws, including fair housing advertising (not required for licensees providing nonresidential brokerage services)
- 3 clock hours on ethics, to include the Maryland Code of Ethics, flipping, fraudulent practices, conflict resolution, public respect, and professionalism
- 3 clock hours on the principles of brokerage relationships and disclosures
- 3 clock hours on broker supervision (required for brokers and licensees designated as branch office manager or team leader)

The remaining required hours may be completed in elective coursework on topics approved by the Commission.

Instruction

Schools and instructors. Continuing education courses are to be taught by qualified instructors with real estate experience. The courses may be offered by qualified real estate professional associations or educational institutions approved by the Commission.

Delivery methods. Courses may be provided by remote satellite access, closed-circuit video, computer/Internet, home study, and other approved delivery systems.

Certificate of completion. The instructor or entity is to issue a certificate of completion, showing the number of hours completed, to the licensee and submit it to the Commission electronically.

BUSINESS ENTITIES

Broker participation
Associate broker and salesperson participation
Ownership interest

Broker participation

Licensed brokers may provide real estate brokerage services through a corporation, limited liability company, or partnership. The broker must be employed by or have a contractual relationship with the entity, have been designated as the entity's broker to provide brokerage services, and notify the Commission of the broker's intent to provide the services through the business entity.

Salespersons and associate brokers may provide brokerage services through the entity if they do so on behalf of the entity's broker with whom they are affiliated.

Salesperson and associate broker participation

With approval from an affiliated broker, one or more salespersons and associate brokers may organize and own a business entity. Each shareholder, member, or owner of the entity must be a licensed real estate salesperson or associate broker. The licensee may direct commissions to be paid directly to the entity.

Ownership interest   No real estate associate broker, salesperson, or combination of the two may directly or indirectly hold more than 50 percent of the interest in a business. That interest percentage includes any interest held by an immediate family member of the licensee unless the family member is also affiliated with the business as a licensee.

PLACE OF BUSINESS REQUIREMENTS

Main office
Branch office
Office signage
Change of address

Main office   **Resident brokers.** Real estate brokers who are residents of and licensed in Maryland are required to maintain an office within Maryland where the broker, affiliated licensees, and employees regularly transact real estate business.

The Commission does not recognize answering services, mechanical message recording devices, mail drops, or any combination of these as a broker's office or place of business.

In their main offices, brokers must

> ▶ display their licenses and those of all affiliated licensees in a conspicuous place
> ▶ keep brokerage and escrow account records in a secure location
> ▶ comply with the Americans with Disabilities Act – provide reasonable accommodations to afford accessibility

Nonresident brokers. Brokers who do not reside in Maryland are required to maintain an office in Maryland only if their resident state requires Maryland residents who are licensed in the other state to maintain an office in that state.

Branch office   Brokers may maintain branch offices within Maryland as long as the broker obtains a branch office certificate for each office. The certificate requires the broker to

> ▶ submit a branch office application
> ▶ pay the application fee
> ▶ submit the name of the qualified licensee who will manage the branch office

The branch office manager must be a licensed associate broker, a salesperson with at least 3 years of experience providing brokerage services, or a salesperson who has completed a broker's course in real estate and passed the broker's examination. The manager is responsible for supervising licensees working out of the branch office. The branch office certificate is renewable every 2 years.

Office signage   Title 17-519 requires brokers to display a sign at each office and branch office. The sign must be displayed conspicuously on the entrance door or outside the premises so as to be easily visible to the public and must contain the phrase "real estate." If the broker is authorized by real estate trade associations, the words "realtor" or "realtist" may also be included on the sign.

Change of address   Brokers must notify the Commission in writing of any change of address of the main office or a branch office. The broker must also submit the office or branch office license certificate and pocket card for the office that is changing location and pay a reissuance fee for a new certificate. A new certificate and pocket card will be issued for the remainder of the broker's current licensure term or the balance of the branch office certificate's current term.

Failure to submit the required notice for address changes will result in the broker's license automatically being suspended until the broker submits the required notice and fee.

26 Maryland Licensing Requirements
Snapshot Review

**ACTIVITIES
REQUIRING
A LICENSE**

**Licensed brokerage
services**

- providing brokerage services for compensation: selling, buying, exchanging, leasing real estate; collecting rent; engaging in any business that regularly deals in real estate

Exceptions

- per court order, public officer duty, power of attorney; as auctioneer, unlicensed property owner, financial institution, attorney, home builder, etc.

**LICENSE
REQUIREMENTS**

License types

- broker, associate broker, salesperson; licensees may affiliate with multiple brokers

General requirements

- good character, 18 years old, completed required education, pay fees, pass license exam and submit results to Commission, submit application, pay Guaranty Fund fee
- convictions are reviewed case by case and do not automatically deny license; applicants may appeal denials
- examinations consist of national and state portions; must pass each with 70% or higher score; must apply for license within 1 year of passing exam; if only one portion passed, applicant must pass the other portion within 1 year; both portions must be passed within 1 year of completing prelicensure education

Salesperson license

- general requirements plus 60 hours of coursework to include 3 hours of ethics; pass salesperson licensure exam; obtain commitment from broker to work as broker's affiliate

Associate broker license

- general requirements plus all broker requirements; obtain commitment from broker to work as broker's affiliate

Broker license

- general requirements plus 135 hours of coursework to include 3 hours of ethics; 3 years as active licensed salesperson without breaks; pass broker licensure exam; submit credit report or fee for Commission to obtain the credit report; notify current affiliated broker of intent to obtain broker licensure or affiliate with an additional broker
- qualified attorneys excused from education and experience requirements but must pass exam
- branch office certificate granted when broker submits application and pays fee for each branch office and indicates who will manage each office; issued for 2-year terms and are renewable

Reciprocal license

- allows nonresident licensees to provide services in Maryland for 2-year terms by submitting application, paying fees, submitting certified license history from resident state, being currently licensed in other state, having no principal place of business in Maryland, obtaining same type of license as in other state; submitting irrevocable consent to the Commission; Maryland's current reciprocal licensing agreements are with Pennsylvania and Oklahoma
- out-of-state licenses may have requirements waived if applicant pays fees, provides evidence of qualifications comparable to Maryland requirements, submits certified copy of comparable license from other state, provide evidence of broker maintaining office in other state

Expedited licensing for military

- military members, military spouses and surviving spouses, veterans qualify for expedited Maryland licensure if have valid license in other state; submit DD 214, military orders, marriage certificate, death certificate, and proof of residence; license is to be issued within 60 days of application

CHANGES IN LICENSE STATUS

Where to file

- all license status may be completed online
- dishonored check-- licensee must pay collection cost in addition to original fee

Affiliated broker

- change affiliation: submit license, pocket card, application, fee, broker statements
- terminate affiliation: broker notifies licensee and Commission, submits form

Contact information

- submit application, fee, license certificate, pocket card

Inactive and active status

- deactivate—submit license certificate, pocket card; end affiliation; expires in 3 years; remains subject to discipline; perform no real estate services
- reactivate-- submit application, pay fee, meet CE requirements; show affiliation

Reinstatement

- within 3 years of license expiration date: submit application at least 30 days before expiration of 3-year period; good character; complete CE; pay past due renewal fees; no reinstatement for expirations longer than 3 years; penalties for misrepresenting CE completion

Upgrading and Downgrading

- exchange of license types-- surrender current license; submit application; submit broker acknowledgment; pay fee; meet license requirements

Death of broker

- death or disability of broker-- immediate family member may continue business for 6 months under broker's license; family member may qualify for 4-year term of broker's license if continuously licensed for 3 years, pass broker exam, surrender current license, surrender broker's license; renewable if education requirements met within the 4 years

LICENSE RENEWAL

Expiration

- licenses expire every 2 years on the month and day the license was originally issued, for both first renewals or subsequent renewals
- failure to renew results in expiration of license with required reinstatement before providing brokerage services

Renewal procedure

- renewal notice sent at least 1 month prior to expiration; licensee renews by paying fee, submitting application, submitting completion certificate for CE; associate brokers and salespersons also to submit names of affiliated broker(s); brokers to submit credit report

CONTINUING EDUCATION REQUIREMENTS

Course hours

- 15 clock hours of CE prior to each license renewal

Exceptions

- licensees with graduate degrees in law or real estate, licensees providing nonresidential services, out-of-state licensees completing CE in other state

Subject matter

- 15 hours of CE is to include changes in laws, fair housing, ethics, brokerage relationships, and broker supervision with additional elective coursework

Instruction

- approved instructors and schools; multiple approved delivery systems; certificate of completion

BUSINESS ENTITIES

Broker participation
- brokers may provide brokerage services through a business entity if the broker is employed by or has contractual relationship with the entity, is entity's designated broker, and notifies the Commission; other licensees may do the same on behalf of the entity's broker

Associate broker and salesperson participation
- broker may authorize affiliated licensees to own a business entity

Ownership interest
- licensees may not hold more than 50% of interest in a business entity

PLACE OF BUSINESS REQUIREMENTS

Main office
- resident brokers are required to maintain an office within Maryland and to display all licenses in conspicuous place in the main office; records are to be kept in the main office; answering services, etc. do not qualify as offices; accommodations are to be made for those with disabilities

Branch office
- brokers may maintain branch offices with certificates for each office obtained by submitting branch office application, paying fee, and submitting name of licensee with 3 years of brokerage experience or with completed broker education and exam who will manage the office; the certificate is renewable every 2 years

Office signage
- brokers are required to display a sign outside of each office and branch office with the sign including the words "real estate"

Change of address
- if office location changes, brokers are required to notify the Commission and obtain new license certificate with new address; failure to notify the Commission will result in automatic suspension of broker's license until the notice is submitted

27 Maryland Regulation of Business Conduct

Key Terms
Compensation
Advertising
Phone, Email, Fax
Handling Trust Funds
Summary Suspensions
Recordkeeping Requirements
Supervision Requirements
Prohibited Acts
Personal Assistants
Real Estate Teams
Offers
Sales Contracts
Condominium Sales Disclosures

KEY TERMS

Broker
Brokerage firm
Providing brokerage services

Broker

A broker is an individual who acts as an intermediary between principals in a real estate transaction without having title to the property. Brokers may work independently or have their own real estate firm and employ affiliated licensees. Either way, they perform on a commission basis and must be licensed to perform certain activities and provide certain real estate brokerage services.

A broker who owns a real estate firm is called a principal broker or managing broker. The broker fulfills a management or supervisory role in a real estate firm by overseeing the acts of affiliated licensees, reviewing contracts, resolving transaction disputes, handling transaction funds, providing training, and so on.

Brokerage firm

A brokerage is a firm or company that employs licensees (as employees or independent contractors) who facilitate real estate transactions based on the brokerage services offered. Brokerages are considered the liaison or middleman in these transactions. The brokerage may be owned by an individual broker or a business entity such as a corporation, a limited liability company, or a partnership.

Providing brokerage services

Providing real estate brokerage services means to engaging in any of the activities for which a license is required (see "activities requiring licensure" in the previous chapter). A broker who chooses to provide services through a business entity must submit notice of the entity to the Commission. Operating as a business entity does not relieve a broker or affiliated licensees of individual liability.

COMPENSATION

Commissions
Incentives

Commissions

Real estate licensees typically receive compensation in the form of a commission, or percentage of the property sale price, for providing brokerage services. Only licensed brokers may accept such compensation from a client. Associate brokers and salespersons may only accept commission or other compensation directly from their affiliated broker and not from a client or customer.

Because the law mandates licensure for receiving such compensation, licensees are prohibited from paying an unlicensed individual for providing brokerage services. Brokers may pay or offer to pay a commission to an attorney for services related to real estate transactions or to an attorney who holds a real estate license but may not pay or offer to pay a commission for an attorney's referrals of potential parties to a transaction.

Brokers are permitted to pay commissions to out-of-state licensees who meet Maryland's licensure requirements and may divide a fee earned in Maryland with an out-of-state licensee if permitted in the other state. Brokers may also pay commissions to recognized professional service corporations, limited liability companies, or other business entities.

Incentives

Inducements to list or purchase. Licensees are prohibited from offering an incentive to influence a party in a real estate transaction. No inducements, prizes, or contests may be offered or used to obtain listings or buyer/broker agreements or to motivate a buyer to purchase a particular property unless the inducements are offered to all consumers on the same basis. No one client or consumer may be offered a prize or cash payment; the offer must be made to all or not made at all. The same holds true for offering free services as an incentive related to a transaction. For example, advertising free appraisals is only allowed if the offer is extended to any person regardless of the purpose for the appraisal.

However, licensees may offer a prize to be given to one of a number of attendees at an open house as long as the only requirement to win the prize is to simply attend the open house. This is not viewed as an inducement or means of influencing a party to purchase the property.

Referrals. An unlicensed individual who refers customers to a licensee may not be compensated in any way or allowed to participate in a drawing for a prize or cash. Referrals are considered a type of brokerage service and, consequently, may not be provided for compensation by any unlicensed person. Allowing the unlicensed person to win a prize for the referral is also considered compensation and is, thus, prohibited.

Rebates. While licensees may not pay unlicensed individuals for providing brokerage services, they may pay individuals who are simply parties to the transaction and are not providing any type of brokerage service. If the licensee agrees to pay a buyer a commission rebate or to compensate the seller with cash or a reduction in the commission rate, the agreement must be in writing. Further, such payments to any party in the transaction must be disclosed to the other party. Inducements in the form of a rebate for a percentage of the property's price are also allowed.

ADVERTISING

Key terms
Advertising requirements
Signs

Key terms

Advertising. Maryland regulations define advertising as "the use of any oral, written, or visual advertisement by a licensed real estate salesperson, licensed real estate broker, licensed associate real estate broker, or other person on behalf of a licensed real estate salesperson, licensed real estate broker, or licensed associate real estate broker."

Advertisement. An advertisement is any oral, written, or printed media advertisement to include any correspondence, mailing, newsletter, brochure, business card, for sale or for lease sign and sign rider, promotional item, automobile signage, telephone directory listing, television announcement, radio announcement, telephone solicitation, and World Wide Web and Internet voice-overs.

Designated name. A designated name is a name used by a licensed broker, associate broker, or salesperson that is other than the licensee's full legal name. The designated name includes a first name, nickname, or last name.

Trade name. A trade name is a trademark or service mark, company name or business name, whether or not the licensee needs to obtain permission from another person or entity who has an existing or continuing right in that trademark or service mark by virtue of any Maryland state or federal law.

Advertising requirements

Usage. The law allows licensed brokers, associate brokers, salespersons, team members, and others acting on behalf of any of these, to use any oral, written, or visual means to advertise brokerage services.

Approval. Every brokerage should have a written advertising policy. The broker, office manager or team leader must approve any advertisement developed by a licensee, team member, or **unlicensed** personal assistant to confirm compliance with the brokerage policies and federal and state law before the ad is placed. The

MREC has created the following checklist for brokers, team leaders, team members, and licensees to ensure compliance with advertising laws.

MREC ADVERTISING CHECKLIST

All advertisements to be placed by or on behalf of a real estate licensee should be submitted to the broker, office manager, or the broker-manager's designee for compliance review prior to release. If the advertisement has been created for a member of – or on behalf of – a team, the team leader should also review and approve the piece using the guidelines below.

Name of Licensee
Does the advertisement include the full name of the licensee exactly as it appears on their real estate license?
☐ YES ☐ NO

License Category
If the advertisement includes a licensee's category, is it correct? The only available options include Salesperson, Associate Broker, or Broker. Terms, such as Associate are not recognized licensing categories.
☐ YES ☐ NO

Brokerage Name
Does the advertisement "meaningfully and conspicuously" display the Brokerage's name, and include the Brokerage's full name as it appears on the MREC license (not solely a company logo or abbreviation of the company name)?
☐ YES ☐ NO

Telephone Number of Broker or Office Manager
Does the advertisement include the identified telephone number of the broker or branch office manager?
☐ YES ☐ NO

Authority to Advertise
Does the licensee have the written authorization of the owner or listing broker to advertise the Property – i.e., a listing contract? For examples, if Broker A has chosen to advertise the listing of Brokerage B in their front office window, Broker A must have written authorization to do so. Another scenario, if a licensee has created advertising that utilizes MLS photos, written permission must be obtained from the MLS to use those photos.
☐ YES ☐ NO

True & Accurate Picture
Is advertisement's content factual and true? Does the advertisement avoid any misstatement or exaggeration of fact? Do(es) the licensee(s) in the advertisement hold an active real estate license registered at the brokerage branch that the advertisement references?
☐ YES ☐ NO

Team Advertising
Does the advertisement include the full name of the licensee as the name appears on the license, as advertising in solely the name of the team is prohibited?
☐ YES ☐ NO

Offering of Inducements
Does the advertisement avoid offering compensation or anything of value through a contest, lottery, drawing or other prize mechanism or element of chance? (Be advised the Commission recognizes an exception to this requirement, for example a drawing at an open house, available to all, not only those who buy/sell the property.)
☐ YES ☐ NO

Payment of Compensation for Referral Fees
Does the advertisement avoid offering compensation or anything of value to an unlicensed person solely for the referral of a prospective client or customer?
☐ YES ☐ NO

Property Owned by Licensees
If the advertisement is for the sale, purchase or lease of real property that a licensee owns, does the advertisement state the fact that the owner is a real estate licensee in the State of Maryland?
☐ YES ☐ NO

Specifications. Among other things, advertisements should provide members of the public the means of contacting brokers and branch office managers for the purpose of asking questions and addressing concerns regarding any licensee and advertisement. Specifically, all real estate advertising in Maryland must meet the following standards:

▸ **name or designated name--** a licensed broker, associate broker, or salesperson's name or designated name, whichever appears on the license certificate, must be "meaningfully and conspicuously" included in the advertisement

    A first and last name must be used and no nickname unless the licensee has applied to the MREC to trade under a nickname or first name other than his or her full legal name.

▸ **trade name--** all advertisements for brokerage services wherein a licensee uses a trade name must also clearly and unmistakably include the licensee's name or trade name as it is registered with the Commission to ensure the licensee's identity is meaningfully and conspicuously displayed to members of the public

    A licensee who uses a trade name on a for-sale sign, business card, office sign, sales contract, listing contract, or other document relating to real estate activities must clearly and unmistakably include the licensee's registered name or trade name on any of these signs or documents.

    A licensee must also clearly and unmistakably include his or her registered name or trade name in any oral conversation with another person to assure the licensee's identity is clear to the other person.

▸ **brokerage name--** the full name of the brokerage with which the licensee is affiliated must be "meaningfully and conspicuously" included in the advertisement

    To qualify as meaningfully and conspicuously displayed, the brokerage name should be at least the same size as the licensee's name, if not larger. The brokerage logo may not be used in place of the brokerage name.

▸ **broker or office manager telephone number--** if a licensee includes his or her office telephone number or e-mail address in the advertisement, the broker or branch office manager's identified telephone number must also be used so the consumer can reach the broker or manager without going through the licensee

    An identified number is one that makes it clear the number is the brokerage office number. Typically, in a single office brokerage, the broker's number would be included while, in a multiple office brokerage, the branch office number would be included rather than the broker's number. The licensee may not use his or her home or cellular number.

- ▶ **teams**-- team advertising must show a direct connection between the team and the brokerage, the brokerage name in a meaningful and conspicuous manner, at least one team member's name, and the broker or branch office manager's telephone number

- ▶ **fair housing**-- the Equal Housing Opportunity logo should be included in all advertising and, when included, must be at least one-half inch by one-half inch in size and the same size as the largest of any other logo used in the advertisement

  No abbreviation may be used for the Equal Housing Opportunity slogan.

  Words or phrases prohibited by HUD may not be used in any advertisement. (See the section on "HUD Fair Housing Advertising" in Chapter 29.)

- ▶ **inducements**-- as previously discussed, offering inducements or compensation through a contest, element of chance, lottery, drawing, or other means of awarding a prize is prohibited, as is compensating an unlicensed person for referring a prospective client

  Coupons offered within an advertisement must include an expiration date and the terms and conditions for redeeming the coupons.

- ▶ **licensee-owned property**-- advertisements for the sale, purchase, or lease of property owned by the licensee or for the licensee's own account must identify the owner as a Maryland real estate licensee

  Such advertisements must also include the name of the licensee's affiliated broker.

- ▶ **authority to advertise**-- the property owner or the listing broker must grant authority to advertise the property

- ▶ **National Association of REALTORS® Code of Ethics**-- advertising properties already sold by other brokerages in a neighborhood without including a disclaimer that the advertising licensee's brokerage was not involved in those sales is a violation of NAR's Code of Ethics

- ▶ **truth in advertising**-- all advertising must be truthful, accurate, and in no way misleading

- ▶ **license category**-- licensees placing advertisements are not required to include their license category (broker, associate broker, salesperson)

However, licensees should avoid using terms that might mislead the public. For example, the term "associate" should only be used by an associate broker and not by a salesperson referring to him or herself as a "sales associate."

Signs   Licensees must obtain a property owner's permission prior to placing any sign on the property. While each locale may have its own regulations for use and placement of signage, typical requirements include signs being placed on the property being advertised and not on public right-of-way easements. Many locales require a permit for posting signage; but temporary signs, such as open house directional signs, may be exempt from needing a permit and may be allowed to be posted on public easements for a limited time.

HOA. Home owners' and condominium owners' associations typically have rules regarding placing signs within the community. Before placing a sign within a community governed by an owners' association, the licensee should become familiar with and comply with the association's rules.

Open house disclosure sign. A licensee conducting an open house must display a disclaimer sign exactly as provided by the Commission, which states the following:

ATTENTION PROSPECTIVE PURCHASERS PLEASE READ THIS SIGN CAREFULLY

This is to advise you that the agent who is conducting this Open House REPRESENTS THE SELLER(S) AND IS REQUIRED BY LAW TO PROMOTE THE INTERESTS OF THE SELLER(S).

ANY INFORMATION YOU GIVE THIS AGENT IS NOT CONSIDERED CONFIDENTIAL under the Maryland Real Estate Brokers Act and could be disclosed to the seller of this property.

You, as a buyer, are entitled to have someone represent you as a buyer's agent if you are interested in this property. The duties of a buyer's agent include helping you to evaluate the property, prepare an offer on the property, and negotiate in your best interests.

Cost and capitalization of ground rent. Ground rent is charged on land that is leased to the owner of the home or improvement located on the land. If a property is subject to ground rent, any sign or advertisement for that property's sale or exchange may include the property's cost and capitalization of ground rent and the price of the property. If both are included, Maryland § 17-606 mandates the lettering used to show the cost and capitalization of ground rent must not be smaller than the lettering used for the property's price.

PHONE, EMAIL, FAX

Telemarketing
CAN-SPAM
Faxes

Telemarketing

Federal telemarketing law. Rules regarding telemarketing across state lines are established by the Federal Trade Commission. In addition to telemarketing use rules, the FTC's Telemarketing Sales Rule (TSR) established the National Do Not Call Registry which allows consumers to register their telephone numbers online at www.donotcall.gov to block unwanted telemarketing calls.

Telemarketers are required to search the Do Not Call Registry every 31 days for numbers they are not allowed to call. Consumers who continue to receive telemarketing calls after registering their telephone numbers can file a complaint at the donotcall.gov website. Telemarketers who fail to honor the registry can be fined up to $40,000 for each call.

Political organizations, charities, and telephone surveyors are exempt from honoring the registry. Businesses with whom the consumer has an established relationship are also exempt from the prohibition against calling the consumer for 18 months after the consumer's last purchase or payment. Companies to whom a consumer has submitted an inquiry or application can also call the consumer for 3 months after the submission.

Federal Trade Commission standards of conduct for telemarketing calls. The TSR prohibits deceptive and abusive telemarketing practices and requires the following:

> ▶ telemarketers must only call between 8 a.m. and 9 p.m.
>
> ▶ telemarketers must promptly identify the seller or charitable organization and state that the call is a sales call or a charitable solicitation
>
> ▶ telemarketers must disclose all material information about the product or service they are offering and the terms of the sale
>
> ▶ telemarketers must be honest about the terms of their offer
>
> ▶ telemarketers must not ask the consumer to pay with a cash-to-cash money transfer, with the PIN from a cash reload card, or with a remotely created payment order (created by the consumer providing bank account information to create a check the consumer never sees or signs)
>
> ▶ telemarketers must obtain a consumer's express informed consent to be charged for any product or service and to have a specific account charged
>
> ▶ telemarketers must connect automatically dialed calls to a sales representative within 2 seconds of the consumer answering the call and must not hang up on an unanswered call before 15 seconds or four rings

- telemarketers must transmit their telephone number to the consumer's caller id service
- businesses using prerecorded messages or "robocalls" must obtain the consumer's permission before calling, must provide consumers with information on how to prevent future calls, and must provide an automated opt-out that can be activated any time during the call
- purely informational prerecorded messages, such as appointment reminders, are allowed, as are political calls and messages from healthcare providers, debt collectors, banks, telephone carriers, and charities

Maryland telemarketing statutes. In addition to federal telemarketing laws, Maryland has its own telemarketing fraud laws with investigations of fraud handled by the Attorney General's Office. The related laws include Business Regulation § 6-101, et seq. and Commercial Law Articles § 14-2203, et seq.

Telemarketers in Maryland must register with the Secretary of State as solicitors. Any contract resulting from a telephone solicitation must be in writing; be signed by the consumer; match the product or service description used in the telephone solicitation; and contain the name, address, and telephone number of the seller as well as the total price of the contract and a description of the product or service. The contract must also contain a disclaimer that the consumer is not obligated to pay any money unless he or she signs the contract and returns it to the seller.

Violations of Maryland's telemarketing laws can result in both criminal and civil penalties. In addition to those penalties, telemarketers who fail to comply with telephone solicitation laws are guilty of a deceptive act which will result in penalties related to the Maryland Solicitations Act as follows:

- misdemeanor willful violation -- a fine up to $5,000 and/or 1 year imprisonment
- misdemeanor gross negligent violation -- a fine up to $3,000 and/or liability for restitution as determined by the court
- noncompliance of registration and other requirements -- revocation of the telemarketer's registration, prohibition against acting as a solicitor for up to 10 years, refund of donations or sales revenue

Consumers who are harmed by telemarketing fraud may also sue the telemarketer in civil court for an unfair or deceptive trade practice under Title 13, Subtitle 3 of Maryland's Commercial Law articles.

The Maryland Office of the Attorney General provides an online brochure called *How to Stop Telemarketing Calls and Junk Mail*. The brochure provides detailed information not only on how to stop telemarketing calls but how to stop receiving junk mail through the U.S. Post Office and can be found online at 96.pdf (marylandattorneygeneral.gov).

CAN-SPAM

In addition to telemarketing calls, many businesses use electronic mail to advertise or solicit business. Electronic mail (email) is sent through a computer or other electronic means to individual people at their unique electronic addresses.

Federal law. The CAN-SPAM Act is a federal law that sets the rules for commercial email. The law establishes requirements for commercial messages, gives recipients the right to opt out of receiving messages, and includes penalties for violations. The law requires all commercial email to comply with the law, including business-to-business emails and emails to former customers. CAN-SPAM requirements include the following:

- the header information must accurately identify the person or business who initiated the message
- deceptive subject lines are prohibited
- the message must be identified as an ad
- the message must provide a valid physical street address, a post office box, or a private mailbox
- the message must include a clear and conspicuous explanation of how the recipient can opt out of receiving emails in the future
- the sender must process and honor opt-out requests within 10 business days without charging a fee, requiring the recipient's personal information beyond an email address, or requiring further steps other than a reply email or visit to an Internet website; the sender must not sell or transfer the opted-out recipient's email address

Violations of the CAN-SPAM Act are subject to penalties of up to $43,280 for each email, and more than one person can be held responsible. Both the company whose product is being promoted and the company who actually sends the email are legally responsible for complying with the law. Further, misleading claims about products or services violate laws regarding deceptive advertising and can result in additional fines and criminal penalties including imprisonment for certain violations.

Maryland's law. Maryland is one of the first states to pass legislation to control junk email. The 2002 Maryland Commercial Electronic Mail Act was passed 2 years before the federal CAN-SPAM Act. Like the federal law, Maryland's law specifically addresses deceptive or fraudulent email. Further, the state's appeals court ruled in 2006 that Maryland's act covers emails sent from another state if they are received in Maryland.

In 2013, Maryland enacted Commercial Law § 14-3001, 3002, and 3003 to address unauthorized, false, or misleading information sent through email and included the penalties for violations.

Under this law, a person may not initiate, conspire, or assist in the transmission of a commercial email that is sent from or received in Maryland, uses a third-party domain name or email address without permission, or contains false or misleading information in the subject line or about the origin of the email. Violators may be liable for reasonable attorney's fees and damages.

Faxes

Maryland Commercial Law Section 14-1313 prohibits intentionally making an electronic or telephonic transmission to a facsimile (fax) device to encourage a consumer to purchase products, realty, or services. However, faxes sent in the course of preexisting negotiations or in the course of a preexisting business relationship with the fax recipient are allowed.

Violations may result in the Attorney General initiating a civil action against the violator and imposing a penalty of up to $1,000 for each violation. Under this statute, each prohibited commercial solicitation is a separate violation.

HANDLING TRUST FUNDS

Trust monies
Trust accounts

Trust monies

Under Title 17-501, trust money is defined as a "deposit, payment, or other money that a person entrusts to a real estate broker or, on behalf of a real estate broker, to an associate real estate broker or a real estate salesperson to hold for the benefit of the owner or beneficial owner of the trust money and for a purpose that relates to a real estate transaction involving real estate in the State."

The beneficial owner is the person for whose benefit the broker or affiliated licensee holds the money.

In a real estate transaction, buyers submit funds to be held in a trust account until they are turned over to the seller at the transaction's closing. Thus, the buyer is the owner of the money while the seller is the beneficial owner of the money.

Trust accounts

Escrow account. Brokers are required to maintain a non-interest-bearing escrow or special account. The account is to be separate from the broker's own accounts and used solely for trust money. The account may be checking, savings, or a combination of both, unless the involved parties provide written instructions for other arrangements. Checks drawn on the account must be signed by the broker, a licensee the broker designates as an alternate signatory, or an unlicensed cosigner who cosigns with a designated alternate signatory.

A broker who receives trust monies must inform the Commission of the bank name and account number where the monies will be held. The broker must also notify the Commission in writing within 10 days of establishing additional escrow or special accounts, changing the account number, or transferring the account to another bank.

The bank where the account is established must be located within Maryland and must have deposits insured by the Federal Deposit Insurance Corporation (FDIC) or another approved insurer as listed in §17–503.

Deposits. An associate broker or salesperson who receives trust money on behalf of a buyer must promptly turn the money over to the affiliated broker. Unless the parties to the subject transaction have provided written instructions to the contrary, the broker must then deposit the funds into the non-interest-bearing escrow account within 7 days after a sales contract has been accepted by both parties to the transaction. The trust monies may not be used for any purpose other than the purpose designated.

Withdrawals and distributions. Trust monies must remain in the escrow account until one of the following occurs:

▸ the transaction to which the funds are related is consummated or terminated

▸ the owner and beneficial owner of the funds direct the broker in writing to withdraw or dispose of the monies in another manner

▸ a court orders a different disposition as a result of the broker filing an interpleader*

▸ the broker decides to distribute the monies to the person the broker believes in good faith is entitled to receive them based on the terms of the contract that established the trust and the fact that either the owner or beneficial owner failed to complete the related transaction

*Note: An interpleader is a civil procedure that allows the broker to file a lawsuit in the appropriate county or circuit court and name the owner and beneficial owner of the funds as defendants. The broker asks the court to allow the trust funds to be deposited in the court's registry and have the funds transferred to the court. At this point, the broker's involvement ceases, and the court will decide the distribution of the funds.

On deciding how to distribute the trust money, a broker must notify both the owner and beneficial owner of the decision in writing, including to whom the money will be distributed. The notice must be in writing and inform both parties that either may prevent such distribution by submitting a written protest within 30 days of the notice. If a protest is received, the broker must distribute the money according to one of the first three bulleted methods listed above. If there is no protest, the broker will distribute the funds as described in the notice.

Distribution disputes. In the absence of provisions for trust money distribution in the sales contract, lease, option agreement, or other document, if a dispute arises over the distribution of the funds, the broker must do one of the following:

▸ hold the funds until all parties have signed releases authorizing the disposition of the funds

▸ file a bill of interpleader in the appropriate court

▸ hold the funds until one party files suit and the court orders the distribution

▸ notify the parties of the broker's decision to distribute the monies according to the broker's good faith opinion as to whom the money belongs, following proper notification procedures and allowing the parties to protest

When the broker's duty to handle the trust money terminates, the broker must promptly account for all money and related transactions.

SUMMARY SUSPENSIONS

The Commission may summarily suspend a licensee's license for committing certain violations of Maryland's real estate law. The Commission must provide the licensee with a written notice of the suspension and the finding leading to the suspension. After the summary suspension is in effect, the Commission must also provide the licensee an opportunity to be heard before the Commission or a hearing board.

The Commission will determine if the summary suspension is to start immediately or at a later date. The suspension will continue until the licensee complies with the Commission's conditions or until a hearing before the Commission results in a different disposition. The Commission may also delay the suspension until after the licensee is provided a hearing.

Grounds for a summary suspension. The Commission may order a summary suspension of a license if the licensee is guilty of any of the following:

▸ failing to promptly account for any money held in trust
▸ failing to comply with the Commission's demand to show all records, books, and accounts of money held in trust

The Commission may also order a summary suspension if a licensee

▸ is convicted of a felony under any federal or state law
▸ fails to notify the Commission within 10 days after a felony conviction or within 10 days of release from incarceration after a felony conviction, whichever is later

RECORDKEEPING REQUIREMENTS

General requirements
E-records requirements

General requirements

Brokers are required to maintain all records of trust money in a secured area within the broker's office. Licensees are required to keep copies of listings and other documents executed or obtained in connection with a brokerage services transaction, including those with electronic signatures. All records and documents must be retained for 5 years after the closing date or 5 years after the listing date if the transaction did not close.

On receiving reasonable notice, a licensee must allow a representative of the Commission to enter the brokerage during business hours to inspect the records required to be kept. The licensee must provide a paper copy of any document to the Commission at the licensee's expense.

E-records requirements

Any record required to be retained may be kept electronically if

▶ the stored record cannot be erased or edited

▶ the stored record is made or preserved as part of and in the regular course of the licensee's business

▶ the original record was made or prepared by the licensee or an employee at or near the time of the activity related to the record

▶ the custodian of the record is able to identify the stored record, the mode of its preparation, and the mode of storage

▶ the electronic storage system contains a reliable indexing system that provides convenient access to the record, appropriate quality control of the storage process, and chronological arrangement of the stored records

---

SUPERVISION REQUIREMENTS

General requirements
Adequate and reasonable supervision
Evidence of compliance

General requirements

The law requires a real estate broker to exercise "adequate and reasonable" supervision over individuals who perform real estate activities on behalf of the broker, and the broker is responsible and can be held liable for the conduct of any such individual.

Both licensed and unlicensed activities fall under the requirement, and the supervisory duty extends to licensed and unlicensed employees, licensed affiliated salespersons, associate brokers, and licensed and unlicensed independent contractors. The broker must also supervise individuals who are not affiliated with the broker but perform activities on behalf of the broker.

A broker's supervision over an individual does not create an employer/employee relationship with the individual, nor does the broker's supervision over an independent contractor alter the independent status of the contractor.

Branch office managers, who are also under the supervision of the broker, are required to exercise reasonable and adequate supervision over salespersons and associate brokers registered to their branch office. The branch office manager's supervision is in addition to, and not in lieu of, the broker's supervision. The same holds true for team leaders.

Adequate and reasonable supervision

The factors defining adequate and reasonable supervision are set out in COMAR 09.11.05.03B. One factor concerns whether the brokerage has a written policies and procedures manual and whether that manual includes guidance on using unlicensed personal assistants. The Association of Real Estate License Law

Officials (ARELLO®) provides a comprehensive guide booklet on creating a policies and procedures manual. The booklet can be found on the Commission's website under the Resources tab at https://www.dllr.state.md.us/license/mrec/mrecarello.pdf.

The factors of adequate and reasonable supervision include, but are not limited to

- training or education sessions provided regularly at least once every 2 months
- experienced supervisory personnel to review and discuss contract provisions, brokerage agreement provisions, and advertising
- written procedures and policies which provide clear guidance in

  - proper and legal handling of deposit monies and other funds
  - compliance with federal, state, and local fair housing laws and regulations
  - advertisement requirements for real estate transactions;
  - review of contracts, leases, and brokerage agreements upon execution by all parties
  - use and limitations of unlicensed personal assistants
  - disclosure of agency relationships by licensees in residential real estate transactions
  - distribution and dissemination of information on new or changed local, state, and federal real estate laws and regulations
  - obligation of all licensees to comply with the Maryland Real Estate Brokers Act, the current Code of Ethics, and all applicable local, state, and federal laws and regulations
  - requirements, restrictions, and limitations applicable to the sale or lease of a licensee's real property and the licensee's purchase or lease of real property for personal use
  - unauthorized practice of law by a licensee

Evidence of compliance

A broker, branch office manager, or team leader may need to prove to the Commission that they are providing adequate and reasonable supervision as required. The following will serve as evidence to provide that proof:

- records of affiliates' attendance at sales meetings
- review by the broker, branch office manager, or either's designee of sale, lease, and brokerage agreements or contracts executed by all involved parties
- review by the broker, branch office manager, or either's designee of advertisements to be placed by affiliated licensees
- compliance with the written policies and procedures
- dissemination of the written policies and procedures to affiliated licensees

If the Commission questions whether a broker has provided reasonable and adequate supervision, it is the broker's burden to show that he or she has done so.

PROHIBITED ACTS

A licensee or license applicant may not

- provide real estate brokerage services without a license
- misrepresent oneself as authorized to provide brokerage services when not holding a real estate license
- lend a broker's license to another individual
- retain an unlicensed individual to provide brokerage services on behalf of the broker
- pay compensation to an unlicensed person for providing brokerage services
- pay a commission to an attorney for referrals
- require a buyer to use a particular title insurance company, settlement company, escrow company, mortgage lender, or title lawyer
- influence a consumer to purchase, lease, or use a particular property based on race, color, sex, religion, handicap, familial status, or national origin (referred to as blockbusting)
- solicit listings to change the racial composition of a neighborhood
- violate a license suspension order
- fraudulently or deceptively obtain or attempt to obtain or use a license
- make false promises or misrepresentations
- intentionally or negligently fail to disclose material facts about a subject property
- fail to inform an affiliated broker in writing about services being provided on behalf of another affiliated broker
- fail to comply with dual agency requirements
- retain the services of an unlicensed individual as an associate broker or salesperson to evade the law prohibiting commission payments to unlicensed individuals
- guarantee or allow another person to guarantee future profits from the resale of a property
- offer inducements to influence or attempt to influence a prospective purchaser
- accept a listing contract with no automatic expiration date or a contract with no notice of the buyer's right of selection
- accept a net listing contract
- solicit another licensee's exclusive listing client to terminate the existing contract and sign a new contract with the soliciting licensee

- ▶ solicit a party to breach an existing contract with another licensee and sign a new contract with the soliciting licensee
- ▶ fail to promptly provide each party to a transaction a copy of the listing contract, the sales contract, or the lease agreement; failing to keep a copy of these executed documents for him/herself
- ▶ influence or attempt to influence a prospective buyer's actions by indicating the proximity of residents of a particular race, color, religion, sex, handicap, familial status, or national origin or by suggesting that their proximity may lower property values, change the character of the neighborhood, increase criminal or antisocial behavior in the area, or decrease the quality of area schools
- ▶ use any materials or documents that contain the name of an organization or association of which the licensee is not a member
- ▶ advertise without including the name of the advertiser and that the advertiser is a licensee; also including the licensee's name without including the affiliated broker's name
- ▶ advertise in a misleading or untruthful manner
- ▶ accept a commission or other compensation from anyone other than the affiliated broker
- ▶ fail to comply with trust money requirements
- ▶ pay or receive a rebate, profit, compensation, or commission in violation of Title 17
- ▶ be convicted of a felony, misdemeanor related to the applicant or licensee's fitness and qualifications under any federal or state law
- ▶ engage in conduct that shows bad faith, incompetency, untrustworthiness, dishonesty, fraud, or improper dealings
- ▶ knowingly associate with a licensee in any violation of Title 17
- ▶ fail to provide required reasonable and adequate supervision over affiliated licensees and branch offices
- ▶ fail to provide a representation disclosure or consent form
- ▶ be disciplined under real estate licensing laws of another jurisdiction
- ▶ violate any provision of Title 17, any regulation adopted under Title 17, or any provision of the Code of Ethics

Penalties. The Commission may deny a license to an applicant, reprimand a licensee, or suspend or revoke an individual's license if the applicant or licensee is investigated for committing any of the prohibited acts and is found guilty in a hearing before the Commission or a hearing board. Some acts may result in imprisonment.

The Commission may instead impose up to $5,000 as a penalty for each violation. To determine the amount of penalty, the Commission considers the seriousness of the violation, the harm caused, the good faith of the licensee, and any history of violations by the licensee.

In the case of a conviction for a felony or misdemeanor, the Commission will consider the nature of the crime, how the crime relates to the licensee's licensed activities, how the crime relates to the licensee's fitness and qualifications as a licensee, the length of time since the conviction, and the licensee's behavior before and after the crime. The Commission will also abide by the Brokers Act in allowing a court of law to impose fines and/or imprisonment for specific violations.

PERSONAL ASSISTANTS

Allowed activities
Prohibited activities

In 1995, the Real Estate Commission issued guidelines for the use of unlicensed employees to assist brokers in performing and supervising transactions for which a real estate license is required. Those guidelines outline what activities an unlicensed employee or personal assistant may and may not perform.

Allowed activities   An unlicensed employee MAY perform the following activities:

- answer the telephone and forward calls to a licensee
- submit listings and changes to a multiple listing service
- follow up on loan commitments after a contract has been negotiated
- assemble documents for closing
- secure documents (public information) from courthouse, public utilities, etc.
- have keys made for company listings
- write and place ads subject to the review and approval of licensee and supervising broker
- type contract forms at the direction of, and for approval by, licensee and supervising broker
- compute commission checks
- place signs on property
- arrange the date and time of home, termite, and well/septic inspection, mortgage application, pre- settlement walk-thru, and settlement
- prepare flyers and promotional information for approval by licensee and supervising broker
- act as courier service to deliver documents, pick up keys, etc.
- schedule an open house
- schedule appointments for licensee to show listed property
- accompany a licensee to an open house or showing for security purposes or to hand out preprinted materials
- contact clients and potential clients using online communication methods such as web-based chat in order to accomplish one of the above-listed tasks

Prohibited activities An unlicensed employee MAY NOT perform the following activities:

▶ prepare promotional materials or ads without the review and approval of licensee and supervising broker

▶ show property

▶ answer any questions on listings, title, financing, closing, etc.

▶ discuss or explain a contract, listing, lease, agreement, or other real estate document with anyone outside the brokerage

▶ be paid on the basis of real estate activity, such as a percentage of commission, or any amount based on listings, sales, etc.

▶ negotiate or agree to any commission, commission split, management fee, or referral fee on behalf of a licensee

▶ discuss the attributes or amenities of a property, under any circumstances, with a prospective purchaser or lessee

▶ discuss the terms and conditions of the real property offered for sale or lease with the owner of the property

▶ collect, receive, or hold deposit monies, rent, other monies, or anything else of value received from the owner or lessee of the real property or from a prospective purchaser or lessee

▶ provide owners of real property or prospective purchasers or lessees with any advice, recommendations, or suggestions as to the sale, purchase, exchange, or lease of real property to be listed or real property presently available for sale or for lease

▶ hold himself or herself out in any manner, orally or in writing, as being licensed or affiliated with a particular company or real estate broker as a licensee

▶ contact the public concerning the availability of real estate brokerage services unless an inquiry about a specific property is immediately referred to a licensee

▶ contact clients or prospective clients using online communication methods such as web-based chat in order to solicit customers with respect to a specific property

▶ contact clients using online communication methods such as web-based chat without first disclosing the broker's name or the company name as it appears on the license at the beginning of the chat session or in text visible on the same web page that contains the chat session

---

REAL ESTATE TEAMS

Definition
Team requirements
Intracompany agent relationships

Definition Title 17 of the Maryland Code of Business Occupations and Professions allows multiple licensees to work together as a group under the label of "team." Title

17.543 defines a team as two or more licensed associate brokers, licensed salespersons, or a combination of both, who regularly work together to provide brokerage services, represent themselves to the public as part of one entity, and use a collective name such as "team" or "group," or use the words "and associates."

Team requirements

Leaders. A team is required to designate a team leader who is either a licensed associate broker or a licensed salesperson with at least 3 years of experience providing brokerage services. The leader must maintain a current list of all members and employees, update the list as necessary, and provide the list to the affiliated broker or branch office manager. The broker or branch office manager must keep copies of the lists and provide them to the Commission on request.

Supervision. Like brokers and branch office managers, team leaders must exercise reasonable and adequate supervision over their brokerage services and team members. Team leader supervision supplements broker and branch office manager supervision. Broker and branch office manager may not delegate their supervisory responsibilities over team members to a team leader. The team leader and members must comply with all office rules, practices, and procedures as established by the broker and branch office manager.

Member requirements. Title 17 mandates the following requirements for teams:

- all licensed team members must be affiliated with the same broker
- all licensed team members must conduct their brokerage activities from the broker's office or the branch office where their licenses are displayed
- no licensed broker may be a member of a team
- no team name may contain the terms "real estate," "real estate brokerage," "realty," or any other term that would lead the public to believe that the team is offering brokerage services independent of the broker

Advertising. Teams advertisements, regardless of type, must show a direct connection between the team and the brokerage. For example:

Services provided by the Blue Team of Red, White, & Blue Realtors, Inc.

All advertising must show the full name of the brokerage in a meaningful and conspicuous way. The ads must also include the name of at least one licensed team member and the broker or branch office manager's telephone number.

Intracompany agent relationships

Dual agency. Intracompany agent (ICA) relationships are formed through dual agency. Dual agency is a type of representation wherein a licensed broker acts as agent for both the seller and the buyer or the lessor and the lessee in the same transaction, making the broker a dual agent. A dual agency is only legal if both parties agree by signing a Consent for Dual Agency form. (Dual agency and the consent form are discussed in more detail in the next chapter.)

In intracompany agency relationships, brokers do not work directly with clients. Instead, the broker or the broker's designee (such as a branch office manager) assigns two members of a team to act as ICAs, with one member representing the seller/lessor and the other member representing the buyer/lessee. Team leaders may not assign the ICAs, and the broker's designee to assign the ICAs may not be a member of the team.

Before ICAs are assigned, both parties must be advised in writing that the ICAs are part of the same team and that the team could have a financial interest in the transaction's outcome. They are notified and indicate agreement by signing the "Notification of Dual Agency within a Team" form shown below and found online on the MREC's website under Forms and Fees at https://www.dllr.state.md.us/forms/mrecdualagency.pdf.

Intracompany agency restrictions. Intracompany agents are held to the duty of maintaining the client's confidentiality. Neither ICA working in the same transaction may disclose any information the client deems as confidential unless disclosure is mandated by law. However, the ICA is allowed to disclose confidential information to his or her affiliated broker, but the broker must keep it confidential. In addition to other confidential information, the ICA is specifically prohibited from disclosing any of the following:

> ▸ the fact that the seller would accept a lower price or agree to other terms
> ▸ the fact that the buyer would pay a higher price or agree to other terms
> ▸ the seller's motivation to sell
> ▸ the buyer's motivation to purchase
> ▸ either party's need or reason to expedite closing quickly
> ▸ either party's negotiation strategy

Client's right of refusal. Either party in a proposed intracompany agency has the right to refuse the dual representation. If one party refuses to consent to the dual agency, the broker may still represent the other party as a single agent in that transaction. The broker may also represent the refusing party as a single agent in another transaction separate from the intracompany agency transaction.

NOTIFICATION OF DUAL AGENCY WITHIN A TEAM

Under Maryland law, a team that provides real estate brokerage services must consist of two or more associate brokers or salespersons, or a combination of the two, who:

1. work together on a regular basis;
2. represent themselves to the public as being part of one entity; and
3. Designate themselves by a collective name such as "team" or "group."

The team operates within a brokerage, and team members are supervised by a team leader as well as by the broker, and, if they work in a brokerage branch office, by the branch office manager.

The law permits one member of a team to represent the buyer and one member to represent the seller in the same transaction only if certain conditions are met. If both parties agree, the broker of the real estate brokerage with which the salespersons or associate brokers are affiliated or the broker's designee (the "dual agent") shall designate one team member as the intra-company agent for the buyer and another team member as the intracompany agent for the seller. No one else may make that designation.

The law also requires that the buyer and seller each be notified in writing that the two agents are members of the same team, and that the team could have a financial interest in the outcome of the transaction in addition to any financial benefit obtained by selling one of the broker's own listings. THIS FORM CONSTITUTES YOUR NOTICE OF THOSE FACTS.

Dual agency may occur only if both parties consent to it, and sign the Consent for Dual Agency form prescribed by the Real Estate Commission. If you have concerns or questions about being represented by a team member when another team member represents the other party, you should address these to the broker or branch office manager before signing the Consent form.

ACKNOWLEDGMENT OF RECEIPT OF NOTICE
I/we acknowledge receipt of the Notification of Dual Agency within a Team.

_____   DATE: _____

_____

OFFERS

An offer is a proposal from a prospective property buyer to purchase a property at a stated price with specific, designated terms. Offers in Maryland use a residential real estate purchase and sale agreement form which includes the specific terms of the sale, an expiration deadline, and information about how the buyer will finance the purchase.

Essential considerations and requirements. When a prospective buyer submits an offer to purchase, the seller may accept the offer as is, completely reject the offer, or counter the offer with additional, fewer, or amended terms. Following are the rules licensees must follow when receiving offers to purchase their client's home:

▸ licensees must present written, signed offers to the seller immediately

Offers may be hand delivered, mailed, faxed, or emailed to the seller's agent. Even if the agent believes the seller will not accept a particular offer, the agent must present it and allow the seller to determine whether to accept it, reject it, or negotiate the terms through counteroffers.

▸ licensees must present all offers to the seller

Licensees must continue to present any additional offers until the seller accepts one offer

▸ buyers may withdraw an offer any time prior to being notified that the seller has accepted the offer

Even if the seller has accepted and signed the offer, the buyer may withdraw it at any time before receiving notice of the acceptance.

▸ once an offer is accepted by the seller and the buyer is notified, the offer becomes a legally binding sales contract.

At this point, the licensee should not present any subsequent offers.

SALES CONTRACTS

Required information
Duties of licensees

Required information

Maryland agreement form. A residential real estate purchase agreement is a binding contract between a seller and buyer for the transfer of ownership of real property. In Maryland, property buyers and sellers use the Maryland Residential Real Estate Purchase and Sale Agreement form for offers and sales contracts and the Maryland Residential Property Disclosure/Disclaimer Statement (found online at Maryland Residential Property Disclosure And Disclaimer Statement) for sellers to disclose property and sale conditions.

Competent parties. Parties who are competent to enter into a sales contract are 18 years of age or older, of sound mind, and have the authority to act.

Written contract. The contract may be written by one of the parties to the transaction or by an attorney. Licensees or others drafting such contracts are engaging in the unauthorized practice of law.

Terms and disclosures. Sales contracts for one- or two-family dwellings must be in writing, signed by both parties, and contain the following:

▶ **seller, buyer, property and transaction details** – principal's names, property legal address and description, agreement provisions, purchase price, and closing details outlining where and when closing is scheduled

▶ **earnest money** -- details on the amount of earnest money and how it will be paid and handled

▶ **mortgage loan information** -- if a mortgage loan is involved, information on the lender and the loan amount

▶ **brokerage commission** -- agreed-upon commission, either a specific amount or a specific percentage

▶ **tax notice** -- printed in conspicuous type or handwritten, the following statement. Failure to include this statement does not invalidate the contract:

> *Section 14-104 of the Real Property Article of the Annotated Code of Maryland provides that, unless otherwise negotiated in the contract or provided by local law, the cost of any recordation tax or any State or local transfer tax shall be shared equally between the buyer and seller.*

▶ **notice of buyer's right of selection** -- printed in bold-faced type, a notice explaining that the buyer has the right to select which title insurance company, settlement company, escrow company, mortgage lender or financial institution, or title lawyer; must include the provision that a seller may not be prohibited from offering owner financing as a settlement condition; failure to include these statements does not invalidate the contract

▶ **critical areas notice** -- the Chesapeake and Atlantic Coastal Bays Critical Area notice informing the buyer of related zoning, land use, and resource protection regulations

▶ **deferred water and sewer charges** -- fee and remaining duration of fee payments if property owner has been charged for connecting the property to a public water and sewer system: failure to include the fee in the contract can result in the seller being responsible for paying the balance of the fee

- **agricultural land transfer tax** -- if the land is subject to this transfer tax, contract must show who is responsible for the tax and state that the tax can be increased if the buyer does not use the land for agriculture

- **ground rent** -- if property is subject to ground rent, contract must state whether the ground rent is redeemable and who is responsible for notice and cost of redemption; contract must include a lien warning for unpaid ground rent

- **required disclosures** -- failure to provide disclosures does not invalidate the contract but may result in a legal suit against the seller if the lack of disclosure causes damages:

  - **licensee buyer or seller** -- licensee must disclose, in writing, the fact that licensee, a family member, licensee's employer, or an entity owned by the licensee or immediate family member is the seller or buyer in the transaction

  - **lead-based paint** -- if home built before 1978, seller must disclose to buyer that lead-based paint may exist on the property; buyer should obtain a copy of the EPA's Lead-Based Paint Brochure to learn the risks of living with lead-based paint or renovating a home that contains lead-based paint

  - **property condition and defects** –seller must provide to buyer the Maryland Residential Property Disclosure/Disclaimer Statement before execution of the purchase agreement

  - **high noise levels** – contract must include the following statement (Allegany, Carroll, Frederick, Garrett, Howard, Montgomery, and Washington counties are exempt from this requirement):

    Buyer is advised that the property may be located near a military installation that conducts flight operations, munitions testing, or military operations that may result in high noise levels.

- **certain conditions** – contract may include agreed-upon repairs, fixture or furnishing inclusions, warranties, claim waivers, and title insurance information

Additional terms and notices based on specific local requirements may be added to the contract or added as addenda as needed.

Contract effectiveness. The sales contract becomes effective on the date the buyer and seller agree to all of the terms and both sign the agreement. All of the obligations included in the contract become binding and enforceable on that date. If the buyer fails to meet any of the included contingencies, such as financing, inspections, insurance, etc., the seller may invalidate the contract.

Duties of licensees   Maryland regulations mandate a licensee's fiduciary duties to clients as well as responsibilities to the general public and other licensees. These duties are discussed in a later chapter. With regard to purchase offers and sales contracts, licensees owe to clients the additional duties to

> ▸ act according to the terms of the brokerage agreement with the client seeking to sell or purchase property
>
> ▸ promptly present all written offers or counteroffers to and from the client
>
> ▸ treat all parties fairly and answer all questions truthfully
>
> ▸ ensure that all agreements are in writing, complete, and signed by the appropriate parties
>
> ▸ comply with all recordkeeping mandates including providing copies of documents to the appropriate parties and retaining copies at the brokerage for the required 5 years
>
> ▸ account for all trust money received in relation to the sale or purchase transaction
>
> ▸ keep the confidentiality of client's confidential information unless the client consents in writing to the sharing of the
>
> ▸ comply with all federal, state, and local laws, including fair housing laws

---

CONDOMINIUM SALES DISCLOSURES

Initial sales
Resales

Disclosure requirements differ for initial condominium sale transactions and resale transactions. Both kinds of transaction require material disclosures, those for an initial sale based on projections for the condominium's future and those for a resale typically based on the condominium's past experience and operations. Both include a declaration describing the condominium's development and individual units, the bylaws, rules, regulations, operating budget, management agreements, and other vital information.

Initial sales. A public offering statement (POS) (required for condominiums created after July 1, 1981) is required for initial sales. The condominium developer must provide the public offering statement to the buyer with the sales contract. The buyer then has 15 days to cancel the contract and receive a full refund of the down payment.

Any material amendments made to the public offering statement after its initial delivery must also be provided to the buyer, who may then cancel the contract within 5 days after receiving the amendments.

The law requires developers to place all down payments in an escrow account, or post a bond, to ensure that funds will be available if a down payment has to be refunded.

Resales. A condominium unit owner reselling a unit must provide the buyer with a resale certificate package that contains the condominium association's declaration, bylaws, rules and regulations, financial statements, which should include a balance sheet, income/expense statements, and an operating budget, as well as any other important information.

Resellers should also disclose whether they have made any alterations to the unit and, if so, if they obtained the necessary authorization from the condominium association. The sales contract will contain a clause above the buyer's signature line that states the buyer has received and read the provided documents.

The package must be provided to the buyer within 15 days of the transaction closing. The buyer may then cancel the sales contract within 7 days after receiving the resale package or until settlement, whichever happens first.

Owners who are reselling their units are not required to set up an escrow account for the buyer's down payment, but they are required to fully refund the monies if the buyer cancels the contract within the allowed time period.

27 Maryland Regulation of Business Conduct
Snapshot Review

KEY TERMS

Broker
- **broker** - an individual who acts as an intermediary between principals in a real estate transaction without having title to the property.

Brokerage firm
- **brokerage** - a firm or company that employs licensees (as employees or independent contractors) who facilitate real estate transactions based on the brokerage services offered.

Providing brokerage services
- engaging in activities requiring a license; business entity must be registered

COMPENSATION

Commissions
- commissions paid as a percentage of a property's sale price; must be licensed to receive commission; licensees may receive commission only from affiliated broker

Incentives
- incentives are prohibited to influence parties in a transaction, to obtain listings, to motivate sales or purchases unless offered to everyone equally; prizes allowed for attendees of open house
- no compensation for referrals by unlicensed individuals
- rebates may be paid outside of brokerage services but must be disclosed in writing to all parties

ADVERTISING

Key terms
- advertising— by a licensee
- advertisement—oral, written, visual; includes mail, newsletter, brochure, signage, promotional item, directory listing, internet
- designated name—name used by licensee that differs from licensee's legal name
- trade name-- trademark, service mark, business name

Advertising requirements
- licensed brokers, associate brokers, salespersons, and team members may use any oral, written, or visual means to advertise brokerage services as long as approved by the broker, office manager, or team leader
- ads must include licensee's name or designated name, applicable trade names, brokerage name, broker phone number, connection between team and brokerage, fair housing logo, identification of licensee as property owner; ads must be truthful and comply with NAR's Code of Ethics

Signs
- placing signs on property, public right-of-way easements, and within HOAs must comply with locale rules; open houses must include disclosure sign; signs for properties with ground rent must comply with lettering size requirements

PHONE, EMAIL, FAX

Telemarketing
- must honor do not call registry or face penalties; political organizations, charities, and phone surveyors exempt from honoring registry; must comply with FTC standards and Maryland statutes or face criminal and/or civil penalties; consumers may sue violators

CAN-SPAM
- commercial emails must comply with state and federal laws regarding deceptive or fraudulent emails or face civil and/or criminal penalties; CAN SPAM requires sender ID within header, honest subject lines, ID email as an ad, provide sender address, provide opt out option to be honored within 10 days

Faxes
- consumer solicitation by fax is prohibited and penalized

HANDLING TRUST FUNDS

Trust monies
- defined as money entrusted to a broker to hold for in relation to a real estate transaction; money is held for the beneficial owner

Trust accounts
- brokers required to have non-interest-bearing **escrow account** separate from personal or business accounts and used solely for trust money; broker must be one of the signatories on the account; broker must inform MREC of the bank and account number and any changes; bank must be within Maryland and be insured by approved insurer
- licensees must turn over trust monies to affiliated broker promptly for deposit into escrow account within 7 days of sales contract acceptance; monies to remain in account until transaction completes or terminates, broker is directed in writing to withdraw the funds, broker files interpleader, or broker distributes funds in good faith
- distribution disputes settled by all parties signing releases, broker filing interpleader with court, one party filing suit for court ordered distribution, or broker distributes funds in good faith

SUMMARY SUSPENSIONS

- imposed against licensee for failing to promptly account for trust money or providing records for MREC review, for being convicted of federal or state felony or notifying MREC within 10 days of felony or release from jail
- MREC to provide written notice of suspension, cause of suspension, and right to a hearing; suspension may start immediately or at a later date and continues until licensee's compliance with suspension conditions

RECORDKEEPING REQUIREMENTS

General requirements
- trust money records and other transaction records to be kept for 5 years in secured area of broker's office; must allow MREC to inspect and receive copies

E-records requirements
- e-records stored so as not erasable, in regular course of business, at the time of activity leading to the record, identifiable, and indexed

SUPERVISION REQUIREMENTS

General requirements
- reasonable and adequate supervision over affiliated licensees and employees required of broker; no relationship created by supervision; branch office managers and team leaders required to supervise in addition to broker's supervision

Adequate & reasonable supervision
- factors for supervision are set in COMAR 09.11.05.03B and included in guidebook on MREC website

Evidence of compliance
- brokers required to maintain evidence of supervision in form of sales meetings records, agreement and contract reviews, advertisement reviews, written policy compliance

PROHIBITED ACTS

- applicant's license may be denied, a licensee reprimanded, a license suspended or revoked, or a monetary penalty imposed if the individual is found guilty of any of several prohibited acts, including but not limited to practicing without a license, misrepresentations, compensating unlicensed individuals to perform brokerage services, violating fair housing laws, making false promises, failing to disclose material facts, noncomplying with dual agency requirements, offering inducements, and more as listed in Title 17 and the Code of Ethics
- licensees may also have fines or imprisonment imposed on them by a court of law for certain violations of the Brokers Act

PERSONAL ASSISTANTS

Allowed activities
- unlicensed employees may answer phones, submit listings to MLS, assemble documents, have keys made, prepare promotional information for broker review, compute commission checks, place signage, schedule property inspections and open houses, assist at open houses, deliver documents

Prohibited activities
- unlicensed employees may not perform brokerage services that require licensure, be paid based on real estate activity, negotiate commission, collect monies, provide transaction related advice, solicit customers, misrepresent self as licensed

REAL ESTATE TEAMS

Definition
- two or more licensees regularly working together to provide brokerage services, representing themselves as part of one entity, and using a collective name; required to designate a leader with 3 years of experience who is to supervise team members

Team requirements
- members to be affiliated with same broker, conduct activities from office where their licenses are displayed, not to include broker as a member, team name not to lead public to think they are performing independent of the broker
- may advertise under team name if direct connection with the brokerage, brokerage name, one team member's name, and broker or branch office manager's phone number are all shown

Intracompany agency relationship
- formed through dual agency wherein broker assigns two team members to act as ICAs for seller and buyer and wherein both parties are advised and sign agreement for dual agency; ICAs must maintain individual client's confidentiality except with broker; must not disclose client's motivation or willingness to pay or sell for other than listing price; must not disclose client's negotiation strategy or need for quick closing; either party may refuse to dual representation

OFFERS
- presented on Maryland's specific form and includes terms of the sale, deadline for the offer, and buyer's financing information; seller may accept the offer as is, reject it, or counter with additions or changes
- licensee must present all written offers immediately until seller accepts one particular offer; if seller fails to respond before offer expiration, buyer may cancel the offer; buyer may withdraw an offer any time prior to being notified the seller has accepted the offer; accepted offers become legally finding sales contract once buyer is notified of the acceptance

SALES CONTRACTS

Required information
- Maryland Residential Real Estate Purchase and Sale Agreement form is used for offers and sales contracts and the Maryland Residential Property Disclosure/Disclaimer Statemen is used by sellers; parties must be of legal age and have authority to act; contracts to be in writing and signed by both parties; required information, clauses, and disclosures must be included with the contract; contract becomes effective on the date both parties sign it; seller may invalidate the contract if the buyer fails to meet any contingency

Duties of licensees
- licensees must comply with terms of brokerage agreement, promptly present all written offers or counteroffers, treat all parties fairly and honestly, assure agreements are in writing and signed, comply with recordkeeping requirements, account for trust monies, maintain client's confidential information, and comply with all applicable laws

CONDO SALES DISCLOSURES

Initial sales
- developer must provide a public offering statement to the buyer with the sales contract; buyer has 15 days to cancel the contract and receive full refund; POS amendments to be delivered to the buyer who can cancel the contract within 5 days of receiving amendments; developer to place all earnest money in escrow account

Resales

- seller must provide a resale certificate package to the buyer, to include the declaration, bylaws, rules and regulations, financial statements, and operating budget, along with proof of authorization for any alterations made to the condo unit; package to be provided within 15 days of closing allowing the buyer to cancel within 7 days after receipt of the package or until settlement, whichever is first; sellers are not required to deposit earnest money into an escrow account but must refund monies if the buyer cancels

28 Maryland Brokerage Relationships and Disclosure

Agency
Listing Agreements
Residential Property Condition Disclosure

AGENCY

Key terms
Agency creation
Representation options
Agency disclosure
Duties to client
Termination of agreement

Key terms

Agency relationship – each relationship in which a licensee acts for or represents another person with the person's authority in a residential real estate transaction.

Brokerage agreement – a written agreement between a broker and a client to provide real estate brokerage services under a brokerage relationship.

Brokerage relationship – an agency relationship under a brokerage agreement between a client and a broker who has been engaged by the client to provide real estate brokerage services in a residential real estate transaction.

Buyer's agent – a licensed real estate broker, associate broker, or salesperson who, in accordance with a written brokerage agreement, represents a prospective buyer or lessee in the acquisition of real estate for sale or for lease.

Client – a person who has entered into a brokerage agreement with a broker and is then represented by the broker.

Common source information company – any person that is a source, compiler, or supplier of information regarding residential real estate for sale or lease or other data, including a multiple listing service.

Confidential information – information that reveals

> ▶ the seller's or lessor's willingness to accept a price or rent less than the price or rent as set forth in the brokerage agreement or terms other than those contained in the brokerage agreement

- the buyer's or lessee's willingness to pay a price or rent higher than the price or rent the buyer or lessee offered or accept terms other than those contained in the offer of the buyer or lessee
- the motivation of a buyer, lessee, seller, or lessor or the need or urgency of a seller to sell, a buyer to buy, a lessee to lease, or a lessor to lease
- any facts that led the seller to sell, the buyer to buy, the lessee to lease, or the lessor to lease
- the negotiating strategy of a client

Customer – a member of the public with whom the licensee has no brokerage agreement and does not represent but to whom the licensee may offer assistance.

Dual agency – each relationship in which a licensed real estate broker or branch office manager acts as a dual agent.

Dual agent – a licensed real estate broker or branch office manager who acts as an agent for both the seller and the buyer or the lessor and the lessee in the same real estate transaction.

Intracompany agent – a licensed associate broker or salesperson who has been designated by the affiliated broker to act as a dual agent on behalf of a seller or buyer or a lessor or lessee in the purchase, sale, or lease of property that is listed with the broker.

Listing agreement – a brokerage agreement between a licensee and a property seller or lessor wherein the licensee agrees to promote the owner's property and find a buyer or lessee.

Material facts – a fact about the property that, if known, may affect the prospective buyer's decision on whether or not to purchase the property or on the price the buyer would be willing to pay; also referred to as defects or latent defects.

Ministerial act – an act that

- a licensee performs on behalf of a client before and after the execution of a contract of sale or lease
- assists a person to complete or fulfill a contract of sale or lease with the client of the licensee
- does not involve discretion or the exercise of the licensee's own judgment

Residential property – property with one to four single-family units or unimproved property zoned for residential use.

Right of confidentiality – a duty owed to a client by a licensee in a brokerage relationship wherein the licensee must keep the client's confidential information confidential; the duty extends past the termination of the relationship.

Seller's agent – a licensed real estate broker who, in accordance with a written brokerage agreement, acts as the listing broker for real estate, or a licensed associate real estate broker or licensed real estate salesperson who is affiliated with the listing broker.

Single agency – a brokerage relationship wherein the broker represents only one party to the transaction

Subagent, aka cooperating agent– a cooperating licensed real estate broker, associate broker, or salesperson who acts on behalf of the client of another broker and who

>   ▶   is not affiliated with or acting as the listing real estate broker for a property
>   ▶   is not a buyer's agent
>   ▶   has a brokerage relationship with the seller or lessor
>   ▶   assists a prospective buyer or lessee in the acquisition of real estate for sale or for lease in a non-agency capacity

Timely – a reasonable time under the particular facts and circumstances.

Agency creation

Agency, or a brokerage relationship, is not created or determined by compensating or promising to compensate a licensee for services. Rather, it is created only when a licensee and a seller, buyer, lessor, or lessee sign a brokerage agreement. Another licensee may also create the relationship by signing a brokerage agreement on behalf of a seller, buyer, lessor, or lessee.

Agreement requirements. The Brokers Act requires the brokerage agreement be in writing and signed by all involved parties. It also requires the following to be included in the agreement:

>   ▶   a definite termination date that is automatically effective without notice from the client
>   ▶   the compensation to be paid to the broker, either as an amount or a specific percentage
>   ▶   when compensation is actually earned and will be paid
>   ▶   whether additional compensation may be paid to the broker by another person
>   ▶   a statement on whether the broker is authorized to cooperate with other brokers, to share compensation with the other brokers, and the amount of the compensation to be shared
>   ▶   an explanation of events or conditions that will entitle the broker to a commission or other compensation
>   ▶   the duties of the licensee to the client
>   ▶   the obligations of the client within the relationship
>   ▶   a provision for cancellation of the relationship by either party

The agreement may also include additional provisions as agreed upon by the licensee and client.

Common source information company. Licensees do not enter into a brokerage relationship with a common source information company simply by participating in or using that company's sources. Licensees also are not deemed to be an agent or subagent of the company or any client of another broker simply by participating in or using that company's sources. Further, a common source information company may not restrict access to its services to any licensee solely based on the type of license he or she holds.

Representation options

Categories of representation. When operating a brokerage company, the broker may choose to limit the company's representation options to

▸ sellers only in a single agency company

▸ buyers only in a single agency company

▸ both buyers and sellers in a single agency company

▸ buyers, sellers, and dual agencies

Within these brokerage companies, agent representation options include the following, based on the type of company:

▸ agents who represent the seller; this includes both the seller's agent and the subagent

▸ agents who represent the buyer

▸ dual agents who represent both the seller and the buyer

The type of representation an individual chooses with a licensee is indicated both in the brokerage agreement and in the agency representation disclosure notice.

Seller's agent. This is a single agency relationship wherein a licensee represents only the seller or lessor in listing and marketing a property for sale or lease. The seller's agent may assist the buyer or lessee, but the licensee's loyalty is strictly to the seller or landlord.

Subagent. This licensee is not the listing broker and is not affiliated with the listing broker. However, a subagent has a brokerage relationship with the seller through the listing broker. Although the subagent does not have a brokerage relationship with the buyer or lessee, the subagent assists the buyer or lessee in acquiring the property. Just as with the seller's agent, the subagent's loyalty is strictly to the seller or landlord.

If an individual is viewing a property for sale or lease and has not signed a brokerage agreement, the individual should understand that the agent showing the property represents the seller.

Buyer's agent. This is a single agency relationship wherein the buyer or lessee has signed a brokerage agreement with a broker who will represent the buyer or lessee in finding a property to purchase or lease. The agent must assist the client in evaluating properties, preparing offers, and developing negotiation strategies. The agent works in the buyer or lessee's best interest and is compensated in compliance with the terms of the brokerage agreement.

Dual agency. In a dual agency, the broker represents both the buyer and seller or the lessee and the lessor. There is no duty of loyalty to one party over the other party. The broker will assign an affiliated associate broker or salesperson to the seller or lessor and another affiliated associate broker or salesperson to the buyer or lessee. Each licensee owes his or her client the duty of confidentiality and must treat the client as though they were in a single agent relationship. The licensees representing the two clients are referred to as intracompany agents.

This agency relationship is only legal if both parties consent to the dual agency by signing the Consent for Dual Agency form found on the Commission's website at https://www.dllr.state.md.us/forms/consentfordualagency.pdf. If one party does not agree with the dual agency, the broker must terminate that party's relationship agreement with the broker. The terminated party will then need to form a brokerage relationship with a broker from another company.

Agency disclosure

When a licensee is in an agency relationship with a seller, buyer, lessor, or lessee to sell or lease residential property or unimproved property zoned for residential use, the licensee must disclose that relationship when approached by another party in relation to the subject property.

For example, if the licensee has a brokerage agreement with a property seller and another party approaches the licensee about the property, the licensee must disclose in writing that he or she represents the seller. This disclosure must occur during the first contact with the other party. If the first contact is not face to face, the licensee must disclose the relationship through the medium in which the contact occurs. Then at the first face-to-face contact, the licensee must provide the written disclosure notice to the party.

At an open house, a licensee complies with this disclosure requirement by posting the open house disclosure sign discussed in a previous chapter. Subagents and buyers' agents are subject to the same disclosure mandate.

Required form. The required disclosure notice can be found under the Forms and Fees tab on the Commission's website (Understanding Whom Real Estate Agents Represent).

The disclosure notice lists and explains the types of representation a licensee may have with a client as well as the licensee's duties to the client. The disclosure also notes that the licensee is qualified to offer advice only on real estate matters and not on legal or tax matters. Both the disclosure form and the dual agency consent form must be written in clear and coherent language, have the various sections divided and captioned, and be printed in at least 10 point type.

When using the form, the licensee will indicate what type of relationship he or she has with the client and will have the other party sign the form to acknowledge receipt of the disclosure. If the other party fails to sign the disclosure, the licensee must add that individual's name to the form and sign below the name, certifying that he or she made the disclosure but was unable to obtain the individual's signature.

Duties to client   Brokerage relationship agreements come with some automatic duties and obligations the broker owes to the client: care, obedience, loyalty, disclosure, accounting, and confidentiality.

An agreement may include such additional duties as the licensee and the client agree upon, but law requires the agent to

> ▸ maintain a client's right to confidentiality by keeping confidential all personal and financial information received from the client during the course of the relationship as well as any other information that the client requests to be kept confidential
>
> The confidentiality requirement ends if the client consents in writing to disclosure of the information or the information becomes public from a source other than the licensee.
>
> The right of confidentiality extends to prospective clients in anticipation of forming a brokerage relationship.
>
> The duty to maintain confidentiality does not apply to the disclosure of material facts about a property.
>
> ▸ treat all parties to a transaction honestly and fairly whether the party is the licensee's client or not
> ▸ exercise reasonable care and diligence
> ▸ refrain from discrimination in the offering of properties
> ▸ promote the interests of the client by seeking a sale or lease of the property complying with the terms in the brokerage agreement and presenting all written offers to and from the client in a timely manner
> ▸ disclose all material facts the licensee knows or should know relating to a property (except those subject to confidentiality)
> ▸ answer questions truthfully
>
> While an agent may not be required to disclose certain information about a property, such as the conditions that label a property stigmatized, the agent must answer truthfully if asked directly about any of those conditions. Agents may not, however, answer questions that would violate the client's confidentiality.
>
> ▸ comply with the terms of the brokerage agreement
> ▸ account for all trust monies promptly
> ▸ comply with all applicable federal, state, and local laws and regulations, including fair housing laws and the Americans with Disabilities Act regulations

Exceptions. Though the foregoing duties may not be waived, the law allows for the following exceptions.

- A licensee is not required to seek additional offers to purchase or lease the subject property after the seller or lessor has accepted an offer or while there is an existing contract of sale or lease.

- An intracompany or dual agent may disclose confidential information to his or her affiliated broker, but the broker may not disclose that information to the other party or the other intracompany agent in the same transaction.

- Licensees may show other available properties to prospective buyers or lessees without breaching their duties to existing clients.

  They may also represent other clients who have or are looking for similar properties for sale or lease and may represent other sellers or lessors with properties similar to the property sought by the buyer or lessee.

  Further, a licensee who has the written consent of the represented seller may discuss other properties with prospective buyers or lessees.

- Licensees may perform ministerial acts for an individual other than the client without violating the licensee's duties to the client as long as the brokerage agreement provides consent for such acts.

  Performing ministerial acts for another person does not form a brokerage relationship between the licensee and the other person.

Termination of agreement

The relationship begins when the client and licensee sign a written agreement and continues until either the terms of the agreement have been fulfilled or any of the following happens:

- the agreement expires on the date the licensee and client agreed on when signing the contract or applicable amendments
- both parties agree to terminate the relationship
- either party defaults under the terms of the agreement
- the broker terminates the relationship when a client refuses to consent to a disclosed dual agency

On termination, the licensee has no further obligations to the client except to

- account for all trust money still in the licensee's possession
- maintain the client's right of confidentiality

LISTING AGREEMENTS

Listing requirements

A listing agreement is both a type of brokerage relationship agreement and a legally binding contract between a property seller and a broker. As discussed in an earlier chapter, a listing agreement may establish

- an exclusive right-to-sell
- an exclusive agency
- an open listing
- a net listing

Note. Maryland § 17-322(b)(11) and COMAR 09.11.01.01 both prohibit licensees from accepting net listings and provide reprimand, license suspension, and license revocation as penalties for doing so.

Standard agreement forms are available for each permitted type of listing. The forms can be modified or amended as needed, but Maryland law includes requirements for every listing agreement.

Listing requirements

Because a listing agreement is both a contract and a brokerage agreement, it must meet the requirements of both along with additional requirements specific to listings. All residential listing contracts which list property for sale, rent, lease, or exchange, either exclusive or open, must

- be in writing and signed by the seller/lessor and the agent
- be given in the form of a copy to the seller or owner before the licensee advertises, shows, or offers the property and retained as a copy in compliance with Maryland's recordkeeping regulations
- include the listing price, terms of the agreement and sale/lease, type of compensation to be provided to the agent (either an amount or a percentage), type of marketing procedures to be used, and beginning and expiration dates of the agreement
- state the conditions under which the broker will be paid and when, whether compensation may be paid by someone other than the client, whether the broker may cooperate with other brokers and share compensation with those brokers, and the amount of compensation to be shared
- state the broker's duties and the client's responsibilities and should include guidelines for handling conflicts or disputes that may arise between the agent and the client
- include a cancellation clause which contains provisions for either party to cancel the contract and what, if any, penalties that party will face for doing so
- may include property information such as address, lot size, age and condition of the structures, all material facts, zoning, and taxing; a

property condition disclosure will cover most of this information and should be include

The agreement should also indicate whether the relationship is a single agency or a dual agency. If a dual agency, the disclosure notice must be signed by both parties and included in the contract.

Out-of-state listings. A Maryland licensee who wishes to list, show, or advertise a property that is located in a state other than Maryland must hold a real estate license in that state.

RESIDENTIAL PROPERTY CONDITION DISCLOSURE

Required form
Exemptions

Required form

A licensee entering into a listing agreement with a residential property owner must have the owner complete a property condition disclosure statement or a residential property disclaimer statement. The licensee must use the statement provided online by the MREC shown at the end of this chapter and at https://www.dllr.state.md.us/forms/propertydanddform.pdf .

Contents. Since licensees are required to obtain and disclose all material facts about the property, the disclosure form aids in meeting that requirement by informing buyers of material defects, if any, affecting the property. Material or latent defects are those a buyer would not reasonably be expected to ascertain on his or her own and those which would pose a direct threat to the buyer or other occupant's health or safety.

The disclosure portion of the form is used to itemize the defects actually known to the seller. Sellers are not required to perform or have performed any investigation or inspection of the property to discover defects not already known to the seller. The disclosure statement form does suggest that a buyer have the property inspected. The disclosure also states that the information included in the form is not a warranty by the seller of the property's actual condition if unknown by the seller.

The disclaimer portion of the form is used when the property is being sold "as is," that is, without offering any warranties as to the condition of the property or any improvements on the property. Even if the property is being sold "as is," the seller must disclose known latent defects in the property.

Time of delivery. The licensee must provide the completed, written disclosure or disclaimer statement to the prospective buyer or the buyer's agent at the time the licensee learns an offer is about to be made or at the time the licensee receives the offer. In case the seller's agent does not automatically deliver the form to the buyer's agent, the buyer's agent should make every effort to obtain the statement before submitting an offer.

Signatures. The seller must sign the form to affirm the accuracy of the information. The buyer signs it to acknowledge receipt of the disclosure and related rights and obligations under §10-702.

Exemptions

Excluded transactions. The disclosure or disclaimer statement is not required in the following transactions:

> ▸ initial sale of a property that has never been occupied or for which a certificate of occupancy has been issued within 1 year before the seller and buyer enter into a contract of sale
>
> ▸ property transfer that is exempt from transfer tax, except land installment contract of sale and option to purchase
>
> ▸ sale of a property by a lender who acquired the property by foreclosure or deed in lieu of foreclosure
>
> ▸ sheriff's sale, tax sale, or sale by foreclosure or by a court appointed trustee
>
> ▸ property transfer by a fiduciary in administering a decedent's estate, guardianship, conservatorship, or trust
>
> ▸ purchase of a single-family residential property that is to be converted to something other than residential use or is to be demolished
>
> ▸ sale of unimproved real property

Stigmatized properties. §17–322.1 declares that the following are not material facts and, therefore, do not need to be disclosed to prospective property buyers:

> ▸ an owner or resident of the property is, was, or is suspected to be infected with human immunodeficiency virus (HIV) or diagnosed with acquired immunodeficiency syndrome (AIDS)
>
> ▸ a homicide, suicide, accidental death, natural death, or felony occurred on the property

MARYLAND RESIDENTIAL PROPERTY DISCLOSURE AND DISCLAIMER STATEMENT

Property Address: _____

Legal Description: _____

NOTICE TO SELLER AND PURCHASER

Section 10-702 of the Real Property Article, *Annotated Code of Maryland*, requires the seller of certain residential real property to furnish to the purchaser either (a) a RESIDENTIAL PROPERTY DISCLAIMER STATEMENT stating that the seller is selling the property "as is" and makes no representations or warranties as to the condition of the property or any improvements on the real property, except as otherwise provided in the contract of sale, or in a listing of latent defects; or (b) a RESIDENTIAL PROPERTY DISCLOSURE STATEMENT disclosing defects or other information about the condition of the real property actually known by the seller. Certain transfers of residential property are excluded from this requirement (see the exemptions listed below).

        10-702. EXEMPTIONS. The following are specifically <u>excluded</u> from the provisions of §10-702:

1. The initial sale of single family residential real property:
   A. that has never been occupied; or
   B. for which a certificate of occupancy has been issued within 1 year before the seller and buyer enter into a contract of sale;
2. A transfer that is exempt from the transfer tax under §13-207 of the Tax-Property Article, except land installment contracts of sales under §13-207(a)(11) of the Tax-Property Article and options to purchase real property under §13-207(a)(12) of the Tax-Property Article;
3. A sale by a lender or an affiliate or subsidiary of a lender that acquired the real property by foreclosure or deed in lieu of foreclosure;
4. A sheriff's sale, tax sale, or sale by foreclosure, partition, or by court appointed trustee;
5. A transfer by a fiduciary in the course of the administration of a decedent's estate, guardianship, conservatorship, or trust;
6. A transfer of single family residential real property to be converted by the buyer into use other than residential use or to be demolished; or
7. A sale of unimproved real property.

Section 10-702 also requires the seller to disclose information about latent defects in the property that the seller has actual knowledge of. The seller must provide this information even if selling the property "as is." "Latent defects" are defined as: Material defects in real property or an improvement to real property that:

    (1) A purchaser would not reasonably be expected to ascertain or observe by a careful visual inspection of the real property; and
    (2) Would pose a direct threat to the health or safety of:
        (i) the purchaser; or
        (ii) an occupant of the real property, including a tenant or invitee of the purchaser.

MARYLAND RESIDENTIAL PROPERTY DISCLOSURE STATEMENT

NOTICE TO SELLERS: Complete and sign this statement only if you elect to disclose defects, including latent defects, or other information about the condition of the property actually known by you; otherwise, sign the Residential Property Disclaimer Statement. You may wish to obtain professional advice or inspections of the property; however, you are not required to undertake or provide any independent investigation or inspection of the property in order to make the disclosure set forth below. The disclosure is based on your personal knowledge of the condition of the property at the time of the signing of this statement.

NOTICE TO PURCHASERS: The information provided is the representation of the Sellers and is based upon the actual knowledge of Sellers as of the date noted. Disclosure by the Sellers is not a substitute for an inspection by an independent home inspection company, and you may wish to obtain such an inspection. The information contained in this statement is not a warranty by the Sellers as to the condition of the property of which the Sellers have no knowledge or other conditions of which the Sellers have no actual knowledge.

How long have you owned the property? _____

Property System: Water, Sewage, Heating & Air Conditioning (Answer all that apply)

Water Supply	☐ Public	☐ Well	☐ Other _____		
Sewage Disposal	☐ Public	☐ Septic System approved for _____ (# bedrooms) **Other Type**			

_____

Garbage Disposal	☐ Yes	☐ No			
Dishwasher	☐ Yes	☐No			
Heating	☐ Oil	☐ Natural Gas	☐ Electric	☐ Heat Pump Age ____	☐ Other _____
Air Conditioning	☐ Oil	☐ Natural Gas	☐Electric	☐ Heat Pump Age ____	☐ Other _____
Hot Water	☐ Oil	☐ Natural Gas	☐Electric Capacity _____ Age____		☐ Other _____

Please indicate your actual knowledge with respect to the following:

1. Foundation: Any settlement or other problems? ☐ Yes ☐ No ☐ Unknown
Comments:_____
2. Basement: Any leaks or evidence of moisture? ☐ Yes ☐ No ☐ Unknown ☐ Does Not Apply
Comments:_____
3. Roof: Any leaks or evidence of moisture? ☐ Yes ☐ No ☐ Unknown
Type of Roof:_____Age_____
Comments:_____
Is there any existing fire retardant treated plywood? ☐ Yes ☐ No ☐ Unknown
Comments:_____

4. Other Structural Systems, including exterior walls and floors:
Comments:_____
Any defects (structural or otherwise)? ☐ Yes ☐ No ☐ Unknown
Comments:_____
5. Plumbing system: Is the system in operating condition? ☐ Yes ☐ No ☐ Unknown
Comments:_____

6. Heating Systems: Is heat supplied to all finished rooms? ☐ Yes ☐ No ☐ Unknown
Comments:_____
Is the system in operating condition? ☐ Yes ☐ No ☐ Unknown
Comments:_____
7. Air Conditioning System: Is cooling supplied to all finished rooms? ☐ Yes ☐ No ☐ Unknown ☐ Does Not Apply
Comments:_____
Is the system in operating condition? ☐ Yes ☐ No ☐ Unknown ☐ Does Not Apply
Comments:_____

8. Electric Systems: Are there any problems with electrical fuses, circuit breakers, outlets or wiring?
☐ Yes ☐ No. ☐ Unknown
Comments:_____
8A. Will the smoke alarms provide an alarm in the event of a power outage? ○ Yes ○ No
Are the smoke alarms over 10 years old? ○ Yes ○ No
If the smoke alarms are battery operated, are they sealed, tamper resistant units incorporating a silence/hush button, which use long-life batteries as required in all Maryland Homes by 2018? ○Yes ○ No
Comments:_____
9. Septic Systems: Is the septic system functioning properly? ☐ Yes ☐ No ☐ Unknown ☐ Does Not Apply
When was the system last pumped? Date_____ ☐ Unknown
Comments:_____
10. Water Supply: Any problem with water supply? ☐ Yes ☐ No ☐ Unknown
Comments:_____
Home water treatment system: ☐ Yes ☐ No ☐ Unknown
Comments:_____
Fire sprinkler system: ☐ Yes ☐ No ☐ Unknown ☐ Does Not Apply
Comments:_____
Are the systems in operating condition? ☐ Yes ☐ No ☐ Unknown
Comments:_____
11. Insulation:
In exterior walls? ☐ Yes ☐ No ☐Unknown
In ceiling/attic? ☐ Yes ☐ No ☐ Unknown
In any other areas? ☐ Yes ☐ No Where?_____
Comments:_____
12. Exterior Drainage: Does water stand on the property for more than 24 hours after a heavy rain?
☐ Yes ☐ No ☐ Unknown
Comments_____
Are gutters and downspouts in good repair? ☐ Yes ☐ No ☐ Unknown
Comments:_____

13. Wood-destroying insects: Any infestation and/or prior damage? ☐ Yes ☐ No ☐ Unknown
Comments:_____

    Any treatments or repairs? ☐ Yes   ☐ No   ☐ Unknown
    Any warranties?   ☐ Yes   ☐ No   ☐ Unknown
Comments:_____

14. Are there any hazardous or regulated materials (including, but not limited to, licensed landfills, asbestos, radon gas, lead-based paint, underground storage tanks, or other contamination) on the property?
    ☐ Yes ☐ No ☐ Unknown
If yes, specify below
Comments:_____

15. If the property relies on the combustion of a fossil fuel for heat, ventilation, hot water, or clothes dryer operation, is a carbon monoxide alarm installed in the property?
    o Yes   o No   0 Unknown
Comments:_____

16. Are there any zoning violations, nonconforming uses, violation of building restrictions or setback requirements or any recorded or unrecorded easement, except for utilities, on or affecting the property?
    ☐ Yes ☐ No ☐ Unknown
If yes, specify below
Comments:_____

16A. If you or a contractor have made improvements to the property, were the required permits pulled from the county or local permitting office? o Yes o No o Does Not Apply o Unknown
Comments:_____

17. Is the property located in a flood zone, conservation area, wetland area, Chesapeake Bay critical area or Designated Historic District?
    ☐ Yes   ☐ No   ☐ Unknown   If yes, specify below
Comments:_____

18. Is the property subject to any restriction imposed by a Home Owners Association or any other type of community association?
    ☐ Yes   ☐ No   ☐ Unknown   If yes, specify below
Comments:_____

19. Are there any other material defects, including latent defects, affecting the physical condition of the property?
    ☐ Yes   ☐ No   ☐ Unknown
Comments:_____

NOTE: Seller(s) may wish to disclose the condition of other buildings on the property on a separate RESIDENTIAL PROPERTY DISCLOSURE STATEMENT.

The seller(s) acknowledge having carefully examined this statement, including any comments, and verify that it is complete and accurate as of the date signed. The seller(s) further acknowledge that they have been informed of their rights and obligations under §10-702 of the Maryland Real Property Article.
Seller(s) _____ Date _____

Seller(s) _____ Date _____

The purchaser(s) acknowledge receipt of a copy of this disclosure statement and further acknowledge that they have been informed of their rights and obligations under §10-702 of the Maryland Real Property Article.

Purchaser _____ Date _____

Purchaser _____ Date _____

Page 3 of 4

MARYLAND RESIDENTIAL PROPERTY DISCLAIMER STATEMENT

NOTICE TO SELLER(S): Sign this statement only if you elect to sell the property without representations and warranties as to its condition, except as otherwise provided in the contract of sale and in the listing of latent defects set forth below; otherwise, complete and sign the RESIDENTIAL PROPERTY DISCLOSURE STATEMENT.

Except for the latent defects listed below, the undersigned seller(s) of the real property make no representations or warranties as to the condition of the real property or any improvements thereon, and the purchaser will be receiving the real property "as is" with all defects, including latent defects, which may exist, except as otherwise provided in the real estate contract of sale. The seller(s) acknowledge having carefully examined this statement and further acknowledge that they have been informed of their rights and obligations under §10-702 of the Maryland Real Property Article.

Section 10-702 also requires the seller to disclose information about latent defects in the property that the seller has actual knowledge of. The seller must provide this information even if selling the property "as is." "Latent defects" are defined as: Material defects in real property or an improvement to real property that:
    (1) A purchaser would not reasonably be expected to ascertain or observe by a careful visual inspection of the real property; and
    (2) Would pose a direct threat to the health or safety of:
        (i) the purchaser; or
        (ii) an occupant of the real property, including a tenant or invitee of the purchaser.

Does the seller(s) have actual knowledge of any latent defects? □ Yes   □ No   If yes, specify:

_____
_____
_____
_____
_____
_____
_____
_____
_____
_____

Seller _____   Date_____

Seller _____   Date_____

The purchaser(s) acknowledge receipt of a copy of this disclaimer statement and further acknowledge that they have been informed of their rights and obligations under §10-702 of the Maryland Real Property Article.

Purchaser _____   Date_____

Purchaser _____   Date_____

Page 4 of 4

FORM: MREC/DLLR: Rev 07/31/2018

28 Maryland Brokerage Relationship & Disclosure Snapshot Review

AGENCY

Key terms
- an agency relationship is one in which a licensee has the authority to represents a client in a real estate transaction

Agency creation
- an agency relationship is formed by the signing of a contract, not by receiving, paying, or expecting compensation
- to be in writing with automatic termination date, details on compensation to agent and other brokers, relationship cancellation provision, duties of both parties
- no brokerage relationship with common source information company simply by using the sources

Representation options
- agents who represent seller – seller's agent and subagent; single agency; loyalty only to seller or landlord; subagent is not listing broker or affiliated with listing broker, assists buyer in acquiring the property, loyalty only to seller or landlord
- agents who represent buyer – single agency; helps buyer find and evaluate properties, prepare offers, and negotiate; works in buyer's best interest
- dual agents – represents both seller and buyer with no loyalty to either over the other; both agents assigned by same affiliated broker; each owes client duty of confidentiality; must treat client same as if in a single agent relationship; called intracompany agents; both parties must agree and sign consent form; if one party disagrees, that relationship is terminated

Agency disclosure
- all agents to disclose existing client relationship to other parties; must be in writing and provided at first contact with the other party; open house disclosure signage meets relationship disclosure requirement

Duties to client
- confidentiality, honesty and fairness, reasonable care and diligence, no discrimination, disclosure of material facts, compliance with agreement, promotion of client's interests, trust monies accounted for, compliance with laws
- exceptions include not seeking additional offers once property under contract, dual agent disclosing confidential information to affiliated broker who may not break confidentiality, showing other properties to prospective buyers or representing other clients with similar properties, performing ministerial acts for other parties with client's consent

Termination of agreement
- expires on date included in agreement; both parties agree to terminate; either party defaults on terms of agreement; client refuses disclosed dual agency
- upon termination, agent has no further duties to client except accounting for trust monies and maintaining confidentiality

LISTING AGREEMENTS

Listing requirements
- types include exclusive right-to-sell, exclusive agency, open listing, and net listing
- net listings prohibited; must be in writing and signed by agent and seller; agent to give seller copy of agreement prior to advertising or showing property; to include listing price, terms of sale, type of compensation and conditions, type of marketing, beginning and ending date; duties of both parties; cancellation clause; property information and condition; type of brokerage relationship
- Out-of-state listings prohibited unless licensee is licensed in the other state

RESIDENTIAL PROPERTY
CONDITION DISCLOSURE

Required form
- required to use MREC disclosure and disclaimer form; required for all listing agreements; provided to prospective buyer prior to offer; disclosure portion of form is for identifying latent defects; disclaimer portion is used when selling property "as is"

Exemptions
- disclosure requirement does not apply to initial sale of never occupied property, transfer exempt from transfer tax, sale of property by lender; foreclosure, tax, or sheriff's sale, transfer by fiduciary, purchase of property to be converted from residential use or demolished, sale of unimproved land
- no requirement to disclose non-material facts or latent defects: stigmatized properties including those with residents with HIV or AIDS; site of homicide, suicide, accidental death, natural death, or felony

29 Ethical Practices and Fair Housing

Fair Housing Laws
Discriminatory Advertising
Agency Relationship Interference
Duties Owed Clients and Public
Predatory Business Practices

FAIR HOUSING LAWS

Federal law
Protected classes and discrimination
Real Estate Brokers Act
Commission on Civil Rights
Enforcement

Federal law

Over the years, several laws have been enacted to address discrimination. The Civil Rights Act of 1866, the Rumford Fair Housing Act of 1963, and the Civil Rights Act of 1964 were the first such laws. The Civil Rights Act of 1866 prohibited discrimination based on race in advertising, sale, and rental of housing, with no exceptions. The Fair Housing Act of 1968, established a week after Martin Luther King, Jr., was assassinated, expanded on the Civil Rights Act of 1964 by addressing discrimination in the sale, rental, and financing of housing. The Act asserted the principle that every American should have an equal opportunity to obtain a home without suffering discrimination for factors outside their control.

In 1988, the Fair Housing Amendments Act was passed with additional protected classes. This law gave enforcement of the Fair Housing Act to the U.S. Department of Housing and Urban Development (HUD).

Protected classes and discrimination

Protected classes. A protected class is defined as a group of people with a common characteristic who are legally protected from discrimination based on that characteristic.

Classes protected under **federal** law include the following:

▶ **color--** pertaining to a person's skin color
▶ **familial status--** families in which one or more children under 18 live with a parent, a person who has legal custody of the child or children, or the designee of the parent or legal custodian with the parent or custodian's written permission; also applies to pregnant women and anyone holding legal custody of a child under 18
▶ **national origin--** country of birth

- ▶ **physical or mental disability**-- an individual who has, has a record of, or is regarded as, having a physical or mental disability that substantially limits one or more major life activities (applies to hearing, mobility, visual impairment, chronic alcoholism, chronic mental illness, AIDS or AIDS-related complex, and mental retardation)
- ▶ **race**-- groupings of human populations on the presumed basis of physical or genetic characteristics
- ▶ **religion**-- participation in one of the world's structured religions; one's spiritual beliefs; inference of religion by place of worship
- ▶ **sex**-- male or female; the Fair Housing Act and HUD, while not naming sexual orientation and gender as protected classes, consider discrimination based on these characteristics to fall under the sex category protected by the Fair Housing Act

Maryland law adds the following classes to the federal classes:

- ▶ **marital status**-- being single, married, separated, divorced, or widowed
- ▶ **sexual orientation**-- the identification of an individual as to male or female homosexuality, heterosexuality, or bisexuality
- ▶ **gender identity**-- consistent and sincere expression of gender-related identity based on appearance, expression, or behavior, regardless of the person's assigned sex at birth
- ▶ **source of income**-- (effective 10/1/2020) any lawful source of money including grants, government assistance, alimony, child support, pensions, annuities, legal gifts, and investment earnings

Local jurisdictions such as counties and cities follow both federal and state laws but often include additional classes such as age, sexual preference, occupation, personal appearance, political opinion, ancestry, and family responsibility.

Discrimination. The Fair Housing Act and the Maryland statute identify discriminatory actions within the following three categories of activities:

- ▶ housing

  - ▪ refusing to rent housing, sell housing, or negotiate for housing
  - ▪ making housing unavailable or lying about housing availability
  - ▪ denying housing
  - ▪ establishing different terms or conditions in home selling or renting
  - ▪ providing different housing accommodations or amenities
  - ▪ requesting information about birth control and/or family planning practices
  - ▪ refusing to consider both applicants' incomes when seeking to buy or rent

- committing acts of prejudice, violence, harassment, intimidation, or abuse directed against families or individuals or their residential property
- refusing to permit reasonable house modifications that are necessary for the daily life of a person with a mental or physical disability
- refusing to make reasonable accommodations or adjust rules, policies, services, or practices that hamper the use of a dwelling by a person with a physical or mental disability, such as allowing a service dog in housing that does not allow pets
- offering multi-family housing that does not have accessible units and access routes (wide doors and hallways), accessible public and common areas, and effective communication as needed by a disabled person

▸ mortgage lending

- refusing to make or purchase a mortgage loan
- setting different terms, conditions, or requirements on the loan, such as interest rates or fees
- refusing to make information about the loan available
- using discriminatory practices in property appraising

▸ advertising and other discriminatory activities

- making discriminatory statements or advertisements indicating a preference, limitation, or discrimination or excluding a protected class; this applies to those who are otherwise exempt from the fair housing act, such as owner-occupied four-unit homes
- threatening or interfering with anyone's fair housing rights

Exemptions. Under certain conditions, the following situations may not be subject to compliance with the Fair Housing Act. The Civil Rights Act of 1866, however, disallows any exemptions involving discrimination on the basis of race:

▸ single-family homes rented or sold without a broker's assistance-- advertising must comply with the act and the seller/landlord may not own three such houses at one time
▸ owner-occupied single-family homes or those with no more than four units (Maryland allows up to five units)-- landlord may deny rentals based on sex, marital status, and/or sexual orientation
▸ members-only private clubs or organizations-- may give preference to members only
▸ religious and nonprofit organizations-- may limit sales, rentals, and occupancy to one sex or members of the organization
▸ rentals and sales-- owners may deny rentals or sales to individuals with convictions for the manufacture or distribution of illegal drugs

- local government ordinance-- owners may limit rental occupancy based on the size and number of rooms in the residence according to local governments
- age restricted housing—seller/landlord may require all residents be at least 62 years of age or that at least 80% of the units be occupied by someone at least 55 years of age with no children living in any of the units

Enforcement of federal laws

The Department of Housing and Urban Development (HUD) is responsible for enforcing the Fair Housing Act. HUD uses fair housing testers to pose as renters or home buyers to interact with landlords, real estate licensees, and individuals selling homes to identify instances of discrimination. HUD also investigates complaints of housing discrimination, determines if the complaint is valid, and decides if further legal action is needed.

Complaints. Complaints must be filed with the Secretary of HUD within 1 year after the alleged discriminatory act. The secretary may refer the complaint to an appropriate public agency, attempt to mediate the dispute and reach a conciliation agreement with the involved parties, or refer the complaint to the Attorney General for court action.

An aggrieved individual may file a civil action within 2 years of the alleged act or after a conciliation agreement has been breached. The individual may be granted actual and punitive damages, attorney fees, and temporary or permanent injunctions.

Real Estate Brokers Act

In addition to following the federal fair housing laws, Maryland covers fair housing within Title 20-702 and Title 17 of the Annotated Code of Maryland, the Real Estate Brokers Act. These laws expand protection by including additional protected classes and prohibited discriminatory acts.

The Brokers Act prohibits real estate licensees and other persons from doing any of the following, whether acting for monetary compensation or not:

- refusing to show available residential property based on the racial composition or character of the property's neighborhood
- failing or refusing to show available residential property that is in the buyer's price range and requested area

    Licensees in Montgomery County and Baltimore City are required to maintain a registry of homes they have listed and must categorize the homes by price; they must show any potential buyer the price category of the registry that corresponds with the buyer's price range and show the buyer any home listed in that category.

- blockbusting (convincing property owners to sell cheaply out of the fear of racial, religious, or other minorities moving into the neighborhood)
- unfairly inducing or discouraging the sale or purchase of property by suggesting that property owned by, used by, or located near

individuals of any protected class may result in lower property values, a change of the neighborhood's character, increased criminal activities, or lower quality of schools in the area

▸ denying participation in housing-related services such as a multiple listing service

Commission on Civil Rights

Mission. The mission of the Maryland Commission on Civil Rights (MCCR) is to ensure opportunity for all through the enforcement of Maryland's laws against discrimination in employment, housing, public accommodations, and state contracts; to provide educational and outreach services related to provisions of this law; and to promote and improve human relations in Maryland.

Membership. The Commission is made up of nine members who are appointed by the governor and confirmed by the State Senate. MCCR is responsible for enforcing state level discrimination laws.

Activities. The Commission investigates allegations of discrimination in employment, housing, public accommodations, and state contracts and attempts to resolve issues either by issuing a written finding of No Probable Cause, through conciliation resulting in a written agreement, or by forwarding the matter to the MCCR's Office of the General Counsel.

MCCR also offers education and outreach services to agencies, businesses, and organizations to provide information on equal access and opportunity under Maryland law. The MCCR's brochure on fair housing is available online at 2016 Housing BiFold Brochue.pdf (maryland.gov).

Complaints. Anyone believing he or she has been the victim of discrimination may file a complaint on the MCCR's website at Housing Discrimination (maryland.gov). Complaints must be made within 1 year of the alleged act of discrimination.

Penalties. The MCCR may modify, remove, or renew a suspension. During a suspension, the Commission must inform the affected community of the racial and economic composition of the area, the number of real estate transactions in the area, and the fair market values of affected properties.

Conservation areas. A conservation area is an urban area where racial stability is threatened by the volume of real estate transactions. Once the MCCR has identified a conservation area, the Commission may suspend any real estate advertising except that published in regularly distributed newspapers, magazines, radio, television, or telephone directories. Advertising suspensions are limited to 24 months. Soliciting properties to list for sale or rent is also suspended during the same time frame.

DISCRIMINATORY ADVERTISING

Under the Fair Housing Act, it is illegal to "make, print, or publish… any notice, statement, or advertisement … that indicates any preference, limitation, or discrimination based on a person's race, color, religion, sex, handicap, familial status, or national origin." Further, words, phrases, photographs, illustrations, symbols or forms of any kind which tend to give the impression that a property is available (or not available) only to certain types of people are also prohibited.

Such items as newspaper ads, websites, applications, flyers, deeds, signs, posters, billboards, and even pictures in a business or office are included in this prohibition, as is anything written or spoken about a property. Use of phrases such as "no children" is discrimination based on familial status.

HUD provides a comprehensive list of acceptable and unacceptable words and phrases to be considered when advertising housing. The list can be found at Fair-Housing-Advertising-Words-Phrases-List-1.pdf (fairhousinginstitute.com). HUD also recommends using their Equal Housing Opportunity logo on ads.

AGENCY RELATIONSHIP INTERFERENCE

COMAR 09.11.02.03 mandates appropriate and professional behavior between licensees. The law requires licensees to respect the exclusive agency listings of other licensees. A licensee who has an exclusive listing is required to cooperate with other brokers when it is in the best interest of the licensee's client. Such cooperation includes sharing commissions with another broker if there is a previous agreement to do so.

A broker or licensee who wishes to negotiate the sale of a property that is listed exclusively with another licensee must do so directly with the listing broker and not with the client.

Before placing signs on a property showing the property is for sale, rent, lease, or exchange, the licensee must obtain the property owner's consent.

DUTIES OWED CLIENTS & PUBLIC

Duties owed clients
Duties to the public

Duties owed clients   On signing a brokerage agreement with a client, a licensee undertakes to protect and promote the interests of the client. In addition to fulfilling the duties owed to a client per the brokerage agreement, as discussed in a previous chapter, Maryland licensees must adhere to Maryland's Code of Ethics, which states the general ethical duties a licensee owes to a client. The licensee must

> ▸ be informed regarding laws, proposed legislation, governmental orders, and other essential information and public policies
>
> ▸ refuse to accept compensation from more than one party to a transaction without the full knowledge of all the parties

> ▸ disclose in writing to the seller, lessor, buyer, or lessee the licensee's licensing status when seeking to obtain or sell an interest in a property for him/herself, an immediate family member, an entity owned by the licensee, an affiliated employee, or a team member; disclosure no later than when an offer is submitted

In addition, a licensee owes a client loyalty-- putting the client's interests above the licensee's-- and obedience-- complying with all of the client's lawful directives.

Competitive Market Analysis. In preparing a competitive market analysis (CMA) for a client or prospective client, a licensee must include the following disclosure conspicuously on the first page:

COMPETITIVE MARKET ANALYSIS DISCLOSURE

This analysis is not an appraisal. It is intended only for the purpose of assisting buyers or sellers or prospective buyers or sellers in deciding the listing, offering, or sale price of the real property.

Licensees who include their own property in a CMA must disclose their ownership interest to the individual for whom the CMA is prepared.

Offers. Licensees must present all offers as required in their duties under a brokerage agreement.

A licensee's duty to protect and promote the interests of the client includes ensuring that the prospective property buyer has been provided the property condition disclosure or disclaimer before submitting an offer. Failure to do so could result in a voided or voidable contract.

Duties to the public

In addition to the duties owed to a client, a licensee owes general ethical duties to the public. The licensee must

- ▸ remain informed on matters affecting real estate in the community, the State, and the nation
- ▸ be informed on current market conditions
- ▸ protect the public against fraud, misrepresentation, unethical practices, and those damaging to the public or to the dignity and integrity of the real estate profession
- ▸ assist the commission in its work of regulating the practices of brokers, associate brokers, and salespersons in Maryland
- ▸ make a reasonable effort to ascertain all material facts concerning every property for which the licensee accepts the agency
- ▸ avoid discrimination in the sale, rental, leasing, trading, or transferring of property to any person or group of persons in violation of state law
- ▸ avoid naming a false consideration in any document
- ▸ comply with all advertising laws and guidelines

> ▶ ensure that financial obligations are in writing and express the parties' exact agreement, and that copies are provided to all involved parties within a reasonable time
>
> ▶ sign all documents in the licensee's own name

PREDATORY BUSINESS PRACTICES

Antitrust violations
Predatory pricing
Predatory lending
Fraud

Antitrust violations

Predatory business practices occur when one business attempts to monopolize the market and push out competitors. Businesses might take advantage of competitors or customers by convincing them to enter into contracts or deals without knowing or understanding the clear terms and conditions. Predatory business practices often violate antitrust laws and result in the injury or exploitation of others for the predator's personal gain.

Predatory pricing

Predatory pricing is illustrated by one company setting prices unprofitably low to make competition difficult or impossible for other companies. Predatory pricing may benefit consumers initially by making low prices available. However, in the long run, after establishing a monopoly, the predator can raise prices and limit consumer choice.

Predatory lending

Predatory lending practices include charging excessive costs, hiding payment terms, stripping equity by repeated refinancing, abusing mortgage service terms, and steering consumers to higher cost mortgages. For example, a predatory lender may induce the elderly, minorities, inexperienced consumers, and the uninformed to sign loan documents with no clear idea of the terms of the loan.

Some lenders target home buyers with sub-prime home loans that contain excessive fees, unreasonable interest rates, penalties, and insurance charges. These loans are often offered in disadvantaged neighborhoods and to buyers with low credit scores. Consequently, such loans often lead to foreclosure when the homeowner can no longer afford the high payments.

Fraud

Predatory business practices typically include illegal acts of fraud, misrepresentation, and deception. Companies may be prosecuted for antitrust violations. Consumers may file complaints with the Office of the Commissioner of Financial Regulation at dllr.state.md.us /finance/consumers/frcomplaints.shtml or with the Maryland Attorney General's Consumer Protection Division online at marylandattorneygeneral.gov.

29 Ethical Practices and Fair Housing Snapshot Review

FAIR HOUSING LAW

Federal law
- Civil Rights Act of 1964, Fair Housing Act of 1968, Fair Housing Amendments Act of 1988

Protected classes and discrimination
- Federal: color, familial status, national origin, disability, race, religion, sex; Maryland: marital status, sexual orientation, gender identity, source of income; Local: age, sexual preference, occupation, personal appearance, political opinion, ancestry, family responsibility
- discrimination prohibited in home renting and selling, mortgage lending, advertising, interfering with others' rights
- exemptions – single-family homes sold without licensee, owner-occupied homes, private clubs, religious and nonprofit organizations, illegal drug convictions, some age restrictions

Real Estate Brokers Act
- prohibits acts based on protected classes; refusing to show property, blockbusting, unfair inducements, denying participation in services

Commission on Civil Rights
- enforces state fair housing laws; investigates complaints; resolves disputes through conciliation or referring to General Counsel
- conservation areas-- urban area where racial stability is affected by real estate transactions; MCCR may suspend advertising and listing solicitations; MCCR to notify community affected

Enforcement
- complaints filed with MCCR or HUD within 1 year of prohibited act; fines imposed for discriminatory acts; victim may file civil action within 2 years of prohibited act

DISCRIMINATORY ADVERTISING
- advertising may not indicate preference based on any protected class; HUD provides list of allowable words and phrases

AGENCY RELATIONSHIP INTERFERENCE
- licensees are to respect other licensees' exclusive listings, cooperate with other brokers when in best interest of client, share commission if agreed, must negotiate exclusive listing directly with listing broker, obtain owner's approval before posting signs on property

DUTIES OWED CLIENTS AND PUBLIC

Duties to a client
- code of ethics requires licensees to stay informed on laws and essential information, to accept compensation only from one party unless disclosed to all parties, to disclose licensee's license status when obtaining or selling property owned by the licensee or other close individuals, to remain loyal and obedient to client
- CMA to include required statement, to disclose licensee's ownership of comparable property, to present all offers, to quote correct price, to assure property disclosure or disclaimer is provided to buyer prior to offer

Duties to the public
- licensee to stay informed on local, state, and federal laws and market conditions, to protect public against unethical practices, to assist with regulating licensee practices, to ascertain material facts, to not discriminate, to not name false consideration, to comply with advertising laws, to assure financial obligations are accurate and in writing, to sign own name when signing documents

PREDATORY BUSINESS PRACTICES

Antitrust violations   ● business attempts to establish monopoly or take advantage of customers for personal gain violate antitrust law

Predatory pricing   ● setting low prices to drive out competition, profit from market dominance

Predatory lending   ● hiding or manipulating lending terms; marketing to unqualified borrowers

Fraud   ● misrepresentation, deception

30 Other Maryland Laws and Practices

Real Estate Appraisers Act
Timeshares
Homeowners' Associations
New Home Warranties
Transfer Tax
Ad Valorem Tax
Mechanics' Liens
Environmental Disclosures
Leases

REAL ESTATE APPRAISERS ACT

The procedures for licensing, certifying, and regulating real estate appraisers, appraisal management companies, and home inspectors are found in both the Annotated Code of Maryland, Title 16 and the Code of Maryland Regulations (COMAR), Title 09, Subtitle 19. The regulations include appraiser certification classifications and the activities allowed under each.

The regulations established the State Commission of Real Estate Appraisers, Appraisal Management Companies, and Home Inspectors, which in turn established hearing boards for appraisers, appraisal management companies, and home inspectors.

The Commission is made up of 16 members and has the power to enforce related regulations, investigate alleged violations, refer complaints to the appropriate hearing board, and adopt additional regulations as needed to carry out the provisions of these titles.

TIMESHARES

Timeshare features
Essential characteristics

Timeshare features

Timeshare. A timeshare is property that is owned by a number of people who divide the use of the property into allotments of time, such as one or two weeks a year. The buyers are not purchasing the property itself but rather a time allotment for the property's use.

Management. There is typically a management company that handles the sale of the shares and maintenance of the property. The management company also handles the timeshare agreement that all buyers must sign.

Timeshare agreement. The agreement lays out the type of ownership that is purchased, the policies of the timeshare community, including rules of conduct, amount and due dates of yearly fees, and use schedule. The agreement also must contain the rules and procedures for canceling the agreement.

Essential characteristics

Registration. Maryland timeshares are regulated by the Maryland Real Estate Time-Sharing Act, Title 11A of the Annotated Code of Maryland and COMAR 09.11.04. A developer who wishes to create a timeshare must register with the Real Estate Commission and meet bonding requirements.

Public offering statement. The developer must also file a public offering statement (POS) for the proposed project with the Secretary of State, who will either approve or reject it. The statement must include all information about the time-share project required by § 11A-112 and which, once approved, must be provided to a purchaser prior to the execution of the sales contract.

Project broker. Timeshare developers must designate a licensed real estate broker as the project broker for the timeshare project. This broker may employ unlicensed individuals to contact people to attend sales presentations and to perform other clerical duties such as arranging appointments and distributing promotional materials.

Conversions. Rather than building a new timeshare complex, a developer may choose to convert an existing building into timeshare units. When doing so, the developer must provide any existing residents with a notice of at least 120 days. The developer must also include an architect's or engineer's report on the condition of the major structural, mechanical, electrical, and plumbing systems if the building being converted is more than 5 years old.

Advertising. Advertising for timeshares may not be misleading in any way nor represent any proposed improvements or nonexistent scenes without clarifying that the improvements and scenes do not currently exist.

Sales contract. Sales contracts must contain the purchaser's total financial obligations, the term of the timeshare plan, the estimated date unfinished construction must be completed, as well as the date and signatures of each party. The contract must also contain specified language regarding the purchaser's right to cancel, the illegality of waiving that right, and the refund requirements.

Warranties. Developers must provide purchasers with a 1-year implied warranty on the timeshare's construction and heating and air conditioning systems. The developer must also provide an additional 3-year implied warranty for the common elements' construction and major systems. Breached warranties may result in the timeshare owner or association bringing a suit for enforcement against the developer.

Cancellation rights. When first purchasing a timeshare, the buyer has the right to cancel the sales contract up until midnight on the 10th calendar day following the latest of the contract date, the day the buyer received all of the required documents related to the purchase, or the date the timeshare unit is ready for occupancy. The right to cancel cannot be waived, and closing cannot occur until the cancellation period has expired. Cancellation language must be included in the POS and the sales contract.

An owner reselling a timeshare must provide the buyer a copy of the timeshare instrument and a certificate containing information on rights of first refusal, expenses, fees, and liens. The buyer of a timeshare being resold has the right to cancel within 7 days of receiving the instrument and resale certificate without reason or liability and with a full refund. This right may not be waived.

Deposits. Any purchase money paid by the buyer must be placed in an escrow account that meets the same requirements as a broker's trust money escrow account. The money may be disbursed after the 10-day cancellation period has expired. However, if a buyer cancels the sales contract, the managing company must refund any purchase monies to the buyer within 20 days of the cancellation.

MARYLAND HOMEOWNERS' ASSOCIATION ACT

Regulation
Members' rights
Sales

Regulation	Homeowners' associations are regulated by the Maryland Homeowners' Association Act, Title 11B of the Annotated Code of Maryland. The Act is enforced by the Maryland Attorney General's Division of Consumer Protection.
Members' rights	All members (homeowners) of the association have the right to attend association and board meetings unless the meeting concerns confidential matters, and they have the right to vote on association matters according to the provisions of the governing documents.
	Members may examine any books and records kept on behalf of the association and receive a copy of each year's budget.
	Members may also submit any disputes with the association's board of directors to the Division of Consumer Protection for resolution.
Sales	The sales contract for a lot in a homeowners' association is not valid unless the buyer is provided with the required disclosures and the contract itself contains specific language regarding the sale being subject to the Act, what notices and information the buyer must be provided and when, the buyer's cancellation right and process, and the association's restrictions on the lot.
	The buyer must also be provided with a copy of the association's articles of incorporation, declaration, bylaws, the proposed or actual budget, mandatory fees or assessments and when they are due, and all recorded covenants and restrictions to which the buyer will be obligated.

If the required documents and disclosures are not provided prior to settlement or within 5 days of receipt of the disclosures, a purchaser may cancel the sales contract without reason or liability and with a full refund of deposits and other monies paid.

NEW HOME WARRANTIES

Required disclosures
Warranty provisions

Required disclosures

Warranty plan participation. Builders are required to disclose whether or not they participate in a new home warranty security plan that provides the homeowner with a warranty either at the homeowner's option or as a requirement of the plan.

The disclosure must be in writing on a form approved by the Consumer Protection Division of the Office of the Attorney General (Division) and must be provided to the owner prior to entering into a sale or construction contract.

The disclosure of a builder who does not participate in a warranty security plan must explain to the owner in 12-point type that

- ▶ new home builders in Maryland are required to register with the Division
- ▶ without a new home warranty or other express warranties, only certain limited implied warranties will be provided by law
- ▶ either the builder has knowledge that certain hazardous or regulated materials are present on the site of the new home or the builder is not making any representations or warranties as to whether there are hazardous or regulated material on site; the builder must describe any such materials known to the builder in the disclosure

Buyer acknowledgment. The new home buyer must acknowledge in writing that he or she understands the lack of a new home warranty security plan and has read and understood the builder's disclosure. Contracts that do not contain this acknowledgement are voidable by the buyer/owner.

After acknowledging the disclosure, the buyer may rescind the contract in writing within 5 working days from the contract date and receive a full refund of any money paid to the builder.

Warranty provisions

Authorized business entity. New home warranty plans must be operated by a business entity authorized to do business in Maryland, must demonstrate the plan's financial security to cover claims, and provide mediation of disputes between owners and builders.

Warranty coverage. The warranty must cover the following:

> ▸ material and workmanship defects for 1 year
>
> ▸ major systems for 2 years except for fixtures and appliances with shorter manufacturer warranty length
>
> ▸ structural defects for 5 years

Exclusions. New home warranties have several exclusions, such as negligent damage, personal property damage, normal wear and tear, as listed in § 10-604 (a)(2) of the Annotated Code of Maryland.

Required documents. Builders selling new homes must provide buyers with a warranty notice that contains the "Notice to Purchaser" exact language mandated by § 10-605. The home warranty security plan must provide the homeowner with validated warranty documents within 60 days of the warranty date.

Right to waive. Homeowners have the right to waive the requirement for a new home warranty using the Division's approved form. Owners also have the right to rescind the waiver in writing within 3 working days from the contract date.

Violations. Any person who knowingly misrepresents the existence of a new home warranty is guilty of an unfair and deceptive trade practice and is subject to a fine up to $50,000 or imprisonment up to 2 years or both.

TRANSFER TAX

Taxed transactions
Exempt transactions

Taxed transactions Maryland charges a transfer tax when the controlling interest in a property is transferred to another person.

Tax rate. Maryland's transfer tax is 0.5 percent of the property's sale price and is divided equally between the seller and the buyer.

The sales contract for a one or two single-family residential property must contain the following statement:

> *Section 14-104 of the Real Property Article of the Annotated Code of Maryland provides that, unless otherwise negotiated in the contract or provided by local law, the cost of any recordation tax or any State or local transfer tax shall be shared equally between the buyer and seller.*

Exempt transactions First-time homebuyers purchasing a principal residence are exempt from paying transfer tax, so the total tax for the transfer is 0.25 percent paid by the seller.

Other exemptions include but are not limited to transfers to government agencies, between relatives and domestic partners, between spouses and domestic partners, between business entities, and transfers to trusts and from estates (See Maryland

§ 13-207). Individual counties may provide exemptions or reductions in the tax rate as well.

AD VALOREM TAX

Tax rates
Tax payments
Delinquencies
Owner's rights

Tax rates

The amount of a Maryland ad valorem tax bill is determined by the assessed value of the property and the tax rate which is set by each state, county, and municipal jurisdiction. There are no restrictions or limitations on tax rates; they are typically set at whatever level is needed to fund governmental services.

Rates are expressed as a dollar amount per $100 of the assessed property value. Properties are reassessed every 3 years, and the tax rate is applied to the reassessed value to determine a property's tax bill.

For example, if a property is assessed at $200,000, dividing the assessment by 100 would result in a tax rate being applied to $2,000. If the tax rate for the jurisdiction is $0.98, the tax bill would be $2,000 x 0.98 or $1,960. In some cases, a tax credit may be applied to the bill to lower a homeowner's tax.

Tax payments

Taxes may be paid annually or semi-annually. The first semi-annual payment is due on or before September 30th with the second payment due on or before December 31st. Annual payments are due on or before July 1st. Payments may be made by the homeowner directly to the county's Director of Finance or by the owner's mortgage company from an escrow account.

Delinquencies

Taxes that are due on September 30th become delinquent on October 1st. Those due in December become delinquent January 1st. Annual taxes due on July 1 become delinquent on the following October 1. Final delinquency notices are sent out on March 1.

Lien. Delinquent taxes are subject to interest and penalties and can become a lien on the property. A lien for delinquent taxes remains in effect until the taxes are paid in full, including interest and penalties.

Tax sale. If the taxes are not paid, the state requires the county's tax collector to sell the tax lien as a tax lien certificate through a tax sale at public auction. The tax collector must send the homeowner a notice of the impending sale. Thirty days later, a listing of the properties to be sold must be published in a local newspaper once a week for 4 consecutive weeks.

At a tax sale, it is the unpaid debt that is sold, not the property itself. The highest bidder at the auction buys the debt and the right to foreclose on the property.

Redemption. After the sale, the homeowner still owns the property but must pay off the debt to the buyer within 6 months to retain ownership. The property is redeemed when the homeowner has paid the debt plus additional interest, taxes, and penalties.

Foreclosure. If the homeowner fails to pay the debt within the 6 months and forgoes redeeming the property, the purchaser may file for foreclosure and for a deed to the property. The purchaser has 2 years from the date of the tax sale to foreclose. Failure to do so results in the purchaser losing the right to foreclose. If the court grants the foreclosure, the purchaser becomes liable for the taxes, interest, and penalties.

Owner's rights

A property owner's rights are contained in the Maryland Property Owner's Bill of Rights which is found on the Department of Assessments and Taxation's website at https://dat.maryland.gov/realproperty/pages/bill-of-rights.aspx.

MECHANICS' LIENS

Features and use
Lien creation and release

Features and use

Mechanics' liens are regulated by Title 9, Statutory Liens on Real Property, Subtitle 1 of the Annotated Code of Maryland. A mechanics' lien gives an unpaid party a security interest in the property owned by the person who has failed to pay.

The lien can be used by anyone who provides labor or materials to a construction project. Architects, engineers, surveyors, designers, construction contractors, and suppliers may all use the lien to obtain a guarantee of payment. The lien, for up to 15 percent of the property's value, is available for buildings being newly built or those being repaired, rebuilt, or improved.

Priority. A mechanics' lien has priority based on the order in which other liens have been or will be filed.

Lien creation and release

Notice and filing. A notice of lien claim must be served on the property owner within 120 days after the last time labor or materials were provided. After serving the notice, the Petition to Establish a Lien must be filed with the circuit court within 180 days of the last time labor or materials were provided. The lien claimant then has 1 year to file a Petition to Enforce a Lien.

While lien waivers between the homeowner and contractor are unregulated, Maryland law does prohibit subcontractors and suppliers from waiving their right to file a mechanics' lien.

Establishment. A mechanics' lien attaches to the property when it is formally established by a judicial order.

Release. When the property owner pays the contractor the amount due, the contractor must give the owner a signed release of lien.

ENVIRONMENTAL DISCLOSURES

Chesapeake Bay
Maryland Department of Environment

Chesapeake Bay

Area of critical concern. An Area of State Critical Concern is defined as a specific geographic area of the State which, based on studies of physical, social, economic, and governmental conditions and trends, is demonstrated to be so unusual or significant to the State that the Secretary designates it for special management attention to ensure the preservation, conservation, or utilization of its special values.

With the approval of local governments, the Maryland Division of State Planning designates certain wetlands as Areas of Critical State Concern. The areas then receive special protection regarding activities allowed within their boundaries.

Chesapeake Bay Agreement. The Chesapeake Bay is one such area of critical concern. The Bay is the largest estuary in the United States and is Maryland's largest natural resource. The Bay drains a watershed of greater than 64,000 square miles and contains more than 13 million people and habitats for 2,700 species of animals and plants.

The area's extensive transportation network encouraged the development of commercial activities ranging from fishing, shipbuilding, agriculture, and manufacturing, to chemical production. The extensive development drastically impacted the health of the area's ecosystem and led to research by the EPA starting in 1975.

The EPA's findings resulted in the first Chesapeake Bay Agreement formed by Maryland, Virginia, Pennsylvania, and the District of Columbia, along with the federal government. The agreement was to work together to improve and protect the Bay's water quality and living resources.

The Chesapeake Bay Agreement was updated in 2000 to improve water quality and protect and restore living resources, vital habitats, and water quality through reasonable land use. The updated agreement is designed to build on past restoration actions and continue commitments outlined in previous agreements.

Chesapeake Bay Critical Area Law. In 1984, Maryland approved the Chesapeake Bay Critical Area Law to regulate land use and development activities within 1,000 feet of tidal waters of the Bay. The intent was to improve the water quality and habitat in the Bay and to restrict construction, clearing, and vegetation management within a buffer zone between the shoreline and 100 feet from the shoreline. The law also established land use policies to accommodate growth but recognize that human activities in the critical area can create adverse environmental impacts. The law established the Critical Area Commission with its 29 members appointed by the governor.

To meet the goals of the law, the Commission must update and enforce the law; the state may revoke any builder's license for knowingly violating the law; the no-build buffer zone was increased from 100 feet to 200 feet for new residential construction in rural areas; and rules regarding the location for new housing were made stricter.

Required disclosure. Title 14-117 of the Maryland Annotated Code requires that all contracts and addenda for the sale of property used as a dwelling place for one or two single-family units contain the following notice:

Notice to Buyer Concerning the Chesapeake and Atlantic Coastal Bays Critical Area

Buyer is advised that all or a portion of the property may be located in the "critical area" of the Chesapeake and Atlantic Coastal Bays, and that additional zoning, land use, and resource protection regulations apply in this area. The "critical area" generally consists of all land and water areas within 1,000 feet beyond the landward boundaries of State or private wetlands, the Chesapeake Bay, the Atlantic Coastal Bays, and all of their tidal tributaries. The "critical area" also includes the waters of and lands under the Chesapeake Bay, the Atlantic Coastal Bays, and all of their tidal tributaries to the head of tide. For information as to whether the property is located within the critical area, buyer may contact the local department of planning and zoning, which maintains maps showing the extent of the critical area in the jurisdiction. Allegany, Carroll, Frederick, Garrett, Howard, Montgomery, and Washington counties do not include land located in the "critical area."

Maryland Department of Environment

Purpose. The Maryland Department of the Environment (MDE) was created to protect and preserve the state's air, water, and land resources for the public's health and safety.

Responsibilities and programs. The MDE is responsible for long-term planning and research as well as enforcement of environmental laws and regulations. The Department also provides technical assistance to industries and communities in taking responsibility for pollution, waste disposal, and emergency spills of waste or oil.

The Department has programs addressing cleaner air; regulating asbestos and radiation handling; collecting and disposing of solid wastes and hazardous substances; and improving water quality and providing safe drinking water.

Enforcement. The Department's enforcement and compliance actions are typically limited to helping correct minor violations with no formal enforcement action taken. However, if the violation is more serious or if minor violations recur, then the Department may impose penalties, corrective orders, injunctions, and criminal sanctions.

Lead. The Lead Compliance and Accreditation Division enforces Maryland's lead paint regulations and abatement procedures and accredits contractors who provide lead paint abatement services. The Lead Rental Registry requires property owners to register residential rental properties built before 1978 which may contain lead paint. Each time the occupancy of these rental properties changes, the property owner must obtain a new lead inspection certificate. Residential rentals built after 1977 and those that have been inspected and certified lead free are exempt from registration.

To help prevent lead poisoning, the Lead Poisoning Prevention program oversees community education of parents, tenants, rental property owners, home owners, health care providers, and anyone involved in lead paint abatement services.

LEASES

Lease terminations
Prohibited lease provisions
Withholding rent for tenant safety

Lease terminations   **Landlord notice to tenant.** Both landlords and tenants are required to provide a written notice to terminate a tenancy. If the lease does not specify the notice, the following are the minimum landlord-to-tenant notice requirements by law, not counting the day of delivery:

> ▶   1 week for weekly tenancies
> ▶   1 month for monthly tenancies, tenancies for a definite term, and tenancies at will
> ▶   3 months for yearly tenancies
> ▶   30 days for tenant's breach of lease

The tenancy and liability for rent terminates immediately if the dwelling becomes uninhabitable due to a fire or unavoidable accident.

Tenant notice to landlord. Minimum tenant-to-landlord notice requirements by law include the following:

> ▶   no notice for termination at end of certain term lease
> ▶   notice equal to period of tenancy in periodic tenancy
> ▶   30 days'-notice for victims of domestic violence or sexual assault with a protective; tenant must pay rent for 30 days after notice
> ▶   no notice for termination due to medical condition certified by physician; tenant must pay rent for up to 2 months' after notice

Prohibited lease provisions

Maryland landlords are prohibited from including any of the following provisions in a residential lease:

▸ tenant waives or forgoes any legal right or remedy, including the right to a jury trial

▸ a rental late payment penalty more than 5 percent of the rent due or more than $3 per week or $12 a month for weekly payments

▸ a termination notice shorter than provided by applicable law (longer notice periods are allowed unless the longer period is required of the tenant but not of the landlord)

▸ tenant authorizes landlord to take possession of premises or personal property without termination of the lease by action of the parties or by operation of the law and personal property abandoned without legal process

▸ anything against public policy

▸ landlord may use eviction proceeding or issuance of a termination notice as retaliation for a tenant planning, organizing, or joining a tenant organization to collectively negotiate with the landlord

▸ automatic lease term renewal not set apart from other provisions and not acknowledged by the tenant's written initials, signature, or witness mark

These prohibited provisions are unenforceable and, if an intent to enforce is demonstrated, can result in the tenant recovering incurred actual damages and attorney fees.

Withholding rent for tenant safety

Right to withhold rent. Maryland § 8–211 permits tenants to withhold rent as a remedy when a landlord fails to repair conditions and defects that constitute a fire hazard or serious threat to the life, health, or safety of the occupants of a residential rental unit.

Justifying conditions. Conditions that justify withholding rent include but are not limited to the following:

▸ lack of heat, light, electricity, or hot or cold running water, except if the lack is a result of the tenant failing to pay utility bills

▸ lack of adequate sewage disposal facilities

▸ rodent infestation in two or more dwelling units

▸ structural defect resulting a serious and substantial threat to the occupant's safety

▸ any health or fire hazard

Notice to landlord. The tenant must notify the landlord by certified mail or have an appropriate government agency, such as the local housing department or fire department, notify the landlord.

Rent escrow filing. If the landlord fails to correct the problem within a reasonable time after receiving the notice, the tenant may file a rent escrow action with the District Court who will then hold a hearing on the matter.

Hearing. If the court agrees that rent should be withheld, the escrow account can be established with the court. The tenant will then pay regular rent payments into the account.

During the hearing, aside from establishing the escrow account, the judge may return the rent money in question to the tenant as compensation, return the rent money to the landlord or tenant to pay for the repairs, or appoint a special administrator to ensure the repairs are made. When the landlord makes all necessary repairs, the money in the escrow account may be released to the landlord or distributed as ordered by the judge.

A tenant may not be evicted, the tenancy terminated, or the rent increased as a result of the tenant taking any legal action for repairs.

30 Other Maryland Laws & Practices
Snapshot Review

REAL ESTATE APPRAISERS ACT
- regulates licensing, certifying, and allowed activities for appraisers; established 16-member Commission for appraisers, management companies, and home inspectors

TIMESHARES

Time-share features
- multiple owners divide use of a property by time allotments; management company sells shares and maintains property; agreement specifies rules for use

Requirements
- developers register with MREC, file POS, designate licensed broker, may convert existing building and provide residents with 120-day notice, include required information in sales contract, to provide 1-year implied warranty on construction and heating/AC, 3-year implied warranty on common elements and major systems
- initial purchasers have right to cancel within 10 days with no closing until end of 10 days; purchasers of resales have 7-day right to cancel; cancellations with full refund and buyer waiver not allowed
- deposits to be placed in escrow account

MARYLAND HOMEOWNERS' ASSOCIATION ACT

Regulation
- Maryland Homeowners' Association Act and Division of Consumer Protection

Members' rights
- members' rights to attend HOA meetings, to vote on HOA matters, to examine HOA records, to receive annual budget, to submit disputes with HOA to Consumer Protection for resolution

Sales
- sales contracts to include required disclosures, required information for buyers, buyers' cancellation rights, and HOA restrictions; must include copy of articles of incorporation, declaration, bylaws, budget, fees and assessments, recorded covenants and restrictions
- buyers' right to cancel if documents not received prior to settlement or within 5 days of receipt of disclosures without reason and with full refund

NEW HOME WARRANTIES

Required disclosures
- builders to disclose whether or not they participate in warranty security plan and provisions of not participating; buyer to acknowledge in writing receipt and understanding of warranty plan and disclosure; failure to include acknowledgement can result in voided contract; buyer may rescind contract within 5 working days and receive full refund
- notice to purchaser to be provided to buyers of new homes; validated warranty documents to be provided to buyer within 60 days; homeowners have right to waive warranty or to rescind warranty within 3 working days

Warranty provisions
- plans to be operated by authorized business entity; to demonstrate financial security; to provide dispute mediation; to cover material and workmanship for 1 year, major systems for 2 years except appliances with shorter manufacturer warranty, structure for 5 years; include exclusions

- misrepresenting existence of warranty is unfair and deceptive trade practice with fine up to $50,000, 2 years prison, or both

TRANSFER TAX

Taxed transactions
- 0.5% of sale price charged for transfer tax split between buyer and seller; sales contracts to include language regarding split of tax payment

Exempt transactions
- 0.25% charged only to seller with first-time buyer exemption; government agencies; domestic partners; business entities; trusts and estates; county exemptions

AD VALOREM TAX

Tax rates
- set by local jurisdiction; dollars/$100 assessed value; assessed every 3 years

Tax payments
- paid annually on or before July 1 or semi-annually on September 30 and December 31

Delinquencies
- September 30 payments delinquent on October 1; December 31 payments delinquent on January 1; annual July 1 payments delinquent on October 1; delinquent taxes subject to interest and penalty and become lien on property; final delinquent notice sent on March 1
- lien remains on property until taxes, interest, penalties paid in full; unpaid taxes result in tax sale of the tax lien certificate at public auction; notice of sale to be sent to homeowner; list of properties to be sold published in newspaper 30 days after notice and once a week for 4 weeks
- unpaid debt is sold, not property; highest bidder at auction buys the debt and right to foreclose; homeowner must pay debt within 6 months to redeem property; failure to pay debt results in buyer filing foreclosure and taking on liability for debt within 2 years from sale

Owner's rights
- in Maryland Property Owner's Bill of Rights

MECHANIC'S LIENS

Features and use
- unpaid providers of labor or materials for construction project may file mechanic's lien for security interest in the property owned by person who failed to pay; available for new builds or repairs up to 15% of property value

Lien creation and release
- lien notice to be served on property owner within 120 days after last time labor or materials provided; lien to be filed within 180 days after last time labor or materials provided; lien to be enforced within 1 year
- lien attaches to property with priority based on order other liens have been filed; lien is released when full payment is received by contractor

ENVIRONMENTAL DISCLOSURES

Chesapeake Bay
- designated as area of critical concern where extensive development damaged the area's ecosystem; agreement put in place by Maryland, Virginia, Pennsylvania, DC, and federal government to improve water quality and protect living resources; updated in 2000 to protect vital habitats and water quality through reasonable land use; law approved to restrict construction, clearing, and vegetation management within 100 feet of shoreline and established land use policies; also established 29-member commission to enforce the law and increased buffer to 200 feet; local governments joined the effort

	•	the 100-foot buffer protects environments from man-made disturbances and filters water; it also minimizes damage from human activities
	•	all sales contracts are to include Notice to Buyer language regarding the critical area
MD Department of Environment	•	MDE created to protect and preserve the state's air, water, and land resources; responsible for long-term planning; has programs for cleaner air, asbestos, radiation, solid waste disposal, safe drinking water
	•	enforcement involves correcting minor violations and imposing penalties for serious violations
	•	enforces lead paint regulations and requires property owners to register residential rental properties built prior to 1978 and obtain new lead inspection with occupancy changes

LEASES

Lease terminations	•	landlord to provide minimum written notice of tenancy termination of 1 week for weekly tenancies; 1 month for monthly, definite term, and tenancies at will; 3 months for yearly; 30 days for tenant's breach of lease
	•	tenant to provide termination notice equal to tenancy period; not notice at end of lease; 30 days plus 30 days of rent for domestic violence and sexual assault; no notice plus up to 2 months of rent for certified medical condition
Prohibited lease provisions	•	provisions prohibited from being included in a lease include tenant waiving legal rights, excessive late payments, shorter termination notices, allowing landlord to take possession of premises or personal property without lease termination; eviction or lease termination based on retaliation; automatic lease renewal without tenant's written acknowledgement
	•	prohibited provisions unenforceable and can result in damages and attorney fees to tenant
Withholding rent for tenant safety	•	rent withheld for unrepaired dangerous defects; must notify landlord, file rent escrow if repairs not made within reasonable time; court to hold hearing on matter and order escrow account; tenant then to pay rent to escrow account until repairs are made
	•	tenant cannot be evicted, have tenancy terminated, or rent increased for taking legal action for repairs
	•	only serious and dangerous defects qualify for withholding rent, such as lack of utilities, rodent infestation, fire hazard, etc.

CHAPTER TESTS
Answer Key begins on page 543

CHAPTER ONE: THE REAL ESTATE BUSINESS

1. Property management and real estate asset management are both real estate management professions. The primary distinction between the two is that

   a. property managers always report to an asset manager.
   b. asset managers have greater knowledge of a property's finances.
   c. property managers handle day-to-day operations while asset managers manage portfolios of properties.
   d. asset managers are primarily responsible for maintenance technicians.

2. People in the real estate business who primarily focus on creating new properties are

   a. brokers.
   b. developers.
   c. zoning administrators.
   d. excavators.

3. The term "commercial property" generally refers to

   a. non-owner-occupied properties.
   b. retail, office and industrial properties.
   c. multi-tenant properties.
   d. retail properties.

4. Which of the following professionals involved in the real estate business are most concerned about procuring buyers and sellers for clients?

   a. Brokers and agents
   b. Property managers
   c. Corporate real estate managers
   d. Appraisers

5. Which of the following ways of specializing is common in the real estate brokerage business?

   a. By type of house
   b. By geography
   c. By financial background of client
   d. By type of mortgage

6. What is an advisory service provider?

   a. A broker of fee simple titles
   b. A corporate real estate broker
   c. A broker performing non-transactional services for a commission
   d. A broker who renders real estate services for a fee

7. The level of government which is most active in regulating real estate licensees is the

   a. federal government.
   b. state government.
   c. county government.
   d. municipal government where the person resides.

CHAPTER TWO: RIGHTS IN REAL ESTATE

1. What guarantees the right of private ownership of real estate in the United States?

   a. Common law
   b. Local statutes
   c. The Napoleonic Code
   d. The Constitution

2. Which of the following is the best definition of real estate?

   a. Land and personal property
   b. Unimproved land
   c. Land and everything permanently attached to it
   d. An ownership interest in land and improvements

3. Which of the following is included in the legal concept of land?

   a. The surface of the earth and all natural things permanently attached to the earth
   b. Only the surface of the earth that is delineated by boundaries
   c. The surface of the earth except for lakes and streams
   d. Everything above, on and below the surface of the earth

4. What are the three unique physical characteristics of land?

   a. Fixed, unchangeable, homogeneous
   b. Immobile, indestructible, heterogeneous
   c. Three-dimensional, buildable, marketable
   d. Natural, measurable, inorganic

5. The primary distinction between the legal concepts of land and real estate is that

   a. real estate includes air above the surface and minerals below the surface.
   b. real estate is indestructible.
   c. land has no defined boundaries.
   d. land does not include man-made structures.

6. The primary distinction between the legal concepts of real estate and real property is that

   a. real property includes ownership of a bundle of rights.
   b. real property includes improvements.
   c. real property is physical, not abstract.
   d. real estate can be owned.

7. Which of the following is included in the bundle of rights inherent in ownership?

   a. To inherit
   b. To tax
   c. To transfer
   d. To vote

8. Which of the following is an example of intangible property?

   a. Real estate
   b. Personal property
   c. Artwork
   d. Stock

9. The right to use real property is limited by

   a. the right of others to use and enjoy their property.
   b. the police.
   c. taxation and subordination.
   d. Title 12 of the U.S. Civil Code.

10. Surface rights, air rights and subsurface rights are

    a. inviolable.
    b. unrelated.
    c. separable.
    d. not transferrable.

11. Which of the following terms refers to the rights of a property that abuts a stream or river?

    a. Allodial
    b. Alluvial
    c. Littoral
    d. Riparian

12. What part of a non-navigable waterway does the owner of an abutting property own?

    a. To the low-water mark
    b. To the middle of the waterway
    c. To the high-water mark
    d. None

13. What is the "Doctrine of Prior Appropriation?"

    a. A pre-emptive zoning ordinance
    b. The right of government to confiscate land and improvements
    c. A doctrine that gives the state control of water use and the water supply
    d. A real estate tax applied to owners of water rights

14. Which of the following is considered real property?

    a. A tree growing on a parcel of land
    b. A tree that has been cut down and is lying on a parcel of land
    c. A tractor used to mow grass on a parcel of land
    d. A prefabricated shed not yet assembled on a parcel of land

15. The overriding test of whether an item is a fixture or personal property is

    a. how long it has been attached to the real property.
    b. its definition as one or the other in a sale or lease contract.
    c. how essential it is to the functioning of the property.
    d. how it was treated in previous transactions.

16. What is an emblement?

    a. A piece of equipment affixed to the earth
    b. A limited right to use personal property
    c. A sign indicating a property boundary
    d. A plant or crop that is considered personal property

17. An item can be converted from real to personal property and vice versa by means of which processes?

    a. Assemblage and plottage
    b. Application and dissolution
    c. Affixing and severance
    d. Personalty and severalty

18. The major sources of real estate law are legislation at federal, state and local level, and

    a. court decisions.
    b. professional real estate associations.
    c. real estate commissions.
    d. local practices.

19. What is the primary thrust of federal involvement in real estate law?

    a. Taxation
    b. Licensing
    c. Broad regulation of usage
    d. Zoning

20. Which level of government controls zoning laws?

    a. State
    b. Taxing authorities
    c. Federal
    d. County and local

21. A grocer temporarily installs special fruit and vegetable coolers in a leased grocery store in order to prevent spoilage. The coolers would be considered which of the following?

    a. Trade fixtures that are real property
    b. Trade fixtures that are personal property
    c. Permanent fixtures that are real property
    d. Permanent fixtures that are personal property

22. Under the doctrine of littoral rights, an owner claims ownership of all of the land underlying a lake where there are three other abutting property owners. Which of the following is true?

    a. The owner's claim is invalid, because the state owns the underlying land.
    b. The owner's claim is invalid, because the underlying land is shared equally with the other owners.
    c. The owner's claim is invalid, because he may only own underlying land to the middle of the lake.
    d. The owner's claim is valid, because the lake is navigable.

CHAPTER THREE: INTERESTS AND ESTATES

1. An interest in real estate is best defined as ownership of

    a. the full bundle of rights to real property.
    b. an estate.
    c. one or more of the bundle of rights to real property.
    d. the right to possession and use of real property.

2. Encumbrances and police powers are

    a. interests that do not include possession.
    b. limited forms of an estate.
    c. unrelated to interests.
    d. types of public interests.

3. What distinguishes a freehold estate from a leasehold estate?

    a. A freehold includes the right to dispose or use.
    b. A leasehold endures only for a specific period of time.
    c. A freehold cannot be defeasible.
    d. A leasehold is subject to government restrictions.

4. The highest form of ownership interest one can acquire in real estate is the

    a. dower and curtesy.
    b. conventional life estate.
    c. defeasible fee simple estate.
    d. absolute fee simple estate.

5. The distinguishing feature of a defeasible fee simple estate is that

    a. it can be passed on to heirs.
    b. it has no restrictions on use.
    c. the estate may revert to a grantor or heirs if the prescribed use changes.
    d. it is of unlimited duration.

6. Upon the death of the owner, a life estate passes to

    a. the original owner or other named person.
    b. the owner's heirs.
    c. the state.
    d. the owner's spouse.

7. How is a conventional life estate created?

    a. It happens automatically when title transfers unless a fee simple is specifically claimed.
    b. A fee simple owner grants the life estate to a life tenant.
    c. It is created by judicial action.
    d. It is created by a statutory period of adverse possession.

8. What distinguishes a pur autre vie life estate from an ordinary life estate?

    a. The pur autre vie estate endures only for the lifetime of the grantor.
    b. The pur autre vie estate endures only for the lifetime of the grantee.
    c. The pur autre vie estate endures only for the lifetime of a person other than the grantee.
    d. The pur autre vie estate cannot revert to the grantor.

9. Which of the following life estates is created by someone other than the owner?

    a. Conventional life estate
    b. Ordinary life estate
    c. Legal life estate
    d. Community property life estate.

10. Which of the following is true of a homestead?

    a. A homestead interest cannot be conveyed by one spouse.
    b. A homestead interest cannot be passed to the children of the head of household.
    c. A homestead interest is a form of conventional life estate.
    d. A homestead is a primary or secondary residence occupied by a family.

11. Dower refers to

    a. joint tenancy of husband and wife.
    b. a wife's life estate interest in her husband's property.
    c. a wife's homestead interest.
    d. a child's life estate interest in his or her parents' homestead.

12. Which of the following is an illustration of the legal concept of elective share?

   a. A surviving spouse places a lien on a debtor's property.
   b. A widow who was excluded from a will makes a claim to a portion of the couple's principal residence.
   c. A spouse who loses her home because of her husband's gambling debt sues in court for exemption from the debt.
   d. A widower whose spouse died without a will sues to change the provisions of the will.

13. A one-year lease on a house has expired, but the tenant continues sending monthly rent checks to the owner, and the owner accepts them. What kind of leasehold estate exists?

   a. Estate for years
   b. Estate from period to period
   c. Estate at will
   d. Estate at sufferance

CHAPTER FOUR: OWNERSHIP

1. When a single individual or entity owns a fee or life estate in a real property, the type of ownership is

   a. tenancy in severalty.
   b. tenancy by the entireties.
   c. absolute fee simple.
   d. legal fee simple.

2. Three people have identical rights but unequal shares in a property, share an indivisible interest, and may sell or transfer their interest without consent of the others. This type of ownership is

   a. joint tenancy.
   b. equal ownership.
   c. tenancy in common.
   d. estate in severalty.

3. The "four unities" required to create a joint tenancy include which of the following conditions?

   a. Parties must acquire respective interests at the same time.
   b. Parties must be legally married at the time of acquiring interest.
   c. Parties must be family members.
   d. Parties must have joint financial resources.

4. Unlike tenants in common, joint tenants

   a. own distinct portions of the physical property.
   b. cannot will their interest to a party outside the tenancy.
   c. may own unequal shares of the property.
   d. cannot sell their interest to outside parties.

5. In a community property state, a basic distinction is made between

   a. property acquired together and property acquired separately over the duration of the marriage.
   b. property owned privately versus property owned by the state.
   c. property acquired during a marriage and property already owned by each party at the time of marriage.
   d. property acquired during the marriage and property acquired after the marriage.

6. Who are the essential parties involved in an estate in trust?

   a. Owner, trustor and lawyer
   b. Owner, trustor and trustee
   c. Trustee, title company, and beneficiary
   d. Trustor, trustee and beneficiary

7. The distinguishing features of a condominium estate are

   a. ownership of a share in an association that owns one's apartment.
   b. tenancy in common interest in airspace and common areas of the property.
   c. fee simple ownership of the airspace in a unit and an undivided share of the entire property's common areas.
   d. fee simple ownership of a pro rata share of the entire property.

8. Who owns the property in a time-share estate?

   a. Ownership is shared by the developer and the broker.
   b. The property is owned by tenants in common or by a freehold owner who leases on a time-share basis.
   c. A real estate investment trust holds a fee simple estate.
   d. A general partner holds a fee simple interest and interval estates are owned by limited partners.

9. Which of the following is true of a cooperative?

   a. A cooperative may hold an owner liable for the unpaid operating expenses of other owners.
   b. The owners have a fee simple interest in the airspace of their respective apartments.
   c. Owners may retain their apartments even if they sell their stock in the cooperative.
   d. The proprietary lease is guaranteed to have a fixed rate of rent over the life of the lease term.

10. One difference between a cooperative estate and a condominium estate is that

    a. a default by a coop owner may cause a foreclosure on the entire property instead of just a single unit, as with a condominium.
    b. the condominium owner must pay expenses as well as rent.
    c. the coop owner owns stock and a freehold real estate interest whereas the condominium owner simply owns real estate.
    d. the condominium owner owns the common elements and the airspace whereas the coop owner only owns the apartment.

11. A unique feature of a land trust is that

    a. the trustee controls both the trustor and the beneficiary.
    b. the trustee takes ownership of both land and improvements.
    c. the identity of the beneficiary may not be identified.
    d. the properties in the trust are probated in the states where the properties are located.

CHAPTER FIVE: ENCUMBRANCES AND LIENS

1. Easements and encroachments are types of

    a. lien.
    b. deed restriction.
    c. encumbrance.
    d. appurtenance.

2. An affirmative easement gives the benefited party

    a. the right to possess a defined portion of another's real property.
    b. the right to prevent the owner of a real property from using it in a defined way.
    c. the right to a defined use of a portion of another's real property.
    d. the right to receive a portion of any income generated by another's real property.

3. There are two adjoining properties. An easement allows property A to use the access road that belongs to property B. In this situation, property A is said to be which of the following in relation to property B?

    a. Subservient estate
    b. Servient estate
    c. Senior tenant
    d. Dominant tenement

4. Which of the following describes a situation in which an easement might be created against the wishes of the property owner?

    a. The property has been continuously used as an easement with the knowledge but without the permission of the owner for a period of time.
    b. The owner of an adjoining property asks the property owner for an easement, is refused, and then uses the property anyway without the knowledge of the owner.
    c. The owner of an adjoining property decides he needs to widen his driveway by sharing his neighbor's driveway and sues in court to create an easement by necessity.
    d. The owner of an adjoining property grants an easement to a third party that includes an easement on the first property.

5. What is the primary danger of allowing an encroachment?

    a. An encroachment automatically grants the benefiting party an easement.
    b. The encroached party may be liable for additional real estate taxes to cover the area being encroached upon by the neighboring property.
    c. Over time, the encroachment may become an easement by prescription that damages the property's market value.
    d. An encroachment creates a lien.

6. A property owner who is selling her land wants to control how it is used in the future. She might accomplish her aim by means of

    a. an injunction.
    b. a deed restriction.
    c. an easement.
    d. a land trust.

7. What distinguishes a lien from other types of encumbrance?

    a. It involves a monetary claim against the value of a property.
    b. It lowers the value of a property.
    c. It is created voluntarily by the property owner.
    d. It attaches to the property rather than to the owner of the property.

8. A certain property has the following liens recorded against it: a mortgage lien dating from three years ago; a mechanic's lien dating from two years ago; a real estate tax lien for the current year; and a second mortgage lien dating from the current year. In case of a foreclosure, which of these liens will be paid first?

    a. First mortgage lien
    b. Mechanic's lien
    c. Real estate tax lien
    d. Second mortgage lien

9. The lien priority of junior liens can be changed by a lienor's agreement to

    a. forgive portions of the debt.
    b. assign the note.
    c. foreclose on the note.
    d. subordinate.

10. Among junior liens, the order of priority is generally established according to

    a. the date of recordation.
    b. the amount.
    c. the order of disbursement.
    d. special agreement among lienees.

11. What is meant by a "lien-theory" state?

    a. A state in which liens are given priority over other encumbrances
    b. A state in which a mortgagor retains title to the property when a mortgage lien is created
    c. A state in which the holder of a mortgage lien receives title to the mortgaged property until the debt is satisfied
    d. A state in which liens exist in theory but not in practice

12. A homeowner has hired a contractor to build a room addition. The work has been completed and the contractor has been paid for all work and materials but fails to pay the lumber yard for a load of lumber. What potential problem may the home owner experience?

    a. The contractor may place a mechanic's lien for the amount of the lumber against the homeowner's real property.
    b. The lumber yard may place a vendor's lien against the contractor and the homeowner for the amount of the lumber.
    c. The lumber yard may place a mechanic's lien for the amount of the lumber against the homeowner's real property.
    d. The homeowner has no liability because the contractor was paid for the lumber.

13. The process of enforcing a lien by forcing sale of the lienee's property is called

    a. execution.
    b. attachment.
    c. foreclosure.
    d. subordination.

14. An important difference between a judicial foreclosure and a non-judicial foreclosure is

    a. there is no right to redeem the property in a non-judicial foreclosure.
    b. a judicial foreclosure forces a sale of the property.
    c. a non-judicial foreclosure ensures that all liens are paid in order of priority.
    d. the lienor receives title directly in a non-judicial foreclosure.

15. A defaulting borrower may avoid foreclosure by giving the mortgagee

    a. a promissory note.
    b. a deed in lieu of foreclosure.
    c. a redemption notice.
    d. a lis pendens.

16. A property survey reveals that a new driveway extends one foot onto a neighbor's property. This is an example of

    a. a easement appurtenant.
    b. an encroachment.
    c. an easement by prescription.
    d. a party wall easement.

17. A property owner has an easement appurtenant on her property. When the property is sold to another party, the easement

    a. terminates.
    b. transfers with the property.
    c. transfers with the owner to a new property.
    d. becomes a lien on the property.

18. A brick fence straddles the property line of two neighbors. The neighbors agree not to damage it in any way. This is an example of

    a. a party wall.
    b. an encroachment.
    c. a trade fixture.
    d. a deed restriction.

19. A property owner allows Betty Luanne to cross his property as a shortcut to her kindergarten school bus. One day the property owner dies. What right was Betty given, and what happens to it in the future?

    a. A personal easement in gross, which continues after the owner's death
    b. An easement by prescription, which continues after the owner's death
    c. A license, which continues after the owner's death
    d. A license, which terminates at the owner's death

20. A court renders a judgment which authorizes a lien to be placed against the defendant's house, car, and personal belongings. This is an example of a

    a. specific judgment lien.
    b. general judgment lien.
    c. voluntary judgment lien.
    d. superior judgment lien.

CHAPTER SIX: TRANSFERRING AND RECORDING TITLE TO REAL ESTATE

1. Which of the following best describes the concept of "legal title" to real estate?"

    a. Ownership of the bundle of rights to real estate
    b. The right of a buyer or lender to obtain ownership under certain circumstances
    c. Possession of a deed
    d. Absolute proof of ownership of real estate

2. A person claims ownership of a parcel of real estate to a prospective buyer, stating that she has lived on the property for five years and nobody has ever bothered her. The claimant also shows the buyer a copy of the deed. The legal basis of this claim is referred to as

    a. prescriptive notice.
    b. constructive notice.
    c. hostile notice.
    d. actual notice.

3. Constructive notice of ownership of a parcel of real estate is primarily demonstrated through

    a. direct inspection to see who is in possession.
    b. title insurance.
    c. title records.
    d. a construction permit.

4. An owner transfers title to a property to a buyer in exchange for a consideration. This is an example of

    a. voluntary alienation.
    b. escheat.
    c. hypothecation.
    d. estoppel.

5. For a deed to convey title, it is necessary for the deed to be

    a. on a standard form.
    b. certified by the grantor.
    c. accepted by the grantee.
    d. signed by the grantee.

6. The only required clause in a deed of conveyance is one that

    a. states restrictions and limitations to the estate being conveyed.
    b. states the parties and the type of estate being conveyed.
    c. states that the grantor has done nothing to impair title to the property being conveyed.
    d. states the grantor's intention, names the parties, describes the property, and indicates a consideration.

7. The purpose of a covenant clause in a deed of conveyance is to

    a. state the grantor's assurance or warrant to the grantee that a certain condition or fact concerning the property is true.
    b. state the grantee's promise to use the property in a prescribed manner.
    c. warrant that the grantor has never encumbered title.
    d. describe the consideration that the grantee promises to give in return for title.

8. The type of statutory deed that contains the most complete protection for the grantee is a

    a. guardian's deed.
    b. special warranty deed.
    c. general warranty deed.
    d. quitclaim deed.

9. A person wishes to convey any and all interests in a property to another without making any assurances as to encumbrances, liens, or any other title defects on the property. This party would most likely use which of the following types of deed?

    a. A sheriff's deed
    b. A special warranty deed
    c. A partition deed
    d. A quitclaim deed

10. A one-time tax levied on a property for purposes of recording a transaction is called

    a. an intangible sales tax.
    b. a documentary stamp tax.
    c. an ad valorem tax.
    d. a franchise tax.

11. If a person dies with no legal heirs or relations and has left no valid will, what happens to real property owned by that person?

    a. It is taken by the state according to the process called escheat.
    b. It is reconveyed to the previous owner in the chain of title.
    c. It is taken by the title insurance company according to the process called involuntary alienation.
    d. It is conveyed to the highest bidder at a public auction.

12. Just prior to passing away, a person tells two witnesses that she would like her estate to pass to her husband. One witness records the statement and signs his name. This is an example of

    a. an enforceable holographic will.
    b. an unenforceable holographic will.
    c. an enforceable nuncupative will.
    d. an unenforceable nuncupative will.

13. If a person having several heirs dies intestate, the property will

    a. pass to heirs by the laws of descent and distribution.
    b. escheat to the state.
    c. pass to the surviving spouse through elective share.
    d. pass to the surviving heirs according to the provisions of the will.

14. A property owner can avert the danger of losing title by adverse possession by

    a. recording proof of ownership in county title records.
    b. inspecting the property and evicting any trespassers found.
    c. claiming hostile and notorious possession.
    d. filing a claim of right with the county recorder.

15. A hermit secretly lives in a cave on a 200-acre property. After twenty years, the person makes a claim of ownership to the property. This claim will likely be

    a. upheld through adverse possession.
    b. upheld because of the length of possession.
    c. declined through the doctrine of prior appropriation.
    d. declined because possession was secretive.

16. The fundamental purpose of recording instruments that affect real property is to

    a. prove ownership of the property.
    b. avoid adverse possession.
    c. give constructive notice of one's rights and interests in the property.
    d. assemble all relevant documents in a single place.

17. What is "chain of title?"

    a. The list of all parties who have ever owned real estate.
    b. The bundle of rights linked to the recorded title to a parcel.
    c. A chronology of successive owners of record of a parcel of real estate.
    d. Involuntary conveyance of title by statutory rules of descent.

18. The Torrens System differs from other title recording systems in that

    a. title is conveyed only when conveyance is registered on the title certificate.
    b. the Torrens System requires prior approval of a transaction before it can be registered.
    c. the Torrens System is not recognized by title insurance companies.
    d. it allows unrecorded encumbrances to cloud title.

19. To be marketable, title must be

    a. registered in Torrens.
    b. free of undisclosed defects and encumbrances.
    c. abstracted by an attorney.
    d. guaranteed by a title certificate.

20. With the exception of a Torrens certificate, the best evidence of marketable title is

    a. a signed deed.
    b. a title certificate.
    c. title insurance.
    d. an attorney's opinion.

CHAPTER SEVEN: LEASING ESSENTIALS

1. A lease contract is best described as

    a. a temporary transfer of legal title.
    b. an instrument of conveyance of limited title.
    c. a conveyance of a possessory interest.
    d. a title conveyance in exchange for rent.

2. When a tenant acquires a leasehold estate through a lease, what does the property owner acquire?

    a. A freehold estate
    b. A reduced leasehold estate
    c. A leasehold estate
    d. A leased fee estate

3. When an owner leases her property, she temporarily relinquishes the right to

    a. transfer the property.
    b. encumber the property.
    c. occupy the property.
    d. maintain the property.

4. Which of the following happens when a leased property is sold?

    a. The buyer acquires title subject to the lease.
    b. The lease is cancelled.
    c. The lease expires within thirty days unless renewed.
    d. A new lease is automatically executed.

5. A landlord and tenant complete a one-year lease. The following week, the landlord dies. Which of the following is true?

    a. The lease is cancelled and must be re-written.
    b. The tenant must continue to abide by all lease terms.
    c. The tenant may annul the lease at his or her option.
    d. The landlord's heirs may cancel the lease at their option.

6. If a lease does not state a specific ending date, when does it terminate?

   a. Immediately, since it is an invalid lease
   b. After one year
   c. When either party gives proper notice
   d. Whenever the property is sold

7. In accordance with the Statute of Frauds,

   a. leases in excess of one year must be recorded to be enforceable.
   b. oral leases are not enforceable.
   c. a five-year lease must be in writing to be enforceable.
   d. an unwritten lease is fraudulent.

8. What is one important difference between a sublease and a lease assignment?

   a. In an assignment, responsibility for the original lease is transferred completely to the assignee.
   b. In a sublease, the original tenant retains primary responsibility for performance of the original lease contract.
   c. A sublease does not convey any of the leasehold interest.
   d. A sublease conveys the entire leasehold interest.

9. Which of the following lease types conveys rights other than the rights to exclusive use and occupancy of the entire property?

   a. A rights lease
   b. A percentage lease
   c. A gross lease
   d. A net lease

10. An owner leases a property to a business in exchange for rent. The tenant is required to pay all operating expenses as well. This is an example of a

    a. proprietary lease.
    b. percentage lease.
    c. gross lease.
    d. net lease.

11. The percentage lease is most often used by

    a. industrial landlords.
    b. retail landlords.
    c. residential landlords.
    d. office landlords.

12. Which of the following summarizes the general terms of a ground lease?

    a. The landlord sells the ground to another, then leases it back.
    b. A tenant buys the landlord's ground, then leases the improvements.
    c. The landlord leases the ground floor of the building to a commercial tenant.
    d. The tenant leases the ground from the landlord and owns the improvements.

13. Among the usual remedies available to the injured party if tenant or landlord defaults on the terms of a lease is the right to

    a. sue to compel performance of the contract.
    b. enter a lien against the other's estate.
    c. lock the other party out of the premises.
    d. apply the security deposit to legal expenses.

14. A lease automatically terminates under which of the following circumstances?

    a. The tenant fails to pay rent.
    b. The leased property is foreclosed.
    c. The tenant goes out of business.
    d. The landlord cancels the lease.

15. One of the aims of the Uniform Residential Landlord and Tenant Act is to

    a. create a standard residential lease for use nationwide.
    b. force states to enact tenants' rights laws.
    c. establish uniform rental rates for each type of property.
    d. discourage the use of unfair and overly complex leases.

16. A primary theme of the Uniform Residential Landlord and Tenant Act is that both landlord and tenant

    a. waive their rights to sue for damages.
    b. bargain with each other in good faith.
    c. give sixty days' notice of intent to terminate the lease.
    d. observe the Realtor's Code of Ethics.

CHAPTER EIGHT: LAND USE PLANNING AND CONTROL

1. A central goal of public land use planning is to

   a. balance individual property rights with the community's welfare.
   b. develop an accord between property owners and tenants.
   c. impede development by for-profit developers and construction contractors.
   d. subordinate private interests to the public good.

2. The best definition of a master plan is

   a. an annual review of all land use permits and zones.
   b. a comprehensive analysis of existing land use patterns in a market.
   c. a state or regional land use law requiring compliance on a county-by-county basis.
   d. a fusion of land use laws and local land use objectives and strategies.

3. The principal mechanism for implementing a master plan is

   a. zoning.
   b. referendum.
   c. public elections.
   d. property management.

4. Zoning, building codes, and environmental restrictions are forms of local land use control known as

   a. force majeure.
   b. pre-emption.
   c. police power.
   d. concurrency.

5. If a municipality exerts its power of eminent domain against a certain property owner, what happens?

   a. The owner must pay higher property taxes or give up the property.
   b. The owner must cede an easement without receiving any compensation.
   c. The municipality annexes the property.
   d. The owner must sell the property or grant an easement to the municipality for just compensation.

6. In most jurisdictions, the master plan is managed by

   a. the mayor or county superintendent.
   b. the Board of Equalization.
   c. the planning commission.
   d. the zoning board of adjustment.

7. Counties and municipalities have the legal right to control land use due to

   a. the doctrine of appropriation.
   b. delegation of authority by state-level enabling acts.
   c. custom and tradition.
   d. consensus of the local community through referendum.

8. To be valid, a local zoning ordinance must

   a. reasonably promote community health, safety and welfare.
   b. comply with federal zoning laws.
   c. apply only to unique properties.
   d. be published periodically in the local newspaper.

9. What is the fundamental purpose of a building permit?

   a. To restrict the number of new development projects
   b. To establish the basis for an inspection
   c. To promote certificates of occupancy
   d. To ensure that improvements comply with codes

10. A primary objective of residential zoning is to

    a. control the value ranges of homes in a neighborhood.
    b. regulate density.
    c. ensure that only a limited amount of commercial and industrial activity is permitted in a particular residential zone.
    d. maximize intensity of usage.

11. A non-profit organization wants to erect a much-needed daycare center in a residential zone. Given other favorable circumstances, the local authorities grant permission by allowing

    a. a special exception.
    b. an illegal nonconforming use.
    c. a variance.
    d. a license.

12. A property that conformed with zoning ordinances when it was developed but does not conform to new ordinances is said to be

    a. a special exception.
    b. a variance.
    c. a legal nonconforming use.
    d. an anomaly.

13. One situation in which a zoning board might permit a variance is when

    a. it would cause the property owner unreasonable hardship to bring the property into compliance with zoning ordinances.
    b. the property owner is the one who brings the variance to the attention of the zoning board.
    c. the variance was caused by a contractor rather than by the property owner.
    d. the property is in conflict with no more than one zoning ordinance.

14. The approval process for development of multiple properties in an area includes submission of

    a. a covenant of restriction.
    b. a plat of subdivision.
    c. a court order.
    d. a developer's pro forma.

15. A county or municipal authority usually grants a certificate of occupancy for new construction only after

    a. all contractors have been paid for services.
    b. all work has been completed for at least thirty days.
    c. the construction complies with building codes.
    d. the tax assessor has valued the improvement.

16. In addition to government entities, organizations that may be able to condemn property under the power of eminent domain include

    a. public utilities.
    b. financial institutions.
    c. major employers.
    d. neighborhood associations.

17. A property owner is precluded by deed restriction from developing a thirty foot boat dock. The limitation prompts the owner to sell to another party. The new owner

    a. is free to build the dock since the next door neighbor built a similar dock two weeks later.
    b. takes title subject to the same restriction.
    c. can build the dock with special permission from the zoning board.
    d. may build, since the restriction is extinguished by the sale.

18. A declaration of restriction in a planned unit development is unlike a deed restriction in that

    a. it applies only to aesthetic standards of property use.
    b. it attaches to rights rather than interests.
    c. it cannot be terminated by a single individual.
    d. it takes effect only when approved by a homeowners' association.

19. A deed restriction or declaration of restriction may be enforced by means of a

    a. sheriff's warrant.
    b. zoning commission order.
    c. foreclosure action.
    d. court injunction.

20. A distinguishing feature of a deed condition is that

    a. it gives the grantor the right to re-possess the property if the grantee violates the condition.
    b. it ceases to apply if a violation is allowed to continue for a certain period of time.
    c. it can be filed at any time after title has been transferred.
    d. it restricts who may own the property.

CHAPTER NINE: LEGAL DESCRIPTIONS

1. What is the principal purpose underlying legal descriptions of real property?

    a. To create a consistent, unchanging standard for locating the property.
    b. To eliminate all possible boundary disputes.
    c. To comply with federal laws.
    d. To eliminate cumbersome metes and bounds descriptions.

2. Which of the following is a distinctive feature of metes and bounds descriptions?

    a. They use meridians and base lines.
    b. They identify an enclosed area, beginning and ending at the same point.
    c. They use lot and block numbers.as the street address.
    d. They incorporate elevation into the descriptions.

3. A certain legal description contains the phrase "...southeasterly along Happ Road to the stone landmark..." What kind of description is this?

    a. Plat survey plat of survey is
    b. Government grid
    c. Metes and bounds
    d. Rectangular survey

4. The abbreviation POB stands for

    a. perimeter of boundaries.
    b. point of beginning.
    c. point of bounds.
    d. plat of boundary.

5. What are the approximate dimensions of a township in the rectangular survey system?

    a . Thirty-six miles on a side
    b . Twenty-five square miles.
    c . Depends on the state.
    d . Six miles by six miles

6. The area running north and south between meridians is a

    a . range.
    b . township.
    c . strip.
    d . tier.

7. The area running east and west between base lines is a

    a . range.
    b . tier.
    c . parameter.
    d . parallel.

8. How many sections are there in a township?

    a. One
    b. Six
    c. Twelve
    d. Thirty-six

9. A section contains how many acres?

    a. 640
    b. 320
    c. 160
    d. 40

10. How many acres are there in the S 1/2 of the NW ¼ of Section 3?

    a. 20 acres
    b. 40 acres
    c. 80 acres
    d. 160 acres

11. If a parcel does not have a lot and block number and is too irregular to be described as a fraction of a section, the legal description

    a. is the street address.
    b. will include a metes and bounds description.
    c. will use an estimate of the sectional fraction.
    d. will create a special reference number.

12. The legal description of a parcel in a subdivision that has been recorded with lot and block numbers on a plat of survey is

    a. the lot and block number, with section, township and meridian references.
    b. the standard rectangular survey description.
    c. the subdivision plat map.
    d. the lot and block number.

13. A datum is a reference point used for legal descriptions of

    a. agricultural and ranch properties.
    b. properties that straddle state boundaries.
    c. properties located above or below the earth's surface.
    d. irregularly-shaped properties.

CHAPTER TEN: FUNDAMENTALS OF CONTRACT .LAW

1. An important legal feature of a contract is

    a. it represents a "meeting of the minds."
    b. it must use precise wording in a document.
    c. it is not voidable.
    d. it can be created only by an attorney.

2. According to contract law, every valid contract is also

    a. void.
    b. enforceable.
    c. enforceable or unenforceable.
    d. voidable.

3. The guardian for a mentally incompetent party enters into an oral contract with another party to buy a trade fixture. This contract

    a. does not meet validity requirements.
    b. is possibly valid and enforceable.
    c. must be in writing to be valid.
    d. is valid but unenforceable.

4. A prospective homebuyer submits a signed offer to buy a house with the condition that the seller pays financing points at closing. The seller disagrees, crosses out the points clause, then signs and returns the document to the buyer. At this point, assuming all other contract validity items are in order, the status of the offer is

    a. an accepted offer, therefore a valid contract.
    b. an invalid contract.
    c. a counteroffer.
    d. an invalid offer.

5. As part of a construction contract between a contractor and a buyer, the contractor promises to complete construction by November 20. This promise can be construed as

    a. competency on behalf of the contractor.
    b. mutual consent.
    c. good faith.
    d. valuable consideration.

6. An unscrupulous investor completes a contract with a buyer to sell a property the investor does not own. The sale contract for this transaction

    a. is voidable.
    b. must be in writing.
    c. is void.
    d. is illegal yet potentially enforceable.

7. A homeowner encourages an agent to aggressively persuade a buyer to purchase his house by overinflating historical appreciation rates. The agent and the seller agree that 25% annual appreciation would work, even though this figure is four times actual rates. The pitch succeeds, and the seller accepts the buyer's resulting offer. This contract is

    a. enforceable.
    b. voidable.
    c. void.
    d. valid.

8. The statute of limitations requires that parties to a contract who have been damaged or who question the contract's provisions

    a. must act within a statutory period.
    b. must select a specific, limited course of action for recouping their losses.
    c. must arbitrate prior to taking court action.
    d. must wait a statutory period before they may take legal action.

9. The purpose of the Statute of Frauds is to

    a. invalidate certain oral contracts.
    b. require certain conveyance-related contracts to be in writing.
    c. nullify oral leases and listing agreements.
    d. eliminate fraud in real estate contracts.

10. A seller immediately accepts a buyer's offer but waits eight days before returning the accepted document to the buyer. Meanwhile, the offer has expired. Which of the following is true?

    a. The buyer is bound to the contract since it was accepted immediately.
    b. The buyer has no obligations to the seller whatsoever.
    c. The buyer may not rescind the expired offer.
    d. The seller may sue for specific performance.

11. A buyer agrees to all terms of a seller's offer except price. The buyer lowers the price by $1,000, signs the form, and mails it back to the seller. At this point, the seller's offer

    a. is void.
    b. becomes an executory contract.
    c. becomes a counteroffer.
    d. has been accepted.

12. A buyer submits an offer to a seller. Two hours later, the buyer finds a better house, calls the first seller, and withdraws the offer. Which of the following is true?

    a. The buyer may not revoke the offer in such a short period of time.
    b. The first seller may sue the buyer for specific performance.
    c. If the seller accepted the offer, the buyer must perform.
    d. The original offer is legally extinguished.

13. Real estate contracts that are not personal service contracts

    a. may be assigned.
    b. are not assignable.
    c. must be in writing.
    d. are exempt from the statute of frauds.

14. Which of the following contracts must be in writing to be enforceable?

    a. A parol contract.
    b. A six-month lease.
    c. A two-year lease.
    d. An executory contract.

15. A good example of a unilateral contract is

    a. an option to purchase.
    b. a listing agreement.
    c. a personal services agreement.
    d. a sale contract.

16. A contract is discharged whenever

    a. there is a cooling period.
    b. both parties have signed it.
    c. it is performed.
    d. the parties agree to their respective promises.

17. A contract may be defensibly terminated without damages if

    a. it is abandoned by one party.
    b. it is impossible to perform.
    c. it is deemed to be valid.
    d. both parties breach its terms.

18. A landlord suddenly terminates a tenant's lease in violation of the lease terms. The tenant takes action to compel the landlord to comply with the violated terms. This is an example of a suit for

    a. rescission.
    b. specific performance.
    c. damages.
    d. forfeiture.

CHAPTER ELEVEN: NATIONAL AGENCY

1. The essence of the agency relationship between an agent and a principal can best be described as a relationship of

    a. mutual consent, consideration, and acceptance.
    b. diligence, results, and compensation.
    c. service, dignity, and respect.
    d. trust, confidence, and good faith.

2. In an agency relationship, the principal is required to

    a. promote the agent's best interests.
    b. accept the advice of the agent.
    c. provide sufficient information for the agent to complete the agent's tasks.
    d. maintain confidentiality.

3. A principal empowers an agent to conduct the ongoing activities of one of her business enterprises. This is an example of

    a. limited agency.
    b. general agency.
    c. universal agency.
    d. special agency.

4. A property seller empowers an agent to market and sell a property on his behalf. This is an example of

   a. general agency.
   b. special agency.
   c. universal agency.
   d. no agency.

5. Implied agency arises when

   a. an agent accepts an oral listing.
   b. a principal accepts an oral listing.
   c. a party creates an agency relationship outside of an express agreement.
   d. a principal agrees to all terms of a written listing agreement, whether express or implied.

6. An agency relationship may be involuntarily terminated for which of the following reasons?

   a. Death or incapacity of the agent
   b. Mutual consent
   c. Full performance
   d. Renewal of the agent's license

7. A principal discloses that she would sell a property for $375,000. During the listing period, the house is marketed for $425,000. No offers come in, and the listing expires. Two weeks later, the agent grumbles to a customer that the seller would have sold for less than the listed price. Which of the following is true?

   a. The agent has violated the duty of confidentiality.
   b. The agent has fulfilled all fiduciary duties, including confidentiality, since the listing had expired.
   c. The agent is violating the duties owed this customer.
   d. The agent has created a dual agency situation with the customer.

8. A principal instructs an agent to market a property only to families on the north side of town. The agent refuses to comply. In this case,

   a. the agent has violated fiduciary duty.
   b. the agent has not violated fiduciary duty.
   c. the agent is liable for breaching the listing terms.
   d. the agent should obey the instruction to salvage the listing.

9. An owner's agent is showing a buyer an apartment building. The buyer notices water stains on the ceiling, and informs the agent. The agent's best course of action is to

   a. immediately contract to paint the ceiling.
   b. immediately contract to repair the roof.
   c. suggest the buyer make a lower-price offer.
   d. inform the seller.

10. An agent owes customers several duties. These may be best described as

    a. fairness, care, and honesty.
    b. obedience, confidentiality, and accounting.
    c. diligence, care, and loyalty.
    d. honesty, diligence, and skill.

11. An agent fails to discover flood marks on the walls in the basement of a property. The agent sells the property, and the buyer later sues the agent for failing to mention the problem. In this case, the agent

    a. may be guilty of intentional misrepresentation.
    b. has an exposure to a charge of negligent misrepresentation.
    c. has little exposure, since the problem was not mentioned on the signed disclosure form.
    d. is not vulnerable, since the problem was not discovered.

12. An agent informs a buyer that a clause in a contract is standard language. After explaining the clause, the agent assures the buyer that the clause does not mean anything significant. If something goes wrong with the transaction, the agent could be liable for

    a. violating duties owed a customer.
    b. misinterpreting the clause.
    c. intentional misrepresentation.
    d. practicing law without a license.

13. An outside broker locates a seller for a buyer representative's client. In this instance, the outside broker is acting as

    a. a single agent.
    b. a dual agent.
    c. a subagent.
    d. a secret agent.

14. Agent Bob, who works for Broker Bill, obtains an owner listing to lease a building. Bill's other agent, Sue, locates a tenant for Bob's listing. In the absence of any arrangement to the contrary, Broker Bill in this instance is

    a. an implied agent.
    b. a dual agent.
    c. a single agent.
    d. a subagent.

15. An agent is operating as a disclosed dual agent on a transaction. In this case, the agent

    a. may not represent one party's interests to the detriment of the other.
    b. must withdraw from the relationships.
    c. must be obedient and loyal to both parties.
    d. must require that the principals share equally in paying the commission.

16. The duties of an agent acting as a facilitator are most similar to those of a

    a. subagent.
    b. single agent.
    c. dual agent.
    d. implied agent.

17. The meaning and import of the agency relationship should be disclosed to the client

    a. prior to completing a listing agreement.
    b. prior to or upon completion of an offer.
    c. upon the initial contact with the person.
    d. whenever a dual agency relationship is indicated.

18. Owner agents must disclose their agency relationship to tenants or buyers

    a. immediately prior to the initial contact.
    b. upon initial contact.
    c. whenever substantive contact is made.
    d. immediately following any offer executed by the customer.

19. A tenant representative should disclose his or her agency relationship to the owner's agent

    a. immediately prior to the initial contact.
    b. upon initial contact.
    c. immediately prior to substantive contact.
    d. immediately following any offer executed by the landlord.

20. A transaction broker should disclose his or her agency relationship to the transaction principals

    a. upon first substantive contact.
    b. upon completion of the listing agreement.
    c. immediately following completion of any offer.
    d. upon initial contact of any kind.

CHAPTER TWELVE: LISTING AGREEMENTS: AN OVERVIEW

1. To be valid, a listing agreement

    a. must be in writing.
    b. may be oral or written.
    c. must be an express agreement.
    d. must be enforceable.

2. The type of listing that assures a broker of compensation for procuring a customer, regardless of the procuring party, is a(n)

    a. exclusive right-to sell agreement.
    b. exclusive agency agreement.
    c. open listing.
    d. net listing.

3. An owner agrees to pay a broker for procuring a tenant unless it is the owner who finds the tenant. This is an example of a(n)

    a. exclusive right-to sell agreement.
    b. exclusive agency agreement.
    c. open listing.
    d. net listing.

4. A landlord promises to compensate a broker for procuring a tenant, provided the broker is the procuring cause. This is an example of a(n)

    a. exclusive right-to sell agreement.
    b. exclusive agency agreement.
    c. open listing.
    d. net listing.

5. A property owner agrees to pay a broker a commission, provided the owner receives a minimum amount of proceeds from the sale at closing. This is an example of a(n)

    a. exclusive right-to sell agreement.
    b. exclusive agency agreement.
    c. open listing.
    d. net listing.

6. The most significant difference between an owner representation agreement and a buyer representation agreement is

    a. the client.
    b. the commission amount.
    c. agency law applications.
    d. contract law applications.

7. A multiple listing authorization gives a broker what authority?

    a. To list the owner's property in a multiple listing service
    b. To sell several properties for the owner at once
    c. To sell or lease the property
    d. To delegate the listing responsibilities to other agents

8. A broker is hired to procure a customer for a client. In order to earn compensation, the agent must procure a customer who

    a. has seen the property and reviewed all documents.
    b. is ready, willing, and able to transact.
    c. has completed an acceptable sale or lease contract.
    d. will successfully complete the transaction at closing.

9. One of the most important actions an owner's agent is authorized to perform under an exclusive listing agreement is

   a. showing the property.
   b. assisting the customer in evaluating the relative merits of other properties.
   c. authorizing price adjustments in a timely manner.
   d. executing the sale or lease agreement.

10. An agent's performance of due diligence concerning a listing can best be described as

    a. initiating the marketing plan on or before a deadline.
    b. expending an amount of effort that is commensurate with the nature and size of the transaction.
    c. ascertaining the facts about the client and the property at the onset of the listing period.
    d. helping customers satisfy their needs to the extent they are entitled.

11. The amount of a real estate broker's commission is

    a. established among competing brokers.
    b. established through negotiation with clients.
    c. established by the Board of Realtors®.
    d. established by state real estate license law.

12. A client suddenly decides to revoke an exclusive right-to-sell listing midway through the listing term. The reason stated: the client did not like the agent. In this case,

    a. the client is criminally liable for discrimination on the basis of the cause for cancellation.
    b. the client may be liable for a commission and marketing expenses.
    c. the agent can sue the client for specific performance, even if no customer had been located.
    d. the agent has no recourse but to accept the revocation.

13. A "protection period" clause in an exclusive listing provides that

    a. the owner is protected from all liabilities arising from the agent's actions performed within the agent's scope of duties.
    b. the agent has a claim to a commission if the owner sells or leases to a party within a certain time following the listing's expiration.
    c. agents are entitled to extend a listing agreement's term if a transaction is imminent.
    d. an owner is not liable for a commission if a prospective customer delays in completing an acceptable offer.

CHAPTER THIRTEEN: GENERAL BROKERAGE PRACTICES

1. Which of the following represents the core activity of real estate brokerage?

   a. Prospecting for and qualifying potential customers
   b. Buying and selling properties for one's company
   c. Procuring customers for clients and effecting transactions
   d. Negotiating sale or lease terms for a client

2. What is co-brokerage?

   a. An owner agent and a buyer agent combine efforts to complete a sale.
   b. Outside brokers acting as subagents assist a listing agent in procuring a customer.
   c. An owner or buyer lists with several brokers to complete a transaction.
   d. Agents from a single agency cooperate to generate listings for the broker.

3. Which of the following best summarizes the critical skills in real estate brokerage?

   a. Communications, market knowledge, mathematics, and analysis
   b. Selling skills, law, and qualification
   c. Fiduciary duties
   d. Listing, marketing, facilitating transactions, and managing information

4. Which of the following is a valid distinction between a corporation and a proprietorship?

   a. A corporation has perpetual existence; a proprietorship terminates upon the owner's death.
   b. Proprietorships are liable for their actions, while corporations are not.
   c. Proprietorships may broker real estate, while corporations may not.
   d. Corporations are not subject to taxation, while proprietorships are.

5. One similarity between a general partnership and a limited partnership is that

   a. both are subject to double-taxation.
   b. both may broker real estate if properly licensed.
   c. the partners in both organizations take an active role in managing the business.
   d. all partners bear full liability for debts to the extent of the debt.

6. Two real estate companies agree to conjoin their resources for the development and sale of an apartment complex, for which profits will be shared equally. This is an example of

   a. a cooperative association.
   b. a real estate investment trust.
   c. a limited partnership.
   d. a joint venture.

7. Which of the following characterizes a real estate franchisee?

   a. A local brokerage owned and operated by a national franchisor
   b. A locally-owned brokerage affiliated with a national franchisor for purposes of enhanced image and resources
   c. A national brokerage company which charges local brokers fees for membership
   d. A national firm which contracts with local franchisors to promote the national identity

8. The term "Realtor"

   a. is the generic name used by brokers throughout the country as a trade identity.
   b. is the identity for any duly licensed, active agent or broker.
   c. is the trade identity for all members of any properly chartered real estate trade organizations.
   d. may only be used by brokers belonging to the National Association of Realtors®.

9. Real estate sales agents are legally authorized to

   a. represent their employing broker in procuring clients and customers.
   b. act directly on a client's behalf to discharge the broker's listing responsibilities.
   c. negotiate and execute contracts for sale on behalf of the client.
   d. take on the listing responsibilities for other listings in MLS.

10. An important distinction between an independent contractor salesperson (IC) and an employee salesperson is

   a. the IC is responsible for taxes; the broker does not withhold.
   b. the IC must obtain his or her own training; it is not provided by the broker.
   c. the employee is not entitled to company benefits.
   d. the IC must abide by all office policies and meeting schedules.

11. An important commitment employing brokers make to salespeople is

   a. a pledge of continued employment over a predetermined period.
   b. a guarantee of market-based, competitive commission structures.
   c. providing them with all listings in the agency.
   d. producing a sufficient number of customers through advertising to make a reasonable living.

12. A salesperson's commission rate and structure is established by

   a. state regulation.
   b. competitive conditions.
   c. agreement with other brokers in the market.
   d. negotiations with the client.

13. Three of the most important skills involved in the listing process are

   a. persuasion, appraisal, and market analysis.
   b. communicating, co-brokering, and timing.
   c. marketing, advertising, and conducting open houses.
   d. locating clients, pricing property, and making listing presentations.

14. Pricing property correctly is pivotal to marketing listings, because

   a. underpriced properties do not require the broker's services.
   b. overpricing a property will lengthen the time required to receive compensation for services.
   c. underpricing a property does not serve the best interests of a client.
   d. overpricing a property does not serve the best interests of customers.

15. The objective of the listing presentation is to

   a. explain how the agent and the agency enjoy a competitive advantage over other companies.
   b. condition the owner to price the property at the lowest possible level.
   c. provide all information necessary for the owner to execute the listing.
   d. execute the listing agreement, then explain its provisions.

16. In marketing an owner's property, the objective of an agent's marketing plan is to

   a. actively participate in the multiple listing service.
   b. expose the property to the maximum number of prospects in relation to marketing expenses and efforts.
   c. ensure that a transaction occurs that will compensate the agent.
   d. convince prospects of the property's superiority over other properties.

17. In obtaining offers from a buyer, an agent must be careful to

    a. pursue only those offers which are at or near the listing price.
    b. balance the owner's price expectations with the buyer's opinion of value.
    c. avoid disclosing what price the owner will accept
    d. avoid completing offers that are beneath market value.

18. When a property is "under contract,"

    a. the principals have agreed to an option to purchase, provided the buyer can obtain financing.
    b. the buyer and the seller are engaged in negotiations to complete a sale contract.
    c. the principals have entered into a sale contract and must satisfy any contingencies prior to closing.
    d. certain contingencies must be satisfied before the buyer or seller will agree to sign the sale contract.

19. Conversion is the act of

    a. mixing escrow funds with the broker's operating funds.
    b. appropriating client or customer deposits for use in the agency's business.
    c. converting an offer into a binding contract.
    d. converting escrow funds into equity funds in a property at the closing.

20. Commingling is the practice of

    a. blending escrow funds on a number of properties in one escrow account.
    b. mixing socially with prospects at open houses or other marketing functions.
    c. appropriating client or customer deposits for use in the agency's business.
    d. mixing escrow funds with the broker's operating funds.

21. Real estate advertising is a regulated activity. One important restriction in placing ads is

    a. a broker may only place blind ads in approved publications.
    b. a broker must have all advertising approved by the proper state regulatory agency.
    c. the advertising must not be misleading.
    d. sales agents may only advertise in their own name.

22. The three principal brokerage firms in a market agree to pay sales agents 15% more than any other competitor currently in practice. This is an example of

    a. collusion.
    b. price fixing.
    c. allocation of markets.
    d. steering.

23. Two leading agencies jointly agree to raise commissions charged a certain class of client to 8% of the sales price. Which of the following is true?

    a. This is a perfectly legitimate business practice.
    b. The brokers have illegally fixed prices.
    c. The brokers have allocated markets.
    d. The brokers have engaged in legal collusion.

24. A corporation would like an agent to sell its country grocery store. Included in the sale are the inventory, equipment, and real property. The agent locates a full-price buyer who does not want to acquire any of the business's actual or potential liabilities. To do this transaction, the corporation would most likely

    a. propose an asset sale.
    b. undertake a stock sale.
    c. propose an exchange.
    d. enter into a sale-leaseback transaction.

25. A broker is reviewing the balance sheet of her new listing to sell a business. Three of the entries on the books are licenses, trademarks, and goodwill. These would be examples of

    a. tangible assets.
    b. intangible assets.
    c. short-term liabilities.
    d. long-term liabilities.

26. In business brokerage, the notion of goodwill is best defined as

    a. the commitment by the agent to expend maximum effort on the listing.
    b. establishing pricing levels that will generate the good will of prospective customers.
    c. the value or price of the business over and above the value of its other assets.
    d. the portion of the sale price that is depreciable.

27. A syndication is

    a. a group of general partners who invest in and manage real estate for a profit.
    b. a group of inactive investors who join with a number of active partners to purchase, manage, and sell properties for a profit.
    c. a network of active brokers who purchase and sell properties.
    d. an organization engaged in illegal property acquisition and sale.

28. In order to sell interests in a syndication, an agent must

    a. obtain a Series 39 securities license.
    b. obtain a Series 22 securities license.
    c. obtain a real estate broker's license.
    d. obtain a syndicator's license.

CHAPTER FOURTEEN: OVERVIEW OF CONVEYANCE CONTRACTS

1. Several buyers are competing for the last available home in a desirable new subdivision. One buyer calls the owner-developer directly on the phone and offers $10,000 over and above the listed price. The developer accepts the offer. At this point,

   a. the parties have a valid, enforceable sale contract on the home.
   b. the parties have completed a verbal, executory contract.
   c. the parties may not cancel their contract.
   d. the developer could not entertain other offers on the property.

2. An owner completes a contract to sell her property. Before closing, the seller runs into financial trouble and assigns the contract to her principal creditor. The buyer cries foul, fearing the property will be lost. Which of the following is true?

   a. The buyer can sue the assignee to disallow the illegal assignment.
   b. The buyer can take legal action against the assignor.
   c. The assignor has completed a legal action.
   d. The sale contract is nullified.

3. During the executory period of a sale contract, the buyer acquires an equitable title interest in the property. This means that

   a. the buyer can potentially force the seller to transfer ownership.
   b. both parties own the property equally.
   c. if contract contingencies are not met, the buyer takes legal title.
   d. the buyer owns equity in the subject property to the extent of the funds deposited in escrow.

4. The purpose of an escrow account is to

   a. entrust deposit monies to an impartial fiduciary.
   b. enable the principals to access the funds in escrow without interference from the other party.
   c. ensure that the broker receives her commission.
   d. prevent the buyer from withdrawing the offer.

5. A sale contract contains an open-ended financing contingency: if the buyer cannot obtain financing, the deal is off. Six months later, the buyer still cannot secure financing. Which of the following is true?

   a. The seller may cancel the contract, since it can be ruled invalid.
   b. The buyer can continue indefinitely to seek financing, and the seller's property must remain off the market.
   c. The seller must return the buyer's deposit.
   d. The seller can force a lender to commit to a loan under fair financing laws.

6. In the event of a buyer's default, a provision for liquidated damages in a sale contract enables a seller to

   a. sue the buyer for the anticipated down payment.
   b. force the buyer to quitclaim equitable title.
   c. sue the buyer for all liquid assets lost as a result of the default.
   d. claim the deposit as relief for the buyer's failure to perform.

7. Which of the following best characterizes a conventional sale contract?

   a. Voluntary, unilateral, and executory
   b. Involuntary, bilateral, and contingent
   c. Voluntary, bilateral, and executory
   d. Involuntary, unilateral, and executory

8. A due-on-sale clause in a sale contract puts parties on notice that

   a. the full price of the property is due the seller at closing.
   b. any loans surviving closing become immediately payable.
   c. all of the seller's debts must be retired before or upon closing.
   d. third-party loans surviving closing may be accelerated by the lender.

9. A sale contract may specifically deal with tax withholding responsibility if the seller is a foreigner. What is this responsibility?

   a. The buyer must withhold 15% of the purchase price at closing for the seller's capital gain tax payment.
   b. The buyer must withhold 15% of the purchase price at closing for the buyer's capital gain tax payment.
   c. The seller must withhold 15% of the buyer's funds as a deposit on the buyer's capital gain tax.
   d. The seller must withhold 15% of the sale price to pay the seller's capital gain tax.

10. An important legal characteristic of an option-to-buy agreement is that

   a. the potential buyer, the optionee, is obligated to buy the property once the option agreement is completed.
   b. the optionor must perform if the optionee takes the option, but the optionee is under no obligation to do so.
   c. the contract can be executed at no cost to the optionee.
   d. it is a bilateral agreement.

11. A tenant has an option-to-purchase agreement with the landlord that expires on June 30. On July 1, the tenant frantically calls the landlord to exercise the option, offering the apology that she was busy with a death in the family. Which of the following is true?

    a. Since options contain grace periods, the landlord must sell.
    b. The tenant loses the right to buy, but can claim the money paid for the option from the landlord.
    c. The landlord does not have to sell, but must renew the option.
    d. The option is expired, and the tenant has no rightful claim to money paid for the option.

12. A tenant exercises an option to buy a condominium. The landlord agrees, but raises the agreed price by $3,000, claiming financial distress. The landlord does, however, offer the tenant two months of free rent before closing as an offset. Which of the following is true?

    a. The tenant can force the sale at the original terms.
    b. The landlord has taken a fully legal action which the tenant must abide by.
    c. The option is null, and the optionee may reclaim any option money paid.
    d. The landlord must offer sufficient free rent to equal the $3,000 price increase.

13. Which of the following is true regarding the legal nature of option contracts?

    a. They are not assignable.
    b. They are enforceable, whether written or oral.
    c. They give the optionee an equitable interest in the property.
    d. They must be recorded to be valid.

14. An important distinction between a contract for deed and a contract for sale is

    a. a contract for deed requires no action on the part of the seller.
    b. a contract for deed requires no action on the part of the buyer.
    c. the seller retains legal title in a contract for deed transaction until fully executed.
    d. the buyer acquires legal title in a contract for deed transaction.

15. While a property is under a contract for deed, the seller, or vendor, mortgages her equity in the property, and has a separate judgment lien placed on the property. Faced with financial loss, the vendor assigns the contract to another party, then leaves town. What can the vendee do in this case?

    a. rightfully cancel the agreement and reclaim all deposits.
    b. sue the creditor for removal of the judgment lien.
    c. disclaim the lien and the mortgage due to homestead rights.
    d. comply with the contract and take legal title when its terms are fulfilled.

16. A potential danger involved in a contract for deed is that

    a. the vendor may rightfully sell legal title to another party during the contract period.
    b. the vendor's rights to encumber the property are extinguished.
    c. the vendee may not have a right of redemption.
    d. the vendee must make an inordinately high down payment, which can be lost.

CHAPTER FIFTEEN: REAL ESTATE MARKET ECONOMICS

1. Price is best described as

    a. what suppliers charge for goods and services.
    b. the amount of money consumers are willing to pay for a product or service.
    c. the amount of money a buyer and seller agree to exchange to complete a transaction.
    d. a control placed on prices by the federal government.

2. Four principal determinants of value underlying the price for a product are

    a. durability, quality, scarcity, and materials.
    b. desire, utility, scarcity, and purchasing power.
    c. popularity, utility, quality, and discount.
    d. desire, costs, convenience, and time.

3. A town has a rapidly growing population, but there are no longer any vacant lots around the lake to build more houses. In this case, it is likely that the price of existing homes on the lake

    a. will stabilize, since the population must stabilize.
    b. will increase.
    c. will decline, since no further building can take place.
    d. will not show any predictable movement.

4. If there is a significant undersupply of homes in a market, construction will tend to increase. This is an example of

    a. supply outstripping demand.
    b. overpricing products.
    c. the price mechanism.
    d. the market tending toward equilibrium.

5. If commercial real estate rental prices are falling in a market, it is likely that

    a. demand has outstripped supply of space.
    b. the market is in equilibrium.
    c. the market is over-supplied.
    d. employment is increasing.

6. Which of the following is an important economic characteristic of real estate?

   a. The demand must literally come to the supply.
   b. Real estate is a highly liquid product.
   c. The product is quick to adapt to market changes.
   d. The market is centralized.

7. The foremost factor contributing to commercial and residential demand in a market is

   a. marketing.
   b. base employment.
   c. existing supply of properties.
   d. household income.

8. A construction boom in a market is an indication that prices

   a. have been increasing.
   b. have been declining.
   c. have been in equilibrium.
   d. have exceeded supply.

9. A local government could stimulate the real estate market by

   a. increasing labor costs and curbing the money supply.
   b. increasing taxes and interest rates.
   c. declaring a moratorium on construction.
   d. expanding the sewer system.

10. Two important concerns of retail property users are

    a. trade area population and spending patterns.
    b. quality of life and dwelling amenities.
    c. costs of occupancy and building efficiency.
    d. environmental regulations and access by suppliers.

11. Two important concerns of office property users are

    a. trade area population and visibility.
    b. convenience and neighborhood make-up.
    c. costs of occupancy and building efficiency.
    d. environmental regulations and zoning.

CHAPTER SIXTEEN: APPRAISING AND ESTIMATING MARKET VALUE

1. As a component of real estate value, the principle of substitution suggests that

   a. if two similar properties are for sale, a buyer will purchase the cheaper of the two.
   b. if one of two adjacent homes is more valuable, the price of the other home will tend to rise.
   c. if too many properties are built in a market, the prices will tend to go down.
   d. people will readily move to another home if it is of equal value.

2. Highest and best use of a property is that use which

   a. is physically and financially feasible, legal, and the most productive.
   b. is legal, feasible, and deemed the most appropriate by zoning authorities.
   c. entails the largest building that zoning ordinances will allow developers to erect.
   d. conforms to other properties in the area.

3. The concept of market value is best described as

   a. the price a buyer will pay for a property, assuming other similar properties are within the same price range.
   b. the price an informed, unhurried seller will charge for a property assuming a reasonable period of exposure with other competing properties.
   c. the price a buyer and seller agree upon for a property assuming stable interest rates, appreciation rates, and prices of other similar properties.
   d. the price that a willing, informed, and unpressured seller and buyer agree upon for a property assuming a cash price and the property's reasonable exposure to the market.

4. A significant difference between an appraisal and a broker's opinion of value is

   a. the appraiser tends to use only one or two of the approaches to value.
   b. the broker may not be a disinterested party.
   c. the broker is subject to government regulation in generating the opinion.
   d. the appraiser uses less current market data.

5. A notable weakness of the sales comparison approach to value is that

   a. there may be no recent sale price data in the market.
   b. the approach is not based on the principle of substitution.
   c. the approach is only accurate with unique, special purpose properties.
   d. sale prices cannot be compared, since all real estate is different.

6. The steps in the market data approach are

   a. choose nearby comparables, adjust the subject for differences, estimate the value.
   b. gather relevant price data, apply the data to the subject, estimate the value.
   c. select comparable properties, adjust the comparables, estimate the value.
   d. identify previous price paid, apply an appreciation rate, estimate the value.

7. In the sales comparison approach, an adjustment is warranted if

a. the buyer obtains conventional financing for the property.
b. the seller offers below-market seller financing.

c. a comparable is located in another, albeit similar neighborhood
d. one property has a hip roof and the other has a gabled roof.

8. To complete the sales comparison approach, the appraiser

a. averages the adjustments.
b. weights the comparables.
c. discards all comparables having a lower value.
d. identifies the subject's value as that of the nearest comparable.

9. One weakness of the cost approach for appraising market value is that

a. builders may not pay market value for materials or labor.
b. market value is not always the same as what the property cost.
c. comparables used may not have similar quality of construction.
d. new properties have inestimable costs and rates of depreciation.

10. The cost of constructing a functional equivalent of a subject property is known as

a. reproduction cost.
b. replacement cost.
c. restitution cost.
d. reconstruction cost.

11. An office building lacks sufficient cooling capability to accommodate modern computer equipment. This is an example of

a. physical deterioration.
b. economic obsolescence.
c. incurable depreciation.
d. functional obsolescence.

12. A home is located in a neighborhood where homeowners on the block have failed to maintain their properties. This is an example of

a. curable external obsolescence.
b. incurable economic obsolescence.
c. functional obsolescence.
d. physical deterioration.

13. In appraisal, loss of value in a property from any cause is referred to as

a. deterioration.
b. obsolescence.
c. depreciation.
d. deflation.

14. The first two steps in the cost approach are to estimate the value of the land and the cost of the improvements. The remaining steps are

a. estimate depreciation, subtract depreciation from cost, and add back the land value.
b. subtract deterioration from cost, estimate land depreciation, and total the two values.
c. estimate depreciation of land and improvements, subtract from original cost.
d. estimate obsolescence, subtract from the cost of land and improvements.

15. The roof of a property cost $10,000. The economic life of the roof is 20 years. Assuming the straight-line method of depreciation, what is the depreciated value of the roof after 3 years?

a. $10,000
b. $8,500
c. $7,000
d. $1,500

16. The income capitalization approach to appraising value is most applicable for which of the following property types?

a. Single family homes
b. Apartment buildings
c. Undeveloped land
d. Churches

17. The steps in the income capitalization approach are:

a. estimate gross income, multiply times the gross income multiplier.
b. estimate effective income, subtract tax, apply a capitalization rate.
c. estimate net income, and apply a capitalization rate to it.
d. estimate potential income, apply a capitalization rate to it.

18. Net operating income is equal to

a. gross income minus potential income minus expenses.
b. effective gross income minus debt service.
c. potential gross income minus vacancy and credit loss minus expenses.
d. effective gross income minus vacancy and credit loss.

19. If net income on a property is $20,000 and the cap rate is 5%, the value of the property using the income capitalization method is

    a. $100,000.
    b. $400,000.
    c. $1,000,000.
    d. $4,000,000.

20. The principal shortcoming of the gross rent multiplier approach to estimating value is that

    a. numerous expenses are not taken into account.
    b. the multiplier does not relate to the market.
    c. the method is too complex and cumbersome.
    d. the method only applies to residential properties.

21. If the monthly rent of a property is $3,000, and the gross rent multiplier (GRM) is 80, what is the value of the property?

    a. $45,000
    b. $240,000
    c. $267,000
    d. $288,000

CHAPTER SEVENTEEN: REAL ESTATE FINANCE

1. A homeowner borrows money from a lender and gives the lender a mortgage on the property as collateral for the loan. The homeowner retains title to the property. This is an example of

    a. intermediation.
    b. forfeiture.
    c. hypothecation.
    d. subordination.

2. Which of the following best expresses the mechanics of a mortgage loan transaction?

    a. The borrower gives the lender a note and a mortgage in exchange for loan funds.
    b. The lender gives the borrower a mortgage and receives a note in exchange for loan funds.
    c. The borrower receives a note in exchange for a mortgage from the lender.
    d. The lender gives the borrower a note, loan funds and a mortgage.

3. In a deed of trust transaction, which of the following occurs?

    a. The beneficiary conveys title to a trustee in exchange for loan funds.
    b. The trustee conveys title to a beneficiary in exchange for loan funds.
    c. The trustor conveys title to a trustee in exchange for loan funds from the beneficiary.
    d. The trustee conveys title to a trustor in exchange for loan funds from the beneficiary.

4. A lender lends money to a homeowner and takes legal title to the property as collateral during the payoff period. They are in a

    a. title-theory state.
    b. lien-theory state.
    c. state allowing land trusts.
    d. state where hypothecation is illegal.

5. A lender who charges a rate of interest in excess of legal limits is guilty of

    a. redlining.
    b. usury.
    c. profit-taking.
    d. nothing; there are no legal limits to interest rates.

6. A lender is charging 3 points on a $500,000 loan. The borrower must therefore pay the lender an advance amount of

    a. $1,500.
    b. $3,000.
    c. $15,000.
    d. $30,000.

7. The difference between a balloon loan and an amortized loan is

    a. an amortized loan is paid off over the loan period.
    b. a balloon loan always has a shorter loan term.
    c. an amortized loan requires interest-payments.
    d. a balloon loan must be retired in five years.

8. A distinctive feature of a promissory note is that

    a. it is not assignable.
    b. it must be accompanied by a mortgage.
    c. it is a negotiable instrument.
    d. it may not be prepaid.

9. When the terms of the mortgage loan are satisfied, the mortgagee

    a. may retain any overage in the escrow account.
    b. may inspect the property before returning legal title.
    c. may be entitled to charge the borrower a small fee to close the loan.
    d. may be required to execute a release of mortgage document.

10. In addition to income, credit, and employment data, a mortgage lender requires additional documentation, usually including

    a. an appraisal report.
    b. a criminal record report.
    c. a subordination agreement.
    d. a default recourse waiver.

11. The three overriding considerations of a lender's mortgage loan decision are

    a. points, interest rate, and loan term.
    b. the location of the mortgaged property, the borrower's cash, and the amount of the borrower's equity.
    c. the ability to re-pay, the value of the collateral, and the profitability of the loan.
    d. the amount of the loan, the borrower's income, and the down payment.

12. The loan-to-value ratio is an important underwriting criterion, for the primary reason that

    a. borrowers with no equity will default and abandon the property.
    b. the lender wants to ensure the loan is fully collateralized.
    c. a borrower can only afford to borrow a portion of the entire purchase price.
    d. a fair amount of borrower equity demonstrates good faith.

13. The Equal Credit Opportunity Act (ECOA) requires lenders to

    a. extend equal credit to all prospective borrowers.
    b. consider the income of a spouse in evaluating a family's creditworthiness.
    c. discount the income of a person involved in child-rearing or child-bearing.
    d. specialize lending activity by geographical area for improved customer service.

14. The purpose of an income ratio in qualifying a borrower is to

    a. safeguard against over-indebtedness.
    b. compare one's earnings to one's short-term debt.
    c. identify the highest possible interest rate that the borrower can afford.
    d. quantify the borrower's assets to the fullest extent.

15. A borrower's debt ratio is derived by

    a. dividing one's total debt by one's debt payments.
    b. dividing one's gross income by one's assets.
    c. dividing one's gross income by one's debts.
    d. dividing one's debts by one's gross income.

16. A lender's commitment to lend funds to a borrower in order to retire another outstanding loan is called a

    a. conditional loan commitment.
    b. firm loan commitment.
    c. take-out loan commitment.
    d. lock-in loan commitment.

17. At the closing of a mortgage loan

    a. the borrower pays off the note and receives clear title.
    b. the lender issues a firm loan commitment.
    c. the parties complete all loan origination documents and the loan is funded.
    d. the borrower's loan application is complete and the file closed.

18. Which laws or regulations require mortgage lenders to disclose financing costs and annual percentage rate to a borrower before funding a loan?

    a. The Equal Credit Opportunity Act
    b. Truth-in-Lending laws
    c. The Real Estate Settlement Procedures Act
    d. Federal Fair Housing Laws

19. Which laws or regulations prevent mortgage lenders from discriminating in extending credit to potential borrowers based on race, color, religion, national origin, sex, marital status, age, and dependency on public assistance?

    a. The Equal Credit Opportunity Act
    b. Truth-in-Lending laws
    c. The Real Estate Settlement Procedures Act
    d. Federal Fair Housing Laws

20. Which laws or regulations require mortgage lenders to provide an estimate of closing costs to a borrower and forbid them to pay kickbacks for referrals?

    a. the Equal Credit Opportunity Act.
    b. Truth-in-Lending laws.
    c. the Real Estate Settlement Procedures Act.
    d. Federal Fair Housing Laws.

21. The Federal Reserve System regulates the money supply in which of the following ways?

    a. Selling securities, printing money, and controlling lending underwriting requirements
    b. Buying securities, changing the discount rate, and controlling banking reserves
    c. Printing money, changing interest rates, and selling T-bills
    d. Controlling the prime rate, trading securities, and purchasing loans

22. One of the primary purposes for the secondary mortgage market is to

    a. cycle funds back to primary lenders so they can make more loans.
    b. issue second mortgages and sell them in the home equity market.
    c. lend funds to banks so they can make more loans.
    d. pay off defaulted loans made by primary mortgage lenders.

23. The major players in the secondary mortgage market are

    a. Fannie Mae, Freddie Mac, and Ginnie Mae.
    b. Fannie Mae, GMAC, and MGIC.
    c. Freddie Mac, FHA, and VA.
    d. Fannie Mae, Freddie Mac, and the Federal Reserve.

24. A principal role of FNMA is to

    a. guarantee FHA-backed and VA-backed loans.
    b. insure FHA-backed and VA-backed loans.
    c. purchase FHA-backed and VA-backed loans.
    d. originate FHA-backed and VA-backed loans.

25. The primary role of the Federal Housing Authority in the mortgage lending market is to

    a. guarantee loans made by approved lenders.
    b. insure loans made by approved lenders.
    c. purchase loans made by approved lenders.
    d. originate loans made by approved lenders.

26. The principal role of the Veteran's Administration in the mortgage lending market is to

    a. guarantee loans made by approved lenders.
    b. insure loans made by approved lenders.
    c. purchase loans made by approved lenders.
    d. originate loans made by approved lenders.

27. A graduated payment loan is a mortgage loan where

    a. loan funds are disbursed to the borrower on a graduated basis.
    b. the interest rate periodically increases in graduated phases.
    c. the loan payments gradually increase.
    d. the loan payments gradually increase and the loan term gradually decreases.

28. A buydown is a financing arrangement where

    a. the lender lowers the interest rate on a loan in exchange for a prepayment of principal.
    b. the borrower pays additional interest at the onset in order to obtain a lower interest rate.
    c. the lender requires the borrower to buy down the price of the property by increasing the down payment.
    d. the borrower pays the lender additional funds to buy down the term of the loan.

29. The key feature of an adjustable mortgage loan is that

    a. the interest rate may vary.
    b. the monthly payment increases over the life of the loan.
    c. the principal balance does not amortize.
    d. the loan term can be shortened or lengthened.

30. One feature of a wraparound mortgage loan is that

    a. the loan is a senior loan.
    b. the seller offering the buyer a wraparound can profit from a difference in interest rates.
    c. the underlying loan must be retired.
    d. the second mortgage borrower may make payments directly to the first mortgage lender.

31. A builder is required to secure a loan with mortgages on three properties. This is an example of

    a. a participation mortgage loan.
    b. a blanket mortgage loan.
    c. a permanent mortgage loan.
    d. a bridge loan.

32. Which of the following is true of a loan with negative amortization?

    a. The loan is an interest-only loan.
    b. Payments are not sufficient to retire the loan.
    c. The loan balance is diminishing, or going negative.
    d. Additional interest is being added to the monthly payment.

CHAPTER EIGHTEEN: REAL ESTATE INVESTMENT

1. All investors desire their investments to increase in value. However,

    a. the degree of return is inversely related to the degree of risk.
    b. the more the investor stands to gain, the greater the risk that the investor may lose.
    c. investments requiring intense management have lesser returns.
    d. the more liquid an investment is, the greater the chances are that the investment will not appreciate.

2. Two of the rewards that investments offer are

    a. income and tax benefits.
    b. negative leverage and appreciation.
    c. appreciation and taxation.
    d. positive leverage and prestige.

3. An investor invests in fifteen diversified bond funds. This is an example of an investment in

    a. money.
    b. equity.
    c. debt.
    d. real estate.

4. A real estate investment can take a long period of time to sell. For the investor, this means that real estate is

    a. management intensive.
    b. insensitive to marketing.
    c. vulnerable to seller's markets.
    d. relatively illiquid.

5. Compared to a stock portfolio, a real estate investment would be considered

    a. a riskier investment.
    b. a more management-intensive investment.
    c. a shorter-term investment.
    d. a more leveraged investment.

6. Six investors purchase a shopping center. One investor manages the tenants and another handles the marketing and leasing. Two investors manage accounting and finance, and the remaining two run the management office. This is a possible example of

    a. a general partnership.
    b. a limited partnership.
    c. a real estate investment trust.
    d. an investment conduit.

7. Taxable income produced by an income property is

    a. gross income minus expenses plus land and building depreciation.
    b. gross income minus expenses minus land and building depreciation.
    c. gross income minus building depreciation plus land depreciation.
    d. gross income minus expenses minus building depreciation.

8. As a general rule, in deriving taxable income on an investment property, it is legal to

    a. deduct principal and interest payments from income.
    b. deduct principal payments from income.
    c. deduct interest payments from income.
    d. deduct principal and interest payments from income and capital gain.

9. Which of the following is true of the tax treatment of a principal residence?

    a. The owner may deduct the property's interest and principal from ordinary income.
    b. The owner may depreciate the property and deduct depreciation expenses.
    c. The owner can deduct any capital gain when the property is sold.
    d. The owner may be able to exclude capital gain from taxable income when the property is sold.

10. An investment property seller pays $14,000 in closing costs. These costs

    a. may be deducted from personal income.
    b. may be deducted from the property's income.
    c. may be deducted from the sale price for gains tax purposes.
    d. may be deducted from the adjusted basis for gains tax purposes.

11. Capital gain tax is figured by multiplying one's tax bracket times

    a. the sum of the beginning basis plus gain.
    b. the difference between net sale proceeds and adjusted basis.
    c. the sum of net sale proceeds and capital gain.
    d. the difference between net sale proceeds and capital gain.

12. Cash flow is a measure of how much pre-tax or after-tax cash an investment property generates. To derive cash flow it is therefore necessary to exclude

    a. cost recovery expense.
    b. interest expense.
    c. loan principal payments.
    d. net operating income.

13. One way investors measure the yield of an investment is by

    a. dividing net operating income by cash flow.
    b. multiplying the investor's required yield times after-tax cash flow.
    c. dividing cash flow by the investor's equity.
    d. multiplying cash flow times the price paid for the property.

CHAPTER NINETEEN: REAL ESTATE TAXATION

1. Which of the following is true with respect to real property taxation by the federal government?

    a. It may impose ad valorem property taxes and capital gain tax.
    b. It may not impose property taxes nor tax liens.
    c. There are no federal ad valorem taxes on real property.
    d. It may impose ad valorem tax, but not capital gain tax.

2. According to law, states

    a. may not levy real estate taxes.
    b. may not impose tax liens.
    c. may delegate taxing authority to county governments.
    d. may prevent federal taxation of real estate within their respective jurisdictions, if properly legislated.

3. The role of local tax districts is to

    a. levy income, sales, and property taxes to meet their budget requirements.
    b. manage their budgeted portion of real estate tax revenues levied and distributed by the state.
    c. impose property taxes for specific municipal services.
    d. place tax liens on its facilities.

4. A special tax district might be created to

    a. construct and manage a park district.
    b. create a two-mile extension of county sewer facilities.
    c. establish and maintain a public library.
    d. create a fire department.

5. Ad valorem taxes are based on

    a. the replacement value of property.
    b. the assessed value of property.
    c. the millage value of property.
    d. the broker's estimate of value.

6. The ad valorem tax base of a municipal jurisdiction is equal to

    a. the jurisdiction's annual budget times the tax rate.
    b. the total of all assessed values of properties minus exemptions.
    c. the total amount of ad valorem taxes required by the budget.
    d. the municipality's budget multiplied times the millage rate.

7. As part of the assessment process, many taxing entities utilize equalization boards in order to

    a. adjust millage rates within the district to ensure fairness.
    b. modify the tax rate from one neighborhood to the next.
    c. ensure that property owners have nearly equal tax bills.
    d. smooth out wide discrepancies of assessed values within the district.

8. A homeowner receives a tax bill that she feels is outrageous. This taxpayer may

    a. appeal to adjust the millage rate.
    b. appeal to adjust the district's budget.
    c. appeal to adjust the assessed valuation.
    d. not appeal.

9. The purpose of a homestead tax exemption is

    a. to exempt qualified property owners from ad valorem taxation.
    b. to offer an amount of tax relief on an owner's principal residence.
    c. to encourage multiple property investment.
    d. to exempt owners of principal residences who rent their properties.

10. A millage rate is derived by

    a. dividing the tax requirement by the tax base.
    b. multiplying the tax base times the tax requirement.
    c. adding an inflation factor to the prior year's tax rate.
    d. dividing the tax base by the tax requirement.

11. A homeowner's total tax bill is derived by

    a. dividing the tax requirement by the tax base.
    b. multiplying each district's tax rate times the assessed value of the property.
    c. multiplying each district's tax rate times the taxable value of the property.
    d. averaging the tax rate for each tax district, and multiplying the average tax rate times the assessed value.

12. A unique characteristic of a special assessment tax is that

    a. it only applies to properties which will benefit from the public improvement.
    b. the equalization board discounts levies for properties not affected by the public improvement.
    c. more valuable properties which stand to benefit will pay proportionately more taxes.
    d. it creates an involuntary junior lien on the property.

13. A tax certificate

    a. certifies to tax collectors that a property owner has paid all ad valorem taxes on the property for the calendar year.
    b. entitles its holder to apply for a tax deed after a certain period.
    c. exempts its holder from paying taxes on the particular property referenced by the certificate.
    d. waives a property owner's rights of redemption in a foreclosure.

14. An equitable right of redemption

    a. allows a holder of a tax certificate to redeem it for a tax deed.
    b. gives a delinquent taxpayer a grace period prior to the tax sale to pay property taxes.
    c. gives a holder of a tax deed the right to acquire the property named in the tax certificate.
    d. gives a delinquent taxpayer a grace period after the tax sale to pay property taxes.

CHAPTER TWENTY: PROFESSIONAL PRACTICES

1. The principal theme of federal fair housing laws is to

    a. ensure all Americans a fair chance to own a home.
    b. prohibit discrimination in housing transactions.
    c. ensure that housing transactions are negotiated fairly.
    d. prohibit agents from dealing unfairly with clients and customers.

2. It is illegal to discriminate in selling a house based on race, color, religion, or national origin. This is provided for through

   a. the Civil Rights Act of 1866.
   b. Executive Order 11063.
   c. the Civil Rights Act of 1968.
   d. the Fair Housing Amendments Act of 1988.

3. Which of the following laws or rulings extended discrimination to include gender, handicapped status, and family status?

   a. Executive Order 11063
   b. the Civil Rights Act of 1968
   c. the Fair Housing Amendments Act of 1988
   d. Jones v Mayer

4. An agent informs numerous families in a neighborhood that several minority families are planning to move into the immediate area, and that the trend could have adverse effects on property values. This activity is

   a. blockbusting.
   b. legal but unprofessional redlining.
   c. discriminatory misrepresentation.
   d. negligent misrepresentation.

5. A minority family would like to buy a home in a certain price range. The agent shows the family all available properties in a neighborhood of families with similar backgrounds. The agent did not mention a number of homes in the family's price range in other neighborhoods. This agent could be liable for

   a. blockbusting.
   b. providing unequal services.
   c. steering.
   d. nothing; his services were legal and acceptable.

6. An agent does not like a particular minority buyer, and is very short with the person, refusing to engage in lengthy conversation or show him any properties. A second minority party visits the office the next day. The agent is very forthcoming, and shows the person five prospective properties. This agent could be liable for

   a. providing unequal services.
   b. steering.
   c. misrepresentation.
   d. nothing; both parties were minorities, and therefore no discrimination occurred.

7. Following the client's recommendation, an agent conceals the availability of a property from an employed but pregnant and unmarried minority woman. This agent could be liable for

   a. discriminatory misrepresentation.
   b. steering.
   c. violating fiduciary duty.
   d. nothing: an agent may show or not show any property at his or her discretion.

8. A condominium complex prohibits ownership of any unit by persons under 55 years of age. The association claims it has made the prohibition properly. Which of the following is true?

   a. They are violating the Civil Rights Act of 1866.
   b. They are violating the Fair Housing Amendments Act of 1988.
   c. They are guilty of age discrimination.
   d. The prohibition may be legal.

9. An owner suddenly pulls a property off the market after hearing from the agent on the phone that the agent had received a full-price offer from a minority party. The agent then informs the offeror that the home has been removed from the market and is unavailable. Which party or parties, if any, have violated fair housing laws?

   a. The agent only
   b. The owner only
   c. The agent and the owner
   d. Neither agent nor owner

10. Real estate trade associations promote a code of ethics primarily to establish

   a. minimum standards of practice as imposed by law.
   b. fair housing law.
   c. high standards of practice for all facets of the business.
   d. grounds for license revocation.

11. The parts of the Americans with Disabilities Act that most concern real estate agents are those that deal with

   a. telecommunications and insurance.
   b. public accommodations and employment.
   c. state and local government.
   d. agency and public service.

12. If a licensee knows a negative material fact about a client's property that the client has not disclosed, the licensee must

   a. keep the fact confidential.
   b. report the seller to the local real estate board.
   c. disclose the information to others.
   d. change the seller's disclosure form.

13. How does CERCLA concern real estate agents?

   a. It may cause them to be held liable for improper disclosure of potential violations.
   b. It requires them to conduct Phase II Environmental Site Assessments.
   c. It makes them subject to Environmental Protection Agency orders.
   d. It absolves them of any responsibility for knowing about environmental hazards.

14. Which of the following is a fact about home warranties that an agent should be sure a client knows?

    a. If the homeowner has paid an annual fee for the warranty, there are no additional charges for service.
    b. Conditions that pre-existed the coverage date of the warranty will not be covered.
    c. Any item that is not specifically excluded in the warranty contract may be assumed to be covered.
    d. Warranties are usually purchased to cover the full term of the mortgage loan.

15. What is an agent's duty regarding inspections?

    a. Personally conduct a detailed inspection of all major structures and systems
    b. Accompany all inspectors as they inspect the agent's listed property
    c. Disclose the result of any inspection, if known to the agent
    d. Interview and hire inspectors for clients.

CHAPTER TWENTY-ONE: CLOSINGS

1. The purpose of the closing event is to

    a. confirm that the buyer has fulfilled all contract requirements prior to title transfer immediately after closing.
    b. ensure that the seller has marketable title before monies are transferred.
    c. conclude the process for loan approval.
    d. exchange legal title for the sale price.

2. A buyer's financing arrangements are often concluded at closing, because

    a. lenders do not fund loans unless title is being transferred.
    b. the lender wants to ensure proper handling of the collateral for the loan.
    c. the loan term must coincide with title transfer.
    d. the deed will be held as collateral for the loan.

3. The Real Estate Settlement Procedures Act prescribes closing procedures that must be followed whenever

    a. a first, second, or third mortgage lien is involved.
    b. the loan is to be sold to the FNMA.
    c. the buyer pays all cash for the property.
    d. the property is a residential complex in excess of four units.

4. A sale contract stipulates that a buyer is to pay the seller's title insurance expenses. This practice is not customary in the area. In this case,

    a. the buyer and seller must amend the contract before closing.
    b. the contract is voidable, since the seller must pay the expense.
    c. the buyer may pay or not pay the expense, at his or her option.
    d. the buyer must pay the expense.

5. A prorated expense on the settlement statement is

    a. a debit to the buyer and seller
    b. a credit to the buyer and seller
    c. a debit and credit to the buyer and seller
    d. a debit to one party and a credit to the other.

6. The amount a buyer owes at closing is equal to

    a. the excess of the buyer's debits over the buyer's credits.
    b. the excess of the buyer's credits over the buyer's debits.
    c. the excess of the seller's debits over the seller's credits
    d. the excess of the seller's credits over the seller's debits.

7. Which of the following are examples of closing items not prorated between buyer and seller?

    a. Taxes and rents
    b. Inspection fees
    c. Utilities and hazard insurance
    d. Condominium assessments and special assessment payments

8. Which of the following items are paid in arrears?

    a. Taxes and insurance
    b. Rents and interest
    c. Taxes and interest
    d. Rents and insurance

9. Which of the following items are paid in advance?

    a. Taxes and insurance
    b. Rents and interest
    c. Insurance and interest
    d. Rents and insurance

10. If a sale contract indicates that the day of closing is "the seller's day," this means that

    a. the seller must pay prorated expenses inclusive of the day of closing.
    b. the seller does not own the property on the day of closing.
    c. the seller may elect the proration method on the day of closing.
    d. the seller must pay the buyer's portion of prorated expenses instead of the seller's portion.

11. Documentary stamps are used to

    a. document the procedures employed to close a transaction.
    b. document the payment of a transfer tax.
    c. certify that a transaction was recorded.
    d. mail closing documents to principal parties after closing.

12. What is the Internal Revenue Service's Form 1099-S?

    a. The buyer's and seller's capital gain form
    b. A form that summarizes and reports transaction data from a closing
    c. A form brokers must submit if the buyer or seller is a foreigner
    d. A lender's tax form showing that a loan was funded for a buyer

13. Assume a seller at closing must pay transfer taxes at the rate of $1.00 for every $500 of purchase price, or fraction thereof. If the sale price is $345,600, how much tax must the seller pay?

    a. $69.12
    b. $70.00
    c. $691
    d. $692

14. If a seller paid $488 for transfer taxes at closing, and the rate was $1.00 for every $400 or fraction thereof of the sale price, what was the sale price?

    a. $195,500
    b. $1,950,000
    c. $195,200
    d. $1,952,000

CHAPTER TWENTY-TWO: OVERVIEW OF LICENSING AND REGULATION

1. In which of the following cases would a person probably be required to have a real estate license?

    a. As a favor, John Smith helps his sister locate an apartment, since he knows the area.
    b. Mary performs secretarial duties for her boss, a real estate investor.
    c. Bruce gets hired to find an office suite for a friend who is relocating her business.
    d. Laura lands a new job managing the reservations desk at a new hotel.

2. A license applicant signs up to take the state examination, but has failed to obtain an employer prior to the exam date. In this case, the applicant

    a. must re-schedule the exam.
    b. must find an employer before taking the exam.
    c. may take the exam, but must find an employer before a license can be issued.
    d. may take the exam and receive an inactive license.

3. A broker operates an office in a town on the state line. A buyer from the adjoining state wants to see homes on both sides of the border. In this case, the broker

    a. may operate in both states since the market's boundaries overlap state lines.
    b. may not show the buyer homes in the other state without a non-resident license.
    c. may show homes in the other state so long as the closing takes place in his home state.
    d. may not show homes in the other state unless accompanied by a licensee from that state.

4. A principal role of the real estate commission is to

    a. enact the state's real estate license law.
    b. administer state licensing requirements.
    c. adjudicate violations of license law in lieu of the state court system.
    d. institute a system of private real estate schools to fulfill educational requirements.

5. License regulators, empowered by state law to oversee brokerage practices, may

    a. take punitive actions against fraud or misrepresentation.
    b. limit the size of a brokerage to prevent possible monopoly.
    c. dictate the commission structures of practicing brokers and salespeople.
    d. disapprove a broker's branch office location to maintain competitive balance in an area.

6. A broker has her license suspended for violating state license law. In such a case, the licenses of her three salespeople are

    a. automatically activated.
    b. not valid.
    c. placed temporarily under the control of the state.
    d. unaffected.

7. The purpose of a recovery fund is to

    a. protect damaged licensees from clients who fail to pay earned commissions.
    b. assist in the liquidity of a troubled brokerage through low-interest loans.
    c. ensure that judgments against licensees will be collectible.
    d. replenish losses in escrow accounts of brokerages found to have mismanaged impounded monies.

CHAPTER TWENTY-THREE: RISK MANAGEMENT

1. Of the following risk management strategies, the one that aims at minimizing both the severity and the likelihood of loss is

    a. avoidance.
    b. reduction.
    c. transference.
    d. retention.

2. Insurance is a method of

   a. risk elimination.
   b. risk mitigation.
   c. risk outsourcing.
   d. risk acceptance.

3. How does disclosure manage risk?

   a. It deflects and reduces risk by preventing others from claiming they were misled.
   b. It eliminates the risk of committing an error.
   c. It accepts the risk of revealing confidential information.
   d. It transfers the risk of a code violation to the client.

4. Which of the following statements about a company procedures manual as a risk management device is true?

   a. It places all the responsibility for compliance on the broker.
   b. It relieves the licensee of responsibility for knowing and obeying the law.
   c. It can be a guide to compliance with the law.
   d. It adds to the risk of misleading the public.

5. In what sense is the use of standardized forms a risk management procedure?

   a. It eliminates the risk of being unable to draft a contract correctly.
   b. It reduces the risk of losing a client by having to make a referral to an attorney.
   c. It reduces the risk of committing an unauthorized practice of law.
   d. It eliminates the risk of wasting valuable time in creating custom forms.

6. Keeping thorough records of every transaction is not only a risk management technique, it is

   a. good for company morale.
   b. necessary for obtaining market share.
   c. a technique for discovering market trends.
   d. a legal requirement.

7. Which of the following communication records must (as opposed to should) be kept?

   a. Notes on every conversation.
   b. Copies of required communications to principals.
   c. Notes from company training sessions.
   d. Business cards of licensees one meets at open houses.

8. The standard E & O policy covers damages resulting from

   a. failure to disclose an environmental condition.
   b. antitrust violations.
   c. mishandling of earnest money deposits.
   d. negligence, error or omission in carrying out professional services.

9. Which of the following is a common risk relating to the agency relationship?

   a. Failing to inform and disclose properly.
   b. Failing to take a personal interest in a transaction.
   c. Acting as an exclusive agent without an oral agency agreement.
   d. Forgetting to record the listing agreement.

10. Even after giving buyer and seller the required information about property condition disclosures, the licensee may still be subject to legal action for

    a. failing to detect customer misrepresentations.
    b. failing to disclose known adverse facts.
    c. relying on publicly available market information.
    d. advising the purchaser to exercise due diligence.

11. In performing a comparative market analysis, a licensee must be careful to

    a. use the term "market value" whenever possible in the report.
    b. show a low suggested selling price to avoid a complaint of misrepresenting the value.
    c. include the results of a certified appraisal in the analysis.
    d. avoid creating a false impression that the licensee is a certified appraiser.

12. In fulfilling a listing agreement, one of the major risk areas is

    a. finding a buyer who turns out to be unqualified.
    b. exceeding the authority of the agreement.
    c. showing the property without the presence of the owner.
    d. cooperating with other licensees.

13. A simple way of reducing the risk of committing an error or omission in the contracting process is

    a. use a checklist of all items, contingencies, dates and responsibilities that must be met.
    b. delegate some of your responsibilities to the licensee who represents the other party in the contract.
    c. call the buyer and seller daily to check on progress.
    d. cut the list of necessary tasks down to a few essentials and concentrate on tracking those.

14. Regarding contracts and forms,

    a. once written and signed they cannot be changed except by a lawyer.
    b. real estate licensees may alter forms but not contracts.
    c. whoever originates them can make changes without the risk of unauthorized practice of law.
    d. the principals may make changes as long as they sign or initial each change.

15. The best way to minimize the risk of violating fair housing laws is to

    a. deal only with consumers who do not belong to a protected class.
    b. obtain education in the content and intent of the laws.
    c. make sure there is always a witness present at all meetings with consumers.
    d. stay away from transactions involving public housing.

16. A licensee risks violating antitrust law by

    a. being present at a conversation where the setting of commission rates is discussed.
    b. being present at a discussion of antitrust laws.
    c. charging a commission rate that happens to be the same as that charged by another firm.
    d. cooperating with another firm to do market research.

17. How is an intentional misrepresentation penalized?

    a. License discipline, fines, and possible incarceration.
    b. License discipline and fines, but no incarceration.
    c. License discipline only.
    d. Fines only.

18. All of the following are areas of risk for unintentional misrepresentation EXCEPT

    a. measuring and reporting property dimensions.
    b. describing properties and amenities.
    c. stating that a client should seek legal counsel.
    d. making statements about the presence or absence of hazardous substances.

19. To reduce risks inherent in reporting transaction progress to a client, the licensee should

    a. make reports orally only, never in writing.
    b. leave progress reporting to the inspectors and other experts.
    c. advise the client that it is company policy to make no progress reports until the contingency period is over.
    d. avoid statements of opinion and speculation in all reports.

20. How does sharing the qualifying function with a lender protect a licensee?

    a. It guarantees that a buyer will have a loan.
    b. It reduces the chance of presenting an offer from an unqualified buyer.
    c. It relieves the licensee of his or her due diligence responsibilities.
    d. It allows the licensee to avoid asking embarrassing questions.

CHAPTER TWENTY-FOUR: PROPERTY MANAGEMENT

1. Property managers have a _____ relationship with the property owner.

    a. non-binding
    b. partnership
    c. fiduciary
    d. subagency

2. One of the property manager's fundamental responsibilities is

    a. obtaining construction loans for the principal.
    b. financial reporting to the principal.
    c. finding a buyer for the property.
    d. maintaining good standing in a managers' professional association.

3. Effective gross income is defined as

    a. the total of scheduled rents.
    b. the total of all rents and revenues generated by a property.
    c. potential gross income minus debt service and reserves.
    d. revenue from all sources minus losses from uncollected rents, vacancies, and evictions.

4. The efficiency of marketing activities can be measured in terms of

    a. cost per tenant prospect generated per lease.
    b. number of ads produced per marketing dollar.
    c. dollars expended per square foot of vacant space.
    d. percentage of reserves expended on marketing.

5. If a property's vacancy rate is significantly lower than market rates, it may be a sign that the manager needs to

    a. lower rental rates.
    b. raise rental rates.
    c. find better tenants.
    d. improve management quality.

6. Why does a manager need to keep tenants happy?

    a. Happy tenants make fewer demands for services.
    b. Managers are contractually required to please tenants.
    c. Unhappy tenants make the owner look bad.
    d. High tenant turnover increases expenses and reduces profits.

7. What are the three kinds of maintenance a manager has to carry out for a managed property?

    a. Constructive, deconstructive, and reconstructive
    b. Routine, preventive, and corrective
    c. Scheduled, planned, and improvised
    d. Emergency, elective, and optional

8. The Americans with Disabilities Act requires property managers to

   a. ensure that disabled employees have the same level of access to facilities that all employees have.
   b. hire the disabled whenever possible.
   c. remove all existing barriers to the free movement of disabled persons within the property, regardless of the cost.
   d. remodel the ground floor of the property in accordance with ADA standards if it was built before 1978.

9. Which of the following statements about the property manager's responsibility for security and safety is true?

   a. The manager has no responsibilities for building safety beyond ensuring that fire doors and sprinklers are working.
   b. The manager's security responsibilities are limited to the common areas.
   c. A court may hold the manager responsible for the physical safety of tenants, employees, and customers in leased premises.
   d. The manager's security responsibilities are limited to tenants and their employees in their leased premises.

10. Commercial fire and hazard insurance policies usually require coverage to equal at least 80 percent of the property's

    a. replacement value.
    b. reproduction value.
    c. original cost.
    d. depreciated basis.

11. Trust funds to be handled by a property manager are likely to include all of the following except

    a. rents collected from tenants.
    b. cash for the management firm's operating expenses.
    c. security deposits.
    d. capital contributions from the property owner.

12. What kind of agency is commonly created by a management agreement?

    a. Universal
    b. Specific
    c. General
    d. Vicarious

13. The rights, duties, and liabilities of the landlord and manager are

    a. apportioned under the terms of the management contract.
    b. dictated by common law.
    c. identical.
    d. regulated by the Universal Landlord Tenant Relations Act.

14. Which of the following describes a gross lease?

    a. The tenant pays a base rent plus some or all of the operating expenses.
    b. The tenant pays a fixed rent, and the landlord pays all operating expenses.
    c. The tenant pays a base rent plus an amount based on income generated in the leased space.
    d. The tenant pays a rent that increases at specified times over the lease term.

15. If an apartment contains a refrigerator that is not included in the lease,

    a. the lessee is required to buy it from the landlord.
    b. the landlord is required to remove it.
    c. the lease is invalidated because of an incomplete property description.
    d. the property manager does not have to maintain it.

16. A basic responsibility of a landlord is to

    a. provide leased space at market rental rates.
    b. deliver a habitable property.
    c. keep the rental space freshly painted.
    d. refrain from entering the leased space at any time during the lease term.

17. How does a constructive eviction occur?

    a. A landlord obtains a court order to force the tenant to vacate the leased premises.
    b. A court officer forcibly removes the tenant from the premises.
    c. A tenant declares a landlord in default and vacates the leased premises.
    d. A landlord declares a tenant in default and takes possession of the leased premises.

18. Among the essential elements of a management plan is consideration of

    a. the competitive market for the property.
    b. the property manager's career goals.
    c. the property owner's net worth.
    d. the management firm's income goals.

CHAPTER TWENTY-FIVE: THE MARYLAND REGULATORY ENVIRONMENT

1. The Maryland Real Estate Commission must include how many professional members?

   a. 9
   b. 4
   c. 5
   d. 3

2. The executive director of the Real Estate Commission is appointed by

   a. the Governor.
   b. the membership of the Commission.
   c. the Chairman of the Commission.
   d. the Secretary.

3. Which of the following is NOT within the Commission's powers?

   a. Administer the Guaranty Fund
   b. Adopt a code of ethics
   c. Allow a conditional license
   d. Revoke real estate licenses

4. When a real estate license is terminated as a result of the licensee's illegal act or omission, the license has been

   a. revoked.
   b. denied.
   c. suspended.
   d. summarily suspended.

5. Which of the following statements is TRUE?

   a. Complaints may be submitted by members of the Commission.
   b. Documents supporting a complaint must be submitted within 10 days of the complaint submission.
   c. All complaints must be made under oath.
   d. Complaints must be filed with the Attorney General's office.

6. A copy of a complaint is sent to an accused licensee, who is asked to respond in writing within

   a. 5 days.
   b. 24 hours.
   c. 30 days.
   d. 10 days.

7. Based on a complaint investigation, the Commission may

   a. issue an award to the complainant up to $10,000.
   b. dismiss the claim.
   c. suspend the accused licensee's license.
   d. deny a hearing.

8. Hearing boards are made up of

   a. 5 members of the Commission.
   b. 2 members of the Commission and 1 member of the general public.
   c. 3 members of the Commission, at least 1 licensed professional and at least 1 consumer member.
   d. 4 members of the general public.

9. Under what condition might the circuit court order a stay of enforcement of a final decision?

   a. The stay is automatic when any petition for judicial review is filed.
   b. The petition for judicial review includes new evidence related to the complaint.
   c. The licensee files a bond up to $50,000.
   d. Under no conditions may the court order a stay.

10. What is the source of funds for the Guaranty Fund?

   a. Fines paid by licensees for violating license laws and regulation
   b. A one-time fee paid by license applicants
   c. Fees paid by licensees at license renewal
   d. Annual licensee assessments

11. Claims for payment from the Guaranty Fund may be made by

   a. the spouse of the licensee who was accused of the act or omission leading to the claim.
   b. an individual who suffered a financial loss as a result of a licensee's misrepresentation.
   c. the personal representative of the accused licensee's spouse.
   d. all of the above.

12. Knowingly making a false statement or material misstatement of fact about a Guaranty Fund matter is

   a. a misdemeanor.
   b. grounds for license revocation.
   c. grounds for license summary suspension.
   d. a felony.

13. John contracted with Broker Bob to sell his house and assist in locating a new house for John to purchase. The two transactions were to be separate. During the sale of John's house, Bob made an error on the sales contract that resulted in a financial loss for John of $10,000. Then during the purchase of John's new house, Bob recommended against a home inspection, resulting in a $25,000 financial loss for John when a foundation problem was discovered after the sale was final. John has filed a claim for reimbursement from the Guaranty Fund. If John's claim is awarded, what can he expect to receive?

   a. $35,000 reimbursement for the total losses
   b. $50,000 reimbursement as the maximum payment allowed
   c. Either $25,000 or $10,000 depending on which loss is being reimbursed
   d. $35,000 for the losses plus $5,000 for attorney fees

14. In the situation described in the preceding question, what penalty will Broker Bob face for the actions leading to John's financial losses?

    a. License revocation
    b. Repayment of the losses
    c. A lien on Bob's property
    d. License suspension and reimbursement of the Fund's payment amount plus interest

15. A licensee's failure to provide records and accounts to the Commission when requested may result in

    a. a $5,000 fine.
    b. the Commission bringing action against the licensee.
    c. license revocation.
    d. summary license suspension.

CHAPTER TWENTY-SIX: MARYLAND LICENSING REQUIREMENTS

1. Which of the following does not require a Maryland real estate license?

    a. An individual who collects rent for use of a property
    b. A consultant to an individual who subdivides and sells real estate lots
    c. A home builder selling a newly constructed house
    d. An individual who assists other people in finding residential real estate to purchase

2. Which of the following statements is TRUE?

    a. Maryland issues five types of real estate licenses.
    b. Salespersons may provide brokerage services on their own behalf as long as they are affiliated with a broker.
    c. Maryland real estate licenses are issued immediately after the applicant passes the licensure exam.
    d. Maryland licensees may affiliate with multiple brokers.

3. In Maryland, credit reports are a requirement for

    a. salesperson licenses.
    b. no licenses.
    c. broker licenses.
    d. all licenses.

4. Which of the following is a licensure requirement only for salespersons?

    a. Complete 60 hours of prelicense education
    b. Complete 3 clock hours of real estate ethics education
    c. Obtain a commitment from a licensed broker to become the broker's affiliate
    d. Be at least 18 years old

5. How many clock hours of broker education must an applicant complete for an associate broker license?

    a. 135
    b. 60
    c. 15
    d. 95

6. If an out-of-state licensed broker has practiced real estate for at least 3 of the 5 years preceding application for a Maryland reciprocal broker license, the applicant is exempt from

    a. submitting an irrevocable consent to the MREC.
    b. completing Maryland's continuing education requirements.
    c. holding a current and active license in the other state.
    d. completing Maryland's broker prelicense education requirements.

7. A reciprocal license is issued for

    a. 1 year.
    b. 2 years.
    c. 3 years.
    d. 4 years.

8. The Veterans Full Employment Act of 2013 mandates that military members, veterans, and spouses who are applying for licensure in Maryland must have their licenses issued within _____ of receipt of their applications.

    a. 30 days
    b. 45 days
    c. 60 days
    d. 90 days

9. If a licensed broker dies or becomes permanently disabled, who may continue the business on the broker's behalf?

    a. Any affiliated associate broker
    b. The affiliated associate broker who has been with the broker the longest
    c. An affiliated licensee who manages one of the broker's branch offices
    d. An adult member of the broker's family

10. To reinstate an expired license, a licensee must apply to the Commission within _____ of the expiration date.

    a. 1 year
    b. 3 years
    c. 2 years
    d. 4 years

11. Brandon obtained his first broker license on January 10 of 2022. When will this initial license expire?

    a. March 1st of 2023
    b. January 10th of 2024
    c. October 1st of 2023
    d. April 15th of 2024

12. Failure to renew a license on time results in

    a. prohibition to provide brokerage services.
    b. license suspension.
    c. license revocation.
    d. need to retake licensure exam.

13. A licensee with a graduate degree in real estate may complete _____ of coursework to meet continuing education requirements.

    a. 15 clock hours
    b. 10.5 clock hours
    c. 7.5 clock hours
    d. 5 clock hours

14. How many hours of ethics instruction does Maryland specify for meeting continuing education requirements?

    a. 1
    b. 2
    c. 3
    d. 5

15. Continuing education coursework

    a. is not required for the initial licensure period.
    b. must be taught in person in a classroom.
    c. is not required for license reinstatement.
    d. must be completed every 2 years.

16. Which of the following is FALSE? Licensed brokers may provide real estate brokerage services through a corporation or other business entity if the broker

    a. is in a contractual relationship with the entity.
    b. is not employed by the entity.
    c. has been designated as the entity's broker to provide brokerage services.
    d. notifies the Commission of his intent to provide the services through the entity.

17. Which one of the following is FALSE? When organizing and owning a business entity, a salesperson must

    a. obtain approval from the affiliated broker.
    b. direct commissions to be paid directly to the entity.
    c. be licensed.
    d. all of the above.

18. Under what circumstances are nonresident brokers required to maintain an office within Maryland?

    a. The broker's resident state requires Maryland residents who are licensed in the other state to maintain an office in that state.
    b. They hold a Maryland reciprocal license and have affiliated salespersons practicing real estate within Maryland.
    c. They are not affiliated with a Maryland licensed broker.
    d. Nonresident brokers are prohibited from maintaining an office within Maryland under any circumstances.

19. To qualify as a branch office manager, an individual needs to be one of the following:

    a. a licensed salesperson.
    b. a licensed salesperson with 3 years of brokerage services experience.
    c. a salesperson who has applied for broker licensure.
    d. a licensed associate broker who no longer wishes to be affiliated with the broker.

20. Failure to submit the required notice to inform the Commission of a main office or branch office change of address will result in

    a. automatic suspension of the broker's license.
    b. automatic revocation of the broker's license.
    c. a $500 fine.
    d. suspension of the branch office certificate.

CHAPTER TWENTY-SEVEN: MARYLAND REGULATION OF BUSINESS CONDUCT

1. A broker who provides brokerage services through a business entity

    a. does not need an individual real estate broker license.
    b. may not employ associate brokers or salespersons to provide services on behalf of the entity.
    c. must notify the MREC of the entity's existence.
    d. is violating the Maryland Brokers Act.

2. Commissions are typically calculated as

    a. a percentage of a property's listing price.
    b. a fee agreed upon between the property seller and the property buyer.
    c. a flat fee charged to the property seller by the brokerage.
    d. a percentage of the property's sale price.

3. Which of the following is legal?

    a. Offering a prize to an individual for obtaining listings.
    b. Offering a free property appraisal in return for an individual signing a listing agreement.
    c. Offering a prize to be given to one of a number of attendees at an open house just for attending the open house.
    d. Offering compensation to unlicensed individuals for referring customers to a licensee.

4. A service mark, company name, or business name used in advertising is called a(n)

    a. trade name.
    b. designated name.
    c. nickname.
    d. alias.

5. To ensure compliance with a brokerage's advertising policies as well as federal and state laws, advertisements created by a licensee, team member, or unlicensed personal assistant must be approved by

   a. the broker.
   b. the office manager.
   c. the team leader.
   d. any of the above.

6. A licensee's nickname may not be used on an advertisement unless

   a. approved by the broker.
   b. a trade name is also used.
   c. placed meaningfully and conspicuously on the ad.
   d. approved by the MREC.

7. Requirements regarding use of the Equal Housing Opportunity logo or slogan in advertising include

   a. the logo being at least ½ inch by ½ inch in size.
   b. the logo being smaller than the largest of any other logo used in the advertisement.
   c. approval from HUD obtained prior to including the logo in any advertisements.
   d. abbreviating the slogan as needed for space within the advertisement.

8. Which type of sign may be allowed on public right-of-way easements even in locales that require a permit for other types of signs?

   a. For Rent signs
   b. For Sale signs
   c. Open House directional signs
   d. No Parking signs

9. The purpose of an open house disclosure sign is to

   a. show the hours of the open house.
   b. inform attendees they may be eligible for winning a prize simply by attending the open house.
   c. provide attendees with the showing licensee's name and brokerage information.
   d. inform attendees that the showing licensee represents the seller.

10. Telemarketers are required to search the national do not call registry every _____ for numbers they are no longer allowed to call.

    a. 7 days
    b. 31 days
    c. 90 days
    d. 6 months

11. Which of the following is exempt from honoring the do not call registry?

    a. Real estate telemarketer
    b. Telephone surveyor
    c. Local government agency
    d. Contest promoter

12. The Federal Trade Commission standards of conduct for telemarketing calls mandates that telemarketers may only call consumers

    a. between 8 a.m. and 9 p.m.
    b. on week days.
    c. on land line telephones.
    d. who are on a national registry.

13. Violations of Maryland's telemarketing laws and the Maryland Solicitations Act can result in

    a. $10,000 fine.
    b. 5 years imprisonment.
    c. liability for restitution.
    d. prohibition of solicitations for up to 15 years.

14. In Maryland, telemarketers are required to register as solicitors with the

    a. Attorney General's Office.
    b. MREC.
    c. Department of Business Occupations and Professions.
    d. Secretary of State.

15. Maryland's law to control junk email is called

    a. the Maryland CAN-SPAM Act.
    b. the Maryland Junk Email Act.
    c. the Maryland Commercial Electronic Mail Act.
    d. the Maryland Electronic Spam Act.

16. Which of the following is NOT a requirement of the CAN-SPAM Act?

    a. The person or business who initiated the message must be identified in the header information.
    b. The message must include a valid telephone number for the initiator of the message.
    c. Subject lines must not be deceptive.
    d. The message must be identified as an ad.

17. Which statement is TRUE regarding penalties for violating the CAN-SPAM Act?

    a. Violations are subject to penalties up to $50,000 for each email.
    b. Certain misleading claims about products or services can result in imprisonment.
    c. Only the company whose product is being promoted is legally responsible for law compliance.
    d. Misleading claims about services violate telemarketing laws and can result in $20,000 penalties.

18. Which of the following commercial faxes is legal?

    a. A fax sent to a property buyer's agent with the seller's counteroffer
    b. A fax sent to a property owner offering real estate brokerage services
    c. A fax sent from one real estate agent to another agent's client to invite the client to an open house
    d. A fax sent to a prospective property buyer offering property inspection services

19. In a real estate transaction, who is the beneficial owner of trust money?

    a. The broker
    b. The seller
    c. The buyer
    d. The bank where the escrow account is held

20. Brokers must deposit trust money in the appropriate escrow account

    a. within 7 days of both parties accepting the sales contract.
    b. within 10 business days of offer acceptance.
    c. prior to closing of the transaction.
    d. prior to both parties signing the sales contract.

21. Which of the following is grounds for a summary suspension of a license?

    a. Failure to complete continuing education requirements
    b. Failing to keep a client's confidential information confidential
    c. Entering into a dual agency relationship without agreement from both parties
    d. Failing to promptly account for any money held in trust

22. If a transaction does not close, how long is a broker required to keep the related records?

    a. 5 years after the transaction terminates
    b. 3 years after the brokerage agreement is signed
    c. 5 years after the listing date
    d. There is no requirement to keep records for transactions that do not close.

23. Which of the following statements is true?

    a. A broker's supervision over an individual creates an employer/employee relationship.
    b. Brokers are not required to supervise nonaffiliated individuals who perform activities on the broker's behalf.
    c. Brokers are not liable for the conduct of independent contractors.
    d. A broker's supervision over an independent contractor does not alter the independent status of the contractor.

24. Maryland law requires brokers to exercise "reasonable and adequate" supervision, which includes which of the following factors?

    a. A written policies manual containing guidance on the use of unlicensed personal assistants
    b. Weekly training sessions
    c. Continuing education tutorials
    d. Instructions on creating a policies manual

25. When a licensee commits a prohibited act that is criminal in nature, the Commission will base the penalty on several factors, including

    a. the good faith of the licensee.
    b. how the crime relates to the licensee's fitness as a licensee.
    c. where the crime took place.
    d. whether or not the licensee was convicted in a court of law.

26. Which of the following activities is an unlicensed personal assistant prohibited from performing?

    a. Computing a commission check
    b. Arranging the date and time of a home inspection
    c. Scheduling an open house
    d. Accepting compensation based on real estate activity

27. Which statement is TRUE?

    a. A real estate team is two or more licensed brokers who work together to provide brokerage services and represent themselves to the public as part of one entity.
    b. A team is required to designate a licensed broker as the team leader.
    c. Teams are supervised by the affiliated broker and not by the team leader.
    d. All team members must be affiliated with the same broker.

28. Which statement is FALSE?

    a. Licensees must present all written offers to the seller immediately.
    b. If an offer does not include an expiration date, the seller must respond within 7 business days.
    c. Buyers may withdraw an offer any time prior to being notified the seller accepted the offer.
    d. An offer becomes a legally binding sales contract once the seller accepts it and the buyer is notified.

29. Several Maryland counties, including Allegany, Carroll, and Montgomery, are exempt from including a disclosure concerning _____ in a sales contract.

    a. lead-based paint
    b. licensee as the buyer
    c. ground rent
    d. high noise levels

30. With the initial sale of a condominium, the developer must provide the buyer with a public offering statement and give the buyer _____ to cancel the contract and receive a full refund of the down payment.

    a. 5 days
    b. 15 days
    c. 20 days
    d. 30 days

CHAPTER TWENTY-EIGHT: MARYLAND BROKERAGE RELATIONSHIPS AND DISCLOSURE

1. Which type of agent has a brokerage relationship with the seller but assists the buyer in acquiring a property being sold?

    a. Seller's agent
    b. Buyer's agent
    c. Subagent
    d. Dual agent

2. A brokerage relationship is formed

    a. when a licensee and consumer discuss representation options.
    b. at first contact between a licensee and customer.
    c. when a customer pays the licensee for brokerage services.
    d. when a customer and a licensee sign a brokerage agreement.

3. Which of the following does NOT belong in a brokerage agreement?

    a. A provision for cancellation of the relationship
    b. The obligations of the client
    c. The date by which a termination notice must be received
    d. The conditions that will entitle the broker to be paid

4. If one party to a transaction does not agree to a dual agency, the broker must

    a. terminate that party's relationship agreement.
    b. terminate both parties' relationship agreements.
    c. assign an intracompany agent to represent that party.
    d. insist the party sign the dual agency consent form and complete the transaction.

5. Broker John represents property seller Samantha in the sale of her property. Recently, Ted approached John to ask questions about Samantha's property. What is the first thing John must do about Ted?

    a. Answer Ted's questions completely and truthfully
    b. Have Ted sign a brokerage agreement with John
    c. Disclose to Ted his agency relationship with Samantha
    d. Refuse to answer Ted's questions since John does not represent him

6. Agency disclosure notices must

    a. be no longer than three pages.
    b. use the appropriate legal terminology that an attorney can interpret for the reader.
    c. include the required information in one concise section.
    d. be printed in at least 10-point type.

7. Which of the following licensee's duties to a client continues after the relationship is terminated?

    a. Loyalty
    b. Confidentiality
    c. Obedience
    d. Diligence

8. Which of the following information is a licensee not required to keep confidential?

    a. Financial information about the client
    b. Personal information about the client
    c. Material facts about the client's property
    d. Willingness of the client to accept a lower price for the property

9. Which of the following is an exception to a licensee's duties to a client?

    a. Exercise reasonable care
    b. Answer questions truthfully
    c. Present all written offers to and from the client
    d. Perform ministerial acts for individuals other than the client

10. Which of the following is not considered a material fact about a property?

 a. Mold in a basement
 b. A murder on the property
 c. A leaking roof
 d. Faulty wiring

11. A brokerage relationship begins

 a. at first contact between the licensee and the client.
 b. when the client and licensee sign the written agreement.
 c. when the client and licensee either enter into an oral or written agreement.
 d. when the client chooses the type of relationship he or she wants with the licensee.

12. Which type of listing agreement is prohibited in Maryland?

 a. Net
 b. Open
 c. Exclusive agency
 d. Exclusive right-to-sell

13. Which statement is FALSE?

 a. All residential listing contracts must be in writing.
 b. Listing agreements must include the type of compensation to be provided to the agent.
 c. The agent must give a copy of the listing contract to the seller when the first offer is submitted.
 d. Listing agreements must state whether someone other than the client may pay the licensee.

14. Under what conditions may a Maryland licensee list property located in another state?

 a. The property owner is a resident of Maryland.
 b. The property owner is not a resident of Maryland,
 c. The Maryland licensee only advertises the property in the other state.
 d. The Maryland licensee obtains a license in the other state.

15. When must a licensee provide a property condition disclosure to a prospective property buyer?

 a. When the listing agreement is signed by the property seller
 b. When the buyer's agent shows the property to the prospective buyer
 c. When the seller's agent learns an offer is about to be submitted
 d. When the seller accepts an offer from the prospective buyer

16. Potentially harmful property conditions that a buyer is unlikely to detect are called

 a. stigmatized conditions.
 b. latent defects.
 c. critical facts.
 d. irreparable defects.

17. Which statement is FALSE?

 a. The disclosure portion of the property condition form is used to itemize the defects actually known to the seller.
 b. Sellers are required to have an investigation or inspection of the property performed to discover defects not already known to the seller.
 c. The property condition disclosure form is not a warranty by the seller of the property's actual condition if unknown by the seller.
 d. The disclosure form is to be signed by the seller who completed it to acknowledge the accuracy of the information.

18. Which statement is TRUE?

 a. The disclaimer portion of the property condition form is used when the property is being sold "as is."
 b. The disclaimer portion of the property condition form is used when the seller is offering a warranty as to the condition of the property.
 c. When using the disclaimer portion of the property condition form, the seller is not required to disclose any known latent defects in the property.
 d. A seller who uses the disclaimer portion of the property condition form is required to have the property professionally inspected for defects.

19. Property condition statements are to be signed by

 a. the seller's agent.
 b. the seller and the buyer.
 c. the buyer's agent.
 d. the property inspector.

20. Which of the following transactions requires use of a property condition disclosure or disclaimer statement?

 a. The resale of a single-family home by the current owner
 b. The initial sale of a property that has never been occupied
 c. The sale of a property in a tax sale
 d. The sale of unimproved real property

21. The law names all of the following as exempt from the requirement to disclose material facts EXCEPT the fact that

 a. a current resident is infected with HIV.
 b. a former resident committed suicide on the property.
 c. the distribution of illegal drugs occurred on the property
 d. a resident is infected with the COVID virus

22. An example of a stigmatized property is one that

    a. is exempt from transfer tax
    b. is to be demolished
    c. has been foreclosed
    d. has had a death in it.

23. Which of the following is not required to be included in a listing agreement?

    a. The type of compensation for the agent
    b. The seller's signature
    c. The agreement expiration date
    d. The subject property's market value

24. If a listing agreement is used to create a dual agency, it must include a disclosure notice

    a. signed by seller and buyer.
    b. stating that the agent's primary duty is to the seller.
    c. stating that the seller and buyer can only speak in the presence of the agent
    d. stating that the agent has no fiduciary duties to either client

25. Which of the following does not legally terminate a brokerage agreement?

    a. The date agreed upon by both parties within the agreement
    b. One party chooses to terminate the agreement
    c. The broker terminates the agreement when one client refuses a dual agency
    d. One party defaults on the terms of the agreement

CHAPTER TWENTY-NINE: ETHICAL PRACTICES AND FAIR HOUSING

1. Which of the following is not a protected class under the federal Fair Housing Act of 1968?

    a. Familial status
    b. National origin
    c. Source of income
    d. Mental disability

2. In addition to protection from discrimination under federal and Maryland state laws, Maryland local jurisdictions often include protection for which of the following classes?

    a. Sexual orientation
    b. Familial status
    c. Gender identity
    d. Age

3. The first class to be protected against discrimination by federal law was

    a. age.
    b. religion.
    c. race.
    d. sex.

4. Which of the following is not discriminatory under federal fair housing laws?

    a. A lender refusing to provide a mortgage loan based on the borrower's source of income
    b. A landlord refusing to rent housing to a single mother with children
    c. An apartment manager refusing to allow a service dog to reside in a "no pets" apartment
    d. A property appraiser indicating a lower-than-accurate value for property owned by a Native American.

5. Which of the following is legal in Maryland?

    a. A landlord rejecting a prospective tenant based on the tenant's prior conviction for illegal drug distribution
    b. A real estate licensee refusing to show a Middle Eastern couple available housing in a predominantly white neighborhood
    c. A licensee discouraging a Jewish couple from purchasing a home in a neighborhood heavily populated with low-income families by indicating the home they're interested in will lose property value due to the makeup of the neighborhood
    d. A licensee convincing property owners to sell their home at a lower price to an Asian family to block Hispanic families from moving into the neighborhood

6. Convincing property owners to sell their properties cheaply by telling them racial minorities will be moving into the neighborhood is called

    a. steering.
    b. inducing.
    c. blockbusting.
    d. sales tactics.

7. If a licensee is not acting for monetary compensation, it is permissible for the licensee to

    a. try to convince a property owner to sell cheaply by warning that racial minorities will soon be moving into the neighborhood.
    b. advise a disgruntled property owner to lodge a discrimination complaint with the Commission on Civil Rights.
    c. dissuade a person from taking advantage of a multiple listing service because of the person's membership in a protected class.
    d. refuse to show a buyer available residential property that is in the buyer's price range in spite of the buyer's membership in a protected class.

8. Who is responsible for enforcing Maryland state discrimination laws?

    a. Department of Housing and Urban Development
    b. Attorney General
    c. Commission on Civil Rights
    d. Administrative Law Judge

9. Federal discrimination complaints must be filed within _____ of the alleged incident.

   a. 30 days
   b. 6 months
   c. 1 year
   d. 2 years

10. An urban area where the racial stability is threatened by the number of real estate transactions is called

    a. a ghetto.
    b. an unstable transaction area.
    c. a conservation area.
    d. an urban instability community.

11. The federal Fair Housing Act is enforced by

    a. MCCR.
    b. HUD.
    c. Attorney General.
    d. US Supreme Court.

12. Which terminology would be legal when used in advertising for housing?

    a. No children
    b. No pets
    c. Not wheelchair accessible
    d. No unmarried couples

13. Which of the following behaviors is required when licensees deal with each other?

    a. Negotiate exclusively listed properties with the property owner only.
    b. Respect another licensee's exclusive listing.
    c. Compensate cooperating brokers with or without an agreement.
    d. Obtain only the affiliated broker's consent to place signs on property owners' properties.

14. If a licensee prepares a competitive market analysis for a client, what must be disclosed on the first page of the CMA?

    a. The recommended offering price for the property
    b. Confirmation the property condition disclosure or disclaimer has been provided
    c. The licensee's license status
    d. The intent of the CMA

15. Which of the following is NOT a predatory business practice?

    a. Setting prices too low for other companies to compete
    b. Providing sub-prime home loans to home buyers
    c. Exploiting consumers for personal gain
    d. Denying home loans to buyers with low credit ratings

CHAPTER THIRTY: OTHER MARYLAND LAWS AND PRACTICES

1. Developers who wish to create a time-share must file a public offering statement with the

   a. Maryland Real Estate Commission.
   b. Maryland Real Estate Time-Share Commission.
   c. Maryland Secretary of State.
   d. Maryland Attorney General.

2. A builder's public offering statement must be provided to a time-share buyer

   a. at the time of showing the property.
   b. prior to submitting an offer.
   c. prior to closing the transaction.
   d. prior to executing the sales contract.

4. Time-share purchasers are actually buying

   a. a percentage of the project.
   b. a specific dwelling unit.
   c. an allotment of time.
   d. a percentage of ownership of a specific dwelling unit.

4. Purchasers of a lot in a homeowners' association may cancel the sales contract

   a. within 5 days of receipt of the required disclosures.
   b. within 7 days of signing the sales contract.
   c. prior to signing the sales contract.
   d. within 10 days of receipt of the public offering statement.

5. Which of the following statements is TRUE?

   a. Builders must disclose their participation or non-participation in a new home warranty security plan.
   b. Builders must disclose that they are not required to register with the Consumer Protection Division.
   c. Builders need not disclose their knowledge of hazardous materials that are present on the site.
   d. Builders must disclose that a new home warranty is required when purchasing an HOA lot.

6. A first-time home buyer must pay a transfer tax of _____ percent of the property's sale price.

   a. 0.25
   b. 0.5
   c. 0.05
   d. 0

7. If a property is assessed at $175,000 and the tax rate for the jurisdiction is $0.80, what would be the amount of ad valorem tax owed?

   a. $1,750
   b. $1,400
   c. $175
   d. $1,350

8. Ad valorem taxes being paid on an annual basis are due on or before

   a. September 30.
   b. October 1.
   c. July 1.
   d. December 31.

9. If ad valorem taxes are not paid and become a lien on the property, the county tax collector is required to

   a. foreclose on the property.
   b. evict the homeowners from the property.
   c. sell the tax lien through a tax sale at public auction.
   d. impose criminal penalties on the homeowner.

10. If a homeowner's tax debt has been sold at a tax sale, the homeowner may redeem the property by paying the debt within

    a. 60 days.
    b. 6 months.
    c. 1 year.
    d. 2 years.

11. Mechanics' liens are available to

    a. automobile repair technicians.
    b. construction laborers.
    c. time-share developers.
    d. homeowners.

12. What caused the damage to the Chesapeake Bay's ecosystem and led to the first Chesapeake Bay Agreement?

    a. Extensive commercial development
    b. Severe weather conditions
    c. Poor water quality
    d. Lack of interstate cooperation between Maryland, Virginia, and Pennsylvania.

13. What law established land use policies within 100 feet of the Chesapeake Bay shoreline?

    a. Chesapeake and Atlantic Coastal Bays Critical Area Act
    b. The Clean Water Act
    c. Chesapeake Bay Critical Area Law
    d. Chesapeake Bay Buffer Protection Act

14. Landlords wishing to terminate a yearly tenancy must give the tenant a notice of

    a. 30 days.
    b. 60 days.
    c. 3 months.
    d. 6 months.

15. Which of the following is a justifiable reason for a tenant to withhold rent?

    a. Rodent infestation in the tenant's unit
    b. Paint peeling from entryway door
    c. A clogged bathroom sink
    d. Broken water heater

CHAPTER TESTS ANSWER KEY

CHAPTER ONE: THE REAL ESTATE BUSINESS
1. c. property managers handle day-to-day operations while asset managers manage portfolios of properties. (8)
2. b. developers. (7)
3. b. retail, office and industrial properties. (9)
4. a. Brokers and agents (10)
5. b. By geography (11)
6. d. A broker who renders real estate services for a fee (11)
7. b. state government. (14)

CHAPTER TWO: RIGHTS IN REAL ESTATE
1. d. The Constitution (25)
2. c. Land and everything permanently attached to it (17)
3. a. The surface of the earth and all natural things permanently attached to the earth (16)
4. b. Immobile, indestructible, heterogeneous (17)
5. d. land does not include man-made structures. (18)
6. a. real property includes ownership of a bundle of rights. (19)
7. c. To transfer (18)
8. d. Stock (19)
9. a. the right of others to use and enjoy their property. (19)
10. c. separable. (20)
11. d. Riparian (22)
12. b. To the middle of the waterway (22)
13. c. A doctrine that gives the state control of water use and the water supply (21)
14. a. A tree growing on a parcel of land (23)
15. b. its definition as one or the other in a sale or lease contract. (24)
16. d. A plant or crop that is considered personal property (24)
17. c. Affixing and severance (25)
18. a. court decisions. (26)
19. c. Broad regulation of usage (25)
20. d. County and local (26)
21. b. Trade fixtures that are personal property (24)
22. a. The owner's claim is invalid, because the state owns the underlying land (21)

CHAPTER THREE: INTERESTS AND ESTATES
1. c. one or more of the bundle of rights to real property. (29)
2. a. interests that do not include possession. (30)
3. b. A leasehold endures only for a specific period of time. (31)
4. d. absolute fee simple estate. (32)
5. c. the estate may revert to a grantor or heirs if the prescribed use changes. (33)
6. a. the original owner or other named person. (33)
7. b. A fee simple owner grants the life estate to a life tenant. (34)
8. c. The pur autre vie estate endures only for the lifetime of a person other than the grantee. (35)
9. c. Legal life estate (35)
10. a. A homestead interest cannot be conveyed by one spouse. (35)
11. b. a wife's life estate interest in her husband's property. (36)
12. b. A widow who was excluded from a will makes a claim to a portion of the couple's principal residence. (36)

13. b. Estate from period to period (37)

CHAPTER FOUR: OWNERSHIP
1. a. tenancy in severalty. (39)
2. c. tenancy in common. (40)
3. a. Parties must acquire respective interests at the same time. (43)
4. b. cannot will their interest to a party outside the tenancy. (42)
5. c. property acquired during a marriage and property already owned by each party at the time of marriage. (44)
6. d. Trustor, trustee and beneficiary. (45)
7. c. fee simple ownership of the airspace in a unit and an undivided share of the entire property's common areas. (48)
8. b. The property is owned by tenants in common or by a freehold owner who leases on a time-share basis. (53)
9. a. A cooperative may hold an owner liable for the unpaid operating expenses of other owners. (52)
10. a. a default by a coop owner may cause a foreclosure on the entire property instead of just a single unit, as with a condominium. (52)
11. c. the identity of the beneficiary may not be identified. (46)

CHAPTER FIVE: ENCUMBRANCES AND LIENS
1. c. encumbrance. (56)
2. c. the right to a defined use of a portion of another's real property. (56)
3. d. Dominant tenement (56)
4. a. The property has been continuously used as an easement with the knowledge but without the permission of the owner for a period of time. (60)
5. c. Over time, the encroachment may become an easement by prescription that damages the property's market value. (61)
6. b. a deed restriction. (62)
7. a. It involves a monetary claim against the value of a property. (62)
8. c. Real estate tax lien (65)
9. d. subordinate. (66)
10. a. the date of recordation. (65)
11. b. A state in which a mortgagor retains title to the property when a mortgage lien is created (67)
12. c. The lumber yard may place a mechanic's lien for the amount of the lumber against the homeowner's real property. (67)
13. c. foreclosure. (68)
14. a. there is no right to redeem the property in a non-judicial foreclosure. (70)
15. b. a deed in lieu of foreclosure. (70)
16. b. an encroachment. (61)
17. b. transfers with the property. (57)
18. a. a party wall. (58)
19. d. A license, which terminates at the owner's death (61)
20. b. general judgment lien. (64)

CHAPTER SIX: TRANSFERRING AND RECORDING TITLE TO REAL ESTATE
1. a. Ownership of the bundle of rights to real estate (72)
2. d. actual notice. (73)
3. c. title records. (73)

4. a. voluntary alienation. (74)
5. c. accepted by the grantee. (74)
6. d. states the grantor's intention, names the parties, describes the property, and indicates a consideration. (76)
7. a. state the grantor's assurance or warrant to the grantee that a certain condition or fact concerning the property is true. (76)
8. c. general warranty deed. (77)
9. d. A quitclaim deed (78)
10. b. a documentary stamp tax. (79)
11. a. It is taken by the state according to the process called escheat. (81)
12. d. an unenforceable nuncupative will. (80)
13. a. pass to heirs by the laws of descent and distribution. (81)
14. b. inspecting the property and evicting any trespassers found. (83)
15. d. declined because possession was secretive. (82)
16. c. give constructive notice of one's rights and interests in the property. (84)
17. c. A chronology of successive owners of record of a parcel of real estate. (84)
18. a. title is conveyed only when conveyance is registered on the title certificate. (85)
19. b. free of undisclosed defects and encumbrances. (85)
20. c. title insurance. (85)

CHAPTER SEVEN: LEASING ESSENTIALS
1. c. a conveyance of a possessory interest. (89)
2. d. A leased fee estate (90)
3. c. occupy the property. (90)
4. a. The buyer acquires title subject to the lease. (90)
5. b. The tenant must continue to abide by all lease terms. (90)
6. c. When either party gives proper notice (91)
7. c. a five-year lease must be in writing to be enforceable. (91)
8. b. In a sublease, the original tenant retains primary responsibility for performance of the original lease contract. (92)
9. a. A rights lease (95)
10. d. net lease. (93)
11. b. retail landlords.(93)
12. d. The tenant leases the ground from the landlord and owns the improvements. (94)
13. a. sue to compel performance of the contract. (95)
14. b. The leased property is foreclosed. (96)
15. d. discourage the use of unfair and overly complex leases. (97)
16. b. bargain with each other in good faith. (98)

CHAPTER EIGHT: LAND USE PLANNING AND CONTROL
1. a. balance individual property rights with the community's welfare. (100)
2. d. a fusion of land use laws and local land use objectives and strategies. (101)
3. a. zoning. (102)
4. c. police power. (103)
5. d. The owner must sell the property or grant an easement to the municipality for just compensation. (109)
6. c. the planning commission. (103)
7. b. delegation of authority by state-level enabling acts. (104)
8. a. reasonably promote community health, safety and welfare. (104)
9. d. To ensure that improvements comply with codes (104)
10. b. regulate density. (105)

11. a. a special exception. (107)
12. c. a legal nonconforming use. (106)
13. a. it would cause the property owner unreasonable hardship to bring the property into compliance with zoning ordinances. (107)
14. b. a plat of subdivision. (108)
15. c. the construction complies with building codes. (108)
16. a. public utilities. (109)
17. b. takes title subject to the same restriction. (110)
18. c. it cannot be terminated by a single individual. (110)
19. d. court injunction. (111)
20. a. it gives the grantor the right to re-possess the property if the grantee violates the condition. (111)

CHAPTER NINE: LEGAL DESCRIPTIONS
1. a. To create a consistent, unchanging standard for locating the property. (119)
2. b. They identify an enclosed area, beginning and ending at the same point. (120)
3. c. Metes and bounds (120)
4. b. point of beginning. (120)
5. d. Six miles by six miles. (123)
6. a. range. (123)
7. b. tier. (123)
8. d. Thirty-six (123)
9. a. 640 (123)
10. c. 80 acres (124)
11. b. will include a metes and bounds description. (123)
12. a. the lot and block number, with section, township and meridian references. (123)
13. c. properties located above or below the earth's surface. (123)

CHAPTER TEN: FUNDAMENTALS OF CONTRACT LAW
1. a. it represents a "meeting of the minds." (128)
2. c. enforceable or unenforceable. (129)
3. b. is possibly valid and enforceable. (130)
4. c. a counteroffer. (134)
5. d. valuable consideration. (131)
6. c. is void. (132)
7. b. voidable. (129)
8. a. must act within a statutory period. (132)
9. b. require certain conveyance-related contracts to be in writing. (132)
10. b. The buyer has no obligations to the seller whatsoever. (135)
11. a. is void. (133)
12. d. The original offer is legally extinguished. (134)
13. a. may be assigned. (135)
14. c. A two-year lease. (135)
15. a. an option to purchase. (136)
16. c. it is performed. (137)
17. b. it is impossible to perform. (137)
18. b. specific performance. (138)

CHAPTER ELEVEN: NATIONAL AGENCY
1. d. trust, confidence, and good faith. (140)
2. c. provide sufficient information for the agent to complete the agent's tasks. (146)
3. b. general agency. (141)
4. b. special agency. (141)
5. c. a party creates an agency relationship outside of an express agreement. (141)
6. a. Death or incapacity of the agent (142)
7. a. The agent has violated the duty of confidentiality. (143)
8. b. the agent has not violated fiduciary duty. (143)
9. d. inform the seller. (144)
10. a. fairness, care, and honesty. (145)

11. b. has an exposure to a charge of negligent misrepresentation. (145)
12. d. practicing law without a license. (145)
13. c. a subagent. (147)
14. b. a dual agent. (148)
15. a. may not represent one party's interests to the detriment of the other. (148)
16. c. dual agent. (149)
17. a. prior to completing a listing agreement. (150)
18. c. whenever substantive contact is made. (150)
19. b. upon initial contact. (151)
20. a. upon first substantive contact. (151)

CHAPTER TWELVE: LISTING AGREEMENTS: AN OVERVIEW

1. b. may be oral or written. (154)
2. a. exclusive right-to sell agreement. (154)
3. b. exclusive agency agreement. (155)
4. c. open listing. (156)
5. d. net listing. (156)
6. a. the client. (156)
7. a. To list the owner's property in a multiple listing service. (157)
8. b. is ready, willing, and able to transact. (158)
9. a. showing the property. (158)
10. c. ascertaining the facts about the client and the property at the onset of the listing period. (159)
11. b. established through negotiation with clients. (159)
12. b. the client may be liable for a commission and marketing expenses. (159)
13. b. the agent has a claim to a commission if the owner sells or leases to a party within a certain time following the listing's expiration. (160)

CHAPTER THIRTEEN: GENERAL BROKERAGE PRACTICES

1. c. Procuring customers for clients and effecting transactions (170)
2. b. Outside brokers acting as subagents assist a listing agent in procuring a customer. (170)
3. d. Listing, marketing, facilitating transactions, and managing information (171)
4. a. A corporation has perpetual existence; a proprietorship terminates upon the owner's death. (173)
5. b. both may broker real estate if properly licensed. (174)
6. d. a joint venture. (174)
7. b. A locally-owned brokerage affiliated with a national franchisor for purposes of enhanced image and resources (175)
8. d. may only be used by brokers belonging to the National Association of Realtors®. (176)
9. a. represent their employing broker in procuring clients and customers. (176)
10. a. the IC is responsible for taxes; the broker does not withhold. (177)
11. c. providing them with all listings in the agency. (178)
12. b. competitive conditions. (179)
13. d. locating clients, pricing property, and making listing presentations. (180)
14. c. underpricing a property does not serve the best interests of a client. (180)
15. c. provide all information necessary for the owner to execute the listing. (181)
16. b. expose the property to the maximum number of prospects in relation to marketing expenses and efforts. (181)
17. c. avoid disclosing what price the owner will accept. (182)

18. c. the principals have entered into a sale contract and must satisfy any contingencies prior to closing. (182)
19. b. appropriating client or customer deposits for use in the agency's business. (183)
20. d. mixing escrow funds with the broker's operating funds. (183)
21. c. the advertising must not be misleading. (184)
22. a. collusion. (186)
23. b. The brokers have illegally fixed prices. (186)
24. a. propose an asset sale. (187)
25. b. intangible assets. (188)
26. c. the value or price of the business over and above the value of its other assets. (189)
27. b. a group of inactive investors who join with a number of active partners to purchase, manage, and sell properties for a profit. (190)
28. b. obtain a Series 22 securities license. (191)

CHAPTER FOURTEEN: OVERVIEW OF CONVEYANCE CONTRACTS

1. b. the parties have completed a verbal, executory contract. (194)
2. c. The assignor has completed a legal action. (195)
3. a. the buyer can potentially force the seller to transfer ownership. (195)
4. a. entrust deposit monies to an impartial fiduciary. (195)
5. a. The seller may cancel the contract, since it can be ruled invalid. (196)
6. d. claim the deposit as relief for the buyer's failure to perform. (196)
7. c. Voluntary, bilateral, and executory (194)
8. d. third-party loans surviving closing may be accelerated by the lender. (199)
9. a. The buyer must withhold 15% of the purchase price at closing for the seller's capital gain tax payment. (199)
10. b. the optionor must perform if the optionee takes the option, but the optionee is under no obligation to do so. (201)
11. d. The option is expired, and the tenant has no rightful claim to money paid for the option. (201)
12. a. The tenant can force the sale at the original terms. (201)
13. c. They give the optionee an equitable interest in the property. (203)
14. c. the seller retains legal title in a contract for deed transaction until fully executed. (203)
15. d. comply with the contract and take legal title when its terms are fulfilled. (204)
16. c. the vendee may not have a right of redemption. (204)

CHAPTER FIFTEEN: REAL ESTATE MARKET ECONOMICS

1. c. the amount of money a buyer and seller agree to exchange to complete a transaction. (208)
2. b. desire, utility, scarcity, and purchasing power. (208)
3. b. will increase. (208)
4. d. the market tending toward equilibrium. (210)
5. c. the market is over-supplied. (209)
6. a. The demand must literally come to the supply. (211)
7. b. base employment. (213)
8. a. have been increasing. (215)
9. d. expanding the sewer system. (216)
10. a. trade area population and spending patterns. (213)
11. c. costs of occupancy and building efficiency. (213)

CHAPTER SIXTEEN: APPRAISING AND ESTIMATING MARKET VALUE

1. a. if two similar properties are for sale, a buyer will purchase the cheaper of the two. (219)
2. a. is physically and financially feasible, legal, and the most productive. (220)
3. d. the price that a willing, informed, and unpressured seller and buyer agree upon for a property assuming a cash price and the property's reasonable exposure to the market. (222)
4. b. the broker may not be a disinterested party. (223)
5. a. there may be no recent sale price data in the market. (225)
6. c. select comparable properties, adjust the comparables, estimate the value. (225)
7. b. the seller offers below-market seller financing. (227)
8. b. weights the comparables. (227)
9. b. market value is not always the same as what the property cost. (231)
10. b. replacement cost. (232)
11. d. functional obsolescence. (232)
12. b. incurable economic obsolescence. (232)
13. c. depreciation (232)
14. a. estimate depreciation, subtract depreciation from cost, and add back the land value. (233)
15. b. $8,500 (234)
16. b. Apartment buildings (235)
17. c. estimate net income, and apply a capitalization rate to it. (236)
18. c. potential gross income minus vacancy and credit loss minus expenses. (237)
19. b. $400,000 (237)
20. a. numerous expenses are not taken into account. (239)
21. b. $240,000 (239)

CHAPTER SEVENTEEN: REAL ESTATE FINANCE

1. c. hypothecation. (243)
2. a. The borrower gives the lender a note and a mortgage in exchange for loan funds. (243)
3. c. The trustor conveys title to a trustee in exchange for loan funds from the beneficiary. (244)
4. a. title-theory state. (243)
5. b. usury. (246)
6. c. $15,000. (246)
7. a. an amortized loan is paid off over the loan period. (246)
8. c. it is a negotiable instrument. (247)
9. d. may be required to execute a release of mortgage document. (249)
10. a. an appraisal report. (250)
11. c. the ability to re-pay, the value of the collateral, and the profitability of the loan. (250)
12. b. the lender wants to ensure the loan is fully collateralized. (250)
13. b. consider the income of a spouse in evaluating a family's creditworthiness. (251)
14. a. safeguard against over-indebtedness. (254)
15. d. dividing one's debts by one's gross income. (254)
16. c. take-out loan commitment. (256)
17. c. the parties complete all loan origination documents and the loan is funded. (256)
18. b. Truth-in-Lending laws (257)
19. a. The Equal Credit Opportunity Act (258)
20. c. the Real Estate Settlement Procedures Act. (258)
21. b. Buying securities, changing the discount rate, and controlling banking reserves (259)
22. a. cycle funds back to primary lenders so they can make more loans. (261)
23. a. Fannie Mae, Freddie Mac, and Ginnie Mae. (261)
24. c. purchase FHA-backed and VA-backed loans. (262)
25. b. insure loans made by approved lenders. (263)
26. a. guarantee loans made by approved lenders. (264)
27. c. the loan payments gradually increase. (266)
28. b. the borrower pays additional interest at the onset in order to obtain a lower interest rate. (266)
29. a. the interest rate may vary. (266)
30. b. the seller offering the buyer a wraparound can profit from a difference in interest rates. (267)
31. b. a blanket mortgage loan. (268)
32. b. Payments are not sufficient to retire the loan. (266)

CHAPTER EIGHTEEN: REAL ESTATE INVESTMENT

1. b. the more the investor stands to gain, the greater the risk that the investor may lose. (272)
2. a. income and tax benefits. (273)
3. c. debt. (274)
4. d. relatively illiquid. (276)
5. b. a more management-intensive investment. (276)
6. a. a general partnership. (276)
7. d. gross income minus expenses minus building depreciation. (277)
8. c. deduct interest payments from income. (280)
9. d. The owner may be able to exclude capital gain from taxable income when the property is sold. (281)
10. c. may be deducted from the sale price for gains tax purposes. (280)
11. b. the difference between net sale proceeds and adjusted basis. (281)
12. a. cost recovery expense. (282)
13. c. dividing cash flow by the investor's equity. (285)

CHAPTER NINETEEN: REAL ESTATE TAXATION

1. c. There are no federal ad valorem taxes. (288)
2. c. may delegate taxing authority to county governments. (288)
3. c. impose property taxes for specific municipal services. (288)
4. b. create a two-mile extension of county sewer facilities. (289)
5. b. the assessed value of property. (289)
6. b. the total of all assessed values of properties minus exemptions. (289)
7. d. smooth out wide discrepancies of assessed values within the district. (290)
8. c. appeal to adjust the assessed valuation. (290)
9. b. to offer an amount of tax relief on an owner's principal residence. (290)
10. a. dividing the tax requirement by the tax base. (291)
11. c. multiplying each district's tax rate times the taxable value of the property. (292)
12. a. it only applies to properties which will benefit from the public improvement. (292)
13. b. entitles its holder to apply for a tax deed after a certain period. (293)
14. b. gives a delinquent taxpayer a grace period prior to the tax sale to pay property taxes. (293)

CHAPTER TWENTY: PROFESSIONAL PRACTICES

1. b. prohibit discrimination in housing transactions. (296)
2. c. the Civil Rights Act of 1968. (297)
3. c. the Fair Housing Amendments Act of 1988 (298)
4. a. blockbusting. (297)
5. c. steering. (297)
6. a. providing unequal services. (297)
7. a. discriminatory misrepresentation. (297)

8. d. The prohibition may be legal. (298)
9. c. The agent and the owner (299)
10. c. high standards of practice for all facets of the business. (314)
11. b. public accommodations and employment. (301)
12. c. disclose the information to others. (303)
13. a. It may cause them to be held liable for improper disclosure of potential violations. (310)
14. b. Conditions that pre-existed the coverage date of the warranty will not be covered. (310)
15. c. Disclose the result of any inspection, if known to the agent (313)

CHAPTER TWENTY-ONE: CLOSINGS
1. d. exchange legal title for the sale price. (319)
2. b. the lender wants to ensure proper handling of the collateral for the loan. (321)
3. b. the loan is to be sold to the FNMA. (322)
4. d. the buyer must pay the expense. (324)
5. d. a debit to one party and a credit to the other. (326)
6. a. the excess of the buyer's debits over the buyer's credits. (325)
7. b. Inspection fees (326)
8. c. Taxes and interest (327)
9. d. Rents and insurance (326)
10. a. the seller must pay prorated expenses inclusive of the day of closing. (328)
11. b. document the payment of a transfer tax. (331)
12. b. A form that summarizes and reports transaction data from a closing (344)
13. d. $692 (331)
14. c. $195,200 (331)

CHAPTER TWENTY-TWO: OVERVIEW OF LICENSING AND REGULATION
1. c. Bruce gets hired to find an office suite for a friend who is relocating her business. (348)
2. d. may take the exam and receive an inactive license. (351)
3. b. may not show the buyer homes in the other state without a non-resident license. (349)
4. b. administer state licensing requirements. (351)
5. a. take punitive actions against fraud or misrepresentation. (352)
6. b. not valid. (350)
7. c. ensure that judgments against licensees will be collectible. (353)

CHAPTER TWENTY-THREE: RISK MANAGEMENT
1. b. reduction. (356)
2. c. risk outsourcing. (356)
3. a. It deflects and reduces risk by preventing others from claiming they were misled. (356)
4. c. It can be a guide to compliance with the law. (357)
5. c. It reduces the risk of committing an unauthorized practice of law. (358)
6. d. a legal requirement. (359)
7. b. Copies of required communications to principals. (358)
8. d. negligence, error or omission in carrying out professional services. (359)
9. a. Failing to inform and disclose properly. (361)
10. b. failing to disclose known adverse facts. (364)
11. d. avoid creating a false impression that the licensee is a certified appraiser. (364)
12. b. exceeding the authority of the agreement. (365)

13. a. use a checklist of all items, contingencies, dates and responsibilities that must be met. (367)
14. d. the principals may make changes as long as they sign or initial each change. (367)
15. b. obtain education in the content and intent of the laws. (367)
16. a. being present at a conversation where the setting of commission rates is discussed. (368)
17. a. License discipline, fines, and possible incarceration. (371)
18. c. stating that a client should seek legal counsel. (371)
19. d. avoid statements of opinion and speculation in all reports. (372)
20. b. It reduces the chance of presenting an offer from an unqualified buyer. (372)

CHAPTER TWENTY-FOUR: PROPERTY MANAGEMENT
1. c. fiduciary (377)
2. b. financial reporting to the principal. (378)
3. d. revenue from all sources minus losses from uncollected rents, vacancies, and evictions. (378)
4. a. cost per tenant prospect generated per lease. (379)
5. b. raise rental rates. (380)
6. d. High tenant turnover increases expenses and reduces profits. (380)
7. b. Routine, preventive, and corrective (381)
8. a. ensure that disabled employees have the same level of access to facilities that all employees have. (382)
9. c. A court may hold the manager responsible for the physical safety of tenants in leased premises. (383)
10. a. replacement value. (384)
11. b. cash for the management firm's operating expenses. (384)
12. c. General (385)
13. a. apportioned under the terms of the management contract. (386)
14. b. The tenant pays a fixed rent, and the landlord pays all operating expenses. (389)
15. d. the property manager does not have to maintain it. (390)
16. b. deliver a habitable property. (391)
17. c. A tenant declares a landlord in default and vacates the leased premises. (392)
18. a. the competitive market for the property. (394)

CHAPTER TWENTY-FIVE: THE MARYLAND REGULATORY ENVIRONMENT
1. c. 5. (398)
2. d. the Secretary. (399)
3. c. Allow a conditional license (399)
4. a. revoked. (403)
5. a. Complaints may be submitted by members of the Commission. (401)
6. d. 10 days. (402)
7. b. dismiss the claim. (402)
8. c. 3 members of the Commission, at least 1 licensed professional and at least 1 consumer member. (402)
9. c. The licensee files a bond up to $50,000. (403)
10. b. A one-time fee paid by license applicants (404)
11. b. an individual who suffered a financial loss as a result of a licensee's misrepresentation. (404)
12. a. a misdemeanor. (406)
13. c. Either $25,000 or $10,000 depending on which loss is being reimbursed (406)
14. d. License suspension and reimbursement of the Fund's payment amount plus interest (406)
15. d. summary license suspension. (407)

CHAPTER TWENTY-SIX: MARYLAND LICENSING REQUIREMENTS

1. c. A home builder selling a newly constructed house (411)
2. d. Maryland licensees may affiliate with multiple brokers. (412)
3. c. broker licenses. (414)
4. a. Complete 60 hours of prelicense education (413)
5. a. 135 (413)
6. d. completing Maryland's broker prelicense education requirements. (415)
7. b. 2 years. (416)
8. c. 60 days (417)
9. d. An adult member of the broker's family (419)
10. b. 3 years (418)
11. b. January 10th of 2024 **(Error! Bookmark not defined.)**
12. a. prohibition to provide brokerage services. (420)
13. c. 7.5 clock hours (421)
14. c. 3 (422)
15. d. must be completed every 2 years. (421)
16. b. is not employed by the entity. (422)
17. b. direct commissions to be paid directly to the entity. (423)
18. a. The broker's resident state requires Maryland residents who are licensed in the other state to maintain an office in that state. (423)
19. b. a licensed salesperson with 3 years of brokerage services experience. (423)
20. a. automatic suspension of the broker's license. (424)

CHAPTER TWENTY-SEVEN: MARYLAND REGULATION OF BUSINESS CONDUCT

1. c. must notify the MREC of the entity's existence. (429)
2. d. a percentage of the property's sale price. (429)
3. c. Offering a prize to be given to one of a number of attendees at an open house just for attending the open house. (429)
4. a. trade name. (430)
5. d. any of the above. (430)
6. d. approved by the MREC. (432)
7. a. the logo being at least ½ inch by ½ inch in size. (433)
8. c. Open House directional signs (434)
9. d. inform attendees that the showing licensee represents the seller. (434)
10. b. 31 days (435)
11. b. Telephone surveyor (435)
12. a. between 8 a.m. and 9 p.m. (435)
13. c. liability for restitution. (436)
14. d. Secretary of State. (436)
15. c. the Maryland Commercial Electronic Mail Act. (437)
16. b. The message must include a valid telephone number for the initiator of the message. (437)
17. b. Certain misleading claims about products or services can result in imprisonment. (437)
18. a. A fax sent to a property buyer's agent with the seller's counteroffer (437)
19. b. The seller (438)
20. a. within 7 days of both parties accepting the sales contract. (438)
21. d. Failing to promptly account for any money held in trust (440)
22. c. 5 years after the listing date (440)
23. d. A broker's supervision over an independent contractor does not alter the independent status of the contractor. (441)

24. a. A written policies manual that includes guidance on using unlicensed personal assistants (442)
25. b. how the crime relates to the licensee's fitness as a licensee. (445)
26. d. Accepting compensation based on real estate activity (446)
27. d. All team members must be affiliated with the same broker. (447)
28. b. If an offer does not include an expiration date, the seller must respond within 7 business days. (450)
29. d. high noise levels (452)
30. b. 15 days (453)

CHAPTER TWENTY-EIGHT: MARYLAND BROKERAGE RELATIONSHIPS AND DISCLOSURE

1. c. Subagent (461)
2. d. when a customer and a licensee sign a brokerage agreement. (461)
3. c. The date by which a termination notice must be received (461)
4. a. terminate that party's relationship agreement. (463)
5. c. Disclose to Ted his agency relationship with Samantha (463)
6. d. be printed in at least 10 point type. (463)
7. b. Confidentiality (465)
8. c. Material facts about the client's property (464)
9. d. Perform ministerial acts for individuals other than the client (465)
10. b. A murder on the property (468)
11. b. when the client and licensee sign the written agreement. (461)
12. a. Net (466)
13. c. The agent must give a copy of the listing contract to the seller when the first offer is submitted. (466)
14. d. The Maryland licensee obtains a license in the other state. (467)
15. c. When the seller's agent learns an offer is about to be submitted (467)
16. b. latent defects. (467)
17. b. Sellers are required to have an investigation or inspection of the property performed to discover defects not already known to the seller. (467)
18. a. The disclaimer portion of the property condition form is used when the property is being sold "as is." (467)
19. b. the seller and the buyer. (468)
20. a. The resale of a single-family home by the current owner (467)
21. d. a resident is infected with the COVID virus. (468)
22. d. has had a death in it. (468)
23. d. The subject property's market value (466)
24. a. signed by seller and buyer. (467)
25. b. One party chooses to terminate the agreement (465)

CHAPTER TWENTY-NINE: ETHICAL PRACTICES AND FAIR HOUSING

1. c. Source of income (475)
2. d. Age (476)
3. c. race. (475)
4. a. A lender refusing to provide a mortgage loan based on the borrower's source of income (476)
5. a. A landlord rejecting a prospective tenant based on the tenant's prior conviction for illegal drug distribution (476)
6. c. blockbusting. (478)
7. b. advise a disgruntled property owner to lodge a discrimination complaint with the Commission on Civil Rights. (478)
8. c. Commission on Civil Rights (479)

9. c. 1 year (478)
10. c. a conservation area. (479)
11. b. HUD. (478)
12. b. No pets (479)
13. b. Respect another licensee's exclusive listing. (480)
14. d. The intent of the CMA (481)
15. d. Denying home loans to home buyers with low credit ratings (482)

CHAPTER THIRTY: OTHER MARYLAND LAWS AND PRACTICES

1. c. Maryland Secretary of State. (486)
2. d. prior to executing the sales contract. (486)
3. c. an allotment of time. (485)
4. a. within 5 days of receipt of the required disclosures. (488)
5. a. Builders must disclose their participation or non-participation in a new home warranty security plan. (488)
6. d. 0 (489)
7. b. $1,400 (490)
8. c. July 1. (490)
9. c. sell the tax lien through a tax sale at public auction. (490)
10. b. 6 months. (491)
11. b. construction laborers. (491)
12. a. Extensive commercial development (492)
13. c. Chesapeake Bay Critical Area Law (492)
14. c. 3 months (494)
15. d. Broken water heater (495)

Real Estate Mathematics

Basic Formulas and Functions
Real Estate Applications

Answer Key is on page 572

BASIC FORMULAS AND FUNCTIONS

Adding and multiplying fractions
Converting decimals and percentages
Converting fractions and percentages
Multiplying percentages
Calculating area

Adding and multiplying fractions

Adding

1. Formulas:

    Same denominator: $\dfrac{a}{c} + \dfrac{b}{c} = \dfrac{a+b}{c}$

    Different denominator: $\dfrac{a}{c} + \dfrac{b}{d} = \dfrac{ad+bc}{cd}$

2. Examples: $\dfrac{2}{5} + \dfrac{6}{5} = \dfrac{8}{5}$

    $\dfrac{3}{4} + \dfrac{4}{7} = \dfrac{(3 \times 7) + (4 \times 4)}{(4 \times 7)} = \dfrac{37}{28}$

    Problem 1: $\dfrac{3}{19} + \dfrac{2}{7} = ?$

Multiplying

1. Formula:

$$\frac{a}{c} \times \frac{b}{d} = \frac{ab}{cd}$$

2. Example:

$$\frac{4}{9} \times \frac{2}{3} = \frac{8}{27}$$

Problem 2:

$$\frac{4}{14} \times \frac{3}{8} = ?$$

Converting decimals and percentages

Converting a decimal to a percent

1. Formula: (decimal number) x 100 = percent number

2. Examples:
   .473 x 100   = 47.3%
   3.456 x 100   = 345.6%
   .0042 x 100   = .42%

Problem 3: Convert the following decimals to percentages:

   2.65 =   %
   0.294 =   %
   0.005 =   %

Converting a percent to a decimal

1. Formula:

$$\frac{percent\ number}{100} = decimal\ number$$

2. Examples:

$$\frac{47.3\%}{100} = .473$$

$$\frac{345.6\%}{100} = 3.456$$

Problem 4: Convert the following percentages to decimals:

   72.1% =
   90.2% =
   5.79% =

Converting fractions and percentages

Converting a fraction to a percent

1. Formulas:

   (1) $\quad\dfrac{a}{b}$ = a divided by b = decimal number

   (2) $\quad$ decimal number x 100 = percent number

2. Examples: $\quad\dfrac{4}{5}$ = 4 divided by 5 = 0.8 = 80%

   $\dfrac{9}{3}$ = 9 divided by 3 = 3.0 = 300%

Problem 5: Convert the following fractions to percentages:

$\dfrac{8}{9}$ = $\quad$ %

$\dfrac{3}{6}$ = $\quad$ %

$\dfrac{14}{42}$ = $\quad$ %

Converting a percent to a fraction and reducing it

1. Formula: $\quad X\% = \dfrac{X}{100}$

   $\dfrac{X \div a}{100 \div a}$ = reduced fraction

   where "a" is the largest number that divides *evenly* into numerator and denominator. If unknown, try 2, 3, 5, or 7.

2. Example $\quad 45\% = \dfrac{45}{100} = \dfrac{45 \div 5}{100 \div 5} \div \dfrac{9}{20}$

Problem 6: Convert and reduce the following percentages:

40% =

16% =

Multiplying Percentages

1. Formulas:

   (1)   convert percent to decimal by dividing by 100

   (2)   whole amount x decimal = partial amount

2. Example: 33% of 400

   (1)   33% divided by 100   = .33

   (2)   400 x .33   = 132

   Problem 7:   What is 75% of 280?

Calculating area

To find the area of an irregular shape, try dividing it into triangles, rectangles, squares or trapezoids and calculate the areas of those parts; the area of the whole shape is then the sum of the areas of all of its subparts.

Base and height

1. Formulas for area of three- and four-sided shapes use a product of base and height. In the formulas, a represents area, b represents base, h represents height, SF represents square feet.

2. The base of a triangle, square, or rectangle may be any side; a trapezoid has two bases, its two parallel sides.

3. The height of a triangle is the length of a perpendicular line from the base to the triangle's opposite point. Height in a square, rectangle or trapezoid is the length of a line which is perpendicular to the base line(s).

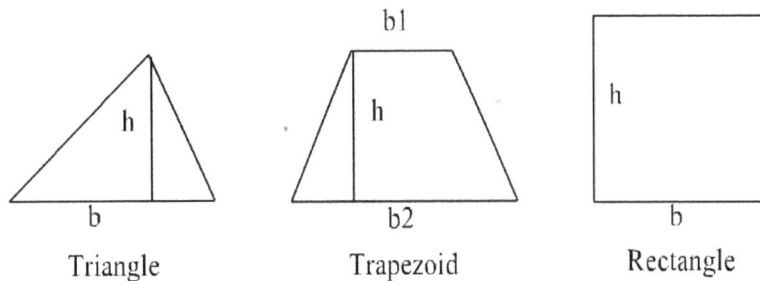

Triangle   Trapezoid   Rectangle

Area of a square or rectangle

1. Formula:

   area (a) = base (b) x height (h) $a = bxh$

2. Example:

   A square measures 3 feet on each side.

   Its area is: 3 x 3 = 9 SF

Area of a triangle

1. Formula:

   $$a = \frac{b \times h}{2}$$

2. Example:

   A triangle has a 20' base and a 4' height.

   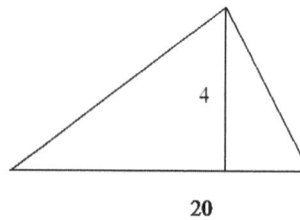

   Its area is: $a = \frac{20 \times 4}{2} = 40$ *SF*

Area of a trapezoid

1. Formula:

   $$a = \frac{a\,(b1 + b2)}{2}$$

2. Example:

   A trapezoid's two bases are 10' and 15', and its height is 7'.

   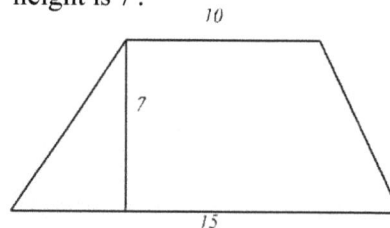

   Its area is: $a = \frac{7\,(10 + 15)}{2} = 87.5$ *SF*

Problem 8: Calculate the areas of the following shapes:

a rectangle with height of 4' and base of 36'

a =

a square with a side of 16'

a =

a trapezoid with height of 5' and bases of 6' and 8'

a =

REAL ESTATE APPLICATIONS

Legal descriptions (Chapter 9)
Listing agreements (Chapter 12)
Brokerage business (Chapter 13)
Sales contracts (Chapter 14)
Appraisal (Chapter 16)
Finance (Chapter 17)
Investments (Chapter 18)
Taxation (Chapter 19)
Closings (Chapter 21)

**Legal descriptions
(Chapter 9)**

Linear measures

(cm = centimeter; m = meter; km = kilometer)

1 inch	=	1/12 foot	=	1/36 yard
1 foot	=	12 inches	=	1/3 yard
1 yard	=	36 inches	=	3 feet
1 rod	=	16.5 feet	=	1/320 mile
1 mile	=	5280 feet	=	1760 yards = 320 rods

1 centimeter	=	1/100th m		
1 meter	=	100 cm	=	1/1000th km
1 kilometer	=	1,000 m		

Area measures

1 square inch	=	1/144th square foot
1 square foot	=	1/9th square yard
1 square yard	=	9 square feet

1 acre	=	1/640 sq. mi	=	43,560 SF	=	208.71 ft x 208.71 ft
1 square mile	=	640 acres	=	1 section	=	1/36 township
1 section	=	mile x 1 mile	=	640 acres	=	1/36 township
1 township	=	6 mi x 6 mi	=	36 sq. mi.	=	36 sections

Metric conversions

(cm = centimeter; m = meter; km = kilometer)

1 inch	=	2.54 cm				
1 foot	=	30.48 cm	=	.3048 m		
1 yard	=	91.44 cm	=	.9144 m		
1 mile	=	1609.3 m	=	1.60 km		
1 centimeter	=	.3937 inch				
1 meter	=	39.37 inches	=	3.28 feet	=	1.094 yards
1 kilometer	=	3,281.5 feet	=	.621 mile		

Fractions of sections, acres, and linear dimensions

Fraction	# Acres	Feet X Feet
1 section	640 acres	5280 X 5280
1/2 section	320 acres	5280 X 2640
1/4 section	160 acres	2640 X 2640
1/8 section	80 acres	2640 X 1320
1/16 section	40 acres	1320 X 1320
1/32 section	20 acres	660 X 1320
1/64 section	10 acres	660 X 660

Calculating area from the legal description

1. Formula:

    (1)   First multiply all the denominators of the fractions in the legal description together

    (2)   Then divide 640 by the resulting product.

2. Examples:

    N 1/2 of the SW 1/4 of Section 6:

    $$\frac{640}{(2 \ x \ 4)} = \frac{640}{8} = 80 \ acres$$

    W 1/2 of the NW 1/4 of the NE 1/4 of Section 8

    $$\frac{640}{(2 \ x \ 4 \ x \ 4)} = \frac{640}{32} = 20 \ acres$$

Problem 9:   Calculate the acreage of the following:

SW 1/4 of the N 1/2 of the E 1/2 of Section 14

SE 1/4 of the NW 1/4 of the SE 1/4 of Section 20

Listing agreements (Chapter 12)

Co-brokerage commission

1. Formulas: sale price x commission rate = total commission

    total commission x split rate = co-brokerage commission

2. Example: A house sells for $600,000. The commission is 6%, and the co-brokerage split is 50-50.

    $600,000 x 6% = $36,000 total commission x 50% = $18,000 co-broker's commission

Agent's commission

1. Formula: broker's commission x agent's split rate = agent's commission

2. Example: Assume an $18,000 broker's commission and a 60% - 40% agent-broker split rate.

    $18,000 x .6 = $10,800 agent's commission ($7,200 to broker)

Problem 10:   A property is co-brokered by listing broker Schroeder and selling broker Hobson for $425,000. The co-brokerage split is 50-50. Schroeder's agent, Joachim, is on a 65% split schedule. Hobson's selling agent, Wallace, splits 50-50 with her broker. If the total commission rate is 7%, what are the participants' commissions?

Broker Schroeder: $

Broker Hobson: $

Schroeder's agent, Joachim: $

Hobson's agent, Wallace: $

Brokerage business
(Chapter 13)

Goodwill calculation

1. Formula: Goodwill = Price - Value of assets

2. Example: A seller wants $1 million for a business. Assets in the
business, including inventory, furniture, equipment,
leasehold improvements, and working capital, have a total
value of $750,000. The goodwill is:

$1,000,000 - 750,000 = $250,000 goodwill

Problem 11: A prospective purchaser complained to a seller that the
selling price had far too much goodwill: $200,000. After
all, the assets only totaled $352,000. What was the price?

Sales contracts
(Chapter 14)

"Percentage of listing price" calculation

1. Formula: Percentage of listing price = offer divided by listing price

2. Example: A property listed for $400,000 receives an offer for
$360,000. The percentage of listing price is:

$360,000 divided by 400,000 = 90%

Problem 12: A seller receives an offer of $674,000 on a property listed
at $749,000. How much is the offer as a percent of the
listing price?

Earnest money deposit calculation

1. Formula: Deposit = Listing price x required percentage

2. Example: A seller requires a 2% deposit on a property listed for
$320,000. The required deposit is:

$320,000 x 2% = $6,400

Problem 13: A seller requires a 1.5% deposit on all offers. A buyer
wants to offer $312,000 for the property. What must the
deposit be?

Rent escalations

1. Formula: New rent = current rent x (100% + escalation rate)

2. Example: An apartment's rent is scheduled to increase by 6%. If the current rent is $1800, the new rent is:

$1800 x (100% + 6%) = $1,800 x 106% = $1,908

> **Problem 14:**   A tenant's rent is currently $650 per month. This rent is scheduled to increase 5% per year. What will the tenant's rent be at the beginning of the **third** year from now?

FIRPTA withholding

1. Formula: FIRPTA withholding = gross proceeds from sale x 15%

2. Example: Gross proceeds on a FIRPTA-regulated property sale are $340,000. The required withholding amount is:

$340,000 x 15% = $51,000

Appraisal (Chapter 16)

Adjusting comparables

1. Rules:
    a. NEVER adjust the subject!
    b. If the comparable is better than the subject, subtract value from the comparable
    c. If the comparable is **worse** than the subject, **add** value to the comparable

2. Examples:
    a. A comparable has a pool and the subject does not. The appraiser estimates the value contribution to be $25,000. Adjust the comparable by entering -25,000 in the CMA.
    b. A comparable has 3 bedrooms and the subject as 4. The appraiser estimates the value contribution of a bedroom to be $15,000. Adjust the comparable by entering +15,000 in the CMA.

Problem **15:**   Identify the proper adjustments for the following:

(a) The subject has a two-car garage, while the comparable does not. Value of garage is $33,000.

Adjustment:

(b) A comparable has a fireplace, and the subject does not. Value of fireplace is $8,000.

Adjustment:

(c) The subject has 1,500 square feet. The comparable has 1,600 square feet. The value of extra square feet is $200/SF.

Adjustment:

Income capitalization

Gross rent multiplier (GRM)

1. Formula: gross rent x multiplier = value

2. Example: $20,000 x 9 = $1,800,000

Net income capitalization

1. Formula: net income (NOI) ÷ capitalization rate = value

$$\frac{net\ income\ (NOI)}{capitalization\ rate} = value$$

2. Example: $50,000 ÷ 10% = 50,000 ÷ .10 = $500,000

Problem **16:**   A property grosses $450,000, nets 350,000, and has a capitalization rate of 9%. Prevailing GRMs are 8.

(a) What is the property value using the GRM?

(b) What is the property value using net income capitalization?

Finance
(Chapter 17)   **Interest only loans**

1. Formulas: interest payment (I) = principal (P) x interest rate (R)

annual interest payment ÷ 12 = monthly interest payment

monthly interest payment x 12 = annual interest payment

$$I = P \times R$$
$$R = \frac{I}{P}$$
$$P = \frac{I}{R}$$

2. Examples: A $300,000 interest-only loan @ 10% has annual payments of $30,000 and monthly payments of $2,500.

Annual interest = $300,000 x 10% = $30,000
Monthly interest = $30,000 ÷ 12 = $2,500

The loan amount of an interest-only loan that has an annual interest rate of 8% and a monthly interest payment of $700 is $105,000.

Annual interest = $700 x 12 = $8,400
Loan amount = $8,400 ÷ .08 = $105,000

Problem 17:

(a) A $250,000 loan carries a 7% rate. What is the monthly interest payment?

(b) A $300,000 loan has monthly payments of $2,000. What is its annual interest rate?

(c) A 12% loan has annual payments of $15,000. What is the loan amount?

Loan-to-value (LTV) ratio

1. Formulas: loan amount = market value x LTV

    LTV = loan amount ÷ market value

2. Example: A 75% LTV will allow a lender to make a loan of $375,000 on a $500,000 property.

    loan amount = $500,000 x 75% = $375,000

    LTV = $375,000 ÷ $500,000 = 75%

Problem 18:

(a) A lender requires $90,000 down on a $400,000 property. Calculate the lender's required LTV.

(b) A property is valued at $600,000. The lender will allow a maximum LTV of 75%. How much can the buyer borrow on the property?

Income underwriting ratio calculation

1. Formulas: Conventional:

    monthly PITI = (25-28%) x monthly gross income

    FHA:

    monthly PITI = 31% x monthly gross income

2. Examples: A borrower has monthly gross income of $2,000. Conventional lenders are using a ratio of 28%. The borrower can afford the following monthly PITI payments:

    Conventional:

    PITI = 28% x $2,000 = $560

    FHA:

    PITI = 31% x $2,000 = $620

Problem 19: A borrower earns $4,000/month and pays $600/month in debt repayments. A conventional lender requires a 26% income ratio, and an FHA lender requires 31%. What monthly PITI can this person afford based on the income ratio?

Conventional: $

FHA: $

Debt underwriting ratio calculation

1. Formulas: Conventional:

   Expense = (36% x gross income) – monthly debt

   FHA:

   Expense = (43% x gross income) - monthly debt

2. Example: An individual has a monthly gross income of $6,000, and has monthly debt payments of $900. The borrower can afford the following monthly housing expense:

   Conventional:

   Expense = (36% x $6,000) - 900 = $1,260

   FHA:

   Expense = (43% x $6,000) – 900 = $1,680

Problem 20: A borrower earns $4,000/month and makes monthly debt payments of $600. What monthly payment for housing can this person afford based on the debt ratio?

Conventional: $

FHA: $

Points

1. Formula: 1 point = 1% (.01) of loan amount

2. Example: A lender charges 3 points (3%) on a $350,000 loan. The points charges are:

   3 points = 3%
   .03 x $350,000 = $10,500

> **Problem 21:**   A lender is charging 2.75 points on a $240,000 loan. How much must the borrower pay for points?

Investments (Chapter 18)

Appreciation

1. Formulas: total appreciation = current value – original price

   Error! Bookmark not defined.total appreciation rate = total appreciation / original price

   one-year appreciation rate = one-year appreciation / prior-year value

2. Example: A house bought for $500,000 appreciates $50,000 each Year for 3 years.

   total appreciation = $650,000 - 500,000 = $150,000

   total appreciation rate = $150,000 ÷ $500,000 = 30%

   first- year rate = $50,000 ÷ $500,000 = 10%

> **Problem 22:**   A property is purchased for $360,000. A year later it is Sold for $410,000. What is the amount of appreciation, and what is the appreciation rate?

Equity

1. Formula: equity = current value – current loan amount

2. Example: A buyer bought a property for $600,000 with a loan of $450,000. The house has appreciated $60,000 and the buyer has reduced the original loan by $30,000. The buyer's current equity is:

    Equity = ($600,000 + 60,000) - ($450,000 - 30,000) = $240,000

Problem 23:   A property is purchased for $450,000 with a $75,000 downpayment. Five years later the property is worth $540,000, and the loan balance has dropped $12,500. What is the owner's new equity?

Pre-tax cash flow

1. Formula
    and example:

potential rental income	$50,000
- vacancy and collection loss	3,000
= effective rental income	47,000
+ other income	2,000
= gross operating income (GOI)	49,000
- operating expenses	20,000
- reserves	3,000
= net operating income (NOI)	26,000
- debt service	15,000
= pre-tax cash flow	11,000

Problem 24:   An apartment building has a potential income of $300,000 and vacancy of $12,000. Its bills total $128,000, and $12,000 has been reserved for repairs. Payments on the loan total $88,000. What is the property's pre-tax cash flow?

Tax liability

1. Formula
    and example:

	net operating income (NOI)	26,000
+	reserves	3,000
-	interest expense	15,000
-	cost recovery expense	5,000
=	taxable income	9,000
x	tax rate (28%)	
=	tax liability	2,520

> **Problem 25:** The property from the previous problem has annual cost recovery of $28,000. Out of the annual debt service, $8,000 is non-interest principal payback. The property owner's tax rate is 28%. What is the property's annual tax?

Annual depreciation (cost recovery) expense

1. Calculation:
    a. identify improvements-to-land ratio

    b. identify value of improvements: ratio x property price

    c. divide value of improvements by total depreciation term

2. Example:
    A property was bought for $400,000. 75% of the value is allocated to the improvement. The property falls in the 39-year depreciation category.

    (1) improvements-to-land ratio = 3:1, or 75%

    (2) improvement value = $400,000 x 75% = $300,000

    (3) annual depreciation = $300,000 ÷ 39 = $7,692

> Problem 26: A property is purchased for $400,000. Improvements account for 80% of the value. Given a 39-year depreciation term, what is the annual depreciation expense?

Capital gain

1. Formula
   and example: (residential property)

	Selling price of property	$300,000
-	Selling costs	24,000
=	Amount realized (ending basis)	$276,000
	Beginning basis (price) of property	$250,000
+	Capital improvements	10,000
-	Total depreciation expense	0
=	Adjusted basis of property	260,000
	Amount realized (ending basis)	$276,000
-	Adjusted basis of property	260,000
=	Capital gain	$ 16,000

Problem 27:   A principal residence is bought for $360,000. A new tile roof is added, costing $15,000. Five years later the home sells for $440,000, and the closing costs $35,000. What is the homeowner's capital gain?

Return, rate of return, and investment amount

1. Formulas:

$$\frac{net\ operating\ income}{price} = return\ on\ investment\ (ROI)$$

$$\frac{cash\ flow}{cash\ invested} = cash\text{-}on\text{-}cash\ return\ (C\ on\ C)$$

$$\frac{cash\ flow}{equity} = return\ on\ equity\ (ROE)$$

2. Example: A property is bought for $200,000 with a $50,000 down payment and a $150,000 interest-only loan. The property has a net income of $20,000 and a cash flow of $8,000. In addition, the property has appreciated $30,000.

ROI	=	$20,000 ÷ $200,000 = 10%
C on C	=	*$8,000 ÷ $50,000 = 16%*
ROE	=	$8,000 ÷ $80,000 = 10%

Problem 28: A multi-unit rental property was bought four years ago for $1,200,000 with a $200,000 down payment. The property now rents for $8,500 per month. Expenses and debt service are $1,000/month and $6,500/month respectively. An appraiser estimates the property's current value at $1,450,000. The investor pays off her principal balance at a rate of $5,000 per year. Compute the following investment returns for the investor:

ROI   =

C on C =

ROE   =

Taxation (Chapter 19)

Tax rate calculation

1. Formula: $\text{tax rate (millage rate)} = \dfrac{\text{tax requirement}}{\text{tax base}}$

2. Example: A municipality has a revenue requirement of $10,000,000 after accounting for its revenues from sale of utilities. This requirement has to be covered by property tax. The real estate tax base, after homestead exemptions, is $300,000,000. The tax rate will be:

$$\frac{10,000,000}{300,000,000} = .0333 \quad 33.33 \text{ mills}$$

Problem 29: Barrington has an annual budget of $25,000,000 to be paid by property taxes. Assessed valuations are $300,000,000, and exemptions total $25,000,000. What must the tax rate be to finance the budget?

Homestead exemption calculation

1. Formula and example

assessed value	$360,000
- homestead exemption	50,000
taxable value	$310,000

Taxing the property

1. Formulas: taxable value of property x tax rate (mill rate) for each taxing authority in jurisdiction

        total tax = sum of all taxes by taxing authority

2. Example: The taxable value of a property after exemptions is 400,000 and tax rates are as shown. The property's tax bill will be:

School tax:	$400,000 x 10 mills	=	$4,000
City tax:	$400,000 x 4 mills	=	1600
County tax:	$400,000 x 3 mills	=	1200
	Total tax:		$6,800

Problem 30:   A homeowner's assessed valuation is $225,000. The homestead exemption is $25,000. Tax rates for the property are 8 mills for schools; 3 mills for the city; 2.5 mills for the county; and .5 mills for the local community college. What is the homeowner's tax bill?

Special assessments calculation

1. Formula: a. Identify total costs to be assessed

        b. Calculate prorated share for each property impacted

        c. Multiply cost x prorated share

2. Example: A canal will be dredged at a cost of $200,000. The improvement affects 30 properties with a total canal frontage of 4,000 feet. One property has 200' of frontage. Its assessment bill will be:

        (1) 200' ÷ 4,000' = 5% share

        (2) $200,000 x 5% = $10,000 assessment

Problem 31:   A street beautification project is to cost $25,000. The project affects 20 properties having a total of 2,000 front feet. One owner's lot has 75 front feet. What will this owner's special assessment be?

Closings
(Chapter 21)   **Prorations**

1. Formulas
    and rules:

Accounting for common items paid (or received) in advance vs arrears

	arrears	advance	debit	credit
real estate taxes	x		seller	buyer
rents received by seller		x	seller	buyer
utilities	x		seller	buyer

Whose share is charged to whom?

- if buyer pays taxes in arrears: charge seller, credit buyer for seller's portion

- if seller received rents in advance: charge seller, credit buyer for buyer's portion

- if seller pays utilities in advance: credit seller, charge buyer for seller's portion

Calculating the proration: 360-day method and 365-day method

1. **Calculate the daily proration amount**

    a. 360-day method: divide the annual amount by 360 or monthly amount by 30

    b. 365-day method: divide the annual proration amount by 365, or monthly amount by # days in that month

2. **Calculate # of seller's days**

    a. 360-day method: use 30 days for each month; actual number of seller days within the month, counting (or not counting) the day of closing

    b. 365-day method: use actual number of days for each month and partial month

3. **Calculate the seller's share**

    Multiply the daily amount times the number of seller's days – both methods

4. **Calculate buyer's share (both methods)**

    Subtract seller's share (from #3) from total share

2. Example: A rental property closes on January 25 and the closing day is the seller's. The 365-day method will be used for the prorations. Monthly rent already received by seller is $2,400. Annual real estate taxes to be paid in arrears by buyer are $4,000. Round to the nearest cent.

1. **Rent proration**: (monthly; 365-day method)

Daily amount:	$2,400 monthly rent ÷ 31 days in January = $77.42
# Seller's days:	25
Seller's share:	$77.42 x 25 = $1,935.50
Buyer's share:	$2,400 – 1,935.50 = $464.50

    Credit buyer and debit seller for buyer's share of $464.50

2. **Tax proration**: (annual; 365-day method)

Daily amount:	$4,000 ÷ 365 = $10.96
# Seller's days:	25
Seller's share:	$10.96 x 25 = $274
Buyer's share:	$4,000 – 274 = $3,726

    Credit buyer and debit seller for seller's share of $274

Problem 32: A rental property closes on March 15th. Proratable income and expenses are: rental income of $1,800/month, received in advance by seller, March 1; annual taxes of $4,800/year, to be paid in arrears by buyer, January 1 of the year after sale. The day of closing is the seller's. February has 28 days. Prorate the items using the 365-day method, and assign debits and credits.

rent:	seller's share	$
	buyer's share	$
	debit seller/credit buyer	$
	debit buyer/credit seller	$
taxes:	seller's share	$
	buyer's share	$
	debit seller/credit buyer	$
	debit buyer/credit seller	$

REAL ESTATE MATHEMATICS: ANSWER KEY

Problem 1: $\dfrac{3}{19} + \dfrac{2}{7} = \dfrac{21+38}{133} = \dfrac{59}{133}$

Problem 2: $\dfrac{4}{14} \times \dfrac{3}{8} = \dfrac{12}{112}$

Problem 3: 2.65 = 265%
0.294 = 29.4%
0.005 = .5%

Problem 4: 72.1% = .721
90.2% = .902
5.79% = .0579

Problem 5: 8/9 = 88.8%
3/6 = 50%
14/42 = 33.3%

Problem 6: 40% = 40/100 = 2/5
16% = 16/100 = 4/25

Problem 7: 210

Problem 8: 144 SF
256 SF
35 SF

Problem 9: 40 acres
10 acres

Problem 10: Schroeder: $5,206.25
Hobson: $7,437.50
Joachim $9,668.75
Wallace: $7,437.50

Problem 11: $552,000

Problem 12: 90%

Problem 13: $4,680

Problem 14: $716.63 keep or change?

Problem 15: (a) +33,000 to comparable
            - 8,000 to comparable
            - 20,000 to comparable

Problem 16: (a) $3,600,000
            (b) $3,888,888

Problem 17: (a) $1,458
                8%
                $125,000

Problem 18: (a) 77.5%
            (b) $450,000

Problem 19: Conventional: $1,040/month
            FHA & VA: $1,240/month

Problem 20: Conventional: $840
            FHA: $1,120

Problem 21: $6,600

Problem 22: $50,000; 13.89%

Problem 23: $177,500

Problem 24: $60,000

Problem 25: $14,560

Problem 26: $8,205

Problem 27: $30,000

Problem 28: (a) ROI   = 7.5%
            (b) C on C = 6.0%
            (c) ROE   = 2.55%

Problem 29: 90.9 mills, or 9.09%

Problem 30: $2,800

Problem 31: $937.50

Problem 32:

rent: seller's share		$870.96
buyer's share		$929.04
debit seller/credit buyer		$929.04
taxes: seller's share		$973.16
buyer's share		3,826.84
debit seller/credit buyer		$973.16

PRACTICE EXAMINATION

Answer Key is on page 582

1. Which of the following professionals involved in the real estate business are most concerned about managing real estate for clients?

   a. Brokers and agents
   b. Property managers
   c. Corporate real estate managers
   d. Appraisers

2. Real estate can be defined as

   a. land and all property contained therein.
   b. unimproved land.
   c. land and everything permanently attached to it.
   d. air, surface, and subsurface rights.

3. Which of the following is included in the bundle of rights inherent in ownership?

   a. To tax
   b. To encroach
   c. To possess
   d. To inherit

4. The overriding test of whether an item is a fixture or personal property is

   a. whether the owner owns the property the item is affixed to.
   b. how it is described in a sale or lease contract.
   c. what the title records on the property indicate.
   d. how the buyer defines the item.

5. An owner of a lakefront property tells a fisherman that he cannot fish in a boat within fifty feet of the owner's shoreline. The fisherman protests that the owner cannot prevent him. Which of the following is true?

   a. The fisherman is correct because the water and the land underlying it are public property.
   b. The owner's prohibition is valid, since the underlying land belongs to abutting properties to the middle of the lake.
   c. The owner can prevent the fisherman from fishing within ten feet, but not beyond.
   d. The owner's prohibition is valid if all lakefront property owners have agreed to it.

6. The distinguishing feature of a defeasible fee simple estate is that

   a. it only endures for the lifetime of the defeasee.
   b. it has no restrictions or conditions on use.
   c. it may revert to a grantor if the prescribed use changes.
   d. it is of limited duration.

7. Dower can best be defined as

   a. a grant of foreclosure immunity extended to a homestead claimant.
   b. a wife's life estate interest in her husband's property.
   c. a husband's homestead exemption.
   d. a grantor who endows property to heirs.

8. A distinct feature of a joint tenancy is that joint tenants

   a. may elect to have any percent of ownership in the property.
   b. cannot will their interest to a party outside the tenancy.
   c. own separate physical portions of the land.
   d. cannot lease the property.

9. Interests in a condominium differ from those in a cooperative, in that

   a. a default by a condominium owner may cause a foreclosure on the entire property instead of just a single unit, as with a cooperative.
   b. the condominium owner owns the common elements and the airspace, whereas the coop owner owns only the apartment.
   c. the coop owner owns stock in the cooperative association, whereas the condominium owner simply owns real estate.
   d. the cooperative owner must pay a pro rata share of the cooperative's expenses as well as rent.

10. There are two adjoining properties. An easement allows property A to use the access road that belongs to property B. In this situation, property B is said to be which of the following in relation to property A?

    a. Dominant tenement
    b. Subordinate tenant
    c. Servient estate
    d. Conditional life tenant

11. Title records of a property reveal several recorded liens: a one-year old judgment lien; a mechanic's lien dating from two years ago; a special assessment tax lien recorded last month; and a first mortgage lien recorded five years ago. In case of a foreclosure, which of these liens will be paid first?

    a. First mortgage lien
    b. Special assessment tax lien
    c. Mechanic's lien
    d. Judgment lien

12. A lender may terminate foreclosure proceedings if the defaulting borrower executes

    a. a wraparound mortgage.
    b. a lis pendens.
    c. a waiver of redemption.
    d. a deed in lieu of foreclosure.

13. A person has occupied a property for seven years, and no one has ever attempted to evict her or co-occupy the parcel. In this case, the person might base a claim of legal ownership on

    a. her prescriptive easement.
    b. title records.
    c. constructive notice of possession.
    d. tenancy in severalty.

14. A person wishes to convey any and all interests in a property to another with full assurances against encumbrances, liens, or any other title defects on the property. This party would most likely use which of the following types of deed?

    a. A quitclaim deed
    b. A general warranty deed
    c. A deed in lieu of warrant
    d. A guardian's deed

15. The chain of title to a property refers to which of the following?

    a. An abstract of the condition and marketability of title
    b. The genealogy of successive heirs to a property
    c. The list of all current encumbrances and clouds "chained" to title
    d. A chronology of successive owners of record

16. A leased property is conveyed to a new owner. What happens to the lease?

    a. It remains in effect.
    b. It is cancelled.
    c. It automatically renews at closing for its original term.
    d. It moves with the owner to a new property, if purchased within one year.

17. The Uniform Residential Landlord and Tenant Act fundamentally attempts to

    a. promote the rights of tenants, particularly in lease defaults.
    b. standardize rental rates.
    c. encourage fairness and simplicity in lease forms and provisions.
    d. minimize rent escalations in economically depressed zones.

18. A primary objective of residential zoning is

    a. regulate rates of appreciation and depreciation of residences.
    b. promote the value and planned land use of a neighborhood.
    c. eliminate nonconforming uses, variances, and special exceptions.
    d. disperse intensity of usage.

19. A shop was originally built in a commercial zone. The zone has since been changed to a residential zone. Zoning authorities permit the use, most likely as

    a. a variance.
    b. a special exception.
    c. an illegal nonconforming use.
    d. a legal nonconforming use.

20. Authorities conduct comprehensive land use planning in order to

    a. balance public interests with individual property rights.
    b. prevent the public from exercising police powers.
    c. ensure positive market conditions for development projects.
    d. limit growth.

21. The purpose of a formal legal description of a property is to

    a. eliminate encroachments.
    b. locate and identify the property reliably.
    c. eliminate the possibility of surveyor error.
    d. qualify for title recordation.

22. A parcel is described as the SW 1/4 of the N 1/2 of the E 1/2 of Section 14. What is its acreage?

    a. 160 acres   b. 80 acres
    c. 40 acres   d. 20 acres

23. A suburb has a growing need for single-family housing, but the land available for new construction is running low. In this case, it is likely that the price of existing homes

    a. will decline.
    b. will increase.
    c. will stabilize.
    d. will not show any predictable movement.

24. The demand for homes in a market is best expressed in terms of

    a. square feet of housing required.
    b. number of contracts signed with developers.
    c. number of houses listed in the multiple listing service.
    d. number of households seeking housing.

25. What is the significance of base employment in a real estate market?

    a. It gives the basic number of people who will need housing.
    b. It indicates the number of people at the low end of the buying power spectrum.
    c. It drives total employment and population growth, which lead to demand for real estate.
    d. It indicates the number of people who want to move into the market.

26. The concept known as substitution states that

    a. buyers will not substitute the quality of one home for the price of another.
    b. the replacement cost of an item cannot be substituted for the item's original value.
    c. a new improvement will only increase market value to the extent of the cost of a similar improvement.
    d. buyers will not pay more for a certain house than they would for another, similar house.

27. The "price that a willing, informed, and unpressured seller and buyer agree upon for a property, assuming a cash price and reasonable exposure of the property to the market" describes which of the following concepts of value?

    a. Highest and best value
    b. Substitution value
    c. Desirability
    d. Market value

28. A warehouse building lacks sufficient ceiling height for the operation of modern forklifts. This is an example of

    a. non-conforming use.
    b. functional obsolescence.
    c. overimprovement.
    d. economic obsolescence.

29. To derive value using the income capitalization approach, one must

    a. divide the capitalization rate by net income.
    b. multiply net income times the capitalization rate.
    c. divide the capitalization rate into net income.
    d. multiply cash flow by the capitalization rate.

30. An office building rents for $600,000, has expenses of $400,000, and a cash flow of $100,000. The prevailing gross rent multiplier is 8. Using the GRM, what is the value of the building?

    a. $800,000   b. $1,600,000
    c. $3,200,000   d. $4,800,000

31. An owner obtains a loan and gives the mortgagee a mortgage on the property as collateral. The mortgagor/owner retains title to the property, and the mortgagee records a lien. This is an example of

    a. intermediation.
    b. contracting for deed.
    c. subordination.
    d. hypothecation.

32. An important characteristic of a promissory note is that

    a. it is assignable.
    b. it must be secured by collateral.
    c. it is not a negotiable instrument.
    d. it must be recorded to be enforceable.

33. Disclosure of estimated closing costs is required of a lender in order to comply with

    a. the Equal Credit Opportunity Act.
    b. Truth-in-Lending laws.
    c. Federal Fair Housing Laws.
    d. the Real Estate Settlement Procedures Act.

34. The secondary mortgage market organizations do all of the following EXCEPT

    a. guarantee performance on mortgages.
    b. buy pools of mortgages from primary lenders.
    c. sell securities based on pooled mortgages.
    d. directly originate loans.

35. Negative amortization of a loan occurs whenever

    a. monthly payments are interest-only.
    b. a payment does not pay the interest owed.
    c. the principal loan balance is diminishing.
    d. the interest rate increases on an adjustable rate loan.

36. A borrower earns $3,000/month and makes credit card and car note payments of $500. A conventional lender requires a 27% income ratio. What monthly amount for housing expenses (principal, interest, taxes, insurance) will the lender allow this person to have in order to qualify for a conventional mortgage loan?

    a. $810   b. $675
    c. $972   d. $1,040

37. A $250,000 interest-only loan carries a 7% rate. Monthly payments are

    a. $1,750.
    b. $1,458.
    c. $17,500.
    d. Cannot be determined without loan term data.

38. A lender is charging 2.75 points on a $240,000 loan. How much must the borrower pay for points?

    a. $550.   b. $5,500.
    c. $6,600.   d. $660.

39. Which of the following is generally true of a real estate investment?

    a. The lower the price, the lower the liquidity
    b. The greater the return, the greater the risk
    c. The more management, the less return
    d. The more liquidity, the greater the return

40. The capital gain on sale of an investment is computed as

    a. beginning basis plus gain.
    b. sale price minus beginning basis.
    c. net sales proceeds minus beginning basis.
    d. net sales proceeds minus adjusted basis.

41. The formula for return on equity is

    a. cash flow divided by equity.
    b. required yield times gross income.
    c. net operating income divided by equity.
    d. cash flow times the capitalization rate.

42. Mary Bright bought a home for $80,000, paying $10,000 down and taking a mortgage loan of $70,000. The following year she had a new roof put on, at a cost of $2,000. What is Mary's adjusted basis in the house if she now sells the house for $300,000?

    a. $12,000   b. $218,000
    c. $230,000   d. $82,000

43. An office building has a potential income of $500,000 and vacancy of 10%. Its cash-paid bills total $300,000, and annual depreciation is $5,000. Payments on the loan total $100,000. What is the property's pre-tax cash flow?

    a. $45,000   b. $50,000
    c. $150,000   d. $155,000

44. A property is purchased for $200,000. Improvements account for 75% of the value. Given a 39-year depreciation term, what is the annual depreciation expense?

   a. $3,846   b. $5,128
   c. $6,410   d. $8,294

45. An income property is bought for $500,000. Gross income is $100,000, and net operating income is $60,000. Cash flow is $10,000. What is the return on investment (ROI)?

   a. 2.00%   b. 12%
   c. 10.00%   d. 60.00%

46. Which of the following is the formula for deriving the tax base of a jurisdiction?

   a. The total tax required divided by assessed values
   b. The total of all assessed values minus exemptions
   c. The annual budget times the tax rate
   d. The annual budget divided by the millage rate

47. The purpose of a homestead tax exemption is

   a. to exempt owners from ad valorem taxation.
   b. to offer tax abatement on a principal residence.
   c. to encourage owners to finance their principle residences.
   d. to exempt owners of principal residences who rent their properties.

48. A homeowner's tax bill for a taxing district is derived by

   a. dividing the tax base by the district's needed revenues.
   b. multiplying the tax rate times the assessed value of the property.
   c. multiplying the tax rate times the taxable value of the property.
   d. multiplying the millage rate times the equalization factor.

49. The village of Parrish has an annual budget requirement of $20,000,000 to be funded by property taxes. Assessed valuations are $400,000,000, and exemptions total $25,000,000. What must the tax rate be to finance the budget?

   a. 4.70%   b. 5.33%
   c. 5.00%   d. 11.25%

50. A canal dredging project is to cost $100,000. There are 40 properties along the canal, and 40 others across the street from the canal. The total canal footage to be dredged is 2,500 feet. How much will the assessment be for a 150-foot property on the canal?

   a. $1,250   b. $2,500
   c. $3,000   d. $6,000

51. A prospective homebuyer offers to buy a house if the seller agrees to pay financing points at closing. The seller gets the offer, signs it, and gives it to his agent to deliver. At this point the status of the offer is

   a. a valid contract.
   b. an invalid contract.
   c. still an offer.
   d. an invalid offer.

52. One aim of the statute of frauds is to

   a. set time limits for disputing contract provisions.
   b. require certain conveyances to be in writing.
   c. prevent fraudulent assignments of listing agreements.
   d. make all oral agreements unenforceable.

53. A buyer agrees to all terms of a seller's offer and sends notice of acceptance back to the seller. The seller now tells the buyer the deal is off because he has learned that the home was underpriced. Which of the following is true?

   a. The buyer must offer the new price to get the property.
   b. The seller may counteroffer.
   c. The contract is cancelled.
   d. The buyer has a binding contract.

54. A principal discloses to the listing agent that she must sell a property within two months to avoid a financial problem. Nearly seven weeks later, a buyer's agent hears of the seller's difficulty from the listing agent and advises his buyer to submit an offer for 80% of the listed price. The buyer complies, and the seller accepts the offer. Which of the following is true?

   a. The buyer's agent has violated fiduciary duties owed the customer.
   b. The listing agent has violated fiduciary duties owed the customer.
   c. The buyer's agent has violated fiduciary duties owed the client.
   d. The listing agent has violated fiduciary duties owed the client.

55. An owner's agent is showing a buyer an apartment building. The buyer questions the agent as to whether some cracking paint contains lead. The agent's best course of action is to

   a. contract to re-paint the cracked area.
   b. assure the buyer the paint is lead-free.
   c. suggest the buyer make a lower-price offer to cover the possible problem.
   d. inform the seller of the inquiry and test the paint.

56. Agent Jerry, who works for Broker Lucy, obtains an owner listing to lease a building. Lucy's other agent, Linda, a tenant representative, locates a tenant for Lucy's listing. If there is no arrangement to the contrary, Broker Lucy in this instance is

   a. an implied agent.
   b. a dual agent.
   c. a single agent.
   d. a cooperating agent.

57. A transaction broker should disclose his or her agency relationship to the transaction principals

    a. before receipt of any offer.
    b. upon completion of the listing agreement.
    c. upon first substantive contact.
    d. upon initial contact of any kind with either principal.

58. An agent obtains a listing which ensures compensation for procuring a customer, provided the agent is the procuring cause. This agent has entered into a(n)

    a. exclusive right-to sell agreement.
    b. exclusive agency agreement.
    c. open listing.
    d. net listing.

59. A landlord promises to compensate a broker for procuring a tenant, provided the landlord's brother decides not to rent the property within a month. This would be an example of a(n)

    a. exclusive right-to-lease agreement.
    b. exclusive agency agreement.
    c. open listing.
    d. net listing.

60. The amount of a real estate brokerage commission is determined by

    a. state license law guidelines.
    b. negotiation with the client.
    c. the Board of Realtors®.
    d. agreement among competing brokers.

61. Real estate sales agents are legally authorized to

    a. represent buyers on their broker's behalf.
    b. enter into approved listing agreements.
    c. execute lease contracts for less than one year.
    d. transfer listings to other MLS agents.

62. In eliciting an offer from a buyer, an owner's agent must be careful to

    a. avoid an overpriced offer that will cause buyer's remorse or lawsuits.
    b. complete any offer the buyer might decide to make.
    c. disclose what price the owner will accept.
    d. avoid completing an offer that contains contingencies.

63. An example of conversion is

    a. depositing escrow funds in a business operating account.
    b. spending a customer deposit on a surety bond for the agency.
    c. spending operating income from an apartment on roof repairs.
    d. depositing a commission into an escrow account.

64. Three leading agencies charge identical commission rates for brokering office properties in Phoenix. Which of the following is true?

    a. This is a perfectly legitimate business practice.
    b. The brokers have engaged in legal collusion.
    c. The brokers have allocated the Phoenix market.
    d. The brokers have illegally fixed prices.

65. A business owner insists on a price for his enterprise that exceeds the value of the tangible assets, claiming that it is a well-known family business with a loyal clientele. The excess value is known as

    a. the buyer's premium.
    b. goodwill.
    c. the risk factor.
    d. the profit margin.

66. An agent informs owners in an area that a decline in property values over the past five years is due to an influx of minority families. He suggests that the trend will continue, and advises them to sell before it is too late. This agent is probably guilty of

    a. blockbusting.
    b. redlining.
    c. discriminatory misrepresentation.
    d. negligent misrepresentation.

67. An agent spends two hours with a minority buyer, then shows the buyer five available properties all over town. Later, a similarly qualified minority couple enter the office. The agent spends twenty minutes with the couple, gives them the MLS book to review, and encourages them to drive by the listings on their way home. If they like anything, they should come back the next day to discuss terms. This agent could be liable for

    a. misrepresentation.
    b. steering.
    c. providing unequal services.
    d. nothing.

68. An owner suddenly pulls a property off the market after hearing from the agent that a minority party has made a full-price offer. The agent then goes back to the minority party and reports that the seller has decided to wait until next year to sell the home. Who, if anyone, has violated fair housing laws?

    a. Both owner and agent.
    b. The owner.
    c. The agent.
    d. No one.

69. An owner completes a contract to sell her property. Before closing, she runs into financial trouble and assigns the contract to her mortgagor. Which of the following is true?

    a. The owner has defaulted.
    b. The buyer can sue to nullify the mortgage.
    c. The assignment can take effect only after the closing.
    d. The sale contract remains valid.

70. Buyers and sellers rely on escrow accounts in order to

    a. allow a third party fiduciary to handle the funds.
    b. have access to the funds without interference from the broker.
    c. prevent the broker from receiving a commission until after closing.
    d. earn equal interest on their funds.

71. An option-to-purchase expires. The landlord agrees to extend it in exchange for a higher price. The optionee claims he can exercise the option within the redemption period. Which is true?

    a. The landlord must honor the option and sell immediately.
    b. The landlord can extend the option term, but cannot raise the price.
    c. The landlord must extend the option but is allowed to raise the price.
    d. The landlord is under no obligation, since options do not have a redemption period.

72. RESPA requires specific closing procedures whenever

    a. the loan is to be guaranteed.
    b. the loan is to be sold to the FNMA.
    c. the commercial property is to be bought by FHLMC.
    d. a borrower does not fully understand closing costs.

73. When an item is prorated between buyer and seller on a settlement statement, the closing officer must

    a. debit the buyer and seller.
    b. credit the buyer and seller.
    c. debit and credit both buyer and seller.
    d. debit one party and credit the other.

74. Which of the following items are paid in arrears?

    a. Taxes and insurance
    b. Rents and interest
    c. Taxes and interest
    d. Rents and insurance

75. A sale transaction on rental property closes on December 16. The landlord received the December rent of $713 on December 1. Assuming the closing day is the seller's, and that the 365-day method is used for prorating, which of the following entries would appear on the settlement statement?

    a. Debit seller $345.00
    b. Credit seller $713.00
    c. Debit buyer $345.00
    d. Credit buyer $368.00

76. The most common form of risk transference in brokerage firms is

    a. continuing education.
    b. errors & omissions insurance.
    c. company rules and regulations.
    d. self control.

77. Which of the following is a major risk in the fulfilling of listing agreements?

    a. Exceeding the limits of the authority granted by the agreement
    b. Disclosing a material defect without the seller's permission
    c. Failing to receive proper compensation
    d. Putting the client's interests above those of the customer

78. In the contracting process, a licensee must be careful to avoid

    a. giving the principal any advice about the transaction.
    b. describing the normal requirements of a contract to a client.
    c. drafting a contract illegally.
    d. pointing out to the principals the importance of meeting contingency deadlines.

79. If a licensee is found guilty of obtaining a real estate license under false pretenses, the most likely penalty will be

    a. paying a punitive fee.
    b. civil suit for damages.
    c. extra continuing education.
    d. license revocation.

80. A broker responsible for handling a trust account is violating the law by

    a. depositing an earnest money check in a personal account.
    b. following the seller's instructions to hold an earnest money check uncashed.
    c. removing an earned commission from a trust account without permission of the depository institution.
    d. opening an account that names the licensee as the trustee of the account.

81. In order to set rents and to estimate the expected return on a managed property, a property manager needs to prepare a(n)

    a. cash reserve statement.
    b. operating budget.
    c. expense report.
    d. rent roll.

82. Why is it important for a property manager to maintain good relations with tenants?

    a. If tenants like the manager they will like the owner.
    b. Happy tenants are easier to work with.
    c. The manager owes the landlord the fiduciary duty of pleasing the tenants.
    d. Unhappy tenants lead to expensive tenant turnover.

83. While physical maintenance of the property is a primary function of the property manager, the level of maintenance performed must be balanced with

    a. the cost of services and the time available.
    b. the manager's monetary incentives.
    c. owner objectives and tenant demands.
    d. the manager's skills and the condition of the property.

84. What kind of insurance would provide coverage for loss of income when a rental property is damaged so badly that it cannot be used?

    a. Casualty
    b. Consequential loss
    c. Fire and hazard
    d. Liability

85. Property managers are usually considered to be

    a. general agents empowered to perform a wide range of duties for the landlord.
    b. special agents empowered to perform a specific task for the landlord.
    c. dual agents serving both the landlord and the tenants.
    d. employees who have no agency relationship with their employer.

86. Which of the following transactions is not eligible for a recovery payment from the Guaranty Fund?

    a. The purchase of undeveloped land for the purpose of building condominiums
    b. The purchase of interest in a limited partnership formed for investing in real estate
    c. The purchase of a private family home
    d. The purchase of a duplex as rental property

87. Sales contracts provided by a broker must include a statement that the buyer is protected by the Guaranty Fund for losses up to

    a. $250,000.
    b. $25,000.
    c. $5,000.
    d. $50,000.

88. A licensee who has been investigated for misconduct and disagrees with a proposed order from the Commission may file an exception within _____ of the dismissal.

    a. 30 days
    b. 10 days
    c. 3 years
    d. 1 year

89. Which of the following statements is true?

    a. Maryland licensees may affiliate with one broker only.
    b. A licensure applicant with a felony conviction will automatically be denied a Maryland real estate license.
    c. Individuals who pass only one portion of the licensure examination must pass the second portion within 1 year.
    d. Both portions of the licensure examination must be passed with a score of 75% or higher.

90. Which of the following is required of a broker license applicant but not of a salesperson applicant?

    e. Be of good character
    f. Submit a credit report
    g. Complete 3 clock hours of ethics coursework
    h. Pay a Guaranty Fund fee

91. An out-of-state licensed broker is exempt from completing Maryland's broker education requirements if the broker has practiced real estate for at least _____ immediately preceding application for a Maryland reciprocal broker license.

    a. 5 years
    b. 2 of the 3 years
    c. 4 years
    d. 3 of the 5 years

92. John's initial salesperson license was issued on June 30 of 2023. By what date must John renew his license to prevent it from expiring?

    a. June 30 of 2025
    b. March 1 of 2026
    c. June 30 of 2024
    d. April 1 of 2025

93. On what type of advertising are licensees required to include their license category?

    a. Ads placed by teams
    b. Ads that include inducements
    c. Ads that include the Equal Housing Opportunity logo
    d. None. Licensees are not required to include their license status on any advertising.

94. Maryland law requires brokers to exercise _____ supervision over individuals who perform real estate activities on behalf of the broker and even set out the factors that establish such supervision.

    a. consistent and concise
    b. thorough and sufficient
    c. careful and diligent
    d. reasonable and adequate

95. Which of the following is not considered a prohibited act?

    a. Requiring a buyer to use a particular title insurance company
    b. Lending a broker's license to another individual
    c. Affiliating with two brokers
    d. Guaranteeing future profits from the resale of a property

96. Dual agency may occur only if

    a. a team leader assigns two team members to act as intracompany agents in the transaction.
    b. the assigned ICAs are from different teams within the brokerage.
    c. each party waives his or her right of confidentiality.
    d. both parties' consent in writing.

97. What document includes disclosures based on projections for a condominium's future?

    a. A condominium resale package
    b. A condominium public offering statement
    c. A condominium declaration
    d. A condominium contract of sale

98. Which statement is FALSE?

    a. A listing agreement is a type of brokerage agreement.
    b. A listing agreement must include the conditions under which a broker will be paid.
    c. A listing agreement must be signed by the seller and the buyer.
    d. A listing agreement must state the client's responsibilities.

99. A property's latent defects are those

    a. easily seen by anyone viewing the property.
    b. the seller is required to repair prior to closing the sale.
    c. the seller regards as confidential.
    d. a buyer is not likely to know about or discover.

100. When a brokerage agreement terminates,

    a. the licensee owes no further duties to the client.
    b. the licensee owes the client only the right of confidentiality.
    c. the licensee owes the client only the duties of answering questions truthfully and treating the client fairly.
    d. the licensee owes the client only the duties of accounting for trust money and maintaining confidentiality.

101. A buyer's agent primarily represents the interests of

    a. the agent's affiliated broker.
    b. the buyer.
    c. the seller.
    d. the seller's agent

102. If a licensee has a brokerage agreement with a property seller and another party approaches the licensee about the property, the licensee is required to

    a. enter into a brokerage relationship agreement with the other party.
    b. disclose in writing the he or she represents the seller.
    c. have both parties consent in writing to a dual agency.
    d. show the seller's property to the other party.

103. A house on the market has a handsome stone fireplace that the agent knows hasn't been used in years because of a clogged chimney. A potential buyer asks the seller's agent if the fireplace works. What kind of response should the agent make?

    a. The agent must answer truthfully and reveal the material fact that it doesn't work in its present condition.
    b. The agent must protect the seller's confidentiality by saying he doesn't know.
    c. The agent must act in the seller's best interests and say that it does work.
    d. The agent must exercise reasonable care and advise the buyer to seek an expert opinion.

104. When the Maryland Commission on Civil Rights investigates a discrimination complaint, what option does the Commission have other than issuing a No Probable Cause finding or obtaining a written conciliation agreement between the parties?

    a. Forward the complaint to the Attorney General
    b. Forward the matter to the Office of General Council
    c. Forward the case to the Administrative Law Judge
    d. Forward the complaint to HUD

105. The Fair Housing Act of 1866 prohibited discrimination based on which protected class without exception?

    a. Race
    b. Religion
    c. Sex
    d. National origin

106. An 18-year-old pregnant woman receiving government financial assistance falls into several protected classes, but not that of

    a. source of income.
    b. sex.
    c. familial status.
    d. physical disability.

107. Time-share developers are required to provide purchasers with a _____ implied warranty on the time-share's construction.

    a.   6-month
    b.   1-year
    c.   30-day
    d.   18-month

108. To redeem a property after a tax sale, the homeowner must

    a.   allow the new owner to foreclose.
    b.   file a release-of-lien action with the court within 2 years of the sale.
    c.   have the buyer sign the deed back to the homeowner.
    d.   pay the tax debt within 6 months of the sale.

109. Mechanics' liens are available for buildings being repaired for up to _____ of the property's value.

    a.   15%
    b.   20%
    c.   25%
    d.   35%

110. Tenants may withhold rent for unrepaired serious defects by

    a.   depositing the rent monies into a personal savings account.
    b.   establishing an escrow account through the District Court.
    c.   notifying the landlord in person.
    d.   filing a lawsuit against the landlord.

PRACTICE EXAMINATION ANSWER KEY

1. b. Property managers (8)
2. c. land and everything permanently attached to it. (16)
3. c. To possess (18)
4. b. how it is described in a sale or lease contract. (24)
5. a. The fisherman is correct because the water and the land underlying it are public property. (21)
6. c. it may revert to a grantor if the prescribed use changes. (33)
7. b. a wife's life estate interest in her husband's property. (36)
8. b. cannot will their interest to a party outside the tenancy. (42)
9. c. the coop owner owns stock in the cooperative association, whereas the condominium owner simply owns real estate. (51)
10. c. Servient estate (56)
11. b. Special assessment tax lien (65)
12. d. a deed in lieu of foreclosure. (70)
13. c. constructive notice of possession. (73)
14. b. A general warranty deed (77)
15. d. A chronology of successive owners of record (84)
16. a. It remains in effect. (90)
17. c. encourage fairness and simplicity in lease forms and provisions. (97)
18. b. promote the value and planned land use of a neighborhood. (105)
19. d. a legal nonconforming use. (106)
20. a. balance public interests with individual property rights. (100)
21. b. locate and identify the property reliably. (119)
22. c. 40 acres (124)
23. b. will increase. (209)
24. d. number of households seeking housing. (212)
25. c. It drives total employment and population growth, which lead to demand for real estate. (213)
26. d. buyers will not pay more for a certain house than they would for another, similar house. (219)
27. d. Market value (222)
28. b. functional obsolescence. (232)
29. c. divide the capitalization rate into net income. (237)
30. d. $4,800,000 (239)
31. d. hypothecation. (243)
32. a. it is assignable. (247)
33. d. the Real Estate Settlement Procedures Act. (258)
34. d. directly originate loans. (261)
35. b. a payment does not pay the interest owed. (266)
36. a. $810 (254)
37. b. $1,458. (246)
38. c. $6,600. (246)
39. b. The greater the return, the greater the risk (272)
40. d. net sales proceeds minus adjusted basis. (281)
41. a. cash flow divided by equity. (285)
42. d. $82,000 (281)
43. b. $50,000 (282)
44. a. $3,846 (277)
45. b. 12% (285)
46. b. The total of all assessed values minus exemptions (289)
47. b. to offer tax abatement on a principal residence. (290)
48. c. multiplying the tax rate times the taxable value of the property. (292)
49. b. 5.33% (291)
50. d. $6,000 (292)

51. c. still an offer. (133)
52. b. require certain conveyances to be in writing. (132)
53. d. The buyer has a binding contract. (133)
54. d. The listing agent has violated fiduciary duties owed the client. (143)
55. d. inform the seller of the inquiry and test the paint. (144)
56. b. a dual agent. (148)
57. c. upon first substantive contact. (151)
58. c. open listing. (156)
59. b. exclusive agency agreement. (156)
60. b. negotiation with the client. (159)
61. a. represent buyers on their broker's behalf. (176)
62. b. complete any offer the buyer might decide to make. (182)
63. b. spending a customer deposit on a surety bond for the agency. (183)
64. a. This is a perfectly legitimate business practice. (186)
65. b. goodwill. (189)
66. a. blockbusting. (297)
67. c. providing unequal services. (297)
68. a. Both owner and agent. (299)
69. d. The sale contract remains valid. (195)
70. a. allow a third party fiduciary to handle the funds. (195)
71. d. The landlord is under no obligation, since options do not have a redemption period. (201)
72. b. the loan is to be sold to the FNMA. (322)
73. d. debit one party and credit the other. (325)
74. c. Taxes and interest (327)
75. a. Debit seller $345.00 (330)
76. b. errors & omissions insurance. (356)
77. a. Exceeding the limits of the authority granted by the agreement (365)
78. c. drafting a contract illegally. (367)
79. d. license revocation. (370)
80. a. depositing an earnest money check in a personal account. (374)
81. b. operating budget. (378)
82. d. Unhappy tenants lead to expensive tenant turnover. (380)
83. c. owner objectives and tenant demands. (381)
84. b. Consequential loss (384)
85. a. general agents empowered to perform a wide range of duties for the landlord. (385)
86. b. The purchase of interest in a limited partnership formed for investing in real estate (405)
87. d. $50,000. (405)
88. a. 30 days (405)
89. c. Individuals who pass only one portion of the licensure examination must pass the second portion within 1 year. (413)
90. b. Submit a credit report (414)
91. d. 3 of the 5 years (415)
92. a. June 30 of 2025 (Error! Bookmark not defined.)
93. d. None. Licensees are not required to include their license status on any advertising (433)
94. d. reasonable and adequate (441)
95. c. Affiliating with two brokers (443)
96. d. both parties consent in writing. (447)
97. b. A condominium public offering statement (453)
98. c. A listing agreement must be signed by the seller and the buyer. (461)
99. d. the seller must disclose on a property condition statement (467).
100. d. the licensee owes the client only the duties of accounting for trust money and maintaining confidentiality. (465)

101. b. the buyer. (462)
102. b. disclose in writing the he or she represents the seller. (463)
103. a. The agent must answer truthfully and reveal the material fact that it doesn't work in its present condition. (464)
104. b. Forward the matter to the Office of General Council (479)
105. a. Race (475)
106. d. physical disability. (476)
107. b. 1-year (486)
108. d. pay the tax debt within 6 months of the sale. (491)
109. a. 15% (491)
110. b. establishing an escrow account through the District Court. (496)

GLOSSARY OF STYLE AND CONSTRUCTION TERMS

HOUSE STYLES

bungalow Originally a one-story house with prominent roof and large overhangs.

Cape Cod A small one-story or one-and-a-half-story house with gable roof, clapboard or shingle siding, and no dormers (originally).

contemporary A modern house that emphasizes materials and structure rather than any traditional or derivative style.

Dutch colonial revival A house with a gambrel roof where the lower slope of the roof flares into the eave with a gentle curve.

Elizabethan A house using or simulating half-timber construction; cross gables; steeply pitched roof; large chimney stacks.

English colonial A saltbox, Cape Cod or other simple style with no ornamentations or classical details.

Federal An adaptation of classical and Georgian styles, featuring tall windows, curved stairs, elliptical rooms, bowed projections and octagonal bays, virtually flat roof, balustrade along the eave line, fanlight transoms, decorated sidelights, porticoes and columns.

Georgian A style characterized by symmetry, aligned windows, and conventional details; gambrel, gable or hip roof; windows capped with cornices or crown moldings; classical cornices on the eaves; pilasters often frame the doorway, but there is no covered porch at the front door; balustrade set high on the roof; building material varies regionally.

Gothic revival A variety of irregular, picturesque, rambling designs; steeply-pitched gable and cross-gable roof, vertical siding in earthy colors; carved ornamentation; verandas and balconies.

Greek revival A style based on the forms of the classical Greek temple; shallow-pitched gable roof, with gable end usually oriented toward the road; portico with columns; recessed front entrance with wide casings; white clapboard with dark green shutters.

Mansard A modern style featuring the mansard roof; often has arched dormer windows, double front doors, smooth stucco covering, and decorative corner features.

modern A house built with up-to-date materials. May be contemporary in style, or a reproduction or derivative style.

neoclassical revival A style featuring a two-story classical portico with columns, restrained decorative details, smooth exterior wall surfaces, often a hip roof.

Prairie Characterized by a low-pitched hip roof with wide overhangs; bands of casement windows; stucco covering; strong horizontal emphasis; low, heavy and solid appearance.

Queen Anne A multi-story, wood-framed and (usually) clapboarded style featuring turrets, towers, verandahs, wrap-around porches, gazebos, scrollwork, varied shingle patterns.

ranch Typically one-story; simple gable roof; built on a slab or shallow foundation; materials, coverings, ornamentation vary.

Romanesque A style featuring masonry construction, massive walls, round arches, masonry mullions, steep multi-gabled roof, turrets.

saltbox A two-story house with a gable roof, the back slope of which is elongated down to a one-story height; usually covered in clapboard siding.

Spanish mission Characterized by red tile roof, wide eaves with exposed rafter ends, open porches with rectangular piers, a dominant curved parapet, and stucco.

split-level A ranch-type house with a one-story section meeting a two-story section midway.

Tudor A masonry or stucco building with parapeted gables, stone mullions, large leaded windows, and a Tudor arch.

Victorian Not a single style; often used to refer to Queen Anne or Gothic revival styles.

Williamsburg colonial A modern style featuring symmetrical facade, steeply-pitched gable roof with dormers; clapboard or brick covering.

DOOR TYPES AND PARTS

bifold A two-paneled folding door mounted in a track, usually used with closets.

bypass Doors set in a track so as to open by sliding past each other, usually used with closets.

Dutch A two-part door divided horizontally.

French A two-part door divided vertically.

hollow core A door constructed of exterior surfaces with air-space and filler between them.

jamb The sides and top member of a door frame.

raised panel A door constructed of shaped solid panels set into a solid frame.

sidelight Narrow window next to an entry door.

solid core A door constructed of exterior surfaces with solid wood blocks filling the space between them.

steel A door constructed of steel as a fire-proofing or security barrier.

threshold The bottom part of a doorway.

ELECTRICAL

240 volt service The type of electrical supply required by such household appliances as air conditioners, washers and dryers. Usually separate from the normal household supply of 120 volts.

amperage A measure of the overall capability of the household supply. 100 amp service is the modern minimum standard.

bus bar A solid metal bar in a service entrance panel or subpanel. A hot bus bar is connected to the main power source. A neutral bus bar provides a terminal for all neutral wires and is part of the grounding connection.

BX A flexible, metal-armored type of self-contained wiring that is installed without conduit. Also called AC (armored cable).

circuit breaker A resettable device that interrupts a circuit when there is an overload or fault on the line.

conduit Metal piping used to carry flexible wiring.

fuse A device that interrupts a circuit when there is an overload or fault. The fuse must be replaced after it has performed the interruption.

ground fault circuit interrupter A device that monitors the current entering and leaving a receptacle or circuit. When incoming and outgoing currents are unequal, the device instantly opens the circuit. Used particularly in bathroom, garage and outdoor receptacles.

junction box A box that contains wire splices or cable connections, but devices.

outlet box A box that protects wire connections and holds a device such as a switch or receptacle.

rheostat A dimmer switch that allows gradient control of current.

Romex A type of nonmetallic, sheathed, multi-conductor cable.

service entrance panel The main control box for a household electrical system, containing the connection to the power supply, the main disconnect, circuit breakers, and the grounding connection.

subpanel A panel containing hot and neutral bus bars to distribute power coming from the service entrance panel.

switch A device installed on a hot wire to break the connection between the hot bus bar and a device connected beyond the switch.

EXTERIOR COVERINGS

beveled siding Siding consisting of horizontally overlapped boards that are thinner on the upper edge than on the lower.

board and batten Siding that is applied in vertical panels or boards with the vertical joints covered by narrow strips.

brick Outside structural wall or veneer consisting of brick and mortar. In residences, generally regarded as low-maintenance, fireproof and decorative.

clapboard A type of smooth beveled siding, generally narrow, that is common in older frame houses.

redwood siding Siding, usually beveled, made of cedar or redwood. Noted for resistance to weather, it may be installed with rough or smooth side out, and may be stained, painted, or only sealed.

shingle A type of thick, wooden shingle, also called a shake, which can be applied vertically as siding.

shiplap A type of wooden siding milled on both edges so that the edge of one board overlaps the edge of the next board.

siding Exterior finish or "skin" of a wall; typical types are vinyl, aluminum, beveled wood, shingle, and board and batten.

stucco A cement-based material applied in semi-liquid form over metal lath. A kind of false stucco is sometimes applied to plywood panels.

tongue and groove A type of wooden siding milled with a groove on one edge and a protruding "tongue" on the other so that the edge of one board fits into the edge of the next board.

FOUNDATION TYPES AND PARTS

brick A foundation of brick laid on a concrete footing, found in some older houses.

cement block A foundation of cast blocks laid on a concrete footing.

footing The base on which the foundation walls sit. Usually poured concrete, twice the thickness of the walls.

poured concrete A foundation in which the walls consist of concrete poured into forms.

slab A horizontal concrete section used as a foundation.

stone A foundation of field stone.

GENERAL STRUCTURE

balloon frame A house framing method in which studs extend from foundation to roof. Floor joists are hung on the studs. Generally replaced by platform framing after 1945.

basement An area below grade level, generally accessible from inside the house, with sufficient clearance that a person can stand up in it. A full basement covers the area of the entire first floor.

bay A portion of a building that projects beyond the face of the building.

beam A horizontal structural member. May be solid timber, laminated wood, or metal.

bearing wall A wall that supports part of the load above it.

blueboard A type of rough gypsum board used for sheathing interior walls.

bridging Diagonal bracing between floor joists to spread load.

building paper An asphalt-saturated paper used as a covering over wall sheathing, roof decking, or a subfloor.

casing Finish trim around a framed wall opening.

crawl space The area between first floor joists and ground in a house without a basement. Often filled with gravel. Clearance is not sufficient to allow a person to stand up.

deck A horizontal wooden surface attached to the exterior of a house.

dormer A windowed structure with its own roof that projects from the main roof of a building.

downspout An externally mounted vertical tube that carries rain water from gutter to ground or drain tile.

drain tile An underground tube that carries water away from the foundation footing or from the top of the foundation wall at the downspout.

drywall A type of smooth gypsum board used as an interior wall covering. Also called sheetrock and plasterboard.

eave The part of a roof that hangs beyond the external supporting wall.

facade The front face of a building.

fascia A board that covers the ends of the roof rafters.

flashing Metal sheets or strips installed as waterproofing at roof edges and around junctures of roof surfaces and other wall and roof locations where leakage must be prevented.

girder A horizontal beam that supports other beams.

greenboard A water-resistant type of gypsum board.

gutter A trough at the roof eave or other low point that collects rain water from the roof and carries it to a downspout.

gypsum board A wall paneling material composed of a core of gypsum between outer layers of heavy paper.

half-timber A type of timber framing in which the timbers and filled space between timbers are left exposed on the exterior surface.

joist One of the parallel, horizontal beams that supports a floor or ceiling.

knee wall A short wall from floor to rafter in a room with a sloped ceiling, such as an attic.

lath A wood or metal support for a semi-liquid wall covering material such as plaster or stucco.

lintel A horizontal supporting member across the top of a door or window opening.

masonry Construction using brick, stone, or concrete block..

partition A dividing wall, usually not a bearing wall.

plaster A mixture of gypsum, sand and lime applied by trowel over lath, plasterboard, or other plaster layer.

plate The top or bottom horizontal element of a stud wall.

platform frame A house framing method in which each floor is built up individually and serves as the foundation for stud walls. Also called western framing.

post A vertical structural member that supports a beam or girder.

rafter One of the parallel supporting members that holds the roof decking. Usually 2 x 6 or 2 x 8 solid timber (2 x 4 in some older houses).

rise The number of vertical inches per horizontal foot (run) of a sloped roof; the height of a flight of stairs; the height of one step.

riser The vertical board that covers the front of a stair.

run The horizontal dimension of a roof or stairway.

sheathing The rough covering of the shell of a structure, fastened to studs, rafters or joists as a support for a finish covering; typically composition board, plywood, or solid lumber (in older houses).

sheetrock Drywall.

shoe Sole plate; finish trim around edges of a finished floor.

sill Bottom horizontal member of a door or window frame; horizontal framing member bolted to a slab or foundation wall.

soffit The horizontal under-surface covering the area between the exterior wall and the end of rafters; the boxed-in area between the top of a row of cabinets and the ceiling

sole plate The bottom plate of a stud wall, attached to subfloor or slab.

span The distance between vertical supports.

stringer One of the side, supporting members of a staircase.

stud One of the vertical, parallel structural elements of a framed wall. Metal or wood.

subfloor Sheathing applied to floor joists as rough flooring.

suspended ceiling A ceiling supported by hangers attached to joists rather than being attached directly to the joists.

termite shield A metal or other barrier placed around foundation walls and wall penetrations to impede termites.

terrazzo A type of finished flooring composed of stones or stone chips imbedded in a hard medium.

top plate The upper plate of a stud wall, supporting joists or rafters.

tread The horizontal surface of a stair.

trim Woodwork, millwork, molding and other finishing material.

underlayment Plywood or other type of panel applied to a subfloor as a support for finished flooring.

wallboard Gypsum board or composition board used as an interior wall covering.

HEATING AND COOLING

central air An airconditioning unit, mounted outside a house, that cools the entire house by way of ducting.

duct work Sheet metal shafting and piping that carries hot and cold air in a house.

electric Heating by electric resistance cable or panels in floors, walls, or ceilings, or some other electrically powered radiation system.

forced air Heating by hot air blown by a furnace fan and carried in ducts.

gas Heating by means of a furnace powered by natural gas. May be forced air or hot water.

heat pump A device for recirculating heated air.

hot water Heating by means of hot water carried through pipes to heating coils, floor radiators, or baseboard radiators.

oil Heating by means of a furnace powered by fuel oil. May be forced air, hot water or steam.

register A grating in wall or floor to permit heated or cooled air to enter a room.

return A grating in wall or floor to remove cooled or warmed air from a room.

solar Heating by means of collection of solar radiation.

steam Heating by means of steam carried through pipes to radiators.

window unit A self-contained airconditioning unit installed in a window.

INSULATION

asbestos A fibrous mineral used for fireproofing, electrical insulation, around heating pipes and ducts, also applied as a spray covering on walls and ceilings; now regarded as a hazardous substance subject to environmental regulation.

batting Fibrous material, usually fiberglass, wadded together, backed with foil or paper, and formed into a roll; designed to fit between studs of a standard stud wall.

blown Loose insulating material blown into spaces between studs and wall surfaces.

fiberglass A cotton-like material consisting of glass and resin.

firestop A fire-resistant material used to impede the spread of flames.

foam Polystyrene or other expanding foam sprayed into gaps.

foam board Light-weight solid board composed of polystyrene foam and cut to fit between studs.

R-factor A measure of the efficiency of insulation

against heat transfer.

vapor barrier A waterproof material that prevents warm, moisture-laden indoor air from meeting colder outdoor air and condensing.

PLUMBING

cleanout A removable opening in a drain pipe that allows cleaning out of clogging material.

cast iron Material traditionally used for soil stack and soil pipe, with joints poured of hot lead.

copper Material traditionally preferred for piping hot and cold water supply within a house, with soldered joints.

lead Material once commonly used to seal water supply pipes, now regarded as hazardous and subject to environmental regulation.

PVC Polyvinyl chloride, a thermoplastic resin used for piping, with glued joints.

soil stack Large-dimension vertical pipe that vents sewer gases through the roof

soil pipe Drain pipe that carries waste to sewer or septic system.

sump pump A pump installed in a basement to remove water from around and under the foundation and floor of the basement.

trap A U-shaped section of drain pipe that holds water as a barrier against sewer gases and odors.

vent pipe A pipe that allows sewer gases to vent above the roof line and prevents back pressure from building up; connects to a vent stack.

vent stack A soil stack.

well and septic A water supply and waste removal system that is self-contained on a parcel, usually in rural areas where city services are not available.

ROOF TYPES AND ELEMENTS

asphalt shingle Heavy felt impregnated with asphalt and coated with mineral granules; come in a range of colors; life span of approximately 15 years.

built-up A low-pitch or flat roof covered with layers of roofing felt laminated with tar, pitch or asphalt and topped with hot tar and gravel.

cross gable A gable roof that intersects another gable roof at right angles.

decking Boards or panels applied to the rafters as a support for the roof covering.

felt Asphalt-impregnated paper installed over decking as an underlayment for the roof covering.

flat A roof with little or no pitch; not suitable for shingles; requires a built-up or membrane type of covering.

gable A triangular end wall defined by the two slopes of a roof and a line joining the eaves; a pitched roof that creates a triangular end wall.

gambrel A roof that has two slopes on each side, the lower slopes being steeper than the upper slopes; typical of barns.

Gothic A ridged roof with sides that curve, often ending in a flair.

hip The outside corner formed by the perpendicular meeting of the outside edges of two roof slopes; a roof that ends in hips rather than gables or other end walls.

mansard A roof that has two slopes on all four sides; the upper slope is close to horizontal and the lower slope is close to vertical.

membrane A vulcanized sheet of rubber or other seamless material applied with adhesive directly to decking; used on flat and low-pitch roofs.

pitched A roof that has a slope; pitch is usually stated as a ratio of rise (vertical distance) in inches per 12 inches of run (horizontal distance).

rafter One of the parallel beams that supports the decking of a sloped roof.

rake The slope of a gable.

ridge The horizontal line formed by the juncture of two roof slopes; the board to which the upper ends of the rafters of two slopes are nailed.

roll roofing Mineral-coated, asphalt-impregnated felt produced in long rolled-up sheets instead of as individual shingles; typically installed in overlapped pieces which are the length of the entire roof.

roofing paper Felt.

shake A wooden shingle, usually redwood or cedar, that can be installed as a roof covering or wall covering.

shed A pitched roof with a single slope.

slate A fine-grained rock that splits into thin, smooth layers that can be used as shingles; very heavy, but long-lasting.

tile Curved ceramic or concrete elements that fit together in such a way as to form a waterproof roof covering.

truss A framework of rafters and connecting beams installed as a unit to support part of a roof and tie together the opposite walls.

valley The inside corner created where two roof slopes meet; the opposite of a hip.

WINDOW TYPES AND PARTS

awning A window hinged along the top edge and designed to swing at the bottom.

bay A window or group of windows in a structural bay.

bow A curved window or a group of windows built as a unit to project beyond the surface of a wall.

casement A window hinged along one of the vertical edges.

casing Finish trim around a window opening.

double-hung A window with an upper and lower sash that slide vertically in separate slots.

eyebrow An arched window set in a rounded dormer that has no side walls.

fanlight A semi-circular transom window with muntins that fan from the center.

French A pair of casement windows hinged on the outer vertical edges so that they open inward or outward together.

hopper A window hinged along the bottom edge.

jalousie A window with adjustable, pivoting overlapped horizontal glass slats.

light A single pane of glass in a window; windows are described as two-light, four-light, six-light, etc.

louver A jalousie window, or one of the glass elements of the same.

mullion A vertical post or double jamb that divides two window sashes or large fixed panes.

muntin The horizontal and vertical cross-members that hold individual panes of glass within a single sash.

oriel A bay window on an upper floor.

rail One of the horizontal elements of a sash.

sash The frame which the panes of a window.

sill The base of a window jamb.

stile One of the vertical elements of a sash.

stool The ledge that sits on the sill of a window.

transom A small window above a door or a larger window; the horizontal divider is, technically, the transom.

GLOSSARY OF GENERAL REAL ESTATE TERMS

absorption The consumption of available vacant property in a building or market.

abstract of title A written, chronological record of the title records affecting rights and interests in a parcel of real property.

acceleration A right granted through a loan clause enabling the lender to call all sums immediately due and payable on a loan should the borrower violate certain provisions of the loan agreement.

accretion An increase in land caused by natural phenomena, for example a deposit of sand on a beachfront property due to a tropical storm.

actual notice Knowledge given or received directly through demonstrable evidence. Actual notice of ownership: reading a bill of sale, inspecting a deed, searching title records. See also *constructive notice*.

adjustable rate mortgage A mortgage loan having an interest rate that can be periodically raised or lowered in accordance with the movement of a financial index.

adjusted basis The beginning basis, or cost, of a property plus the costs of capital improvements, minus all depreciation expense.

ad valorem tax A real property's annual tax levied by taxing entities according to the property's assessed value.

adverse possession The entry, occupation, and use of another's property without the consent of the owner or where the owner took no action to evict the adverse possessor. May lead to loss of legal title if the adverse possessor fulfills certain requirements.

agency A fiduciary relationship between an agent and a principal where respective rights and duties are prescribed by laws of agency and by the agency agreement executed by the two parties. See *universal agency*, *limited agency*, and *fiduciary*.

agent The party in an agency relationship who is hired by the principal to perform certain duties. In so doing, the agent must also uphold fiduciary duties owed the principal.

air rights Rights in real property as they apply to the property's airspace, or all space above the surface within the parcel's legal boundaries.

air space The air portion of real property. In a condominium unit, the freehold space enclosed by the unit's outer walls, floor, and ceiling.

alienation A transfer of title to real property by voluntary or involuntary means.

allocation of markets An act of collusion where two or more competitors agree to limit competitive activity in portions of the market in exchange for reciprocal restrictions from the others.

amortization A partial or complete reduction of a loan's principal balance over the loan term, achieved by periodic payments which include principal as well as interest. See *negative amortization*.

annual percentage rate (APR) The total cost of credit to a borrower inclusive of finance charges and the stated interest rate, expressed as an annual rate of interest.

antitrust laws Legislation aimed at preventing unfair trade practices and monopoly, including collusion, price fixing, and allocation of markets.

appraisal An opinion of value of a property developed by a professional and disinterested third party and supported by data and evidence.

appraiser A duly trained and licensed professional authorized to perform appraisals for other parties.

appreciation An increase in the value of a property generally owing to economic forces beyond the control of the owner.

appurtenance A right, interest, or improvement that attaches to and transfers with a parcel of real property, such as an easement or a riparian right.

arrears Payment that occurs at the end of a payment term rather than at the beginning. Examples of items paid in arrears include taxes and interest.

assemblage A combining of contiguous parcels of real estate into a single tract, performed with the expectation that increased value will result.

assessed value The value of a property as established by assessors for the purpose of ad valorem taxation.

assessment A periodic charge payable by condominium owners for the maintenance of the property's common elements.

asset A tangible or intangible item of value.

asset sale A sale of a business involving the transfer of assets as opposed to the liabilities or stock.

assignment A transfer of one's entire interest in an item of real or personal property. The assignor transfers the interest to the assignee.

assumption In a sale of real property, the transfer of the seller's mortgage loan obligations to the buyer. Requires, in most cases, the approval of the lender.

balloon payment A lump sum payment on any loan which retires the remaining loan balance in full.

base line An imaginary latitude line within the rectangular survey system that is designated in relation to a principal meridian for purposes of identifying townships.

beginning basis The original cost or market value of an acquired asset.

benchmark A registered marker denoting an official elevation above sea level; used by surveyors to identify other elevations in the area.

beneficiary A party named to benefit from the yield or disposition of an asset identified in a trust, insurance policy, or will.

bilateral contract A contract where both parties promise to perform in exchange for performance by the other party. See *unilateral contract*.

binder A temporary agreement to buy a property evidenced by a valuable deposit. Receipt of the deposit binds a seller to a good-faith agreement to sell a property, provided a complete sale contract is executed within a certain period.

blind ad An advertisement that does not contain the identity of the advertiser.

blockbusting Inducing property owners to sell or rent their holdings due to an impending downturn in their property values, often owing to a change in the area's ethnic or social composition.

broker A direct agent of the principal who is hired for compensation to perform a stated service such as procuring a customer.

broker's opinion of value An estimate of a property's value rendered by a party who is not necessarily licensed, objective, or qualified. The estimate may not be a complete appraisal.

brokerage The business of procuring customers on behalf of clients for the purpose of completing a real estate transaction.

business brokerage The brokerage of a business enterprise in addition to any real property it may own or lease.

building code A specific standard of construction or maintenance of any aspect of an improved property established by local government officials.

bundle of rights A set of rights associated with ownership of property, including the rights to possess, use, transfer, encumber and exclude.

business trust See *syndication*.

buydown A loan arrangement where the borrower pays extra interest in advance for the future benefit of a lower interest rate over the loan term.

buyer representation agreement A broker's listing with a buyer to locate a suitable property for purchase or lease.

buyer's market A market characterized by an excess of sellers over buyers.

capital gain (or loss) The difference between the net sales proceeds of an asset and its adjusted basis.

capital improvement An upgrading of improved property having sufficient magnitude to constitute an addition to the property's basis. Contrasts with repair and maintenance.

capitalization rate The rate of return on capital an investor will demand from the investment property, or the rate of return that the property will actually produce.

cash flow The remaining positive or negative amount of income an investment produces after subtracting all operating expenses and debt service from gross income.

certificate of occupancy A document confirming that a newly constructed or renovated property has fully complied with all building codes and is ready for occupancy and use.

certificate of title A document expressing the opinion of a title officer or attorney that a property seller is in fact the owner of good title based on a review of title records.

chain of title Successive property owners of record dating back to the original grant of title from the state to a private party.

chattel An item of personal property.

closing A meeting of principal parties where a seller transfers title and a buyer pays monies owed the seller and lender.

closing statement A financial summary and settlement of a property transaction indicating sums due and payable by the buyer and seller.

cloud An encumbrance or claim on title to property impeding or diminishing its marketability.

co-brokerage A brokerage practice where agents and brokers outside of the listing broker's agency assist as subagents in procuring a customer in exchange for portions of the commission.

collateral Property liened by a lender as security for a loan.

collusion An unlawful agreement between competitors to monopolize a market, disadvantage other competitors, or otherwise undertake activities in violation of fair trade laws.

color of title A defective title transfer or the transfer of a defective title where the new owner is originally unaware of the defect. Color of title may be used as a grounds for adverse possession, which, if successful, would nullify the original defect.

commingling An unlawful practice of mixing escrow funds with the agency's operating funds.

common elements 1. Portions of a condominium property that are owned by all unit owners, for example the grounds, parking facilities, lobby, and elevators. 2. Portions of a commercial property used by all occupants as well as the public, for which the tenants may have to share in the repair and maintenance costs.

common law A body of law developed by court judgments, decrees, and case decisions.

community property A system of property ownership established by law which generally defines rights of property ownership of spouses; community property is co-owned by spouses, and separate property is owned by a single spouse. Generally, property acquired during the marriage with jointly held funds is community property.

comparable A property having similar characteristics to a subject property in an appraisal. The value or sale price of the comparable is used to estimate the value of the subject.

comparable sales approach See *sales comparison approach*.

comparative market analysis (CMA) A method used by brokers and salespeople for estimating the current value of a property using sale price data from similar properties. Not to be confused with a bona fide appraisal performed by a licensed appraiser.

concurrency A local, county, or regional planning policy that requires developers to correct foreseen negative impacts of a development during the construction period of the project itself rather than afterwards; for example, widening a road during construction to accommodate a future increase in traffic.

condemnation 1. A decree by a court or municipal authority that a parcel of private property is to be taken for public use under the power of eminent domain. 2. A government order that a particular property is no longer fit for use and must be demolished.

condominium estate An estate distinguished by fee simple ownership of the airspace of a unit plus an undivided interest with the other unit owners in the overall property's common elements.

consideration An item of tangible or intangible value, or one's promise to do or not do some act which is used as an inducement to another party to enter into a contract.

constructive notice Knowledge one could or should have, according to the presumption of law; a demonstration to the public of property ownership through title recordation, "for all to see." See *actual notice*.

contingency A condition that must be satisfied for a contract to be binding and enforceable.

contract A potentially enforceable agreement between two or more parties who agree to perform or not perform some act. If valid, the contract is enforceable, with limited exceptions.

contract for deed A financial contract where a seller retains legal title to a property and gives the buyer equitable title and possession over a period of time. During the contract period, the seller finances all or part of the purchase price. If the buyer makes timely payments and abides by all contract provisions, the seller conveys legal title at the end of the contract period.

contribution The increment of market value added to a property through the addition of a component or improvement to the property. Not to be confused with the cost of the component.

conventional loan A permanent long-term loan that is not FHA-insured or VA-guaranteed.

conversion 1. Changing real property to personal property, and vice versa. 2. An illegal act of appropriating escrow funds for payment of an agency's operating expenses.

conveyance A voluntary transfer of real property interests.

cooperative estate Ownership of shares in a cooperative association which acquires a multi-unit dwelling as its primary asset. Shareholders also receive a proprietary lease on a unit for the duration of their share ownership.

cost approach A method for determining value that takes into account the cost of the land and the replacement or reproduction cost of the improvements net of estimated depreciation.

cost recovery See *depreciation*.

counteroffer Any new offer or amended offer made in response to an offer. See *offer*.

covenant A written warrant or promise set forth in a contract or other legal document by one or both of the parties to the contract.

credit 1. An accounting entry on a closing statement indicating an amount a party has paid or is to receive. 2. Loan funds advanced to a borrower.

credit evaluation A lender's opinion of a borrower's ability to repay a loan in view of financial capabilities and past repayment patterns.

curtesy A widower's life estate claim to portions of his deceased spouse's real property. See also *dower*.

customer In agency law, a party outside of the fiduciary relationship of client and agent. If an agent treats a customer as a client, an implied agency may result.

datum A standard elevation reference point used by surveyors to measure elevations of property in an area.

debit An accounting entry on a closing statement indicating an amount a party must pay.

debt coverage ratio An underwriting equation reflecting how much debt service an investment property can reasonably afford to pay out of its net operating income; used to identify how large a loan the property can afford given an interest rate and loan term.

debt ratio An underwriting equation that is used to determine how much debt an individual can reasonably afford in view of the party's or household's income.

debt service Periodic payments of interest and/or principal on a mortgage loan.

deed in lieu of foreclosure An instrument used to convey mortgaged property back to the lender rather than have the lender foreclose on the property.

deed in trust An instrument used to convey real property to the trustee of a land trust. The trustor is also the beneficiary. See *land trust*.

deed of trust An instrument used by a borrower to convey title to mortgaged property to a trustee to be held as security for the lender, who is the beneficiary of the trust.

deed restriction A provision in a deed that limits or places rules on how the deeded property may be used or improved.

defeasible fee A fee estate where ownership is perpetual, provided that usage restrictions or other conditions stated in the deed are upheld. If not, the fee reverts to the grantor either automatically (determinable fee) or by the grantor's actions (condition subsequent).

deficiency judgment A court order enabling a damaged lender to attach a lien on the defaulted borrower's property for an amount equal to the difference between the debt and the proceeds of a foreclosure sale.

demand A quantity of a product or service that is desired for purchase, lease, or trade at any given time.

density A measure of the degree of residential land use within a given area for purposes of residential zoning and land use control.

deposit Valuable consideration accompanying an offer to purchase real estate that signifies the offeror's good faith intention to complete a sale or lease contract.

depreciable basis The portion of a property's total basis that may be depreciated, generally the basis of the improvements, since land cannot be depreciated.

depreciation 1. A non-cash expense taken against the income of investment property that allows the owner to recover the cost of the investment through tax savings. 2. A loss of value to improved property.

descent and distribution, laws of A body of state-level laws that stipulates how an estate will be passed on to heirs in the absence of a valid will.

determinable fee A defeasible fee estate where title automatically reverts to the grantor if usage conditions stated in the deed are violated.

devise A transfer of real or personal property from the devisor to the devisee(s) by means of a will.

discounting A financial practice of reducing the value of dollars received in the future by an amount that reflects the interest that would have been earned if the dollars had been received today. Performed to measure the present value of an investment's future income.

discounted cash flow analysis A financial analysis to identify the discounted value of the cash flow of an investment over a given number of years. See *discounting* and *cash flow*.

discrimination in housing A failure to provide equal opportunity for persons to acquire or finance housing based on race, color, religion, national origin, sex, handicapped status, marital status, or family status.

disintermediation Direct investment without the intermediation of a bank or other depository institution to make loans and other investments.

documentary stamp A tax stamp affixed to a property document or record as evidence that the owner has paid taxes related to the financing or transfer of real property.

dominant tenement The property that benefits from the existence of an easement appurtenant. The holder of the easement is the dominant tenant. See *servient tenement*.

dower A widow's life estate interest in portions of her deceased spouse's real property.

dual agency Representing both principal parties to a transaction.

due on sale A loan provision defining the lender's right to accelerate a note upon the transfer of collateralized property.

earnest money escrow An impound account used for the safekeeping of a buyer's earnest money deposit; accompanied by specific instructions to the escrow agent for holding and disbursing the funds.

easement An interest in real property giving the interest holder the right to use defined portions of another's property. May or may not attach to the estate.

economic life The period during which an improvement is expected to remain useful in its original use. Establishes the improvement's annual depreciation amounts in appraisal. Depreciation in tax accounting is determined by a property's cost recovery class, which is related to economic life.

economic obsolescence A loss of value in a property because of external factors generally beyond the control of the owner, for example, a municipality's lack of funds to improve deteriorated roadways. Also called external obsolescence.

effective gross income The actual income of an investment property before expenses, expressed as total potential income minus vacancy and collection losses.

elective share A right of a surviving spouse to claim a prescribed portion of the decedent's real and personal property in place of the provisions of the decedent's will.

emblements Plants and crops considered personal property, since human labor is required for planting, growing and harvesting.

eminent domain A power of a government entity to force the sale of private property for subsequent public use.

encroachment An unauthorized physical intrusion of one's real property into the real property of another.

encumbrance An interest, right or intrusion that limits the freehold interest of an owner of real property or otherwise adversely effects the marketability of title.

enforceability Legal status of a valid contract or other document that a court of law will force to be performed.

equalization An averaging of assessed valuations in an area to compensate for ad valorem tax inequities.

equilibrium A theoretical market state in which the forces of supply and demand are in balance.

equitable title An interest that gives a lienholder or buyer the right to acquire legal title to a property if certain contractual conditions occur.

equity That portion of a property's value owned by the legal owner, expressed as the difference between the property's market value and all loan balances outstanding on the property.

equity of redemption A mortgagor's right to pay off a defaulted mortgage and reclaim the property, provided the redemption occurs before the completion of the foreclosure sale.

escalator clause A lease clause providing for an increase in rent.

escheat A reversionary transfer of real property to the state or county when the legal owner dies without a will and without heirs.

escrow 1. A trust or impound account used for the proper handling of funds and documents in the closing of a real property transaction. 2. An account that a lender requires a borrower to establish to ensure that adequate funds will be available for payment of taxes and insurance on a mortgaged property.

estate 1. A set of rights to real property that includes the right of possession. 2. The totality of one's personal and real property ownership.

estate in land An estate.

estoppel A legal restraint to prevent a person from claiming a right or interest that is inconsistent with the person's previous statements or acts. An estoppel certificate documents the party's initial position or act, which cannot be contradicted later.

ethics Standards governing proper and professional business practices.

eviction Removal of a tenant from a property because of a lease default.

evidence of title Actual or constructive notice of real property ownership, including opinion of title, certificate of title, and title insurance.

exclusion One of the bundle of legal rights to real property enabling the owner to prevent others from entry or use.

exclusive agency A listing agreement which pays the listing broker a commission if anyone other than the property owner procures a customer..

exclusive right to sell A listing agreement which pays the listing broker a commission if anyone at all procures a customer.

executory contract A completed agreement which enjoins one or both principal parties to perform certain actions in order for the contract to become fully executed.

facilitator A transaction broker who assists principal parties in completing a transaction without acting as a fiduciary agent of either party.

fair financing laws Anti-discrimination legislation designed to ensure that all parties have equal access to mortgage financing.

fair housing laws Anti-discrimination legislation designed to ensure equal opportunity in housing to all home buyers.

Federal Deposit Insurance Corporation A quasi-governmental agency that insures deposits of depository institutions and otherwise develops regulations for the banking industry.

Federal Home Loan Mortgage Corporation (Freddie Mac) A major secondary mortgage market organization which buys conventional, FHA, and VA loans and sells mortgage-backed securities.

Federal Housing Administration An agency of the Department of Housing and Urban Development which insures permanent long-term loans that meet certain qualifications.

Federal National Mortgage Association (Fannie Mae) A government-sponsored agency in the secondary mortgage market which buys conventional, FHA, and VA loans, sells mortgage-backed securities, and guarantees payment of principal and interest on the securities.

Federal Reserve System The principal regulator of the money supply as well as of the American banking system.

fee simple An estate representing the highest form of legal ownership of real property, particularly the fee simple absolute estate.

fiduciary The agent in an agency relationship; receives the trust and confidence of the principal and owes fiduciary duties to the principal.

fiduciary duties Duties of an agent to the principal in an agency relationship, including skill, care, diligence, loyalty, obedience, confidentiality, disclosure, and accounting.

fixture An item permanently attached to land so as to be defined as real property.

foreclosure A procedure for forcing sale of a secured property to satisfy a lienholder's claim.

freehold estate An ownership estate of indeterminable duration; contrasts with a leasehold estate.

full-service lease A lease requiring the landlord to pay all of a property's operating expenses, including those that pertain to an individual tenant.

functional obsolescence A loss of value in an improved property because of design flaws or failure of the property to meet current standards. May be curable or incurable.

general agency A fiduciary relationship which authorizes the agent to conduct a broad range of activities for the principal in a particular business enterprise. May or may not include authority to enter into contracts.

general lien A lien against any and all property owned by a lienee.

general partnership A for-profit business where two or more co-owners agree to share management responsibilities and profits. Does not involve silent partners, as in a limited partnership.

general warranty deed A bargain and sale deed containing the assurance that the grantor will defend against any and all claims to the title.

goodwill An intangible business asset valued at the difference between the sale price and the value of all other assets of the business.

Government National Mortgage Association (Ginnie Mae) A division of HUD which guarantees FNMA mortgages and securities backed by pools of VA-guaranteed and FHA-insured mortgages.

government survey system See *rectangular survey system.*

grantee A party who receives a right, interest, or title to real property from another.

grantor A party who transfers a right, interest, or title to real property to another.

gross easement A personal right to use another's property, granted by the owner; does not attach to the estate, and there are no dominant or servient tenements.

gross income multiplier A shortcut method for estimating the value of an income property. The procedure involves multiplying the property's gross annual income times a multiplier that reflects the ratio between gross annual income and sale price that is typical for similar properties in the area.

gross rent multiplier A shortcut method for estimating the value of an income property. The procedure involves multiplying the property's gross monthly rent times a multiplier that reflects the ratio between gross monthly rent and sale price that is typical for similar properties in the area.

gross lease See *full service lease.*

ground lease A lease of the land-only portion of a parcel of real property

hazard insurance Insurance against loss or damage to real property improvements; required by most mortgage lenders to protect the collateral.

highest and best use A theoretical use of a property that is legally permissible, physically possible, financially feasible, and maximally productive, usually in terms of net income generation.

holographic will A will prepared entirely in the testator's handwriting, complete with date and signature.

home equity loan A junior mortgage loan on a residence, secured by portions of the owner's equity in the home.

homestead laws Laws that protect a homeowner against loss of the homeowner's principle residence to a sale forced by creditors to collect debts. Homestead laws also protect the interests of individual spouses by requiring both spouses to sign any conveyance of the homestead property.

homestead tax exemption An exemption of a portion of the assessed value of a homeowner's principal residence from ad valorem taxation.

hypothecation Use of real property as collateral for a mortgage loan.

implied agency An agency relationship that arises by implication from the actions and representations of either agent or principal.

implied contract An unstated or unintentional agreement that may be deemed to exist by implication because of acts or statements by any of the parties to the agreement.

implied listing See *implied agency*.

improvement Any manmade structure or item affixed to land.

income capitalization A method of appraising the value of a property by applying a rate of return to the property's net income.

income ratio An underwriting ratio that relates a borrower's gross or net income and the debt service of a loan; used to determine how large a loan a borrower can reasonably afford.

independent contractor A sales agent who works for a broker but is not legally an employee. The employer exerts only limited control over the contractor's actions, does not provide employee benefits, and does not withhold taxes from the contractor's pay.

inferior lien A lien whose priority is subordinate to that of a superior (tax) lien. Priority among inferior liens is established according to the time of recordation, with the exception of the mechanic's lien. Also called junior lien.

installment contract See *contract for deed*.

interest 1. A right to real property. 2. A lender's charge for the use of the principal amount of a loan.

interest rate The percentage of a loan amount that a borrower must pay a lender annually as interest on a loan amount.

intermediation Investment by a depository institution on behalf of depositors.

internal rate of return The rate at which inflows from an income property investment must be discounted in order for the total inflows over time to equal the initial outlay, expressed as a percent; may include projected proceeds from the future sale of the property as an inflow.

interval ownership See *time-share*.

intestate Legal condition of a person who dies without leaving a will.

investment Expenditure to purchase an asset with the expectation of deriving a future profit or benefit from the asset.

involuntary alienation A transfer of title to real property without the consent or against the will of the owner, for example, eminent domain, foreclosure, and adverse possession.

involuntary lien A lien imposed by legal process irrespective of the owner's wishes or consent.

joint tenancy A form of real property ownership in which co-owners share all rights and interests equally and indivisibly; entails right of survivorship. Parties must establish tenancy at the same time and with a single deed.

joint venture A partnership created for a specific, pre-determined business endeavor, after which the joint venture is usually dissolved.

judgment A court decision resulting from a lawsuit. If a creditor sues to collect a debt, a favorable ruling is followed by a judgment lien against the defaulting borrower's property.

judicial foreclosure A court proceeding triggered by a foreclosure suit. Involves notice, debt acceleration, the termination of the owner's interests in the property, and a public sale where proceeds are applied to the debt.

junior lien See *inferior lien*.

land The surface area of the earth, all natural things permanently attached to the earth, and everything beneath the surface to the earth's center and above the surface extending upward to infinity.

land contract See *contract for deed*.

land trust A trust in which a trustor conveys a fee estate to a trustee and names himself or herself as beneficiary. The beneficiary in turn controls the property and the actions of the trustee.

land use control Regulation of how individual owners use property in a municipality or planning district. Control patterns are generally in accordance with a master plan.

landlocked A parcel of property lacking legal access to a public thoroughfare; requires a court-ordered easement by necessity to relieve the condition.

law of agency A body of law defining roles, duties and responsibilities of an agent and a principal. Laws also set forth standards of conduct agent and principal owe to a customer.

lease A legal contract and instrument of conveyance which transfers to the tenant, or lessee, a leasehold fee for a certain duration. The lease contract sets forth all tenant and landlord covenants, financial terms, and grounds for default. The landlord is referred to as the lessor.

legal life estate A life estate established by operation of law rather than by the actions or wishes of the property owners. Examples are homestead law, dower, curtesy, and elective share.

legal title Full legal ownership of property and the bundle of rights as they apply to it. Contrasts with equitable title.

leasehold estate An estate that entails temporary rights of use, possession, and to an extent, exclusion, but not legal ownership. Compare *freehold estate*.

legal description A description of a parcel of property which accurately locates and identifies the boundaries of the subject parcel to a degree acceptable by local courts of law.

leverage The relationship between the yield rate of an investment and the interest rate of funds borrowed to finance the investment. If the yield rate is greater than the loan rate, positive leverage results. If the yield rate is less than the loan rate, negative leverage results.

liability 1. An accounting entry representing a claim against the assets of a business by a creditor. 2. A condition of vulnerability to lawsuits seeking redress for potentially wrongful acts or statements.

license 1. Legal authorization to conduct business. 2. An individual's personal right to use the property of another for a specific purpose. Revocable at any time at the owner's discretion. Does not attach to the property and terminates upon the death of either party.

lien A creditor's claim against real or personal property as security for a property owner's debt. A lien enables a creditor to force the sale of the property and collect proceeds as payment toward the debt.

lien priority The order in which liens against a property are satisfied; the highest priority lien receives sale proceeds from a foreclosure before any other lien.

lien theory state A state whose laws give a lender on a mortgaged property equitable title rather than legal title. The mortgagor in a lien theory state retains legal title. See *title theory state*.

liquidated damages In a contract, a clause that expressly provides for compensation a defaulting party owes the damaged party. In the absence of such a clause, a damaged party may sue for unliquidated damages.

liquidity The degree to which an investment is readily marketable, or convertible to another form of asset. If immediately salable, an investment is liquid; the longer it takes to sell, the more illiquid the investment. Real property is relatively illiquid in comparison with other types of investment.

lis pendens A public notice in a foreclosure proceeding that the mortgaged property may soon have a judgment issued against it. Enables other investors to join in the proceeding if they wish to collect their debts.

listing A legal contract that establishes and controls the dynamics of the agency relationship between principal and agent. The principal to the listing may be buyer, seller, landlord, or tenant.

littoral rights A set of water rights defined by state law relating to properties abutting navigable bodies of water such as lakes and bays. Generally, a property owner enjoys usage rights but owns land only to the high water mark. See *riparian rights* and *prior appropriation*.

living trust A trust established during one's lifetime in which the trustor conveys legal title to property to a trustee and names another party as beneficiary. The trustee discharges management duties and the beneficiary receives all profit and gain net of the trustee's fees.

loan commitment A lender's written pledge to lend funds under specific terms. May contain deadlines and conditions.

loan-to-value ratio (LTV) An underwriting ratio that relates the size of a loan to the market value of the collateral. The closer the loan value is to market value, the riskier the loan is for the lender , since the lender is less likely to recover the debt fully from the proceeds of a foreclosure sale.

lot and block system A method for legally describing property in a subdivision where lots are identified by block and number. A recorded metes and bounds or rectangular survey description of the subdivision underlies the lot and block system.

market 1. Buyers and sellers exchanging goods and services through the price mechanism. 2. The totality of interactions between supply and demand for a specific set of products or services in a particular geographic area.

market equilibrium See *equilibrium*.

market value An opinion of the price at which a willing seller and buyer would trade a property at a given time, assuming a cash sale, reasonable exposure to the market, informed parties, marketable title, and no abnormal pressure to transact.

marketable title A condition of title to a property where there are no claims, liens, or encumbrances clouding title or impeding the property's transferability.

marketing plan An agent's design for procuring a customer for a client, including selling and promotional activities.

life estate A freehold estate that is limited in duration to the life of the owner or other named person. On the death of this person, legal title passes to the grantor or other named party.

limited agency An agency relationship which restricts the agent's authorizations to a specific set of duties. The relationship usually terminates on performance of these duties, as in a real estate broker's listing agreement. Also called special agency.

limited partnership A business enterprise consisting of general and limited partners: general partners manage the affairs of the business while limited partners are silent investors.

master deed A deed used to convey land to a condominium developer.

master plan An amalgamated land use plan for a municipality, county, or region which incorporates community opinion, the results of intensive research, and the various land use guidelines and regulations of the state. Acts as a blueprint for subsequent zoning ordinances and rulings.

materialman's lien See *mechanic's lien*

mechanic's lien A junior lien enabling property builders, suppliers, and contractors to secure debt arising from labor and materials expended on a property. Distinguished by its order or priority, which is based on when the work was performed rather than when the lien was recorded.

meridian A north-south line used in the rectangular survey system of legal descriptions.

metes and bounds A method of legally describing property which utilizes physical boundary markers and compass directions for describing the perimeter boundaries of a parcel.

millage rate The ad valorem tax rate of a taxing district, derived by dividing revenues required from taxpayers by the district's tax base. If the millage rate is 30, the tax rate is 3%, or $3.00 per $100 of assessed valuation (net of exemptions).

mill One one-thousandth of a dollar ($.001). Used to quantify the ad valorem tax rate in dollars.

mineral rights Separable subsurface rights to mineral deposits; transferrable by sale or lease to other parties.

misrepresentation A statement or act, or failure to make a statement or act, that misleads a party in a transaction. May be intentional or unintentional. May warrant legal recourse or license revocation.

monument A fixed, artificial or natural landmark used as a reference point in a metes and bounds legal description.

mortgage A legal document wherein a mortgagor pledges ownership interests in a property to a lender, or mortgagee, as collateral against performance of the mortgage debt obligation.

mortgage financing Financing that uses mortgaged real property as security for borrowed funds.

multiple listing service An organization of brokers who agree to cooperate in marketing the pooled listings of all members.

mutual consent Consent by all principals to a contract to all provisions of the contract. A requirement for validity.

negative amortization A situation in which the loan balance of an amortizing loan increases because periodic payments are insufficient to pay all interest owed for the period. Unpaid interest is added to the principal balance.

negotiable instrument A legal instrument that can be sold, traded, assigned, or otherwise transferred to another party, such as a promissory note.

net lease A lease which requires a tenant to pay rent as well as a share of the property's operating expenses to the extent provided for in the lease contract.

net listing A listing which states a minimum sale or lease price the owner will accept, with any excess going to the broker as a commission. Professionally discouraged, if not illegal.

net operating income The amount of pre-tax revenue generated from an income property after accounting for operating expenses and before accounting for any debt service.

non-conforming use A land use that is not consistent with the current zoning ordinance. May be legal or illegal.

non-judicial foreclosure A forced sale of mortgaged property without a formal foreclosure suit or court proceeding. Authorized through a "power of sale" clause in a mortgage or trust deed document.

non-prorated expense An expense incurred by buyer or seller in closing a real estate transaction that is not shared with the other party. Examples include attorney fees, documentary tax stamps, and lender fees.

note An agreement to repay a loan of an indicated amount under certain terms.

notice of title Actual or recorded public evidence of real property ownership. See *actual notice* and *constructive notice*.

null and void Without legal force or effect. See *void*.

obsolescence A loss of property value because of functional or economic (external) factors. See *functional obsolescence* and *economic obsolescence*.

offer A proposal to enter into a binding contract under certain terms, submitted by an offeror to an offeree. If accepted without amendment, an offer becomes a contract.

offer and acceptance A process that creates a contract. Acceptance is the offeree's unequivocal, manifest agreement to the terms of an offer. The offer becomes a contract when the acceptance has been communicated to the offeror.

open listing A non-exclusive listing which pays an agent a commission only if the agent is procuring cause of a ready, willing, and able customer.

operating expense A recurring or periodic expense necessary for the operation of an income property. Examples include utilities, management, and ad valorem tax expenses. Excluded are debt service and the property's income tax liability.

opinion of title An attorney's or title officer's opinion of the condition and marketability of title to a parcel of property based on a recent search of title records by a competent party.

opinion of value See *broker's opinion of value*.

option A unilateral contract in which an owner, or optionor, grants a buyer or tenant, the optionee, a future right to be exercised before a deadline, in exchange for valuable consideration. The terms of the right, such as a right to purchase or lease, must be clearly stated and cannot be changed during the option period.

origination fee A lender's charge for funding a loan.

parallel See *base line*.

parol contract An oral agreement. Potentially enforceable if validly created.

partition suit A lawsuit requesting the court to alter or cancel the interests of a co-owner in a parcel of real property. Initiated when co-owners do not agree to make the change voluntarily.

party wall easement An easement appurtenant where owners of two adjacent properties share an improvement along the property boundary. The parties agree not to perform acts that would adversely affect the other party's interest in the shared improvement.

percentage lease A retail property lease which requires a tenant to pay a minimum amount of rent plus an additional increment that reflects the sales achieved by the tenant.

performance Fulfillment of the terms of a contract.

periodic tenancy A leasehold interest for a lease term where, in the absence of default, the term automatically renews itself until proper notice of termination is provided by either party.

personal property All property that is not considered real property; all property that is not land or permanently attached to land, excepting trade fixtures and emblements.

physical deterioration A loss of value to property because of decay or natural wear and tear. Exacerbated by deferred maintenance, or the failure to repair or maintain property on a regular basis.

planned unit development (PUD) A multi-use development project requiring special zoning and involving deed restrictions.

plat A map of one or more properties indicating each parcel's lot and block number, boundaries, and dimensions.

plottage An increment of value added by the assemblage of contiguous properties.

point One-percent of a loan amount, a lender's finance charge.

point of beginning (POB) The origination and termination point in a metes and bounds legal description.

police power A state's or local government's legal authority to create, regulate, tax, and condemn real property in the interest of the public's health, safety, and welfare.

potential gross income The maximum amount of revenue a property could generate before accounting for vacancy, collection loss, and expenses. Consists of total rent with full occupancy at established rent rates, plus other income from any source.

power of attorney An authorization granting a fiduciary the power to perform specified acts on the principal's behalf. Used to establish a universal agency relationship.

present value The discounted value of an amount of money to be received in the future that accounts for the interest that would have been earned if the money had been received in the present.

price fixing An act of collusion where competitors agree to establish prices at certain levels to the detriment of customers or other competitors.

price mechanism An interaction of supply and demand that determines a price a buyer and seller agree is the value of a good or service to be exchanged. A quantification of value in a transaction.

primary mortgage market Lenders and mortgage brokers who originate mortgage loans directly to borrowers.

principal 1. The employer in an agency relationship, to whom the agent owes fiduciary duties. 2. The loan balance to which interest charges are applied.

principal meridian A designated meridian in the rectangular survey system that is used in conjunction with a base line to identify ranges, tiers, and townships.

prior appropriation A legal doctrine granting a state the power to control and regulate the use of water resources within state boundaries.

priority See *lien priority*.

private grant A voluntary conveyance of property by a private party.

private mortgage insurance (PMI) An insurance policy, purchased by a borrower, that protects a lender against loss of that portion of a mortgage loan which exceeds the acceptable loan-to-value ratio.

probate A court proceeding to validate and distribute a decedent's estate to creditors, tax authorities, and heirs.

procuring cause A party who was first to obtain a ready, willing, and able customer, or a party who expended the effort to induce the customer to complete the transaction.

promissory note See *note*.

property An item that has a legal owner, along with the attendant rights to legal ownership.

property management The business of managing the physical and financial condition of an investment property for an owner.

proprietary lease A cooperative owner's lease on a unit in the cooperative building. The lease runs concurrently with the owner's ownership interest in the cooperative.

proration Apportionment of expense and income items at closing. Examples of items prorated between buyer and seller include interest, insurance, taxes, and rent.

public grant A voluntary conveyance of property by a government entity to a private party.

pur autre vie A life estate where the grantee's interest endures over the lifetime of another party named by the grantor.

purchase money mortgage A mortgage loan where a seller lends a buyer some or all of the purchase price of a property.

qualification 1. A mortgage underwriting procedure to determine the financial capabilities and credit history of a prospective borrower. 2. A listing and marketing procedure to determine the needs and urgency of a client or customer.

quiet enjoyment A right of an owner or tenant to use a property without interference from others.

quiet title suit A court proceeding to clear a property's title of defects, claims, and encumbrances.

quit claim deed A deed which conveys one's possible ownership interests to another party. The grantor does not claim to own any interest and makes no warrants.

range A north-south area bounded by consecutive meridians.

real estate Land and all manmade structures permanently attached to it.

real estate investment trust (REIT) An investment in which owners purchase shares in a trust which owns or acquires real property. Investors receive income and gain on a per-share basis.

real property Real estate and the bundle of rights associated with ownership of real estate.

reconciliation An appraiser's weighted blending of the results of different approaches to value into a final value estimate.

recording An act of entering into public title records any document or transaction affecting title to real estate. Recording gives constructive notice of one's rights and interests in a property and establishes the priority of inferior liens.

rectangular survey system A method of legally describing real property which uses longitude and latitude lines to identify ranges, tiers, and townships. Also called government survey system.

redemption period A statutory period after a foreclosure sale during which the foreclosed owner may buy back the property by paying all sums due the lender. See also *equity of redemption*.

redlining The illegal lending practice of restricting loans by geographical area.

refinancing Obtaining a new loan to replace an existing loan, usually to take advantage of lower interest rates, to obtain a longer-term loan, or to liquidate equity.

Regulation Z A fair financing law applying to residential loans; lenders must disclose financing costs and relevant terms of the loan to the borrower.

remainder A future freehold interest in a life estate held by a third party remainderman named by the grantor. When the life tenant dies, the estate passes to the remainderman. See also *reversion*.

replacement cost The cost of constructing a functional equivalent of a property at current labor and materials costs using current construction methods.

reproduction cost The cost of constructing a precise duplicate of a property, at current labor and materials prices.

reserve allowance An amount of money allocated from a property's income to cover future repair and maintenance costs.

restriction A limitation on the use of a property imposed by deed, zoning, state statute, or public regulation.

reversion 1. A transfer of title from a life estate tenant back to the grantor. 2. Proceeds from the sale of a property at the end of a holding period in a cash flow analysis.

revocation 1. Cancellation of a contract. 2. Cancellation of a real estate license.

right of redemption See *equity of redemption*.

riparian rights Water rights of a property that abuts a watercourse (stream, river).

sale contract A contract for the purchase and sale of real property containing all terms and provisions of the sale and describing the responsibilities of the parties.

sale leaseback A sale of a property executed simultaneously with a lease on the property from the buyer back to the seller as tenant.

sales comparison approach A method of appraising property that relies on the principle that a property is generally worth what other, similar properties are worth. See *substitution*.

salesperson A licensed employee or independent contractor hired by a broker to perform authorized activities on behalf of the broker's client.

scarcity The degree of unavailability of a product or service in relation to demand for the product or service. A critical element of value.

second mortgage A mortgage loan whose lien priority is subordinate to a senior, or first, mortgage.

secondary mortgage market Lenders, investors, and government agencies who buy, sell, insure, or guarantee existing mortgages, mortgage pools, and mortgage-backed securities.

section An area defined by the rectangular survey system and consisting of 1/36th of a township, or one square mile.

securities license An authorization to broker securities. The Series 39 and 22 securities licenses authorize licensees to broker real estate securities.

security 1. Collateral for a loan. 2. A type of personal property investment, for example, bonds, stocks, and mutual funds.

seller financing Any financing arrangement where a seller takes a note and mortgage from the buyer for all or part of the purchase price of the property.

seller's market A market condition characterized by an excess of buyers over sellers.

senior lien See *superior lien*.

servient tenement A property containing an easement that must "serve" the easement use belonging to a dominant tenement.

severalty See *tenancy in severalty*.

severance A conversion of real property to personal property through detachment of the item from the land.

sole proprietorship A business entity with an individual as sole owner. The death of the owner terminates the business.

special agency See *limited agency*.

special assessment lien A lien against property to secure a tax levy for a specific public improvement, such as a new road or sewer. Only properties benefitting from the improvement are taxed and liened.

special exception A land use in conflict with current zoning that is nevertheless authorized because of its perceived benefit to the public welfare.

specific lien A lien placed against a specific item of property rather than against all of an owner's property.

specific performance Forced performance of one's obligations in an agreement, to the letter of the agreement. A legal remedy for a damaged party to take against a defaulting party.

statute of frauds A law requiring certain contracts to be in writing in order to be enforceable. Examples are real property conveyances, listing agreements, and longterm leases.

statute of limitations A law which restricts the period during which a damaged party may seek to rescind or disaffirm a contract or take other legal actions.

steering The prohibited practice of channeling prospective buyers and tenants toward or away from a particular area..

stock sale A conveyance of an incorporated business through the purchase of the stock. Entails the purchase of all liabilities as well as assets. See also *asset sale*.

straight-line cost recovery An accounting method for deducting depreciation expense from income. Periodic cost-recovery charges are made in equal amounts over a depreciation period. For example, the straight-line cost recovery of a $5,000 item over 5 years would be $1,000 per year.

strict foreclosure A court proceeding which gives a creditor legal title to a liened property rather than cash proceeds from a court-ordered sale.

subagency An agency relationship between the client of a listing broker and other brokers and salespeople who have agreed to assist the broker in procuring a customer for the client. The assisting brokers are agents of the listing broker and subagents of the listing broker's client.

sublease A transfer by a tenant of portions of the rights and obligations of a lease to another party, the sublessee. The original tenant, who is sublessor in the sublease, is still lessee in the original lease and remains primarily liable to the landlord for fulfilling lease obligations.

subordination A voluntary or involuntary placing of a lien's priority below that of another. A mortgage lien, for example automatically subordinates to a real estate tax lien.

substantive contact Contact between an agent and others that is deemed relevant to a transaction; used as a benchmark to define when an agent should disclose agency status to a prospective client or customer . If a contact is substantive, the agent must disclose agency status at the time of the contact.

substitution An appraisal principle that holds that a buyer will pay no more for a property than the buyer would pay for an equally desirable and available substitute property. Forms the foundation for the sales comparison approach to value.

subsurface rights Rights and interests to whatever is beneath the surface of one's parcel of real property.

suit for possession A landlord's formal legal avenue for evicting a tenant.

superior lien 1. One of a class of liens that by law have a higher priority than any junior lien; all are tax liens. 2. A junior lien whose priority is higher than that of another lien.

supply The quantity of a product or service available for sale, lease, or trade at any given time.

surface rights Rights to the surface area of a parcel of real estate.

survey A formal measurement of the boundaries, dimensions, and elevations of a parcel of real estate performed by a professional surveyor. Required by lenders to identify possible encroachments, easements, and flood hazards.

survivorship, right of A surviving joint tenant's right to receive all rights and interests in the property enjoyed by another joint tenant in the event of the latter's death.

syndication A real estate investment structure in which investors provide capital and organizers provide management expertise to develop or acquire and manage investment real estate for profit.

tax base The total of the assessed valuations of real properties within a taxing jurisdiction, less the total of exemptions.

tax certificate An instrument that gives the holder the right to apply for a tax deed after paying taxes on a property and after a statutory period.

tax deed A deed used to convey title to property sold in a tax foreclosure.

tax district A local government entity authorized by state, county, or municipality to levy taxes for a particular purpose.

tax rate See *millage rate*.

tax sale A court-ordered sale of a property to satisfy unpaid real estate taxes.

tax shelter An investment that produces depreciation or other non-cash losses that a taxpayer can deduct from other income to reduce tax liability.

taxable gain Capital gain subject to taxation. See *capital gain*.

taxable income Annual income from an investment property that is subject to taxation, generally equal to net operating income plus reserves minus depreciation and interest expense.

taxable value The assessed value of a property net of all exemptions.

tenancy A freehold or leasehold estate held by a tenant.

tenancy in common An estate where each co-owner owns an electable share of the property and can transfer this share to any other party. Does not include right of survivorship; interests of deceased owners pass to heirs.

tenancy in severalty An estate in real property owned by a single party.

testate The legal condition of a person who dies leaving a valid will.

tier An area between consecutive parallels, as defined in the *rectangular survey system*.

time share A fee or leasehold interest in a property that is shared by owners who have use of the property at different times.

title Ownership of real property as well as evidence of such ownership; legal title.

title insurance A policy that protects the holder against loss arising from defects in title or documents conveying title.

title plant A duplicate set of title records copied from public records and maintained by a title company

title records Public records of real property documenting the history of ownership, claims, ownership, conveyances, legal descriptions, and surveys.

title theory state A state whose laws give legal title of a mortgaged property to the mortgagee until the mortgagor satisfies the terms and obligations of the loan. See *lien theory state*.

Torrens System A title recording system that registers title to property, as well as liens and encumbrances, on a title certificate. The certificate is the title and reflects everything there is to be known about the condition of the title.

township An area six miles square, bounded by two consecutive parallels and two consecutive meridians in the rectangular survey system. Contains 36 sections.

trade fixture A fixture necessary for the conduct of a business. Although affixed to the land, it is personal property.

trust A fiduciary relationship between a trustor and trustee. The trustor conveys legal title to property to the trustee, who holds and manages the estate for the benefit of another party, the beneficiary (in a land trust, trustor and beneficiary are the same person).

underwriting 1. A process of investigating the financial capabilities and creditworthiness of a prospective borrower and granting credit to a qualified borrower. 2. The act of insuring or financing a party, business venture, or investment.

unequal services Services that differ in nature or quality from those normally rendered, with the alteration based on race, color, sex, national origin, or religion.

unilateral contract An agreement in which only one party promises to perform, contingent on the other party's performance of an optional action.

universal agency A fiduciary relationship which empowers an agent to perform any and all actions for a principal that may be legally delegated.

usury Excessive or illegal interest charged on a loan.

utility A determinant of the value of an item reflecting the item's ability to perform a desired function.

vacancy A measure of the unoccupied supply of exiting space in a building or market at any point in time. A vacancy rate is the amount of vacant space divided by the total amount of existing space.

validity Legal status of a contract that meets requirements of: competence of parties, mutual consent, valuable consideration, legal purpose, and voluntary good faith. A prerequisite for enforceability.

value In general, the worth of an item as determined by its utility, desirability, scarcity, affordability, and other components and quantified as price.

variance A land use that conflicts with current zoning but is authorized for certain reasons, including undue hardship to comply and minimal negative impact to leave it alone.

void Without legal force or effect; unenforceable and null, such as an illegal contract.

void contract An agreement that is null and cannot be enforced.

voidable contract An agreement that is subject to being nullified because a party to the agreement acted under some legal disability. Only the disadvantaged party can take action to void the contract.

water rights Rights of a property that abuts a body of water to own or use the water. See *littoral rights*, *riparian rights*, and *prior appropriation*.

will Last will and testament; a written or verbal statement by a testator instructing how to distribute the testator's estate to heirs.

yield Investment return expressed as a dollar amount or a percent of the original investment amount

zoning ordinance A municipal land use regulation

INDEX